A GERMAN OFFICER
IN OCCUPIED PARIS

EUROPEAN PERSPECTIVES
A SERIES IN SOCIAL THOUGHT AND CULTURAL CRITICISM

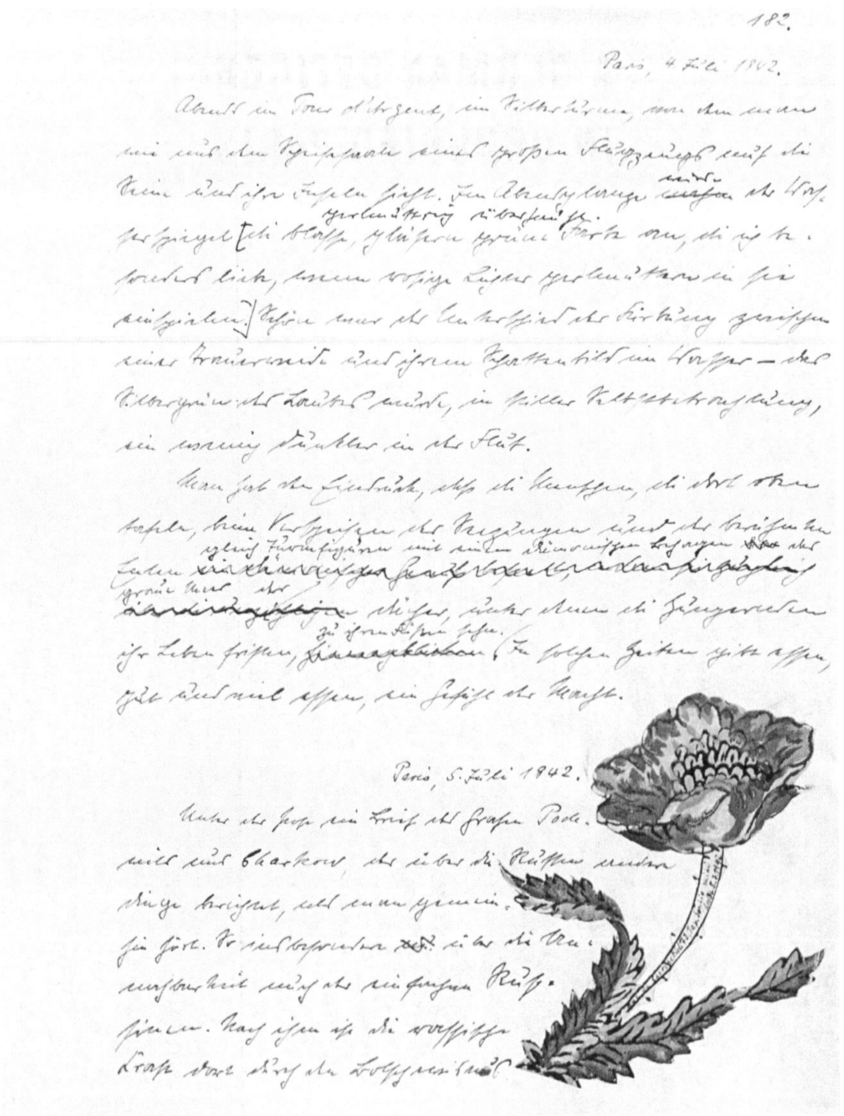

182.

Paris, 4 Juli 1942.

Paris, 5. Juli 1942.

Facsimile page from the First Paris Journal (4–5 July 1942)

EUROPEAN PERSPECTIVES
A SERIES IN SOCIAL THOUGHT AND CULTURAL CRITICISM
LAWRENCE D. KRITZMAN, EDITOR

European Perspectives presents outstanding books by leading European thinkers. With both classic and contemporary works, the series aims to shape the major intellectual controversies of our day and to facilitate the tasks of historical understanding.

For a complete list of books in the series, see the Columbia University Press website. https://cup.columbia.edu/series/european-perspectives-a-series-in-social-thought -and-cultural-criticism

ERNST JÜNGER

A GERMAN OFFICER IN OCCUPIED PARIS

THE WAR JOURNALS, 1941–1945

INCLUDING "NOTES FROM THE CAUCASUS"
AND "KIRCHHORST DIARIES"

FOREWORD BY ELLIOT NEAMAN
TRANSLATED BY THOMAS S. HANSEN AND ABBY J. HANSEN

COLUMBIA UNIVERSITY PRESS
NEW YORK

Columbia University Press wishes to express its appreciation for assistance given
by the Pushkin Fund in the publication of this book.

Columbia University Press
Publishers Since 1893
New York   Chichester, West Sussex
cup.columbia.edu

Strahlungen:
Das erste Pariser Tagebuch, Kaukasische Aufzeichnungen,
Das zweite Pariser Tagebuch, Kirchhorster Blätter by Ernst Jünger
Klett-Cotta
© 1949, 1979 Klett-Cotta - J.G. Cotta'sche Buchhandlung
Nachfolger GmbH, Stuttgart
For the English language translation
© 2019 Columbia University Press

Library of Congress Cataloging-in-Publication Data
Names: Junger, Ernst, 1895–1998, author. | Hansen, Thomas S. (Thomas Stansfield), translator. |
Hansen, Abby J., 1945– translator. | Neaman, Elliot Yale, 1957– writer of foreword.
Title: A German officer in occupied Paris / Ernst Junger ; translated by Thomas Hansen
and Abby J. Hansen ; foreword by Elliot Y. Neaman.
Other titles: Strahlungen. English
Description: New York : Columbia University Press, [2018] | Translation of: Strahlungen. |
Includes bibliographical references.
Identifiers: LCCN 2018020094 (print) | LCCN 2018042867 (e-book) |
ISBN 9780231548380 (e-book) | ISBN 9780231127400 |
ISBN 9780231127400(hardback; alk. paper) | ISBN 9780231548380 (e-book)
Subjects: LCSH: Junger, Ernst, 1895–1998—Diaries. | Authors, German—20th century—Diaries. |
Junger, Ernst, 1895–1998—Homes and haunts—France—Paris. |
Paris (France)—History—1940–1944. | Paris (France)—Intellectual life—20th century. |
Germany—History—1945–1955. | LCGFT: Diaries.
Classification: LCC PT2619.U43 (e-book) | LCC PT2619.U43 S813 2018 (print) |
DDC 838/.91207—dc23
LC record available at https://lccn.loc.gov/2018020094

Columbia University Press books are printed on permanent
and durable acid-free paper.
Printed in the United States of America

Cover image: Photograph of Ernst Jünger by Florence Henri (1942).
Courtesy of the private archives of Ernst Jünger.

Cover design: Chang Jae Lee

CONTENTS

FOREWORD

ELIOT NEAMAN

Memories bear traits of an inverse causality. The world, as an effect, resembles a tree with a thousand branches, but as memory it leads downwards into the tangled network of the roots. When I confront memories, it often seems like gathering a bundle of seaweed from the ocean—the tiny bit visible from afar, when slowly dragged up into the light, reveals an extensive system of filaments.

> —Ernst Jünger, *A German Officer in Occupied Paris*, 5 July 1942

Take yourself back in time to the summer of 1942, in Nazi-occupied Paris. A middle-age German officer in a gray uniform strolls down the Avenue Wagram, an army eagle insignia perched above his right breast pocket. The man is of medium height, of compact build, with chiseled thin features and graying hair around the temples. He turns to follow the Right Bank and inspect the *bouquinistes*, whose antiquarian books, cards, journals, and prints overflow from small well-worn shacks. Walking north, past the *Arc de Triomphe*, he stops at a stationery store on the Avenue Wagram and is jolted by the expression on the face of the girl behind the counter. Later he will write in his journal,

It was clear that she was staring at me with deep hatred. The pupils of her light blue eyes were like pinpoints; she met my gaze quite openly with a kind of relish—a relish with which the scorpion pierces his prey with the barb in his tail.[1]

He leaves the shop in deep thought. The walk ends at the nearby Hôtel Majestic, the headquarters of the German High Command in Paris. Captain Jünger takes a seat at a table overflowing with mail written by German soldiers to friends and loved ones at home. He reads each piece carefully, marking out lines of sensitive information before placing the envelope in one pile or another bound for the home front. As a military censor, he is tasked with reading French newspapers and other publications for signs of insubordination. A not uninteresting assignment for a writer whose job it is to enter the minds of others.

Who was this man?

He was born in 1895 under the Wilhelmine empire, marched off to war in 1914, and ended service as a highly decorated hero. He worked as a writer in Berlin at the height of Weimar Germany's cultural rebirth, beginning in 1927, and stayed in the capital just long enough to see Hitler seize power. He fought as a captain in World War II, spending much of his time in occupied Paris close to a resistance circle of aristocratic Prussian generals. He lived out much of the rest of his life in a small Swabian village through the period of the cold war and after the downfall of communism. He lived long enough to see Germany reunified and died in 1998, a celebrated centenarian and Olympian figure.

Jünger was the oldest of six children, two of whom did not survive infancy. From his father Ernst Georg, a chemist, he inherited the sharp analytical skills of a scientist, and from his mother Karoline Lampl, he received artistic capacities and an eye for natural beauty.[2] Jünger's family moved from place to place, partly in search of a good school for Ernst, who got into trouble and received poor grades. His father went in search of a stable income, abandoning ambitions to work as a scientist and opening an apothecary in a small town in the Erzgebirge, near the eastern border of today's Czech Republic. Jünger retained fond memories of the pristine landscape of forests and meadows in the surrounding area that he remembered as enigmatic and magical. The family did not enjoy the idyll very long. Between 1905 and 1913, the boy was sent to various educational institutions, including boarding schools, which rendered him even more alienated from adults and their rules. He and his brother joined the *Wandervogel* movement in 1911, one of the many prewar youth groups that had sprung up across Germany, offering adolescents an escape from the benevolent tyranny of regimented life in late imperial Germany.[3]

In 1913 Jünger realized his first youthful desire for actual adventure. He crossed the French border, fibbed about his age, and joined the Foreign Legion. He was shipped off to Algeria but had no desire to become a legionnaire. Escaping from the camp in Oran, he darted off to discover Africa on his own. Quickly captured by Foreign Legion soldiers, he was held until his father arranged for his release through the German Foreign Office. The furtively proud father instructed the boy to have a photograph taken before departing. The *adventure*, as we will see, will come to play a central role in his life experiences, then distilled into ice-clear form in his writings.

Jünger's father promised the precocious young man an adventure excursion to Kilimanjaro, the highest mountain in Africa, as long he finished school. Then came the war fever of August 1914. Jünger rushed to Hanover and volunteered for the Seventy-Third Regiment of General Field Marshal Prince Albrecht von Preussen. After hurrying through an alternative high school degree, he shipped out at year's end and was in battle by early January 1915 on the western front. Promoted the following autumn to lieutenant, in the latter stages of the war he was part of a new group of assault troops, sent in small numbers to infiltrate enemy trenches. This innovative "shock" strategy was more effective than mass lines of infantry, which were chewed up by the enemy's machine guns, but required more skill and individual initiative. After suffering fourteen battle wounds, Jünger received the Pour le Mérite on 22 September 1918, the highest honor awarded by the Prussian military, rarely given either to soldiers of the infantry or to warriors of his tender age.

THE GENERATION OF 1914

The venturesome boy was exhilarated by the war experience. He carried a copy of Homer in his pocket and imagined himself a Greek hero of the Trojan War. The copious notes he took of these battle experiences were self-published in 1920 as *In Stahlgewittern (Storm of Steel)*. The work was picked up by various publishers in the decades that followed and, along with several other essays from the 1920s, established Jünger's reputation as one of Germany's foremost authors of the war generation. He was recognized as a leader of the New Nationalists, intellectual veterans of the postwar period who inflated the memory of the war into mythic proportions and pitted themselves against the liberal tendencies of the Weimar Republic, especially against its fulfillment policies such as the payment of reparations, downsizing the army, and regaining good standing among the nations of Europe.

The Treaty of Versailles forced the German government to reduce its standing army to one hundred thousand troops. Although now under a republican government, it retained the imperial adjective to designate the *Reichswehr* and was filled with antidemocratic aristocrats. Jünger enthusiastically wrote treatises on storm trooper tactics, but he was put off by the empty socializing and boozing of the fraternizing officers. While studying the natural sciences in Leipzig, he joined the illegal paramilitary *Freikorps* and the legal veterans' group *Stahlhelm* and began a career in journalism, writing for a score of right-wing newspapers, including the Nazi *Völkischer Beobachter*. He became a leading exponent of the young German intellectual right, which advocated for an authoritarian alternative to the Weimar democracy. These "Ideas of 1914" had been foreshadowed by Oswald Spengler in his 1918 bestseller, *The Decline of the West* and Moller van den Bruck's *The Third Reich*, published in 1923. The young nationalist critique of parliamentary political systems followed in many ways the path laid out by Carl Schmitt in his seminal 1923 treatise, *The Crisis of Parliamentary Democracy*.[4] They advocated a form of "Prussian Socialism," as a new dictatorship, not monarchical, which would replace the nineteenth-century ideologies of liberalism, socialism, democracy, and anarchism. The new state would be run by steely-eyed workers and soldiers in full mobilization to restore Germany to its status as a world power. Jünger embraced these ideas in various forms, albeit often in a meta-historical and epochal rather than parochial German context, as one of three editors of the weekly *Die Standarte* (later *Arminius*), which included the writers Friedrich Hielscher, Franz Schauwecker, Hans Friedrich Blunck, and his brother Friedrich Georg Jünger, all intellectuals who his secretary Armin Mohler would identify as proponents of a "Conservative Revolution" in Germany.[5]

In these years, Jünger worked to establish a Central Council that would unite workers and soldiers until a Führer could be found who could put the revolution into practice. This was a "National Bolshevik" strategy and explains his close friendship with Ernst Niekisch, a politician and writer from Saxony who founded the journal *Widerstand*, with the aim of grafting Soviet Bolshevism onto Prussian nationalism. In the *War Journals*, Niekisch is referred to twelve times under the pseudonym "Cellaris." He was a key figure for understanding the ambiguous position Jünger held on the right-wing spectrum of pre-Nazi politics in Germany. Jünger was deeply concerned about Niekisch's fate during World War II and received updates from military contacts who knew how he was being mistreated by the Nazis. (Niekisch was arrested in 1937 and spent the war years in a Gestapo jail, where he was liberated by the Red Army in 1945, a broken, nearly blind man).[6]

By 1927 Jünger became disillusioned with the various nationalist groups fighting one other as the Weimar government entered a relatively stable period, which lasted until the Great Depression doomed Germany's first experiment with democracy. He decided to move to the bustling capital city.

THE TOTAL MOBILIZATION

In 1927 he took his wife and infant son to Berlin to settle down as a full-time writer. He had married Gretha von Jeinsen, ten years his junior, in 1925. With the Great War now almost a decade past, he became less focused on strident German nationalism and the battles of his youth. Residing in the humming metropolis, which began to eclipse Paris as the center of European cultural innovation, Jünger's curiosity turned to more expansive themes of modernity, technology, and cultural disruption. As Marcus Bullock has noted, he was particularly fascinated by the pulsating sexuality of the city, the intoxication experienced by the breaking of taboos and bourgeois norms.[7] Here he wrote the first version of his surrealist work, *The Adventurous Heart*, "notes written down by day and night."[8] The literary scholar Karl-Heinz Bohrer has strikingly labeled Jünger's style an "aesthetics of shock" because this book contains a phantasmagoria of scientific and poetic vignettes, a collage of wild associations and ghostly images that recall the war-inspired art of painters of the era like René Magritte, Salvador Dali, and Max Ernst, as well as the expressionists Otto Dix and George Grosz.[9]

Jünger's circle of friends and literary acquaintances expanded in Berlin as he moved beyond his ties to war veterans. On the left, he interacted with Bertolt Brecht, Ernst Toller, and the anarchist Erich Mühsam. On the right, he associated with Gottfried Benn, Ernst von Salomon, and Arnolt Bronnen. Around this time, his intellectual infatuation with France and French culture began. He made frequent trips to Paris, making contact with French literary circles, facilitated by the well-connected German-French author Joseph Breitbach.

As the Nazis began their final ascent to power after winning 107 seats in the Reichstag in the elections of September 1930, Jünger distanced himself from the party. He simultaneously advocated his own political vision, which in some ways was a more radical version of the nationalist revolution: authoritarian and ruthless, but not racist. Despite Goebbels's attempt to win him over to the Brown Revolution before and even after 1933, Jünger steadfastly declined any offers to become involved in Nazi politics and forbade the propaganda minister from using any of his works without permission. Although Goebbels transmitted the Führer's avid wish to meet him, Jünger did not reciprocate.[10] Apart from one unfortunate essay on "Jews and the National Question," in which he stressed the impossibility of Jews and Germans sharing the same national culture,[11] he resisted the Nazi "Blood and Soil" ideology.[12]

In 1932, the same year Aldous Huxley published *Brave New World*, Jünger's *The Worker* appeared in print. As the war journals indicate, Huxley was one of the few modern authors Jünger prized. Huxley's novel and Jünger's social analysis shared a dystopian vision of the future resulting from economic and political breakdown. Whereas the former was read as a warning of the end of the liberal order in western societies, Jünger's tract affirmed a Nietzschean reevaluation of and triumph over the liberal order. Nevertheless, the Nazis had little use for Jünger's treatise because it lacked any connection to the German *Volk* community or racial hierarchies. The book heralded a collective new age of the laborer in epochal terms, while the Nazis concentrated on the specific situation of Germany's supposed superior racial characteristics. National Socialism appeared to Jünger as a purely technical execution of the "total mobilization" (the title of another of his short treatises of this period). He later said that Nazism "lacked metaphysics."[13] As a political platform *The Worker* was considered useless by the new regime. In fact, it was explicitly denounced in the *Völkischer Beobachter*, the Nazi party newspaper.[14]

Jünger was well aware of what could befall an opponent of the new regime, regardless of his war hero status. Around this time, he began burning many personal papers and letters. Because of his ties to the anarchist Erich Mühsam, the Gestapo searched Jünger's apartment in early 1933. At the beginning of December 1933, Jünger's family left Berlin for Goslar, in Lower Saxony on the slopes of the Harz Mountains. During the so-called Röhm Purge at the end of June 1934, in which the *Schutzstaffel* (SS) eradicated the leadership of the unruly Brown Shirts, as well as nearly one hundred political opponents of the regime, Jünger was vacationing on the island of Sylt but felt the threat palpably. The mood was ominous, wrote Jünger's wife.[15]

GOODBYE TO ALL THAT

Jünger now entered a period of "inner emigration," a term possibly coined by Thomas Mann, but one Jünger never embraced.[16] He published a series of essays based on his travels, and revised *The Adventurous Heart*, removing large parts of the book that were political in nature. He rejected membership in the Nazified Prussian Academy of the Arts, which was "synchronized" (*gleichgeschaltet*) in the spring of 1933, forcing out many luminaries, including Thomas Mann and Alfred Döblin. The Nazis filled the writing (*Dichtung*) section with party hacks, although the Academy was headed by Gottfried Benn, a major poet who was on friendly terms with Jünger.[17] In 1934 Jünger published a collection of his essays on philosophically esoteric topics, which stood in stark contrast to the "Blu-Bo" (a contraction for *Blut und Boden*, blood and soil) popular literature of the period. In 1936 he published the diversionary *Afrikanische Spiele* (African Games), a novel about his short adventure in the French Foreign Legion.

The Jünger family moved several times in the 1930s, once down to Überlingen, on the north shore of Lake Constance, to be near his brother Friedrich Georg. But Jünger didn't like the mild climate there, and so they finally settled in Kirchhorst near Hanover in 1939, where Gretha had found a large, somewhat run-down old house with a large garden, which would be very useful since food would soon be rationed in Germany. Jünger would live there until 1948, although he was away for much of World War II. He had another reason for moving back to Lower Saxony: unit assignments were based on residence, and he wanted to be back in his old regiment if war broke out.

Just before the outbreak of World War II, Jünger published *On the Marble Cliffs*, which he began writing in February 1939 on the balmy shores of Lake Constance and finished quickly in Kirchhorst at the end of July. The book was written as an allegory on the abuse of power. A peaceful seaside agricultural people are threatened by a primitive nomadic tribe from the hinterland and by the followers of an unscrupulous tyrant named the Head Ranger, whose thugs torture their enemies in a ghostly camp called Köppelsbleek. Skulls and the flayed skins of the victims surround the site. Two brothers, modeled after Jünger and his brother Friedrich Georg, are shaken from their peaceful existence and forced to flee their domicile, which the Head Ranger destroys in a violent *Götterdämmerung*. Jünger later denied that the novel was a cryptic assault on National Socialism, but the descriptions of the main characters in the novel are too suggestive to be pure coincidence. The Head Ranger dresses ostentatiously and throws lavish parties on his estates, just like Goering, who was in fact in charge of Germany's forests during the Third Reich.[18] In the war journals, Jünger repeatedly ruminates on his novel, whose readers understood it as a contemporary allegory.

CAPTAIN IN THE CITY OF LIGHT

Jünger was conscripted as a lieutenant soon after the war broke out and reached the rank of captain. He participated in the invasion of France in the spring and summer of 1940. Then, in April 1941, his regiment was ordered to occupied Paris. Jünger was granted considerable privileges in his military posting, not the least of which was due to the fact that he did not face much physical danger apart from some English bombing raids over Paris. His office was at the Hôtel Majestic, under the command of General Otto von Stülpnagel and later his distant cousin Heinrich von Stülpnagel. He served there with Hans Speidel, a lieutenant general and later chief of staff to the famed General Erwin Rommel, as well as with Werner Best, an SS officer who was a deputy to Reinhard Heydrich, one of the main architects of the Holocaust.

Jünger had much free time to wander around the metropolis, often in civilian clothing, although he didn't see his situation as without peril. "When I think about the difficulties of my situation compared with other people—especially those in the Majestic—I often get the feeling," he wrote on 23 May 1942, "that you are not here for no reason; fate will untie the knots it has tied, so rise above worries and see them as patterns." In other words, he was surrounded by opponents of the Hitler regime, who are named in the journals. With a tinge of guilt and self-reflection, he added, "thoughts like that seem almost irresponsible." Almost but not quite irresponsible because he saw himself as part of the resistance to Hitler even though he believed that active opposition was pointless. Others around him were to pay dearly for their convictions, whereas Jünger managed to survive the war unscathed.

The lavish Hôtel Majestic is still situated on the Avenue Kléber, five minutes by foot from the Arc de Triomphe. Jünger was billeted nearby, at the luxury hotel Raphael on the Avenue des Portugais. He worked in Majestic's Division Ic, responsible for gathering military intelligence on enemy and oppositional activities. Another of his assignments was to keep notes about the rivalry between the Nazi party and the army, which he kept, along with a diary and other writings, safely locked away in a vault at the Majestic. The diary entries formed the basis for his later published collected war journals *Strahlungen* (*Emanations*). The first World War II diaries, *Gardens and Streets*, were published in Germany in 1942 and were translated the same year into French, published by Plon, so that his fame in occupied France spread among readers in that country. The translated war diaries included in this current volume contain the two journals from his tour of duty in Paris, his sojourn in the Caucasus, and his visits and then homecoming to the house in Kirchhorst.

As a well-known author, Jünger was welcome in the best salons of the capital city. There he met with intellectuals and artists across the political spectrum. The *First Paris Journal* was written as the Third Reich reached the fullest extent of its continental expansion. Through reports passed on by Speidel, Jünger was privy to the brutal facts of the Russian campaign,[19] and the German army was still deep inside Soviet territory until well after the end of the Battle of Stalingrad in February 1943. Not surprisingly, some conservative Parisian intellectuals greeted the *Pax Germanica* with cheers, hailing the demise of the disorganized and highly fractured French Third Republic. The sympathizers of the New Order included the dramatist Sasha Guitry and the writers Robert Brasillach, Marcel Jouhandeau, Henry de Montherlant, Paul Morand, Jean Cocteau, Drieu la Rochelle, and Paul Léutaud. To call these intellectuals antirepublican "collaborators," however, depends on the word's definition and on whether or not they played any official role in cooperating with the German authorities. The word "collaborator" is thrown around too loosely, even by historians today. But that a Franco-German intellectual alliance between 1940 and 1944 was forged, can hardly be doubted. That the Germans often understood that relationship differently from their French counterparts must also be considered when reading these journals.

Jünger frequented the Thursday salon of Paris editor for Harper's *Bazaar*, Marie-Louise Bousquet, who was married to the playwright Jacques Bousquet. Pablo Picasso and Aldous Huxley frequented the meetings, as well as the pro-Nazi Pierre Drieu la Rochelle and Henry de Montherlant. Drieu La Rochelle was editor of the collaborationist journal *Novelle Revue Française* and hoped that a uniquely French form of fascism would contribute to an international fascist order. He had already befriended the German ambassador to France, Otto Abetz, before the war.[20] Montherlant was deeply Catholic, hated the former French Third Republic, and was pro-German but not overtly fascist. However, he did write for the reactionary Catholic journal *La Gerbe*, which tried to synthesize Catholicism and racism and was subsidized by the Nazis through Otto Abetz. Through the ambassador to Bucharest, Paul Morand, Jünger met Benoist Méchin, who was a member of the Vichy government, and Ferdinand Céline, the fascist sympathizer who Jünger calls Merline in the Paris journals.[21] Céline was a vicious anti-Semite, and Jünger judged the brutality of his character harshly. But he was quite friendly with another more sympathetic writer, Marcel Jouhandeau, whom he visited often in these pages. Jouhandeau was a repressed homosexual and observant Catholic who wrote a number of anti-Semitic diatribes for the journal *Le Péril Juif* (*The Jewish Peril*). In 1938 Jouhandeau had accepted an invitation from Josef Goebbels, the minister of propaganda, to visit Germany.[22]

Another key contact in Paris for Jünger was the salon of Florence Gould (Lady Orphington in the journals),[23] where he rubbed shoulders with Braque, Picasso, Sacha Guitry, Julien Gracq, Paul Léautaud, and Jean Paulhan, one of the founders of the resistance newspaper *Lettres Françaises*.[24] Paulhan was arrested and jailed by the Gestapo during the war.

Jünger frequented the luxury hotel George V, where a roundtable of exclusive French and German intellectuals met, including the writers Morand, Cocteau, Montherlant as well as the publisher Gaston Gallimard. The renowned legal scholar (and early exponent of the Nazi regime) Carl Schmitt often attended, as did Speidel and the Paris correspondent of a Frankfurt newspaper, Friedrich Sieburg, who had written a bestseller about France in the interwar years, *Like a God in France*. Jünger operated on the edge of politics in Paris, rather like a butterfly fluttering among both resistors and collaborators. He didn't trust the generals, who had taken a personal oath to Hitler, to be able to carry out a coup. Jean Cocteau later quipped: "Some people had dirty hands, some had clean hands, but Jünger had no hands."[25]

Cocteau's witticism notwithstanding, the accusation was not entirely fair. When Jünger saw an opportunity to help save Jews at an acceptable level of risk, he did act. He passed on information, for example, through intermediaries to the French Resistance about upcoming transports and thus saved Jewish lives. The German playwright and novelist Joseph Breitbach, who lived in Paris from 1931 through the end of the occupation, was one of them. He publicized this fact after the war.[26]

In addition to the secret diaries, Jünger also worked during the war on an essay that was published after the war (in Amsterdam, after being denied publication rights by the occupation authorities). It was called *The Peace*. In this unapologetic, religiously infused essay, Jünger conceived of the period from 1918 to 1945 as a long European civil war. He discussed the explosion of technology that had brought with it an exponential increase in the ability to create destruction. He described the failure of the League of Nations and the harsh terms of the Treaty of Versailles. The victors, he warned, should not take revenge on the vanquished. The war was won by one side, he intoned, but the peace must be won by all. History was represented as a vale of tears and all of mankind as equal subjects of suffering (the line between victim and victimizer thereby diminished). Jünger had read the Bible, both Old and New Testaments, from beginning to end twice during the war years. *The Peace* was imbued with a Christian sense that the new world must be accompanied by a religious revival, the only means to conquer the nihilism of the previous decades. Jünger divided his own work into Old Testament writings of his nationalist phase followed by a new gospel of religiosity and humanism.

DEPORTATIONS

Beginning in the spring of 1941, Jünger complained in his journals of insomnia, depression, and general exhaustion. When he started losing weight in early 1942, a physician "friend," the *Doctoresse*, ordered various cures for his ills. Despite his weakened condition, he was ordered to tour the eastern front in October 1942 and decided he had no viable grounds to back out. The mood in the Caucasus was grim, as the Russian army began to encircle the German Sixth Army in the city of Stalingrad (today Volgograd). Hitler had taken over tactical planning on the eastern front and began making dilettantish and fatal mistakes, such as prohibiting his generals from undertaking strategic retreats. Clausewitz must be turning over in his grave, Jünger thought to himself. Death, human and animal suffering, and devastation littered the military landscape, more like the Thirty Years' War, Jünger mused, than World War I.

At a New Year's Eve party at staff headquarters, Jünger heard direct confirmation that Jews were being exterminated in trains that carried them into tunnels filled with poison gas.[27] Jünger mentioned the harsh treatment of Jews in Paris several times and the shame he felt about being in uniform, when he noticed three young girls wearing yellow stars.[28] On 27 March 1942, the first transport of Jews left Compiégne for Auschwitz. In July, thousands of French police were seen rounding up Jews on the streets of Paris. He noted on 18 July,

Never for a moment may I forget that I am surrounded by unfortunate people who endure the greatest suffering. What kind of human being, what kind of officer, would I be otherwise? This uniform obligates me to provide protection wherever possible.

To his credit, he never attempted to justify or explain away the Holocaust, even though the brutality of the eastern front did not affect Jews alone. But he did place these "wicked crimes" in a cosmic context that deprived individual actors of agency. "Ancient chivalry is dead; wars are waged by technicians," he wrote. Two years to the day after the commencement of Operation Barbarossa, he observed with bitterness that demagogues brought Germany into a war with the Soviets that could have been avoided, leading to atrocities against the Jews, which "enrage the cosmos against us."[29] At the end of 1942, he made three New Year's resolutions, the second of which reads, "Always have a care for unfortunate people."

A TOUR OF HELL

Jünger's tour on the eastern front is notable for its sharp contrast to his privileged existence in Paris. There he was able to enjoy the luxury of French comforts, good food, and socializing among refined company, despite increased rationing of almost all commodities as the war progressed. But even on the eastern front, he discovered that his reputation as an author was a tremendous help:

I had no idea that little things like a pocket mirror, knife, sewing thread, or string are precious items here. Luckily I constantly come across people who help me. Not infrequently they are some of my readers, whose help I count among my fortune.[30]

On 11 January 1943, Jünger took the night train from Lötzen (today Giżycko in northeastern Poland), stopping in Leisnig, halfway between Leipzig and Dresden. He arrived home in Kirchorst on 9 February. He calls his wife "Perpetua" in the diaries, and she frequently appeared in his dreams while in Paris. But marital troubles dominated the visit in Kirchorst. Many female accomplices are mentioned in the diaries, including Camillea, Charmille, Mme. d'Armenonville, Mme. Dancart, and most often the *Doctoresse*.[31] These were probably all the same person, Sophie Ravoux, with whom Jünger had an intimate affair.[32] The Russian writer Umm El-Banine, who opened many doors for him in Paris, was also probably a lover.

When he departed again for Paris on 18 February, he left behind letters and diary entries that his wife Gretha read with an eagle eye and sharp intuition. Gretha had already been upset about his pleasurable lifestyle in Paris while she had to manage a household and deal with Allied bombing raids. She might have forgiven his sexual escapades were it not for an emotional coldness she felt in his presence during his stay. "Perpetua" turns out to be an apt nickname because it recalls those women who did housekeeping chores in Catholic monasteries. She wrote him on

20 February 1943, threatening a divorce. Jünger managed to patch things up with her but not without many protestations of his love and devotion, as well as some soul-searching. She demanded that he completely cut off contact with the despised Sophie Ravoux, the relationship with whom, Jünger maintained, was entirely platonic.

All of this is barely mentioned in the war journals. One has to read between the lines, as in this diary entry:

> A word to men. Our position with respect to two different women can re-semble that of the judge pronouncing a Solomonic verdict, yet we are also the child. We deliver ourselves into the custody of the one who does not want to cut us in half.[33]

Gretha was not the only observer to resent Jünger's Nietzschean penchant for turning his life into a work of art. Although the war journals offer a unique per-spective from "inside the Belly of the Leviathan" as Jünger put it, some critics have accused the writer of posing as a *flâneur* and dandy while others suffered. In one famous scene, Jünger climbed up to the roof of the Hotel Raphael and, holding a glass of red burgundy, observed bombers flying over Paris, as fires engulfed the city and "its red towers and domes, was a place of stupendous beauty, like a calyx that they fly over to accomplish their deadly act of pollination."[34] On 27 May 1943, however, there were no air strikes over Paris. The strawberry swimming in red burgundy may have been, as Tobias Wimbauer speculates, derived from an erotic impulse rather than an actual observation of events.[35]

Whatever moral judgment one wishes to make about the aesthetics of violence, which is evident in many places in the journals, Jünger's account is an indispens-able firsthand reflection of Paris under the German occupation and provides sharply observed portraits of contemporaries as they struggled with the destruc-tion of Europe at the end of a second Thirty Years' War.

A CHRISTIAN HEART

In the winter of 1943–1944, Jünger's reflections turned gloomy and often apocalyp-tic as he systematically studied the entire Old and New Testaments. Jünger viewed the war through the lens of God's judgment for the evil perpetrated by mankind, as well as the promise, with the return of God through Christ, of everlasting grace and renewal. He was too sophisticated to take the gospels literally, and further-more he had been brought up by his positivist, scientifically trained father to be skeptical.[36] Nevertheless, he viewed the period as if the two world wars were a test for mankind. He held out hopes for a renewal of Christianity after a descent into nihilism. His "Appeal to the Youth of the World," *The Peace* treatise, was written in this spirit and was suffused with his Bible studies. Throughout 1944 he tinkered with the script, and the intended audience expanded beyond youth, to include a general appeal for a postwar metahistorical transformation of all nations.

In 1944 news of Allied armies conquering Italy and the Soviets pushing into Eastern Prussia and Poland confirmed his worst fears about Germany's fate. He noted with deep sadness the destruction of German cities, of which he learned through letters from friends and saw firsthand during his travels by train from Paris back to Kirchhorst while on furlough.

THE RIDE OF THE VALKYRIES

On 27 March 1944, Jünger was visited in Paris by Lieutenant Colonel Cäsar von Hofacker, a liaison between Carl Heinrich von Stülpnagel and the group of officers around Hofacker's cousin, Colonel Claus Schenk Graf von Stauffenberg, who was the central figure in the failed assassination attempt on Hitler's life on 20 July 1944. On that afternoon, Hofacker took a walk with Jünger on the Avenue Kléber and informed him that Stülpnagel was under observation and Jünger himself was viewed with suspicion. Hofacker suggested he leave Paris and go to Marseilles for a while. The young colonel also filled him in on many of the details of the plot, called *Operation Valkyrie*, and listed the main conspirators. On 20 July 1944, Stauffenberg brought a bomb in an attaché case into Hitler's "*Wolf's Lair*" in East Prussia. Stauffenberg left just before the explosion, which injured but did not kill Hitler, shielded as he was by a heavy concrete table.

Jünger had also came into contact with officers involved in the Rommel Plan to arrest and replace Hitler.[37] In fact, Rommel had been given Jünger's treatise *The Peace* through an intermediary, was impressed by the ideas, and may have been spurred to act by them.[38] The *Westlösung* (or Western Solution) envisaged imprisoning Hitler sometime in May 1944, when he was inspecting the Atlantic Wall, an extensive system of fortifications built to defend against the expected Allied landing in the west. Inexplicably, Hitler continued to direct the war effort from Berchtesgaden, his outpost and home in the Bavarian Alps. After the invasion of Normandy, Hitler announced an unexpected visit for 19 June to Rommel's headquarters at La Roche-Guyon, fifty-eight kilometers from Paris. Speidel and Rommel had an ideal opportunity to strike. But as so often in Hitler's life, he was spared by a lucky intervention. The bombing of England with V-1 rockets had begun from French territory on 15 June. On 18 June, one of the rockets strayed off course and came down near Margival, nearly hitting the Führer's headquarters Wolfschlucht II, where Hitler was meeting with General Rundstedt. Shaken by the near miss and depressed about the viability of his new wonder weapons, he returned abruptly to Bavaria.

The failed Rommel plan to arrest Hitler was now replaced by the Stauffenberg plot to kill the dictator. On the early evening of 20 July, Hofacker called Stülpnagel and reported that Hitler was dead.[39] Thereupon Stülpnagel ordered the arrest of more than a thousand SS and *Sicherheitsdienst* agents. He had already set in motion plans to have them face mass executions. But at twenty to eight the same evening, the German radio reported that Hitler had survived. Chaos now reigned in the Hôtel Majestic. Jünger spent the day hunting butterflies in the forest around

Saint Cloud[40] and made only veiled references in the journals to the sense of heightened danger when he came back to headquarters.

The news from Berlin was contradictory. Was this a trick by Goebbels to buy time? The commanding general in the west, Hans Günter von Kluge, would have to make a decision without knowing the true state of affairs. Kluge had known about the plot through one of its instigators, Henning von Tresckow, but when it came time to act he decided that there could be no coup while Hitler was still possibly alive. General Rommel, the only military leader in Nazi Germany who could have led a rebellion against the living Führer, had been badly injured just three days before Operation Valkyrie. All of the prisoners were released, including the top SS commanders Carl-Albrecht Oberg and Helmut Knochen.

Jünger's confidante Hofacker was arrested by the Gestapo in Paris on 26 July, brutally tortured. and eventually sentenced to death by the infamous People's Court. Under torture, he revealed details about General Rommel's involvement in the German Resistance, but he did not disclose the participation of Jünger and the officers around Stülpnagel in Paris.

Field Marshal Wilhelm Keitel, a servile mouthpiece of Hitler, ordered Stülpnagel to fly to Berlin. Stülpnagel sent Jünger regrets through his secretary for having to cancel a scheduled breakfast and then, instead of flying, ordered a driver to take him by car past the battlefields of Verdun where he had fought in the Great War. During a fierce rainstorm, Stülpnagel shot himself in the temple on the banks of the Meuse River. His driver rescued him from the water, still alive. He had blinded himself but was brought to an army hospital, guarded by the SS, and then taken to Plötzensee in Berlin, where he was tried by the notorious Peoples Court's judge Roland Freisler on 30 August and hanged six weeks later. Kluge was replaced by General Walter Model on 17 August and ordered to report to Berlin. He took his own life with cyanide pills near Metz on 19 August.

Kluge's representative in Paris, General Günther Blumentritt, may have saved the day for Jünger and others in the group that met at the Hotel George V. On the evening of 20 July, he sat down with Oberg and Knochen in the Salon Blue of the Hotel Raphael and, in a scene seemingly out of a tale by Rabelais, ordered several bottles of fine champagne to placate them. Blumentritt tried to frame the entire affair as a gross misunderstanding. Having been caught flatfooted by the plot that developed on their watch, it was in the SS commanders' self-interest not to delve too deeply into the extent of the German *Wehrmacht* officers' involvement in the botched coup.[41]

With Jünger having been so close to key members of the German Resistance, the question must be posed how he survived the brutal crackdown by the SS in Paris after 20 July. It is widely claimed that Hitler protected him, saying "Nothing happens to Jünger" ("*Dem Jünger geschieht nichts*"). There is only one source for this supposed utterance, namely Friedrich Hielscher, who heard it from Wolfram Sievers, an SS officer who was hanged after the war, in June 1948.[42] (Hielscher and Jünger carried on an extensive correspondence for fifty-eight years).

The Hielscher-Severs source seems credible, but it is uncorroborated. According to one biographer, Jünger was to have been called before Roland Freisler's

Peoples' Court in the spring of 1945. Only the chaos of the final months of the war saved him.[43] Hitler is not known to have made compassionate exceptions, to say the least, even for war heroes. Erwin Rommel would be a good example. The more likely explanation is that Jünger was inordinately careful. He burned his manuscripts and letters on sensitive matters, as noted above, and he was in fact opposed to any attempt to assassinate Hitler or work against the party dictatorship, as much as he disliked both. He expressed his opposition to assassinations of dictators several times in his journals. He argued from historical precedents in which the aftermath of such killings had produced greater tyranny. In the specific case of Germany, he feared that a successful elimination of Hitler would lead to a new Stab-in-the-Back Legend.[44]

LAST KNIGHTS OF THE MAJESTIC

By early 1944, the liberation of Paris was imminent. Jünger noted that the Americans were in Renne on 5 August. He climbed up to the top of Sacré-Coeur to bid goodbye to his beloved Paris as the cobblestones baked in the hot sun. "Cities are feminine and only smile on the victor," he noted enigmatically. On 10 August, he visited Florence Gould for the last time. Three days later he took a walk with Charmille on the banks of the Seine. The Paris journals end there. The next day, 14 August, the evacuation of the German army began, and Jünger was seated on one of the first military transports out of the city.

He received news of the liberation of Paris back home in Kirchhorst. On 17 August, the German army began placing explosives around the French capital, not only intending to hold off the Allied advance but also honoring Hitler's orders to destroy Paris if necessary. Columns of German military vehicles were on the move everywhere in the metropolis. The French Resistance plastered the capital with posters calling for a general strike and mobilization against the Germans. The war journals are curiously silent about all this frenetic activity. On 20 August, he visited a cemetery and ruminated about short life spans. On 21 August, he joined some boys in a fishing expedition. Finally, on 23 August he noted that "the Americans have entered Paris" and then went off for a swim and sunbathing. Attacks on collaborators in Paris began at this time, and Jünger noted with bitterness how many of his Paris friends were arrested, beleaguered, or attacked by mobs. "They say Montherlant is being harassed. He was still caught up in the notion that chivalrous friendship is possible; now he is being disabused of that idea by louts."[45]

ON PAIN

On 25 October, before departing for the Italian front, Jünger's son Ernstel visited Kirchhorst for the last time. On 27 October, Jünger was formally decommissioned from military service. He returned to his books and his garden, although constant Allied bombing made life difficult and dangerous even in rural areas in Germany.

On 12 January 1945, Jünger received the dreadful news that his eldest son, his namesake Ernstel, had been killed on 29 November 1944 in, of all places, the marble cliffs of Cararra, Italy. The boy had been overheard talking to a friend, Wolf Jobst Siedler (later an important writer and publisher in the Federal Republic), expressing "defeatist" remarks about the Hitler regime. Ernstel was also caught listening to foreign radio broadcasts. A spy denounced both boys, and they were arrested in January 1944. Hitler had recently given orders that fresh recruits (Ernstel was eighteen) were to be trained not only in the best military tactics but also as sharp ideological warriors. The actions of Ernstel and Wolf could therefore have led to death sentences.

Jünger had received permission to leave Paris in February 1944 and met with the authorities in Berlin, displaying his Pour le Mérite medal ostentatiously at his neck. In April, Ernst and Gretha visited the presiding judge in Ernstel's case, Admiral Scheurlen,[46] who reduced an initial harsher penalty to *Frontbewährung*, which meant the boy was allowed to return to military service to prove his worth and was given a dangerous assignment in the Italian mountains. Jünger was never sure whether his son had been shot by the enemy or executed by the SS, with a shot to the back of the neck.[47]

For the most part, the war journals consist of dispassionate, precise observations, showing little emotion and only limited introspection, as when, for example, Jünger ruminates about his tendency to fall into depression, *la frousse*. By contrast, for weeks after he and Gretha received news of the boy's death, he returned repeatedly to ruminating on the poignant pain of losing his eldest son. "I cannot stop thinking about Ernstel. So much about his life is a riddle that is hard to solve."[48]

The war journals end with Jünger unenthusiastically commanding the local *Volkssturm*, the national militia of males between sixteen and sixty not already serving in the army, which had been announced by Hitler in the fall of 1944. As refugees streamed through the countryside, some billeted in his house, Jünger retreated as much as possible into his books and letters, hiding out in a garden cottage or upstairs in his attic. Perpetua took command of the household and kept intruders at bay. On 29 March, on his fiftieth birthday, he heard news from his publisher that Goebbels had forbidden mention of his name in the press, "the only honor that I prize."[49] His final thoughts in these journals were about his dead son. As he watched American army tanks and other armored vehicles pass by on a road nearby, with jets streaming overhead, a "parade of dangerous toys," he sensed the "incursion of a superpower into a completely crushed region."[50] The only saving grace, at least Ernstel did not see this, for "it would have hurt him too much."

THEMES AND FORMS

As important as historical context is for a full appreciation of these war journals, it is necessary before concluding to pay some attention to Jünger's idiosyncratic style. Nothing derogatory is meant by the term "idiosyncratic," deriving from the Greek words "idio" and "sunkratikos," or mixed together in a way particular to an individual. An "idiot" in Greek was someone who did not participate in the public sphere, but by inference was someone who took a singular path. Jünger was certainly no idiot, but he did very much march to the beat of his own drum. His depth of experience and knowledge was astounding, especially considering that he was still in his late forties when he wrote these journals. Furthermore, he was an autodidact who, despite some university study, lacked specialized academic training. Very few observers could have predicted at the time that by the 1980s he would be compared to Goethe.[51] The journals give many indications of why that judgment was not off the mark, not only because of the bountiful evidence of polymathy but also because of Jünger's unique style and form. The following sections briefly address three key aspects of his writing that are essential for revealing the inimitable fabric, the *texture* that links words to reality in these pages.

1. THEMATIC: ADVENTURE

Jünger's thirst for adventure was played out in his short stint in the French Foreign Legion and his four-year, life-changing service in the Great War. It was also imaginary, as in his reflections on books, dreams, plants, and animals. These offer a key that can unlock many of Ernst Jünger's writings. In these war journals, for example, Jünger returns repeatedly to adventure books about shipwrecks, a metaphor for the situation in which he finds himself, logging the events leading to the inevitable downfall of Germany.

Adventure is perhaps the oldest of all literary genres. Gerhard Nebel, who worked as a translator in Paris in 1941 and is mentioned in the war journals, explored the concept in his early post–World War II book, describing Jünger's spiritual and metaphysical thirst for adventure as the glue that holds together such disparate endeavors as militant nationalism and Christian spiritualism.[52] Gerhard Loose also picked up the adventure theme in his Jünger biography, emphasizing the pitfalls inherent in the *cult of self* (*Ichbezogenheit*), which reduces the natural world, foreign lands, war, or just about any phenomenon to objects of speculation for Jünger's aesthetic imagination.

In one of the most insightful essays ever written on the topic, the sociologist Georg Simmel defined the adventure as a self-contained experience, without reference to all the neighboring parts of life: "it is like an island in life, which determines its beginning and its end according to its own visionary powers (*Bildungskräfte*), and is not at the same time determined, as in the case of a part of a continent, by the one side or the other."[53] Both world wars were (by Simmel's definition) islands in Jünger's life, and both provided ample material for his visionary imagination.

2. FORM: STEREOSCOPY

In the mid and late 1930s, Jünger's adventures continued, but in a different key. In 1934 he published a collection of essays, *Leaves and Stones*, which marked a turn away from militant politics. The collection contained a travel diary, an essay on pain, a surrealist take on the "Man on the Moon," and a piece on language, "In Praise of Vowels." The volume also contained theoretical tracts on military subjects, in particular a reprint of "'The Total Mobilization." He revised *The Adven-turous Heart*, which in tone and substance was so distant from the kind of litera-ture published in Germany at the time that it might as well have been penned by a foreign author. In 1938 Jünger cut most of the autobiographical details of the first edition and replaced them with metaphysical reflections and dream sequences that would avoid the censor's blue pencil in Hitler's Germany. The method was "stereoscopic," a journey into dreamlike realms below quotidian existence.[54]

"Stereoscopic perception" has a technical meaning for Jünger. In *The Adventur-ous Heart*, he noted that it involved "extracting two sensual qualities from one and the same object, through—and this is essential—the same sense organ."[55] One sense organ has to take over a function of another. Thus, a red, fragrant carnation is not stereoscopic as it involves merely sight and smell separately. But a velvet carnation that emits the fragrance of cinnamon is stereoscopic because the nose both smells and tastes the qualities of spice simultaneously. The device has roots in French decadence and symbolism, as evidenced by repeated occurrences in the poems of Arthur Rimbaud and Charles Baudelaire. Jünger may have possessed synesthesia, or at least was able to create it poetically, by separating and mixing dif-ferent sensory qualities in an object. "I thought I was seeing sounds that no painter had ever observed," he wrote in an entry on 9 April 1942.

In the *Paris Diaries*, Jünger's recollection of his dreams, as well as his zoological observations and recurrent descriptions of long walks and visits to cemeteries, parks, libraries, bookstores, antiquarian shops, galleries, and museums of Paris, partake of some of the same magical-realist method.[56] The diaries, one must add, are meant to be actual descriptions of events, not phantasmagoria. Jünger's analogies are imaginative, but in these pages usually not technically "stereoscopic," such as when he compares receiving a typhus vaccination to Holy Communion.[57] The method is stereoscopic in a broader sense, the way Jünger described, in an essay from the 1930s, the magical effect of perceiving a man's face on a brightly lit moon.[58] As Jünger explains, "the real is just as magical as the magical is real"[59]—or to put it another way, the enchanted and the mundane are stereoscopically equal and present in Jünger's optics.

3. FORM: *DÉSINVOLTURE*

A key term Jünger borrowed from the French was *"désinvolture,"* the casual and innocent observation of actuality from a distance, which embraces the Heraclitian flux, the "innocence of becoming" of all things that come in and out of existence, beyond good and evil.[60] In the harsh environment of the two wars, the applied method enabled Jünger to keep an emotional distance from the horrors he experi-enced and translate them into objective descriptions.

For Jünger there is no single mode of consciousness but rather multiple layers of experience, which must be uncovered below the Veil of Maya, the surface illu-sions of reality. For that reason, he was fascinated by hallucinatory substances. In the war journals, he refers to the effects of ether in an essay by de Maupassant on 17 September 1942 and to the *Veil of Maya* on 2 October 1942. In the 1920s, Jünger had an intense interest in hallucinogenic drugs, magic, and the supernatural.[61] In the early 1950s, Jünger would experiment under medical supervision with LSD with Albert Hoffman, its inventor. He dedicated an entire book, *Annäherungen: Drogen und Rausch* (*Encounters: Drugs and Intoxication*) to the subject, which was published in 1970.

REENCHANTMENT OF THE WORLD

In 1995 on Jünger's hundredth birthday, his friends contributed to a collection of essays under the title *The Magic of Serenity*.[62] For the editors, Jünger's work was so valuable because it demonstrated that "one can only understand one's own time when one is not captivated by it" (*wenn man sich ihr nicht ausliefert*).[63] Both Jünger's many admirers and his equally numerous critics recognize this attribute. For the former, Jünger's distance to the events of his time and his familiarity with the occult traditions of occidental culture are an admirable antidote to the sicknesses of modernity, resisting ecological destruction, the loss of the sacred, unfettered consumerism, and the triumph of instrumental reason. For the latter, Jünger's ambivalence about modern culture, his cold gaze, renders his Olympian stance suspicious, or worse, reactionary. Both sides in this long simmering feud fail to grasp that Jünger's optics are informed much more by epistemology than politics. Although fully alert to the scientific and technological revolutions around him, Jünger's aesthetic sensitivities were self-consciously old-fashioned—with the one exception of modern art, which fascinated him and led to friendships with avant-garde artists such as Picasso and Alfred Kubin.[64] One notices immediately when reading the war journals that the predominant books Jünger collected and read were published before his own era. He sought to rehabilitate an older version of science, organic and holistic, without jettisoning the value of scientific rigor.

In sum, Jünger was concerned with reversing Max Weber's diagnosis of modernity as an iron cage, and he attempted to open doors for a reenchantment of the world, seeing, writing, and relating to reality in a way that supersedes the "modern." Not unlike Heidegger and Nietzsche, who pined for the pre-Socratics, Jünger sought to recover the supposed epistemological primordial relationship to being as "awe," which was closed off with the advent of abstract-rational thinking. Like another Nietzschean, Michel Foucault, who foresaw the eclipse of the modern episteme and the consequent "death of man," Jünger conceived of modernity as a passing epoch, a cognitive horizon bound, one day, to yield to a return of new mythologies. The word "antimodern" fails to describe his fundamental project. An "alternate" or transcended modernity, in contrast to the flabby phrase "postmodernity," better hits the mark.[65]

After 1945, Jünger would explore the posthistorical mood of a dissolved occident, that old Enlightened Europe that reached a zenith of development just as it destroyed itself in the process. If every document of civilization is at the same time a document of barbarism, as Walter Benjamin famously observed, then the World War II chronicles of Ernst Jünger are surely one of the brightest and most enduring testaments to that Janus-faced history.

TRANSLATORS' PREFACE

English-speaking readers who seek access to Ernst Jünger's works have a long tradition of translations to explore. Over a dozen of his titles have appeared in English since 1929. *In Stahlgewittern* (*Storm of Steel*), his World War I memoir and probably his most famous book, has been translated twice into English and received serious attention from readers and critics alike. Four of Jünger's six World War II journals, on the other hand, are presented here in English in their entirety for the first time. These texts first appeared in German in 1949 collected under the title *Strahlungen*, which is roughly equivalent to the English for "rays," "beams," (of light), "radiations," or "emanations."

In his original preface Jünger explains the concept behind this title as the combination of themes that radiate across historical events to illuminate the mind of the observer like waves of light and dark patterns fluctuating with the extremes of existence. To the dark sphere belong the horrors of war and destruction; the realm of light encompasses moments of love, family, nature, and art to uplift and guide us. Jünger imagined his journals capturing such emanations and reflecting them back to the reader. He conceived of this interplay as a decidedly moral—not to say metaphysical—dynamic that epitomizes the function of art, which conveys a lesson couched in words and parables that challenge the reader to fathom through careful, disciplined reading. Indeed, for Jünger this reading process represents an almost sacred duty. In the tradition of the romantic poet, he endows his texts with spiritual value and his literary mission with the promise of salvation: whosoever shall read these words and experience excitement of the will or of the emotions, shall be granted insight into the core of the message.

The personal reflections in these four journals are based on the definitive German edition of Jünger's works and cover the period when he joins the staff at military headquarters in Paris in February 1941 at the rank of captain, and continue through the events when he and his family endure Allied bombing raids on their village beginning in 1944. Finally, he records the effect of witnessing American tank divisions roll through his damaged town on their eastward course in the spring of 1945.

Ernst Jünger's journals are remarkable for several reasons, but chiefly because he was an articulate observer of life and nature whose diaries record three historical areas of experience. The first of these is at the personal and cultural core of the two separate Paris journals, which detail his interaction with the French people, particularly writers, artists, and other figures who attached themselves to the German cause during the occupation. Those entries document his genuine Francophile excitement at the beauties and secrets of the city as well as his lightly disguised romantic affairs during this tour of duty. We also watch him interacting with his comrades, other officers who are carrying out their administrative duties and frequently discussing political opinions with him. Such material is, in fact, most revealing when it places him on the fringe of the group of Wehrmacht conspirators plotting to assassinate Hitler on July 20, 1944, a group he may have inspired but declined to join.

The second area of historical importance comprises first-hand experiences from Jünger's interlude on the eastern front. His brief tour of duty covered in *Notes from the Caucasus* describes a risky posting in hostile, mountainous territory at the moment when German forces are beginning their retreat in the face of the Russian victory at Stalingrad. Here he witnesses the chaos and horror of a routed army and the suffering of its soldiers, though he is also always completely candid about the torment perpetrated by his own compatriots.

The third area of historical and human interest covered in these journals records what it was like to experience the allied bombings of German cities, particularly of Hannover and its outlying villages. He had spent his childhood in Hannover and in 1939 moved back to the region, settling in the village of Kirchhorst, fifteen kilometers to the northeast of the city. He had witnessed aerial bombing raids on Paris from the spring of 1943 onwards, but always from a safe distance. After the German retreat from Paris, he reaches Kirchhorst in September 1944 where he is no longer the detached observer enjoying a position of power and capable of finding appealing traces of grandeur in carnage. Rather, he is a reduced to the role of threatened civilian struggling to protect his family and several refugees as they prepare for the inevitable capitulation.

In addition to documenting topical events, Jünger's journals also record the inner life of the man. He was a voracious reader, a prolific writer, a passionate entomologist, and a thinker given to mystical speculation who also suffered occasionally from depression. As a result, these journals are filled with notes on reading that record his subjective responses to French, Russian, English, and American writers, both classical and contemporary. They chronicle his musings and his intellectual growth—and closely related—his avid book collecting activity among the antiquarian booksellers of Paris. As he reads, he frequently takes issue with the thought processes of the writers who fascinate him. These often stimulate his personal brand of mysticism regarding the nature of the cosmos and the relationship of man to God. After finishing his first reading of the Bible, he begins again, this time consulting scholarly commentary to explicate the texts. These traditions reinforce his own piety and encourage mystical and mythically tinged speculation about history, linguistics, and science. In fact, this restless and deeply irrational aspect of Jünger's mind conflicts with his scientific training to the extent that piety ultimately motivates a skeptical rejection of Darwin that sounds quaint today.

Science, however, is always central to Jünger's activity and world view. In 1923 he began to study zoology and philosophy in Leipzig, and although he abandoned his studies to concentrate on writing, his life-long passion for insects—especially collecting beetles—never waned. These journals detail how his curiosity about nature provides both a respite from human company and a glimpse of creation in a microcosm. Jünger's aesthetic appreciation of nature—for example, the exhilaration he finds in the rich iridescence of a dung beetle's carapace—is essentially the same reflexive aesthetic he records at the sight of a bomber squadron at sunset. His next stage of reflective thought, however, quickly juxtaposes the first impression with the reality of mechanized death.

The literary style of these journals—particularly of this translation—requires a few remarks. Readers of Jünger sometimes become impatient when they perceive a putative coldness, apparent distance, or lack of emotional engagement with people and events. This objective detachment in his style correlates with the principles of the man himself. The cool, sometime impersonal tone of many journal entries are devices to maintain the rhetorical defenses of a military man trained to endure hardship with stoic discipline and respond to the world with strict categories. Such training can color many facets of life, not just those moments that demand endurance. Jünger's laconic notations may strike some readers as callous in situations when sentiment might seem more fitting. Yet Jünger preferred not to commit too much sentiment to his journal, which he conceived as a manuscript for public consumption and not as a therapeutic exercise. We hear in his style the attempt to maintain an authoritative literary voice that is personal and dynamic but seldom genuinely confessional. This deliberate pose can be corroborated in another work, specifically by tracing the stylistic redactions Jünger made over the course of the several editions of *Storm of Steel*, his World War I narrative. He drastically edited the style of that memoir by toning down or removing indications of his youthful, subjective voice. Something similar happens to the compositional process of these wartime journals. He states candidly that he does not necessarily consider the first draft of any memoir to be the most authentic and admits that he has edited, expanded, and redacted this material over time.

One stylistic trait that helps to create Jünger's remote narrative voice is his frequent use in German of the impersonal pronoun *man*. English can translate this as "one," e.g., "One can see from the example. . . ." Jünger's style thus often has a generalized impartiality that could be avoided by using the first-person pronouns I or we (which he used less frequently). An English translation that respects this feature in every case produces a stilted, awkward manner alien to English readers. As a result, we have adopted the tendency followed by other English translators of Jünger and in places chosen more colloquial English pronouns in order to create an idiomatic and readable English text appropriate to journal writing. To be sure, this may at times produce expressions like "You can see this when you examine. . . ." instead of "One can see this when one examines. . . ." Similarly: "I feel a sense of disbelief," rather than, "One feels a sense of disbelief."

Counter examples abound in these journals that contradict the charge of emotional detachment. Passages show the writer—the man—expressing deep filial piety, familial devotion, love and affection toward women, delight in nature, pervasive melancholy, despair at the destruction of his culture by war, empathy for victims, or outrage at the cruelty perpetrated by the National Socialist regime. Especially moving are those journal entries during the weeks made after the death of his son, Ernstel, who is killed in action in November 1944.

Many of Jünger's conventions are familiar from journal-writing style. For example, he omits pronouns to produce a shorthand entry like, "Was in the city yesterday." Furthermore, his entries frequently do not separate the world of real experience from that of dreams. His dream journal is thus sometimes integrated into the narrative of the day and given the same weight as the account of waking activity, with the result that a paragraph about familiar routines might shift without warning to a setting of classical ruins teeming with snakes.

The journals use distinctly different levels of style for different subject matter. Jünger's appreciation of natural beauty can border on the lyrical, while descriptions of military or daily routines can have the crisp concision of objective reportage. When he speculates on mystical themes, however, his vocabulary frequently uses neologisms—or employs familiar vocabulary in personal and metaphorical ways—to create allusions to arcane or imagined reality. Furthermore, his command of French often permeates his native German and introduces concepts that depart from traditional German vocabulary. This translation renders idiosyncratic inventions with more familiar terms to enhance clarity.

Occasional footnotes have been added to explain particular historical references or unfamiliar linguistic features. The index of personal names (as well as nicknames and pseudonyms) will be helpful in establishing identities of persons mentioned. Brief explanations of possibly obscure concepts, foreign words and phrases, as well as translations are inserted in brackets in the text. Dates of historical events may also be included if they clarify the context. All material within square brackets is the work of the translators, not the author.

We wish to express our gratitude to Ms. Jennifer Crewe of Columbia University Press for her perseverance in undertaking this ambitious project, as well as to professors Barry Lydgate, Randall Colaizzi, and Jens Kruse for their advice on aspects of French, Latin, and German passages respectively.

Mr. Tobias Wimbauer of Hagen, Germany, whose knowledge and appreciation of Ernst Jünger and his works is as deep as it is wide, deserves special mention for his support and suggestions. He helped clarify many a puzzle.

Thomas S. Hansen and Abby J. Hansen
Wellesley, Massachusetts
December 2017

A GERMAN OFFICER
IN OCCUPIED PARIS

1

FIRST PARIS JOURNAL

1941

SARS-POTERIES, 18 FEBRUARY 1941

Arrived before dawn at the railroad freight yard in Avesnes, where I was jolted out of a deep sleep. This made me aware of a beautiful dream: I was both a child and a grown man traveling along my old route to school from Wunstorf to Rehburg, a trip we always took by narrow-gauge railroad. I got out in Winzlar and followed the tracks on foot. It was night, for in the area around my father's house I could see shots being fired, high and bright, through the darkness. But at the same time, it was also day, and to my left the fields were bathed in sunshine. One of them was covered with green seedlings, and I could see my mother waiting there, a magnificent young woman. I sat down beside her, and when I got tired, she picked up the edge of the field like a green blanket and pulled it over us.

The dream image made me very happy and warmed me for a long time afterward while I stood on the cold loading ramp and supervised the work.

March to Sars-Poteries; billeted there. I was assigned to two old ladies. One was eighty-two years old and had already seen three wars. I was able to contribute a bit of sausage to their evening meal, but it was still little better than meager. It consisted essentially of three large potatoes that had stood on the stovetop under a clay dome. This little device was called an *étouffoir*, probably because the food inside is steamed by closing off its air supply.

Sars-Poteries, 20 February 1941

Strolled near the railroad station. In the ceramics factory, I inquired about the source of the clay that gave the town its reputation. A little beyond the tracks, I reached the pits and saw that these had been excavated from the lovely brown and white sand. I did not discover any of the fossils I was hoping to find. At the bottom of one old abandoned excavation, there were puddles that must occasionally flood with water. There I came upon willows growing at the bottom of one of the pits, taller than a man and covered with tiny, hairy roots. These sprouted like moss from the trunk and branches—a nice example demonstrating that each individual part of a plant can reproduce others. The whole organism is suffused with concentrated powers of generation. We humans have lost this art, and once our cultures display leaves and blossoms, we will never again see roots. Yet, when danger mounts in moments of sacrifice, we send out different, more spiritual organs, aerial roots, into the void—naturally at the expense of individual lives. All of us benefit from this new growth.

As I walked back, a storm of heavy wet snow dappled the landscape. Yet in the gardens, I could still see hazel and laurel blossoms covering the bare branches like swollen lilac blooms. In protected places, I noticed clusters of snowdrops. These seemed quite early, especially after the harsh winter. Here they are called *fleurs de Saint Joseph* [Saint Joseph's flowers], whose day is celebrated on 19 March.

Sars-Poteries, 21 February 1941

During my early morning sleep, I was in a little pharmacy where I was buying various things. Then Rehm woke me up. Before my eyes were open, I briefly noticed a paper bag labeled Braunschweiger Rubber Cement. It is always strange how we focus on such details.

Currently reading *Reine* [Queen] by Julius [*recte* Jules] Lermina, a book lent to me by the lady who owns my living quarters; it rather amusingly describes the factionalism around 1815 in the style of *The Three Musketeers*. Here you come across passages like the following that surpass the quality of the popular novel: "There is something childlike to be found in every conspirator." I can confirm that judgment from personal experience.

Sars-Poteries, 22 February 1941

Dozed in the early morning hours and pondered exotic books like *Die Geheimnisse des Roten Meeres* [*The Secrets of the Red Sea*] by Henry de Monfreid. The work is bathed in the gleam of coral and mother of pearl and the delicate breath of the sea. Also pondered Mirbeau's *Le Jardin des Supplices* [*The Garden of Torments*]. This garden, with its paths paved in red brick dust, is filled with green vegetation and great masses of blazing peonies. It draws its luxuriance from the countless corpses of coolies who created it under conditions of murderous toil and have moldered anonymously in its depths. This book deserves praise for clearly delineating the beauty and savagery of the world—as the two forces whose combination and interplay remind us of sea monsters. Veiled in iridescence, these camouflage the terrifying dangers of their weaponry with alluring hues. In such intense coalescing of hells and heavens, the eye cannot differentiate the details of desire and suffering any more than it can the tangled chaos of a jungle island. Here our planet reveals a most incredible drama to our spirit.

Then about Wagner, who appeared to me in a new, more meaningful light for our age. I thought I spotted the error of Baudelaire, who possessed an authentic relationship to the ancient, eternal verities. Thoughts about the mighty mind of the dramatist who breathes artificial breath into past ages and dead cultures so that they move like corpses we can quote. A sorcerer of the highest order who conjures with real blood at the gates of the underworld.[1]

Things assume colors that make it hard for even the sharpest eye to distinguish truth from illusion. The actor steps into reality, becomes a historical person, achieves triumphs, garners laurels as green as real ones. What good does it do to contradict or debate with him? He has arrived because his time has come. In this alone lies his guilt, which runs deeper than any guilt based on individual action. Art as a hothouse of past ages—it is like a promenade through winter gardens or salons where palm trees bloom. It is hard to take issue with this, for the terrors of destruction are so great, so horrifying, that the will to rescue a single shade is all too understandable. Nietzsche presents a contrast that stands and falls in wintery tempests. These are the exemplars that our youth, like Heracles, beheld at the crossroads.

The case of Nietzsche *contra* Wagner[2] reminds me of those little toy houses we used to have with their different figures that would emerge depending on the weather conditions. One little figure would stand outside and forecast the weather, prophetically correct but out of step with the moment. The other showed the prevailing climate conditions, whether or not signs of a downturn could be sensed. For that reason, this figure waits in safety, away from the bright light. And yet they both were attached to one and the same little strip of wood fashioned by the carver of the little weather house.

SAINT-MICHEL, 24 FEBRUARY 1941

Departed from Sars-Poteries, in particular from my eighty-two-year-old maiden lady, whom I thanked before dawn while she was still in bed. Then marched to new quarters near Saint-Michel, at first in a light frost and then through damp snow. The numerous destroyed or abandoned houses make the town a forbidding place. A tank juts out of the little river that flows through it. Myths are already being created: people say the driver plunged off the bridge to deprive the Germans of their prize. Wherever the inhabitants have moved back again, they have attached strips of white linen to the doors of their houses to signal their presence. They give an impression of being poorer and more famished than the people of Sars-Poteries. Swarms of children with bare legs frozen blue huddle at the field kitchens. Rats can be heard scampering in the houses; cats stare from the empty windows.

I am living with Rehm in the house of a landlady whose husband is a prisoner of war in Germany. She is probably around forty but is still attractive, lively, and hospitable and likes to talk about her husband, whom she provides for diligently. Still, I'd like to think of her as available; she is filled with high spirits stimulated by fresh and vibrant experiences. Such things often dwell in one and the same heart, for the moral world cannot be called to account or dissected as neatly as the physical world. By the same token, most men do not behave like Othello (something I never understood before) but know how to forgive, especially in long-lasting marriages.

Saint-Michel, 27 February 1941

Vivid dream images, as usual, in the early morning hours. I was taking part in a meeting where people were amusing themselves by imitating dead or forgotten politicians. They were improvising in the spirit of the moment. Here and there someone in the company would rise from his seat and provoke hilarity with his histrionic gestures. I saw a large stout man pretending to be Bismarck; he enjoyed loud applause. It occurred to me that many a subtle gesture elicited much surprise and laughter, but only among a few people. I concluded from this that the people here were my contemporaries, probably my colleagues. But the survivors of small forgotten cliques could be seen wildly applauding figures whose humor was lost upon anyone but them.

The group gave the superficial impression of being high-level civil servants or retired generals, types known from anecdotes and lost personal accounts that show them carousing in their clubs. There was an undercurrent with a different tone, this time concerning the drama of human history, but one devoid of bitterness, producing mirth instead. It was suffused with a trace of childlike innocence, like the kind that comes as no surprise in dignified old retired gentlemen. Also a little bit of *plaudite, amici* [Give me your applause, friends], if we take the meaning in an ironic or self-deprecating sense.

Saint-Michel, 1 March 1941

Significant warming over the past two days. At first accompanied by showers, then by sunshine. The snow disappeared in no time with the warm breeze. Water levels rose, and the trees gleamed in the play of color that marks early spring.

As for animals: I saw large *Timarcha* beetles [bloody-nosed leaf beetles] crawling on the hard earth yesterday in the rain; noticed especially how the male of the species showed very broad tarses [leg joints]. I imagine that this chrysomelid [member of leaf beetle family *Chrysomelidae*] is related to the early onset of warmer days. When I was a young boy, I noticed this as one of the first signs of life in the bare quarries near Rehburg as it glistened blue in the February or March sun. In Algeria and Morocco, I saw them in their large forms as early as December, and their appearance always correlated with a certain mood of melancholy that overcomes me during this period of the year and then disappears when the trees turn green.

Then as I was riding my bicycle along the road to Hirson, I brushed past a salamander—a female recognizable by the greatly enlarged *mons veneris* [mound of Venus] visible at this time of year. Its gentle swelling terminates in the brown-spotted abdomen tinged with a faint red pigmentation. I carried the little lady, who twisted gently in my fingers, to a damp meadow—thereby saving her life. How many times has the sight of such creatures filled me with new strength, like a source of life?

SAINT-MICHEL, 7 MARCH 1941

Yesterday Rehm and I called on Madame Richardet's aunt, who had invited me for a meal. We talked about being thunderstruck—that *coup de foudre* [love at first sight]—as a form of love to be avoided.

Field maneuvers in the morning in the vicinity of Ferme La Butte; during these, I meditated on the theme of worlds—for example, reflections of human relationships in other dimensions—to visualize them better. One might think of polished spheres—such as cloudy opals or rock crystals—that reflect the drama more minutely, intensely, and deeply. It could all play out in a large house that can be explored from cellar to attic.

SAINT-MICHEL, 27 MARCH 1941

In Charleville, I was a witness at a military tribunal. I used the opportunity to buy books, like novels by Gide and various works by Rimbaud, who was born here and—as I was told by the bookseller—where a small circle of poets preserves his memory. On the return trip I read a beautiful passage about the kaleidoscope in *Si le grain ne meurt* [*If It Die*, 1924].

PARIS, 6 APRIL 1941

Saturday and Sunday in Paris. Spent the evenings in the company of Lieutenant Colonel Andois in the Rôtisserie de la Reine Pédauque near the Saint-Lazare railroad station and, after that, in Tabarin. There, saw a floorshow of naked women before an audience of officers and bureaucrats of the occupying army seated in the front rows. They fired off a volley of champagne corks. The women's bodies were well proportioned except for their feet, which had been deformed by their shoes. Perhaps a further thought: the foot as a kind of degraded hand. Performances like this are geared to the mechanism of the sex drive—the point is inescapable, although it is always one and the same. The rooster-like quality of the Gallic race was powerfully evident. *Les poules* [the sluts].

Then went to Monte Cristo, an establishment where patrons luxuriate on low cushions. Silver chalices, fruit bowls, and bottles glinted in the twilight as in an Orthodox chapel. Companionship provided by young girls, almost all of them born in France to Russian emigrés. They chattered away in several languages. I sat beside a small, melancholy twenty-year-old and, through the champagne haze, carried on conversations about Pushkin, Aksakov, and Andreyev, whose son [Daniel] had been a friend of hers.

Today, Sunday, uninterrupted rainfall. I went to the Madeleine twice; its steps were covered with fallen beech leaves. Was at Prunier at noon and in the evening. The city is like an old familiar garden that now lies desolate but where paths and passageways are still recognizable. Its state of preservation is remarkable, almost Hellenistic; clearly, special ploys of the High Command are at work. It is alienating to see the white signs on the signposts that the troops have placed throughout the city—gashes in an ancient, organic stand of timber.

SAINT-MICHEL, 12 APRIL 1941

New plans, new resolutions: "It is not yet too late." During the night a beautiful woman appeared to me. She kissed me many times gently on my eyes, which I kept shut. Afterward, I went to a horrible place, where the door that I opened was bound with barbed wire. An ugly old woman was singing vulgar songs. When she turned her back on me, she lifted her skirts.

On the previous night, it was a journey to Tibet. The houses, rooms, and furniture didn't seem to be original anymore. An influence of foreign forms was already discernible, yet the change was slight. I walked through the houses without noting the inhabitants, yet I felt their presence in rooms I did not enter. The dream was malevolent in that I was an invisible, demonic being. Czarist officers appeared as adversaries. *We* saw and recognized each other from a distance—there was a hierarchy of visibility.

SAINT-MICHEL, 13 APRIL 1941

Easter Day stroll. The brown fields, as yet unplowed, seem bare, but in some places, they are blanketed with delicate low-growing nettle blossoms—almost invisible, approaching ultraviolet—where bumblebees forage as if on a tissue of dreams.

The narrow, deeply rutted woodland paths. Even these possess northern and southern slopes where the different plant species grow at different rates.

PARIS, 24 APRIL 1941

Got up early for transport to Paris. The regiment has been ordered there for guard duty.

The reveille sounded during one of those dreams that are like living tableaux, posed groups full of tension. In them, the dreamer savors a first-rate insight, for he soon sinks into them, into the hopes and suffering of the figures; soon he emerges from their constituent parts and sees them integrated into one static image. Thus, the complexity of the content and the poverty of movement contradict each other; the actions remain under the spell of the meaning, and this repression unleashes a feeling of dizziness that often becomes a nightmare.

In this state, I saw José with the high-ranking doctor and his wife, along with me and four orderlies in a room where the furniture reminded me of a hospital. José was suffering from rabies and had sunk his teeth into the doctor's wife's neck to infect her, and without a doubt, he had succeeded. I saw his victim, who was being held down on a hospital bed by two orderlies and also saw the wounds from the bite; a slight film of pus was already forming on their red edges. The high-ranking doctor was about to give her an injection because she was nearly mad. As he tested the solution in the hypodermic, his glance fell upon José—serious, pained, yet in complete control of his passion. José was also being forcibly sub-dued by two orderlies, half in the twilight state that follows an attack and half in triumph because his assault had succeeded. I had both hands around his powerful neck, stroking him the way one pats a horse's flanks. Yet at the same time, had he tried to escape, I could have choked him. The little room where we were suffering was so full of radiation that I comprehended his inner being like the text of a book. The remarkable thing about the attack was that after all the years of secret infidel-ity, José now wanted to unite with the high-ranking doctor's wife in death. And in the husband's eyes, I read that he completely understood the gravity of the deed. Although he felt he had been bitten by a viper, he remained conscious and main-tained his medical objectivity. In this context, José's vicious action was a sign of illness, a symptom of fury. The will to heal was the appropriate response. It struck me as great and wonderful that this master controlled himself calmly in the face of such an onslaught of passion.

And yet during this struggle, I felt myself on José's side; I patted his broad neck as I would that of a good horse that I might watch streak across the finish line in a storm. I felt that his moral sense was still intact. Nonetheless, he seemed to be like one of those ancient chieftains who took everything of value—gold, weapons, slaves, and women—when they crossed into the realm of death. This body was already inhabited by death, but I sensed in it the immense power of life.

Once again, I was the observer of the image as a whole, constructed by my mind in contemplation out of sense and nonsense like a pattern in the wallpaper.

Departure from Saint-Michel; perhaps, we may eventually return to this place. The gentle willows will stay in my memory along with their hawthorn hedges, whose still-leafless thickets shelter green globes of mistletoe and dark magpies' nests. The celandine and violets were already blooming among the dead leaves, and nettle shoots were beginning to sprout. This is an undulating landscape; here and there it conceals large farms with stables and barns. The shiny slate roofs reflect like mirrors from its valleys. My thoughts upon gazing at these farmsteads: the age of magic has past, yet we still possess the keys to bring it to life. But then there are stages when man loses the memory of goodness and truth. There he does not recognize the sources of his unhappiness.

In Laon by midday. We drove around the lower portion of the old city. It was with a sense of joy that I saw the cathedral again. From the distance, the perforated spires make an especially powerful impression. I imagine it is possible to grasp the internal structure of the work, the pillars and shafts of the shell, the intellectual aspect of the whole plan. It presents a wealth of kaleidoscopic variations to the eyes of those who drive past, as if the building were turning gently on its axis to the sound of a music box.

We reached Paris very late and then marched through dark and desolate streets to Fort Vincennes, where the troops will be billeted. After a walk through the quarters in the early morning hours, I took a room in the Hotel Moderne at the Porte de Vincennes. In the early light, a glimpse of the huge pillars on the Place de la Nation. Behind it, in the distance, a hazy view of the Eiffel Tower. Monumental traits become ever more exaggerated when they appear *en masse*.

VINCENNES, 27 APRIL 1941

First Sunday in Paris. In the meantime, I have moved to an apartment that provides a lovely view of the Donjon des Forts. Powerful feeling of melancholy. Afternoon, to the zoo in Vincennes. Giraffes were eating dried acacia leaves from a high trough, picking them out with their long, pointed tongues. Black bears, a pride of cheetahs, Alpine rams from Corsica posing on the crags of a mighty cliff. The stupendous aspect of these pageants: they speak, but we no longer understand their divine nature.

VINCENNES, 28 APRIL 1941

Stroll through the streets and alleys of Vincennes. Details: a man with a slender sickle mowing the grass of a railroad embankment next to a busy street and stuffing the clippings into a sack, probably collecting fodder for rabbits. In his other hand, he held a small basket to collect little snails that fell out of the grass as he worked. In the outskirts of the big cities, scenes of Chinese frugality are often evident—they bring to mind the grasses and herbs that grow in the crevices of a wall.

VINCENNES, 29 APRIL 1941

Hôtel de Ville and Quais de la Seine;[3] took stock of expenditures. *Tristitia* [melancholy]. Looked for solutions; only doubtful ones presented themselves. The monsters of Nôtre-Dame are more brutish than those of Laon. These incarnations stare so knowingly out over the roofs of the cosmopolitan city, surveying realms of lost knowledge—the knowledge, yes, but its existence as well?

At Prunier, Rue Duphot. The little room on the first floor is cool and cheerful, with its aquamarine atmosphere, very inviting for the enjoyment of seafood. The round church very nearby; a fig tree flourishes at its wall. Then the Madeleine—a church despite everything. Boulevard des Capucines. The *Blitzmädchen*[4] whom I had noticed the day before yesterday on the Place de l'Étoile,[5] a tall West Slavic type with long wavy hair. The strange feeling when we begin to notice and pay attention to each other. It is we who beget relationships; a new human being is like a seed that originates deep inside us. An alien image inhabits us; it is like a small wound, a gentle pain when it marks us. How well women know this phenomenon; it always intensifies when the encounter is repeated.

Telephoned Schlumberger. But like almost all my earlier acquaintances, he is not staying in Paris. When I looked for an escape route between the Pont Neuf and the Pont des Arts, it became clear to me that the labyrinthine nature of our position resides only inside us. This makes the use of force destructive; that would demolish walls, chambers in ourselves—that is not the path to freedom. The hours regulate themselves from the inner mechanism of the clock. When we move the hand, we change the numbers but not the course of fate. No matter where we desert to, we carry the full military kit with us, inborn. Even in suicide, we cannot escape ourselves. We must ascend, sometimes by suffering; then the world becomes more comprehensible.

Vincennes, 1 May 1941

Sacré Coeur. Chevalier de la Barre was gruesomely executed at a very early age for not showing proper respect during a procession. I recently read his story in Voltaire. A statue of him at the martyr's stake stands in the consecrated area of the church as an altar to Freemasonry. The choice of the space lends the monument a dialectical flavor and disrupts commiseration with the fate of the unfortunate man. We raise our finger in warning as we leave him.

Then Place des Ternes. I bought a small bouquet of lilies of the valley in celebration of the day. These were probably responsible for my encounter with Renée, a young office clerk in a department store. The city effortlessly produces such couplings, but then one can't help notice that it was founded on the altar of Venus. It's in the water and in the air. I now sense that more clearly than when I lived here for the first year and a half of the war isolated in barracks and garrisons and billeted on farms. In long periods of asceticism when we tame our thoughts, we get a foretaste of the wisdom of old age, of serenity.

Ate, then went to the cinema; there I touched her breast. A hot iceberg, a hill in the spring, filled with myriad seeds of life, perhaps something like white anemones. During the newsreel, the room remained illuminated to prevent any demonstrations. Our offensives in Africa, Serbia, and Greece were shown. The mere glimpse of the weapons of annihilation produced screams of fear. Their automated nature, the way the steel plates of the tanks glide, the way the ammunition belts with their bright projectiles are swallowed as they fire. The rings, hinges, armor, observation slits, sections of the tank, the arsenal of life-forms that harden like crustaceans, toads, crocodiles, and insects—Hieronymus Bosch had already envisioned them.

Subject for study: the ways propaganda turns into terror. The beginnings in particular contained much that people are going to forget. That is when power walks on cats' paws, subtle and cunning.

We said goodbye at the opera, probably never to meet again.

Vincennes, 3 May 1941

In the sunshine in front of Brasserie Lorraine on the Place des Ternes. These are the moments when I can breathe, like a drowning man. Opposite me a girl in red and blue who combines absolute beauty with an icy manner—a pattern of frost crystals. Whoever thaws her, destroys the form.

When I turn off the light I am gladdened by the thought that I shall now be alone for eight, nine hours. I seek solitude as my cave. I also like waking up now and then to enjoy it.

Vincennes, 7 May 1941

On the Place des Ternes in front of the Brasserie again—a pleasant spot I find so appealing. I usually sit here in the sun drinking a cup of tea and enjoying some paper-thin sandwiches—almost wafers, which I dedicate to the memory of past abundance. Then, across the Champs-Élysées to Rue Duphot. I always enjoy seeing the fig tree at its entrance in front of the small church.

The cliffs of porphyry. Even plants and animals have to differentiate themselves from everything else on the earth.

Vincennes, 10 May 1941

Jardin des Plantes. A jujube tree in full bloom. Some of the blossoms sprang directly from the trunk, so that they gleamed from afar in like coral branches or clumps of pink bees.

Large black or amber-colored cats can be seen napping in the shop windows. Then the Paulownia [princess tree; foxglove tree] trees, still without leaves, blooming in the *allées* or in large groups on the squares. Their delicate violet veils cast a spell over the silver-gray stone. Amethysts on elephant hide.

Vincennes, 11 May 1941

I drove to the Place des Ternes as usual. At the Bastille, I was overcome by the desire to get out. I found myself in a crowd of thousands, the only one in uniform, not to mention that it was the Feast of Joan of Arc. Still, I took a certain pleasure in walking around and meditating, the way one would walk through a powder magazine, dreaming while holding a burning candle. I later discovered that there had been a few disturbances at the Place de la Concorde.

Vincennes, 12 May 1941

They placed us barefoot around a bright fire and moved us close to it so we could see the skin first reddening, then becoming like parchment, and then cracking open. Then they scourged them with whips. Bundles of vipers were attached to the handles instead of cords. They sank their teeth into the raw flesh, and I experienced the bites as relief when compared with the pain of the fire.

On what slave ships do such images occur to us?

Vincennes, 17 May 1941

In the night I lay anxious in the dark for a long time, counting the seconds and then counting them again. Then came a horrible morning in the barracks yard of Vincennes. I was like someone who is very thirsty: during a break, I slaked my thirst with the foamy freshness of white blossom clusters up against the fortress wall. When I see the blossoms spreading out so peacefully in the sunlight, their serenity seems infinitely deep. I feel that they speak to me in words and sentences that are sweet and comforting, and I am always seized with pain because no sound from any of them can penetrate my ears. We are summoned, but we do not know where to.

At midday the colonel arrived with Captain Höll, who will be staying here for a while and is supposed to paint a portrait of me. I was with him in the evening in the area around the Madeleine and bought gifts for Perpetua.[6] In the shop of a Negro; conversations about cola nuts and white rum. It was a strange afternoon and confirmed my opinion that it is *we* who control experience; the world provides us with the means. We are endowed with a certain kind of power that activates the appropriate objects. Thus, if we are males, women will appear. Or, when we are children, presents are showered upon us. And when we are pious—

Paris, 20/21 May 1941

At noon my company took over guard duty in the Hotel Continental. Before that, mounted guard duty on Avenue Wagram. I had my company perform the drill that we had been practicing for a month and then pass the Monument to the Unknown Soldier in parade step. We went by the monument to Clémenceau, who had clearly foreseen these things. I nodded to him, as though to a prophet.

The night was troubled, even turbulent, as more than forty men who had been detained by patrols on the streets or in bars and hotels were brought before me. These were mostly cases of inebriation or soldiers without leave who had been picked up in the little *hôtels de passe* [brothels]. The prostitutes they had been enjoying themselves with were brought along too. After brief interrogations, I entered them all in the large incident log and then had them confined in little cells that had been built on the first floor in great numbers, like bathing cabins. Anyone who had slept with a "companion" was first disinfected. Breakfast was doled out in the morning, and then the whole group was brought to a disciplinary judge in the same building for sentencing. Along with one of the wagonloads that had been picked up on Montmartre, there was a little eighteen-year-old prostitute who stood at attention just like the soldiers. Because this little person was especially cheerful and showed *bon moral* [morale], I had her sit and chat with us in the guardroom. By doing so, I was keeping her like a pet canary in this depressing place.

Vincennes, 24 May 1941

In the morning in the Hotel Continental as an associate justice on a military tribunal. Three cases. The first involved a drunken driver who had knocked over a gas lamppost with his car. A second before, he had "seen something dart across street." Four weeks confinement under close guard. When asked if he had any response to the sentence:

"I am surprised that the sentence is so lenient."

Then a second driver who came to blows with four of his shipmates in a bar and passively resisted arrest: sentenced to forty-three days in military jail. During the cross-examination one of the sailors said, "he rarely sets foot on land," to characterize the sobriety of a crewmate. He also differentiated between strong inebriation, "a big trip," and simple tipsiness, "a little trip."

Finally, a corporal who went berserk in front of the Metro station Jean Jaurès, attacked several pedestrians, and stabbed people with his bayonet until he was arrested by the military patrol. Postponement because several of those involved did not appear, probably out of fear.

In this last case, the perpetrator's fury was evident in the hearing. The proceedings had to be patched together from bits and pieces, leaving a series of gaps. The differences between the testimony of the French witnesses and the translation by the interpreter were informative. The method revealed a person as a sensory organ, receiving and transmitting. This practice shows how much gets changed and lost in the process.

In the evening in the Ritz with Count Podewils, whom I met for the first time today, although I have been corresponding with him and his wife for years. He brought First Lieutenant Grüninger along with him, who reminded me of characters from *Ardinghello*. Höll joined us. Colonel Speidel, chief of the General Staff of the Supreme Military Command, showed up late for a moment.

VINCENNES, 25 MAY 1941

The morning visit. Two friends in silk costumes stand in front of a table made of mother-of-pearl and ivory. They have a folder with colored etchings open in front of them and are viewing the pictures through lorgnettes. The room is colorful, splendid, cheerful. I notice especially the rich intarsia in the table. Yet there's also something unusual about it. When I take a closer look, I discover a woman kneeling beneath it. Her heavy silk dress, delicately powdered face, colorful hat with feathers, blend so perfectly with the furniture that the concealed woman reminds me of one of those butterflies camouflaged to resemble the blossom it perches on. I now become aware of the mood of terror underlying the cheerfulness of the room that streams with morning light, and I realize that this puzzling figure is frozen with fear. The enigmatic nature of the scene was latent in the title: it was not only about the visitor but also about his wife, the female visitor who was all too lovely and all too near.

VINCENNES, 26 MAY 1941

Called on Höll in the afternoon on the fifth story of a house on Rue de Montreuil. There three of us raised several glasses, first to his model, Madeleine, then to a magnificent rainbow over the roofs of Vincennes where it formed a double arch of happiness.

Conversations related to the girl's profession; she was an *entraîneuse*, whose job it was to lead clients to a nightclub. She was no beauty but education, a good background, and clearly also good nature would be superfluous to this job. There was a sick mother to be provided for and other things like that. As usual with types like her, I am moved by the mixture of superficiality and melancholy.

Thus, we navigate toward destruction on ships festooned with garlands. This artificial enhancement that helps to disintegrate these middle-class lives merits closer inspection. In the final analysis, this is the last stage of a more general decline. Money holds one of the supreme secrets. If I place a coin on the table and receive a piece of bread for it, this act reflects not only the order of the state but also the universe. It would be worth researching to what extent numismatics, in the higher sense, gets expressed in the symbols stamped on the coins. My contact with Höll does me good and has pulled me back from the brink of those dangerous thoughts that have engulfed me since the beginning of the year. I reached a low point in February when I refused nourishment for a week and in every sense drew down the capital I had accumulated in the past. My situation is that of a man who dwells in the desert between a demon and a corpse. The demon urges him to action; the corpse, to sympathy. In life it has often been the artistically gifted person who came to my aid during such crises. He distributes the treasures of the world.

PARIS, 29 MAY 1941

To add to the flood of repugnant things that oppress me comes the order to be present at the execution of a soldier sentenced to death for desertion. My first inclination was to report in sick, but that seemed cheap to me. Furthermore, I thought to myself: maybe it is better that *you* are present rather than someone else. And in truth, I was able to accomplish many things much more humanely than could have been expected.

Basically, it was exaggerated curiosity that was the deciding factor. I have seen many people die, but never at a predetermined moment. How will the situation present itself that today threatens every one of us and spreads and spreads its shadow over his existence? And how should we act in this situation?

Therefore, I looked at the records that culminated in his sentencing. The matter concerns a corporal who left his unit nine months ago to disappear into the city where a French woman gave him shelter. He moved around, sometimes in civilian clothing and sometimes in the uniform of a naval officer as he went about his affairs. It seems that he felt a false sense of security and not only made his lover jealous but also beat her. She took her revenge by reporting him to the police, who turned him in to the German authorities.

Yesterday after this, I accompanied the judge to a little spot in the forest near Robinson, the appointed location. In a clearing, an ash tree, its trunk splintered by previous executions. Two groups of bullet holes are visible—a higher one for the head and a lower one for shots to the heart. In among the delicate filaments of the exploded fibers of the tree's heartwood layer, some dark blowflies are resting. They objectify the feeling that I brought with me to this spot: no place of execution can be sufficiently sanitized to efface all vestiges of the knacker's yard.[7]

We drove a long distance today to reach this spot in the forest. The staff doctor and a first lieutenant who was in command were in the car. During the journey, conversations had a particular quality of closeness and intimacy characterized by things like "imagine being in a fix like this."

In the clearing we meet the detail. We form a sort of corridor of two rows in front of the ash tree. The sun is shining after the rain that fell on our way here; drops of water glisten on the green grass. We wait a while until shortly before five o'clock. Then a car pulls up the narrow forest road. We watch the condemned man get out, followed by two prison guards and the clergyman. Behind them a truck appears, driving the burial detail and military issue coffin: "cheapest model, standard size."

The man is led between the two rows; at that moment, I am overcome with a feeling of trepidation, as if it were suddenly difficult to breathe. He is placed before the military judge, who stands beside me: I note that his arms have been secured behind his back with handcuffs. He is wearing gray trousers made of good material, a gray silk shirt, and an open military tunic that has been draped over his shoulders. He stands erect and is well built, and his face bears pleasant features of the sort that attract women.

The sentence is read aloud. The condemned man follows the procedure with the highest degree of attention, and yet I still have the impression that he doesn't understand the text. His eyes are open wide, as though drinking it all in, large, as if his body were suspended from them; he moves his full lips as if he were spelling. His gaze falls on me and stays there for a second on my face with a penetrating, questioning tension. I can tell that the agitation lends him an air of something confused, florid, even childlike.

A tiny fly plays about his left cheek and alights several times close to his ear. He shrugs his shoulders and shakes his head. The reading takes barely a minute, but the time seems extraordinarily long to me. The pendulum becomes long and heavy. Then the guards lead the condemned man to the ash tree; the clergyman accompanies him. Heaviness increases in this moment. There is something staggering about it, as if heavy weights had been lowered. I remember that I am supposed to ask whether he wants a blindfold. The clergyman answers yes for him while the guards tie him to the tree with white ropes. The clergyman softly asks him a few questions; I hear him answer them with *jawohl* [yes sir]. Then he kisses a small silver cross while the doctor pins a piece of red cardboard the size of a playing card onto his shirt over his heart.

In the meantime, the firing squad has followed a signal from the first lieutenant and has taken up their positions standing behind the clergyman, who still blocks the condemned man. He now steps back after running his hand down the prisoner's side once more. The commands follow, and with them I again awaken into consciousness. I want to look away, but I force myself to watch. I catch the moment when the salvo produces five little dark holes in the cardboard, as though drops of dew had landed upon it. Their target is still standing against the tree; his expression shows extraordinary surprise. I see his mouth opening and closing as if he wanted to form vowels and express something with great effort. This situation has something confusing about it, and again time seems attenuated. It also seems that the man is now becoming menacing. Finally, his knees give out. The ropes are loosened and now at last the pallor of death quickly comes over his face, as if a bucket of whitewash had been poured over it. The doctor rushes up and reports, "The man is dead." One of the two guards unlocks the handcuffs and wipes the glistening metal clean of blood with a cloth. The corpse is placed in the coffin. It looks as if the little fly were playing around him in a beam of sunlight.

Return trip in a new, more powerful state of depression. The staff doctor explains to me that the gestures of the dying are only empty reflexes. He did not see what was most gruesomely clear to me.

Vincennes, 30 May 1941

At the Ritz this noon with Colonel Speidel, Grüninger, and Clemens Podewils. I have counted Grüninger among my most insightful readers, and probably pupils as well, and it was his idea that I would be in a better position here in Paris than I would be elsewhere. In truth, it's quite possible that this city has not only special gifts but also inspirations for work and other influences for me. Almost more important is the sense that earlier it was always a capital, symbol and fortress of an ancient tradition of heightened life and unifying ideas, which nations especially lack nowadays. Perhaps I'm doing the right thing if I take advantage of the possibility of establishing myself here. The opportunity presented itself without my instigation.

In the evening, I was visited by the two sisters who were acquaintances from my lodgings in Noisy[Noisy-le-Grand]. The three of us chatted together. The older one is getting divorced from her husband, who squandered her dowry. She speaks of his misconduct and of her lawsuit with Gallic certainty, using the phrases of a canny notary. I gather that there are no insoluble problems here. It seems that she is not obsessed with enmity toward men, but just toward marriage, and that in her own way she wants to introduce the younger woman, who looks like an Amazon, to life. In all this there is a remarkable contrast between pedagogical dignity and epicurean subject matter.

Vincennes, 3 June 1941

In the afternoon, went to the little patisserie of Ladurée on Rue Royale to say goodbye to the Amazon. Her red leather jacket, the green shoulder bag on its long strap. The mole over the left corner of her mouth rises nervously, appealingly, when she smiles and exposes her canine tooth. On Sunday she will be eighteen years old.

Of all the things we used to refer to as style in the old days—the instinctive extravagance that a man displays openly in his own milieu—all that remains is the company of a beautiful woman, and she alone gives the feeling of this vanished condition.

The great cities not only refine the senses, they also educate us to things that belong to their own *genera*—things we would otherwise enjoy only in isolated or specialized contexts. For example, in Barcelona, I noticed that there were specialty shops for all things salted. The pastry bakeries, antiquarian bookshops selling only eighteenth-century bindings, and others, only Russian silver.

Current reading: Anatole France, *Sur la Pierre Blanche* [*On the White Stone*]. Alexandria—the thoughts have lost all their organic components, thereby permitting a linear analysis that is clearer and more mathematical. The style is filtered through all the strata of skepticism; in this way, the clarity of distilled water communicated itself to him. Prose like this can be read at twice normal speed just because every word stands in its logical place. That is its weakness and its strength.

MONTGÉ, 8 JUNE 1941

Took leave of my little apartment in Vincennes. In the bedroom there hangs a photograph of its owners who fled—a photograph I found unpleasant from the start. Their expressions had something strained, distorted, and agitated about them. They bore the marks of a querulous spirit, which is reflected in the contents of their library. I often thought of removing the picture, especially in the evenings, and only the reluctance to change anything about the furnishings prevented me from doing so. It now seemed as if I were discovering a new character trait in the face of this unknown and involuntary landlord, as though from beneath the mask there gleamed and smiled something different, a glimmer of understanding, of sympathy. That struck me as odd—almost as a reward for the fact that in this apartment I had always behaved like a human being. On the other hand, maybe it was a sign that of my own accord I had penetrated the individual surface to that core where we are all united and can understand each other: penetrated to the pain, the suffering, that is the universal substrate.

On the afternoon of 5 June, we marched off. The girls of Montreuil and Vincennes formed two columns in front of the gates of the fort as the beauties of old had when Alexander's troops departed from Babylon. Höll also said goodbye to me. My contact with artists of a free and lighthearted style of life has always been the most valuable.

We marched through the woods of Vincennes, then via Nogent, Chelles, Le Pin, Messy, and Vinantes to Montgé, where I spent three days with the company. The name of the town is supposedly derived from *Mons Jupiter*. I am living here in the house of a Monsieur Patrouix and his wife, both of whom are quite aged yet energetic and vivacious. The man is an engineer who carries on his business in Paris during the week. The woman takes care of the house as well as the large garden, which is watered by seven springs and produces a rich fruit and vegetable harvest. As we chatted about flowers and fruits, I recognized in her a dilettante in the best sense. Evidence for this is that she likes to give away the extra produce from her abundant harvest, but never sell it. Monsieur Patrouix is a Catalan born in Perpignan. We discussed his language. He told me that of all living tongues, it is closest to Latin.

In order to reach old age, he says, people must work. Only the lazybones dies early. I tell him that in order to grow old, we have to stay young.

VILLERS-COTTERÊTS, 9 JUNE 1941

Marched through the great, steaming woods in heavy rain as far as Villers-Cotterêts. There I warmed myself at the stove of a doctor in whose house I was billeted. I conversed with him as we ate together, and when he was called away to an urgent case, he left his daughter behind to keep me company. I found her—the wife of a surgeon—to be well read and well traveled. We conversed about Morocco and the Balearic Islands, then about Rimbaud and Mallarmé, especially about the first strophe of *"Brise Marine"* ["Sea Breeze"]. Here the study of literature always refers to a finite canon and its contents, while back home, ideally, we speak of specific individual works, naming distinct schools and often distinguishing them by their political sympathies. Things are similar when it comes to painting. In Paris, I saw ordinary people stop in front of art dealers' windows and heard them make sound judgments about the pictures on display. Literary appreciation surely corresponds to that of painting. Yet it is remarkable that in a musical people like the Germans, the corresponding sensitivity to sculpture is so poorly developed.

SOISSONS, 10 JUNE 1941

We marched as far as Soissons, where I got some sleep in the Lion Rouge. The house façades were riddled with bullet holes. Often it remained unclear whether these were from the last war or this one. Perhaps this is the way the images of each one coalesce in memory.

NOUVION-LE-COMTE, 11 JUNE 1941

Strenuous march to Nouvion-le-Comte. High up on the right, the massive ruin of Coucy-le-Château. Rested at noon in the glass factory of Saint-Gobain. The inclement weather forced us to eat inside the building among huge piles of bars and sheets of glass. The sterile quality of this material impressed me. In the evening, despite my fatigue, I did a little hunting for *subtiles* [brown mushroom beetle].[8] Such entertainments are like a bath that washes off the dirt of duty; there is freedom in it.

We spent the rainy twelfth of June resting. I wrote letters, updated my diary, and worked. In the evening, slightly tipsy from white Bordeaux as I read Giono, *Pour saluer Melville* [*Melville: A Novel*, 1941]. In such moods, we are more receptive to books. We also read more into them; we fantasize over them, as over a piano keyboard.

SAINT-ALGIS, 13 JUNE 1941

Regimental march with combat training. In the Bois de Berjaumont. At around eleven o'clock at night, we reached our quarters in Saint-Algis. I sat for another hour around the stove with my landlord's family, enjoying cider, cheese, and bread. We had a good conversation. Finally, the woman made us coffee and offered sugar and a little glass of brandy.

I particularly liked the *paterfamilias*, a fifty-six-year-old man who wore the same vest at the table that he had worn in the fields. I wondered how such a simple, good-hearted, childlike creature could still exist in this day and age—maybe only because he is so completely disarming. His face, especially in the gaze of his blue eyes, communicated not only inner joviality but also an exceedingly gracious quality. I could easily imagine myself being in the company of a vassal from olden times. I sensed this especially at several of his questions, which were directed to me with great delicacy, such as, "Vous avez aussi une dame?" [Do you also have a lady?], and his eyes lit up when he heard that I possessed one, as well as property.

SAINT-MICHEL, 14 JUNE 1941

In the morning, I had coffee in the company of my hosts, and then we marched to Origny for a combat exercise. During the final discussion on a hot hill, General Schede took me aside and informed me that I had been promoted to the staff of the High Command. I could see that Speidel had been thinking of me. Time resembles a hot object whose temperature cannot be reduced but can be endured for longer and longer periods by shifting it from one hand to the other. The situation I find myself in reminds me of someone who has a supply of gold coins he needs to change into smaller denominations. He searches in vain in his pockets for the smaller coins. On several occasions, especially back in Dielmissen and during the first half of my stay in Paris, I got swept into the rapids, but I always maintained the minimum amount of breath to make it possible to swim, or at least float. I predicted this situation years ago, but the ways it has come about have surprised me.

In the afternoon, we entered our old Saint-Michel again. Madame Richardet welcomed me with such delight that I found it touching. She said that the time since we had last seen each other had passed so slowly. After the milking was over, Ma Tante[9] came by with her little basket as usual and asked me whether I had experienced the *coup de foudre* in Paris. In this mood of mutual domestic familiarity, we all then drank a bottle of wine with Rehm.

Read my correspondence; among it a letter from Höll sent from Rue Montreuil in which he recalled the rainbow. It bears a postscript from Germaine, expressing the hope of seeing her two captains again, who had turned up at a crossroads in her life. In general, I have to say that one reason my stay in Paris was so fruitful was that it brought me such a wealth of human contact. People still preserve much of their seed corn, which can sprout again as soon as the weather becomes milder and returns to more humane temperatures.

Lovely letters from Perpetua. I note the following from 10 June:

Last night I had a strange dream again. In association with young Meyer and Lahmann I caught a burglar who had hidden in our armoire during the night as you were coming upstairs. Your face, when you heard those men's voices, was the one you usually put on when you encounter unpleasant things. I showed you the thief and you had a good laugh. Then, after you had a good long look at me, you said, "You will recall my remark about Hölderlin, when he says that the fear that holds all our senses in extreme tension gives a person's expression a strange demonic look. When that dissipates, the expression relaxes and a happy serenity spreads over the face. That is what's happening to you at this moment, and I like you better than ever."

I am writing these lines at the semicircular table where I have so often read and worked before. Madame Richardet has picked some peonies from her garden and placed them in a tall vase among the letters, diaries, magazines, and manuscripts. Once in a while, one of the dark red or pale purple petals falls from one of the open blossoms so that the material disorder of the space is exaggerated by a second, colorful one, but at the same time that disorder is negated.

Incidentally, I don't usually update my notes until the following day, and I do not date them on the day of their writing but rather the day they occurred. Nonetheless, it happens that some overlap can occur between both dates. That remains one of the imprecisions in perspective that I don't attend to very strictly. This applies all the more to what I have just said about the flowers.

SAINT-MICHEL, 17 JUNE 1941

Spent Saturday on the banks of the Glandbach stream, where I have organized sports for the men, the first time this year. While they were doing that, I hunted for *subtiles* along the beautifully tree-lined banks. In a tree fungus where I once found a reddish-brown *Orchesia* [darkling beetle] before our stay in Paris, this time I discovered a related species with orange spots, and a little bit later on the stump of an old alder tree, a variety *Eucnemidae* [false click beetle]. I also glimpsed the dark, otherwise inconspicuous *Staphylinidea* [rove beetle]. In the bright sunshine, they danced with their abdomens pointed upward like black flames upon the fresh crust of river mud in a wild celebration of life. When their armor glistens, the nobility of their black color becomes obvious.

I gave some more thought to my project about Black and White. For a long time, it has seemed that I must still establish a method before beginning it.

For anyone who wants to pursue this. A youth once came to an old hermit and asked him for a rule to guide him through life. The hermit imparted this advice: "Strive for the attainable."

The youth thanked him and asked whether it would be immodest to ask for a second word of wisdom as sustenance for his journey, whereupon the hermit added another piece of advice to his first: "Strive for the unattainable."

In the evening, in Madame Richardet's garden. A bee approached a pink lupine and alighted upon the lower lip of the blossom, which drooped obligingly under its weight. In this way, a second narrow sheath, deep dark red at its tip, opened up. This section holds the pollen receptacles. The bee feasted on this sideways, right at the point indicated by the dark shading.

I stood for a long time before an iris with a tripartite crown. Entry to its chalices lay across a golden fleece leading to an amethyst cleft.

You flowers, who dreamed you up?

Höll arrived late by car. Because it was my sergeant's birthday, I took him along to see the junior officers. It was a hearty feast. At around two o'clock, we pledged our close friendship over toasts.

He brought along the photograph from Rue Montreuil. The likenesses and also the view had come out well, but the rainbow was missing, that symbol of our attachment. The inert lens does not capture those authentic and miraculous qualities.

SAINT-MICHEL, 18 JUNE 1941

In a dream I was sitting with my father at a table heaped with food. It was at the end of the meal where others were present. He was in a good mood and posed the question to what extent every gesture—especially a man's gestures in conversation with a woman—carries erotic significance. In doing so, he revealed the structure of gestural language and produced a cynical effect, yet this impression was mitigated by his astonishing erudition. Concerning the gestures, he mentioned those men use to indicate their experience and prowess; he cited Juvenal's reference to the two books of Anticatones.[10]

Before the roundtable broke up he passed a goblet holding bright red wild strawberries on a mound of white ice cream. I heard him comment on it, but I have unfortunately forgotten what he said, although it was rather more profound than jocular.

PARIS, 24 JUNE 1941

Departure to Paris in the very early morning. I was warmly embraced on Rue de la Bovette by Madame Richardet and her aunt, who warned me again about the *coup de foudre*.

Laon again with its cathedral, which I love especially. In the woods, the place where the chestnut bushes are beginning to bud marks the boundary of a growing zone. Just on the outskirts of the city there are tall stands of marvelous wild cherries that glowed the color of coral as they ripened. That surpasses the limits of the gardener's art, encroaching into the realm of precious stones and jewelry— just like those trees that Aladdin found in the grotto of the lamp.

For three days now we have been at war with Russia—strange how little the news has touched me. But the ability to absorb facts in times like these is limited unless we do so with a certain callousness.

PARIS, 25 JUNE 1941

Standing in front of La Lorraine again on the Place des Ternes. I reencounter the same clock that has so often been the focus of my gaze.

When I take up my position in front of the troops to say goodbye, as I did on Monday, I notice the urge to stand off-center. That is a trait that denotes an observer and a prevalence of contemplative leanings. In the evening, bouillabaisse with Ziegler at Drouant. I waited for him on Avenue de L'Opéra in front of a store displaying rugs, weapons, and jewelry from the Sahara. Among these were heavy silver armbands and ankle bracelets, fitted with locks and spikes—ornaments common to lands where slaves and harems are found.

Then Café de la Paix. Took stock of the situation as it comes into focus more clearly.

PARIS, 26 JUNE 1941

Toward morning, dreams of earthquakes—I saw houses swallowed up. The scene was as confusing as a maelstrom and threatened to make me dizzy and even lose consciousness. At first I struggled against the urge, but then I threw myself into the vortex of annihilation, as into a swirling shaft. The leap produced desire, which was part of the horror, yet also transcended it as the body dissolved into malevolent, fragmented music. Sadness prevailed, as when a flag is lowered.

Had a further conversation about the situation with Ziegler in the Ambassador. Also talked about second sight, a trait inherited in his wife's family. She saw the explosion of the zeppelin[11] three hours before it was announced on the radio, as well as other things. Yes, there are strange springs that feed our knowledge, for she also saw Kniébolo[12] lying on the floor, his face spattered with blood.

PARIS, 27 JUNE 1941

At the table, I joked around with a beautiful three-year-old child I had grown fond of. Thought: that was one of your own children, unbegotten and unborn.

In the evening I accompanied the sisters to Montmartre, which was glowing like a volcanic crater. They complement each other like a centaur, a twin being in spirit and flesh. While half asleep I ardently entered into the spirit of language. The consonant groups *m-n m-s m-j* that express the exalted, the masculine, and masterful became especially distinct.

PARIS, 5 JULY 1941

I met Morris on the Place d'Anvers, a man still mentally alert and physically active at age seventy-six. He has spent his life guiding rich Englishmen, Americans, and Scandinavians through the city. He has intimate familiarity with all of its far-flung districts. His experience is also extensive in clandestine matters, in the vices of the rich and powerful. Like the face of all who have passed through such regions, his own betrays a somewhat demonic aspect. While we ate together on the Boulevard Rochechouart, he gave me a lecture on various techniques of making amorous advances. At a glance, he can tell women who expect money from those who don't, almost infallibly. I find that a rather coarse trait. Despite all his debauchery, I found something pleasant, even lovable in him. At the same time, I also sensed an icy chill in this person, who has spent years unattached relying on himself alone in this metropolis.

PARIS, 12 JULY 1941

Strolled with Madame Scrittore to the Place du Tertre opposite the old Mairie near Sacré Coeur. I showed her a mullein flower blooming in a dry crevice in a wall. She said she thought it had grown thanks to *"collaboration du Saint-Esprit"* [collaboration with the Holy Spirit]. Conversation about the men who are good husbands and bad lovers. In such cases, women tend to take comfort in the thought that "I have always led a double life." I wondered about the reason for such confidences. It can probably be attributed to the loneliness felt by two people who live near each other—a loneliness imbued with something terrifying.

Men live there as if suspended over chasms lightly covered with flowers but which conceal snakes and small carcasses in their depths. But why? Ultimately, only because they instill fear and mistrust. If we possessed perfect, divine understanding, our fellow human beings would reveal their secrets to us like children, without suspicion.

We ate together in a wine bar on the Place d'Anvers. Here I allowed myself the pleasure of interrogating my companion about details of French history, such as the heraldic significance of the lilies. At the next table, there sat a married couple, obviously "people who smell well-educated," as the Chinese say. They were becoming increasingly disturbed by our conversation. Several times the man had to restrain his wife with effort when she wanted to interrupt and give me a piece of her mind.

PARIS, 14 JULY 1941

Bastille Day. The streets were very crowded. When I crossed over the Place des Ternes in the evening, I felt someone touch my hand. A man carrying a violin under his left arm gripped my hand powerfully as he passed, while giving me a silent but genial look. There was something strangely invigorating about it, and it immediately improved my melancholy mood.

The city as sweetheart. Her streets, her squares, as bounteous places where we are surprised by gifts. I get special joy from seeing loving couples who walk with their arms around each other and occasionally pull each other closer for a kiss.

PARIS, 19 JULY 1941

Went to the flea market with Speidel in the afternoon. I spent several hours in this jumbled maze in the kind of mood produced by reading *Aladdin and the Magic Lamp*. A place where East and West mingle and combine in the most outlandish way.

The impression of this fairytale world is evoked by all the treasures of metalwork, stones, pictures, fabric, and antiquities mixed in with a lot of rubbish. Treasures can be found in cheap market stalls, precious items among the piles of bric-a-brac.

This is the final collecting point for things that have spent their dreamy lives for years, decades, and centuries among families and households. They pour out of the rooms, the attics, and the storage rooms and bring anonymous memories with them. They fill the whole market with the emanations of household gods.

PARIS, 8 OCTOBER 1941

My transfer to Paris left a lacuna in these entries. Even more than that, the events in Russia are responsible for it; these started around the same time and evoked a kind of mental exhaustion, not just in me. It seems that this war is deteriorating in stages organized according to the rules of some unidentified dramatic structure. Of course this sort of thing can only be guessed at because events are sensed by those who are living through them in all their anarchic spirit. The maelstroms are too close, too violent, and nowhere, not even on this ancient island, are there any places of safety. The breakers are surging into the lagoons.

At noon Speidel and I went to see Ambassador de Brinon, on the corner of Rue Rude and Avenue Foch. They say that the little *palais* where he received us belongs to his Jewish wife, but that did not prevent him from making jokes at table about the *youpins* [Yids]. There I made the acquaintance of Sacha Guitry, whom I found very pleasant. His dramatic side also far outweighs his artistic side. He possesses a tropical personality of the sort I imagine Dumas Père had. On his little finger there gleamed a monstrous signet ring with a large embossed monogram SG on the gold surface. I conversed with him about Mirbeau, and he told me that the man had died in his arms as he whispered into his ear: "*Ne collaborer jamais!*" [Never collaborate!] I am recording this for my collection of last words. What he meant was collaborating on comedies, for in those days, the word did not have the odor that it does now. Sat next to the actress Arletty at table. At the moment, she can be seen in the film *Madame Sans-Gêne* [*Brazen Lady*]. Just the word *cocu* [cuckold] is enough to make her laugh, which means that in this country she is almost always in a state of merriment. Orchids in a vase: smooth, stiff, with a lip that divides into trembling feelers. Their color, a shimmering white luster, as though enameled for insects' eyes in the jungle. Lasciviousness and innocence are wondrously united in these blossoms.

Pouilly, Burgundy, champagne, just a thimbleful of each. On the occasion of this breakfast, around twenty policemen were stationed in the vicinity.

PARIS, 11 OCTOBER 1941

Went to the Monte Carlo with Nebel in the afternoon, where we discussed the matter of the safe. He had just returned from leave and told me that a novel by Thomas Mann, *Ein Tag aus dem Leben des alten Goethe* [*A Day in the Life of the Aged Goethe*][13] was being circulated clandestinely.

Later called on Consul General Schleier on Avenue Suchet. Conversation with Drieu La Rochelle, editor of the *Nouvelle Revue Française*, focusing on Malraux, whose career I have followed ever since I got my hands on his novel *La Condition Humaine* [*The Human Condition*] many years ago. Since then, I've considered him one to be of those rare observers with an eye for the war-ravaged landscape of the twentieth century.

Went to see Speidel in the evening, who had just been on the telephone with the quartermaster general. Snow has already fallen in the central area of the eastern front.

PARIS, 13 OCTOBER 1941

The morning was brisk, but I spent a pleasant hour in the Tuileries Gardens in the afternoon. It is impossible to be bored out in the sunlight. There we bathe in the fountain of time. Then went to the Quais de la Seine, where I bought a large-format "Temptation of Saint Anthony" by Caillot in good condition. At the same stall, I pored over a colored drawing of the familiar motif of the bird that must be coaxed back into its cage. The pair of lovers who reclined, half-exhausted and half-revived, on a Biedermeier sofa, wore thin, tight clothes. Details of their anatomy were not exactly obvious, but nevertheless could be discerned in the contours of the cloth, resembling impressions of shells and ammonites. In this genre, it is especially important to set a trap for the imagination. This is the art of the embarrassing moment.

Herpetology Museum—first in the empirically zoological section, then to works of art and ethnographic collections. Finally, the snake as symbol of magic and cultic power. All this in a southern landscape between labyrinthine gardens and ranges of cliffs crisscrossed with dazzling, winding paths. A flight of marble steps leads upward, and on it black, bronze, and multicolored bodies laze in the sunlight. The entrance is treacherous, discovered only by the initiated. In the background, near caves, are further buildings—like baths and a temple of Asclepius.

The snake as primeval power is an archetype, a Platonic idea. The images, whether of life or of the mind, advance toward it without ever reaching it. There is a similarity here to worms, round fish, reptiles, and dinosaurs or to Chinese dragons and fabulous creatures of all sorts.

It would good for the "house" [project] to put the world into architectonic order—from its dark cellars to its observatories. The staircases where encounters occur are important. Life takes place in the rooms, chambers, and halls. This is visible in all its detail, as if in pictures painted in shimmering dreamy hues. We move as though on stage but at the same time remain spectators. "Pilgrim's Progress." The manuscript would have to be kept partly in the form of stage directions. Add to this the audial dimension: cries, which significantly simplify life's relationships. "*On tue les nôtres.*" [They are killing our own.] "They're interrogating the children." The populated area would have to be paced off; anyone doing so would need to be of advanced age and have extensive experience.

Individual rooms: the chamber of irrevocable decisions as a Platonic ideal of all courtrooms. The declassification office. Elevators for the more sophisticated who no longer need steps. A cabinet of mirrors.

PARIS, 14 OCTOBER 1941

Went to the [Hotel] George V in the evening with Speidel. Sieburg was here, who with his pleasant nonchalance personifies all the skills of the cosmopolitan journalist and, even more important, with pronounced self-confidence that underscores and magnifies his talent. To judge by his horoscope, I can only assume the middle of the transit of Jupiter plus a good position of the sun. As is common with this kind of aspect, the shape of the face departs from oval and approximates round. This impression is intensified by the hair sticking straight out from his head.

He thinks the defeat of France is irreversible, but on the other hand, he believes in the continued predominance of this country in matters of taste and culture.

PARIS, 15 OCTOBER 1941

Went with Speidel to Sacha Guitry's for lunch on Avenue Elisée Reclus. In front of the house, on city property, there stands a bust of his father, the actor Lucien Guitry and in the garden, a female torso in sexual ecstasy by Rodin.

When he welcomed me, Guitry handed me a folder containing one letter each by Octave Mirbeau, Léon Bloy, and Debussy—the three authors whom we had discussed at our first meeting—and he told me to add these pieces to my collection. The little sheet by Bloy is especially lovely, with its personal comments and the oversize penmanship typical of him.

We then looked at books in manuscript, among them Flaubert's *Éducation Sentimentale* [*Sentimental Education*, 1869]. In a work by Bergson, he showed me the author's dedication "*À Sacha Guitry, un admirateur*" [To Sacha Guitry from an admirer] and pointed out the *un* [an] as opposed to *son* [his] as being especially choice. Molière's travel case filled with first editions of his plays, Napoleon with all his marshals of the Empire cast in lead, and many other things.

In the bedroom. Over the bed, the wall has been broken through, as in dining rooms, so as to let plates be passed through from the kitchen. This opening leads to his wife's bed—"but it is a bit tight for her, master," says one of the guests. "Being Madame Guitry comes at a price," he is promptly informed by the slender lady of the house.

A colleague from the theater arrives late: "the most beautiful woman in Paris—twenty years ago," Guitry whispers to me before greeting her.

At the table. The salad was served on silver, the ice cream on a heavy gold service that had belonged to Sarah Bernhardt. I was again astonished by his effusive personality, especially when he told anecdotes of his encounters with royalty. When talking about different people, he would accompany his words with expressive gestures. During the conversation, he used his large horn-rimmed glasses to great dramatic effect.

It dawns on me that in the case of such talent, the whole reservoir of personality that a marriage can possess gets used up by the man. And yet my first impression is corrected, because at the same time, this is surely a human being with real heart. I caught a glimpse of the fecund *materia prima* [primal material] that is the root of all character. It is true that we enjoy ourselves in the aura of such idiosyncrasy, and this feeling of well-being produces the climate that promotes his personality.

PARIS, 18 OCTOBER 1941

At noon in the Ritz with Carl Schmitt who gave a lecture the day before yesterday on the different significance of land and sea under international law. Colonel Speidel, Grüninger, and Count Podewils also there. Conversation about current scholarly and literary controversies. Carl Schmitt compared his situation to that of the white captain in Melville's *Benito Cereno*, who was held captive by black slaves, and he quoted the proverb: "*Non possum scribere contra eum, qui potest proscribere.*" [I cannot write against him who can proscribe.][14]

Walked along the right bank to the Trocadéro. We discussed the matter thoroughly while doing so. Carl Schmitt finds significance in the fact that layers are beginning to peel away from the human stock and ossify beneath the region where free will exists—similar to the way that animals are the cast-off masks of the human image. Man is evolving a new zoological order from himself. The real danger of privilege lies in whether or not one is included in it.

I added that this ossification had already been described in the Old Testament and can be seen in the symbol of the bronze serpent. In that age, law represented what technology does today.

Finally, we went to the Musée de l'Homme and viewed skulls and masks.

PARIS, 19 OCTOBER 1941

Visited Port-Royal with Grüninger and Carl Schmitt. There on top of Pascal's books, I found the little bird's nest again that had so amused me during my first visit. Even in their state of dilapidation, such places still hold more life than when they are preserved as museums. We picked a leaf from Pascal's dying nut tree, then had breakfast in Moulin de Bicherel, and spent the night in Rambouillet and Chartres where I saw the cathedral for the very first time. The colorful stained glass had been removed, and as a result, a dimension was lacking.

PARIS, 21 OCTOBER 1941

The Doctoresse called on me in the Majestic[15] to discuss matters of the safe. It concerned letters I had written from Switzerland to Joseph Breitbach in 1936 that had been confiscated along with other papers in a bank safe, but not yet read. They contained references to further correspondence, such as the one with Valeriu Marcu. I am cautiously attempting to gain control of these matters through the financial office of the Army High Command.

I am keeping my personal papers and journals under lock and key in the Majestic. Because I am under orders from Speidel to process not only the files concerning Operation Sea Lion,[16] but also the struggle for hegemony in France between the military commander and the Party, a special steel file cabinet has been set up in my room. Naturally, armor like this only symbolizes personal invulnerability. When this is cast in doubt, then even the strongest locks spring right open.

Paris, 22 October 1941

Went for a walk with a milliner from the South who grew up near the Spanish border; she had come to me to make inquiries about a comrade. I had the pleasure of buying her a hat in a salon not far from the Opéra—a little number the size of a hummingbird's nest with a green feather on top. It was remarkable to see how this little person seemed to grow and change with her new adornment, the way a soldier swells with pride after receiving a medal. It wasn't so much a head covering as a decoration.

We strolled and chatted through the twilit alleys near the Madeleine. It was Morris who first made me aware of this quarter. During such encounters, a strong feeling of curiosity makes me want to eavesdrop on people I don't know, get into strangers' gardens, or gain entrance to hallways of houses otherwise locked. And thus, I got a glimpse into an ancestral village—*a noste*, as they say here—with its groves of chestnut trees (*châtaigneries*), sheltering mushrooms and ring-necked doves.

The wolf breaks into the fold, slaughters two or three sheep confined there, but several hundred die in the stampede.

Paris, 23 October 1941

Discussion with the Doctoresse at Crémaillère [restaurant]. A doctor with deft, precise, mercurial intelligence. At first, we conversed about the matter of the secure storage cabinet, then about grammar, then acquaintances we had in common, like Hercule.

Finished reading Huysmans, *A Vau l'Eau* [*With the Flow*, 1882] in a beautiful edition that I bought from Berès with a dedication from the author to his friend Rafaëlli, if I interpret the handwriting correctly.

The hero of the book, Fromentin, is a bourgeois Des Esseintes.[17] The tone of the book is filled with powerful disgust at the counterfeit nature of civilization—every page contains perceptions and judgments that presuppose a nervous dyspepsia. As I read this, the thought occurred to me once again that certain maladies resemble magnifying glasses. They enable us to see more clearly the conditions they correspond to. One could categorize the literature of decadence accordingly.

How much further we have sunk in the meantime, and how delectable those things have become that nauseate Fromentin—the leathery meat of the food stall, the blue wine, all that muck in general.

Huysmans describes one of those points where we begin to delve into all these defects. This is the reason he is experiencing a renaissance today

Paris, 25 October 1941

Lunch with Ina Seidel at Prunier. She was worried about her son-in-law, whom Hess employed as his astrological advisor but who has been arrested. That surprised me, since I thought that the flight to England had happened with Kniébolo's knowledge and possibly even on his orders.[18] One could counter this by saying that, with the rediscovery of *raison d'état* [reasons of state], even having knowledge of certain secrets has become objectively more dangerous than before. Surely, that's the case here. This daredevil exploit gives an idea of the spirit of the roulette game that controls us. The return of the structures of the absolute state, but without aristocracy—meaning without objectivity—makes catastrophes of unimaginable dimensions possible. Yet they are anticipated in a feeling of fear that tinges even the victories.

I heard something from Ina Seidel that I have occasionally heard from other intelligent women, namely that in certain figures of speech and images the precision of language leads us deep into forbidden regions that give the impression of imminent danger. We should always listen to such warnings, even when we must follow our own precepts. Like atoms, words contain a nucleus around which they orbit, vibrating, and they cannot be touched without unleashing nameless powers.

PARIS, 2 NOVEMBER 1941

Where people do intellectual battle, death is part of their strategy. This gives them something impregnable, and the thought that the enemy is intent upon taking their life loses some of its power to instill terror. On the other hand, it is of the highest importance that this should happen in the correct manner, and in a situation heavy with symbolism in which such people can be reliable witnesses. At times, they might give the impression that they shrink from death. In doing so, they resemble a field marshal who hesitates at length until the time is ripe before giving the signal to attack. There are different ways to conquer.

The enemy who senses this in his obtuse way feels appalling, frenetic anger when confronted by real intellect. This explains the effort to try to overpower him in vanguard action, bribe him, or somehow distract him. These encounters produce moments that erase the incidental or historical nature of the enmity, and something evolves that has existed since the beginning of our earth. The roles are reversed in a remarkable way. It almost seems as though the fear were transferred to the side of the attacker, as if he were trying to corrupt his victim by all means possible, but postponing the death that he has prepared for him. A hideous triumph accompanies the butchery. History records situations in which men clutch death like a staff of office. So it was in the Templars' ritual where the Grand Master and the judges suddenly reveal themselves in their true characters. Then a ship dispels the phantasm as it comes into our astonished view, flying flags and showing its cannons. In the evening, it would then be burned, but during the night, the site of the conflagration would be guarded so that people could not steal any of the holy relics. The ashes instill fear in the tyrant, who knows he must perish.

PARIS, 5 NOVEMBER 1941

Judges at bloody assizes. When they cross the corridors and enter, they have a perfunctory aura about them, the erstwhile dignity of macabre marionettes. They are Duk-Duk dancers.[19]

"That which does not kill me, makes me stronger."[20] And what kills me makes me incredibly strong.

In history, ideas do not proceed in linear fashion. They create reactions like the falling weight of a clock as it moves not only the hands but its counterweight as well.

This establishes equilibrium. The ideas that correspond to forms are prevented from developing into monstrosities or from persisting within them. In the realm of free will, it's the same kind of pruning that in zoology trims the developing tendrils.

Roland has returned from Russia and describes the hideous mechanism for executing prisoners. This is done under the pretext of wanting to measure and weigh them, for which they must strip. Then they are taken to the "measuring apparatus," which in reality positions the air gun for delivering the *coup de grace*.

PARIS, 10 NOVEMBER 1941

In every age, there are two theories of evolution. One of these seeks our origin above, and the other, below. Both are true; human beings may be categorized based on whether they accept one or the other.

PARIS, 11 NOVEMBER 1941

Regarding illnesses. There are differences here in the way these affect the imagination that do not correlate with the severity of the malady. I feel that I tend to ignore disorders of the lungs and heart more than those of the stomach, liver, and lower body in general. Purely with regard to the flesh, it seems there are also qualities of dying. Flames are reserved for unbelievers; thus, not only is cremation increasing but also immolation of the living.

PARIS, 12 NOVEMBER 1941

History is also made up of atoms, and it is impossible to imagine a single one different without changing the entire course of its progress. Marat would have made quite a different impression if his name had been something like Barat, or if when his assassin entered, he had been spending that hour at his desk instead of in the bath. It is precisely assassinations that often cause the greatest changes, and yet essentially they depend on such a concatenation of chance. Sarajevo provides us with a very good example here.

When we look back, it is hard to imagine a single pebble in a different position. Should we be able to draw conclusions from this about the future? Should we conclude that the intellect is only capable of finding such seamless progression intelligible if we see all of the future inexorably folded in upon itself? Or is it the present that causes a change in the aggregate condition of the age by monumentalizing and fossilizing everything it touches? The future is fluid; the past is fixed. The whole resembles a game of cards: we have to distinguish between the ones on the table and the others, which are still in play.

These observations form a mosaic. Yet we have to see those little pebbles of chance in a higher vision as Boëthius does, a vision that endures unchanged in his mind. Genuine morality lies outside of time.

In the afternoon, read the farewell letters of Count d'Estienne d'Orves, who was executed by firing squad. I received these from his defense attorney. They are reading matter of the highest order; I had the feeling that I was holding an enduring document in my hand.

PARIS, 13 NOVEMBER 1941

Contrast between the graphs of morale and physical health: even in good physical condition we often may be depressed, whereas the opposite is also true. We experience an upsurge, a spring tide, when our whole potential comes into play.

It is good when an important date or significant meeting happens to fall on such days.

To the George V, in the evening. I brought the maxims of René Quinton for Colonel Speidel. When he asked me for an inscription, I chose, "*La récompense des hommes, c'est d'estimer leurs chefs*" [Men's reward is to honor their leaders]. Under his aegis, here deep in the military machine, we formed a kind of cell of intellectual chivalry, meeting in the belly of the beast, trying to preserve regard and compassion for the weak and vulnerable.

Conversation with Grüninger about soldiers' obedience and its relation to absolute, even constitutional, monarchy. After a while, this virtue resembles an instinct that continues to exert an influence, but can damage the man who possesses it by making him a tool of unscrupulous forces. This brings him into conflict with the second pillar of chivalry: honor. This, the more delicate virtue, is the first extinguished, leaving behind a kind of automaton, a servant without a real master, who is finally little more than a pimp.

In such times, the best characters founder upon the rocks, while more cunning intellects cross over into politics. In some lucky cases, a general from an old patrician family who finds himself in this situation laughs at those who try to command him, putting them in their place as the *pourriture* [rot] they are.

PARIS, 14 NOVEMBER 1941

Visit from Dr. Göpel this morning; he brought me greetings from Carlo Schmid from Lille. Afterward, with Grüninger in the print collection of the Louvre, where we viewed lovely old pictures of flowers and snakes.

The hour of twilight—night announces its presence like a tide that, murmuring and barely noticed, sends forth its first waves. Strange beings arrive with it. This is the hour when owls ready their wings and lepers come out on the street.

We may demand of people no more than what is commensurate with their essence; from women love, not justice.

PARIS, 15 NOVEMBER 1941

Invitation to the birthday party for Jacqueline, the milliner from the South. Quai Louis-Blériot. A narrow back staircase led to the fifth floor, and a warren of low garret rooms reminiscent of the catwalks of a theater. There was her apartment: a tiny bedroom almost completely filled by one of those large beds and as on small ships, a still smaller kitchen where her friend Jeannette—a tall, gaunt, slightly demonic person—prepared the feast. She conjured up seven courses. In addition, there was Bordeaux, Chianti, *café au rhum*.

In the corner, there hung one of those wooden stakes overgrown with the interlocking coils of a hardy vine. The wood was the sort that carpenters' apprentices at home traditionally use to cut walking sticks for themselves. This had also been trained to curl around the trunk so that the vine resembled a snake. The dimensions of the body, created by the play of muscles, worked well, probably because there are similar forces at work in the plant. The color was also very natural, a yellowish brown, speckled with black of the sort found in swamp-dwelling species.

In this vein, there was a conversation about snakes in general. Her friend said that when she was a child *a noste* in the Béarnaise region, she was once sitting in the garden with her mother who was nursing her little sister. Because the smell of milk attracts snakes, a gigantic adder slithered slowly and unnoticed out of a nearby hedge, up to the chair, and frightened her. Her father came out and killed the creature.

She recounted that quite graphically in a mythical way.

Paris, 18 November 1941

Concerning this journal. It captures only a certain layer of events that take place in the intellectual and physical spheres. Things that concern our innermost being resist communication, almost resist our own perception.

There are themes that interweave themselves mysteriously through the years, such as that of the inevitability that consumes our age. This is reminiscent of the grand image of the wave of life in Asian painting, or of the maelstrom in E. A. Poe. There is something extremely instructive in this, for when there is no escape or hope, we are forced to stand still. Our perspective changes.

It is nonetheless remarkable that confidence animates me most profoundly. The star of fate shines through the foam of the breaking waves and tattered clouds alike. I don't mean this only personally, but generally. During the past weeks, we reached the nadir and have gotten past it.

The efforts we must make to survive our times and gain strength take place out of sight, deep in the mineshafts. So it was in the decisive dream upon the heights of Patmos on my journey to Rhodes. Our life is like a mirror; although it is smudged and hazy, it reveals meaningful things. One day we shall enter into this world of reflections and then attain perfection. The measure of perfection that we shall be able to bear is already implied by our lives.

During the lunch break, went to the sales division of the print collection [of the Louvre], where I had ordered a few copies of etchings that were out of print. Among these was the beautiful image of a cobra, coiled and erect with its neck flared. The sales clerk, a gaunt dark-haired girl roughly in her thirties, told me that she always placed this sheet face down on the pile. When she wrapped it up for me, she bade it goodbye muttering "*sale bête*" [filthy beast].

Otherwise an amusing person. When I made a comment that she seemed to find unusual, she was taken aback for a moment, and looked me up and down and said, "*ah bon*" in acknowledgment.

During this brief visit, I leafed through the large folder of etchings by Poussin. Although I have had an English reproduction of his *Heracles at the Crossroads* hanging over my desk for years, it was only today that I truly realized the mighty, even regal spatiality of this master. This is absolute monarchy.

PARIS, 19 NOVEMBER 1941

Paid a visit to the Doctoresse in the afternoon; an amethyst-tinged flight of stairs leads to her apartment. I climb the steps through violet light in the spiral whorl of a seashell. In such centuries-old houses, time itself is still part of the continuing construction process. There are small depressions, dislocations, and curvatures of the beams, and these change the proportions in a way that no architect could imagine. The Doctoresse thinks that families who rent apartments here never move out but simply become extinct in this place.

We then went out to eat on Place Saint-Michel. Had garfish served on ice and seaweed. Long strings of the plant covered the plate, and its color was extraordinary. At first glance it appeared black, but closer inspection revealed a dull, dark, malachite green, yet without any mineral hardness—one of life's great delicacies. Accompanying this were oyster shells with their green slate mother-of-pearl encrustations amid the reflections of silver, porcelain, and crystal.

PARIS, 21 NOVEMBER 1941

At Weber's for half-an-hour in the evening; the Doctoresse taught me how to open the safe. She also mentioned a doctor who took pictures of the dying so as to capture and study the agonies produced by various illnesses—a thought that I found both astute and repugnant. For some minds, taboos no longer exist.

PARIS, 23 NOVEMBER 1941

Lunch at the Morands' on Avenue Charles-Floquet. There I also met Gaston Gallimard and Jean Cocteau.

Morand epitomizes a kind of worldly sybarite. In one of his books, I found a passage comparing an ocean liner with a Leviathan infused with the aroma of *Chypre*.[21] His book about London is commendable; it describes a city as a great house. If the English were to build pyramids, they would include London in the decoration of their tombs.

Cocteau: amiable and at the same time, ailing, like someone who dwells in a special, but comfortable, hell.

With intelligent women it is very difficult to overcome physical distance. It is as though they girded their alert intellects with a belt that foils desire. It is too bright within their orbit. Those who lack specific erotic orientation are most assertive. This could be one of those chess moves that ensures the continuity of our species.

One can ask advice of a subaltern in a matter, but not regarding the ethical system fundamental to that matter.

The dignity of man must be more sacred to us than life itself.

The age of humanity is the age in which human beings have become scarce.

The true leaders of the world are at home in their graves.

In moments of inescapable disruption, individuals must proclaim their allegiance like a warship hoisting its colors.

By choosing certain circles in life, such as the Prussian General Staff, one may gain access to certain elevated spheres of inside information but exclude himself from the highest.

PARIS, 25 NOVEMBER 1941

I sometimes spend my noon hour in the little cemetery near the Trocadéro. Moss has grown over many a gravestone and edged the names and inscriptions with borders of green velvet. Things glow in their after-image and often more beautifully in memory before they dissolve into the nameless void.

After such visits, I usually have a half-hour left over when I drink coffee in my room and read books or look at pictures. Today I admired Memling's series on the procession of the ten thousand virgins. These paintings give a hint of the transfiguration that man can attain, as well as what the artist can perceive.

Reading matter: *Fumée d'Opium* by Boissière,[22] a book that Cocteau recommended and sent to me. Furthermore, this strange story of the island of Juan Fernandez, a present from Doctor [Werner] Best.

PARIS, 26 NOVEMBER 1941

Dropped in on the print and book dealers on Rue de Tournon in the afternoon. In the antiquarian bookshop of Lechevalier, with whom I have been corresponding for years. Admired entomological volumes, among them one by Swammerdam.

Went to the Brasserie Lorraine in the evening with Nebel and Poupet. When Poupet wants to characterize something trivial, like a book that's creating a stir, he says, "*cela n'existe pas*" [that does not exist]. He likes to work in bed, and then in the morning when he wakes up, he continues his work where he left off. He sleeps with his books spread out around him on the bed and turns over carefully at night so as not to touch them.

PARIS, 29 NOVEMBER 1941

In the afternoon, I met Grüninger at Countess Podewils'; he had just returned from the Pyrenees. He said he had dreamed about me. In the dream, he asked whether he should depict an ivy-covered ruin. I answered yes and added, "That suits you. I, on the other hand, want to represent an elephant." This bothered him as a reference to Romanticism.

In the evening, went to the Grand Guignol with the Doctoresse to cheer her up. I didn't find it as amusing as I had before the war, which is probably because horrors have replaced everyday life in the world, and so the presentation has lost its remarkable quality.

Montmartre—dark, foggy, and locked down tight by police and soldiers because of an assassination that had taken place there.

Paris, 30 November 1941

Conversations among men should be conducted like those among gods, among invulnerable beings. To duel with ideas is to use swords of the intellect that cut through matter without pain or effort. The deeper the cut, the purer the enjoyment. In such intellectual encounters, one must be indestructible.

Paris, 3 December 1941

At the shop of Lechevalier on Rue de Tournon in the afternoon. While studying engravings and colored plates in books on insects, I was overcome by a feeling of disgust, as though the presence of cadavers had diminished my enjoyment. There are transgressions that touch the world in its entirety and its whole logical context. At such points, the aesthetic person must turn away from beauty and devote himself to freedom. The terrible thing nowadays is that it cannot be found in any of the parties, and so one has to do battle alone. On the other hand, it is the day laborers of this war we must envy; they fall with honor on a small patch of ground. And yet they too enter another, greater world.

Later, at Charmille's on Rue de Bellechasse. The street is quiet, and when I cross the stairwell time stands still in the twilit forecourts. This brings a feeling of security: "No one knows my name and no one knows this place of refuge."

"*Voyage autour de ma chamber*" [voyage around my room] in the old easy chair, as on the flying carpet from *One Thousand and One Nights*. We chat, mostly about words and their meanings, and sometimes look things up in books. The library is rich, especially in theological and reference works.

Charmille. What I admire about her: her sense of freedom, which is evident in the shape of her forehead. Among human beings there exists a type that is salt of the earth, people who always prevent history from sinking completely into stifling servitude. Individuals know by instinct what freedom is, especially when they are born among policemen and prisoners. You can always find those who belong to the race of the falcon or eagle; they are recognizable even behind prison bars.

I had to reach this age to find enjoyment in the intellectual encounter with women, just as Kubin, the old sorcerer, prophesied of me. The change has meant something startling for me, precisely because I had been satisfied with the course of my life, like a specialist in ballistics who has watched his shot traverse its prescribed trajectory and then seen it take a new direction into a limitless dimension. He had not known the laws of the stratosphere.

In addition, the hunger for human beings grows significantly. In prisons, men see clearly their companions' latent merits. We can do without anything as long as we have other people.

Ended the evening late at the Raphael:[23] Boissière, *Fumeurs d'Opium*. This book from 1888 was a treasure trove for me. It not only describes life in the Annamese [Vietnamese] swamps and forests but also has intellectual appeal. In the opium dream, there towers above the febrile tropical zones another, crystalline, world. Viewed from this level, even cruelty loses its horror. There is no pain here. That is perhaps the most exquisite quality of opium: it animates the mind's creative power and begets enchanted castles in the imagination. Upon those towers the loss of the swamps and foggy realms of this earth can never inspire fear. The soul creates levels for our passage to death.

PARIS, 4 DECEMBER 1941

Went to the theater at Palais-Royal in dense fog. I returned the Boissière to Cocteau. He lives nearby on Rue de Montpensier in that very house where Rastignac[24] received Nucingen's wife. Cocteau was entertaining guests. Among his furnishings, I noticed a slate blackboard he uses to illustrate aspects of his conversation with swift chalkmarks.

I sensed the danger on the way home, especially when the doors in the narrow old streets near the Palais-Royal opened onto hazy red-lighted areas. Who knows what is brewing in such kitchens, who knows the plans the *lemures*[25] are hatching? We pass through this sphere in disguise, for if the fog were to lift, we would be recognized by these creatures, and the result would be disaster.

"*L'homme qui dort, c'est l'homme diminué.*" [A man who sleeps is a man diminished.] One of Rivarol's errors.

PARIS, 7 DECEMBER 1941

At the German Institute this afternoon. Among those there was Merline. Tall, raw-boned, strong, a bit ungainly, but lively during the discussion—or more accurately, during his monologue. He speaks with a manic, inward-directed gaze, which seems to shine from deep within a cave. He no longer looks to the right or the left. He seems to be marching toward some unknown goal. "I always have death beside me." And in saying this, he points to the spot beside his seat, as though a puppy were lying there.

He spoke of his consternation, his astonishment, at the fact that we soldiers were not shooting, hanging, and exterminating the Jews—astonishment that anyone who had a bayonet was not making unrestrained use of it. "If the Bolsheviks were in Paris they would demonstrate it, show how it's done—how to comb through a population, quarter by quarter, house by house. If I had a bayonet, I would know what to do."

It was informative to listen to him rant this way for two hours, because he radiated the amazing power of nihilism. People like this hear only a single melody, but they hear it uncommonly powerfully. They resemble machines of iron that follow a single path until they are finally dismantled.

It is remarkable when such minds speak about the sciences, such as biology. They apply them the way Stone Age man did, transforming them only into a means to slay others.

They take no pleasure in having an idea. They have had many—their yearning drives them toward fortresses from which cannons fire upon the masses and spread fear. Once they have achieved this goal, they interrupt their intellectual work, regardless of what arguments have helped them climb to the top. Then they give themselves over to the pleasure of killing. It was this drive to commit mass murder that propelled them forward in such a meaningless and confused way in the first place.

People with such natures could be recognized earlier, in eras when faith could still be tested. Nowadays they hide under the cloak of ideas. These are quite arbitrary, as seen in the fact that when certain goals are achieved, they are discarded like rags.

The announcement came today of Japan's declaration of war. Perhaps the year 1942 will be the one when more people than ever before will pass over and enter Hades.

PARIS, 8 DECEMBER 1941

Walked through the deserted streets of the city in the evening. Because of the assassinations, the populace is under curfew in the early evening. Everything lies lifeless in the fog. The sound of radios and chattering children came from the houses, as if I were walking among birdcages.

In the course of my work about the struggle between the army and the Party for authority in France, I am translating the farewell letters of the hostages[26] who have been executed in Nantes. These came to light in the files. I want to preserve them because they would otherwise be lost. Reading them has given me strength. When faced with imminent death, man seems to emerge from his blind will and realize that love is the most intimate of all connections. Except for love, death is perhaps our only benefactor in this world.

In my dream I felt Dorothea returning from my early childhood days. I felt her approach and touch me with her delicate and slender fingertips. I felt each individual finger, especially at the point where the fingernails begin as she trailed her hands over me. Then she stroked parts of the face, the eyelids, the corners of the eyes, the zygomatic arches.

That was a very pleasant characteristic of this being and her whole conception. She performed the most detailed physical survey on me; it almost seemed as though she were trying to sculpt me, for she moved her fingers as though molding a fine pastry dough.

Then she turned her attention to the hand, but she seemed to make a mistake as she made long strokes across the back of my hand. While this was happening I noticed in the magnetism of this contact that she was now caressing the imaginary hand whose fingers were a bit longer than those of the physical one.

In parting, she placed her hand upon my forehead and whispered, "My dear friend, say your farewell to freedom."

For a long time I lay awake in the dark, sad as never before, at least since the days of Vincennes.

PARIS, 9 DECEMBER 1941

The Japanese are attacking with fierce determination. Perhaps because time is most precious for them. I surprise myself by changing allegiances. Sometimes I am overcome by the mistaken belief that they have declared war on us. It is impossible to untangle, like a sack full of snakes.

PARIS, 10 DECEMBER 1941

Floods. I was in the nineteenth century with a party of people on an outing who had taken refuge upon toppled oak trees to escape the mud. At the same time, great numbers of snakes were struggling to get to these dry spots. The men lashed out at the creatures with their walking sticks and flung some of them high into the air, so that some smashed when they fell but others landed in the crowd, biting. That caused an outbreak of panic, and people threw themselves into the mud. I was bitten by a living cadaver as it hit me. I thought: if these brutes left the animals alone, we would all be safe.

As I translate the letters of the executed hostages as a document for future ages, I notice that the most frequent words are "courage" and "love." Perhaps "farewell" is even more frequent. It seems that in such situations man senses a compassionate power and abundance of generosity, and he can comprehend his actual role as that of victim, as that of benefactor.

KIRCHHORST, 24 DECEMBER 1941

On furlough in Kirchhorst. Here I feel hardly any urge to write—a good sign for the gravitational pull that Perpetua exerts on me. Why carry on a monologue? Visitors, including Carl Schmitt. He stayed here for two days.

During the night, images in the style of Hieronymus Bosch: a crowd of naked people, among them executioners and victims. In the foreground a woman of wonderful beauty whose head the executioner struck off with a single blow. I saw the torso stand for a moment before it crumpled—yet even headless, it seemed desirable.

Other henchmen dragged their victims along on their backs so as to slaughter them somewhere else, in private. I saw that they had bound the chins with cloth to prevent any obstruction to the blow.

The ducks in the garden. They mate in the puddles on the lawn left by the rain. Then the duck stands in front of the drake and flaps her wings, puffing out her chest—a primeval courtship ritual.

1942

ON THE TRAIN, 2 JANUARY 1942

Returned to Paris at midnight. Before that, dinner on Stephansplatz with Ernstel and Perpetua.[27] Looking at the boy in profile, I noticed the genteel but also pained quality his face has acquired. In these times, the two go hand in hand. The year will be extraordinarily perilous; we never know whether we are seeing each other for the last time. Every farewell includes the confidence in a higher reunion.

In the compartment, conversation with a lieutenant returning from Russia. His battalion lost a third of its men to the freezing temperatures, in part because of the amputations. The flesh turns white, then black. Conversations like this are now quite common. He says there are field hospitals for soldiers with frostbitten genitals, and even their eyes are endangered. Frost and fire conspire like the two blades of a vicious pair of shears.

PARIS, 4 JANUARY 1942

At Ladurée's in the company of Nebel and the Doctoresse. We spent the afternoon chatting in the [Hotel] Wagram. I have the impression that, given the nature of the situation, we can no longer continue as caution dictates. As in the act of childbirth, we are forced onward. This is the effect of the reviews of *On the Marble Cliffs*[28] in the Swiss papers.

I like the euphony of the *Ei* in *bleiben* [remain, stay], in the same way that I like other vowel sounds, such as in *manere* [Lat. remain], *manoir* [Fr. country house, manor]. This is the way we must rediscover language.

Grüninger, about his conversation with a theologian: "Evil always appears at first as Lucifer, then evolves into Diabolus, and finally ends as Satanas." This is the way the Bringer of Light develops, from the one who divides to the one who destroys—or, to express this with the quality of vowels, we see the triad: *U, I, A*.

PARIS, 5 JANUARY 1942

During the midday break bought paper for my manuscript about peace. Began with the outline. Also tested the safe for its security.

PARIS, 6 JANUARY 1942

Stavrogin.[29] His disgust with power. No corrupt authority ever tempts him. By contrast, we have the man who comes from below, Pyotr Stepanovich,[30] who understands quite well that under such conditions power becomes a possibility for him. Thus, the humbler man rejoices when he sees the magnificent woman he desires shamed, for only then does she become attainable for him.

This also shows up after the fact, in the regiment. Where villains reign, they can be seen exercising infamy without restraint and disregarding the tenets of statecraft. This infamy is celebrated like a mass; in its depths, it conceals the mystery of popular power.

Read the manuscript of Maurice Betz's translation of *Gärten und Straßen* [Gardens and Streets]. For the word *freilich* [certainly] I found *il est vrai* [it is true], which in this instance does not sound right to me. *Freilich* can precede a qualifier; on the other hand, it can also signal emphasis. The closest to it is probably "my opinion boils down to . . . ," or "when we consider this properly, we find that . . . " You could say that it's an intensifier, but it also makes you put your cards on the table. Yet something else is in play here as well, namely a note of exhortation, a kind of cheerful affirmation implied for the reader's benefit. The reader's assent has been tacitly assumed.

At the George V in the evening. Among those present were Nebel, Grüninger, Count Podewils, Heller, and Maggi Drescher, a young sculptress. Nebel declaimed the poem to Harmodios and Aristogeiton, to whom there stands a magnificent statue in the Museo Nazionale [Naples]. He followed this with verses by Sappho, Sophocles, and Homer. He easily accesses the extraordinary memory he has at his disposal, giving the impression that he is actively creating the poetry. That's the way to quote: by incantation . . .

PARIS, 7 JANUARY 1942

In the afternoon at Poupet's on Rue Garancière. In these narrow streets around Saint-Sulpice with their antiquarian bookshops, book dealers, and old workshops, I feel so at home, it's as though I had lived among them for five hundred years.

When I entered the building, I recalled that I had first crossed this threshold in the summer of 1938 coming from the Palais du Luxembourg just as today via Rue de Tournon. And so, the circle of years gone by has closed like the clasp of a belt.

When I entered I tried to convey this feeling to Poupet, the feeling that overwhelms me so often when I glimpse old familiar things and people—this feeling from the past, bounteous as a net full of fish, becomes clear when we encounter it again. Even though this was difficult to express in a foreign language, I had the impression that he understood me.

Charmille. We talked about Proust, and Poupet gave me one of his letters. Then about acquaintances whom she characterized in acerbic detail. Also about the influence of Eros upon physical development. Related to this, the word *souplesse* [flexibility], like *désinvolture* [detachment], seems untranslatable.

The first letter from Perpetua. As I had sensed, after they had brought me to the station, the two of them continued talking about me for a long time on their way home through the dark streets. She might buy a house for us near Uelze, that region in the heart of the [Lüneburg] Heath would be just right for the solitary life we both long for.

In addition, a letter from Wolfgang, who—the third of us four brothers— has been called up. As a corporal, he has been put in charge of a prison camp in Züllichau. The prisoners will be in good hands there. He writes this curiosity: "Yesterday I was sent on official business to Sorau in the Lausitz [area], where I had to deliver a prisoner to the field hospital. While there, I also had to pay a visit to the asylum. There I encountered a woman whose only tic consisted of continuously murmuring 'Heil Hitler.' At least it's a fitting, topical form of insanity."

Even when viewed tactically, exaggerated prudence increases danger. People listen most carefully to those who disguise their voices. There is, incidentally, an aristocratic as well as a Jacobin instinct for anyone not party to this. There are degrees of subtlety and simplicity that are dissembled, and ultimately, what is prudence without providence?

PARIS, 9 JANUARY 1942

In the evening, another bottle of Beaune with Weinstock, who is going to Angers. In him, as well as in Nebel and Friedrich Georg,[31] I can observe the powerfully formative influence that ancient Greek culture still exerts upon modern Germans. Their language, history, art, and philosophy will always remain indispensable for the training of elites.

I was thinking again with great animation about *The Marble Cliffs*. The book is open-ended, unfinished; it finds its continuation in events. On the other hand, the events harken back and change the book. In this sense, it resembles an ellipse with two foci. One of these marks the author's place; the other, the place of facts. Filaments connect these two as in nuclear fission. Thus, it can change fate, but it's also possible for it to determine the fate of the author. This indicates that he had been working in other realms than language—for example, where dream imagery is powerful.

PARIS, 10 JANUARY 1942

Tea with the Doctoresse. In the evening we went to a small cellar restaurant on Rue de Montpensier to meet Poupet and Cocteau. Cocteau was delightful, ailing, ironic, fastidious. He complained that people were sabotaging his plays, letting rats loose, and throwing teargas bombs onto the stage.

Among the anecdotes he recounted, I found the one about the bad-tempered coachman especially good. When he was a student in school, he had taken a cab home in the pouring rain after seeing a play in the theater. Unfamiliar with the standard rates of tipping, he gave the coachman too little and then approached the door of the building where the family, who were friends of his parents, was standing in the rain because the lock was difficult to open. As he greeted them, the coachman called after him: "What kind of tip is this—what if I were to tell them where I picked you up?"

Read a little more back in the Raphael. I finished the novel by Countess Podewils, then started *Confession* by Kanne. It is a significant work, recommended to me by Carl Schmitt, its editor. Kanne's experiences at prayer. He feels it when his prayers "get through." His own little cog of destiny turns in conformity with the course of the universe.

Woke up at five o'clock. I had dreamed that my father had died. Then I thought about Perpetua for a long time.

In the morning, Maurice Betz came and brought his translation. We looked through a series of questionable passages and normalized some of the less common words, particularly names of animals and plants. In such cases it is best to go back to the Latin of Linnaeus's system. That logical, conceptual system makes it possible to elucidate philosophical and poetic differences.

Paris, 13 January 1942

Birthday party at the Raphael. It dawned on me for the first time that the inhabitants of this hotel are trustworthy. That kind of thing is only possible today when the circle is the result of an unspoken self-selection. A vicious joke that Phillipps told about Kniébolo gave the signal for candid conversation. Coercion and caution separate people like masks; when these are stripped off, exuberant merriment breaks out. I got into a serious conversation with Merz and Hattingen and explained the main ideas of my manuscript about peace to them.

Conversation with Luther about surveillance. He said it had been difficult to recruit Englishmen for the job, yet before the war, he had succeeded in recruiting a man of good social position whom they equipped with a shortwave radio that he still uses to transmit weather reports from London. He said this was crucial for the aerial attacks. This Englishman had recently given shelter to an agent who had broken his leg in a parachute landing. For weeks he had to hide and care for the man in his apartment. The first time this agent went out, he was arrested and later executed without ever having betrayed his host.

These things have an almost demonic nature, especially when we consider the terrible loneliness such people endure in the midst of a population of millions. For this reason, I can't commit any details to these pages.

Paris, 14 January 1942

Charmille. There are conversations that can only be compared to smoking opium together. Part of this is the lighthearted, effortless back and forth, like the gracefully coordinated movements of acrobats. She, incidentally, praises something in my own conversation that others have criticized: that I am almost always thinking of other things and often reply to sentences after my partner makes some good observation—once they have long since dissolved into the greater context.

Paris, 15 January 1942

In the mail, a letter from Feuerblume with a note about the Hippopotamus:[32]

"I think that your princess has been a bit influenced by 'The Fall of the House of Usher,' but she also shows the path to healing. That is good. Poe showed only the decline."

The fact is, when I conceived of this story in a dream before visiting Kubin, I experienced a powerful longing to emerge from the maelstrom. We have to view such things as prognostication, for these imagined figures begin the circle dance of destiny, keeping it going, sometimes smiling and sometimes terrified. And literature is invisible history, as yet unlived—but also its corrective.

In addition, a letter from Perpetua who in the meantime has taken a look at the house near Bevensen. During the trip she got into a political discussion with the driver. To her amusement, he ended it with the comment: "Anything but a group where the chairman has lice."

By the way, it is one of her greatest qualities that she can converse on all social levels. When she presides at table she puts everyone at ease.

PARIS, 17 JANUARY 1942

In my dream, I was at Emmerich Reitter's in Paskau looking at insects. He showed me a case filled with examples of the species *Sternocera*. Instead of showing their typical cylindrical form, all of them were broad and flat. I nonetheless recognized their classification at first sight. I love these variations that still preserve the species. These are the adventurous journeys of an idea across archipelagoes of matter.

In the afternoon, Charmille picked me up to go swimming. Magnificent sight in the pond. I saw one of the large and marvelous fishes cloaked in tiny bubbles, hovering in the green water. I perceived this from above, foreshortened, as is frequently the case with magical things.

PARIS, 18 JANUARY 1942

A restless night. Sleep interrupted by long period of wakefulness. I spent the time thinking of Carus, my imaginary son.

In the evening, I saw Armand, who wants to go underground. We ate together in the Brasserie Lorraine. After walking up Rue du Faubourg Saint-Honoré, where I always feel good, he asked me whether I wanted to meet his friend Donoso, and I said no. Later he responded to a comment about both our countries: "*Ah, pour ça je voudrais vous embracer bien fort.*" [Ah, for that I'd like to give you a big hug.] Said goodbye on Avenue de Wagram.

I then put my uniform on and went to the George V. Speidel, Sieburg, Grüninger, and Rörecht, chief of the General Staff of the First Army, with whom I had discussed Rimbaud and similar things in Hamburg right after World War I. Then Colonel Gerlach, who has come to us from the East as a quartermaster, and in whose conversation one can study the pungent wit of Potsdam.

There are always the same conversations in these gatherings, sometimes more, sometimes less emphatic, as though we were in the antechambers of the inevitable. In these situations, I always have to think of Bennigsen and Czar Paul. Gerlach, in particular, was informed about the lack of winter clothing in the East. This—like the execution of hostages in the West—will become one of the major themes of later research, whether that research is focused on the history of the war or on adjudicating it.

On optics. In the afternoon in the Raphael, looking up from my reading, I stared at a round clock. When I turned my gaze away, it remained as a pale, round after-image on the wallpaper. I kept my eye focused on a projection from the wall that was closer than the part the clock was fastened to. Here the after-image appeared much smaller than the clock. But when I moved my eyes so that my gaze got very close to the clock, then its after-image merged with it, and they both overlapped. And finally, when I projected it to a point farther away, I had the impression that it grew bigger.

This is a nice example for the mental alteration that we project based on distance. By straining the retina in the same way, we enlarge a familiar object in the distance, and we minimize it when it seems closer. E. A. Poe bases his story "The Sphinx" upon this law.

Nowadays when I wake up at night in the Raphael, as often happens, I can hear the deathwatch beetle in the wooden paneling. It knocks louder and slower—and with greater significance—than the ones I heard in the dead wood of my father's pharmacy. These somber signals probably come from a large dark *Anobiid* [wood borer beetle]. I found a specimen of one on the staircase last summer and now have it in my collection in Kirchhorst. I could not identify it; it is probably an imported species.

These sounds announce a tremendous remoteness from everyday life—sounds from a creature active nearby in the dry wood. And yet, in comparison to other distances, it is close and familiar. We are passengers on one ship.

PARIS, 20 JANUARY 1942

In the evening with Doctor Weber in Palais Rothschild. Thanks to his clandestine gold purchases, he has a thorough knowledge of all the occupied territories and the neutral countries. I asked him if he would pay a visit to Brock in Zürich regarding the matter of the Swiss newspapers. He can also be useful to me in other ways. I enjoy talking with him, especially because he's a compatriot who exemplifies the dry humor of the Lower Saxon type. He leaves the impression that the world is not about to end all that soon.

Incidentally, it is instructive to see a gathering of intellects like those assembled during that remarkable meeting of national revolutionaries at Kreitz's at the Eichhof [Conference] and to consider them in a European and global context. One can sense what lies at the core of the human being—sometimes it is the tyrant in the petty bookkeeper or the mass murderer in the ridiculous swaggerer. These histrionics are rare because it takes extraordinary circumstances for this core to reveal itself. It is also remarkable to reencounter marginalized characters and literary types whose chaotic nocturnal rantings are impossible to forget. How amazing to meet them again in positions of authority where their word is law. There are times when the flimsiest dreams force their way into reality. Yet when Sancho Panza[33] was governor of Barataria, at least he didn't take himself seriously. That's still his most attractive attribute.

In yesterday's dispatch, the Russians claim that when they try to remove the boots from German prisoners, the feet come off too.

A typical snippet of propaganda from that icy hell.

PARIS, 21 JANUARY 1942

Visit to Charmille on Rue de Bellechasse.

The clock runs faster during our chats, as in the primeval forests of old. Various factors converge to create this effect: beauty, complete intellectual comprehension, and the presence of danger. I attempt to slow the pace through reflection. This retards the delicate clockwork.

I find a human being—that's like saying, "I discover the Ganges, Arabia, the Himalayas, the Amazon River." I saunter through that person's secluded places and vast expanses; I note the treasures I find there, and in doing so, I change and grow. In this sense, especially in that person, we are formed by our fellow human beings, our brothers, friends, women. The atmospheric conditions of other climates remain in us—so powerfully that after some encounters I feel: "This person must have known this or that other one." Contact with human beings stamps us like goldsmiths' hallmarks on precious objects.

PARIS, 24 JANUARY 1942

In Fontainebleau with Röhricht, the commander of the First Army. He lives in the house belonging to the Dolly sisters. I spent the night there. Reminisced about old times, the Hanoverian Riding School, Fritsch, Seeckt, and the aged Hindenburg—in those days, we lived in the embryo of the Leviathan. The stone floor of the dining room is tiled in green-veined marble and lacks a carpet. According to the old custom, it is uncarpeted so that diners could toss bones and scraps of meat onto the floor for the dogs. Fireside chat, first about Mommsen and Spengler, and then about the progress of the campaign. Our conversation reminded me of the damage Burckhardt caused with his *Renaissance*,[34] especially those Nietzschean impulses that spread among the educated class. These were intensified by theories from natural science. It is strange how pure speculation can be transformed into will, into passionate action.

Simplification corresponds to complication—weight and counterweight in the clock of destiny. Just as there is a second religiosity, there is a second brutality, more pallid and neurotic than the original.

I always work hard at such conversations—you have to be less focused on the individual than on the hundreds of thousands of people he represents.

In the morning Lieutenant Rahmelow showed me the castle.

Charmille. Concerning dreams of flying. She told me that she often thinks she can fly, and demonstrated this with a graceful sweep of both arms. Yet when she does so, she has the feeling of being anchored by a weight hanging from her body. She calls the compulsion to fly a persecution that is always a variety of fear. That could apply to many situations, even to our contemporary one.

The upswing that she described with her arms was less that of a bird than one of a delicate dinosaur. Or maybe the gesture contained a hint of both. It makes me think of the winged rowing motion of the Archaeopteryx.

PARIS, 25 JANUARY 1942

In the Madeleine Theater in the afternoon to see a play by Sacha Guitry. Enthusiastic applause: "*C'est tout à fait Sacha.*" [That's pure Sacha.] Cosmopolitan taste is always a matter of perspective and delights in scene changes, mistaken identity, and unexpected characters, as in a house of mirrors. The complications are so intricate that they are already forgotten on the staircase. Who did what to whom seems irrelevant. The nuances are pursued to such an extreme that nothing is spared.

A painting of Eleanora Duse in the foyer. It's only in recent years that I seem to have gained an appreciation for this kind of beauty. Her otherworldliness surrounds her like an impenetrable aura. The reason for this may be that we sense a kinship, a relationship in such beings; incest is part of it. It is easier to approach Aphrodite than Athena. When Paris handed over the apple, he created great desire and great suffering by speaking with the natural appetite of the shepherd, the warrior. At a more mature level, he might have discovered that an embrace can also bestow power and wisdom.

As always, before turning out the light, I read the Bible, where I have gotten to the end of the books of Moses. There I read the horrible curse that reminds me of Russia: "And thy heaven that is over thy head shall be brass, and the earth that is under thee shall be iron" [Deuteronomy 28:23].

My brother-in-law Kurt [von Jeinsen] laments in a letter that his nose and ears have almost frozen. Young recruits whose feet have frozen get dragged along. For all that, he had originally set out in a huge column of vehicles. In their last dispatch, the Russians claim that the week's fighting has cost us seventeen thousand dead and several hundred prisoners. And who would not prefer to be among the dead?

PARIS, 27 JANUARY 1942

In a letter, Feuerblume writes about her reactions to reading my *Gardens and Streets* and particularly to passages she has noted. For example, "that one must read the prose as if through latticework." To that, a female friend commented, "You have to be able to see the lions behind the bars."

It's curious that such images often produce concepts quite contrary to those intended. I meant, namely, that words form a lattice as they yield a glimpse of the unutterable. They engrave the setting for the gem, but the stone itself remains invisible. But I too shall adopt the image of the lion. Refraction produces one of the errors, but also the advantages of *style imagé*.[35]

PARIS, 28 JANUARY 1942

Reading through a text, my personal sensations and thoughts are always at work like an aura imparting a luster to this strange light.

In some sentences or images thoughts come to my consciousness in profusion. I then deal with the first one and leave the others out in the waiting room, but occasionally I open the door, just to see if they're still standing around. All the while, I continue reading.

While I'm reading, I always have the feeling that I am essentially dealing with my own material. This is what an author is supposed to produce. In doing so, he serves himself first, and only then, others.

The mail included a letter from Schlichter containing nine drawings for *One Thousand and One Nights*. An image of the City of Bronze is wonderfully successful—full of mourning for death and glory. The sight awakened in me the desire to possess the piece; I'd like to have it to complement his *Atlantis Before Its Destruction*, which has hung in my study for years. Early on my father developed a sharp eye for the magic of the tale of the City of Bronze, which is among the most beautiful in this wonderful book. Emir Musa is a man of profound spirit, a connoisseur of the melancholy of ruins, of the bitter pride that goes before a fall, which in our culture is at the heart of all archaeological effort. Musa considers this to be pure and contemplative.

PARIS, 29 JANUARY 1942

Wrote to Schlichter concerning the picture of the bronze city. In doing so, I thought of other tales from *One Thousand and One Nights*, especially the one about Peri Banu. That tale has always seemed like a description of an exalted love affair that makes people willing to foreswear or sacrifice inherited royal prerogative for its sake. It is beautiful the way the young prince disappears in this realm, as though into a more spiritual world. In this fairytale work, he and Musa stand out as princes from ancient Indo-European empires, far superior to the Oriental despots and quite comprehensible to us. Right at the beginning the archery competition with the bow is beautiful—the bow, a life symbol with metaphysical tension for Prince Achmed. His arrow thus flies incomparably far into the unknown and beyond all the others.

The castle of Peri Banu is the spiritualized Mountain of Venus. The invisible flame is everlasting, but the visible one consumes.

PARIS, 30 JANUARY 1942

Today's mail brought a letter from Friedrich Georg, who in reference to *Gardens and Streets*, quotes the sentence of Quintilian: "*Ratio pedum in oratione est multo quam in versu difficilior.*" [The principles governing metrical feet are much more difficult in prose than in verse.] Here he touches upon a question that has occupied me in recent years, namely how to take prose a step further, give it a new dynamic that unites both strength and grace. We must find new keys to unlock the enormous legacy that lies concealed there.

PARIS, 1 FEBRUARY 1942

Nebel visited me this morning to discuss an incident that occurred at his listening post. He certainly could not say that nobody had warned him. After he had incurred suspicion through his essay about the insect people (published by Suhrkamp), he now provoked denunciation.[36] In the hallways during the New Year's Eve festivities, they had made fun of the "Head Forester."[37] Nebel has to disappear for a while, but the departure of such a clever mind from this city saddens me.

In the afternoon at Madame Boudot-Lamotte's where Cocteau read aloud his new play *Renaud et Armide*. It was a magical combination of supple and melodious sound, and he was more than up to the task. His lilting voice had both lightness and strength and was especially fitting when describing how the sorceress Armida enchants and snares the bewitched Renaud. He let out cries of "*file file file*" [run run run], launching them into the air like autumnal gossamer.

There, in addition to Gaston Gallimard, I met Heller, Wiemer, the Doctoresse, and the actor Marais, a plebeian Antinous. Afterward, conversation with Cocteau while he recounted amusing anecdotes about a play that used painted human hands representing snakes rising up out of a basket on stage. Actors then lashed out at these beasts with sticks, but it happened that when one of the snakes was struck particularly hard, "*merde!*" [shit] was heard from beneath the trap door from a bellowing extra.

In Drouant, near the Opéra. It's one of my old failings that the days when I especially love my neighbors and those when I actually express this to them rarely coincide. At times the spirit of contradiction grips me powerfully.

Dreams at night—in deepest sleep, the meaning of the chambers became apparent to me. They bordered on the room where I was sleeping, and each had a door: one for the mother, one for the wife, for the sister, the brother, the father, the mistress. And in the silent power and influence of these rooms, in their over-whelming nearness and grand detachment, there lay something both solemn and fearfully clandestine.

"—and then the mother entered."

PARIS, 2 FEBRUARY 1942

At the Ritz in the evening with the sculptor Breker, who had invited me and his wife, an intelligent Greek woman—a true bohemian. Madame Breker devoured our appetizer of sardines without leaving a trace: "*J'adore les têtes, vous aussi?*" [I just love the heads, don't you?] Nebel was there as well, again with his typical Parnassian joviality. When it comes to things he likes, he possesses a delicate touch, as though he were lifting a curtain with a smile to reveal precious objects.

He called our modern savagery unique, insofar as it maintains no belief in the indestructibility of the human race and, in contrast with the Inquisition, is deter-mined to destroy and obliterate us all forever.

His case, incidentally, was decided with leniency: he was transferred to Étampes.

PARIS, 3 FEBRUARY 1942

In the morning, Jessen called on me in my room in the Majestic. As soon as I saw him, I remembered those good, or rather, precise predictions that I had heard about him a year ago when most people had not given any thought to a Russian war. The value of a clear, highly focused intellect that perceives the inherent logic of things is evident. You can see that in him, in his eyes, and especially upon his brow you see evidence of a consummately rational intellect. Men like him and Popitz, who was also present at the time, are the last specimens that German ideal-ism has driven into this desert.

New predictions. We talked about the rigidity that has made itself felt since the beginning of this year. I perceive it very clearly, as if I carried a gauge inside me that measures currents and countercurrents.

Then Valentiner, a son of the U-boat captain, the old Viking. As a corporal here, he has a minor post as an interpreter for the airmen. He spends most of his time with books or with friends in a studio that he has rented in a garret on the Quai Voltaire. He invited me there, and I had the feeling that the visit was going to be the first in a long friendship. It was gratifying to note his intellectual courage when he entered the room.

Stokers in a boiler room where pressure of a million atmospheres throbs behind the escape valves. The manometers rise gently beyond the last red line on the gauge. Things are suddenly silent. Flames flare up behind the tempered glass.

PARIS, 4 FEBRUARY 1942

Finished reading *La Faustine* by Edmond de Goncourt. A few weeks ago, I bought a copy of the book signed by the author from Berès. As I read it, I was slightly displeased whenever I came upon a fact that I was familiar with from Goncourt's journals. Things like that can be annoying in artistic works, which should incorporate life experiences more profoundly and unobtrusively. Otherwise they remind us of the sort of picture that disrupts painted imagery with an overlay of collage.

A word about the author's method of connecting with the reader: In his preface, Goncourt invites his female readers to send him *documents humains* [personal documentation] revealing private details of their lives that could be useful to him as an artist. This gesture is improper; it oversteps the boundaries of the genre that should constrain the work.

Faustine shows little composition, and the characters make entrances where they are not necessary, but the author happens to need them. Furthermore, the decadence is so far advanced that it is tolerable only in very well-written descriptions.

PARIS, 5 FEBRUARY 1942

New poems by Friedrich Georg arrived from Überlingen. In "Zelina," I recognize his old love for female tightrope walkers and circus performers. I had already known "Peacocks," so full of bright sunshine, as though reflected from faceted gems, and the poem "Sundial." A man's true masculinity does not begin to show until he has reached his fortieth year.

PARIS, 6 FEBRUARY 1942

This morning's dreams were of a pond or lagoon edged in stone. I stood there to watch the creatures in the water. Birds would dive beneath the surface and fish would jump out. I listened to a gray speckled coot as it swam over the rocky bottom. Stone-gray fishes rose to the surface, dreaming and becoming ever more visible. I watched this from my vantage point on domes that protruded from the water's surface and twice gave way underneath me: I had been standing on the shells of tortoises.

Paris, 8 February 1942

At Speidel's this morning. There was a large crowd in his outer office because of the Sunday signatures. He had just returned from headquarters and showed me the notes he had made on the files. These altered my opinion that strategies of elimination—those efforts to murder by shooting, starving, and exterminating—are produced by a general nihilistic tendency in our age. Of course that is also true, but behind the swarms of herrings, there are sharks driving them on.

No doubt there are individuals responsible for the blood of millions, and they go after bloodshed like tigers. Aside from their vulgar instincts, they have an inherently satanic will that takes cold pleasure in destroying human beings, perhaps even humanity. A deep sorrow seems to come over them, a wail of fury when they sense that some power prevents them from devouring as much as their lust demands. You can see them preparing massacres when these seem unnecessary, even when they threaten their own security. It was horrible to hear what Jodl reported about Kniébolo's objectives.

Let's not forget that many Frenchmen support such plans and are eager to provide the hangman's services. But here in our organization there are regulations in force that restrain the participation of our partners and even put a stop to clandestine activities. Most of all, it is crucial that any semblance of humanity be diligently avoided.

Went to the X-Royal in the afternoon with the Doctoresse. After that, to visit Valentiner on the Quai Voltaire. An ancient elevator supported by a cable alarmed us all the way up as it let out creaking wails of protest. In the garret, we found several little rooms full of old furniture; books were strewn about on tables and easy chairs. The owner received us in casual civilian attire. Whenever time permits, he sneaks off to this hideaway and changes his life with a change of clothes as he wiles away the hours in reading and introspection or in the company of friends. The degree to which he succeeds is a testimony to his freedom and imagination. In this place Cocteau felt himself reminded of times he had spent similarly during World War I. We enjoyed fine conversation in his little lair and were able to gaze out over the ancient roofs of Saint-Germain-des-Prés.

Paris, 10 February 1942

Called on Nostitz in the evening on Place du Palais-Bourbon. Among the guests, I noticed the young Count Keyserling,[38] although he spoke not a word the whole evening. He reclined in an easy chair half languishing and luxuriating dreamily like a cat. The old families still have a sense of security, even intrinsic elegance, in the most intellectual circles.

Paris, 12 February 1942

Took a walk down Avenue des Ternes in the middle of the day. After these past weeks of bleakness, the first glimmer of spring filled the air with life. Underfoot the black, hard-packed snow still lay on the streets. I was feeling nervous, excited, and whimsical, which often happens when spring approaches.

On the catastrophe of human life: the heavy wheel that grinds us to a pulp, the shot of the murderer or fanatic that cuts us down. The tinder had accumulated inside us long enough, and now the spark has just been ignited. The explosion comes from inside us.

This caused so many of the wounds in World War I. They corresponded to the fiery spirit that exhilarated me and found escape valves because it was too powerful for the body. The same is true of the wild escapades and affairs that result in wounds and often, suicide. Life leaps into the barrel of a revolver.

Went to the Raphael. Met Major von Voss, in whom a bit of the fifteenth century is visible, like a vein of silver in a rock. His bloodstream carries something of the troubadour, something of the old free and easy sorcery. There is always good company there. From encounters like this, you can learn history right from its source.

PARIS, 15 FEBRUARY 1942

I dropped in to see the Doctoresse, who was laid up with sciatica. Conversation about the human body, then about its specific anatomy. She told me that in the early days on her way home from the dissection lab after staring at the deep red color of human flesh, she often felt ravenous.

PARIS, 16 FEBRUARY 1942

Andromeda. In the case of such regal daughters, it's the same as with the Germanic tribes: They had to be broken before they embraced Christianity. They can love only when they are prey to the dragon in the abyss.

The love of a particular woman is twofold, because on the one hand, she shares what she has in common with millions of other women, and at the same time, she alone possesses what differentiates her from all others. How strange it is that both aspects meet so perfectly in the individual—the chalice and the wine.

PARIS, 17 FEBRUARY 1942

Visited Calvet in the evening at a party that included Cocteau, Wiemer, and Poupet, who gave me an autograph of Proust for my collection. That prompted Cocteau to tell about his association with Proust. He would never let anybody dust his rooms; the layer of dust on the furniture was as "thick as chinchilla." Upon arrival, you would be asked by the housekeeper whether or not you had brought flowers, whether you were wearing scent, or had been in the company of a woman wearing perfume. He was usually to be found in bed, but dressed and wearing yellow gloves to prevent him biting his nails. He spent a lot of money making workers in the building stop because their noise disturbed him. It was never permitted to open a window. The night table was covered with medicines, inhalers, and sprays. His refined taste did not lack macabre aspects: he would go to the slaughterhouse and ask to be shown how a calf was killed.

Concerning poor style: This becomes most apparent in moral contexts, such as when a bad writer tries to justify the shooting of hostages. That is far worse—far more flagrant—than any mere aesthetic offense.

Style is essentially based on justice. Only the just man can know how he must weigh each word, each sentence. For this reason, we never see the best writers serving a bad cause.

PARIS, 18 FEBRUARY 1942

Visit from Baron von Schramm, back from the eastern front. The colossal loss of life in the gruesome cauldrons[39] awakens a longing for the old death—death that was other than being trampled. Schramm expressed the opinion that not everyone was dragged into these lethal rings, just as fate did not send everyone to the Manchester bone mills.[40] The crucial distinction is ultimately whether you die a humane death in either of these. Then you draw on personal strength to make your own bed and altar. In those depths, many of our grimmest dreams come true; things become historical reality that we have seen coming for a long time—for more than seventy years.

PARIS, 22 FEBRUARY 1942

Called on Klaus Valentiner on the Quai Voltaire in the afternoon. There I met Nebel, the "Outcast of the Islands,"[41] who is being sent to one of the islands tomorrow, just as in the days of the Roman Emperors. Then visited Wiemer, who is leaving. While I was there, Madeleine Boudot, Gallimard's secretary, handed me the page proofs of the translation of *Marble Cliffs* by Henri Thomas.

In the Raphael I woke up to a new attack of melancholy. This just comes, like rain or snow. The enormous distance that separates us human beings became clear to me, a distance that we can gauge in our relationships with our nearest and dearest. We are separated from each other by endless distances like the stars. But that will all change after death. The most beautiful part of death is that it erases this distance while extinguishing the physical light. We shall be in heaven.

An idea that makes me feel better: maybe Perpetua is thinking of me at this moment.

The struggle of life, the burden of individuality. On the other hand, all that is universal, with its ever-rising high-water mark. In moments of embrace, we submerge ourselves in it, sink down into strata penetrated by the roots of the tree of life. Of course, there is also superficial, transitory lust—combustible as kindling. Above and beyond this lies marriage—"you shall be one flesh." Your sacrament: one bears only half the burden. Finally death, which tears down the walls of individuation. That will be the moment of greatest genius (Matthew 22:30). All of our true bonds have laid aside the mystical knot tied in eternity. We are granted sight when the light is extinguished.

Books. It is wonderful to find thoughts, words, and sentences in them that make the reader suspect that the narrative is leading him down a man-made trail through uncharted forests, deep and unfamiliar. Thus, he is led through regions with unknown borders, and only occasionally do tidings of plenty reach him like a breath of fresh air. The author must seem to be distributing unlimited treasure, and by paying in hard currency, he introduces foreign coins—doubloons, with the coats of arms of unexplored lands. Kipling's phrase, "but that is another story" must be weighed carefully in the text.

PARIS, 23 FEBRUARY 1942

This afternoon went to the Palais Talleyrand for a tea in honor of the departing commander-in-chief, General Otto von Stülpnagel.

He shows a remarkable combination of delicacy, grace, resilience, reminiscent of a court dancer, with traits that are also wooden and melancholy. He uses phrases of elaborate courtliness, wears high patent leather boots and gold buttons on his uniform.

He summoned me to talk about the hostage question, as he is concerned about how posterity will judge the exact description in the historical record. This is the reason for his present departure. In his position, one can see only the grand trappings of proconsular power from the outside, not the clandestine plots and other palace intrigues. This problem is fraught with tensions between the embassy and the Party in France, which is gradually gaining ground without the support of the High Command. On Speidel's orders, the development and continuation of this struggle—wrangling over the lives of the hostages—will be part of my report in the confidential files.

The general first touched upon the human, all too human, aspects of the matter. People could see that things had affected his nerves and shaken him to the core. Then he went into the tactical reasons for his resistance. He was of the opinion that it was necessary to tread a middle way, especially considering the damaging potential of the situation. The industries would produce more, the better this matter were managed here. In view of the unexpected course of the eastern campaign, he deemed this to be of the highest importance. He argued that our influence in Europe must transcend the current age in which we are a presence brandishing bayonets. He claimed that he had always remained on the side of reason, with never a shred of weakness, which the political leadership had accused him of. Like many old professional soldiers, he was particularly hurt by the allegations of weakness and unreliability.

In view of the tremendous superiority of the enemy, he considered retreat to be the only possible tactical option. For this reason, he tried to give special emphasis to the fact that acts of collective retribution were only doing the *résistance* the greatest favor. This explains the sentence that frequently appeared in his brief communiqués to the High Command: "The reprisals are getting out of hand." With a single revolver shot, a terrorist could incite a powerful ripple effect of hatred. The result was a paradoxical subterfuge of concealing the majority of the assassinations in the report to the High Command.

The pervasive weakness of the middle class and the aristocracy shows in these generals. They have enough vision to recognize the way things are going, but they lack the authority and ability to oppose minds motivated only by violence. The new masters exploit them like wardens. But what if these last props were to fall? Then horrible leaden terror like the Cheka[42] will spread over the land.

There is always something timeless in these situations. In this case, it's the figure of the proconsul, one of whom was Pilate. The *demos*[43] vehemently demanded the blood of the innocents from him as they cheered the murderers on. And from afar the emperor, who enjoyed divine status, threatened with his thunderbolt. That makes it difficult to maintain the dignity of a senator—he passes judgment as he washes his hands or, as in this case, he disappears like an air-raid warden into a Berlin apartment block.

Death. A few, too refined for this life, dare to disobey. They seek the void, isolation. Some beings who cleanse the filth of their natures with light often show their noble character in their death masks.

What I love about man is his essence beyond the grave and the fellowship with it. Here, love is nothing more than a pallid reflection. "*Was hier wir sind, kann dort ein Gott ergänzen.*" [What we are here, a god can augment there.][44]

How did Pontius Pilate enter the Creed?[45]

We would have to ask the Copts; they honor him as a martyr.

In my dreams at night, I am climbing cliff fortifications. Their foundations are so weak that my weight dislodges them, and my every movement brings the threat of a terrible plunge.

As soon as I sensed that I could no longer keep my balance, I tried to open my eyes and switch off the dream. My action was like that of someone showing a film in which he is also acting: when catastrophes approached, I cut off the electricity.

In this respect, I have learned a lot that should stand me in good stead for my daytime life. We generate the world from dreams and, if necessary, must dream more intensely. For these years there was a dream in which my behavior was significant: I was sailing to Rhodes when Kniébolo appeared and engaged me in a test of will.

Report on how things unfolded chronologically during the night at Gerstberger's in Ermatingen. Vesuvius opened up for a moment; the insight followed that historical forces could not reverse things. The dogs howled outside the house. That must have been preceded by Trott's nighttime visit to the vineyard. "They want to confront the dragon and are awaiting the order from you." By daylight, clouds form above the fearsome crag.

PARIS, 24 FEBRUARY 1942

Visited Fabre-Luce in the evening on Avenue Foch. There I met two professors of philosophy who are brothers and a Monsieur Rouvier.

The host told a story about an acquaintance who hated priests. Often when the man came home he would fold his hands and say, "My God, I thank you for not making me a believer. I thank you."

He was once sitting on a bench in the forest in Upper Bavaria looking at the mountains when a tree crashed to the earth beside him. He left because he no longer found the view as pleasant. "*Il y a des choses, qui rompent le charme.*" [There are things that break the spell.]

We ate in the study, which was paneled halfway up in dark wood. A large map of the world was mounted in one of the walls. It was completely white, like terra incognita, and only the places that its owner had seen were painted in.

PARIS, 28 FEBRUARY 1942

Letters. Mother writes to me from Obersdorf that she is disturbed by the little word *nichts* [nothing], which is beginning to appear with ever-greater connotations. For example on posters: *"Das Volk ist alles—du bist nichts."* [The nation is everything—you are nothing.] That would then be a totality composed of zeroes. You certainly get that impression at times. The game that the nihilists play is becoming more and more transparent. The high stakes force them to show their cards and often for no reason.

Otte reports that in Hamburg there is talk of pulping the remaining copies of Kubin's *Andere Seite* [*The Other Side*]. That would merely achieve a destruction of paper, whereas with people, it would be a destruction of the flesh.

Finally a letter from Henri Thomas, who is all worked up about the translation of some proper names and place names that have allusive meaning in the *Marble Cliffs*. An example is "Fillerhorn," which derives from the obsolete verb *fillen*, meaning to maltreat, abuse, or skin. He choses *corne aux tanneurs* and says that this guild is one of the oldest and that mentioning it would convey a dark, medieval tone as well as one of suspicion. Köppelsbleek—or better, Köppelesbleek—is a place of bleached skulls.[46] For that he uses the expression *rouissage* [retting]. Here I was using a place name of a landscape feature in the region of Goslar. In Germany, the name has already changed to Göbbelesbleek. For Pulverkopf, he wanted to use *hauteflamme* of *brusqueflamme*, but that choice did not seem to connote enough irony to answer the old artillery soldier whose name is not even known. He had boasted of having a cannon in reserve to use against Christendom. I suggested calling him *le vieux pétardier* [the old artilleryman], which seemed too coarse for Thomas. He suggested *boute feu*, which as well as fuse, can also mean arsonist—a word that over time has gained an ironic note. *Soit.* [So be it.]

I have the impression that he was being a little bit devious as he translated, for he knows how to walk like a hunter or trapper along the fault lines of language. Translation demands passion.

PARIS, 1 MARCH 1942

Finished reading Frédéric Bouyer *La Guyane Française* [French Guyana] a description of a journey the author took in 1862–1863. Good account of the flora, fauna, and people of the swamps. Even back then, the native people knew about a kind of vaccine against snakebite. One such young man, who thanks to this vaccine thought himself invulnerable, found a delicate coral adder while he was digging a grave and without listening to any warnings, draped it around himself like a necklace. He was bitten and died immediately. Another man who had also been vaccinated against snakes let pit vipers bite him for money. He also kept a number of them slithering around his dwelling, thus eliminating the need for lock and key, since everyone gladly avoided the place.

PARIS, 2 MARCH 1942

Visit from Grüninger, who has returned from the East. He commanded a battery there. A selection of his *capriccios* [anecdotes, sketches]:

The 281st Division, deployed with inadequate winter gear, was almost immediately wiped out by the frost and was dubbed "The Asthma Division."

At a crossing in a trench, a commissar who had been killed in hand-to-hand combat by a German corporal, had frozen solid in a standing position. This corporal, whose frequent duty it was to lead captured officers through the lines, used to take them past his frozen commissar, rather like a sculptor displaying his work.

A Russian colonel was captured with the remnants of his regiment, which had been in the cauldron for weeks. When asked the source for his troops' rations, he answered that they had nourished themselves from corpses. When reproached, he added that he himself had eaten only the livers.

PARIS, 3 MARCH 1942

Today was the first spring day after this grim winter. Joy and exhilaration animated the crowds on the Champs-Élysées. The sound of countless shovels removing the slabs of black snow from the streets was almost like Easter bells that aroused an agreeable feeling.

In the bookstore at 8 Rue de Castiglione I bought a three-volume page-turner, which promises to offer many an enjoyable hour during future winter nights on the Lüneburg Heath. It is a story of shipwrecks, winter survival, exposure to the elements, Robinson Crusoe–like adventures, firestorms, famine, and other calamitous incidents on the high seas. The book was published by Cuchet, Rue et Maison Serpente, in the third year of the Republic. A stamp reveals a former owner of the book to have been a Jesuit priory.

In this great chess match, women do not always consider the endgame, yet they appreciate it when intimations first suggest that direction with subtle clarity and nuance. That is the spice of seduction.

In the evening at Ramponneau with Abt, who had been a cadet with Friedrich Georg. After dinner, we heard a distant sound that reminded me of an explosion, so I wrote down the exact minute. When we heard further rumblings, we concluded it was a spring storm, not unusual around here at this time of year. When Abt asked the waiter whether it was raining, the man answered with a discreet smile, "The guests think it is a storm, but I'd prefer to believe that it's bombs." Hearing that, we decided to leave, and outside we heard that anti-aircraft fire really was in progress. The orange-yellow flares of the English hovered over the cityscape. Bombers occasionally darted over the roofs like bats.

The shooting continued for a long time after I had gone to bed. I read the essay by Du Bos about the Goncourts and a chapter in the Book of Samuel. The shelling provided contemporary atmosphere.

Paris, 4 March 1942

Last night's attack targeted the Renault works and by this evening has cost five hundred lives, mostly workers. Ten German soldiers were mortally wounded, and more than a thousand casualties have been admitted to the field hospitals. Although huge factories and two hundred dwellings were destroyed, from the vantage point of our quarter, the whole thing looked like stage lighting for a shadow play.

Paris, 5 March 1942

Yesterday the Doctoresse and I dined on one of the hens sent by dear Madame Richardet from Saint-Michel. Afterward, I consulted her about a bad cold I felt coming on. After drinking some hot rum in the Raphael, I lay awake most of the night in a semifeverish state. Such hours are not lost. I have the impression that when the temperature is elevated, body, and mind work better and faster as a unit, and one *surges* like water over a weir. For me, feverish nights are always highly creative. I'd like to assume that they have transformative power. In addition to distinguishing sickness from health, they also mark spiritual eras, the way festivals mark the seasons.

In the evening, paid a visit to Valentiner in his studio apartment on the Quai Voltaire. He had turned up a beautiful copy of Tocqueville for me; he also gave me the *Contes Noirs* by Saint-Albin. Heller, Rantzau, and Drescher also there; conversed with them about Tocqueville.

From delicate souls like Rantzau, I hear the opinion that in dangerous times like these leadership belongs in the hands of impulsive, brutal types and should be left up to them. *Après on verra.* [We'll see later on.] That's the point of view of a traveler who has landed in a flophouse and hopes that downstairs they will all kill each other while he is asleep upstairs. It doesn't always work out that way.

Paris, 6 March 1942

Went to lunch at Prunier with Mossakowsky, who used to be a colleague of Cellaris. If I can believe him, there are certain butchers in the large charnel houses[47] they have built in the border states on the eastern frontier, men who have single-handedly slain enough people to populate a midsize city. Such reports extinguish the colors of the day. You want to close your eyes to them, but it is important to view them like a physician examining a wound. They are symptoms of the monstrous lesion that must be healed—and I believe that it can be healed. If I did not retain that hope, I would immediately go *ad patres*.[48] This, of course, goes much deeper than anything political. Its infamy is unremitting.

Went with Weinstock and Grüninger to the Raphael in the evening, where the air was full of *capriccios* from the eastern front. Perhaps one day there will arise a new Goya to depict these *Desastros*,[49] an artist who understands the whole spectrum of human cruelty, including its absolute nadir.

Wounded Russians in the forest who screamed for help for hours drew their pistols and fired on German soldiers who finally came to rescue them. This is a sign that the struggle has reached the point of bestiality. An animal shot and lying where it fell begins to bite when it is touched.

People have seen corpses lying on the tarmac that have been crushed by thousands of tanks until they are as flat as sheets of paper. The march goes right over them, as if over decals or designs visible in the icy depths of the roads.

Grüninger represents the precursor of a type who is "above it all": able to cope with a high level of pain and at the same time more subtle in his perceptions. A paradoxical combination, but one that is probably the basis for this development in general, which arises from a pattern of converging forces.

At the table, there was a major who had lived in Moscow long before World War I and told stories of sleigh rides, fine furs, varieties of caviar, and dinners of Asiatic splendor. Today that sounds like a dreamland from a sumptuous fairytale realm, perhaps out of medieval Persia. One of the rich merchants had champagne served in silver chamber pots but immediately ordered it removed when he noticed a guest with an expression of disgust on his face. An example of fusion of coarseness and gentility that has probably changed very little.

Read further in the Book of Samuel. The rivalry between Saul and David gives us the pattern for every conflict between youthful strength and legitimate power. There is no negotiation here.

PARIS, 8 MARCH 1942

A letter from Friedrich Georg in the mail. Among other things, he gives an account of his visit to the Straubs in Nussdorf—in the very house we used to pass so often on our walks to the Birnau Forest. He describes the light in the apartment as having something flower-like about it, "as if the shapes of very bright blossoms formed in the air."

After dinner visited a young sculptor, Gebhardt, with Weinstock. He partially counts as an émigré and receives clandestine support from people here in the building. On the way, we discussed the situation as usual. It looks as though the three commanders-in-chief in the West are of one mind, and that we can expect the result in the form of a spring offensive. During such discussions, we passed by the catafalque that had been erected on the Place de la Concorde to honor the victims of the English aerial bombings. Dense crowds of Parisians file past the place.

At Gebhardt's we met Princess Bariatinski. Viewed the sculptures and thought the head by young Drescher particularly striking. The countess said of Claus Valentiner, "He is like a bee: everything he touches, he turns to honey."

The Doctoresse then arrived to pick me up, and I accompanied her through the quarter where the antiquarian bookshop are; these have always have the power to inspire me to dream, purely through the accumulated historical matter that they radiate.

In the night, I dreamed of various animals. Among them, a salamander with a blue back and a white abdomen speckled in blue and yellow. The exquisite nature of the colors lay in the fact that they were suffused with the glow of life, like fine damp leather. The freshness and delicacy of this palette melted into the creature.

The slate blue and somewhat yellowish white of the underbelly dominated the whole effect. Such glorious luster is only possible when animated by life—like the flames that consume love.

Woke up with thoughts of my old plan about the *Teoria dei Colori* [*The Theory of Colors*], which will treat color as a function of surface.

The fact that I love the most elusive, and probably also the best, in them—that may be the source of the coldness they perceive in me.

We live life merely at its edge: it is but a battlefield where the struggle for life is fought. It is a remote fort, hastily built in the dimension of the citadel into which we shall retreat in death.

The goal of life is to gain an idea of what life is. In the absolute sense, of course, that changes nothing, according to the priests—but it helps our journey.

We bring our chips to the table and gamble for infinitely high stakes. We are like children who play for beans without knowing that each one of them contains the potential for the marvels of blossoms and May.

PARIS, 9 MARCH 1942

In the evening, with the Doctoresse who invited me to the Comédie Française: *Les Femme Savantes* [*The Wise Women*]. There are still islands where one can find a mooring. In the foyer, Houdon's sculpture of the seated Voltaire, combining the traits of age and childhood in a wonderful way. It is beautiful how intellectual liveliness easily triumphs over the gravity of years.

PARIS, 10 MARCH 1942

The work of art must reach a state that renders it superfluous—when eternity illuminates it.

Its intangible stature increases as it approaches the highest beauty and deepest truth. The thought becomes less and less painful that, as a work of art with its ephemeral symbols, it must perish.

The same applies to life itself. There we also have to reach a stage in which it is possible for it to cross over easily and osmotically, a stage in which it *earns* death.

In the evening in the round salon with the new commander-in-chief, Heinrich von Stülpnagel.[50] We talked about botany and Byzantine history, a subject in which he is well read. Andronikos is a name that keeps coming up even today. He attributed this and other bits of learning to his frequent poor health. He was often bored in the field hospitals and supplemented the Spartan cadet training with his own studies. In contrast to his brother and cousin, he possesses an unmistakable *désinvolture* [detachment, unconcern] and, on top of that, an aristocratic bearing. His steady smile makes him appealing. This is noticeable even in the way the staff treats him.

PARIS, 11 MARCH 1942

Carlo Schmid called on me this morning. Years ago, I spent a whole night drinking with him in Tübingen, and now he is in Lisle with the commander-in-chief of

Belgium. We talked about his Baudelaire translation, from which he read aloud "Les Phares" ["The Lighthouses"].

Then, about the situation. He felt that nowadays it is less a struggle *between* human beings than a struggle *about* them. For him, it is possible to see very concretely how they are caught up and led either to the right or the wrong side.

Visited Gallimard after dinner. Had a conversation with the head of the firm, its director, Stameroff, and Madeleine Boudot-Lamotte about the *Falaises de Marbre* [*On the Marble Cliffs*]. Gallimard gives the impression of a spiritual as well as intellectual and commanding force—all traits of a good publisher. There must also be something of the gardener in him.

Read on in Samuel. With David something new enters the law—a trace of elegance. You can see how the law changes when mankind observes it differently, without challenging it. The forms remain in place, but they are danced.

Baal—Jehovah had to be merciless with such rival gods. Even today, we should really try to imagine them in a way that lets us see them, even though their altars have long since fallen into ruin. They are not mere milestones on humanity's path. Dostoevsky saw Baal in London's railroad stations.

In peacetime, I plan to rearrange my reading matter according to a new plan, with theology as its basis.

PARIS, 12 MARCH 1942

It is said that since the sterilization and extermination of the mentally ill, the number of children born with mental illness has increased. Similarly, with the suppression of beggars, poverty has become more widespread. And the decimation of the Jews has led to the spreading of Jewish characteristics in the world, which is exhibiting an increase in Old Testament traits. Extermination does not extinguish the primeval images; on the contrary, it liberates them.

It seems that poverty, sickness, and all evil rest upon certain people, who support them like pillars, and yet they are the weakest in this world. They are like children who need our special protection. With the destruction of these pillars, the weight of the vault topples. Its collapse crushes the false economists.

Feast Days of the *lemures*, including the murder of men, women, and children. The gruesome spoils are hurriedly buried. Now there come other *lemures* to claw them out of the ground. They film the dismembered and half-decayed patch of land with macabre gusto. Then they show these films to others.

What bizarre forces develop in carrion.

PARIS, 14 MARCH 1942

Tristitia. Took a walk this afternoon with Charmille along Avenue du Maine to Rue Maison-Dieu, then back across the Montparnasse Cemetery. There we stumbled upon the graves of Dumont-d'Urville and the aviator Pégoud.

After a bowl of soup, to the Comédie Française. *Le Misanthrope.* During the intermission, I went to take another look at Houdon's Voltaire. This time I was struck by its combination of malicious and childlike qualities.

A hairdresser talking with the Doctoresse about the bombing:

"I'm not afraid of it. The dead are better off than we are."

"But you don't know that."

"Yes, I do. I'm sure of it because a not a single one of them has ever returned."

PARIS, 15 MARCH 1942

Took a walk with Armand in the Bois [de Boulogne] in the beautiful sunshine. I waited for him under the Arc de Triomphe beside the tomb surrounded with yellow narcissus and purple anemones. Bees were ducking into their blossoms. Thought: in this sea of stone, do they survive on nothing but cut flowers?

I now regard the human being as a "man of sorrows" who has been crushed by the gears and rollers of a machine that has broken him rib from rib and limb from limb. But that does not kill him as a human being—maybe it even does him good.

PARIS, 16 MARCH 1942

Colonel Speidel came to my room in the evening. He brought me an essay that Sternberger had published about me in the *Frankfurter* [*Allgemeine Zeitung*]. He also let me have a look at orders. Kniébolo's shift from Diabolus to Satanas is now more obvious.

It is miraculous that the motion of the atom's nucleus spins in every stone, every crumb, and every scrap of paper. All matter is alive, and even when we think things are inert, we simply aren't comprehending their true state. We see only shadows of the absolute, of the undivided light.

PARIS, 28 MARCH 1942

In the evening, paid a visit to Madame Gould in the Bristol; also present were Heller and Jouhandeau, whose *Chronique Maritales* I had read years ago.

Air-raid alarm. We were sitting together by daylight drinking a champagne from 1911 when the airplanes began to roar and the thunder of the artillery shook the city. As tiny as ants. Conversed about death during all this. Madame Gould had some good observations on this subject, namely that the experience of death is one of the few that no one can take from us. And also that it is one that often enriches us, even though it means us the greatest harm. Fate, she went on, can deprive us of all great encounters, but never of the one with death.

She mentioned the fundamental premise of any correct political attitude: "Have no fear." On a tropical evening, she once saw a butterfly land on the back of a gecko in the light of a garden lamp. For her that symbolized great safety.

Then we talked of Mirbeau. I had the impression that this landscape of terror had an attraction for her—a certain appeal that is still potent after all other pleasures of luxury are exhausted.

I talked with Jouhandeau about Bernanos and Malraux and then about the features of civil war in general. He said that nothing makes it more comprehensible than Cicero's biography. He stimulated my desire to go back and focus on that historical period again.

The images surface that surface within us: I often see myself on the edge of the Überlingen Forest on a lonely, foggy evening; then again in early spring in Stralau, or as a boy in Braunschweig staring at patterns on the wall. I have the feeling that I have made some significant decisions while I was just dreaming or brooding.

It may be possible now and then, though far from all activity, to perceive the rhythms of life's melody. They only emerge in the silences. In them we can then sense the composition, the whole that is the foundation of our existence. This explains the power of memory.

It also seems to me that the totality of life does not dawn on us sequentially, but rather as a puzzle that reveals its meaning here and there. Some fantasies of childhood are worthy of old age; on the other hand, some phenomena of old age tap directly into childhood.

Perhaps our constitution is at its strongest when we encounter ourselves in the tranquil dreams of solitude—nothing enters; and yet we enter into a new house.

PARIS, 30 MARCH 1942

Klaus Valentiner returned from Berlin. He described a horrifying young man, formerly an art teacher, who boasted about commanding a death squad in Lithuania and other border territories where they butchered untold numbers of people. After the victims were rounded up, they were first forced to dig mass graves and then lie down in them, where they were shot from above in layers. Before that they were robbed of their last possessions and the rags they were wearing, right down to their shirts.

Grotesque pictures of famine in Athens. At the climax of a large Wagner concert, the trombones gave out because the weakened brass players ran out of breath.

PARIS, 4 APRIL 1942

Walked through the Élysée Gardens, where a first gentle breath of blossoms and young greenery permeated the darkness. The pods of the chestnut buds were especially aromatic.

Dropped in at Valentiner's studio in the afternoon to take my mind off things for a while. The former studio of Ingres is off the courtyard, and a tall, slender ash grows beside it, struggling upward to the light as if from out of a mineshaft.

Klaus recounted that his father, the old Viking, had once promised him 500 marks if he would gratify him by producing a grandchild with the beautiful Frenchwoman who lived with them.

PARIS, 5 APRIL 1942

Visited Valentiner with Heller and Podewils, where we also met Rantzau. Conversation focused on whether the war would be over by the autumn, as many augurs predict. In the evening, a spring storm brought hail over the high roof ridges. Then a double rainbow on a blue-gray background arched over the ancient roofs and church spires.

A fierce bombardment raged during the night or early morning. At breakfast, I discovered that the attack had caused many fires, among them one at the rubber factory of Asnières.

PARIS, 6 APRIL 1942

Conversation with Kossmann, the new chief of the General Staff. He briefed us on the frightening details from the forests of the *lemures* in the East. We are now in the midst of the bestiality that Grillparzer foresaw.[51]

PARIS, 7 APRIL 1942

Said farewell to the Paris Committee on the Quai Voltaire. Drieu la Rochelle, Cocteau, Wiemer, Heller, Drescher, Rantzau, Princess Bariatinski, two German lieutenants, and a young French soldier who distinguished himself during the last campaign. Madeleine Boudot-Lamotte, who is from Mauritania, wore a hat with black-red-black cockerel feathers. I would like to have seen Poupet, but unfortunately he is ill.

These people make it clear to me the way many and varied branches of my life flow into this city as if into a bay.

PARIS, 8 APRIL 1942

Dinner at the home of Lapeyrouse with Epting and Gros-Meunier, whose face has taken on a powerfully demonic aspect that has replaced joy with the dark, brooding strength of Lucifer. He explained that blood would soon have to flow in France like the bloodletting that revives a patient. One would have to consider carefully whom these measures would apply to. As far as he was concerned, he had no doubt about the parties in question. I certainly had that impression as well.

Then about Japan, which he called the real victor in this war.

MANNHEIM, 9 APRIL 1942

Departure from the Gare de l'Est at seven o'clock this morning. Rehm drove me to the station. The sky was a crisp blue; I noticed especially the magical play of color in the water of the rivers and canals. I thought I was seeing sounds that no painter had ever observed. The blues, greens, and grays of the water gleamed like clear, cool stones. The color was more than just color: it was the symbol and essence of the mysterious deep glimpsed in the play and reflection of the surface.

Somewhere beyond Coolus, a bright russet falcon landed on a thornbush. Fields full of high glass domes for raising melons and cucumbers—retorts for the finest fermentation in the area of horticultural alchemy.

Before reaching Thiaucourt, I read a little of the *Faux-Monnayeurs* [*Counterfeiters*] in the sunshine. After the sun had disappeared behind a mountain, the letters began to glow with a deep phosphorescent green.

Reached Mannheim in the evening, where Speidel picked me up at the station. I stayed with him. Little Hans, an artist in the way he enjoys things. Such children attract love and presents like magnets. There is also a little daughter, very delicate. When there has been a night air raid, she will not eat the next day. Who knows the burden that weighs upon the shoulders of women?

KIRCHHORST, 10 APRIL 1942

The Speidels took me to the station in the morning. The shift in social stratification was apparent in the interaction of people on the trains, especially the staff in the dining car or in the hotels; inevitably, differences are being eradicated. This is particularly apparent when you arrive here from France.

Late arrival in Hannover. Perpetua picked me up from the station in the car.

KIRCHHORST, 22 APRIL 1942

On the moor with the children. Our little boy called a salamander a "water lizard" when he saw it for the first time, which tickled me, as though he had addressed the creature by name. In doing so, he demonstrated an ability to differentiate, which is the foundation for knowledge as surely as gold is the security for paper currency.

KIRCHHORST, 24 APRIL 1942

When I woke up at six I wrote down a fragment from an extensive dream negotiation:

I: "It's best that I proceed with my old subject, the comparative physiology of fishes."

Perpetua: "If the results turn out favorably, he will be in such a good mood that he will frighten his friends."

I: "That indicates to me that the future is going to be horrible."

Pale, moon-shaped fishes lay on the ground. I inserted my index finger into the mouth of one of them to find a gland, which I could feel as a little bump.

KIRCHHORST, 9 MAY 1942

On the moor. I heard the first call of the cuckoo, that oracular crier, although I had plenty of money on me.[52] On the other hand, we haven't just cut into the ham but almost finished it up. That's a good indication of the way things stand this year.

I took a sunbath by a peat-cutting bank. The color of the old walls that had been sliced by the shovel changes from a rich black to a soft golden brown. Just above the water level, there is a long mossy band; the sun creates red embroidery upon the dew. All this shows order and necessity. Thought: This is only one of the countless aspects, just one of the gashes in the harmony of the world. We must look beyond such formations to perceive the power of its form.

It is a fine feeling to stride across the damp peat interpenetrated with a deep, ruddy glow. Here you walk upon layers of the pure stuff of life, more precious than gold. The moor is a primeval landscape and therefore the repository of health and freedom. I sense this so gloriously in these northern refuges.

I found a letter from Valentiner in the mail; he states that Gallimard had printed the second edition of *Falaises de Marbre*. He also reported on a visit of the Outcast of the Islands [Gerhard Nebel] to Quai Voltaire.

Reading matter: Tolstoy's short stories, including the "Recollection of a Billiard-Marker." It's a good narrative technique that a basically noble but dissipated life is captured and observed in a diary of a servant, as though in a cheap mirror. Between the cracks, we can sense the tragic and authentic image.

Unfortunately, I could not find my favorite story, "The Death of Ivan Ilyich" in the edition.

KIRCHHORST, 12 MAY 1942

Drive to the barber's. Had a conversation there about the Russian prisoners who are being sent from the camps to work here.

"They say there are some tough customers among them. They'd steal the dogs' food."

Noted verbatim.

KIRCHHORST, 17 MAY 1942

Frau Lukow brought a letter from Grüninger in which he bewailed the demise of our Arthurian round table in the George V. Other than that, the usual *capriccios*. After capturing a Russian reconnaissance patrol, his soldiers had discovered among the dead a seventeen-year-old girl who had fought fanatically. How that was possible, no one could say, but the next morning, her naked corpse was lying in the snow. Because winter is a brilliant sculptor who preserves shapes in their firm, fresh state, the occupying troops had plenty of opportunity to admire the beautiful body. When the base was later recaptured, many a volunteer reported for duty to take pleasure in the sight of that splendid form.

My departure from Kirchhorst approaches. I quickly adjusted again to the house and study and also to the garden where I'm leaving behind the beds in good order. Perpetua thinks that I should move into the parsonage again in the autumn. Well, we shall see. How I would like to live here beside her and grow old slowly, but I yearn to get back to work.

She, incidentally, found an expression for the remarkable relationship between me and the *lemures*. She says that I am [swimming] in a different current.

KIRCHHORST, 18 MAY 1942

I treated Astor, the dog, very badly for constantly running through the garden beds. He has just walked up to me wagging his tail as I sit beneath the old beech trees. He's not looking at me reproachfully, but rather inquisitively, thoughtfully: "Why are you like this?" And like an echo I hear inside me: "Yes, why *are* you like this?"

My current reading: James Riley, *Le Naufrage du Brigantin Américain Le Commerce* [*Authentic Narrative of the Loss of the American Brig "Commerce,"* 1817], published by Le Normant (Paris, 1818). Some of the shipwrecked sailors are murdered, some are stripped naked by brutal nomads and are driven through the Mauritanian deserts under horrible conditions. They come upon deserted cities bleaching in the sun reminiscent of the visions of Emir Musa. The breach in the wall is visible as well as the abandoned siege machinery in front of it, like an oyster-shucking knife lying beside a plate. A scene that Poe could have described plays itself out on a sheer cliff wall rising into the clouds from the sea. A path barely as wide as a hand has been carved into it, and before traversing that terrifying track, people call out from a precipice to make sure that nobody is approaching in the opposite direction. A small caravan of Jews once neglected to do this. They wanted to reach their camp before twilight and, as fate would have it, a group of Moors, who thought no one was on the path, came toward them from the opposite direction. They met in the middle of the path above the terrifying abyss where it was impossible to turn around. After long and useless negotiations, they set upon each other one by one, falling to their deaths in pairs.

Riley's attitude, and even his fate, are proof of the power that rational belief still possesses. In the midst of the most horrible suffering, trust directs itself to God and his guidance as though to an effective system of curves in a superior form of higher mathematics. For an intelligent being like Riley, God is the highest intelligence that inhabits the cosmos. Mankind is sustained all the more powerfully, the more logically he thinks. That is reminiscent of the "strongest battalions" of Old Fritz.[53]

PARIS, 20 MAY 1942

Scholz picked me up in his car at eleven o'clock for the return trip to Paris. Perpetua waved to me in the darkness by making circles with the flashlight.

During the trip, read about the Panama scandal, then a biography of the Berlin entomologist Kraatz, and last, a collection of classical letters; among these Pliny's appealed to me most of all. Whenever I glanced up, I caught a glimpse of the way fields and gardens were laid out, inspiring in me new aesthetic ideas for the design in Kirchhorst.

Rehm and Valentiner welcomed me at the station in Paris even though the train was delayed. I went to Valentiner's studio for a cup of tea and to contemplate the ancient roofs, which after a rainstorm stood out in glistening clarity.

Today's mail brought a letter from Grüninger with some new *capriccios*. As I read it, I thought again about this intellect and its sense of the geometric expansion of power. Such types are perhaps unknown in other cultures, although foreshadowed by Dostoevsky. When Bolshevism is measured against the strongest of these fictional characters, its decline is obvious.

It is certain that only such characters who understand the fundamentals of power on which the world is based, and are dictated to "from above," are capable of confronting the horrible popular revolution that is destroying the world. They are like snakes who have joined a swarm of rats bent on gnawing everything to bits. Where others retreat, they are attracted. Calmly, and with satanic joy, they approach the terrifying ceremonies used by the *lemures* to spread their horror, and they join in the game. They are also drawn to the Muses as Sulla was. That is the essence that Pyotr Stepanovich recognizes in Stavrogin.

In the clandestine power struggle in this area, it was Grüninger who delayed—not to say prevented—Kniébolo's attempts to establish himself and his agents here by about a year. Like Stavrogin, such characters fail because the rot attacks even the small class of leaders that would be necessary to shield the operations—in this case, the generals.

PARIS, 22 MAY 1942

In the afternoon, went to Plon on Rue Garancière with Poupet who seemed to be ailing. He described the most beautiful dedication he'd ever read in a book: "À Victor Hugo, Charles Baudelaire." Absolutely, for no invention can attain that profundity of substance. In this sense, to make a name for oneself means to give it substance by giving each of its letters the greatest weight and importance.

The same applies to language in general. Anyone can say "more light,"[54] but only in the case of Goethe do those two syllables contain such richness. Thus, the poet bestows with language what the priest does with wine. In doing so, the poet contributes something to all.

In the evening sat in the Raphael reading *Routes et Jardins*[55] over a strong grog. I find the translation by Betz a little too polished, but it reads smoothly.

PARIS, 23 MAY 1942

When I think about the difficulties of my situation compared with other people—especially those in the Majestic—I often get the feeling: "You are not here for no reason; fate will untie the knots it has tied, so rise above worries and see them as patterns."

Thoughts like that seem almost irresponsible. Of course, when we face dangers in dreams, it is certain that waking up will dissolve them into smoke—but by day, we are not permitted to see though the charade too clearly. We have to take it seriously, or people will take advantage. We must dream along with the rest, for better or worse.

Someday we will be astonished by the fact that the living do not see us, just as we are puzzled that no signal from the spirit world reaches us today. Perhaps these realities are aligned, but with different modes of seeing like the reflecting and opaque sides of a looking glass. The day will come when the mirror is turned around, and its silvered side is covered in the black crepe of mourning. We can only gain the night when we have penetrated it with our antennae.

PARIS, 24 MAY 1942

On the Quai Voltaire this afternoon. The sight of the ancient roofs is wonderfully relaxing for the mind. It tarries there far from our fragmented age. In addition to Valentiner, I met Rantzau, Madeleine Boudot-Lamotte, Jean Cocteau, and the actor Marais.

During our discussions about plants, Cocteau told me the most wonderful poetic description for *Zittergrass* [quaking grass]: *le désespoir des peintres* [the painters' despair].

PARIS, 30 MAY 1942

Between two and four this morning the English flew over the city dropping bombs within the river bend of the Seine. I awoke at four from dreams of islands, gardens, and animals and kept dozing, but was jolted awake now and then when one of the airplanes approached under fire. But I stayed asleep during these events, as I monitored the danger. When dreaming, it is almost possible to think that you are in control.

The crack of the shrapnel in the empty streets—like that of meteorites on a lunar landscape.

Went to Parc de Bagatelle[56] in the afternoon, where I admired a range of clematis species whose blue and silver-gray star-shaped blossoms decorated the wall. The roses were already in bloom. I noticed especially a Mevrouw van Rossem. The bud was still closed and showed at its base a hue of tea rose yellow with flaming veins of peach-red radiating out toward its point. It resembled a delicately curved breast pulsating with red wine, its aroma sweet and pungent.

PARIS, 1 JUNE 1942

Took an afternoon walk to the Place des Ternes, with its clock on the pharmacy. Then, to the Majestic. Today, I move among officers as formerly among zoologists in the aquarium in Naples. We each perceive the same situation and take completely different sides.

In the evening, I met Henri Thomas at Valentiner's for the first time.

PARIS, 2 JUNE 1942

Kossmann, our new boss, told me that our old comrade N. had committed suicide recently. On the shooting range where he was in charge, he suddenly took his drawn pistol, put it to his head, and pulled the trigger.

Although more than ten years have passed since my last encounter with N., even back then I noticed the pressured, mercurial, exaggeratedly ethical component of his character. In personalities like this, suicide is as predictable as the breaking of overstretched strings on a violin.

PARIS, 3 JUNE 1942

In the Bois de Vincennes. I was thinking about my walks and my worries of last year and paid a call on the woman who was my old concierge who lives opposite the fort. You talk to these simple people the way you talk to children, without creating any subtle disparity between words and their meanings. In times like these, it is desirable to keep a small coterie of such people. There are situations in which they can be more helpful than the rich and powerful.

PARIS, 4 JUNE 1942

In the morning, Carlo Schmid paid me a visit; he had just returned from Belgium. We talked about his translation of *Les Fleurs du Mal* [*The Flowers of Evil*]. Then about the world and its erotic hierarchy. Then about dreamcatchers, which he takes to be a kind of person who can capture other people's dreams like a concave mirror and then fulfill them. These people can either elevate or degrade the dreamers.

As we walked, he mentioned his fourteen-year-old son who writes letters about stylistic differences in sentences of Tolstoy and Dostoevsky; the boy is also a remarkable draftsman. I was amazed as I listened because, during the times that we've been together, we have talked about so many different subjects, and for the first time the father was now mentioning such an important relationship in his life.

PARIS, 5 JUNE 1942

In the morning, Rehm reported in his field uniform. He has accompanied me as my adjutant since the beginning of the war. Contact like this evolves into something like the relationship between knight and squire, which is why I shall find it hard to part from him. Went to Valentiner's in the evening where the time passed unobserved and painlessly as we contemplated the ancient towers and roofs.

Among today's letters there was one from the Comtesse de Cargouët that bespeaks highbrow audacity: "My family has lived in the same house for five hundred years. My forebears were corsairs in the royal fleet and later famous Chouans.[57] So we've remained quite untamed."

She then asks why I emphasize that women are becoming more intelligent. She says that in France they have always been more intuitive and have grasped things more quickly. Based on their intellectual gymnastics, many men have seemed to think and speak intelligently, but how few of them have truly acted and lived in an intelligent manner.

Perpetua writes to me that the garden is thriving. In her letter, she enclosed a pressed blossom of bleeding heart from it. I also find beautiful her statement that people can never get used to the loss of freedom. That is the basic difference between free men and slaves. By freedom, most people mean new forms of slavery.

PARIS, 6 JUNE 1942

During World War I we confronted the question of whether man was more powerful than machines.

In the meantime, things have gotten more complex. We are now concerned with the problem of whether humans or automatons will dominate the earth. The issue brings up further divisions beyond the imprecise ones that partition the world into nations and groups of nations. All around us men stand fully armed at their battle stations. The result is that we never completely agree intellectually with any partner; there is only greater or lesser rapprochement. Above all, we must fight against that tendency within our breast to harden, calcify, ossify.

Concerning marionettes and automatons—the decline in that direction is preceded by loss. This hardening is well depicted in the folktale about the glass heart.

The vice that has become commonplace leads to automatism, as it did so terribly in the case of the old prostitutes who became pure sex machines. Something similar is emanating from the stingy old men. They have sold their souls to material things and a life of metal. Sometimes a particular decision precedes the transition; man rejects his salvation. A widespread vice must be the basis for the general transition to automatism and its threat to us. It would be the task of the theologians to explain this to us, but they are silent.

What an image of a superman, cowering on the tattered cushions in his carriage with a bullet in his spleen and horsehair stanching his wounds. Such news burns through the hell he has created like a lugubrious, celebratory bonfire. Anyone who would assume the role of the despot has to be invulnerable and insensitive to pain, or else he becomes a burden in the hour of his destruction.

PARIS, 7 JUNE 1942

Went to Maxim's at noon, where I had been invited by the Morands. The conversation included a discussion of American and English novels like *Moby Dick* and *A High Wind in Jamaica*, a book I read years ago in Steglitz with acute suspense, like someone who watches children who have been given razors to play with. More talk about Bluebeard and Landru, who killed seventeen women in a suburb near here. A railroad official finally noticed that he always bought only one round-trip ticket. Madame Morand said that she had been his neighbor. After the trial, a small-time innkeeper bought the house where the murders had been committed and named it Au Grillon du Foyer [The Cricket on the Hearth].

On Rue Royale, I encountered the yellow star for the first time in my life. Three young girls who were walking past arm in arm were wearing it. This badge was distributed yesterday, and those who received it had to part with a point from their clothing ration card in return. I then saw the star more frequently that afternoon. I consider things like this, even in my own personal history, a significant date. Such a sight is not without consequence—I was immediately embarrassed to be in uniform.

PARIS, 9 JUNE 1942

Perhaps the least miraculous thing about the cosmos is that most things astonish the mind. There is no difference among miracles, whether one or a billion worlds exist.

PARIS, 14 JUNE 1942

Went to Bagatelle in the afternoon. There Charmille told me that students had recently been arrested for wearing yellow stars with different mottoes, such as "idealist," and then walking along the Champs-Élysées as a demonstration.

Such individuals do not yet realize that the time for discussion is past. They also attribute a sense of humor to their adversary. In so doing, they are like children who wave flags while swimming in shark-infested waters: they draw attention to themselves.

PARIS, 18 JUNE 1942

Reading matter: *Le Martyrologue de l'Église du Japon* [*The Martyrdom of the Church in Japan*, 1549–1649] by Abbé Profillet (Paris, 1895).

The book contains the example of an answer that trumps the threat it elicited. In December 1625, Monika Naisen appeared before the court because, along with her husband and her little daughters, she had given asylum to the Jesuit priest Jean-Baptiste Zola. When the judges threatened to strip her naked, she tore off her girdle herself, crying "There is nothing you can do to me that will make me deny Christ. I would strip off not only my clothing, but my skin."

Called on the Comtesse de Cargouët. We talked about the end of the war, and she said she is betting on the Germans. Then we discussed English society and Churchill, whom she has met a few times. She said that all the whiskey he drinks was preserving him like plums in brandy.

PARIS, 22 JUNE 1942

Went to Berès's at midday, where I bought *Mon Journal* by Léon Bloy. The epigraph that he included after the title reads, "*Le temps est un chien qui ne mord que les pauvres.*" [Time is a dog that bites only the poor.] This is debatable, for our age bites everyone. This is the democratic principle contrasted with the aristocratic one. For this reason, time cannot be leased, and no one adds a single second to his own life.

I then leafed through an edition of epigrams and poems by Johan Christoph Friedrich Haug (Unger, 1805). I thought the motto preceding the epigrams wasn't bad: *In brevitate labor* [Concision is hard work] because, like a good pedagogue, it furnishes the existential example. Although the price of both volumes was not cheap, I bought them because of the epigram about the bridge, which first caught my eye:

> *Die Brücke hier, wie künstlich, stark und hoch!*
> *Nur Wasser mangelt noch.*

[Here stands a bridge, ingenious, strong, and high! / It lacks but water nigh.]

PARIS, 24 JUNE 1942

At Bagatelle in the afternoon. Extensive contact with individuals reveals their stories, which accumulate pebble by pebble from chats and anecdotes. Some secrets we share with them alone, and we become intimate.

Reading matter: the memoirs of Alexander Dumas and *Les Jeunes Filles* [*The Girls*] by Montherlant. In order not to forget passages that have struck me as I read, I have found it most useful to put a check mark beside them and note the page numbers at the back of the book along with keywords. I could paste in a sheet of paper for the same purpose, something like the bookplate that identifies the owner. These are methods that can save a lot of searching.

PARIS, 27 JUNE 1942

Went to Gruel in the afternoon to inquire about a case for my journals. There I held in my hand a small skull very artfully carved out of beech wood from the period of Henri IV. Half the head was still covered in skin, while the other was depicted as the bony skull. A snake emerged from an eye socket. While I was admiring it, I was surprised by Wiemer and Madeleine Boudot-Lamotte, who happened to be standing in front of the shop window. The larger a city is, the more exhilarating and meaningful such an encounter seems.

Visited Valentiner afterward, who brought me greetings from Carl Schmitt. Went from there to Florence Henri, the photographer on Rue Saint-Romain, who lives on the top floor where she tends a lovely roof garden. She asked me to prune her tomatoes, and the aroma of the curly leaves clung to my hands afterward, awakening a longing for Kirchhorst.

PARIS, 29 JUNE 1942

Took a Sunday excursion yesterday to Saint-Rémy-lès-Chevreuse. From my dreams during the night, I can recall the wall of an ancient fortification. I was standing there with Perpetua, and we watched as a pale adder emerged from a cavity in the crumbling stonework. The creature was pale as the moon with an oval patch of hair at the back of its neck, parted in the middle. We watched as it slowly climbed up among the decayed stumps of the hazel shrubs along the fortress until it disappeared into a rectangular pit that had been formed when an embrasure collapsed.

There had to be another reason why this scene was so disturbing. I believe that we had known the wall for ages, and that we had never noticed an inhabitant like this one, although the walls and fortification had always seemed mysterious.

In the morning, the dream had almost vanished, become as transparent as the snakeskin itself, but then in the middle of the day, it came back into focus.

The patch of hair must probably be understood as a symbol of rank, like a crown, or at least as some human trait. Yet it looked repugnant, the way humans have always degraded animals.

Truhe [coffer, chest, box] from *truen* "*anvertrauen*" [confide, entrust]. Then there is the word *hüstrue* for "female spouse," "housewife," which I have seen on northern European gravestones. Then there is *trude*, meaning "witch." Here the concealed, hidden aspects take on negative connotations. The word *trudeln* [trundle, spin] belongs to this family and describes how witches navigate through the air.

Received news that our little fellow is better. I had been very disturbed by reports of his fever, his cough, and his weight loss. Nowadays, despite all our radio and telegraph technology, we are still unable to offer any help from a distance. We probably accomplish more in certain dreams than with all the technology in the world.

A second letter from 26 June came from Perpetua around noon. She writes that during the night nine bombs hit Kirchhorst, exploding on the meadow behind the Kähne bakery, where they blew the heads off several cows. When considering whether she should take our little boy downstairs or stay where they were, she chose to do the latter. It seemed too risky to get him out of bed.

Paris, 1 July 1942

The proximity of the *lemures* and their bleak rites awakened homesickness for the archipelagoes and the worlds of fixed stars, whose expanse is revealed to the initiate beyond the cliffs and narrow mountain passes of death. We feel that our home is there, and here we dwell in a strange land.

Paris, 2 July 1942

Maggi Grüninger brought me a letter from Friedrich Georg that shows, to my joy, that he is in better condition now.

Current reading: Montherlant, *Les Jeunes Filles* [*The Girls*], one of the books that Comtesse de Cargouët sent me; it reminds me of *Les Liaisons Dangereuses* [*Dangerous Liaisons*]. Certain aspects of the hunting scenes high in the mountains are well done, particularly the cold-blooded observation tempered with fascination. The perfect proportion of innocence and consciousness in the creation of molecules from these two elements produces one of the aspects of our age. This combination is seldom successful, because each half destroys the other if they are not joined in a very specific way.

The book tells the story of a girl who drinks water from a fountain and swallows a snake's egg. Years later, X-rays reveal the body of a snake deep inside her. This hybrid image shows elements of the primeval within the conscious world.

Then I read the memoirs of Alexander Dumas. Connoisseurs prefer these to his novels, which—although I don't like to put aside books I have just begun to read—I have grasped only minimally. The annoying thing about such texts is that their author avoids describing nuanced and gentle impressions while recording and exaggerating lurid ones. Reading them is like walking through meadows thronged with larger-than-life blossoms, while grasses and moss are absent.

Ebb and flow. When we exhale, sleep, dream, the tidal zone is visible with its seaweed and shells, sea stars, and aquatic life among the colored pebbles. Then the mind appears like a quick white bird with red feet and snatches up its prey.

The longing for death can become wild, sensual, like the light green sea as it cools upon the beach.

Paris, 4 July 1942

Went to the Tour d'Argent in the evening, that silver tower where Henri IV dined on egret pies. Sitting in the dining room is like being in a large airplane looking out over the Seine and its islands. In the rays of evening light, a film of mother-of-pearl covered the surface of the water. The contrast between the coloration of a weeping willow and its reflection in the water was lovely—in silent introspection the silver-green foliage became imperceptibly darker in the water.

The people up there on the balcony dining on *suprême* of sole and the famous duck seem like tower sculptures looking down from their demonic comfort upon the gray sea of roofs at their feet, beneath which the starving eke out their living. In times like this eating—eating well and much—brings a feeling of power.

PARIS, 5 JULY 1942

In the mail I found a letter from Clemens Podewils from Kharkov describing the Russians and other things we frequently hear about. He mentions, in particular, the aloofness of the simple Russian women. Bolshevism has barely dented the surface of the innate strength of the people.

Certain dreams cannot be recorded. They go back before the Old Covenant and dismantle the primitive raw materials of humanity. We must suppress what we have seen there.

Memories bear traits of an inverse causality. The world, as an effect, resembles a tree with a thousand branches, but as memory it leads downward into the tangled network of the roots. When I confront memories, it often seems like gathering a bundle of seaweed from the ocean—the tiny bit visible from afar, when slowly dragged up into the light, reveals an extensive system of filaments.

As past and future intersect in the narrow neck of the hourglass, there must be a point from which they look like mirror images. In ethics, guilt and retribution refer to this point, and so does the iron-clad law of causality in logic. An artistic person senses unity in the conflict, the innermost identity of the world. It is his calling to proclaim this in poetry. We recognize him thus:

O Fittiche gib uns, treuesten Sinns
Hinüberzugehn und wiederzukehren.

[O give us wings of most steadfast minds / To cross over and to return.][58]

PARIS, 7 JULY 1942

Reading matter: Léon Bloy, *Mon Journal*, bound in purple leather and pleasing to the touch. His mind has a certain condensed quality of something boiled down, like a soup made from extinct fishes and mussels whose flavor has intensified. Good to read when the appetite has been destroyed by too much bland food. Incidentally, this time the association, or rather the correspondence, with Hamann occurred to me. This lies in a penchant for absolutes; a comparison between these two authors would produce a good study.

Twice he mentions that the dead wake him up at night, sometimes knocking at his door, or sometimes he simply hears their names. At that point, he gets up and prays for their salvation. Maybe today we are experiencing the power not only of past but also of future prayers that will be said after we die.

This spirit is strongest in its relationship to death. I am thinking here of a beautiful passage in another of his books, in which he says that dying has no greater significance for us than being dusted off has for a piece of furniture.

But I find his wild pamphleteering repugnant. For example, when he describes people as barely worthy of cleaning the chamber pots in hospitals or scraping off the residue on the latrines of a Prussian infantry barracks. He reaches levels of hatred that veer off into lewdness, for example, when he describes a former cleric who suggested in a newspaper article that he had made such an impression on women by wearing his cassock that he would have had no trouble seducing one or more of them if he had wanted to.

PARIS, 8 JULY 1942

Went to Prunier for lunch with Grüninger and his young wife. He was brimming with new *capriccios* and passed around some photographs from Russia. I found one quite touching: a young girl who had been injured was lying down having her wound dressed. In order to give her an injection in the buttock, the medic had pulled up her clothing. In the photograph, she is crying, not from pain, but because soldiers were standing around looking at her like an animal caught in a net.

In the evening I read the poem by Friedrich Georg about the blue flints—a Stone Age hymn.

PARIS, 9 JULY 1942

When I close my eyes, I sometimes see a dark landscape of stones, cliffs, and mountains at the edge of infinity. In the background, on the shore of a black sea, I recognize myself, a tiny little figure that almost seems to be drawn in with chalk. That is my forward posting, at the edge of the void. Over there at the abyss, I am fighting for myself.

The linden blossoms these days—I don't think I've ever smelled them so powerfully and fervently.

I read Carlo Schmid's translation of Baudelaire's "The Cats." The second stanza is especially effective:

Nach Wissen gierig und nach tiefen Lüsten,
Sind ihnen lieb das Schweigen und die Nacht;
Zu Rennern hätte Hades sie gemacht,
Wenn sie der Knechtschaft sich zu beugen wüssten.[59]

The two last stanzas beautifully describe not only the 1–0 advantage of cats over dogs but also the moment of general stillness before action.

PARIS, 11 JULY 1942

Dropped in on Valentiner in the afternoon, where I met Henri Thomas with his wife. Thomas shows the synthesis of youth, poverty, and dignity, which—when combined with intelligent insight—lends his judgment a certain incorruptibility. His wife, who still lives with her parents, is remarkably gracious. That was evident when she said to me, "You want to find an expression in language that describes things with greater clarity than reality does. I try to do the same thing in the theater, but using my entire body, not just the head."

I encouraged Thomas to support her talent, but he said that was difficult, and when it comes to realizing an individual's talent, human beings are basically all alone.

"Yet support can be useful to other people."

"I believe rather that it is talent that creates support."

Concerning Montherlant, whom I compared to a cannonball, Thomas said:

"Yes, but he doesn't penetrate things very deeply."

Again, the ancient roofs were magnificent. I often sense that it is the pressure of time that distills beauty. Every day I have to tell myself that the signal to evacuate could come at any moment, at which point I, like Bias, will take what is mine and leave the rest behind—if need be, even my skin.

Then at Charmille's, where I ate dinner and studied the calendar.[60]

PARIS, 12 JULY 1942

Was with a woman in a shop that sold edible snakes. The merchant opened a drawer and, without looking, reached in and yanked out the creatures by the middle of their bodies. Before handing them over, he put miniature muzzles on them, through which the little vipers' horns quivered. We paid twelve or fourteen marks for a medium-size specimen.

Once I had awakened, I kept scratching my head over who the woman had been. Such apparitions are vaguely familiar, often combining several people like a sister, mother, or wife—all the primeval elements of femininity combined. We grope our way through a dark web and do not recognize each other.

Visited Valentiner in the afternoon. Before I entered, I rummaged around in the displays on the Quai. I picked up a 1520 copy of *Doctrina Moriendi* [*Doctrines of the Dying*], which according to a handwritten entry by the chancellor of the church in Paris, Jean de Gerson, was written in the fourteenth century. A further notation by Baluze, the librarian of Colbert, documents that this volume once stood in the *Biblioteca Colbertina*.

Then went to the Louvre with the Doctoresse to look at the sculpture. We ate dinner together and enjoyed lively chitchat.

PARIS, 14 JULY 1942

What I ought to have is a reserve of good books printed on newsprint—books to be read in the bath or while traveling that can then be tossed away.

Daily schedule in Kirchhorst. I need two hours in the evening to unwind, time to go through and organize books, clippings, manuscripts, diaries, correspondence. *Cura posterior* [secondary tasks].

PARIS, 16 JULY 1942

Five gladioli in a vase on the table in front of me—three white, one pale red, and one salmon colored. Gladioli tend to have hues of a concentrated quality; the life force within the blossoms almost retreats behind the powerful flash of the pure extract of their tint. When looking at these flowers—as with anything of a pure, all too pure, nature—a feeling of emptiness and ennui is hard to avoid. Yet the white examples especially stimulate theological questions.

During the noon break, went by Berès's shop and rummaged through the books. I picked up the *Monographie du Thé* [*Monograph on Tea*] by J. G. Houssaye (Paris, 1843). It had nice engravings, even if the binding does show some worm-holes. Also *La Ville et la République de Venise* [*The City and Republic of Venice*] by Saint-Didier (Paris: De Luyne, 1660). The binding is beautiful and indestructible, full vellum with mitered corners and vellum bands on the spine. Finally, Lautré-amont's *Préface à une live future* [*Preface to a Future Book*], published in 1932, again in Paris, the great city of books.

On the way I was overcome by the desire to write something, even if it were nothing more than a short story or two. I thought about Riley's shipwreck,[61] and then about the story of the bootblack of Rhodes, which I've been pondering for quite a while.

PARIS, 18 JULY 1942

Architectural dreams in which I saw old Gothic buildings. They were standing in abandoned gardens; not a soul grasped their meaning in the midst of the solitude, and yet I thought them even more beautiful in a cryptic way. They showed a clear sense of structure like that intrinsic to plants and animals—it is their higher nature. Thought: that had been built in for God.

Visited the photographer Florence Henri in the afternoon. Just before that, rummaged around in books on the corner, where I bought, among other things, *Les Amours de Charles de Gonzague* [*The Loves of Carlo Gonzaga*] by Giulio Capoceda and printed in Cologne in 1666. There was an old bookplate inside that read, "*Per ardua gradiar*" [I forge ahead through adversities]. I underscored my agreement by writing my own, "*Tempestatibus maturesco*" [Storms have made me the man I am].

Jews were arrested here yesterday for deportation. Parents were separated from their children and wailing could be heard in the streets. Never for a moment may I forget that I am surrounded by unfortunate people who endure the greatest suffering. What kind of human being, what kind of officer, would I be otherwise? This uniform obligates me to provide protection wherever possible. One has the impression that to do that one must, like Don Quixote, confront millions.

PARIS, 19 JULY 1942

Visited the Père-Lachaise Cemetery in the afternoon. There I wandered around among the monuments with Charmille. Now and then we stumbled upon famous names in the labyrinths of this necropolis without looking for them. We found the gravestone of General Wimpffen holding a sword with a ribbon curled around it bearing the word "Sédan?"[62] The question mark on grave inscriptions was new to me. Then we found Oscar Wilde, whose monument had been paid for by one of his wealthy lady readers. Tasteless. You can see the tormented spirit who hovers on it being borne aloft by wings that weigh tons. Then we went down a mossy path canopied with green, which leads like the Street of Forgetting[63] into the valley among crumbling monuments. There we found the grave of Cherubini crowned by an urn, an adder coiled around its foot. Beside this was Chopin's grave with an oval marble relief.

The derelict parts of this cemetery are the most beautiful. Comforting epitaphs occasionally gleam from the toppled stones, like *obitus vitae otium est* [Death is life's rest]. Thoughts about the multitudes resting here. There are no spaces large enough to accommodate their ever-increasing armies. A different principle must be applied. They shall find space in a hazelnut.[64]

This contact with a being who then disappears with the dark scepter is surely the most wonderful thing in the world. This cannot be compared with birth, which is merely the budding of life already familiar to us. Life lies in death like a small green island in the dark ocean. To fathom this—even at the edges and tidal zones—means real knowledge, compared to which physics and technology are mere trifles.

Returned to the city by the back streets. Every time I see the winged spirit of the Bastille with his torch and the broken chain in his hands, the sight reinforces the notion of highly dangerous and still potent energy. He combines the impression of great speed with stasis. He represents the spirit of progress raised on high, embodying the triumph of future conflagrations. Just as the rabble and the merchants united in spirit to erect this column, the vengeance of the Furies unites here with Mercury's cunning. This is no longer a symbol, but an actual idol surrounded by the terrible tempest that has always illuminated such bronze columns since time immemorial.

PARIS, 21 JULY 1942

Finished reading Lautréamont, *Préface à un livre future* [*Preface to a Future Book*]. I'm going to read the complete works of this author, which are collected in one volume, to deepen my understanding of him. In this preface, a new version of optimism is predicted, one without God, but differing from notions of progress by taking the perspective of the consciousness of perfection rather than some Utopian recollection of it. This gives his argument a metallic quality, gleaming in technological glory and conviction. He writes in an easygoing style, as if we were on a beautiful, fast ship devoid of other passengers—propelled by consciousness rather than electricity. Doubt has been abolished as has air resistance; all that is worthwhile and good is to be found in the material, which the structure makes visible.

Our age shows strong evidence of this attitude. An early example among the painters would be Chirico, whose cities are deserted and whose human beings are constructed from bits of armor plate. This is the optimism that our machine technology brings with it and which it cannot do without. The message must be heard in the voice of a speaker who delivers news of a metropolis that has been reduced to rubble and ashes.

PARIS, 22 JULY 1942

Called on Picasso in the afternoon. He lives in a spacious building in which the floors have been designated as storage rooms and depots. The building on Rue des Grands-Augustins appears in Balzac's novels; Ravaillac was brought here after he committed the assassination. In one corner, a narrow spiral staircase with steps of stone and ancient oak twisted upwards. A piece of paper bearing the little word *ici* [here] in blue pencil was pinned to a narrow door. I rang, and the door was opened by a short man in a simple worker's smock: Picasso himself. I had met him briefly once before and again had the impression that I was looking at a magician—an impression that was only intensified by the little green pointed hat he wore.

The household consisted of a small dwelling and two further storage rooms, one of which was in the garret. He appeared to use the lower one as a sculpture workshop and the upper one as a painting studio. The floor was tiled in a honeycomb pattern. The walls were colored with a yellow wash and supported by dark oak beams. Ribs of black oak ran across the ceilings. The rooms seemed to be perfectly laid out as a workspace. The sense that time stood still lay heavy in the air.

First we looked at old papers downstairs, and then we went up to the second story. Among the pictures standing around, I liked two simple female portraits and then, most especially, a beach scene that blossomed in tones of red and yellow the more I looked at it. We talked about his views on painting and writing from memory. Picasso asked whether there was a real landscape behind the *Marble Cliffs*.

I found other pictures, like a row of asymmetric heads, quite monstrous. We have to grant such remarkable talent its own objectivity when we watch it develop such images over years and decades, even when they differ from our own perceptions. He is essentially showing us things as yet unseen and unborn; they are like alchemical experiments, and the word retort was mentioned several times. It had never dawned on me so powerfully and oppressively that the homunculus was more than just an idle fiction. The image of man is predicted magically, and few can sense the terrifying profundity of the decision that the painter makes.

Even though I tried more than once to draw him out on this subject, he avoided the topic, perhaps intentionally: "There are chemists who spend their whole lives investigating the elements concealed in a piece of sugar. So I would like to know what color is."

On their impact: "My pictures would have the same effect if, after they were finished, I were to wrap them up and seal them without showing them to anyone. These are manifestations of the most intuitive nature."

Concerning the war: "Both of us sitting here together would be able to negotiate peace over the course of this afternoon. In the evening people would be able to turn their lights on again."

Paris, 23 July 1942

I began reading the Book of Esther, where Herodotus's ancient world of splendid pageantry still reigns supreme. Right there in the first chapter we have the feast at Susa lasting months in the Asiatic palace of Ahasuerus, who reigned over 127 empires, from India to the land of the Moors. Anyone who appears before him unbidden must die unless he raises his golden scepter, as he did to Esther. Nowadays the only remnants of this terrible magical kingdom are the Jews—the unbending bronze serpent of the old life. I witnessed this once quite clearly. It was the sight of a Polish Jew at the *Schlesischer Bahnhof* [Silesia Station] in Berlin. My thought: "That is how you must have stood back then under the Ishtar Gate of Babylon."

My mail contains more and more letters from survivors writing to me about readers of mine who have been killed in the war. It often seems as though the dead appear as voices from a reading public *in tenebris* [in darkness].

Visit from Kurt, who was the model for traits in my character Biedenhorn.[65] He could be called a sort of Falstaff who mingles good living with a sense of entitlement. He's back from the East, where he commands a tank company. He carries his official seal in his pocket so he can issue courier's identification cards, tickets, ration coupons, and whatever else he wishes at will. He uses it to stretch out in special train cars along with his pilfered "courier baggage," which he orders the conductors to guard. When hotel staff do not jump to attention, he demands a room, service, and wine in his thundering voice—leaving the hoteliers quaking and apologizing. If he wants to force his way into a room that's off limits, as he did today when he wanted to get into the commissary of the military academy, he doesn't use subterfuge; he inspects the guards in order to find fault with them. Then he has people brought in to carry the merchandise he purchases. All this gives him material to joke about over wine.

I talked with him for a long time in the Raphael, partly because his conversation embodies a cynical but elemental power, and also because he is significant as a type. He seems to have instinctive insight into our situation. He thinks it is old fashioned of me, one of my whims, that the injustice of this world still grieves me. He says that will never be eradicated, and at this point, I discover a gentle trait in him: the concern of the stronger for the weaker man, which is how I seem to him. This concern is quite specific: he would not feel it if I were under fire with him or attacking someone in authority of the sort that he, as an old OC-man,[66] well knows. On the other hand, it would distress him to see me come to grief as a result of my "good nature." He has political ideas of the sort you'd find in a herd of big game. You have to avoid the dominant stags and protect yourself as long as they're in power.

While we were conversing so casually about the temper of the times, I wondered whether or not he might still be preferable to those officers who are blindly obedient while honor goes to hell. The *Landsknecht*[67] represents an authentic type, a powerful contrast to the flaccid idealism that soldiers on as if things were all in order. One gets the feeling that he was, is, and will always be in all regions and at all times, and that he has nothing in common with those living corpses. As danger increases, he feels happier and becomes more necessary.

PARIS, 24 JULY 1942

Beautiful images appear before my closed eyes while dozing. Today it was a honey-yellow agate with sepia moss-shaped inclusions. It drifted slowly past like a blossom falling into the abyss.

Those red flowers one sees now and then in the windows of darkened rooms—they are like cut gems that sparkle in the sunshine.

PARIS, 25 JULY 1942

The tiger lily on the table in front of me. While I am observing it, all at once the six petals and six stamens fall from it like a magnificent robe rudely ripped off, leaving behind only the desiccated pistil with the ovules. At that moment, I become very aware of the force that destroys the flower. O reap your fruit, for thus do the Fates cut you down.

Went to the Latin Quarter in the afternoon, where I admired an edition of Saint-Simon in twenty-two volumes. Such a monument to historiographical passion. The work represents one of those points where modernity comes into focus.

Tea with the Doctoresse at her place. Afterward we went to see Valentiner, who had invited us to dinner. In addition to him, des Closais was there. We talked about Picasso and Léon Bloy. Des Closais told an anecdote about Bloy that I don't believe, but have written down nonetheless because it gives a hint of the profound and perhaps not undeserved hatred of the literary establishment for this writer:

> As was his habit, he once also asked Paul Bourget for money, without success. After this, Bloy publically gave Bourget the cold shoulder. Some time passed before Bourget received another letter from Bloy with the request for the immediate loan of 500 Francs because his father had died. Bourget puts the money in his pocket and makes his way personally to Montmartre where Bloy lives in one of the obscure hotels. When the porter takes him to Bloy's room, Bourget hears music inside, and when he knocks, Bloy opens the door completely naked.
>
> He could see naked women and cold meats and wine on the table. Bloy mockingly invited Bourget to enter, and he accepts the invitation. He first puts the money on the mantelpiece and has a look around.
>
> "Monsier Bloy, I believe you wrote me that your father had died?"
>
> "So, you are a pawnbroker?" Bloy answers, and opens the door to the next room, where his father's corpse is lying on the bed.

What makes the story especially suspect is the setting, which is actually not one where anyone would die. It's also remarkable that Bloy hardly ever mentions his father in his voluminous journals, despite the fact that they are otherwise overly rich in detailed family description.

On his own deathbed, Bloy was asked what he felt as he faced death: "*Une immense curiosité*" [enormous curiosity].

That's very good. He had the habit of disarming his listeners by making the first thrust.

Then there was talk about celebrities. The Contesse de Noailles had invited Marshal Joffre.

"That must have been so boring just before the Battle of the Marne."

When he was serving, the porter clicked his heels every time he presented a platter. He had spent World War I as a trench fighter with a combat patrol. A German had bitten off one of his thumbs in hand-to-hand combat. He forbids his wife to call the Germans "*Boches*," adding, "I'm allowed to say '*Boche*' because I fought them."

PARIS, 26 JULY 1942

Visited Montparnasse Cemetery in the afternoon. After searching for a long time, I finally found the grave of Baudelaire, with its tall stele showing a gigantic bat with furled wings.

In the midst of all these dilapidated monuments, I paused a long time in front of the gravestone of Napoléon Charles Louis Roussel, who died on 27 February 1854 at the age of nineteen, having been an "artist" for half a year. Over the slab that his friends had paid for lay an urn that had fallen from its pedestal. It was covered with moss that gushed from it like a green life force.

I am always fascinated by the mystery surrounding such tombs of ordinary people in this sea of graves. Like tracks in the sand, they are soon erased by the wind.

In the Raphael, I read Heinrich Hansjakob, *Der Theodo*. I sense such a narrative gift springing from the popular imagination is now running dry. With it dies the compost of literature, the mossy flora on the roots and at the base of the trunks, and for that matter, the whole range of descriptive powers. Then the treetops start to dry out.

In the night, I dreamed about a beautiful snake; its iridescent, steel-blue scales showed labyrinthine wrinkles like those on a cherry pit. The creature was so large that I could barely put my arms around its neck; I had to carry it a long way because no cage was available.

I thought I would like to build a beautiful garden for it, but how could I construct it without having to charge an entrance fee?

PARIS, 27 JULY 1942

The mail brought me a surprise in the form of the *Griechische Götter* [*Greek Gods*] by Friedrich Georg. These are the page proofs published by Klostermann. Even though I was familiar with the images and thoughts from conversations we had in

Überlingen, reading them in this format had a very powerful effect upon me. It is beautiful how the ancient and modern worlds meet here—primeval thoughts are grasped with the perspective of our time. One feels that the German has nourished them step by step along their way and that they have reciprocated. The mythical universe is omnipresent here; it resembles the abundance that the gods conceal from us. We wander as beggars in the midst of inexhaustible riches, which the poets pay out to us in coin.

PARIS, 28 JULY 1942

The unfortunate pharmacist on the corner: his wife has been deported. Such benign individuals would not think of defending themselves, except with reasons. Even when they kill themselves, they are not choosing the lot of the free who have retreated into their last bastions, rather they seek the night as frightened children seek their mothers. It is appalling how blind even young people have become to the sufferings of the vulnerable; they have simply lost any feeling for it. They have become too weak for the chivalrous life. They have even lost the simple decency that prevents us from injuring the weak. The opposite is true: they take pride in it.

After writing these lines before lunch, I called on Potard, that good fellow, and took him a prescription that the Doctoresse had written for me. When he brought it to me, he gave me a small bar of soap as a gift, as if he sensed that I had been directing good wishes to him. I never allow myself to forget that I am surrounded by sufferers. That is more important than any fame achieved through military or intellectual exploits, or the empty applause of youth, whose taste is erratic.

I then went to the shop on the Rue du Faubourg Saint-Honoré that belongs to the lady bookseller with the limp. There I examined an illustrated volume about a journey up the Nile by Carl Werner from about 1870. Looking at pictures does me good when I'm upset.

PARIS, 2 AUGUST 1942

Visited Père Lachaise [Cemetery] in the afternoon. Here in the city center, not far from the overpopulated neighborhoods around the Bastille, you can enjoy one of the most tranquil walks. On a mossy path among the graves beneath the canopy of ash and acacia, I came upon an obelisk erected to the memory of the great entomologist Latreille. Just under the scarab above the inscription of his name, a silkworm larva had established itself. The scarab lifted up the ball like a sun disk. I laid a blossom on this grave and as I picked it, a small weevil fell out into my hand as a reward. It was one I lacked for my collection.

Such an old cemetery is like a quarry. Many generations have contributed to the richness of its variety as well as its individual monuments. When I was looking at many different types of granite and porphyry, I had the thought that in the world of stones, the polished finish embodies what the blossom does for plants, or the mating display for animals. It provides the place where the hidden glory and order that reside deep in matter are visible. By contrast, the crystal structure bursts forth in flowers.

A bell rings in the evening to remind visitors to leave the cemetery. You then see them pushing toward the exit, either one by one or in little groups. Their pace is faster than when they wandered around the cemetery. It is almost as though the thought of being locked into this labyrinth of death awakens a dark terror in them.

Large cemeteries like this make the unity of culture visible, especially through their power, which rests beyond all struggle. The dead have returned to their maternal ground and are now unassailable; instead of feuding with each other, the names merely accumulate. Here we can see the inviolate nature of people, like a glimpse into rooms behind the stage. Whereas there the actors become people again, here they are transmuted into spirit. The mighty dead—how could this insight ever be lost?

I returned by way of Rue de la Roquette, from which you can sometimes see the guardian spirit of the Bastille gleaming like one of the Furies in the distance.

Back in my room in the Raphael, I met a Miss Vilma Sturm who had come to seek me out for advice. Then I read some Renan and a little of the biography of the Brontës, then finally some of the Book of Job. Chapter 28 contains a foreshadowing of the immense distance separating man from wisdom: "Destruction and death say, we have heard the fame thereof with our ears."

PARIS, 3 AUGUST 1942

Finished reading Renan, *Das Leben Jesu* [*The Life of Jesus*] and in addition Robert de Traz, *La Famille Brontë* [*The Brontë Family*].

The Brontës are significant because they seem to possess an intelligence unlike that of other people—one that flows to them indiscriminately, like electric current. You can almost imagine knowledge being conducted through the earth and through the trunk of the tree until it reaches the bird's nest and the young brood in it. Such power could endow heavenly bodies with intelligence.

This extraordinary side of the Brontës suggests that it is the rule on other stars, in other profound thought systems. In this sense, prophetic dreams that come true, second sight, and prophecies are all extraordinary. In the same way that colors exist outside the visible spectrum, there also exists a dark body of lore that is seldom individuated. The harmony and subtle interaction of our life cycles depend on its invisible influence.

PARIS, 4 AUGUST 1942

This morning a Herr Sommer dropped in to see me at the Majestic and brought me greetings from Federici. We spoke about China, which he knows well, having been born there. Then, about Japan. His father, who wanted to have a pair of polo breeches made, entrusted a tailor with the task by giving him a garment purchased in England as a sample. He made it especially clear to the Japanese tailor that he was allowed to cut this model apart so that the new breeches would fit him perfectly. On the day of delivery the tailor arrived with six pairs, all matching their model like mirror images—he had even included the two patches and a worn spot on the inside of one of the knees.

PARIS, 5 AUGUST 1942

Perpetua writes me that bombs fell on Hannover in the afternoon of 2 August, killing many people. When the fires started, she heard the old gravedigger Schüddekopf yelling from the cemetery, "What do you know? Now they're coming in broad daylight!" In the parsonage, she keeps a suitcase ready, packed with some underwear and the manuscripts.

Dinner at the Morands. He did not appear because he was made a minister today. His wife represented him; I also saw the new prefect of police and Princess Murat. I had a conversation with the prefect about what the underworld was up to on Rue de Lappe. He was not pleased to hear that I take walks there.

PARIS, 6 AUGUST 1942

Tallemant des Réaux. I am reading his *Historiettes* [*Brief Histories*] right now, and I find they surpass Saint-Simon's history when it comes to meaty substance. They give a kind of social zoology.

Yesterday I heard an amusing anecdote about the Marquis de Roquelaure. It conveys the comedy well and exposes the source of the humor as the clash between social conventions and natural artistic relations. During a ball, Madame Auber took Roquelaure by the hand, whereupon he plucked a steward's sleeve and asked him whether it was permissible to dance with this bourgeois woman. The event was turned into a satirical rhyme:

> *Roquelaure est un danceur d'importance;*
> *Mais?*
> *S'il ne connoist pas l'alliance,*
> *Il ne dancera jamais.*

[Rocquelaure is a dancer of importance; / But? / If he does not understand [how to make] the connection / He will never dance at all.]

PARIS, 8 AUGUST 1942

Dropped by Valentiner's in the evening. There, in addition to des Closais, I met a young pilot who is commanding a tank company on the islands. Darkness fell gradually during our conversation; bats fluttered about the old gables, and swifts settled into their nests. A city like this has its animal element, like a coral reef.

Walked back to the Étoile with des Closais. We talked about the obelisks and the way they seem to stand in the great squares as magical cynosures, symbols of spiritual rectitude. They imbue the world of stone with meaning. I sometimes think I see sparks shooting from their tips. It is lovely when they glow in different colors, perhaps red, or are illuminated by an errant ray of light, but glimpsing them can also be frightening. In them we sense the life of cities devoid of people, where their shadows count the hours like a gnomon.

Conversed about Boëthius and in that context about the threats of our own age, which, despite everything, need not distract individuals from their normal mode of life—the stillness at the heart of the waterfall. Des Closais observed that this presumed a reference to some point of stasis. He recalled that this was how he had always braved his fear of thunderstorms as a child, sustained by the thought that, high above the clouds the blue heavens were shining unchanged.

D.—an appalling man. Made aware of this because every day six to ten people in his forced labor camp die from lack of nourishment and medication, and yet relief is supposed to be provided: "Have them enlarge the cemetery."

PARIS, 9 AUGUST 1942

I wonder whether we ever agreed to our fate at some decisive point in our pre-existence. Perhaps we selected it, as if from among a pile of costumes before a masked ball. But the light in which we rummaged around in the anteroom where we made this hasty decision showed the material with its true meaning in the game of life. Perhaps then the beggar's tattered garment appeared more desirable than a regal robe.

I'm reading *Diable amoureux* [*The Devil in Love*, 1772] again and find that the most significant passage is the one in which Biondetta explains that the world is not ruled by chance, but by a system of finely balanced inevitabilities, from the course of the stars down to the petty trifles of the gaming table. It seems that cosmic events are determined by a secret law of numbers, which explains why the future is unknowable.

After this explanation, she gives Alvarez a few signals that help him win at faro. Even though he takes no money from her, he does not consider this sort of help to be cheating.

That is a subtle detail, for in the Kabbala the devil actually reaches his greatest heights when all traces of his origin are obliterated. By such means, it would be possible to form holy names, the Lord's Prayer, or passages of scripture by applying automatic calculations to create infinite sequences of numbers and combinations. Texts generated in this manner would, of course, merely have the semblance of the letters in common with the true ones, but not possess their meaning and healing power.

Although Alvarez does not recognize all these connections, his reaction is a nice countermove that shows his basically healthy character: after a winning streak, he tires of the game of faro.

Human beings are privileged in not knowing the future. That is one of the diamonds in our diadem of free will. If we were to lose it, we would become automatons in a world of machines.

PARIS, 10 AUGUST 1942

In the night, I dreamt of the trenches of World War I. I was in the dugout, but this time the children were sitting with me, and I was showing them picture books. I then went outside and stretched out in a bomb crater. The earth had been turned to powder by the shelling. I rubbed the soft crumbs together in my hands, recognizing it as I did so as the material from which we are made and to which we shall return. I could hardly tell the difference between the soil and my own hand. I lay there like a mummy surrounded by concentrated essence of mummies.

PARIS, 11 AUGUST 1942

A letter from Schlichter containing photos of some powerful new pictures and drawings. I look forward to good things from his illustrations for *One Thousand and One Nights*.

PARIS, 12 AUGUST 1942

I was with Friedrich Georg on a cliff at the edge of a desert. We were throwing stones at a little piece of something the size of a snail shell that glistened like a piece of lapis lazuli. We talked about the distance we had to keep from it because it was such highly explosive material. It is odd that our dream conversations so often have to do with the physical world, while in our waking state our discussions are about art.

We then made our way down and gathered insects at the damp grassy edge of the desert. They were unlike any genus I was familiar with. I considered whether I should even be taking them, for they differed so greatly from the structures inherent in their type that I took no pleasure in collecting them. I found myself confronting the demiurge like a child who says, "I'm not playing anymore."

Went to the Bagatelle in the afternoon to admire the beautiful flowers, among them the *Dolichos* vine [hyacinth bean] with its magnificent broad, purple-lilac seedpod—this living thing that does not flaunt its blossoms but rather its fruit.

Then the Virginia jasmine with its large, slit blossoms that reach upward like blazing trumpets—a decoration for garden gates in *One Thousand and One Nights*. Star clematis—the flower flies, in their tiger colors, hovered around them, suspended in space, quivering spasmodically over the sea of blossoms.

Resting in the grotto. It stands over dirty green water, where a large golden orfe with its dark, scaly back, was swimming. It went past like a dark shadow in the depths, shimmering ever brighter as it rose lazily and then broke the surface with a burst of incandescence.

Probably influenced by these things, I dreamed at night of a bookplate that I would like to own. It showed a swordfish breaking the surface of the water from a matte black background in India ink; it was delicate, Japanese, with an antique gold border. When I woke up, I felt so joyous from the sight of this image that I wanted to have an engraving made, but by daylight this charm faded. The joy we feel in dreams is like the joy of childhood. Within minutes after awakening, we grow into adulthood.

PARIS, 13 AUGUST 1942

Finished reading Jean Cocteau, *Essai de Critique Indirecte* [*Essay of Indirect Criticism*]. It contains the prophetic dream that the author had already recounted to me when we met at Calvet's. As for me, I can't remember dreams like that, and experiences often seem as though I had just dreamed them. At one point they were experienced most profoundly as Platonic ideas—that is far more important than their literal fulfillment. This is the way one should consider death so as to become used to the idea of it.

I noted the following good observations: "*Surnaturelle hier, naturel demain.*" [Supernatural yesterday, natural tomorrow.] Certainly true, for the natural laws with their consistency that Renan makes such a fuss about will always adjust to reality. They are like the musical accompaniment that falls silent as soon as things become dramatic. Existence knows no law.

One could probably put that a bit more cautiously: natural laws are those that we perceive. At all points, when we ourselves enter the equation, we can no longer perceive them.

Technology has now been so profoundly implemented that even after the domination of the technicians and their major premises has been broken, we are going to have to deal with its remnants. The terrible fate of its victims is built into this system. Thus, it will remain, in the same way that the ancient law still held sway after the appearance of Christ—as one of our memories, along with its human residue. The real question is whether these memories curtail freedom. Probably a new form of slavery is the result. This can be reconciled with comfort and even the possession of power—but the chains remain in place. Nonetheless, free men know each other and are recognizable by a new nimbus that suffuses them. Perhaps we are talking only about small groups that preserve freedom, probably among its victims, yet the spiritual gain compensates for its losses many times over.

The flowers, the birds, the gems—those things of glowing color or pungent aroma. The sight of them fills us with longing for their places of origin.

PARIS, 16 AUGUST 1942

Saturday and Sunday in Vaux-de-Cernay at the house of Rambouillet, as a guest of the commander-in-chief, who is using this old monastery as his summer residence. My stay here has the advantage that I can do and say what I think is right and not be seen by any *lemures*. The woodsy surroundings are damp, even swampy, which reflects the rule of the Cistercians, who built like beavers. I saw the venerable and unpretentious gravestone of the early abbot Theobaldus, known as Saint Thibaut de Marly.

While there, I read Joseph Conrad's *An Outpost of Progress*, a story that superbly describes the transformation of civilized optimism into utter bestiality. Two Philistines come to the Congo to make money, and there they adopt cannibalistic habits. In broader contexts, Burckhardt described this process as "rapid decay." Both men heard the overture of our age. Conrad perceives something more clearly than Kipling, and that is Anglo-Saxon constancy in transitional situations. That is a remarkable and unpredictable trait in our world, which might sooner have been prophesied of the Prussians. The difference between them, however, lies in the fact that the Englishman can tolerate a significantly greater dose of anarchy. If the two were innkeepers in squalid neighborhoods, the Prussian would expect the regulations to be followed in every room. In doing so, he would actually be preserving a certain veneer of order while the entire building was being devoured by nihilism from the inside out. The Englishman would turn a blind eye to the growing disorder at first and just keep on filling the glasses and collecting the money until finally, when the racket on the floor above got out of hand, he would take a few of the customers upstairs, and together they would beat the others to a pulp.

From the standpoint of character analysis, the Englishman has the advantage over the Prussian in being phlegmatic, while the other is sanguine; objectively, he has the advantage of the seaman over the landlubber. Seafaring people are used to greater fluctuation. Add to this the frequently noted superiority of the Norman genetic material, which is more favorable for the creation of a leader class than the common Germanic stock. In any case, it is better that such cousins stand back to back, or rather shoulder to shoulder—as they did at Belle-Alliance [Waterloo]— instead of nose to nose. This was always the goal of Prussian policy, which was good as long as landowners were in charge of it, and not people elected by a democratic plebiscite. Naturally, the influence of the soil diminishes when population numbers rise and there is a shift to the large cities. But the influence of the seas grows. That is an important difference. We talked about these things over dinner, and then about the situation in general.

Took a walk later in the woods with Herr Schnath, the director of the Hanoverian Archives. The conservation and lore of strange old things, especially those of Lower Saxony reminds one of ritualistic purification rites with smoke, or of a world of images still present in the moor and the turf, redolent with the smell of fire and earth. The tradition relates to the demons of the landscape, and turns into a sort of ghost hunt. Historical fact intrudes into this twilight realm, as in the case of the Battle of the Teutoburg Forest.[68] Without any outside sources, that event would have been woven into mythology long ago. In the midst of the tools of the peat-cutting culture in the Hanoverian Museum, the silver treasure of Hildesheim shone brilliantly. Its character appeals to me; it indicates the superiority of the Norns over the formulaic history depicted on it. No matter how colorfully and richly the thread may be dyed, they spin and cut it, and then the pattern fades down the river of time, and only the warp of the fabric remains—that ancient, gray sensibility common to us all since time immemorial.

The general came around to the topic of the Russian cities and said that it was important for me to be aware of them, especially with respect to particular corrections in "the figure of the worker."[69] I responded by saying that for quite a while I have been considering a visit to New York for my sins, but that I was not opposed to a command on the eastern front.

PARIS, 17 AUGUST 1942

Visit to the Bois in the afternoon, then tea at Madame Morand's in her garden, where the top of the Eiffel Tower looks down over the tallest trees onto the marble paving stones. Heller, Valentiner, Rantzau, and the Marquise de Polignac were there; she and I compared memories of the Capuchin catacombs in Palermo. She said that the sight of this morbid parade of death awakened in her a mad lust for life, and that when she emerged into the daylight, she felt tempted to throw herself at the first decent man to cross her path. Perhaps that was why mummies were thought to have aphrodisiac qualities in ancient times.

Capriccio: I wonder whether these ancient arts of embalming might still provide nourishment nowadays, and whether in the necropolises you could give a feast with bread made of wheat from the pyramids, broth from the steer god Apis. Then one could excavate carbonized flesh from the necropolises the way we do carbonized plants from coal in coalmines. That would be an inferior form of nourishment, just as coal is an inferior fuel source.

PARIS, 18 AUGUST 1942

Destroyed papers in the morning, including my plan for an effective peace that I had composed last winter.

Conversation with Carlo Schmid, who came to my room and told me about his son again, as well as about his dreams and the Baudelaire translation he has now finished.

I bought a notebook in a stationery shop on Avenue Wagram. I was in uniform. I was struck by the expression on the face of a young girl behind the counter: it was clear that she was staring at me with incredible hatred. The pupils of her light blue eyes were like pinpoints; she met my gaze quite openly with a kind of relish—a relish the scorpion uses to pierce his prey with the barb in his tail. I felt that this intensity of human emotion had not existed for a long time. The shafts of such glaring looks can bring us nothing but ruin and death. I sense that it wants to spread like an epidemic or a spark that can be extinguished only deep inside, with difficulty and self-control.

PARIS, 19 AUGUST 1942

To the Ritz at noon with Wiemer who wants to visit Poupet and Hercule in Marseille in the next few days. Discussion of the situation. "*Nous après le déluge*" [We (shall be here) after the deluge.].

Called on Charmille for tea right after that. We ate on the Rue de Duras and afterward, crossed the Rue de Faubourg Saint-Honoré to the Étoile under strong sheet lightning. On our way, we occasionally heard the crickets chirping in the bakeries; our conversation was wide-ranging and retrospective in nature.

Current reading: Schlegel's *Lucinda*, which gives me the impression that here Romanticism could have turned into a way of life, the way details have become perpetuated in bad style through Gentz and Varnhagen [von Ense]. Here there are just intimations and foreshadowing. Perhaps one day they will form a melody. Then Romanticism would emerge as an intricate prelude to exquisite and refined attainments of our later culture. Today, one can still sense the urge with which it tries to capture talented individuals; it resembles a spirit that influences us with its design and demands to find form in flesh and blood. These individuals can also transform anything into the Romantic mode, as Ludwig II did to the Versailles of Louis XIV, or the way Wagner transformed the world of the Norse gods. The Romantic key fits ninety-nine treasure houses; madness and death lurk in the hundredth.

PARIS, 26 AUGUST 1942

Friedrich Georg writes to me that during the last attack on Hamburg, the type for his second edition of *Illusionen der Technik* [*Illusions of Technology*] was melted in the fire.

The Doctoresse picked me up in the evening for a walk through the old neighborhoods by the light of the full moon. At the monument to Henri IV, we went down to the Square du Vert-Galant, where we saw lights in the ships' galleys, and it smelled of stagnant water. We talked about Platen's poetry, whose beauty she compared to the harsh brilliance of the moonlight—secondhand light. Let Eros bathe in reflected light.

At times I have difficulty distinguishing between my conscious and unconscious existence. I mean between that part of my life that has been knit together by dreams and the other, by the day. It's similar when I try to create images and characters—when I work as an author, many things coalesce into flesh and blood and develop lives of their own.

Man could disappear into the images that he himself has invented in the role of sorcerer, but actually the opposite must happen: the images must raise him up into the light, and then they can fall from him like petals from the fruit.

At the moment, we are in the process of implementing the exact opposite dynamic from that of the Romantics. Where they dove deep into things, we rise upward. This new, clearer vision is still painful, still unfamiliar.

"*Les tape-durs*" [the stubborn, hard-headed ones]. This is what the *Septembriseurs*[70] call themselves. The word contains a frightening tenderness, evoking something of the world's malicious child's play.

PARIS, 28 AUGUST 1942

Still no news of my journey to the East. At noon had a conversation with Weinstock about Plato and his contemporary appeal. These ideas come to me after having read Friedrich Georg's *Griechische Götter* [*Greek Gods*].

In the afternoon, I had a visit in the Majestic from a Herr S., an owner of factories that make electrical equipment. He posed the question whether moral man is prepared to enter reality today and whether there is any prospect for this. We discussed this a long time, calling to mind Nietzsche, Burckhardt, and Stavrogin.

My visitor seemed to be animated by a certain pragmatic moralism, or Utopianism, a kind of substantiated rationality like that of the Jesuit fathers who commissioned the vault in Saint Michael's Church in Munich. The philosophical tract that was popular one hundred and fifty years ago, *The Economy of Human Life*,[71] came to mind.

It's good to keep the concrete world in sight and close at hand when having such abstract discussions. It's like a great machine in which the momentum of our conversation sometimes powers a piston and at others, a flywheel.

We can seek another person with the intention of being particularly cordial or particularly intimate that day, yet that is no protection against annoyance. The tuning of the strings to produce a harmonious chord is not controlled by our will. This often happens to me with encounters I've been looking forward to—they seem chilly, and the proper harmony is not reestablished until days or weeks later.

Dreams of clouds last night. They looked like massive ribbons of snow, with edges of soil, like the clumps of earth children used to roll along the ground in wet weather in the spring thaw.

Paris, 29 August 1942

In the afternoon I went to visit le Moult on the sixth floor of a house on Rue Duméril to examine his insect collection. The door was opened by a stout gentleman sixty years old with a full white beard who had obviously been debilitated by his many years in the tropics. He left me alone for a moment in a large room; its walls were covered with cases full of butterflies the way a library would be with books. I saw an aquarium, and a ring-necked dove flew down toward me from the top of one of the cabinets. It cooed at me and hopped onto the index finger of my hand. Then le Moult returned and showed me his magnificent butterflies from the Solomon Islands and other archipelagoes of the world. Here I was again reminded of the strange enterprise of accumulating hundreds of thousands of tiny colorful mummies—there is something Egyptian about the activity. These arts, he says, seem so tenuous in our world of destruction. A single such case often represents the result of many years of the most painstaking work. That explains why le Moult poured out his heart with a distraught account of an anti-aircraft shell that had quite recently exploded nearby.

At night I dreamed of climbing a mountain. From a small rivulet, I picked out a green fish with seven pairs of eyes, those in the front were blue, the ones at the back still in an indistinct embryonic stage. When I ascended higher into the icy mountain terrain, the fish stopped moving and froze in my hand. I then entered a mountain chapel.

Paris, 30 August 1942

Visited Bagatelle in the afternoon with Charmille. There was a yellow lantana blossom with a red center. The bloom is like velvet and gives forth a delicate velvet aroma. This attracts the butterflies, especially the swallowtail, which hovers over it with outspread wings as it inserts its proboscis into the colorful recesses. I've seen these in the Azores, but they were violet, and I'm always overcome by a feeling of homesickness when the sight reminds me of those Hesperides. On those islands and on the Canaries and on the mountains of Rio de Janeiro, I spent hours that revealed to me that there must have been a paradise—so solitary and beautiful, often majestic.

Even the sun seemed to shine with a different light, more divine. In such hours, out of all the evils of our modern age, only one remained: that the moment had to pass.

PARIS, 31 AUGUST 1942

Went by the new antiquarian bookshop I have discovered: Gonod on the Rue de Miromesnil. A new bookdealer means a new hobbyhorse. I especially liked a little square room completely lined with books. I bought the memoirs of Baron Grimm, whose writing, in addition to his letters, will always remain a choice morsel for connoisseurs. Each volume bore the bookplate of a Baron de Crisenoy, "*Je regarde et je garde*" [I watch and I guard]—a proud motto. In addition, I picked up a detailed account of the shipwreck of the American brig *La Sophie* (Paris, 1821). And finally, *L'Art du Duel* [*The Art of the Duel*] by Tavernier signed by the author to A. Gerschell, whom he identifies as the "king of photographers." Just to poke around among all these things is informative; memory retains in passing a mass of names and dates, and although these facts erode, they deposit a kind of compost in the mind, which nurtures later growth of diffuse knowledge. This can be superior to precision, as it consists of nuances of contour and intellectual currents. Thus, none of my many walks along the quais is ever in vain—just as the appeal of the hunt lies in the chase, not in bagging the prey.

PARIS, 1 SEPTEMBER 1942

The first of September—along the Quais de la Seine, there already extends a pattern of yellow, jagged, heart-shaped poplar leaves. We are now entering the fourth year of this war.

Called on Valentiner in the evening to watch darkness climb over the rooftops. The swallows and swifts had already moved on. Later, to the Tuileries with Charmille. We sat on a bench as the big dipper sparkled overhead and talked about the flower with the golden calyx, the flower of imagination.

My current reading: Paul Morand, *Vie de Guy de Maupassant* [*The Life of Guy de Maupassant*]. These are bouquets, flowers interlaced with variegated spiders and snakeheads. Incidentally, one should not become the biographer of anyone one does not love.

PARIS, 2 SEPTEMBER 1942

Visited Parc de Bagatelle in the afternoon. The leaves are turning yellow and asters are coming into bloom. Intimate conversation in the pavilion.

Slept poorly at night. There is a sort of dream in which only thoughts form instead of images. We cannot seem to penetrate the deeper vaults of the structure to find solutions.

PARIS, 8 SEPTEMBER 1942

Went to Valentiner's in the evening; Henri de Montherlant was there, as well as Nebel, who had come from the islands. Nebel told us about a prophecy from the sixteenth century that had foretold the destruction of Cologne for our time. He claimed that it had been fulfilled quite literally and concretely, for only the city center within its sixteenth-century limits had been demolished. Then, a discussion of American values, which will be further promoted by the obliteration of our old cities.

Further conversation about de Quincey; Nebel had brought an English edition with him that made my mouth water. Talk of bullfighting, which had encouraged Montherlant to run away from home when he was a boy. About the Duke of Saint-Simon and the memoirs of Primi Visconti from the court of Louis XIV. Montherlant told the anecdote about the Comte de Guiche that he had run across and which he mentions in one of his books.

Paris, 9 September 1942

Breakfast at the Morands', where, in addition to them, I also saw Benoist-Méchin. Talked about Maupassant on the occasion of Morand's biography. He said he owned a large number of unknown letters by this author. Then talk about d'Annunzio, whom Benoist-Méchin once visited on his island. On his little battleship, d'Annunzio fired off salutes to honor various nations after toasting each of them briefly. At the end, after a particularly heartfelt acclamation of France, the powder from the guns settled into a ring around the ship, which gradually rose into the air. At this d'Annunzio said to his guests, "Do you now believe I am a poet?"

Benoist-Méchin then talked about the recruitment of the 650,000 workers that Germany is demanding of France, and about the prospects and disadvantages that await them. Among these he listed the increased dangers for central Europe that such an accumulation of rootless individuals brings with it from a purely technical aspect, and for France, particular danger by virtue of proximity.

This cabinet minister gives the impression of incisive intelligence. His error lies in the fact that he made the wrong decision at the crossroads. He now finds himself upon a path that is becoming ever narrower and more impassable. In this situation, he has to step up his activity, although the results will diminish. In this way his energies are dissipated: his desperate measures will ultimately lead to his downfall. Europe resembles a beautiful woman with too many suitors. She is holding out for the right one.

Then I met Charmille at the Eiffel Tower in the Parc de Bagatelle. The asters are beginning to bloom, one in particular bears myriads of pale gray buds hardly larger than pinheads on its bushes. The flower thus brings honor to its name, as if it were reflecting the firmament in a microcosm.

Paris, 10 September 1942

Went to the Ritz in the evening with Humm to hear the correspondent for the *Kölnische Zeitung* [Cologne newspaper], Mariaux and his wife. Mariaux reported that in the turmoil of this war, fire had destroyed all his notes and manuscripts, the result of thirty years of work. He compared the condition he's been in since then to that of Peter Schlemihl, the man who lost his shadow.[72]

His misfortune made me wonder whether or not I should publish certain of my unpublished materials, like my travel journals, earlier than I had planned to. Appearing in print is a safety measure against these types of losses.

During these past years, solipsism has emerged as a particularly difficult hurdle in the evolution of my thought. This is not only a product of isolation, it is also related to a temptation to embrace misanthropy, a trait that one cannot resist strongly enough in oneself. When surrounded by these crowds who have renounced free will, I feel more and more alienated, and sometimes it seems as if these people were not even there or that they were merely specious outlines constructed of half-demonic, half-mechanical materials.

Active solipsism: the power that lets us dream the world. We dream ourselves into health or death; if we could dream more powerfully, we would become immortal. That is seductive, yet you always have to think of the dangers, the way Ruysbroeck L'Admirable saw them and described them in his *Mirror of Eternal Salvation*: "One finds other, evil, and diabolical men who say they are God, that heaven and earth were made by their hands, and that they received Him along with everything else that exists."

These are the temptations of theological speculation, like those visible in the *Thebais*.[73] How puny by comparison is the entire world of technology.

PARIS, 13 SEPTEMBER 1942

Sunday stroll to Saint-Rémy-lès-Chevreuse. It is my habit to have a leisurely breakfast there in the inn Chez Yvette. Then I walk up the hill to a large park abandoned by its owner. A good cigar for its gatekeeper, the disabled veteran who opens this overgrown garden. I rest on a solitary slope overgrown with low chestnut bushes with a view of green stands of fir and oak, the jays and woodpeckers flying back and forth among them. In the rhythm of resting and thinking, the afternoon passes all too quickly.

PARIS, 14 SEPTEMBER 1942

The riddle of life—before it, blocking the way, hangs the combination lock of the mind doing its job. The outrageous aspect of this job is that the contents of the safe change according to the method applied to gain access to it. If the lock is ever broken open, it evaporates.

Doucement! [Carefully!] The more delicately we finger it, the more remarkable are the combinations that are revealed. By the same token, they also become simpler. Ultimately, we begin to sense that we are gaining access to our own breast, to our self, and that the riddle of the world is a reflection of the riddle of life. The treasures of the cosmos now pour in.

PARIS, 15 SEPTEMBER 1942

Current reading: Progressing in the Bible, which I have been engaged in systematically for a year. Among the Psalms, Psalm 139 struck me especially, for it is an expression of divine physics. This can be called monistic, because *one* trunk bears a branched system of contradictions. God is present as far as the depths of hell, and the darkness illuminates Him as the light. He inhabits matter, sees our bones growing in the womb, and knows their future.

For our thought processes, this psalm sets itself completely apart from the others by its perfect intelligibility. Compared with others, such as the powerful Psalm 90, it is more modern in the same sense that Thucydides is more modern than Herodotus. In contrast with the other songs of destiny, it is composed of the highest spiritual content. Verses 19–22 seem to break down and, if I am not mistaken, appear to be by a different author. On the other hand, verse 14 is lovely, when man thanks God for having created him "wonderfully made." It makes sense that piety is only imaginable between wonderful beings. The animals express their praise through their behavior and their magnificent coloration, but for this purpose, man has been given the Word.

Further reading includes the story *Quitt* by Fontane. As I was reading, the thought came to me that a powerful narrative gift can sometimes be a detriment to an author, since delicate intellectual plankton cannot thrive in a swift flood of writing. The fact is that narrative talent was originally a rhetorical gift and thus does not conform to the pen but drags that instrument too quickly in its wake. Of course, it usually reveals a healthy nature, yet lends itself equally easily to a kind of optimism that assays men and things too superficially. But when poetic and narrative power remain in equilibrium at a high level, incomparable creations result— as in Homer. The ancient bards did not separate rhetorical and poetic craft, and fiction was born spontaneously of the quill. This presupposes that poetry is the mother tongue of the human race, as Hamann suggests.

Finally, Maurice de Guérin. In many respects, he represents the highest quality. For example, in the way that his language not only mediates feelings and sensations but is in itself a thoroughly sentimental, animated presence that requires taste to its last syllable. Because Guérin is master of this free spirit, which transforms clay into flesh and blood, his language is called as no other to delineate and describe a pantheistically animated world.

I noticed that in a journal entry of 6 February 1833, Guérin gives a list of German poets, yet he does not mention Novalis, whose life and works possess many similarities to his own.

PARIS, 16 SEPTEMBER 1942

Wednesday afternoon in the Jardin d'Acclimatation. Among the combined stock of the pheasant house, I noticed a small pair of Sumatra chickens—black, with a deep green luster, making a magnificent display in the full sunshine. The male is powerful and does not only carry the long, curved tail plumage upright in a crescent form as our roosters do but can also drag it like an Oriental train. This finery especially befits an animal perched in a tree, as it can then display a cascade of metallic green.

Why do we feel such a strong sense of delight when something so familiar, like our good old domestic rooster, reappears in an unexpected guise—transformed on islands beyond the charted seas? This has such a powerful effect on me that I sometimes find myself close to tears. I believe that in such moments, the unimaginably concentrated essence inherent in familiar images is revealed to us. Such a creature seems to be gravid with life, even down to his last cell, and flourishing there magnificently in those zones, it unfurls its profusion. It is the one thing, the archetype visible to us in these bewitching games. The sight even induces a giddy feeling: we plunge from the iridescent effect of the plumage down to the animal's very essence. The hierarchy of rainbows: it is imaginable that the whole universe was built according to an archetype and finds its variation in a myriad of solar systems.

Herein lies the charm of collecting, not in any sense of completeness. It's a matter of finding points of reference in all this multiplicity that indicate a creative energy. That is both the meaning of gardens and ultimately the meaning of the path of life itself.

Then tea in the shade of the trees in the Pavillon d'Armenonville at the edge of the tiny pool of the same name. The gentle strokes of the fishes' fins or the fall of a ripe chestnut drew delicate circles of ripples across its surface; they crisscrossed to form an exquisite latticework that reflected the magnificent green of the trees. This network seemed to become ever more delicate at the edges, so that the leaves of a tall catalpa tree in the center were reflected in ovals, only to blur into green bands at the shore and then flutter like flags in a breeze before returning to the deep.

Thought: "This is the way we ought to spread the new message—pedagogically, using images that reflect familiar concepts. In this focused area the less restrictive law holds sway." But isn't this the way it is? Innovation works by attaching itself to what is acceptable as a gentle contradiction, a possible gradation. Then it turns things inside out. We should be able to trace this in the history of painting, using examples that evolve from the use of shadow, mirrors, twilight, or darkness. Incidentally, history shows something similar: innovation bides its time in reflections and at the creative margins; it influences intellectual games, utopias, philosophical theories—and then it gradually becomes concrete, finally seeping in as if by osmosis. The boats that bring the prophets of destiny land in the twilight on distant shores.

Not to be forgotten are both of those kingfishers whizzing around here at the edge of the metropolis over cushions of duckweed. They make their nests in the small tributary that feeds the little pond. Of all the facets of this gemlike animal, I find its display of tail feathers most beautiful—their azure blue backs flash like turquoise dust.

PARIS, 17 SEPTEMBER 1942

Current reading: Harold Begbie, *Pots Cassés* [*Broken Earthenware*, 1909]. This book, translated from the English, describes the lives of a series of proletarian

Londoners. They have all fallen—physically, spiritually, and morally—into the mire and then have been converted. The book makes it clear just how far an institution like the Anglican Church has strayed from its original mission and how it forsook the pure practice of saving souls. In the terrible chaos of decline, we need guides who know exactly what the drowning man is struggling to breathe. This is where we can learn from the sects, especially the Salvation Army, which can be viewed as the most recent of our great holy orders. As the Benedictines built on the heights and the Cistercians down in the swamps, they have chosen the big cities as their sphere of influence, and from these desperate wastelands, developed their rule of conduct and their tactics.

The efforts of these men and women are even more important for their pioneering than for the huge treasure of good works that they have performed. Just as pioneers throw themselves into the breach of an attack, the salvation and conversion of the individual precede the onslaught of faith on the masses. The masses lead superficial lives, ignorant of their innermost nature. Yet they crave knowledge of this, and to relish it better than their means would allow, they accept a little piece of spiritual bread.

The details included a passage about alcohol that I liked. Long quotations without sources are included claiming that the irresistible attraction of alcohol is not caused by physical enjoyment, but by its mystical power. It is thus not depravity that leads the unfortunate man to it, but rather hunger for spiritual power. Drink gives the poor and uneducated what others derive from music and libraries: it provides them with enhanced reality. It leads them from the edges of reality into its innermost workings. For many, this narrow zone in which they experience a breath of air is a place close to the realm of inebriation. Consequently, people make a considerable mistake in thinking they can combat drunkenness as a species of gluttony focused on liquid.

The air and nitrogen oxide are cited as keys to this mystical insight. They give us a glimpse of a deeper truth that is revealed as one falls from precipice to precipice. This is absolutely correct, and is also described in the little study by Maupassant about the ether that I translated many years ago. The author considers the possibility that there does not have to be only a single condition of consciousness, but rather many different ones, separated by membranes—membranes that can be permeable in a state of hallucination.

I pursued some similar thoughts when I was studying various kinds of hallucinatory states. I pictured normal consciousness as a disk attached horizontally to an axis. Depending on the drug administered, the varieties of intoxication change the angles of the axis, and with that the orientation of the plane, and with that the characters, which light up. One full revolution of this disk completes the sum of these changes, and with it the entire mental universe in spherical form. Once I have voyaged across all the seas of hallucination, rested upon all its islands, passed time in all its bays, and explored all its archipelagoes and magical cities, then I have completed that great circle—that journey around the earth in a thousand nights and have traversed the equator of my consciousness. That is the grand tour, the excursion into the mental cosmos, that place where countless adventurers have come to grief.

PARIS, 18 SEPTEMBER 1942

I sat on a bench near the Étoile during the afternoon and fed pigeons; they were so trusting that they perched their little coral-colored feet on my hand. The sight of a pigeon's neck always carries me back to childhood. It was a time when nothing seemed more wonderful than this green, golden, and purple play of color that the tiny feathers produce when the bird pecks grains from the earth, or when the male parades before the female making his cooing sound. In this dazzling display, the modest gray pigmentation is transmuted into a higher opalescent hue igniting the light concealed deep within.

Walked along the Rue du Faubourg Saint-Honoré in the company of Charmille, who encouraged me to buy a little paperback she saw lying in the window of an antiquarian bookshop. It was apparently a translation from a manuscript by an ancient Brahmin.[74] In fact, a casual glance revealed it to be a good find. In addition, I also bought the *Histoire Générale des Larrons* [*General History of Thieves*] by d'Aubricourt in the *editio princeps* [first printed edition] of 1623.

We sat for a while on the Place du Tertre in the garden of Mère Cathérine and then ambled around Sacré Coeur in lazy spirals. The city has become my second spiritual home and represents more and more strongly the essence of what I love and cherish about ancient culture.

PARIS, 21 SEPTEMBER 1942

At the age of three, children display the full dignity of the moral person, combined with exhilaration, which they later lose.

Visited Vincennes in the afternoon, where a particular reason led me to pay a call on the old woman who used to be my concierge. Our acquaintances are like colored strings that fate has placed in our hands. When we combine and braid them, we see patterns whose value and order determine the measure of harmony granted to us. Not everybody knows how to husband these resources.

PARIS, 23 SEPTEMBER 1942

Walked with Charmille in the Forest of Vincennes. We discussed what these years had brought and the chaos we see approaching. The weather was rainy; the damp paths were strewn with shiny chestnuts.

In the night I dreamed about the soldiers I was with. They were wearing small round medals on their chests, awarded for having shot the wounded. I concluded from their conversation that these were awarded by some international organization and had the endorsement of something like the Red Cross: "Quite right. That is the point on which you still agree."

PARIS, 24 SEPTEMBER 1942

Poupet and Heller paid me a visit in the Raphael. We talked about the memoirs of Caillaux, which have just appeared with Plon. Poupet said that at a recent dinner he had seen Madame Caillaux, who had shot the publisher Calmette in 1914. She appeared wearing elbow-length red gloves.

Objects that have absorbed aromas for years have particular appeal: mortars, bath towels, spice grinders, or sometimes whole buildings, like the ancient pharmacies or tobacco storehouses that I saw in Bahia.

PARIS, 25 SEPTEMBER 1942

Have been reading documents and contemporary accounts of events during the French Revolution. The fate of the royal family is so melancholy and opens up such depressing insights into the shame of the human race. It is as if one were seeing swarms of rats surrounding defenseless victims, ultimately to pounce on them.

In the afternoon, Claus Valentiner dropped by the Majestic and gave me an edition of the works of Vico issued by Michelet in 1835.

PARIS, 27 SEPTEMBER 1942

Walked in the rain through the Forest of Vincennes. We took the path around Lac des Minimes with its islands and, at the edge of the woods, watched people bowling. Their casual nonchalance had amused me greatly once when I was here with Höll. There you encounter men between forty and sixty years of age, mostly lower-level civil servants and businessmen. From behind a pair of boundary lines on a cement lane, they pitch metal balls approximately the size of their open hand and try to hit a smaller ball roughly the size of a pomegranate. They give the impression that the fall of empires, the collapse of military campaigns, are here only vaguely comprehended. It is restorative to watch these games—like being among philosophers.

We then visited the stalls of a small circus and watched a jack-of-all-trades who was in makeup as he was energetically scrubbing three elephants in the courtyard before their performance. The rain ran down the tent and formed puddles at the edges. One of the elephants furtively used his trunk to fish out chopped straw that had been washed into them by the rain. He formed little balls of his pickings and crammed them contentedly into his mouth. To make them completely presentable, after their toilette was finished, this jack-of-all-trades forced them to relieve themselves. When he cracked his whip and shouted "chi-chi-chi," the obedient beasts stood up on their hind legs and produced tremendous amounts of water and excrement.

The jack-of-all-trades was apparently afraid that he was not going to finish the cleaning process before the beginning of the performance. This increased the humor of the process significantly. In general the comical nature of such absurd activities, like making elephants move their bowels, is enhanced by the level of seriousness motivating the pursuit. This is also the key to the real comedy in *Don Quixote*, which is raised to the third power there when the narrator seems to take the adventure seriously.

PARIS, 29 SEPTEMBER 1942

Very wakeful night, tossed and turned feverishly, but still the hours fly by. I glide across the surface of sleep without sleeping, the way one does on black ice.

As is my habit, I traced the paths of times past, step by step. When I do this, I land on an island and awaken memories. This time I was again climbing the mountains of Las Palmas. The air was filled with the spray of a heavy, warm rain, and I saw the fennel in all its wondrous freshness—its green sap pulsing through the delicate gossamer of its emerald veins. The heart of the plant was revealed. These were perhaps my most exalted moments on this earth, more yielding than the embraces of beautiful women. When I bent down over such a miracle of life, I had to fight for breath, as though submerged by a wave rising from a blue sea. A small star-shaped blossom is no less an object of veneration than the entire firmament.

Thought: All night we sleep with our bodies in the same position, but our state of mind is always making its way through new underbrush, encountering a new ambush. Thus, we often lie in sinister places on isolated terrain, infinitely far from our goal. This accounts for the often inexplicable fatigue after deep sleep.

Perpetua writes me that the most recent attack on Munich destroyed Rodolphe's studio. Fortunately, none of his pictures were stored there. The loss of the portrait that I sat for in Überlingen would not have bothered me much.

Siegler dropped by in the morning and told me about the attack on Hamburg. The firebombs were dropped in batches of up to seventy pieces. To keep the fire brigades from extinguishing them, every tenth bomb was packed with explosives. When the print shop was in flames, fifteen hundred fires were already raging in the city.

In the evening heard a lecture by a little Mauritanian with a certain cynical complacency who spoke about propaganda techniques used to influence the masses. This type of man is certainly novel, or at least in comparison to the nineteenth century, downright new. The advantage that people like this truly possess lies in their negative qualities. They have thrown off the moral baggage sooner than the majority of other people and introduced the laws of mechanical engineering into politics. But this advantage will be overtaken—not by moral human beings, who are necessarily inferior to them relative to their unrestrained violence—but rather by people just like them who have learned at their feet. Ultimately, the stupidest man says to himself, "if he respects nothing, then why should he insist we respect him?"

It is, therefore, an error to expect religion and piety to restore order. Animalistic tendencies are produced at the zoological level, and demonic ones on the demonic level. This means that the shark is devoured by the leviathan and the Devil by Beelzebub.

Paris, 30 September 1942

Corrected the *Letters from Norway*.[75] I had doubts about "molten rivers of lead." Unjustified, because rivers can also be frozen and solid.

The flaw that I sense here is incidentally inherent in language itself and is a result of one of the tiny spaces in the mosaic. Language lacks the concept "solid river" as an independent noun.

The ventral side of many terrestrial animals, such as the flat fishes, the *turbellaria* [flatworms], and the snakes, is drab. Nature is a frugal painter.

Visited the National Library in the afternoon. The catalogue room—I often wished I could possess folios where I could look up every printed book. But here one sees the research tools no individual could own, no matter how rich he might be. These match the stature of the Great Man, that is to say, the state. So it is with this system of catalogues. Standing before them, one senses an intellectual mechanism designed by a methodical mind.

Here I spoke with Dr. Fuchs, who is working on a comprehensive catalogue of German libraries, which will represent a major work of human industry worthy of the bee. The enterprise of collecting and cataloguing on a grand scale seems to be in its infancy; here we stand before a new style of Chinoiserie, a Mandarin culture devoid of creativity that nonetheless knows how to conjure the existing ideograms. In the area of archives, we can look forward to the emergence of a more severe, more modest, but also more enjoyable scholarship that possesses downright anarchic traits when compared to that of the nineteenth century. Many of the strands of this scholarship will connect with that of the eighteenth century, to Linnaeus, to the Encyclopedists, and to the Rationalist school of theology. It will be easier to live with intellectuals like these; they can be manipulated. They are the conservators in the world of carnage. We have new pyramids and catacombs in our future—the subterranean bustling of an ant colony. In the days of the pharaohs, priests tried to protect the king and his household from the world of transience; today this is happening with methodically organized material of inquiring minds, down to the last trivial detail.

Afterward visited the manuscript room where magnificent objects were on display, such as the Gospel of Charlemagne, the Bible of Charles the Bald, and the book of hours of the Duc de Berry, which was opened to the calendar for August and September. The space was like a shrine where tiny motes of dust hovered in the clear air, as if we had entered a picture by Memling. Archival order achieves its highest form when the choicest pieces also have the power of relics; the precious nature of these things is intensified by the aura of ancient authority. This is where one should counter historical developments and install a new clerisy to be the custodians of such things. Of course, their way must be prepared by a new sense of responsibility. One cannot expect that of a state that uses its police to protect its Monument to the Unknown Soldier.

Among the musical pieces, there was the score to Debussy's opera *Pélleas et Mélisande*, which revealed something amazingly precise. It resembled the blueprint for an electrical circuit; the heads of the notes were little glass insulators arranged on wires.

In the evening, we went to the Rôtisserie Nique on Avenue Wagram with Heller and Siegler, whose visits to Paris are always a pleasure. We discussed the situation and for the last ten years have agreed in our appraisal of it. Then we spoke about acquaintances, among them Gerhard [Nebel], whose wife is so-called one-quarter Jewish. For this reason, the house committee of the building where she lives has banned her from the air-raid shelter. It's hard to imagine that a sense of purity of blood is so finely developed among the secondary school teachers of Hamburg who live there. To compensate for that, however, they are uncannily acute at sniffing out scapegoats.

Later I read *The Wisdom of Solomon* and then slept very little and poorly, which has been typical recently. Sleep is the principle opposed to the will, which is why I am becoming more alert the more I try to force it. For its part, thought stays on the path of the will. One can thus think of all those things one wants to think of, but on the other hand, we cannot banish thoughts we do not want to think. Here is where the anecdote about the farmer belongs: he was promised treasure but only on the condition that he would not think of a bear when he dug it up. The joke is deeper than it seems; it shows the path leading to the treasures of the earth.

PARIS, 2 OCTOBER 1942

Perpetua writes to me that the end of our century will perhaps be even more terrible than the beginning and middle have been. I do not tend to believe that, and I have often thought that people will look back upon it like the baby Herakles who strangled the snakes in his cradle. But she's quite right when she says that in an age like ours, we must develop the habits of lizards: we must learn to seek out those rare sunny spots and use them. This is also true of the war; we cannot always be wondering uselessly when it will end. We have no control over that date. Yet we still have the capacity to spread joy in the teeth of the storms, joy for ourselves and for others. When we do so, we hold a tiny shred of peace in our hands.

I've also heard from her that the astrologer's father has been missing for some time. It is assumed that Russian prisoners of war murdered him for his clothes. That reminds me of the terrible fate of old Kügelgen. Years ago, incidentally, I predicted the resurgence of gangs of robbers without imagining precisely *how* history would fulfill my prophecy. I was simply deriving my prediction from negative evidence, such as overweening power and the nationalization of injustice.

I met the Doctoresse in the evening at the Place des Ternes for one of those cups of lemon verbena tea she has prescribed for me. Since I have started to worry about the state of my health, this hour together is also an office visit.

When I got to bed, I read in the journals of Léon Bloy and then a bit further in the Book of Wisdom. The inclusion of a document of such great skepticism in the canon, and the assumption that it is one of the authentic books, is surprising and only comprehensible when we view the Bible as landscape, a piece of creation where different sections complement and balance each other. In this sense, one ascends to heights where the old golden eagle with his white crown builds his aerie. The air has become thinner, and the earth reveals its design. No gaze is more piercing than that of the wise king, yet Job penetrated deeper. In old age, he still brought forth fruit, for pain cultivated his soil.

The preacher sees pain as vanity. In doing so, he has ignored the life of Lear while enjoying that of the aging Faust. He transformed lands into lush gardens, planted forests and vineyards, and in his pleasure domes lived with multitudes of female slaves and singers. But all that was as vain as the wind, and this notion is more terrible than the one that sees it as the veil of Maya.[76]

Each life holds a certain number of things that, out of consideration, a human being does not confide to his dearest friend. They are like the stones you find in chickens' stomachs that are not digested along with everything else. Man preserves the basest and the best so anxiously. Even when confession has relieved him of the burden of evil, he still wears his best for God alone. The part of us that is noble, good, and holy resides far from the social sphere; it cannot be communicated.

Incidentally, women are significantly more secretive in this respect. They are often the true graves of past love affairs, and does there exist even one of them about whom a husband, a lover, knows everything—even when she is lying in his arms? Anyone who has encountered an old lover after many years has been frightened by this mastery of silence. Daughters of the earth indeed! Some knowledge that finds sanctuary in our breast is terrifying and lonely; fatherhood is one such. The horrors of Medea rear up in a thoroughly middle-class world. Thus, the dilemma of the woman who watches her husband cherish a child through the years—a child that is not his.

"Two people who love each other should tell each other everything." But are they strong enough to do so?

"I would like to confess something to you, but I'm afraid you'll hear me as a priest in your own right and not someone who listens with wisdom, as a representative of God. I fear you might become my judge."

That is the prodigious—but also healing—significance of prayer, namely that for a moment it opens the recesses of the heart and lets light shine in. For human beings, especially in our northern latitudes, it opens the only portal to truth, to the ultimate, radical honesty. Without it, people could not live with their nearest and dearest without suspicion and dark thoughts. And at times, when caution would not silence our tongues, then consideration would do so.

Thoughts about negating consonants, those that convey something pejorative, especially *N* and *P*. *Pes, pejus, pied, petit, pire.* The *P* is also used as a sound denoting pure contempt. The foot as a symbol of the lesser human being, as a degraded hand. After the war, I want to work on these connections, especially the way in which the human body is represented by language. To do so it would, of course, be a good idea if I were to move in again with Friedrich Georg, who animates conversation a great deal.

PARIS, 3 OCTOBER 1942

In the afternoon, I dropped by the bookshop in the Palais Royal, where I bought the 1812 Crébillon edition printed by Didot. One can see from the green calf bindings what a powerful sense of style the Empire possessed. It naturally had access to the guild of artisans of the *Ancien Régime*, and that's more important than the style; that is a matter of substance. Today France still enjoys this advantage of traditions passed down from hand to hand, and will certainly retain these thanks to its largely rational policies. But what is important in this country at the moment is that its old haunts, the cities, will not be plowed under and on its ruins chain stores from Chicago would be built—which is what will happen in Germany. To activate the huge potential slumbering here, to consign it to the flames, that is the goal of both warring parties, and only a small group of people is keeping the scales in balance. That this could have succeeded for this long is all the more astonishing, since it contradicts the brutal politics of the day.

I decided not to erase the comments of the bookdealer on the inside of the flyleaf. His notes about the condition, plates, the value of the various editions, et cetera, contribute a note to what Feltesse calls the authenticity of the book. I make my own note on the bookplate regarding the time and place of my purchase, or of the giver, and occasionally other special circumstances.

Dinner in the Doctoresse's apartment. Watched her cook. The way in which she goes about it shows something of the *femme savante*, especially in the way she times things and plans the sequence of the various tasks and procedures. In this way, cooking has the appearance of a well thought-out process, rather like a chemical experiment. Incidentally, just the acquisition of ingredients has become a feat in itself; the shops are almost empty, and hunger is spreading.

Currently reading: Conan Doyle. We reach an age when even good mysteries bore us. Our appreciation for the kaleidoscopic shifting of facts begins to wane; the elements are all too familiar.

This is also true of life. We reach a point when we master the facts that satiate us. "We number our years as threescore and ten . . . " One could add to that: and that is quite sufficient. Anyone who, up to then, has not learned enough to be promoted to the next grade must go back to the beginning and make it up.

This explains the childish aspect of broken-down old men, especially the lecherous, stingy, cruel, and petty ones. In them chaos has displaced the awareness that promotes successful old age, which carries quite precise external signs.

PARIS, 4 OCTOBER 1942

Outing to Saint-Rémy-lès-Chevreuse. Rambled through the woods after breakfast. The mushrooms are thriving in all this moisture, their caps gleam in the moss among the spiderwebs heavy with dewdrops. I saw a round puffball that had long white spines on its cap, obviously the hedgehog member of this outlandish group.

A squirrel was romping high in a chestnut tree, a lovely burnished red against the wet green foliage. It had tossed shiny nuts down for the winter; we shared in his harvest.

Quite melancholy because I am becoming more unhappy with my physical condition. I have been losing weight for weeks. I often grow weary of this business and treat the body as a mutineer, but it is better to open my ears and listen to what it wants.

In the evening read further in *La Porte des Humbles* [*The Gate of the Humble*] by Léon Bloy. I always find his writing satisfying despite his maniacal and indiscriminate diatribes against everything Germanic. He would like to destroy London with a single bomb, while he sees Denmark as a kind of filthy Sodom. I think, however, that by this time I've learned to value people's intellect, although their motivations are different from mine, and to see them in their pure state devoid of contradictions.

Read further in the Song of Songs.

PARIS, 5 OCTOBER 1942

In the afternoon, I thumbed through *Pyrrhus* by Crébillon. The method by which language is revealed here seems unparalleled. It is so smooth and perfectly burnished that it cannot be improved. For language to attain new sounds or new colors, we would have to penetrate words with chemical processes. *Décadence* would be the inevitable result.

The verses follow upon one another with a beautiful lightness and move toward the rhymes with such unforced grace—here in poetry language is at play more naturally, not more artfully. What makes these verses so supple is surely the wealth of one-syllable words, which creates the dactylic meter.

La nuit est plus clair que le fond de mon coeur.

[The night is more clear than the depths of my heart.]

Back to the Quai Voltaire in the evening, where I met the Valentiner brothers and Poupet. Silver-gray mists cloaked the houses, and above them slate blue clouds with a brown ring of dusk. Some tones had already been drained away; the shaft of light from Saint-Germain-des-Prés looked washed out, and only the dark tower roof shone through.

The light grey limestone used to construct so many houses, pavement, bridges, and quais shows countless concave impressions made by the shell of the slender whorl snail. I am always pleased when my eye falls upon one of them: they are part of those secret heraldic beasts, the microcosmic embellishments of this city.

PARIS, 6 OCTOBER 1942

Finished reading *La Porte des Humbles* by Léon Bloy. I can sense the old lion mellowing. Such hard cider takes seventy years to lose its kick.

Reading provides me with such pleasure, especially during the noonday break. The true appeal of journals is not their strange or extraordinary content. Much more challenging is the description of simple daily routines, familiar rules that govern life. That is done very successfully here; a reader is a participant in everyday activity. Thus do the passing years repay us once more, in the same way that many a summer has provided the wood that warms us as it burns in the fireplace.

The book contains predictions, including one that concerns the Russian Revolution. This period actually provides us with an apocalyptic vision of our own. From one of the final sentences, we hear the sage say: "I am expecting the Cossacks and the Holy Ghost." Then, shortly before the end, on 16 October 1917, we read an oracular utterance: "I am no longer eating. I lack appetite. Everything about me needs to change." Death was to accomplish this and left its stamp on Bloy's features, which were then judged to be "majestic, serene, and commanding."

His life demonstrates that it is not our errors that threaten our authority when we pass through the final gate of honor that our spirit has yearned for. It could more likely be our shortcomings, which are taken as nakedness there. We shed them as Don Quixote his armor, and our disrobing is greeted with laughter.

Visited the bookshop of Jean Bannier in the afternoon, at 8 Rue de Castiglione. There I picked up *Roma Subterranea* [*Underground Rome*] by Aringhus, a work containing many plates and inscriptions from the catacombs that can be seen as a predecessor to Rossi's *Roma Sotteranea*. In our zones of fire and devastation, the peace offered by such tombs hewn into the rock holds great appeal for its promise of eternal slumber in the earth's womb.

But, even more important, however, was the beautiful copy of Breton's *La Chine en Miniature* [*China in Miniatures*], which I bought. I had tiptoed around this several times like the fox around the bait before the trap springs shut. The purchase was beyond my means, but what we gain from books makes the investment worthwhile, although I have the feeling that I am stacking them up for the heap of rubble that the house could someday all too easily be reduced to. Still, I am browsing with great enjoyment in these six volumes with their miniatures that are more than 130 years old yet still glowing in the brightest colors. The distances created by deserts and oceans are hardly greater than the space of heaven, and therefore life in these foreign realms often seems to us like images from a distant planet.

Concerning abnormalities: below all the soft-soap artists and snake oil salesmen that authors write about there lies a deep-seated atavistic stratum—the memory of a time when our whole skin was still mucus membrane. This membrane is a precursor of skin, evolutionary remnant from the ocean's cradle and of our Neptunian origins. Here the sense of touch struggles to grasp similar states, like those that open to our vision when we perceive the color red. But one can also find types different from the sanguine solarian, namely lymphatics with little pigmentation, a preference for steam baths, hairdressers' salons, and mirrors; for the lunarians, it is the world of caves. They exhibit blood disorders and a tendency toward eczema and pruritus. Exaggerated symptoms—often manic cleanliness, occasional albinism, fear of microbes, and loathing of snakes—are common.

These abnormalities are not really disorders—they are elements that have been released, elements that are present in all of us, latent and potent. In our dreams, they often climb up from the chasms. The deeper these things lie concealed within us, the more powerful is our alienation, our horror when nature works as a chemical analyst to reveal them in their pure form. With that, the snake emerges from its hole. This explains the terrible excitement that can grip a metropolis in response to news of a rape-murder. When this happens, we all feel the sound of the bolt sliding shut in our own netherworld.

The misguided attempts of certain doctors are surely questionable when they try to protect a perpetrator from justice by portraying him as sick. That point of view would be defensible if the sickness were not the sickness that afflicts us all but is merely manifest in him and could be surgically removed. Like an ancient human sacrifice, he is immured under the bridge buttresses of the community. What's at stake here is less the poor criminal than the millions of his brethren.

PARIS, 7 OCTOBER 1942

Slept poorly. Was awakened in the early hours by a strange but gentle rain inside me. I have the impression that the body is trying to say something, yet in the artificial lives we lead, we understand its sentences and vocabulary hardly any better than we would those of an old tenant farmer conversing with us at our city address about things like parish fairs, harvests, and stunted crops. We can dismiss him with money, but we have to give the body pills. In both cases: back to the land—that means to the earth and its elements.

Read in the newspapers: "A book that reaches an edition of 1,000,000 copies is always something unusual—a remarkable event in the intellectual world. It is evident that a deep need exists for such a work. The success of *Mythus*[77] is one of those signs that lets us perceive the latent will of a coming era." Thus speaks the wise Kastor in the *Völkischer Beobachter* of 7 October 1942 about the *Mythus* by Rosenberg, the dullest collection of hastily copied platitudes imaginable. The same Kastor argued in the same publication almost ten years ago, "Well, didn't Herr Spengler read the newspapers?" Thus, a philosopher refers another philosopher to the newspapers for his source of inspiration—and this in Germany and quite openly. That simply never should have been articulated so blatantly. And let it be noted that this Kastor is considered the most prominent voice in his field, the chief spokesman of the heroic school of philosophy. This is but one small example of the quality of the air we have to breathe.

People like this Kastor, incidentally, belong to the type of truffle-hunting pigs found in any revolution. Because their coarse fellow ideologues are incapable of identifying their most exquisite opponents, they co-opt the corrupt higher-level intellects to sniff them out. And once their opponents have been exposed, they can then be attacked—when possible through police intervention. Whenever I noticed him referring to me, I expected the police at my house with a search warrant. Kastor even called on the police to go after Spengler, and there are those in the inner circle who say he has that on his conscience.

PARIS, 8 OCTOBER 1942

Went to Berès in the evening, where I looked at books. I bought the old *Malleus Maleficarum* [*Hammer of Witches*] by Sprenger in the Venice edition of 1574. The purchase would have excited me more twenty years ago, when I was studying hallucinogens along with magic and Satanism.

PARIS, 9 OCTOBER 1942

In the afternoon, rode through the Bois de Boulogne, where the leaves are turning. Colonel Kossmann told me that my command posting to Russia could get serious in the next few days. Preliminary orders have already been received. Since my life here has taken on a new form, this disruption could be a welcome one. While pondering this, I knocked a glass off the washstand, and it smashed to pieces.

I shall try to have Rehm assigned to me as my adjutant.

PARIS, 11 OCTOBER 1942

Sunday, went to the Rue de Bellechasse in the afternoon. Perhaps my last time crossing this threshold into the stairwell where the amethyst spiral always gives me a feeling of anxiety, the kind one feels when keeping tremendous secrets. I noticed the pattern of the tiny snail shells on the stone threshold; the sight of these in this city has often brought me such delight.

PARIS, 12 OCTOBER 1942

Slept very poorly, which is certainly the result of illness. At the moment when I am supposed to go to Russia, I can't simply report to the infirmary. Such coincidences have often arisen in my life; they create a real dilemma.

Among my letters was one from Umm-El-Banine, an Azerbaijani writer who enclosed her novel *Nami*. A beautifully pressed lily of the valley falls out as I thumb through the volume. From its dark brown stalk, ten yellow ones branch off into little bell-shaped blossoms as if embossed on heavy paper.

SURESNES, 13 OCTOBER 1942

Slept very poorly again. In the morning I went to the senior staff doctor, who recommended a short stay in the infirmary in Suresnes, which can still be arranged before my marching orders come through. Have just arrived there. I am spending my time partly lying on the bed reading, and partly looking out the window, which provides a view of Mont Valérien. Its foliage is still mostly green but sprinkled with patches ranging from copper-hued to fiery red and yellow. Foliage also covers the fort, the ancient Bullerjan from 1871, up to its roof.

The images from last night are still in my mind. I recall standing in the parlor with my father, along with several siblings, one of whom was squirming in a laundry basket. I wanted to make a comment about this and turned to my father several times. He seemed to ignore me deliberately. I was finally able to make myself heard: "You were not successful in achieving the optimal combination in any of us. My conclusion is based on the virtues that I see in us as a whole, but are not present in any one of us individually."

The old man thought about this for a few seconds, vacantly gazing with an acid stare, and then said dryly: "You may be right."

Similar things as well that I would like to have written down, but I was afraid I would become wide awake if I turned on the light.

Deep melancholy. Rehm arrived yesterday, so I am not at a loss for someone to run errands.

SURESNES, 14 OCTOBER 1942

I called on the Doctoresse in the evening and brought her red zinnias. She didn't stop pestering me about going to the staff doctor. She even had a meeting with the head medical officer here.

To return to yesterday's dream: the document about death should perhaps begin with a chapter that emphasizes the operation of chance in our individual lives. We would not exist had our father married a different woman, or our mother a different man. Assuming this marriage continues, we are chosen from among millions of embryos. We are thus random combinations of the absolute. We resemble winning lottery tickets with values written on them in the characters of fate are then paid out in earthly currency, in the form of talent that we should make the most of.

We could draw the conclusion that as individuals we are imperfect, and that eternity is neither suitable nor bearable to us. Moreover, we have to revert to the absolute, and this possibility is offered to us by death. Death has both an external and an internal form; the latter is usually visible in the physiognomy of the dead. Death has its mysteries, which the mystery of love nonetheless transcends. We become adepts when he takes us by the hand. The smile of surprise is a spiritual one, yet its reflection penetrates the physical world as far back as the features of the dying man.

Consider here what I wrote about the wheel of fortune and the number disk.

Current reading: Paul Bourget, *Voyageuses* [*Women Travelers*, 1917], a collection of short stories that introduces the author in a way that does not invite a second reading. The thick shell of convention is hardly scratched here to reveal the human content beneath.

Read further in the book of Chinese miniatures, where I noticed a description of a snake merchant. At the bottom of his basket is a bowl filled with a concentrated brew of viper flesh. And above this, a container holding live snakes. In the ancient pharmacies of the West, we also attribute particular healing powers to risking our lives. The serpent, a tellurian animal, is a powerful medicine.

I again found the journals of Emperor Kang-hsi mentioned, as I have so often in the course of my reading over the past years. I have been eager to find this work for a long time. The attraction of such power of mind transcends empires and centuries.

Read further in Isaiah, the prophet of destruction, whose "heart laments for Moab like a harp." A good visionary for our age as well.

I have a tendency to distance myself from people I love. It's as if their images developed such power in me that their physical presence becomes intolerable.

The man who murders his mistress chooses the opposite path: to possess her he extinguishes her likeness. Perhaps this is how immortals treat us.

A shared death is always a significant act—beautifully described in *Axel* by Villiers de L'Isle-Adam. In this respect, Kleist seems like someone in a hurry; he took the first good one that came along.[78]

"I say to you today you will be with me in Paradise." That also applies to the unrepentant thief. We're just not supposed to say that too loudly.

Suresnes, 15 October 1942

Had a bad night. I dreamed of doctors who had treated me, including an imaginary one whose waiting room seemed quite familiar. After waking up, it took a long time for me to distinguish this mirage from reality; perhaps its specificity was nurtured by memories of earlier dream visions.

Very worn out in the morning, but still mentally alert. I appreciated the natural vault presented to my eyes by the green and yellow trees in the gardens.

Got further in Isaiah, who luxuriates in images of destruction. His essential vision is one of the obliteration of the historical world, its old cities, fields, and vineyards, and of the triumph of the elements. This produces recovery and preparation for the new, indestructible reconstitution by the divine spirit. Men and empires will someday become just as the inner eye perceives them.

This imagery could be seen as a sort of three-field system of agriculture: the tilling of the earth; the fallow period; harvesting the fruits of the spirit. The centerpiece of the triptych when the earth lies dormant has its own inherent beauty, painted by a connoisseur of blooming deserts and fecund wildernesses. To this field, God has applied his measuring rod.

Was weighed and found to have gotten very thin. But this morning, I measured my mental weight against the sight of the trees. This is not the first time in my life that the ebb of the body and the flow of images coincide—as if sickness made things visible that were otherwise concealed.

Had a visit from Valentiner and the Doctoresse in the afternoon. She placed a purple cattleya orchid with bearded lower lip and vanilla yellow calyx on my table. It's good to see the way the little nurse from Holstein, who likes to see me reading the Bible, avoids this flower like a dubious insect as she works.

Suresnes, 16 October 1942

Another night of distress. In one dream image, I was waiting with Friedrich Georg in a room where the floor was tiled in white porcelain. The walls were built of glass bricks, and in the room stood cylindrical vessels of glass and ceramic, roughly in the shape and size of our water heaters.

We were playing a game, throwing glass balls the size of snowberries, but only one in ten was white like these. The others were colorless and invisible in flight. The balls hit the ground with a dry smack and then bounced against the walls and the vessels, creating mathematical designs of angles and straight lines as they did so. The path of the invisible balls delighted our imaginations, while the white ones resembled guidelines whose network gave the sensual connection to the all-too-intellectual, all-too-abstract game.

Thought: that must have been one of the weightless cells deep inside the cloister of the workaday world.

Read further in Isaiah, accompanied by Lichtenberg's aphorisms and Schopenhauer's *Parerga*, two reliable old sources of comfort when in need. I read these while walking up and down in the room with the tube that they had forced down my throat hanging out of my mouth.

Lichtenberg's judgment on Jean Paul: "If he starts over again from the beginning, he will become great." Even though this presupposes an impossibility, from an individual standpoint, it still points to the procreative, spermatic force of Jean Paul's prose. Many stories by Stifter bring forth such shoots. I have always regretted that Hebbel could not start over again "from the beginning," especially by adding greater potency to his journals.

We say, "That's as certain as two times two equals four," but we don't say, "as one times one equals one."

The first version is actually clearer; it has already overcome the hurdle of the identity theorem.

How to counter the objection that I no longer use certain expressions that I formulated years ago, expressions that have now become common, such as the word "total":

"Gold is withdrawn in times of inflation."

That comes from a letter to Grüninger, who enjoys such ripostes.

SURESNES, 18 OCTOBER 1942

Sunday. In the morning, the top of the Eiffel Tower was shrouded in fog.

Friedrich Georg wrote yesterday, mainly about reading Isaiah, which I notice he began to read at about the same time as I did. There are so many invisible threads uniting us.

Visit from Charmille, who brought me flowers. What is it that attracts me to her so? Probably the childlike nature that I recognize in her. We meet people who awaken in us the desire to give them presents—that is the reason I regret not having been blessed with worldly goods.

Toward evening Sacré Coeur emerged, at times beaming brightly from atop its hill and at others half-hidden in a violet haze. There is something phantasmagorical about this structure. Distance increases its magic, letting us see it as a symbol of all that is miraculous in it.

SURESNES, 20 OCTOBER 1942

Intense air raids in the night: *La frousse* [extreme dread]. Then comes the reckoning: from Charlemagne to Charles V, from the Reformation to the chaos of World War I.

I was fishing on the seashore and caught a giant sea turtle. Once I had landed it, it got away from me and dug itself into the earth. While in pursuit, I not only injured myself on the fish hook, but a disgusting sea creature crawled out of the turtle and right over me with its many feet. That was the first time that a turtle had appeared to me in a figure in a dream, and with such significance at that.

I was discharged at noon with an entry in my service record that read "alkaline gastritis." I think the Doctoresse was fearing much worse. She was pleased at the diagnosis and conferred again with the senior doctor, whom she knows from Bergmann's clinic. Rehm then picked me up, and we drove together to the Majestic to prepare for the journey.

PARIS, 21 OCTOBER 1942

In a volume that appeared in 1757, I read the court records of the case brought against Damiens. The assassination attempt took place in the first month of this same year. The historical introduction also includes a detailed description of the horrible execution.

Louis XV's demeanor during the attack upon his person was regal. He identified the perpetrator, recognizable as the only man who kept his head covered. The king commanded that he be arrested and decreed that no harm should be done to him.

Went to Chez Nique in the evening where we played American roulette [pinball].

PARIS, 22 OCTOBER 1942

Bad night. *La frousse.* Since I can't possibly report in sick now, I went to a French doctor on Rue Newton whose assurances were very helpful—more helpful than the doctors in the infirmary with all their equipment. When he heard that I was off to Russia, he didn't want to take any payment. Telephoned Ritter von Schramm.

Dropped by Morin's in the afternoon and poked around in his books one last time. I spent a further enjoyable hour in his little antiquarian bookshop. There I discovered something I had been seeking for a long time, the work by Magius, *De Tintinabulis* [*On Bells*], including the tract *De Equuleo* [*On the Rack*] bound with it in one volume. Then *De Secretis* [*On Secrets*] by Weckerus—a treasure trove. *The Spanish Journey* by Swinburne bound in red morocco. Among other things, I finally came upon the trial of Charles I, where I browsed in the description of the execution, which showed the king's great dignity, far above bodily concerns, like a ship's passenger standing on the gangplank, taking his leave of friends and entourage before a long journey.

I shall miss the world of books; I have spent precious hours in it—oases in a world of carnage. Walking along either bank of the Seine represents perfection in its own right; time flows by easily. It is hard to imagine how to improve on this, and it would not be anywhere near as beautiful if the books cost nothing. The water is part of it all.

In Chez Nique in the evening. Conversation there about little Alcor, "the rider on the wagon shaft."[79] This was punctuated by a brief air-raid alarm and a few rounds of gunfire in the darkness. Played some more American roulette, a maze where the course of nickel balls lights up electric bulbs and rows of numbers. It's the old game of chance under the guise of technology.

PARIS, 23 OCTOBER 1942

Reporting for leave today, so I called on Kossmann and the commander-in-chief who told me that on his staff there would always be a little "*Wartburgstübchen*" [little Wartburg room][80] waiting for me. I found everybody more cordial; maybe that was just a reflection of my own improved morale. "Life is opinion," says Marcus Aurelius. The general is one of those people who entered my life as an unexpected gift at a time when it had become hard to breathe. He circulated books of mine here that could no longer be published in the Fatherland, and he still has high hopes for me.

The morning passed with the transfer of current business to Neuhaus; I locked the rest up in the safe and am taking the key with me.

As a farewell, I visited a church: Saint Pierre-de-Chaillot. I took it as a good sign that a red carpet had been laid down on the steps, and the large portal decorated with curtains. But this was closed, and I had to enter through a side door. Upon leaving, however, I found it open, and once I was outside, after having thoughtlessly walked through it, noticed that it had been decorated and prepared for a funeral. This convoluted configuration revived me; I was able to find a kind of irony in it superior to the Socratic. *Rebus*, "by means of things"—that could be a motto.

Paid a visit to Rue de Faubourg Saint-Honoré once again. There I walk across patterns in the carpet of my past. Also went to Rue de Castiglione, where I bought a seal as a memento of this day.

It's strange how often I come across the image of a turtle on my walks after having dreamed of it. All these signs surround us, yet the eye chooses but a few of them.

Departure from Charmille at Chez Nique near the Place des Ternes. Air-raid alarm, but fortunately it was soon lifted; otherwise, I would have missed the train to Berlin.

2

NOTES FROM THE CAUCASUS

KIRCHHORST, 24 OCTOBER 1942

Passed through Cologne in the middle of the day. I gazed from the window of the dining car at the city's destroyed neighborhoods. The buildings and rows of houses radiated a grim, palatial grandeur through their destruction. We glide through this alien, colder world: this is the dwelling of death.

Düsseldorf also looked mournful. Fresh ruins and red roof tiles bore witness to the firestorm. This too is one of the stepping-stones to Americanism; in place of our old haunts, we shall have cities that are the brainchildren of engineers. But perhaps only herds of sheep will graze upon the ruins, as in those old pictures of the Roman Forum.

Perpetua picked me up at the station in the evening. Schulz had been saving fuel for a long time for this trip. I sent Rehm home to his wife in Magdeburg for a few days' leave.

KIRCHHORST, 2 NOVEMBER 1942

Back in Kirchhorst, where I am less tempted to write entries in my journal. This is the setting to recover. That is perhaps the best claim to be made for any place.

Upon arrival, I noticed that the quantity of books, correspondence, and collections was making me uneasy. They demanded my immediate attention and, thanks to my more relaxed state, I realized that everything lives from and depends upon involvement, upon mental, and physical responsibility. We *possess* things thanks to a special virtue, a kind of magnetic power. In this sense, wealth is not merely a gift but also an aptitude corresponding to the scope of one's reach. It is clear that most people lack the inner capacity for wealth or even modest property. If it should nonetheless come to them from some outside source, then it disappears without a trace. It may be that this even brings misfortune with it. For this reason, old wealth is crucial so that not only the gift, but also the talent necessary to keep and use it freely, may be bequeathed to the child and subsequent generations.

Diet—even in relation to things and possessions that we acquire. Otherwise, instead of making our life easier, we must assume the role of guardians, servants, and custodians in life. The weather is autumnal, occasionally gray, punctuated by sunshine. The soft golden yellow of the poplars along the road to Neuwarmbüchen fits beautifully with the pale blue sky that arches over our unremarkable landscape.

Kirchhorst, 5 November 1942

At night dreams of ancient cave systems on Crete, where soldiers were swarming like ants. An explosive charge had just obliterated thousands of them. When I woke up, it occurred to me that Crete was the island of the Labyrinth.

Foggy day. Heavy fringes of dew accumulated on the reddish-black cabbage leaves like those little silver bubbles that form on the ruddy seaweed from deep in the ocean. Brockes was the first to note this, just as his oeuvre is rich in examples of the way a new sense of nature emerges from the *gravitas* of the baroque, although it is often indistinguishable from it. Thus, the ever-changing fabric of the ages becomes interwoven, like the color gradations on the throat of a pigeon.

Thought: Nature has forgotten the hydrogen animals, those lighter-than-air creatures that swim through the atmosphere like whales through the seas. In doing so, she deprived us of the true giants by adopting the more elegant solution of flight from the outset.

Concerning the habit of touching wood to avert some inauspicious omen. This can probably be traced back to some particular event, yet some customs become engrained only when they possess inherent symbolism. This might lie in the organic nature of wood. We reach out to it as something that has grown, and transposing the gesture to suggest fate, we imply our life span with its own destiny, in contrast to the lifeless mechanism of seconds, which merely count the *tempus mortuum* [time of death].

The breaking of glass as a symbol of luck could then be interpreted as a corollary—as an explosion of mechanical form and a release its living essence.

Kirchhorst, 6 November 1942

Friedrich Georg writes to me from Überlingen about lilies and the *Eremurus* [foxtail lily] bulbs that he planted in the garden in Leisnig. It gives me great joy to learn that he has finished not only a new collection of poems but also a second work on mythology with the title *Die Titanen* [*The Titans*]. He seems to be hard at work. At times in happy hours, I sense that fate has granted me not only the gratitude of a person who enjoys good fortune but also a sense of wonder that I have benefited equally from our camaraderie.

Walked across the lonely fields in the evening through the fog and drizzle. Clumps of trees shimmered hazily in the distance and between them and old farms, like gray arks carrying their cargoes of man and beast.

Finished reading Louis Thomas, *Le Général de Galliffet* [*General de Gallifet*, 1909], in an edition enriched by both an autograph of the author and one of the general. Galliffet offers a model of the sanguine temperament appropriate to a good cavalryman and especially a commander of the hussars. It is the temperament of a man who must be able to move and make decisions quickly, easily, and forcefully. Sanguine optimism drives vigorously toward its goals, albeit goals that are usually short term and narrow in their perspective. The world spirit propels characters like this to the fore wherever quick intervention is called for—as at Sedan and during the riots. Galliffet is also typical for the history of modern brutality and for the rediscovery of bestial methods. He got his early training in Mexico.

As I read, I recalled an old project of mine: the diagram of a historical process showing the order proceeding from left to right according to natural law. It starts at one end with the rank of tribune and moves to that of senator with Marius and Sulla, with Marat and Galliffet. Someday I would like to venture a brief typology of history—it would resemble a description of the tiny crystals in a kaleidoscope.

What did Galliffet lack to make him a Sulla, and what differentiated him from a Boulanger?

I read further in Chamfort, sampling him in small doses. His maxims are much more pointed and less appealing than those of Rivarol.

In the afternoon, I harvested carrots, celeriac, and red beets, and put them in the cellar. This kind of work, with the earth, makes me feel my health returning.

KIRCHHORST, 9 NOVEMBER 1942

In the morning, dreams about future air raids. A hybrid machine the size of the Eiffel Tower flew through the fire above a settlement; beside it was a structure resembling a radio tower. On its platform there stood an observer wearing a long coat; he was taking notes and throwing these down in smoke canisters.

In the afternoon, I attended the burial of old Frau Colshorn. As always happens at such events, I noticed a group of five to seven middle-age men wearing morning coats and top hats. These were the village fathers of Kirchhorst. Because the community does not own a hearse, neighbors carry the casket to the cemetery. This is announced in the following way: "*Jur Vadder mot mit an'n Sarg faten*." [Your father has to help carry the casket.][1]

Visit to the neighbors in the evening, but just as we were beginning to chat, the air-raid sirens started up in Hannover. We gathered in a downstairs room with our coats and suitcases, as if we were in the cabin of a ship in distress at sea. People's behavior during these attacks has changed. It shows how close the catastrophe has come.

Through the window, I could see the bright red tracer bullets being fired from the Bul [section of Hannover] into the cloud cover, as well as the flickering illumination of the shells and the fires in the city. The house was shaken to its foundation several times, although the bombs were falling far away. The presence of children lends the events an even more oppressive and gloomy feeling.

KIRCHHORST, 10 NOVEMBER 1942

We hear that yesterday's attack involved only about fifteen aircraft. I am bothered by the landing of the Americans in North Africa even more than by these things. As I respond to contemporary events, I perceive a level of empathy in myself that marks a man who realizes he is caught up less in a world war than in a global civil war. For that reason, I find myself entangled in very different conflicts from those of the hostile nations. The solution to those conflicts is secondary.

BERLIN, 12 NOVEMBER 1942

Departed this morning along with Mother and Perpetua. As I was saying goodbye, I showed our little boy a lovely drake that was swimming happily around in a puddle near the train stop. Never before have I embarked on a journey knowing so little about the course it will take or what it might achieve. I am like a fisherman casting his net into murky waters on a winter's day.

Studied some physiognomy during the trip: the subtle, almost imperceptible trace of experience that I saw at the corner of the mouth of a young girl. Lust etches its presence in the face as sharply a diamond.

In Dahlem in the evening; we are staying with Carl Schmitt.

BERLIN, 13 NOVEMBER 1942

Friday, the thirteenth of November. The day brings the first snow of the year. Strolled with Carl Schmitt through the Grunewald Forest in the morning.

BERLIN, 15 NOVEMBER 1942

My reading matter, the journal *Zalmoxis*, was named for a Scythian Herakles mentioned by Herodotus. I read two articles. One about the customs involving methods of digging up and using the mandrake root, and a second one about the *Symbolisme Aquatique*. They discussed the connections among the moon, women, and the sea. Both are by Mircea Eliade, the editor. Carl Schmitt filled me in on him as well as on his mentor, René Guénon. The etymological associations between seashells and the female genitalia are very informative. Latin *conca* and Danish *kudefisk* for "mussel" reflect this, whereas *kude* is synonymous with *vulva*.

The agenda evident in this journal is very promising; instead of following strict logic, pictograms emerge. This gives the impression of caviar, of fish roe. Every sentence contains fecundity.

Carl Schmitt also gave me a book by de Gubernatis, *La Mythologie des Plantes* [*The Mythology of Plants*]. Sixty years ago, the author was a professor of Sanskrit and mythology in Florence.

Strolled through Dahlem during the evening blackout. We talked about the daily Bible verses of the Moravians; the quatrains of Nostradamus; about Isaiah and prophecies in general. The fact that prophecies come true—even transcending distant ages—is the mark that lets us recognize the real prophetic power of their vision. With the passage of time, what the seer observes in the elements repeats as though refracted through a prism. His gaze does not pause on the history, but rather on the subject matter; nor on the future, but on the law. It is justifiable then that the mere knowledge of future dates and conjunctions betrays symptoms of a sick mind or of vulgar magic.

It was late when we visited Popitz, where I also met Sauerbruch, the surgeon. Conversation about the difference between military and medical authority as embodied in the role of the military physician, where they are more or less united but also produce tensions. There followed a discussion about the large edition of classical writers that the minister[2] is planning.

Sauerbruch said goodbye early to go see a first lieutenant whose pelvis had been fractured by a Russian shell. He feared that his art would be of little use here; in the best-case scenario, however, the pieces of bone would knit themselves together again like the shards of a clay pot. As he put it: "Still, a visit during this crisis might have a positive effect upon the patient."

Lötzen, 17 November 1942

Departure from the Silesian Station [Berlin] yesterday at nine o'clock. Perpetua accompanied me there; we sat in the waiting room for a while. Brother Physicus[3] was at the train along with Rehm, whom I am forced to leave behind. After leaving the station, I was soon fast asleep and did not wake up until we reached Masuria[4] in the late morning. The land reminded me somewhat of deer—there was something modestly furtive about the brown pelt of the earth and the tranquil eyes of the lakes.

Spent the day at the camps in the forest around Angerburg and Lötzen, where I was issued identification papers and tickets, and am now in Lötzen in a downright dingy hotel room.

Lötzen, 18 November 1942

I have stayed in Lötzen because all the seats in the airplane to Kiev were full. They have been reduced because of a crash caused by ice on the wings three days ago.

Visited the bleak cemetery in the morning. To the museum in the afternoon, a place that is more of a hero's shrine since memorabilia from combat in East Prussia in 1914 are collected there. The visit made me uneasy; the memory of all this is still too fresh. The corpse of this war has not yet decomposed, which explains the ghostly resurrection of so many of its apparitions. Specters in graveyards.

LÖTZEN, 19 NOVEMBER 1942

Went to the airfield in the morning, but several seats in the plane were eliminated because of the weather. I'll be staying here until tomorrow.

Before eating, I took a short walk through the fields, where I observed two crested larks in front of an abandoned barn.

Thought: When traveling, we have to be as warmly insulated as these birds are by their plumage. How often I envy them when I see them in the snowy woods sitting upon a branch, solitary but not abandoned. Feathers have been given to them, whereas we have received the spiritual aura that protects us from the loss of warmth. This bolsters and nourishes man through prayer, and for this very reason is beyond price.

In the afternoon, I drove with Major Dietrichsdorf to Widminnen, where we had been invited by a comrade who owns an estate there. It was almost dark. Illuminated by the rays of the setting sun, there lay a placid lake covered with brown and purple mists; by morning, these displayed a gentle, cool, green reflection. Along its shores stood young birch trees; their white trunks glistened through the soft brown of the surrounding thicket.

In Widminnen we were welcomed with coffee and mountains of cake. We then drank East Prussian *Bärenfang*, a concoction of honey and alcohol. The honey is supposed to appeal to the sweet tooth, but it is then anaesthetized by the high-octane alcohol. During the evening, there appeared sausages, with cooked drumsticks and breast of goose. Along with this came conversation, mainly about the delicacies. Life in these eastern provinces revolves more slowly, with greater gravitational force, greater lethargy, with easy enjoyment. Here we approach bear country.

Our host was a great hunter. I noticed a spotted nutcracker among the stuffed animals in his room. I had never seen one before: a brown bird with pale speckling and tail feathers with whitish tips—perfectly camouflaged for a seamless disappearance into Nordic conifer forests at dusk.

LÖTZEN, 20 NOVEMBER 1942

In the morning strolled around the Boyen Fortress;[5] its angular redoubts are wreathed by sparse woods of birch and elder. Flocks of crows swarmed in the bare treetops. I reached the hill on the lake where there stands a tall iron crucifix as a memorial to Bruno von Querfurt, a missionary to this region, who suffered a martyr's death on 9 March 1009.

Current reading: Got further in Jeremiah and also thumbed through Henri Bon, *La Mort et ses Problèmes* [*Death and its Problems*]. There I found quoted the morbid opinion of Parmenides who attributes sentience to corpses. They are supposedly aware of silence, cold, and darkness. As I read this, I thought of the uncanny changes I saw on the faces of the dying horses during our advance.

In the evening, I went back out into the dark to visit the lake, as the moon shone through the clouds. I felt a renewed inner strength and was immediately more curious about the course this journey would take.

KIEV, 21 NOVEMBER 1942

Takeoff at nine o'clock through low-lying cloudbanks and light snowfall. Once we had gained altitude, I could again see the lakes around Lötzen bounded by birches and bands of pale rushes. Then fields under a dusting of snow that revealed the brown earth and green shoots beneath this blanket. Conifer forests followed, and yellowed cracks in the land with networks of branching streams gleaming blue against the frost. And then the shiny dark earth of the peat ditches. In between, separated by large expanses in brownish-gray islands, lay the cultivated earth with some solitary settlements, or others stretching along the roads. The cottages or stables seemed to be fast asleep, yet tracks in the snow leading out from them were evidence that their inhabitants had already fetched hay, straw, and provisions from their barns, haystacks, and vegetable stores.

The clouds grew heavier toward noon, and our aircraft flew low over the ground. I had dozed off for a while; then I woke up to notice a change in our situation. A long, pale red flame trailed from the engine cowling. At the same time, the aircraft struggled to land but not, as I thought, due to a carburetor fire, but because we had reached Kiev. Amazement and terror combined at the sight of all this to create a state of petrified attention. At such moments, something primeval and familiar awakens within us.

Once we were on the ground, I spoke with the pilot about the crash that had happened the previous week on this runway. The aircraft had burned out. The corpses of the passengers were found pressed against the door, which had sealed tightly shut.

In Kiev I was billeted in the Palace Hotel. Although the sinks lacked hand towels and the study had no ink, and several marble steps were missing from the stairs, this is supposed to be the best hotel in occupied Russia. No matter how long you turned the faucets, they produced no water, let alone warm water. The same was true of the flush toilets. As a result, the whole Palace Hotel was filled with a noxious odor.

I took advantage of the hour that was still left before dark to walk through the streets in the city—and was glad to return after this sojourn. As true as it is that our earth harbors enchanted lands, we also encounter others, where disenchantment reigns and nothing magical remains.

ROSTOV, 22 NOVEMBER 1942

I shared my room with a young artillery captain. Despite my objections, he insisted on covering me with his coat when it got cold. When I woke up, I saw that he had made do with a thin blanket. He also frightened away a big rat that had emerged from the crannies of the hotel and made for my paltry rations.

Reveille before dawn. Departure through hazy weather around six in the morning. The flight took us across the huge expanse of the wheat fields of the Ukraine, where in some places the fields were still covered in faded stubble, while on most of them the fresh topsoil already glistened. Very few trees, but on the other hand, frequent deep branching, washed-out gullies that give the impression that the good soil reaches immense depths here and only its uppermost, thinnest layer is cultivated.

Reached Stalino[6] at nine o'clock, and after another hour we were in Rostov. There the weather became so unsettled that the pilot thought it advisable to take only the courier baggage to Voroshilovsk and leave the passengers behind—all the more so because a thick crust of ice was already forming on the wing sections of his aircraft.

I decided to travel on to Voroshilovsk the following day by train and then spent the night in the officers' quarters. That is what they call one of these squalid buildings where sacks of straw are laid out in rows in the rooms and a stench lingers in the hallways.

Stroll through city: images of despair repeat themselves. In Rio on Las Palmas, or on many an ocean beach, the walks I have taken have seemed like beautifully composed melodies. But here dissonance assaulted my heart. I watched some ragged children playing as they slid along the ice, and I marveled as if I had glimpsed a colored light in Hades.

The only products for sale are black sunflower seeds, offered in shallow baskets by women from the steps of burnt-out houses. High atop the trees in the middle of the busy avenue I noticed clusters of crows' nests.

Unfortunately, I did not pack enough equipment. I had no idea that little things like a pocket mirror, knife, sewing thread, or string are precious items here. Luckily I constantly come across people who help me. Not infrequently they are some of my readers, whose help I count among my fortune.

ROSTOV, 23 NOVEMBER 1942

I was able to scare up a bowl of soup in the soldiers' mess this morning.

Changed money; the Russian banknotes still bear Lenin's portrait. To compute the exchange rate, the female civil servant used an abacus with large balls that she flicked back and forth. I am told these machines can't be compared to the ones children at home use. Anyone who can master them can supposedly achieve a result more quickly than with pencil and paper.

In the afternoon, went to one of the few cafés permitted to operate on the free market. A small piece of cake costs two marks there, and an egg, three. It makes me sad to see people dozing and killing time, as though in waiting rooms before their trains depart for some terrible destination. And it's the privileged few sitting here.

I continue to study people on the street, which again reinforces my impression of the Orient as a place of disenchantment. The eye has to grow accustomed to the most unpleasant sights imaginable—there is no oasis, no respite. Technology is the only thing that functions in good order: the railroad, the cars, the airplanes, loudspeakers, and naturally everything belonging to the world of weaponry. Otherwise, there is a complete absence of everything organic, of nourishment, clothing, warmth, light. This is even more pronounced for the higher aspects of life—for joy, happiness, and cheer, and for any benevolent power of art. And all this on some of the richest soil on the globe.

The story of the Tower of Babel always seems to repeat itself. In this place, however, we do not find it under construction, but rather in the stage after its collapse and the confusion of languages. These rational constructs always contain the seeds of their own destruction. They have an icy chill that attracts fire the way iron attracts lightning.

The empty windows of the burnt-out office buildings show red calcination near their rooftops where the pure flame leapt out. Along each side, they bear the dark traces of the escaping smoke. The floors have collapsed; the steam radiators dangle on the bare walls. A tangle of twisted metal rises from the cellars, and neglected children comb through the heaps of ashes with hooks looking for bits of wood. One walks through a world of rubble that is home to rats.

When it comes to commerce here, all one sees except for women selling sunflower seeds are boys with shoe-cleaning brushes or people who have constructed little carts so they can carry soldiers' gear. They prefer bread to cigarettes or money.

People's clothing here looks like disguises, as if they have put on every garment they own and don't take them off at night. Coats are rarer than thickly padded jackets. Like so many other things, these are reduced to rags. For head covering, they wear caps with earlaps or trimmed flaps. You also see Soviet caps made of tan cloth and with a high crease in the center. Almost all these people, and especially the women, carry sacks over their shoulders. The sight of them indicates a burdensome, onerous existence. They bustle about hurriedly, restlessly but without any noticeable purpose, as if they were in an anthill that has been pried open.

Among all these you see many uniforms, even Hungarian and Rumanian, as well as ones that are completely unknown, like those of Ukrainian volunteers or of the local security service. After nightfall, you can hear gunfire from the desolate factory yards over near the railroad station.

In the afternoon, vacationers waiting for their trains were stopped and sent to the front in hastily assembled marching units. There is news that the Russians have broken through north of Stalingrad.

Voroshilovsk, 24 November 1942

Toward evening, I continued on my journey, heading toward Krapotkin, where we arrived at four in the morning. There I slept on the counter in the waiting room until the train left for Voroshilovsk. Within two short days, I have adjusted to this existence in cramped train compartments, in cold halls, without water, without service, without warm rations. But I observe others who are worse off, such as the Russians standing in open freight cars or on the running boards in the icy wind.

Our route leads through the fertile Kuban steppe;[7] the crops have been harvested, but the fields are mostly untilled. Their dimensions are huge and the boundaries are out of sight. From this treeless expanse now and again there arises a cluster of silos, tanks, or warehouses. These contain heaps of yellow or brown wheat that gleam like some higher power created by the fertility of the good earth. There are still traces of the cultivation of wheat, corn, castor bean, sunflowers, and tobacco. The edges of the train embankment are covered with the desiccated, parched brown flora of thistles and other composite blossoms. There is also a plant that resembles a horsetail, but in the form and size of a small fir tree. This plant stock reminds me of the Japanese tea blossoms that I used to dissolve in warm water when I was a child. Then, too, I would try to guess their species by attempting to imagine them in bloom.

Arrival in Voroshilovsk after dark. I am billeted in the office building of the GPU,[8] a place of gigantic dimensions like everything else under the authority of the police and prison systems. I have a little room here with a table, a chair, a bed, and, most important, intact windowpanes. For shaving, I have even found a piece of broken mirror to use. After my experiences of the past few days, I recognize the value inherent in such objects.

VOROSHILOVSK, 25 NOVEMBER 1942

The weather is rainy; the streets are covered with mud. I am going to be stuck here for a while. A few streets I have walked down have made a more positive impression than the things I've seen up until now. In particular, the houses from the Czarist period radiate a certain warmth, while those monstrous Soviet boxes oppress the country for miles around.

In the afternoon, I climbed the hill where the Orthodox church stands—a crudely finished Byzantine-style building with its onion dome half blown away. The old buildings always project something primitive, but it is still more pleasant than the abstract nullity of the new construction. Here one can quote Gauthier: "*La barbarie vaut mieux que la platitude*" [Barbarism is better than a platitude], where *platitude* is best translated as nihilism.

In the afternoon the commander-in-chief of the Army group, General Colonel von Kleist,[9] appeared and dined with us. I knew him already from my years in Hannover. Discussed Giraud, the French general now in command in Tunis. Right after his retreat, Hitler is supposed to have said that further unpleasantness could be expected from him.

The women's voices, especially those of the girls, are not actually melodious, yet they are pleasant. They convey strength and serenity; one could almost imagine them resonating with the deep tones of life's music. Mechanical and impersonal changes seem to pass over such natures without affecting them. I noticed something similar among South American Negroes; their deep, enduring joy after generations of slavery. Incidentally, the staff doctor, von Grävenitz, told me that physical exams showed the great majority of the girls to be virgins. This is also apparent from their faces, but it is difficult to say [whether] this is more readable from their foreheads or their eyes. A silver glow of chastity suffuses the face. Its light does not have the glow of active virtue, but more a second-hand reflection, like moonlight. It lets us perceive the sun, the source of such serenity.

VOROSHILOVSK, 26 NOVEMBER 1942

Snow flurries accompanied by high winds. I tried to climb the church tower to have a look around, but I found the upper steps badly charred. Thus, I had to make do with a view from halfway up. Then I made my way toward a sparse wood that I had spied.

Unfortunately, I found it to be impassable, so I had to be satisfied with the captivating sight of a flock of birds swooping nimbly through the bushes and hedges. They resembled our titmouse but seemed to my eyes to be larger and more brightly colored.

At lunch, I saw Major von Oppen, the son of my former regimental commander. Among other things we discussed the poem "Der Taurus," which Friedrich Georg dedicated to the memory of Oppen's father, who is buried there.[10]

In the afternoon got a vaccination for typhus. Inoculation remains a remarkable act. I used to like to compare it to baptism, yet the more precise analogy to the spiritual world is perhaps represented by holy communion. We use the living experience that others have collected for us through their sacrifice, sickness, or through snakebite. The lymph of the lamb that has suffered for us. Miracles are prefigured and preserved for us in matter—they are its most exalted expression.

In the evening, Lieutenant Colonel Schuchardt explained the situation to me. Using the large map, he showed me the recent Russian breakthrough of the lines formerly held by our adjoining army group. The thrust destroyed the sections of the front held by the Rumanians and let the Sixth Army be surrounded. A cauldron like this has to be supplied by air until a land bridge can be established.[11]

Life in these areas surrounded by carnage presents the most extreme challenges. The threat resembles that of a besieged city from classical times when no one could expect mercy. This is true of morale as well. For weeks and months, death could be seen approaching from afar. Many scores are settled this way, for the political structures that the states had assumed have been turned inside out.

Voroshilovsk, 27 November 1942

Visited the city museum in the morning. This had been founded under the Czars and is mainly a zoological collection that has suffered over time. I saw snakes faded by sunlight, curled around branches as white, scaly forms, and others as desiccated mummies in display jars because the alcohol had evaporated. Yet at one time all these objects had obviously been displayed with love and a certain joy in design. Informed viewers can discern such things from little clues. My gaze also fell upon a small label that indicated the activity of groups of local amateurs: *Acta Societatis Entomologicae Stauropolitanae*, 1926 [*Proceedings of the Entomological Society of Stavropol*, 1926]. Stavropol is the old name of Voroshilovsk.

Among the taxidermy specimens, I noticed two double-headed animals, a goat and a calf. The goat showed a deformity resembling a Janus head, whereas in the case of the calf, two snouts but only three eyes had formed with the extra one located like that of Polyphemus[12] in the center of the forehead. This intrusion was not without its aesthetic elegance. It gave the impression of an intentional composition, rather than one of a zoological, mythological creature.

Incidentally, it would be a good project, either for the natural scientist or for a humanist, to work on the concept of two-headedness. The conclusion reached would probably be that the phenomenon is part of the lower strata of life, either the vegetative or the demonic. The advantages one could imagine—such as a special synesthetic intelligence or the ability to converse with oneself in the most astonishing way—were allotted to us more simply and cleverly in the form of the hemispherical structure of the brain. The Siamese twins were not so much connected with each other as they were shackled together.[13]

Despite the early hour, I noticed a number of visitors in rapt attention at the display cases. I observed two women in peasant clothing conversing about the objects. One of them seemed particularly enchanted by some of them, such as a pink shell that was armed with long spikes, like a hedgehog.

In the evening I was a guest of Lieutenant Colonel Merk, the quartermaster, a man who excels in that precise businesslike style characteristic of people in charge of supplies. Two Korean women, twin sisters, served us with elegance. Conversation with Captain Dietloff, who had managed a large estate here before the war. We discussed crops and yields that were possible on the soil types here. The fertility is enormous, but as always in such cases, this also applies to the blights. Icy winds can ruin the budding cereal crop in minutes, and wheat rust forms such thick clouds during the harvest that the horses are blinded. Furthermore, there are legions of grasshoppers and June beetles, and thistles with stalks that can grow as thick as a man's arm. Farmers fear a thorny vine that rolls up into a ball when it reaches maturity and, after rotting at the root, separates and is carried across the fields by the autumn winds, casting its seed as it goes.

VOROSHILOVSK, 29 NOVEMBER 1942

Visited the large town market in the morning; it was crowded with people, but there was very little merchandise to be had. The prices are those of famine times. I paid three marks for a little spool of thread that I saw for sale in France for a few pennies a short while ago. Listeners were crowded around a singing beggar with a freshly bandaged arm stump. It seemed that they were listening less to the music than to the long, drawn-out text. It was a Homeric image.

A funeral procession then passed by. Two women in front carried a wooden cross decorated with a wreath, and following them were four more carrying the coffin lid on their shoulders as though it were a boat decorated with flowers. Four young men bore the coffin slung from linen cloths. In it lay the dead woman. She was approximately thirty-six years old, had dark hair and a face with sharp features. Her head lay on a bed of flowers. She was carried feet first, and at that end, lay a black book. I had encountered this Orthodox practice most recently on the island of Rhodes in the public display of the dead, and I approve. It's almost as if the deceased were consciously bidding farewell before descending into darkness.

During these days, I conceived of a new project, "The Path of Masirah." The narrator Othfried begins at the moment when he has wandered through the great desert and can make out indications that he is approaching the coast. Salt accretions, grasshoppers, and snakes appear at first—a world of animals and plants that seems born from the arid sand. Then come thorn bushes in bloom, and, finally, palm trees and traces of earlier settlements. Yet the land is desolate and abandoned; now and then, his march goes past destroyed cities whose walls have been breached and huge siege machinery stands in the sand.

Othfried is in possession of a map drawn by Fortunio showing half the text as lettered and the other half consisting of landscape hieroglyphs, all describing the path to Gadamar, where Fortunio had found a mine of precious stones. The study of this map presents difficulties—Othfried wishes he had taken the sea route because each reference leads to the next one like the links of a chain. It seems that Fortunio has given the map's owner a task to be rewarded with the discovery of the treasure. The details of this mission are at first thrilling, but then they involve intellectual powers as they finally emerge as ethical trials.

Each evening, Othfried unfolds this remarkable map like the bellows of an accordion. He would have given up his quest long ago had it not been for the glimpse of one of the jewels that Fortunio showed him as a test—an opal the size and shape of a goose egg, possessing iridescent, mystical depths. Looking at this stone long enough reveals magical scenes and images from the past and future. This stone was mined in the earth's mythical period and offers a last remnant of the vanished riches of the Golden Age.

With his followers, Othfried must traverse the path of Masirah across a frightening track high above the coastal surf. This represents ethical patterns of plot and topography. The track has been cut so steeply and narrowly into the smooth cliff face that no more than a single human foot or mule's hoof can make its way across. The two points of access are invisible to each other, and, to prevent caravans from meeting on the path, there is a kind of turret at each end. From this vantage point, travelers must call out their intention to enter the path. Othfried neglects this warning and thus brings misfortune to a caravan of Jews from Ophir approaching from the opposite direction at the same time. Both parties meet with their mules on the narrowest, most frightening spot above the abyss, the point where any thought of turning around fills the heart with terror. How can this conflict, which threatens to end with the destruction of one or both groups, be solved?[14]

While I was walking across the market square thinking about this subject, it seemed to me a shame to have to delete any piece of it; it lends itself to a parable about the path of life itself. The map would then have to reveal fate, so that we could read it the way we read the lines on someone's palm. The lode of precious stones is the Eternal City described in Saint John's vision in the Book of Revelation: It is the goal that rewards the path. Thinking like this, one could derive much significance from the material.

Of course, this inspiration occurs to me at the least opportune moment, and today I laid aside the first page that I have written. Better days may come when I have more freedom.

VOROSHILOVSK, 30 NOVEMBER 1942

Visited the cemetery, the most derelict one I have ever seen. It is a square area bounded by a half-collapsed wall. The lack of names is striking; there are hardly any inscriptions, whether on the moss-covered grave markers or on weather-beaten Saint Andrew's crosses cut from soft golden-brown limestone. On one of these, I thought I could decipher the word incised in Greek letters, *Patera*. It made me think of Kubin and his dream city Perle, like so much else here.[15]

The grave mounds are choked with brambles; thistles and burrs also run riot everywhere. Among these, apparently without any plan, new places have been dug out, as yet unmarked by either a stone or wooden monument. Old bones are bleaching on the churned-up ground. Vertebrae, ribs, and leg bones are scattered like pieces of a puzzle. I also noticed the greenish skull of a child on top of a wall.

Back through the crumbling suburbs. In the construction of the houses, in the facial features of the people, in countless mostly imponderable details, the senses pick up echoes and hints of Asia. I sensed this especially when I saw a little boy with his hands folded across his body in a distinctive way. Such fundamental things are perceived as subtle, invisible messages. Scholars think they have found traces of the third eye, the eye in the forehead that was perhaps the eye for such primeval images. Originally, we perceived the lands, animals, springs, and trees as figures—gods and demons—the way we nowadays perceive surfaces and shapes.

VOROSHILOVSK, 1 DECEMBER 1942

Visit to the Research Institute for Plague Control, which is staffed by Russian scholars and employees. The fertile soil of this country is an El Dorado for epidemics and sicknesses like Ukrainian fever, dysentery, typhus, diphtheria, and a virulent variety of a jaundice pathogen that has not yet been isolated. They say that the plague returns every ten years. It appeared in 1912, 1922, and 1932, so its time is again fast approaching. It is brought by caravans from the region of Astrakhan. A mass extinction of rodents precedes it heralding its arrival. In such cases, the institute sends out an expedition comprising zoologists, bacteriologists, and collectors to do more thorough research. The advance of the contagion is observed and combatted by means of quarantine in small stations—so-called plague houses. Particular care is given to the extermination of rats, a function fulfilled by specialized rat catchers called "deratizers," who can be found on every collective farm.

Professor Hach, the research director, put me at ease during our conversation. A Frenchman would call this relationship between people humane, but it has a different, more primitive tinge with Russians and springs from deeper currents. In France, the endearing quality of an individual is produced by subtle exertion, by psychological action; here it is the product of lethargy. It has a more feminine, but also a darker, amoral quality about it.

Professor Hach has been placed under a mild form of banishment called Minus Six. This means that he must avoid entering the six largest cities in the country. Because the Plague Research Institute also produces large quantities of vaccine, it was placed under the protection of the German troops after the invasion and assigned the responsibility for a collective farm where, before this, the Russian state had employed and fed 800 mentally ill people. To clear the estate for the

Plague Institute, these patients were exterminated by the Security Service. Such an act betrays the tendency of the technician to substitute hygiene for morality, similar to the way he substitutes propaganda for truth.

VOROSHILOVSK, 2 DECEMBER 1942

Hints of the executioners' presence are often so palpable that all desire to work, to create images and thoughts, dies. Evil deeds have a negating, upsetting consequence: Human growth becomes stunted as if polluted by invisible decay. In its proximity, things lose their magic, their aroma, and taste. The mind is exhausted by the tasks it has set itself, tasks that used to refresh and engage. Yet, it is precisely against such things that it must now struggle. The palette of the flowers along the deadly mountain ridge must never fade from our sight, even though they are but a hand's breadth from the abyss. This is the situation I described in *Cliffs* [*On the Marble Cliffs*].

VOROSHILOVSK, 4 DECEMBER 1942

The foggy weather was sufficiently clear by evening that I could just make out the stars through the veil but not really see them.

The sunflower seeds that they sell everywhere here are black with fine white striation. You see people, young and old, nibbling them whether they are walking or standing, by popping them quickly into their mouths and cracking them deftly. The shell is then spit out and the little seed eaten. On the one hand, this resembles a pastime like smoking, and on the other hand, it seems to be a kind of homeopathic nourishment. The saying goes that these are good for building firm breasts for women. All the paths and pavement are covered with the shells that have been spat out, as if you were walking along behind a procession of rodents.

In my dealings with people, I have noticed that I do not speak much to the middle sort, whether of intelligence or character. My contact with very simple as well as highly developed natures, however, presents no difficulty. I seem to resemble a pianist playing only the keys at the extreme ends of the keyboard and just having to make do without the rest. It's either peasants and fishermen or people of the highest quality. The rest of my social dealings consist of arduous attention to the mundane—rummaging through my pockets looking for change. I often get the feeling that I am moving within a world for which I am not adequately equipped.

VOROSHILOVSK, 6 DECEMBER 1942

Sunday, clear frosty conditions. A little snow lies on the ground. In the morning, I took a walk through the woods and at the site of that light, pure dusting I thought of the wondrous verse that Perpetua once murmured to herself upon waking up in our Leipzig garret:

Es schneet der Wind das Ärgste zu—

[Windblown snowbanks hide the worst—]

In those days, we lived in a studio. At night, we could watch the stars in their course and, in winter, the softly falling snowflakes.

My impressions from the woods were a little more cheerful. There peasant women approached me carrying long, curved yokes with buckets of water or small bundles swinging at the ends. Even the yokes on the small Panje horses[16] dance high over their shoulders and are pleasant to see when they trot. That conjures up a bygone age, times of plenty. I feel that this land has been depleted by abstract concepts and that it would blossom again under the sun of a benevolent paternal force. Especially when I hear the people speak with their vowels that echo deep joy and resonate gentle laughter, I am reminded of winter days when flowing springs were audible beneath ice and snow.

Finished reading Jeremiah, which I had begun on 18 October in Suresnes. My journey takes me through the book of books, and the eventful world provides the evidence for it.

Jeremiah's visions can't quite measure up to those of Isaiah, whose incomparable power towers over his. Isaiah describes the fate of the universe, whereas Jeremiah is the prophet of political configurations. As such, he plays a significant role; he is the professional prophet, the subtlest tool of national sentiment. He still unites the powers of priest, poet, and statesman. He views the decay of the state not as a cosmic catastrophe stimulating horror and lust, but rather as political collapse, the shipwreck of the state that introduces in its wake a deviation from the divine order.

The situation he sees confronting him is that of Nebuchadnezzar's threat, a power that he can assess differently and more accurately than the king can. He advises Zedekiah without success. It is hard for us to discern the difficulties of his office, because we are so far removed from theocracies. To do justice to them, you would have to compare Jeremiah's duties to that of a gifted visionary at the Prussian court in 1805. In that year, he would have to have predicted not only how the year 1806 would end but also 1812 and, then, armed with this knowledge, have warned the king against Napoleon. In such cases, one is not only opposed by the pro-war faction but also by the common man. It is hard to exaggerate the courage that Jeremiah displayed, for it presupposes that there was no doubt of divine guidance. That is what gave him such certainty.

Voroshilovsk, 7 December 1942

Yesterday was a significant day. I got a glimpse of: "This is you." Not since South America have I felt such a force.

Can there be such things as geographical, or better, geomantic influences on character? I don't mean just on behavior as Pascal and Stendhal have understood it, but rather influence upon our essence. That would mean that in other latitudes we could undergo disintegration and then reconstitution. This would correspond to corporeal transformations: at first we are enveloped in fevers, and then we recover our health. We would be world citizens in the highest sense if the globe in its totality were to form and shape us. World leaders are elevated to such status by their nations; the legend of the supernatural conception of Alexander the Great is akin to this. A lightning bolt strikes the mother—strikes the earth in her womb. The great poets like Dante in his excurses and Goethe in the *West-östlicher Diwan*[17] interpret this spiritually. So do the world religions—with the exception of Islam, which is too influenced by climate. Take Saint Peter's vision of the animals: the enjoyment of their flesh symbolizes the assimilation of all the empires and nations of this world.[18]

The evening was crystal clear. The great constellations glittered in a light such as I know only from the southern hemisphere. I wonder whether people in other ages ever felt this sensation of tremendous cold that comes over us at the sight. Lately, I found this most accurately described in a few verses by Friedrich Georg.

I had a dream in which I was engaged in various tasks. The only image that remains is the scene that preceded awakening: a car with a hood that had a small weevil, the hazelnut borer, as radiator ornament. But here it was the size of a lamb and shone like a cherry-red, striated horn, translucent in the sunlight. The impact of seven bombs dropped by a Russian plane at dawn awakened me at the moment when I was admiring this figure.

It was a radiant morning; not a cloud darkened the blue vault of heaven. I climbed the church tower, an octagonal cylinder resting on a square base. The tower supports a squat onion-shaped dome on top. For the first time, I could look out over the town as a whole with all its far-flung, square dwellings of low houses with a few gigantic new buildings sticking up here and there. These are either a barracks or a police station. To build such boxes, several million people had to be exterminated.

In the morning light, Mount Elbrus with its twin peaks seemed to rise up right in front of the gates like shining silver walls of snow, and yet it is several days' march from here. It dwarfs the dark Caucasus range over which it towers. This sight made the earth speak to me again for the first time in a long while, as a work of God's hand.

On my way back, I passed a group of prisoners doing road repair under guard. They had spread their coats out along the edge and passers-by had laid the occasional donation on them. I saw bank notes, slices of bread, onions, and one of the tomatoes they like to pickle in vinegar here when they're still green. This was the first kind gesture I have noticed in this landscape, aside from a few children at play or the fine camaraderie among the German soldiers. All the parts worked together here: the residents who donated, the prisoners who were poor, and the guards who permitted this activity.

KRAPOTKIN, 9 DECEMBER 1942

Departed last night with the courier train to meet the Seventeenth Army. The train resembled an automobile on tracks pulling a freight car. After a short journey, we stopped on the tracks for part of the night due to snow squalls. Because we were able to scare up some wood, a little stove warmed us for an hour or two.

Arrived in Krapotkin in the morning, where I spent the day waiting for the train to Belorechensk. Many hundreds of soldiers were waiting in the huge, bare railroad station just like me. They stood together in silent groups or sat on their gear. At various times, they crowded around windows where soup or coffee was being served. In this vast space, you sensed the presence of powerful forces that drive human beings without ever being revealed to their sight: raw, colossal power. Hence the impression that every fiber of our will is being commandeered, while our comprehension remains idle. If pure intuition were possible—such as on a painter's canvas—that would surely bring great solace and relief. But at this stage, it is as impossible as the interpretation of events by a great historian, or better yet, in a novel. We do not even know the names of the powers that have squared off against each other.

A thought at this moment: "Freedom in the nineteenth century sense cannot be restored, as many people still dream. It must rise up to new and freezing heights of the historical process and higher still: like an eagle soaring above the turrets that tower above the chaos. Even freedom must pass through the pain. It must be earned again."

BELORECHENSK, 10 DECEMBER 1942

I departed from Krapotkin after a fifteen-hour delay. The word "delay" of course loses its meaning here. We have to adjust to a visceral condition that destroys all patience.

The rain was pouring down, so I permitted myself some time to read by candlelight in the compartment. Even with my reading matter, I now live *à la fortune du pot* [by potluck] by having to pick up many an unappetizing item, such as in this case *Abu Telfan* by Wilhelm Raabe. I brought this along from Voroshilovsk, a book I had heard praised by my grandfather, the schoolteacher, although I was never especially curious about it. The constantly repeated ironic embellishments in this prose resemble the gilded metal mounts on imitation rococo of the sort seen on walnut furniture from this period. Things like: "The poplar trees are again showing that they are capable of casting very long shadows."

Or: "The white fog, which had unfortunately already been used by the honest *Wandsbecker Bote*,[19] also made its presence felt upon the meadows."

This provincial irony is one of the symptoms of the nineteenth century; some authors seem to be plagued by its chronic itch. Yet these Russian years claim not only human victims but also books. They turn yellow like leaves before the frost, and someday it will be noticed that whole literatures have silently ceased to exist.

Arrived in Belorechensk in the early morning hours. Waiting on the muddy train platform I studied the magnificent, luminous constellations. It's remarkable how they captivate the spirit in new ways when you are approaching a world of suffering. Boëthius mentions them in this context in his final, most beautiful verse.

In the bed assigned to me, I discovered two drivers whose vehicle had gotten stuck in the mud. The hut had only one room divided in half by a large stove; it contained two more beds where the housewife slept along with her female friend. They crawled into bed together, freeing up a warm berth for me.

I visited the commander-in-chief, Lieutenant General Ruoff, around midday, bringing him greetings from his predecessor, Heinrich von Stülpnagel. Discussion about our positions. Whereas the cold temperatures had been the most dangerous aspect of the first Russian winter, now at least on this section of the front, it's the damp that is even more debilitating. For the most part, the troops in the wet forests are huddled in foxholes, because the advance has been halted for the past three weeks. Tarpaulins offer the only protection. Flooding in the brooks and rivers has washed the bridges away. Supplies are held up. Aircraft cannot even drop anything over these foggy woods. Exertion reaches its extreme limit here, at which point men die of exhaustion.

In the afternoon, I was present at the interrogation of a captured nineteen-year-old Russian lieutenant. His soft, unshaven beard growth looked innately girlish. The boy wore a shearling cap and carried a long wooden staff in his hand. He was a farmer's son, who had gone to engineering school and before his capture had led a mortar unit. The general impression reinforced this: a peasant turned mechanic. There was something ponderous and deliberate in his hand motions. I could imagine that these hands had not forgotten their work with wood, although by now they had grown used to the feel of iron.

Discussion with interrogating officer, a Balt who compared Russia to a glass of milk from which the thin layer of cream had been skimmed off. A new layer will have to rise to the top, or else it won't taste right. That is graphic! The question is, what sort of sweetness remains finely dispersed within the milk? This could be a leavening agent when times are calm again. To put it differently: Has the cruel imposition of technical abstraction penetrated the fertile human substrate? I would say no, based purely on the impression conveyed by the voices and physiognomy of the people.

Relapse. It was extraordinary: at the very moment when I realized it, a heavy piece of the ceiling fell down, leaving a hole shaped like the outline of Sicily.

BELORECHENSK, 11 DECEMBER 1942

Because frost had formed overnight, I took a walk around the town where yesterday the muddy paths were impassable. Today they lay like broad village ponds under sheer ice. The houses are small one-story buildings roofed with reeds, shingles, or tin the color of red lead. The bottommost layers of the reed roofs are constructed of the strong stalks; the upper ones are made from the leafy sections, resembling shocks of yellow hair. A remarkable style of canopy roof decorates the entry doors of the more stately buildings and partially protects the steps from rain, but these structures are also for show. The feature probably harkens back to a time when tents influenced architecture. The decoration of these walkways roofed with tin suggests fringe or tassels.

Inside the cottages, it is not uncommon to see heat-loving plants, such as tall rubber trees or lemon bushes bearing fruit. The small rooms with their large stoves are like greenhouses. Poplar trees grow in profusion out of the gardens and at the edges of the broad streets. The dense branches were glorious in the sunlight.

A small military cemetery contained the dead from a field hospital as well as a few from aircraft that had crashed over the town. As many as thirty graves had been dug and marked with crosses, a number of others had been dug for future use—something that Meister Anton in Hebbel's *Maria Magdalena* decries as a sacrilege.[20]

Outside, on the banks of the Belaya River. It churns with dirty gray floodwaters. Along its banks there extended a field position with barriers and foxholes that were being worked on by groups of women under the supervision of soldiers from the Corps of Engineers. In a narrow gorge lay a dead horse; the last shred of flesh had been scraped from its skeleton. From this vantage point, the city with its wooden huts and roofs covered in green moss doesn't look bad. You can still feel the vitality that comes from handwork and the organic mellowing that make the place livable.

Afterward I spent time with my landlady, Frau Vala, short for Valentina. Her husband had been away since the beginning of the war in the field with a chemical warfare unit. Living with her is a sixteen-year-old friend, Victoria, daughter of a doctor, who spoke a little German and had also read Schiller. Like almost all her other compatriots, she admires him as the archetypal poet: "Oh, Schiller, super!" She is now obligated to go work in Germany and is looking forward to it. She is a high school student, but her classmates who are over sixteen have been mobilized as partisans. She told me about a fourteen-year-old girlfriend of hers who had been shot near the river, conveying this in an unemotional tone that was by no means harsh. That left a deep impression on me.

Had a conversation in the evening with Major K., primarily about the partisans; it is his job to locate and engage them. The fighting is merciless enough between the regular troops. A soldier will go to any extreme to avoid capture. This explains the tenacity with which these cauldrons are defended. Russian orders have been found that place a bounty on captured soldiers who are delivered alive—prisoners the Intelligence Service can then use in its interrogations. Other orders state that the prisoners must first be brought before military officers and only then, before the political officers. This means that they follow a clear sequence for squeezing the lemon.

The opponents expect no mercy from each other and their propaganda only reinforces this opinion. By way of an example, last winter a sleigh carrying wounded Russian officers blundered into the German positions. At the moment the men realized their error, they pulled the pins on the hand grenades they had concealed between their bodies. Prisoners are nonetheless taken in order to increase the workforce and also to attract deserters. But the partisans stand beyond the reach of military law, inasmuch as one can even still speak of such a concept. They are surrounded in their forests like packs of wolves to be exterminated. I have heard things here of the most bestial nature.

On the way home, I pondered these things. In such intervals, a thought forms that I used to spin out in various scenarios. It is this: Where everything is permitted, first anarchy, then tighter order is the result. Anyone, who arbitrarily underestimates his opponent, cannot expect pardon himself. And so new and tougher rules of combat evolve.

That seemed to me like a tempting theory, but in practice, we inevitably confront the moment when we must raise a hand against defenseless noncombatants. This is only possible in cold-blooded combat with beasts or in wars that atheists wage against each other. At that point, only the Red Cross has any clear mission.

There will always be areas where we cannot allow ourselves to accept the rules of the opponent. War is not a cake divided up by the parties until it's all gone; there is always a piece left over to share. This is the divine part that remains outside the fray, separate from the struggle between pure bestiality and demonic power. Even Homer recognized and respected this. The truly powerful man, the one destined to rule, will be distinguished by the fact that he does not appear as an enemy filled with hatred. He also feels responsible for his opponent. That his strength is superior to that of the other's is apparent at more sophisticated levels than physical violence, which serves only to persuade his subordinates.

MAYKOP, 12 DECEMBER 1942

Yesterday's meeting tells me that I am not going to get a full briefing on the status of this country. There are simply too many places that are off limits to me. These include all those where violence is being perpetrated upon defenseless people and also where reprisals and punitive measures are being applied collectively. Incidentally, I have no hope for change. Things of this sort are part of the zeitgeist; we can see that being eagerly embraced everywhere. Adversaries copy each other.

I wonder if it might be good to visit these places of terror as a witness in order to see and remember what sort of people the perpetrators and the victims are. With his *The House of the Dead*, Dostoevsky had enormous influence. But he was not there as a volunteer, but rather as a prisoner.

There are also limits to what we are capable of seeing. Otherwise we would have to be ordained to higher holy orders than our age is capable of bestowing.

The departure for Maykop that was planned for the morning was postponed until dark. I was again the guest of the commander, along with a short Saxon general whose car had gotten mired here in the mud. He described the difficulties he had experienced in Kharkov. At first, seventy-five people starved to death each day, but he had underreported this number as twenty-five. He spoke of police tactics with the attitude of a gamekeeper, for example: "I consider the view quite erroneous that the thirteen and fourteen-year-old youths captured with the partisans should not be liquidated. Anyone who has grown up that way, without a father or mother, will never turn out well. A bullet is the only right thing. By the way, that's what the Russians do with them too."

Citing evidence, he told an anecdote about a sergeant who had picked up a nine-year-old and a twelve-year-old lad overnight out of pity; in the morning, he was found with his throat cut.

Said farewell to Frau Vala. My billet in her parlor with the large stove wasn't bad—a sort of cabbage-soup comfort. Our life's paths lead us to strange way stations.

In Maykop, I was the guest of the supply commander. I was billeted in a house that had no light except for a tiny flame illuminating an icon. But the commander sent me a honey-colored candle that gave off a delightful aroma.

KURINSKI, 13 DECEMBER 1942

I departed for Kurinski before dawn. Just past Maykop the road took a turn into the mountains. Signs at the edge of the woods: "*Achtung*, partisan alert. Keep weapons at the ready."

The wooded areas are secured against the Russians on the opposite side by sparse positions, often no more than outposts; the larger areas beyond are only traversed by troops along the roads. They are not only threatened by partisans—or bandits (to quote the German term used for them)—but also by scouting parties and patrols from the regular forces, as when the car of a division commander was recently ambushed and hit by a high explosive charge.

The ground was frozen solid, making it easy for our car to go uphill. It followed the road to Tuapse, made famous by the German paratroopers' attack and the Russian defense. The track had already been cleared; only heavy vehicles like steamrollers and tractors were occasionally visible on the slopes. In the undergrowth lay a horse frozen to the ground. Its flesh had only been stripped from the upper portion, with the result that its bare ribcage and frozen blue and red intestines made it look like a detail from an anatomical atlas.

The forest was thick and leafy, and untended growths of young oak trees spread out in curtained rows as far as the eye could see to the point where the jagged white peaks of the lofty mountain range met the blue mountains. In some places, woodpeckers flew down from stands of older trees to peck at the brittle wood. Their bright raspberry breasts shone here and there against the snowy tree trunks.

In Kurinski, I am told that these hills are overgrown in part with bushes and, as for the rest, with shoots that propagate directly from the tree stumps. The reforestation took place mostly under Russian authority, since the Circassians who lived here, being cattlemen, kept the land open. Only a few huge surviving trees were spared. These are therefore called Circassian oaks. Other places in these vast forests are still habitats for bears. Here there still exist patches of virgin stock, but otherwise this sea of forest has an inherent primeval power of its own. The eye notices the first thing that will be exploited: nature as yet unspoiled by swarms of people passing through.

At Khadyshenskaya a bridge had been flooded out. Soldiers from the Corps of Engineers conveyed us over the torrential river, the Pshish,[21] in inflatable dinghies. Beside me a young infantryman crouched on his gear: "The last time I sat in a thing like this we got a direct hit that ripped it in half and killed four comrades. I and one other man got away with our lives. That was on the Loire."

And so this war provides generations to come with material for tales to tell their children and their children's children. People will forever hear about how the narrator drew one of the lucky numbers in the terrifying lottery. Of course, it is only the accounts of the survivors we hear, since they are the ones who write history.

In the utterly devastated town of Kurinski, I reported to an Austrian, General de Angelis, the commander of the Forty-Fourth Paratroop Corps. He showed me our positions on the map. The advance along the road from Maykop to Tuapse has brought heavy losses since the Russians have taken cover in the extensive, dense forests and defended them with skill and tenacity. Thus, it happened that—to use the words of Clausewitz—the attack reached its zenith just before the watershed and came to a standstill just short of its strategic goals. Such a situation is fraught with calamity at every step. After tough close-quarter combat in the undergrowth, torrential rainfall destroyed the bridges and made roads impassable. Now the troops have been pinned down for weeks in sodden foxholes, being worn down as much by the cold and damp as by enemy fire and frequent attacks.

In the afternoon went up into the mountain forest that rises above the huts of Kurinski. The undergrowth level consisted of rhododendrons that were already bearing greenish-yellow buds. I returned by way of the narrow valley of a mountain stream that flowed over green marl. It was here that the populace survived the fighting by hiding in small caves. You could still see the remnants and traces of their campsites.

KURINSKI, 14 DECEMBER 1942

Starry night. I spent it in the bare bedchamber of a Cossack hut that was equipped with only a metal bedframe for sleeping. Luckily the large stove built of rough stone was in working condition so that a good fire produced heat for the first few hours. Before falling asleep, I listened for a while to the cricket of this hearth whose voice rang out in full-throated melody, more a chime than a chirp. The next morning was intensely cold. Russian aircraft could be heard circling over the valley in the distance, releasing strings of bombs. This was punctuated by the brisk pumping action of our *Flak* [anti-aircraft guns].

In the morning, the weather was clear, and I went out with First Lieutenant Strubelt to get a view of the terrain on both sides of the road to Tuapse. We drove in a car that had a row of bullet holes at the back of the roof—traces of an attack by partisans.

A railroad line had been built through the Pshish Valley along our road. It looked like a muddy hellhole. The river had reached a high-water mark a few days ago. By now it had fallen to the point where long banks of gravel glittered among the whirlpools. The section where the valley was the widest had room for gun emplacements, command posts, field dressing stations, and ammunition depots. At those spots, the road had been churned by the wheels into thick yellow-brown mire that seemed bottomless. Parts of horses and cars projected from it. Rows of tents and huts had been built a little higher up the slope. Bluish smoke hovered over them, and Russian or Turkoman prisoners could be seen splitting wood in front of their doors. The scene gave the impression of a caravansary that had been built at the edges of a wide current of thick silt. The nature of this material and its dull hue conveyed the essence of lethargic, creeping activity. Streaks of flame blazed up amidst all this as our artillery fired on a battalion position the Russians had breached that morning.

Columns of herded animals and processions of bearers with Asiatic faces crept through the morass. Among them was a large number of Armenians, with their dark penetrating eyes, large hooked noses, and olive skin, often heavily pock-marked. You could also see the Mongol types of the Turkomans, with their smooth black hair and, occasionally, with the beautiful, tall physiques of the Caucasian tribes like the Grusinians and Georgians. A few individuals shuffled by so wearily that one could see their near-fatal exhaustion. Strubelt actually told me that some of them would lie still in holes in the earth in order to expire like animals.

We turned away from the valley and drove farther into the winter forest, climb-ing gradually. High mountain peaks were visible in passing as they shone briefly. Some of them were in Russian hands. In other words, we were visible—but in this region, the enemy is saving his ammunition he must carry with such great effort through the mud to the gun emplacements. For a moment, a plane appeared and then veered away abruptly when two gray clouds of smoke materialized near it. As the pilot banked, the underside of his aircraft shone like the silver belly of a trout, displaying two Soviet stars in place of its red spots.

We stopped at the Elisabeth Polski Pass near a small cemetery, actually just a group of graves. For one of these, the grave of an anti-aircraft gunner, his comrades had constructed a fence of slender yellow shell casings by hand. These were arranged like those bottles sometimes seen stuck bottom up into the earth along the edges of our own garden beds. Nearby the last resting places of three soldiers from the Corps of Engineers had been lovingly fenced with garlands of oak leaves strung in makeshift rows. The grave of a Turkoman bearer was marked by a wooden post with a foreign inscription, perhaps a verse from the Koran.

We ascended the north side of the mountain where a layer of new snow had thawed overnight and frozen again. The new crystal formations produced patterns of broad needles that glistened with a bluish tint. After driving up the mountain for three-quarters of an hour, we reached the ridge, which revealed a view of a sea of forested mountains for miles around. The closest ones had mossy green color-ation that came from the lichen covering the bare branches. The blue mountain ranges got darker and darker, and behind them rose the snow-capped peaks, with their ashen slopes and sharp crags. Opposite us towered Mount Indyuk with a long ridge ending sharply in twin peaks and connecting to a domed ridge. A white cone rose up behind it. On our flank to the right, the Góra Sarai towered upward to a Russian observation post in position at the summit. For that reason, we retreated back into the undergrowth when we unfolded our white maps.

We had reached the ridge at a point where an artillery lieutenant had been directing the fire toward the spot where the Russians had broken through that morning. Far down behind us from the dense forest floor the deep roar of the large guns could be heard. Then their shells spiraled up over our heads, their shrill whistles slowly fading into the distance and finally dying out in the green valleys with the dull, barely audible reports of their impacts. White clouds then billowed up from the conifer groves and hung suspended in the humid air for a long time.

We watched this activity for a while across the broad expanse. Afterward, I walked a bit on the south slope, which was protected from view by dense tree growth. The sun warmed its ridge and dappled the pale foliage as if it were a beautiful spring day. The north side was covered with beech trees. These had grown a layer of moss from all the rain and bore a lush growth of black crescent-shaped tinder fungus. But here on this side, the oak trees predominated. Plants also flourished, such as large bushes of hellebore beside delicate Alpine violets with their light, spotted leaves on a purple background.

It reminded me of home; I felt as though I had often been on such oak-covered slopes. The Caucasus is not only an ancient wealth of peoples, languages, and races; it also preserves animals, plants, and topography of far-flung regions from Europe and Asia. Memories awaken in these mountain ranges. The meaning of the earth seems more palpable, just as the minerals and precious stones are more visible, and water here springs from its source.

Kurinski, 16 December 1942

Inspected our position above Shaumyan with First Lieutenant Häussler. At the outset, we accompanied General Vogel as far as the field headquarters of Regiment 228. We reached this by climbing up a steep and narrow depression made by the melt water as it ripped deep into the forest floor. On each side, huts were pasted into the clay like swallows' nests showing only their front walls facing outward. Inside, these were close and dirty, but brick stoves radiated good heat. There is no lack of wood in this ocean of forests.

We then climbed through the dense but leafless woods and stayed on a path that had been trodden deep into the brown mud by the pack animals and their guides. Walking was difficult; the path had recently come under rocket fire, and one hit had killed one of the animals, a lovely little dark brown horse that lay dead in the mire. Dark blood had flowed into yellowish clay-colored pools of water left by its hoof prints and settled there, undiluted.

The trees, mostly oaks, were thickly covered with liverwort, and thick, silvery green tresses hung from their branches like beards. These gave the forest a soft, swaying quality. In the winter sunlight, the woodpeckers and the agile nuthatches flitted from trunk to trunk as squawking jays flew around. These last, a local Caucasian variant recognizable by the black crests atop their heads, animated the forest. Yet I still felt that the zeitgeist was trying to extinguish all beauty in us. We perceive it as if we were gazing out through the bars of prison windows.

We climbed upward along a trail that had been blazed in order to reach a high-elevation emplacement that jutted out like a nose. Neither barbed wire nor any continuous trench demarcated it from no man's land. All that was visible was a group of molehills scattered through the forest. Each of these hills concealed a small shelter—an excavated hole that had been shored up with tree trunks and then covered in earth. Here and there a tarpaulin had been spread on top, providing only inadequate protection from the rain.

The company commander, a young Tyrolean from Kufstein, showed us around his demesne. Close by on the other slope, the Russians had dug in. We could make out one of their pillboxes from a minor variance in coloration from the gray-green shimmer of the forest floor. As if to prove the point, a loud volley of gunfire whipped across in our direction. The only bullets we heard distinctly were those that whistled as they ricocheted through the branches. One of them tore the sight off a machine gun.

We jumped into the foxholes for cover and let the storm pass over. Such situations make me recognize both their half-comical and half-upsetting aspects. I have long since passed the age, or better said the condition, when I find such things amusing and immediately try to outdo them.

In order to smoke out our foxholes, the Russians had hauled an armor-piercing artillery piece up the mountain. The small shells exploded on impact within the target areas causing many casualties. Countless trees that had been shorn off at mid-height bore witness to their force.

It was dull, melancholy, and dank. After the sleepless night, most of the unit was lying down asleep; individual sentries were scanning the forest. Others were polishing the fresh rust off their weapons. A short fellow from Thuringia had soaped himself from head to foot and was having a comrade slowly pour warm water over his body.

I spoke with these men, who have landed here at the end of the world. They have taken part in the difficult offensive and fought their way forward through these mountains step by step, only to dig themselves in here when the force of the thrust diminished. They have been holding their position under fire and without relief for a long time. Casualties, direct hits, sicknesses like those brought on by exhaustion and damp, deplete their numbers each day—numbers that were low at the outset. They are truly living on the edge of existence.

During the descent to Shaumyan, we again passed by the horse we had seen that morning. In the meantime, it had been butchered down to its bones and small intestines. Turkoman soldiers perform this duty, eaters of horseflesh in huge quantities whose yellow faces could be seen bending over canisters full of bubbling goulash.

Shaumyan was badly battle-scarred; it comes under fire daily. One hit is enough to dismantle the huts like houses of cards so that their construction can be studied: four walls whose flimsy timbers have been covered with a mixture of clay and cow dung; the roofs are covered with wooden shingles split paper thin. Two pieces of furniture protrude from the ruined ground plans: the large stone oven and the metal bed frame.

This town is a way station for our vehicles. Stretcher-bearers carry the wounded down from the mountains to this point. A cemetery with crosses damaged by shelling is evidence that this first station has taken already taken its deadly toll.

At a wound-dressing station (one of the reconstructed huts), we met Dr. Fuchs performing the duties of both doctor and soldier. He hospitably invited us to eat with him. The place is not marked because the Red Cross means nothing here. Just yesterday a rocket struck the adjoining house, severely injuring a stretcher-bearer.

The wounded come in intermittent batches once the battle picks up, and then there's a lot to do. The injured leave the woods at dark and arrive in a state of extreme exhaustion, some even dying on the way. This morning, for example, the doctor heard a cry outside: "Please come help me!" He found a soldier with outstretched hands who had collapsed into the mud and lacked the strength to get up by himself.

After eating, our host treated us to a cup of coffee and a piece of Christmas cake that his wife had sent him. We then took our leave from this unassuming helper, whose shelter even had a cultivated air about it—a trait that people of character seldom lose.

On the subject of mythology. The secret of the Odyssey and its influence lies in the fact that it is a metaphor for life's journey. The image of Scylla and Charybdis conceals a primeval configuration. The man burdened by the wrath of the gods moves between two dangers, each more terrible than the other. In these cauldron battles, he seems to stand between death in battle and death in captivity. He finds he is forced into the tortuous narrow gap between the two.

If a great poet of our age ever wanted to express how human beings long for peace when they are pushed to the limits of destruction, he would have to write a continuation of the Odyssey as a new epic or as an idyll: Odysseus with Penelope.

KURINSKI, 18 DECEMBER 1942

Walk to the Góra Sarai, a peak whose summit the Russians occupy. *Ssarai*, a word of Tatar origin, means "barn," and *gora* is Russian for "mountain."

I got this explanation from a young interpreter, whom Häußler had brought along to carry a machine gun because the region is rife with partisans. He is German-Russian, descended from Swabian emigrants.[22] His parents lived as prosperous farmers in the Crimea near Eupatoria. As "Kulaks,"[23] they were deported to Omsk in Siberia and forced to leave their eight-year-old son behind. He has not heard anything from them since 1936.

We climbed up the mountain through a dense mixed forest growth of young oaks, aspens, and beeches. At times, we made our way through bushes with pink and bright green branches as well as little islands in marshes with tall stands of cattails hung with brown cotton fluff. On the way, a corporal carrying an axe joined us. He was out hunting for a Christmas tree.

After an ascent of two hours, we reached the ridge that concealed a row of pillboxes behind it. The sentries were positioned slightly higher so they could see down into the valley on the other side. We inspected their line, which had been drawn up very carelessly. There was a gaping hole in the right flank, then came a battalion of Turkomen troops. Here the corporal crept forward with his axe and returned after an hour with a beautiful fir tree. Its needles showed pale growth lines on their undersides.

We rested at the quarters of the company commander, who then took us to an elevated point where two weeks ago the Russians had been able to break through. In doing so, they had slaughtered all the men. The graves along the heights were crowned with crosses that had been planted with Christmas roses [hellebore]. From there the summit was visible—a bare peak with bunkers in the nearby undergrowth. At that moment a cluster of rockets hit the earth with a loud explosion. It startled an enormous eagle that soared in lazy circles over the chaos.

During the descent following this, Häußler briefed us about an execution of partisans. Behind us I heard the interpreter laughing, so I studied him a bit more closely. I thought I could tell from his features—the parchment texture of his skin, the grim look in his eyes—that he was the type of person who longs for such bloodshed. The mechanical habit of killing produces the same ravages in the facial features that mechanical sexuality does.

Visited General Vogel for tea; he sent me back to Kurinski with a bodyguard. Just yesterday after dark, two couriers were ambushed, shot, and their corpses stripped to their shirts.

Navaginski, 19 December 1942

Departure at noon for the field headquarters of the Ninety-Seventh Division. The commander, General Rupp, was waiting for me at the demolished bridge over the Pshish. We crossed the silted river of yellow clay in an inflatable dinghy. We had to cross a steep mountain ridge in order to reach staff headquarters because an explosion had made a tunnel through the mountain impassable.

We wriggled our way through dense undergrowth, and then crossed over cliffs through hart's tongue fern, which had opened its long tender leaves. We encountered hundreds of Russian and Asiatic bearers on the narrow path. They were laden with rations, equipment, and ammunition. On the descending slope lay a dead man with long black hair on his face. He was covered with clay from his head to his feet, which had been robbed of their boots. He was barely distinguishable from the mud. The general leaned down over him and then, without a word, continued on his way. Despite any imaginable comment to the contrary, I have never seen a dead body more out of place than here. Flotsam on a loveless sea.

Back in the valley, we again came to the Pshish. The towering railroad bridge had been blown up here as well. High water had rammed driftwood against it, moving the huge structure downstream. Among its trestles hung trees, wagons, gun carriages, and even a dead horse dangling by its halter among the branches of an oak tree. Set among these titanic dimensions, the animal looked as tiny as a drowned cat.

The staff was quartered in a stationmaster's house. I sat beside the general, who was affable, shy, and a bit melancholy. I had the feeling that despite a few peculiarities, he was loved by his officers. Like Chichikov among the landowners in *Dead Souls*, I am driving around with the generals and observing their metamorphosis into workers. One has to abandon the hope that any traits of a Sulla or Napoleon might develop from this class. They are specialists in the area of command technology and as interchangeable and expendable as the next best worker at a machine.

Spent the night in the blockhouse of the ordnance officer. The gaps between the heavy oak beams are packed with moss. Three bedsteads, a card table, and a desk. Two telephones ring in brief succession. Outside a sloshing, scraping sound is audible: people and animals are slogging through the mud. A Russian prisoner cowers by the stove—an "Ivan"—and puts wood on the fire when it dies down.

NAVAGINSKI, 20 DECEMBER 1942

Climbed with Major Weihrauter to an observation point placed high above the valley. In the soggy mist, we passed through clearings of mighty beeches with patches of black fungus on their bark. Among these towered oaks and wild pear trees with light gray crackled trunks. The trail had been marked by blazes on the trees; our steps through the viscous mud exposed the flat tubers of the cyclamen.

Once we had reached our objective—a hut concealed underneath cut branches—we lit a small fire and trained our field glasses on the wooded area. Dense, heavy mists curled through the valleys, obscuring our sight but at the same time making the contours as distinct as on a relief map. Our field of vision was cut off by the highest parts of the watershed. The position at the foot of Mount Indyuk, which towered up to the right with its twin peaks and steep ridge, had come under fire today. To the left is the tallest peak, Mount Semashko, giving a view of the Black Sea. This was under German control but had to be abandoned because it was too hard to supply. The access points to such peaks soon become littered with the corpses of bearers and pack animals.

Up on a bare snow-covered patch, the field glasses picked out a small group of Russians apparently crawling around aimlessly in one direction and then another like ants. Resisting this impression, I saw men for the first time as though through a telescope pointed at the moon.

Thought: "During World War I, we would have been permitted to fire at them."

NAVAGINSKI, 21 DECEMBER 1942

Early departure along the Pshish Valley with Nawe-Stier. The trees along the highest ridges were covered with hoarfrost. From afar, the branches stand out from the mass of darker growth in the valleys as if dusted with silver powder. How remarkable that a small deviation of a couple of degrees from the norm is a sufficient difference to create such enchantment. There is something about this that gives hope both to living and dying.

We rested upon reaching Captain Mergener, the commander of a combat unit. His combat position turned out to be a white house set alone like a forester's hut in a mud-choked clearing. In the midst of this wasteland scattered with the detritus of war, I noticed a number of neatly tended graves that had been especially decorated for Christmas with holly and mistletoe. The farmstead was surrounded by deep craters, but its inhabitants had not yet moved out. The contrast between warm rooms and hostile marshlands is all too great.

The combat unit of the twenty-six-year-old commander consisted of a battalion of engineers, a company of Bicycle Infantry, and a few other units. After a cup of coffee, we made the ascent to the position defended by the Corps of Engineers Battalion. Here I found the conditions somewhat better than in the other sections. Some modest barbed wire was strung between the sentry posts along the steep ridge between the trees. In front of this a triple row of mines was set out.

Laying mines, especially at night, is dangerous business. In order to be found again, the mines must be laid out in a pattern. They also have to be well concealed, because it happens that the Russians sometimes dig them up and bury them in front of their own positions.

The S-mine is the type generally used here.[24] When triggered, the device is launched into the air to approximately a man's height where it then explodes. The trigger mechanism is either a tripwire activated by a footfall or by contact with the three wires that project from the earth like feelers. The zone is paced off very cautiously, especially in the dark, but things often happen anyway.

As an example, a while ago, a cadet was checking the mines with a corporal. They kept their eyes on the tension wire but did not notice that this had frozen to a clump of earth, which pulled the wire away when the cadet stepped on it. The corporal shouted: "Look out, smoke!" and threw himself on the ground. He survived, but the explosion ripped his companion apart. Before the mine springs upward, it makes a hissing noise for a few seconds—just enough time to get down. Sometimes the fuse can also be set off by rabbits or foxes, as happened a few weeks ago when a great stag that had been rutting in the valley for a long time was blown up.

Captain Abt, with whom I talked about these things, recently stepped on a mine himself and threw himself down on the ground. He was not hit: "—because this one had not been placed according to my instructions," as he added. An old Prussian would have enjoyed that additional comment.

The position was thus more secure, but the men were nonetheless thoroughly exhausted. Three men are sheltered in each of the tunnels connected to a small combat position. One of them does sentry duty; then comes the work detail: getting rations, maintaining the trenches, laying mines, cleaning weapons, and cutting wood. All this with no respite since the end of October under heavy fire in a position established after a period of long and intense fighting.

It was easy to see that there had been a lot of shooting in the woods. The forest was pockmarked with many shell craters, new ones as well, which looked freshly greased on the bottom; the earth was rippled at their edges. Inside these hung a knot of mist. The tops of the trees were lopped off. Because the Russians do not spare their rockets, one or another of the lookout patrols always gets picked off.

Visited the battalion commander, Captain Sperling, in his shelter framed in oak timbers. Rougher tree trunks supported the ceiling. Two crude cots, shelves on the walls with canned goods on them, as well as cooking utensils, weapons, blankets, field glasses. The commander was fatigued, unshaven, looking like someone who had tossed and turned all night. He had been jumping from tree to tree in the dark, sodden forest, waiting for an attack while the rocket launchers churned up the dirt and ripped down the treetops.[25] One dead, one wounded, so it went night after night. Our own artillery had even dropped a shell behind his own slope position:

"No talk of being pinned down here. You'll have to answer to me if the shells fizzle out in the trees."

And so, the classic exchange between artillery and infantry.

"Nobody grouses anymore. They're getting apathetic. That worries me."

He talks about his ceiling made of beams that can withstand shells but not survive heavy rocket fire. Losses: "it has happened that some days we don't have any."

Sickness: "rheumatism, jaundice; kidney infection, which makes the extremities swell; the troops die as they march to the field dressing station."

I heard all these conversations in World War I, but in the meantime, the suffering has become more dismal, more compulsory, and is rather the rule than the exception. We find ourselves here in one of those great bone mills that have been familiar since Sebastopol and the Russo-Japanese War.[26] The technology, the world of automatons, must converge with the power of the earth and its ability to suffer in order to give rise to this sort of thing. By contrast, Verdun, the Somme, and Flanders[27] are mere episodes. It is impossible for such images to affect other areas such as air and sea combat. Ideologically, this Second World War is completely distinct from the first. It is probably the greatest confrontation about free will since the Persian Wars.[28] And again the fronts have been drawn up completely differently from the way they look on the map. Germans lost World War I together with the Russians, and it could be that they will lose the second along with the French.

Descent around twelve o'clock. In order to target the men going for rations, the artillery started to pepper the ravines with concentrated shelling, causing Sperling some apprehension about his own shelter. The barrage sounded truly massive—like mountain ranges breaking apart and collapsing with a crash.

Back through the Pshish Valley. A figure of mud lay on the riverbank—a dead Russian face down, his head resting on his right arm as if he were asleep. I saw his blackened neck and hand. The corpse was so swollen that the mud was caked on it like the pelt of a seal or the skin of a big fish. And so there he lay, no better than a drowned cat—a disgrace. In the Urals, in Moscow, or in Siberia, a wife and children have been waiting for him for years. Following this, our own discussion of "that topic" gave me the opportunity to marvel again at the general numbing process, even among educated people. Individuals have the feeling of being passive participants, enmeshed in a huge mechanism.

In the evening, I read a strange phrase in the military communiqué that mentions the danger of a threat to the flanks. This is likely to be a reference to the threat against Rostov, for that is without doubt the strategic target of the Russian attacks.[29] There is always the prospect of being caught up in mass catastrophes like a fish trapped with its school in a net cast by a distant hand. Yet it is up to us whether we too shall suffer mass death, death dominated by fear.

Kurinski, 22 December 1942

Returned to Kurinski in the morning. I again passed the railroad bridge that had been washed downstream. The dead horse—so tiny in the distance—still hung on one of the trees that decorated the structure like bouquets of flowers.

The middle plank of a wooden walkway had just broken where gun carriages were crossing so that a draft horse plunged through the opening and dangled in its harness with its head just above the rough waves. For a few long moments its nostrils kept being submerged in the water while up above the agitated drivers were scrambling around helplessly. Then a corporal with bayonet drawn sprang down onto the bridge from the bank and slashed through the straps, letting the animal tumble into the water and swim to safety. An aura of unease, of abnormality lay over the place—a mood of crisis.

Crossed the ridge with the tunnel again. Omar, a good-natured Azerbaijani who had been looking after me for the past few days, followed with my gear. The dead bearer was still lying there in the mud even though many hundreds of men had passed him by every day. The display of corpses seems to be part of the system—I don't mean the human system, but that of the *daimon* who rules over such places. That tightens the reins.

A bit farther up, I saw two new dead bodies, one of which had been stripped to his underwear. He was lying in the streambed, his powerful chest protruding, blue from the frost. His right arm was crooked behind his head, as though he were sleeping; on his skull glistened a bloody wound. For all I could tell, people had tried to rob the shirt off the other corpse too, but without success. Yet it had been pulled up far enough here to reveal a small, pallid entry wound near the heart. Mountain troops with heavy packs hurried past, and lines of bearers loaded with beams, coils of wire, rations, and ammunition. None of them had shaved in a long time, they were all caked with mud, and the odor of humanity emanated from them—people who had been strangers to soap and water for weeks. They barely glanced at the corpses, but they start with fright when a shot from a heavy mortar down below resounds like a boom out of a large empty kettle. Interspersed were pack animals that had wallowed in muck like great rats with clotted pelts.

On the cable car across the Pshish. At great height on a narrow board swinging over the river, both fists clenched around a cable, I comprehend the landscape like a picture in one of those moments that goes deeper than any painting. The little ripples down below take on something stiff and eternally frozen in time, a bit like the pale edges of the scales on the body of a snake. I am swaying next to one of the tall bridge abutments with Romanesque windows that remains standing like a shattered tower. An officer peers out through one of the fissures in the way people look out of those hollow eggs in Bosch paintings and glimpse bizarre machines. The officer is calling numbers over to the crew of a heavy cannon. Down below, the artillerymen are visible around a gray monster; then they stand back and cover their ears as a red tongue of flame flashes through the air. Immediately afterward, the head calling out numbers emerges from the wall again. Injured men with bright white bandages are ferried across the river and then taken on stretchers to the ambulances, which have driven up en masse. Their red crosses have been camouflaged. Like ants, hundreds and thousands of bearers in long lines bring forward planks and wire. Through all this, melodies of Christmas carols in a supernatural voice fill the enormous cauldron: A propaganda unit's loudspeaker is playing Silent Night, Holy Night. And accompanying this, the constant furious pounding of mortar shelling echoes through the mountains.

KURINSKI, 23 DECEMBER 1942

In the evening, de Marteau brought the first mail from Maykop: a parcel containing Christmas cake, the holiday bread baked by Perpetua with hazelnuts from the vicarage garden. Included were letters from her, from Mother, from Carl Schmitt. He writes about nihilism, which he equates with fire when he considers the four elements. Nihilism, he says, is the urge to be incinerated in crematoria. These ashes then produce the phoenix, that is to say a realm of the air.

Carl Schmitt is among the few people who try to assess the process in categories that are not entirely shortsighted, such as the national, the social, and the economic arguments. Blindness increases with awareness; humans move in a labyrinth of light. They no longer know the power of darkness. Who can even imagine the scale—whose delight requires dramatic effects like those I witnessed yesterday while hanging from my cable? Immensity is triumphantly enthroned at its center. It is obvious that at some level a deep enjoyment is derived from these hells.

Reading matter: *Der Wehrwolf* by Löns, a book I haven't read since childhood.[30] I found a copy here in one of the bunker libraries. Despite its crude and woodcut-like style, traces of the old sagas, of the old *nomos*, shape the description.[31] I am engrossed by the book because the plot is set nearby, actually not far from Kirchhorst.

Then read further in Ezekiel. The vision that introduces his book conceals an insight into the structure of the world. This transcends the boldest thoughts, the most elevated works of art. We enter the region of absolute concepts and explore them in a state of *ecstasis*.[32] In this tangible model is revealed the luster of the world and its overworlds.

KURINSKI, 24 DECEMBER 1942

Dreams last night. I had long talks with Friedrich Georg and others, and I was showing him around Paris. One of them, a short fellow from Saxony: "All people possess the capacity to lead happy lives, but they just never make use of it."

Walk into the Pshish Valley after breakfast to spend a little time for a short beetle hunt. Such activity serves to preserve my dignity, as a symbol of my free will in the world.

Celebrated Christmas in the afternoon. As we did so, we saluted the troops of the Sixth Army. If they were to be defeated by this encirclement, then the entire southern portion of the front would start to crumble. That would correspond exactly to what Speidel predicted to me last spring as the probable consequence of a Caucasus offensive. He said it would open an umbrella, meaning that it would lead to the construction of huge fronts with narrow points of access.

In the evening, we got together in the little space that Captain Dix had set up in town in the former bathhouse. Leather seats from a bus are arranged around the smokers' table; the colossal wooden wheel of a Russian artillery piece hangs from the ceiling as a chandelier. The occasional chirp of a cricket, gentle and dreamlike, comes from the walls of the immense stove now and then. We ate roast duck and had sweet Crimean champagne to go with it.

I soon withdrew to my Cossack hut to devote myself to studying the extensive correspondence that de Marteau had delivered to me during the party. The most important contents were four letters from Perpetua. Friedrich Georg writes about a trip to Freiburg and conversations with the professors there who "observe the passage of time from their Alemannic retreats." Grunert writes about the *Eremurus* [foxtail lily] and lilies and lets me know that he is sending some beautifully blossoming allium species. His letter contains a marginal note referring to the Magister and a meeting with him in a London pub just before the outbreak of war. Claus Valentiner writes about our circle of friends in Paris. Two letters from people I didn't know contain references to authors, one of them to Sir Thomas Browne, who lived from 1605 to 1681; the other to Justus Marckord and his work *Gebete eines Ungläubigen* [*Prayers of an Unbeliever*]. A photocopy of a will informs me that another unknown correspondent who used to write to me, but who in the meantime has been killed in action, has designated me as the heir of his literary remains. There is also a strange message from a Dr. Blum from Mönchen-Gladbach about a passage that he read in my *Gärten und Strassen* [*Gardens and Streets*]. In the description of Domrémy, I mention the grave monument of a Lieutenant Reiners, who was killed there on 26 June 1940. I am now told that this young officer had been a horticultural genius, an enthusiastic breeder of fine fruits and flowers, preferring the amaryllis above all others. Surpassing even the Dutch gardeners, he was often able to achieve eight huge blossoms on one stem—from the purest white to the deepest crimson, and wrote about all of his flowers in a journal. Blum believes it was no accident that I memorialized this rare person, and I agree with him. In addition, letters from Speidel, Stapel, Höll, Grüninger, and Freyhold, who tells me that he is going to send me a salmon from the coast of Finland. Strange, how the game of cat's cradle keeps playing out in life even in the midst of carnage. If there were no more mail deliveries, we would have to confide in the ether.

KURINSKI, 25 DECEMBER 1942

In the morning, I attended a service of a young Catholic cleric who performed his office superbly. Then took communion from the Protestant pastor—also a young corporal—who distributed it with great dignity.

Following this, went to the Pshish to hunt for beetles. In a rotten tree stump found a nest of *Diaperis boleti* [darkling beetles] with red femurs—this is the

Caucasian aberration. The study of insects has consumed much time in my life—but you have to see such things as an arena where you can practice the art of precise differentiation. These provide insight into the most delicate features of the landscapes. After forty years, one learns to read wing covers as texts, like a Chinese scholar who knows a hundred thousand ideograms. Armies of schoolmasters and pedants devised the system, work that took nearly two hundred years.

Visited the Mirnaya ravine in the afternoon with First Lieutenant Strubelt, one of Hielscher's intelligent pupils. When our conversation came around to the predicament of the Sixth Army, I became aware of a bond that had never before seemed so clear: in these cauldrons, each and every one of us is melted down and remolded, even if he is not physically present. Accordingly, neutrality does not exist.

We struggled in the fog through the stands of oak and wild pear trees that enveloped the low hilltops in thick forestation. On one of these slopes we came upon a cluster of graves. Among them was that of Herbert Gogol, killed here as a private in the Corps of Engineers on 4 October 1942. The sight of these crosses in this primeval, foggy, wet forest interwoven with gray lichen, filled me with deep sadness at so much anguish.

Thought: they have huddled together here like children in the sinister enchanted forest.

APSHERONSKAYA, 27 DECEMBER 1942

In Apsheronskaya for two or three days in order to bathe here and have things repaired that were badly damaged by the mountain walking.

The place has been taken over by supply and relief troops and also field hospitals, enclosed by a rapidly expanding wreath of cemeteries. We sow the ground profusely with our dead. Many of those buried here must have died of epidemics, a fact I conclude from the doctors' names that appear frequently on the crosses.

I answer my mail in the evening. I stopped working when a nearby loudspeaker started up. This kind of disturbance has become more and more outrageous since the days when Luther threw his inkwell at a blowfly. I find that they create acoustic images similar to the visual ones found on the great pictures of temptation by Bosch, Brueghel, and Cranach. These brazen, underworld noises, demonic grunts, intrude upon intellectual work like the laughter of fauns peering over the edges of cliffs into the landscape, or like the mad cheers resounding from the depths of the elves' caves. What's more, it can't be turned off—that would be sacrilege.

APSHERONSKAYA, 28 DECEMBER 1942

Walked to the opposite bank of the Pshish across a long narrow suspension bridge that swayed from two cables like vines. At this point, the river is broader than upstream in the mountains, its beautiful stone-green water flows along a bed of dark slate with vertical striations.

Magnificent stretches of woods extend along the other bank. I came upon a settlement of gray wooden houses where smoke emerged from ramshackle shingle roofs and, in spite of the cold, women sat in front of them busying themselves beside little stoves that had been set up outdoors. The settlement seemed medieval, barely spawned from the earth—a world of wood and clay. Add to this the machines, so important here, that were allotted to the white man in America. And so I noticed a sawmill; all around it for quite a distance the forest had been cut down to the ground. Such a sight makes clear the devouring and gluttonous aspect that Friedrich Georg has described in his *Illusions of Technology*. This runs its course as long as it has natural resources and leaves behind a soil weakened and forever infertile. We lack minds like that of old Marwitz, men who will ensure that we take only from the increase of the earth and not from its capital.

KUTAIS, 29 DECEMBER 1942

Dreams last night: Among other things, I was thumbing through a history of this war, which was arranged systematically. It contained a paragraph on Declarations of War dealing with several types, beginning with the simple invasion and including the performance of significant ceremonies.

Departure in the morning, initially from the railroad station in Muk and then via Asphalti and Kura-Zize to Kutais. From Kura-Zize onward, I used a truck because the deep tracks had made the road impassable for light vehicles. It had frozen, but the pressure of the wheels soon thawed the top layer, making the surface resemble a piece of buttered bread. Then came the slopes, potholes, and other obstacles that forced us to push the vehicle through the muck. The driver, a Swabian from Esslingen, was a man of choleric temperament who took all these hardships very much to heart: "If you have any feelings at all for a vehicle, you could just weep." Now and again he would let out particularly strong sighs: "Poor little truck," referring to this enormous behemoth.[33]

Forest enveloped our route, choking it off in places with long green ropes of moss hanging from the branches. The road passed by the ruined drilling towers and other demolished facilities of the oil fields. We could see individuals staggering among the wreckage like ants.

KUTAIS, 30 DECEMBER 1942

This place resembles a mudhole with plank walks connecting individual points with each other—such as the staff quarters, the field hospitals, and the mess. Except for these paths any effort made to get around is almost futile. As a result, deaths from exhaustion are not uncommon.

The deluge of sludge even penetrates the interiors of the buildings. In the morning, I was in a field hospital that rose from the center of a yellowish-brown morass. As I entered, the casket of a first lieutenant was being carried toward me. Yesterday he succumbed to his sixth wound of this war. Back in Poland, he had sacrificed an eye.

Under such conditions you must try to secure at least the three most basic requirements for comfort: to be warm, dry, and fed. This had been accomplished: The patients in their heated shelters could be seen dozing in apathetic groups. Exposure to the cold is the leading cause of ailments, especially in their severest forms like kidney and lung infections. Frostbite was prevalent, caused here by the constant soaking and evaporation even at temperatures above freezing. You get the feeling that every last bit has been drained from the troops. Their bodies completely lack any reserves, meaning that a mere flesh wound can be fatal because the body lacks the capacity to heal. There are also fatal cases of diarrhea.

The countless mines that still carpet this town continue to do damage. For example, recently a Russian was found at the edge of the road with his legs blown off. Because detonators were discovered on him, he was immediately executed—a gesture that may have mingled humanity with bestiality, but which correlates with the decline in our ability to discriminate moral categories. The realm of death becomes a depository: There we stick anything that seems upsetting where it won't be seen again. But that may well be wrong.

KUTAIS, 31 DECEMBER 1942

Dreams at night: I was party to a conversation between a lady wearing a riding costume and a middle-age gentleman. I was carrying on this conversation myself, sometimes as one partner, sometimes as the other; otherwise I just listened. I was individualized in the dialogue. This revealed the true chasm that exists between participant and observer: The unity of this process became clear to me in the vision, then took on a dialectic quality whenever it was my turn to speak. The image captures my situation in general.

In the morning, I visited Herr Maiweg, the commander of a unit in the Technical Petroleum Brigade in Shirokaya Balka. This is the designation for a part military, part technology group; it is their mission to discover, secure, and develop the conquered oil regions. Shirokaya Balka, meaning "the wide ravine," was one of those places that produced considerable quantities. Before their retreat, the Russians were extremely thorough in destroying all oil wells and other equipment. They filled the drill-holes with cement reinforced with pieces of iron, springs, screws, and old drill bits. They also submerged iron mushroom-shaped devices. When these are drilled and lifted up, they spread out and tear apart the mechanism.

After a lengthy conversation, we mounted horses and rode across the terrain. With its toppled drilling towers and exploded boiler houses, it looked like those containers for old iron that plumbers have. Rusted, bent, dismantled pieces lay scattered around and among them stood the blasted machines, boilers, tanks. To get anywhere with this chaos would have been depressing. Here and there across the terrain one saw a lone man or a troop wandering around as if they were in the middle of a puzzle that had been dumped out on the floor. Fresh mine craters gaped, especially over near the drilling towers. The sight of sappers looking for mines as they carefully poked the soil with their pointed iron forks awakened the oppressive feeling that comes when the earth can no longer be trusted. But I still had my good horse under me.

At lunch we drank Caucasian wine and discussed the vast topic of how long the war might last. Maiweg had lived ten years as an oil engineer in Texas and was of the opinion that the war with Russia would create a new *limes* [frontier][34] and also play itself out against America, but at the price of the English and French empires.

I countered by saying that it is precisely the violence of the war that contradicts this. The still undecided conclusion would be the worst imaginable. The widespread prognosis of an infinite continuation derives essentially from a lack of imagination. It occurs to people who see no way out.

Detail: Russian prisoners Maiweg had selected from all the various camps to work on the reconstruction—drilling technicians, geologists, local oil workers. A combat unit had been commandeered at a railroad station as bearers. There were five hundred men; of these three hundred and fifty died along the roads. From the rest, another hundred and twenty died from exhaustion when they returned so that only thirty survived.

New Year's Eve party at Staff Headquarters in the evening. Here again I saw that during these years any pure joy of celebration is not possible. On that note General Müller told about the monstrous atrocities perpetrated by the Security Service after entering Kiev. Trains were again mentioned that carried Jews into poison gas tunnels. Those are rumors, and I note them as such, but extermination is certainly occurring on a huge scale. This put me in mind of the wife of good old Potard[35] back in Paris, who was so worried about his wife. When you have been party to such individual fates and begun to comprehend the statistics that apply to the wicked crimes carried out in the charnel houses,[36] an enormity is exposed that makes you throw up your hands in despair. I am overcome by a loathing for the uniforms, the epaulettes, the medals, the weapons, all the glamour I have loved so much. Ancient chivalry is dead; wars are waged by technicians. Mankind has thus reached the stage described by Dostoevsky in Raskolnikov.[37] He views people like himself as vermin. That is precisely what he must guard against if he is not to sink to the level of the insects. That terrible old saying applies to him as well as to his victims: "This is you."

I then went outside where the stars shone brightly and the artillery shells streaked like sheet lightning against the sky. The eternal symbols and signs—the Great Bear, Orion, Vega, the Pleiades, the band of the Milky Way—what are we human beings and our earthly years before such glory? What is our fleeting torment? At midnight, through the noise of the carousers, I vividly recalled my loves and felt their greetings touch me.

1943

APSHERONSKAYA, 1 JANUARY 1943

Prophetic New Year's dreams—I was waiting in a large inn, discussing other travelers' luggage with a doorman who had silver-embroidered keys on his uniform. He told me that they were embarrassed to admit they did not wish to be separated from their bags because these signified more than just containers for their possessions. Their contents included the rest of their journey and all their reputation and credit. These were like a ship, the last thing we leave behind on an ocean voyage—they were like our own skin. I vaguely understood that the inn was the world and the suitcases, life.

For Alexander, I then carved an arrow from a rose shoot so he could use with his bow. Its tip bore a scarlet bud.

Got up early for the return journey to Apsheronskaya. The sun shone gloriously on the mountains, and the woods breathed the violet palette of early spring. I was in a good mood as well, like a fencer returning to the arena. The minor, mundane tasks on this first day of the year are more precious: washing, shaving, eating breakfast, and making journal entries—all are symbolic acts of celebration.

Three good resolutions. The first, "Live moderately," because almost all the difficulties in my life have been the result of breaches of moderation.

Second, "Always have a care for unfortunate people." It is an innate human trait not to recognize true misfortune. This goes deeper: we avert our gaze from it, and then sympathy gets neglected.

Finally, I want to banish contemplation of individual refuge in this chaos of all potential catastrophes. It is more important to act with dignity. We only secure ourselves shelter at superficial points within a totality that remains concealed from us, and it is precisely such delusions of our own devising that can kill us.

The road surface did not seem quite as bottomless as it had on the way here. As a matter of fact, I probably counted five hundred people working on it. A further five hundred were bringing up supplies on wagons or horses. Such images reflect the gravitational field of the wider area. Within this space, even individual mountains like the Ssemasho take on the burden of Atlas. Spengler's superb prognosis also came to mind.

In Apsheronskaya, Massenbach and I then ate together before taking a walk through the woods. The mountains gleamed white on the horizon. We discussed the atrocities of our age. A third man with us said that he considered them inevitable. He went on: The German *petit bourgeoisie* had been reduced to a state of panic by the slaughter of the Russian middle class after 1917 and by the execution of millions in the cellars—and this turned them into something horrifying. As a result, something emerged from the Right that was an even more hideous threat than when it came from the Left.

Such discussions clarify how deeply technology has already penetrated the moral sphere. Man feels he is inside a huge machine from which there is no escape. Fear reigns everywhere supreme, be it in obfuscation, grotesque concealment, or all-powerful mistrust. Wherever two people encounter one another, they are suspicious of each other—it begins with their greeting.

MAYKOP, 2 JANUARY 1943

Nearly fifty bombs fell on the town during the night. In the morning, I departed for Maykop. The journey led past troops that had been relieved and were pulling medieval supply carts behind them. Generally speaking, I am reminded more of the Thirty Years' War than of the previous one, not just because of the look of things but also because of the obvious religious questions that loom large.

The weather was mild and clear. In the morning, I visited the Cultural Park where plaster figures of modern supermen were crumbling, and then went to the steep banks of the Belaya. In the afternoon, I was received by General Konrad, commander of the Caucasus front. He showed me the large situation map and said that the retreat was in preparation. The pounding suffered by the Sixth Army had shaken the entire southern flank. He was of the opinion that during the last year, our forces had been squandered by people who understood everything except how to wage war. The general continued, saying that their neglect of the concentration of forces was especially dilettantish. Clausewitz would be turning in his grave. People followed their every whim, every fleeting idea; and propaganda goals trumped those of strategy. He said that we could attack the Caucasus, Egypt, Leningrad, and Stalingrad—just not all at once, especially while we were still caught up in secondary objectives.

Teberda, 3 January 1943

When I arrived at the airfield at eight in the morning, a German reconnaissance plane was just landing. On his morning rounds over Tuby, he had taken an anti-aircraft hit in the left wing, where a hole the size of a watermelon could be seen. Four fighters were then on top of him. The gunner on board put a burst of twenty rounds into his own rudder when he swung his gun into position. In the course of the firefight, a hit from a fixed cannon ripped up the right steering mechanism, and over thirty bullets drilled through the plane. Its gray paint peeled off revealing silver furrows in the metal. The fuel tank also showed leaks.

The pilot, a first lieutenant—washed-out, overtired, inhaling cigarettes—explained that the dogfight that had just taken place. The holes in the fuel tank seal off automatically with a layer of rubber. Discussion about getting out of a burning aircraft.

"Impossible over Russian territory. It amounts to the same thing whether you shoot yourself in the head when you're up there or wait until you bale out."

I then got aboard a Fieseler Storch,[38] a small liaison aircraft with room for the pilot and one passenger. As we gained altitude, the dimensions of the settlement came into focus: equilateral squares of houses surrounding garden plots. We swayed slowly over the ground in that direction. I was delighted to be able to observe birds, like the geese hurrying away in formation or the chickens flapping their wings as they ran for the cover of hedges and fences—their typical reaction in response to an actual stork. Birds of prey with the wings of sparrow hawks flew away from us; clouds of titmouse and finch shimmered above the landscape of sunflowers.

I thought of a conversation I had with my father around 1911. His subject was whether the day would come when human beings in flight above us would cause as little surprise as a flock of cranes. In those days, I had a future-oriented, romantic feeling, as if we still had the age of the dinosaurs ahead of us. That is a trait I have shed. The optics at the center of cataracts is different from the optics used to correct them. All this corresponds to our wishes, our great desires; we put all our energy into them.

From the airfield at Cherkessk we went by car up to the Kuban Valley, one of the grand and solemn plains, before reaching the highlands. Its ice green waters bore glacial floes downstream. The broad gorge was surrounded by brown, serrated peaks; those facing the valley were steep and formed white cliffs with smooth or vertically corrugated faces. These patterns alternated with those resembling organ pipes and others like beautifully folded shapes. Then came canyons with mesas of reddish-brown or pink stone in horizontal strata, so that we seemed to be driving past giants' masonry. Down below us the broad riverbed with its white, glossy pebbles.

In Chumarinsk and other villages, little wooden mosque with their crescent moons dominated the town centers. Mounted shepherds drove their sheep and cows along in front of them. Others led donkeys heavily laden with wood down from the forests. They wore the burka, the stiff shearling coat native to the people of Karachay.

The mountains gradually appeared closer and presented jagged openings that permitted glimpses of the blue-white giants of the high mountains. Near Mikoyan-Shachar, the seat of the local government rose out of nowhere. The path turns down into the Teberda Valley. Teberda, a spa town for lung ailments, has a veneer of homey comfort, of affluence of the sort one looks for in the valleys of the Harz region or in the Tyrolean Alps.

With Colonel von Le Suire, who commands a fighting unit of mountain troops, I am a known quantity in the midst of an army of one hundred thousand. He welcomed me cordially into the circle of his small staff. The towering mountains have an invigorating effect, as I have often experienced; they make the blood lighter and freer and communication more candid and comradely.

Keeping a journal: The short entries are often as dry as instant tea. Writing them down is like pouring hot water over them to release their aroma.

Teberda, 4 January 1943

Pushed farther into the Teberda Valley, as far as the field headquarters of Captain Schmidt. With his mountain troops, he is blocking two passes up there. I used the motorcycle, a vehicle for difficult climbs.

The narrow path led between stands of gigantic conifers and upward toward moss-covered boulders. A small brook trickled down it beneath the snowdrops encapsulated under domes of ice. On the right, the waters of the Teberda flowed between pale deposits of scree veined with multiple channels; then came the Amanaus, which is fed by the glaciers. I was buoyant with a sort of high-altitude intoxication.

High above in the Amanaus gorge stand the wooden buildings of a mountain climbing school as well as a sanatorium. Here Schmidt welcomed me to his headquarters, the ice giants towering above us: to the left the massif of the Dombai-Ulgen, then the craggy Karachay needle, the eastern and the western Belaya-kaya, and between them, the unusual pinnacle of the Sofrudshu. The sentries securing the passes are stationed on the mighty Amanaus glacier with its fields of green glare ice, deep fissures, and sparkling crevasses. They still have seven more hours to hike up to their huts of ice and snow. Their path leads among rockfalls, avalanches, and grim precipices. Schmidt explained to me that all the mountaineering dangers are dwarfed by those of the war. During a difficult ascent thoughts are concentrated on the enemy. A message had just reached him: Russian scouts had burrowed into position in dugouts in the snow; a firefight was under way. These dugouts are each papered with newsprint and heated by a candle; that is the only trace of comfort.

I had planned to stay up here as long as possible and to make forays high into the glacier region. I felt at home and sensed that up in these massifs one more of those great sources lived on, as Tolstoy had felt so powerfully. But as I was discussing the details of my stay with Schmidt, a radio message came from Teberda ordering immediate retreat. That can only mean that the situation in Stalingrad has deteriorated. The weather has been clear here for weeks but has suddenly become threatening. It was apparent that the warm Black Sea air was making its way across the passes in eddies and billowing swathes; wafting vapor attached itself to the mountain peaks. I glanced back from the hollow for a last look at these giants— saw their ridges, peaks, precipices. Boldest, highest thoughts, combined with all the dark terrors of power. Such places reveal a blueprint of the world.

In Teberda as well I found everything in a state of agitation. The First Tank Division was abandoning its positions; the Caucasus front is in flux. Within days positions will be abandoned that cost more blood and toil to capture than the brain can comprehend. As a result of the tumult, much will be left behind. The colonel has received the order to explode munitions and destroy supplies. The crosses are also to be removed from the graves and their traces obliterated. Otherwise his mood was philosophical. For example: "I wonder who will be pinching Anastasia's bottom a week from now."

His remark referred to one of the two serving maids who has been waiting on us at table. They were crying and said that the Russians would slit their throats, whereupon the colonel made room for them in the convoy.

TEBERDA, 5 JANUARY 1943

Back in the Teberda Valley again this morning in gentle rain. Who knows when a German's eye will ever gaze on these forests again? I'm afraid that when the war is over large sections of the planet will be hermetically sealed off from each other.

I especially wanted to take in the sight of the ancient trees once more. The fact that they are becoming extinct on this planet is the most alarming sign of all. They are not only the mightiest symbols of pristine terrestrial power but also of the ancestral spirit embedded in the wood of our cradles, beds, and coffins. In them is enshrined a sacred life that is lost to man when they are felled.

Yet here they still stood erect: mighty firs, their trunks clasped by a thick garment of branches; beeches of shimmering silver; thick-barked primeval oaks; and the gray wild pear. I said farewell to these giants like Gulliver before he goes to the Land of Lilliput, where Gargantuan proportions are the product of interpretation rather than natural growth. All this was revealed to me as in a fleeting dream like Christmas marvels glimpsed by a child through a keyhole—yet memory preserves the proportions. We need to know what the world has to offer so that we do not capitulate too easily.

Voroshilovsk, 6 January 1943

Arose early for the journey to Voroshilovsk. Thanks to the heavy snowfall, I saw little of Teberda and then of the Kuban Valley. Trifling, casual thoughts and fantasies, full of intellectual power. I attribute this to the mountain air and to honey, that powerful nectar, the old food not only of the gods but [also] of the hermit and the recluse, food I had practically lived on in recent days. If I could only always have enough of it and, in addition, white bread and red wine—then my mental wings would spread like a butterfly's.

The road was choked with retreating columns. Karachay rode among them in their black coats. They drove their cattle down from the mountain slopes or turned into side valleys. People are in a tough spot because they had welcomed the Germans as liberators. If they do not follow the retreat, they will probably have to flee into the impassable mountains in order to escape slaughter. The terrible part is the changing balance of power and the short-term nature of errors that take an ever-higher toll in blood.

Beyond Cherkessk, the road disappeared completely in the snow as it wound its way between cornstalks and dry sunflower stems. Then these signs gradually petered out too, and the driver followed a wheel track for a long time that was the only visible trail. This led us only as far as a large haystack, then made a loop around it and doubled back upon itself. No choice but to go back. A second attempt ended at a river that wound its dark course through the snow desert. Meanwhile, we were losing the daylight and the mist was rising.

We finally reached a barn where people had been threshing, and a young lad showed us the way by galloping beside us on horseback. He did not want to get in, as he apparently feared we might not let him go. Back on a deeply rutted track, we reached a slope covered in fine clay as brown and glistening as cocoa butter. We tried to push the car forward, but the wheels spun in place covering us with thick mud from head to foot. A couple of peasants working nearby came to help us and threw their backs into the job. In doing so, their broad shoulders pushed in our car windows as they lifted.

Following this, we tried to drive around the spot, with the result that the car broke through a snow-covered layer of ice into a bog hole. I was watching it sink ever deeper when a carter came by, hitched up his horse, and pulled us out of this mess with a rope. We continued to drive through the night as the snowstorm enveloped us with thousands of shining flakes whirled into the field of our headlights and then went dark, as though they had melted away. Arrived late in Voroshilovsk.

Our odyssey gave me an inkling of the power with which the steppes assault the mind. This assault suggests a contradiction felt as a dull, paralyzing anxiety, such as I have never felt at sea.

VOROSHILOVSK, 7 JANUARY 1943

Among the staff officers I found the mood more depressed than among the troops. This makes sense, because they have an overview of the situation. Cauldron battles produce a frame of mind unknown in earlier wars from our history. Inertia sets in when we are about to hit rock bottom.

That cannot be a result of the facts, no matter how terrible the prospects are of dying in frost and snow huddled together with masses of the dead and dying. It is rather the mood of people who believe that destruction is absolute.

At a high-level staff headquarters, you can hear the rustling of the net being tightened; you can observe its mesh closing almost daily. Tempers can be the object of study over weeks as panic sets in gently like placid currents of water predicting the imperceptible but approaching flood. During this phase, people isolate themselves from each other; they fall silent and become reflective as they were during puberty. But the weakest specimens provide evidence of what we can expect. They are the points of least resistance, like the little first lieutenant I found shaking in a fit of weeping when I went to his office.

The populace is also restive; goods they were hoarding appear on the market; the value of the currency rises. The peasants desire the Russian banknotes because they must stay behind; the city dwellers want the German ones because some of them will accompany the retreat. Similar things were reported by the First Tank Division, and also that some people who had set out with them along with their wives and children dropped behind by the second or third day and are now in a much more dangerous situation than before: their attempt to flee will seal their fate.

The Russians are of course trying to blow up bridges and railroads and are deploying numerous troops of saboteurs for this purpose; some infiltrate through gaps in the front, while others are parachuted in. An officer from Military Intelligence told me details about one such troop of six members, three men and three women. Two of the men were officers in the Red Army and one was a radio operator; one of the women was a radio operator, the other a scout and quartermaster; the third was a nurse. They were captured as they spent the night under the cover of a haystack. They had not been able to complete their mission to blow up bridges, because the parachute carrying the explosives had landed in the village. The women, all high school graduates, had served as soldiers in the Red Army and been assigned to a sabotage course. One day, they were told to get ready and to board an aircraft, where there were pushed out behind the German lines without being told their mission. Their equipment consisted of machine guns (even the nurse carried one), a radio, canned rations, dynamite, and a first aid kit.

A sign of humanity: During their arrest, one of the girls ran up to a Russian doctor accompanying the mayor and the German soldiers. She tried to embrace him and addressed him as Father. She then began to cry and said that he looked just like her own father.

The old nihilists of 1905 celebrate their resurrection in such people. Naturally, under different conditions. Their means, their mission, their way of living have remained the same. But nowadays the state provides the explosives.

VOROSHILOVSK, 8 JANUARY 1943

Went to the marketplace early. It was crowded with people. The situation encourages selling, since it's easier to carry money than goods. The food is now sumptuous; the men are wolfing down the supplies. In gardens, I saw soldiers smoking geese; mountains of pork were heaped upon the table. I could sense the whirlwind of terror that announced the approach of the eastern army columns.

At noon, visited the commander-in-chief, Colonel General von Kleist, whom I found anxiously studying his map. Nice to have stepped out of the hubbub of the marketplace right into the center of things. The field marshal's perspective is incredibly oversimplified but at the same time fiendishly detached. The fates of individuals vanish from sight, though they are mentally present—a combination that creates an incredibly oppressive mood.

In the anteroom, the intelligence officer handed me a telegram: my father is seriously ill. At the same time rumors are circulating that the railway to Rostov has been disrupted. I happened to meet First Lieutenant Krause, with whom I've been in contact from earlier matters, especially since the secret meeting at the Eichhof.[39] He was waiting for a plane from Berlin and offered it to me for my return. While we were discussing this, the chief of staff of the commander-in-chief sent word to me that a seat was being reserved for me in the courier aircraft scheduled to take off from Armavir tomorrow morning. A car is leaving for there in two hours.

KIEV, 9 JANUARY 1943

Had vivid thoughts of my father during the night flight. I have not seen him since 1940 when I was on leave in Leisnig after the campaign in France. I have spoken with him a few times on the phone, of course. Now in the fatigue of the early morning hour, I saw his eyes beaming in the dark sky; they were large and had a deeper, more vivid blue than ever before—the eyes that are essentially so appropriate to him. I now saw them gazing on me full of love. One day I would like to describe him like a mother possessing male intelligence—with a deeper sense of justice.

Arrival in Armavir at two o'clock, where I dozed a bit on the full mail sacks. Sleepy secretaries were sorting letters and parcels while bombs were falling on the town. In the midst of this restless slumber, the nocturnal side of the war oppressed me. Part of this is just sleeplessness from all those interminable night watches at the front or back home behind the lines.

At six o'clock took off in a green painted craft that bore the name Globetrotter and was piloted by a prince of Coburg-Gotha. Two hours later, we were flying over the frozen, green Don dotted with white ice floes. The roads were choked with columns of people streaming westward. In Rostov, we landed for a moment on an airfield where swarms of bombers were loading huge projectiles.

In Kiev I spent the night in an old hotel that now seemed very comfortable. Everything is relative. I shared my room with an officer from World War I who had come from the Stalingrad cauldron. It seems that there the airfields are under targeted bombardment. They are clogged with destroyed aircraft. Inmates of a large prison camp that used to be part of the compound at first survived by eating horseflesh, then they turned to cannibalism; finally, they died of starvation. People who escape the cauldrons are disfigured, carry scars—perhaps the stigmata of future glory.

LÖTZEN, 10 JANUARY 1943

Arrived in Lötzen around noon and immediately booked long-distance calls to Kirchhorst and Leisnig. At seven o'clock, I learned from Perpetua that my good father had died, just as I had clearly felt it. He is to be buried in Leisnig on Wednesday, so I have arrived in time, which is a great comfort.

As I have often done in recent days, I spent a long time thinking about him, about his lot in life, his character, his humanity.

IN A SLEEPING CAR, 11 JANUARY 1943

Made some purchases in Lötzen, where it was bitter cold. Departure to Berlin in the evening. Colonel Rathke, head of the department of military affairs, was on the train. Conversation about the situation in Rostov, which he considers reparable. Then, about the war in general. After the first three value judgments, one recognizes someone from the other camp and retreats behind polite clichés.

KIRCHHORST, 21 JANUARY 1943

Looking back. During the trip to Leisnig on 12 January I noticed the faces of the other travelers. They were pale, artificially bloated, the flesh a temptation for serious, debilitating illness. Most people slept, laid low by extreme exhaustion.

The German Greeting[40]—that most potent symbol of voluntary coercion or coerced volunteering. Individuals give it upon entering or leaving the train compartment, that is to say, when they are discernible as individuals. But amidst the anonymity of crowds this gesture gets no response. During a trip like this, there is ample opportunity to study the nuances that tyranny is capable of.

After paying a short visit to my siblings in Leisnig, I went straight to the cemetery where the caretaker gave me the key to the mortuary chapel. It was already dusk when I opened the gate. Far in the distance, high and solemn on a bier in an open casket, my father was laid out wearing white tie. I approached slowly and lit the candles to the right and left of his head. I gazed at his face for a long time. It seemed so unfamiliar. The lower portion particularly, the chin and lower lip, were those of someone else, someone I didn't know. When I went to his left side and stood back to view his brow and cheek, the red line of his familiar saber scar was visible. I was able to make the connection again—I saw him as I had countless times before, chatting after eating while sitting in his easy chair. Such a joy to find him thus before the earth conceals him from me. Thought: "I wonder if he is aware of this visit." I touched his arm, which had gotten so thin, his cold hand, and shed a tear upon it as if to thaw it. What is the meaning of the immense silence that surrounds the dead?

Then I returned for tea in the familiar old dining room where the conversation centered on him. He had gotten sick on the first day of Christmas and gone to bed after having spent a few days on the sofa. "Now you will just have to see how you will manage alone," he said a little while later. His health deteriorated quickly and the doctor ordered him taken to the hospital, where his condition was diagnosed as double pneumonia.

Friedrich Georg had the impression that he was focusing increasingly on himself, and not making any time to see visitors. "Take a seat" and "water" were the last words he heard him say. He saw him on Friday afternoon. During the night, Sunday, at one o'clock according to the nurse, he died. That would make it about the same time I saw his eyes appear during my journey to Armavir. When I looked back through my journals I was also struck by the discovery that precisely one year before to the hour, I had awakened in sadness because I had dreamed of his death.

He was seventy-four years old when he died, ten years older than his father and ten years younger than his mother. This again confirms my view that one of the ways to calculate the age we will probably attain, is to take the midpoint between the lifetimes of our parents—assuming that they died of natural causes.

That night I slept in his room, where he used to read in bed by the soft light or play chess. The books he had been reading during his last days were lying on the night table: Jäger's *History of the Greeks*, works about the deciphering of hieroglyphics, and periodicals about chess. I felt very close to him here and sensed a deep pain when I observed the well-ordered domesticity with its libraries, laboratories, telescopes, and apparatus. In his last days, he had set up a large electrophorus[41] with an X-ray tube in a special room in the attic. The house is our garment—an extended self that we arrange around us. When we pass away, it soon loses its form in the same way that the body does. But here everything was still fresh, as if each object had just been set aside by a human hand.

The burial service was on the following day; only family members attended, just as he had wished. We all took his hand one last time—"so cold," said my mother when she touched it.

I note that when I returned to the house I felt an almost uncontrollable exhilaration. That is a primeval human trait in the wake of mysteries from which we have become estranged.

On Saturday, I traveled to Kirchhorst for several days. On the train, we were subjected to four inspections. Once by police detectives.

KIRCHHORST, 22 JANUARY 1943

I immersed myself in those new publications by Friedrich Georg that we had talked about during our walks in Leisnig. I read the *Titanen* and the *Westwind*, where I found many pieces that were new to me, among them the "*Eisvogel*" ["Kingfisher"] and the "*Selbstbildnis*" ["Self-Portrait"]. His poems about animals are suffused with magical insight and serenity—quite different from impressionistic treatments of such creatures based on external observations. This poetry reveals a dichotomy that has long been observable in painting.

Today's mail included a letter from Feuerblume, who describes a New Year's dream in which she heard the name of a city that sounded like Todos or Tosdo. The recollection of this caused her to avoid taking a particular train to Hannover on 3 January—a train that was then wrecked. She interprets Tosdo as "*So Tod*" [thus death].

KIRCHHORST, 23 JANUARY 1943

Current reading: *Les Aventures de Lazarille de Tormes* [*The Adventures of Lazarillo de Tormes*] in the beautiful edition printed by Didot Jeaune in Paris in 1801 and illustrated by Ransonnette. The paper, printing, binding, and engravings all contribute to my enjoyment of the content.

Then read further in the *Histoires Désobligéantes* [*Offensive Stories*] by Léon Bloy. Here I found the following sentence paraphrasing a fundamental thought in the *Marmorklippen* [*The Marble Cliffs*]: "—I harbored the suspicion that this world is modeled on the perfidious prototype of the charnel house."

This also implies a challenge.

BERLIN, 24 JANUARY 1943

I've been in Berlin since yesterday for a short visit, where I have again been staying with Carl Schmitt. Today, I participated in the traditional wreath laying ceremony of the Knights of the Order *Pour le Mérite* at the monument to Frederick the Great. I had the distinct feeling that this time was to be the last. That splendid utterance of Murat: "I wear medals so that people will shoot at me." I have only to reverse this sentiment in order to comprehend my own situation. They are still talismans.

Heavy damage in Dahlem.[42] The last air raid not only crushed whole blocks of buildings but also lifted the roofs off of entire districts and blew in thousands of windows. Air pressure often acts in strange ways. For example, it penetrated a neighboring house by getting under a balcony door without damaging it, but once inside the room, tore a piano stool in half.

Walk through the park at night. Conversation about the death of Albrecht Erich Günter, and then about dreams. In a dream, Carl Schmitt was involved in a conversation about conditions he finds difficult to accept. To others who marveled at his expertise or even doubted it, he answered: "Don't you know that I am Don Capisco?"

A marvelous expression to capture danger and adventure and absurdity all at once—and one that includes subtle insight.

The day before yesterday Tripoli was evacuated.

KIRCHHORST, 9 FEBRUARY 1943

Back in Kirchhorst, where I'll be on leave until 18 February. I am falling behind in my journal entries. I have been bothered for weeks by a slight migraine, the likes of which I have hardly ever known. This accompanies far-reaching ruminations that the mind is not free of—even when life is most solitary. The effects of these are felt not only in the basic elements of life but even in one's moral core. Aside from moments when the spells are bad, the pain is conducive to a feeling of sympathy.

Today I walked the long circuit through Stelle, Moormühle, Schillerslage, Oldhorst, and Neuwarmbüchen. Even at a quick march this takes three hours.

To the right in the fields stands the shed with writing painted on one side that reads: Burgdorf Asparagus Nurseries. The bright lettering is as readable in the distance as a newspaper headline, making the building itself almost disappear. Such advertising can change arbitrarily until it gets obliterated by wind and weather and the honest old shed in the background is visible again—like an obedient donkey that bore the letters on its back. This is how true forms survive over the course of time.

Thoughts about the link between intoxication and productivity. Although they are mutually exclusive in combination, they correlate with one another like discovery and description, like exploration and geography. In a state of inebriation or euphoria, the mind advances more adventurously and more spontaneously. It experiences things in the realm of infinity. There can be no poetry without such experience.

Incidentally, the jolt that accompanies the conception of poetic works is not to be confused with intoxication—it is like the transposition of molecules just before crystallization. Love materializes in the same way—through vibrations as we become attuned to a higher chord.

The sight of Moormühle made me think of Friedrich Georg and the conversation we had here in 1939 about the "illusions of technology."[43] Since this book evokes the spirit of silence, it was fated to remain unpublished at the time. It was incompatible with events.

Then discussed Schopenhauer and his metaphysics of sexual love. It's a good thing that he finds the magnet of the erotic encounter in the resulting child and not in the individuals themselves. But the child is essentially only a symbol of the higher unity consummated here. In this sense, the fulfillment is the more significant, more direct testimony, expression. Plato unveils the mysteries better in his *Symposium*. Biology obfuscates Schopenhauer's work. Villiers de L'Isle-Adam apprehends the timeless, colorless core of the flame of love more deeply. Weininger's admiration for Axel is understandable.[44]

Finally, some remarks about certain facets of my life in connection with the entries that I recorded about my good father. Among them there is much that I consider taboo; I have not explained the obscure and murky passages. As Rousseau remarked, such things do not require honesty. Honest confession is nothing to be scorned, but in reality, it is more important that the author achieve liberating energy in response to his ephemeral creation. He will succeed at this—whether as poet or thinker—to the same extent that he transcends his individuality.

When coming this way again, one might cross the moor from Schillerslage to Neuwarmbüchen.

KIRCHHORST, 10 FEBRUARY 1943

Had breakfast with stout Hanne [Wickenberg] and Perpetua. Then read Rimbaud whose "Bateau Ivre" represents a last beacon of hope, not only for the literature of the nineteenth century but also for Copernican literature. After this endpoint, all literature must be grounded in a new cosmology, whether it is the product of physics or not. According to such terms the terrifying Isidore Ducasse only appears contemporary; he is modern. The tropical fevers have run their course; the path now leads to the Polar Seas.

Then I worked in the collection, especially with the order of the genus *Galerucca* [beetle]. Specimens can be found in the marshy ground of our terrain. Related species turn up mostly in similar habitats or, to use the language of the hunter, similar territory. Yet there are exceptions, as in the case of the *Scymnus* beetle, where a small group lives on aphids instead of sap. The theories about this focus either on environment or on characteristics, for these are the essential features that drive the struggle for life. Both explanations seem to be one-sided, learned arguments that are futile. All these theories illuminate only layers of reality. We need to lay them all on top of one another like blueprints and peer through them at the colorful map of nature. Of course, we also need new eyes to do this. I described the process in my *Sizilischer Brief [Sicilian Letter]*.[45]

Went to the barber in the nearby county town. He repeated the story of the wicked nature of the Russians who devour the dogs' food themselves, and he had some new thoughts on the subject as well. He said that they shouldn't be given a single seed to plant because they would eat these up right away—they even gobble up raw asparagus. Generally speaking, nothing edible is sacred to them, as he put it. Despite all this, this barber is a good-natured man.

KIRCHHORST, 13 FEBRUARY 1943

Current reading: *Dead Souls* by Gogol after a long hiatus. This novel would be even more powerful without all the musings and the all-too-frequent intrusions of authorial consciousness to remind us that he is painting genre pictures.

Due to the heavy rainstorms, I spent a long time in bed this morning, even having my breakfast there. While doing so, I had thoughts about the protective strategies of plant eaters that are so conspicuous in many classes of the animal kingdom. The oversized and plantlike nature of these defenses can reach branch-like proportions, as in the case of stags and many insects that live on wood. Even the shedding of antlers has a vegetable quality to it. Nothing similar is found among predatory animals. The defensive aspect of these protuberances is probably just a secondary characteristic, a conclusion I draw from the fact that they belong mostly to an animal's sexual characteristics and are produced in species that never use them defensively, such as in many beetles found in dung or others in wood or dry rot. The oversized excrescences are part of their physical structure and form not only the jaws but other parts of the chitinous exoskeleton as well. You get the feeling that these herbivores like to make themselves look more terrifying than they are.

Our kind of life, our essence, is our arsenal; from it we gather our weapons when we need them. This thought stands in significant contrast to the formulaic model of the struggle for life. Different premises apply here, such as "when God appoints a man to an office, He also gives him the wits for it."[46]

There are predators with all the attributes and characteristics of herbivores, such as whales that graze for their prey.

KIRCHHORST, 14 FEBRUARY 1943

Heavy rainstorms. I brought a plum branch in from the garden to force. It is in full bloom indoors. The bare wood is covered with a profusion of small white stars.

Migraine worsening, as if under heavy clouds.

KIRCHHORST, 15 FEBRUARY 1943

Yesterday the Russians captured Rostov. In the mail there was a letter from Edmond's sister [Fritzi], who is contemplating her escape from Poland. We offered her and her children refuge here.

Friedrich Georg writes from Überlingen, "It may be that we are reaching the point when our opponents will have to do the thinking for us. And if they don't do so out of revenge—they will cast us into a black hole."

KIRCHHORST, 17 FEBRUARY 1943

We have beautiful sunshine today after days of stormy, rainy weather. This morning among the gooseberry bushes, I picked fresh parsley—green, mossy, and encrusted in frozen dew.

The Goncourts wrote about Daumier that his descriptions of the middle class had reached a degree of reality bordering on the fantastic. That can be seen wherever realism reaches a climax. The final brushstrokes then add unreal touches.

Yesterday the Russians captured Kharkov. We are expecting Fritzi Schultz, who is fleeing from Alexandrov with her children. Her ancestors settled there over a hundred years ago. Before my departure, I am thinking about how to preserve a portion of my manuscripts. In doing so, I must take into account the possibility of the house being ransacked and plundered, and of protecting them from aerial bombardment and fire. Considering how difficult it is to find suitable hiding places for things, it is quite astonishing how much old paper has come down to us over time.

3

SECOND PARIS JOURNAL

Returned to Paris yesterday afternoon. Perpetua took me to the train and waved for a long time as it pulled out of the station.

On the train, conversation with two captains who offered the opinion that this year Kniébolo was going to attack using new methods, probably gas. They did not exactly seem to condone this, but restricted themselves to that moral passivity typical of modern man. In such cases, arguments relating to technology are the most forceful. For example: given our inferiority in the air, any such undertaking equals suicide.

If Kniébolo is planning anything of the sort, then domestic political concerns are going to be crucial as they are for all his ideas. Propaganda takes precedence over everything else. In this case, it would be important to him to drive a wedge between nations that cannot even be reconciled by the best of intentions. In this he is consistent with his own genius, relying on dissension, partisanship, and hatred. We have come to know the tribunes.[1]

A brief digression here: When people with minds like this hear reports from the other side about such crimes, a trace of demonic joy rather than horror flickers across their faces. The defamation of one's enemy is a cult among the courtiers in the realm of darkness.

After having seen cities like Rostov, Paris holds a new and incomparable glory for me, despite the fact that scarcity has become more widespread—with the exception of books. I celebrated my return to them by purchasing a beautiful monograph on Turner. It contains an account of his remarkable biography, previously unfamiliar to me. Fate seldom beckons so powerfully. In his last years, he stopped painting and turned to drink. There will always be artists who outlive their calling; this is particularly true in cases where talent appears early. Ultimately, they resemble retired civil servants following their own inclinations the way Rimbaud turned to earning money and Turner to drink.

PARIS, 21 FEBRUARY 1943

Went to the Tour d'Argent for lunch with Heller and Kuhn, the painter. We talked about the how books and paintings exert influence even when unobserved. "*Doch im Innern ist getan.*" [In our hearts this is achieved.][2] This thought will be incomprehensible to contemporaries who exalt communication and publication, meaning that they have replaced spiritual connections with technology. Come to that, does it matter whether the prayers of a monk are ever heard by those for whom he is praying? Wieland still knew this. He told Karamsin that he could have written his works on a lonely island with the same zeal, in the certainty that the Muses would be listening to them.

Then we went to Le Meurice, where Kuhn (who is serving as a corporal for the Commandant), showed us pictures. I especially liked a resplendent dove whose rosy and dark palette intermingled with that of the city in the background. It was called Twilight in the City. We discussed this on our way home and also talked about the atmosphere of twilight and about the influence it exerts. Dusk transforms individuals into figures, removes personal details from people, and turns them into general impressions—a man, a woman, or simply a human being. In this way, the light itself resembles the artist, in whom much twilight and darkness must dwell in order for him to perceive figures.

At this moment, in the evening, I am thumbing through an issue of *Verve* from 1939, where I find excerpts by Pierre Reverdy, an author I do not know. I jot down the following: "I wear a protective suit of armor forged completely of errors."

"*Être ému, c'est respirer avec son coeur.*" [To be moved is to breathe with one's heart.]

"His arrow is poisoned; he has dipped it into his own wound."

On the walls of the buildings of Paris, I now frequently see the year "1918 "scrawled in chalk. Also "Stalingrad."[3]

Who knows whether or not they will be defeated along with us?

PARIS, 23 FEBRUARY 1943

In the morning, I looked at a portfolio of pictures taken by the propaganda branch of our troops blowing up the harbor area in Marseille. This was one more destruction of a place that was out of the ordinary and one I had grown to love.

During the midday break, I always permit myself a visual treat. Today, for example, I browsed in my Turner edition; his maritime views, with their shades of green, blue, and gray, convey icy chill. Their reflections lend them a feeling of depth.

Then went to the little cemetery near the Trocadéro, where I again looked at the mortuary chapel of Marie Bashkirtseff, a place where you sense the uncanny presence of the deceased. There were already many types of plants in bloom, such as wallflower and colorful mosses.

In the bookshop on Place Victor-Hugo, I found another series of works by Léon Bloy, whom I wish to study more thoroughly. Every major catastrophe has an effect on the supply of books and casts legions of them into oblivion. Only after the earthquake, do we see what ground the author relied on in times of safety.

I took a short walk in the evening. The fog was denser than I had ever seen it—so thick that the rays of light that penetrated the darkness through cracks looked as solid as beams, so that I was almost afraid I was going to bump against them. I also met a lot of people who were trying to find their way to the Étoile and was unable to give them directions—but we had been standing right there the whole time.

PARIS, 24 FEBRUARY 1943

The true measure of our worth is other people's growth in response to the power of our love. Through this, we experience our own value and the meaning of the terrifying thought: "thou art weighed in the balance and found wanting." This is most obvious when we fail.

There is a kind of dying that is worse than death; it happens when a beloved person obliterates the image of us that lived inside him. We are extinguished in that person. This can occur because of dark emanations that we convey. The blossoms close quietly before our eyes.

PARIS, 25 FEBRUARY 1943

Sleepless night punctuated by moments of waking dreams—first there was a nightmare in which grass was being mowed; then scenes like those in a marionette theater. There were also melodies that reached a crescendo in threatening bolts.

According to the rules of an arcane moral aesthetic, it is more dignified to fall on your face than your back.

PARIS, 28 FEBRUARY 1943

Gave a lecture about my mission. In the meantime Stalingrad has fallen. This has made our predicament more acute. If, according to Clausewitz, war is the continuation of politics by other means, this implies that the more absolute the methods used to wage war, the less politics can influence it. There is no negotiation in battle; no one has a free hand, and no one has the energy for it. In this sense, the war in the East has absolutely reached a magnitude that Clausewitz could never have imagined, even after the experiences of 1812. It is a war of states, peoples, citizens, and religions, with brutal escalation. In the West, we still have a free hand for a little while. This is one of the advantages of the two-front war: it defines the fate of the center with its classic pattern of threat. Apparently, 1763[4] is the ray of hope for those in power. At night they send our columns to paint that date on the walls and cross out 1918 and Stalingrad. But the miracle of miracles lay in the fact that "Der Alte Fritz" ["Old Fritz"][5] enjoyed the sympathy of the world. Not so Kniébolo, who is seen as the enemy of the world, and it would not matter whether one of his three great adversaries were to die—the war would still be prolonged. Wishful thinking focuses less on the idea that one of them could extend the hand of peace, than on the hope that he will capitulate. Thus we are becoming progressively icier, more rigid; we cannot thaw by ourselves.

Imported Cuban cigars in glass tubes stood on the table. In Lisbon, these are traded for the French cognac that high-ranking staff members on the other side hate to part with—but at least it's a form of communication. My duties have been increased to include oversight of postal censorship in the occupied territory— a ludicrous yet delicate business in every conceivable way.

Paris, 1 March 1943

In the evening, I pondered the word *Schwärmen*.[6] This could be a chapter title in a book about the natural history of the human race. Three things constitute *Schwärmen*: heightened vibrancy of life, communal gathering, and recurrence.

The vibrancy of life, or vibration as seen in a swarm of midges, is collective energy; it unites the individual with its species. Their communal gathering serves its purposes in the forms of wedding, harvest, hiking, and games.

In earlier times, the rhythm of *Schwärmen* was surely primeval, determined by the influence of the moon and the sun upon the earth and its vegetation. When we sit beneath large trees in full bloom and filled with the buzzing of bees, we receive the wonderful sensation of what *Schwärmen* means. Times of day, such as twilight and moments when electrically charged air precedes the storm can be important here as well. These natural-cosmic signs are the substrate beneath ever-changing historical periods—they remain as the facts of the ceremonies whose significance seems to change with rituals and cultures. What changes, however, is only the devotional portion, while the primeval aspect remains unaltered. Hence, the pagan side to every Christian festival.

Incidentally, the designation *Schwarmgeister*[7] is well chosen to characterize an aberration, when at its core, there lies a confusion between the devotional and primeval aspects of the rituals.

Paris, 3 March 1943

Midday on the banks of the Seine with Charmille. We strolled down along the quay, from the Place de l'Alma to the Viaduc de Passy and sat down there on a wooden railing watching the water flow by. Milk thistle, with its seven golden crowns, was already blooming in a crevasse of a wall; in one of these blossoms, there sat a large metallic-green fly. Once again, I noticed many examples of ammonites, the small land snail, in the cut stone of the breastwork along the riverbank.

PARIS, 4 MARCH 1943

Heller and I visited Florence Gould for breakfast; she has recently moved into an apartment on Avenue de Malakoff. There we also met Jouhandeau, Marie-Louise Bousquet, and the painter Bérard.

Conversation in front of a vitrine filled with Egyptian artifacts from Rosetta. Our hostess showed us ancient unguent jars and tear vials from classical graves. From these, she playfully scratched off the thin dark purplish-blue and mother-of-pearl layer—the accumulation of millennia—letting the iridescent dust swirl in the light. She even gave some of them away. I could not turn down the gift of a beautiful pale gray scarab with an extensive inscription on its base. She then brought out books and manuscripts that had been bound by Gruel. One of the volumes of old illustrations was missing three pages, torn out so that she could give them to a visitor who had admired them.

While we ate, I picked up details about Reverdy, whom I had mentioned because both Bérard and Madame Bousquet are friends of his. One mind can suggest and reveal itself through a single epigram.

Had a conversation with Jouhandeau about his work methods. Hércule had sent me his *Chroniques Maritales* [*Marital Chronicles*] years ago. He rises at four in the morning after barely six hours of sleep and then sits over his manuscripts until eight. Then he goes to the Lycée where he teaches. Those quiet morning hours that he spends with a hot water bottle on his knees are the most enjoyable for him. Then we talked about sentence construction, punctuation, and especially the semicolon—something he couldn't do without but considers a necessary alternative to the period in cases where the phrasing continues on logically. About Léon Bloy: Jouhandeau heard details of Bloy's life from Rictus that were new to me. Bloy is not yet a classic writer, but some day he will be. It always takes a while for literary works to slough off their contemporary masks. But they must also pass through their own purgatorial fires before they outlast their critics.

PARIS, 5 MARCH 1943

Went to the Trocadéro during the noonday break to admire the crocuses covering the grassy banks in clusters of blue, white, and gold. The colors sparkle like jewels that shine from their slender florets—these are the first and purest lights in the annual blossom cycle.

Today finished reading Léon Bloy, *Quatre Ans de Captivité à Cochons-sur-Marne* [*Four Years in Captivity at Cochons-sur Marne*], including his journals from 1900 through 1904. This time, I particularly noticed how utterly untouched the author is by the illusions of technology. He lives as an antimodern hermit in the midst of the throbbing crowds animated by the excitement of the great World Exposition of 1900. He sees automobiles looming as instruments of death. He generally associates technology with impending catastrophes and thus sees the methods of rapid transport like motorcars and locomotives as inventions of minds bent on escape. It could soon be important to reach other continents quickly. On 15 March 1904, he uses the underground for the first time. In its catacombs, he grudgingly admits a certain subterranean, albeit demonic, beauty. The whole system stimulates in him the impression that the end of idyllic springs and forests, of sunrises and sunsets, has arrived—the general impression of the death of the human soul.

The inscription from a sundial is appropriate for this attitude that awaits judgment: "It is later than you think."

PARIS, 6 MARCH 1943

Visited Poupet in the afternoon on Rue Garancière. His top floor lodgings are stuffed with books and paintings. There I met the novelist Mégret, with whom I had corresponded during peacetime. The Doctoresse was there as well. May such islands of serenity long endure.

Since the beginning of the year, I have been bothered by a mild migraine. Nonetheless, since January, I have been filled with a powerful trust in a turn for the better. In times of weakness and melancholy, we forget that ultimately all will be well.

A word to men. Our position with respect to two different women can resemble that of the judge pronouncing a Solomonic verdict, yet we are also the child. We deliver ourselves into the custody of the one who does not want to cut us in half.

PARIS, 9 MARCH 1943

In the afternoon went to a showing of the old Surrealist film, *Le Sang d'un Poète* [*Blood of a Poet*]; Cocteau had sent me a ticket. Certain scenes reminded me of my plan for the house, in the way it presented glimpses through the keyholes of a series of hotel rooms, but only in its superficial structure. In one of them, we see the execution by firing squad of Maximilian of Mexico, which is then repeated in two more versions; in another, we see a young girl being taught how to fly under threat of corporal punishment. The film shows the universe as a beehive of secret cells where the disconnected progression of scenes of a life condemned to manic rigidity is playing. The world as a rationally constructed insane asylum.

It is appropriate to this genre that the Surrealists discovered Lautréamont and Emily Brontë, as is their curious preference for Kleist, whose *Käthchen von Heilbronn* seems to be the only work of his they know to the exclusion of his *Marionettentheater* [*On the Puppet Theater*],[8] the work in which he conceived his dangerous formula. They never noticed others such as Klinger, Lichtenberg, Büchner, or even Hoffmann. When we look beneath the surface, we have to ask ourselves why the Marquis de Sade is not the grand master of this order.

PARIS, 10 MARCH 1943

Visited Baumgart in the evening on Rue Pierre Charron for our usual chess game. While playing this game, you might not glimpse the absolute superiority of a person's mind, but you do encounter a special form of it. A kind of logical pressure is revealed, as well as the muted reaction of the other player. This gives us an idea of how simpletons must suffer.

On my way home I was running fast, as was my habit, and in the dark I had a painful collision with one of the barriers in front of our office buildings that have been erected to prevent attacks. As long as these things happen to us, we are not completely rational. Such harm comes from inside us. Things that injure us this way surge up as if from the depths of our reflected selves.

"Secret cemeteries"—a concept of modern coinage. Corpses are hidden from adversaries so that they cannot be exhumed and photographed. Such activities among the *lemures* are evidence of an incredible increase in wickedness.

PARIS, 11 MARCH 1943
Visited Florence Gould for lunch. There, Marie-Louise Bousquet described her visit to Valentiner: "With a regiment of young men like him, the Germans could have captured France without a single cannon shot."

Florence then recounted her activity as an operating room nurse in Limoges: "I found it much more bearable to see a leg amputated than a hand."

Then on marriage: "I can live perfectly well within marriage; this is obvious because I have been happily married twice. I would just make an exception in the case of Jouhandeau because he loves appalling women."

Jouhandeau: "But I'm not in favor of tantrums measured out in tiny doses."

PARIS, 12 MARCH 1943
Current reading: *Contes Magiques* [*Magical Stories*] by P'Ou Soung-Lin. One of them has a nice image: a man of letters who feels compelled to go chop wood in distant forests wears himself out to the point where he gets "blisters like silkworm cocoons on his hands and feet."

In one of these tales, we read of a concoction that reveals whether one is dealing with a female demon. We are supposed to take the creature whose humanity is in doubt and place it in the sunlight to see whether part of its shadow is missing.

The importance of this becomes clear in an extremely vicious trick that one of these sorceresses plays on a young Chinese man. She succeeds in beguiling him in a garden so that he embraces her, yet at the same time he falls to the ground with a terrible cry of pain. It is revealed that he has thrown his arms around a huge log with a hole bored into it where there lurks a poisonous scorpion with a sting in its tail.

A word about the jokes that go around the table in the Raphael. A couple are quite witty, for example: "*Die Butterquota wird steigen, wenn die Führerbilder entrahmt werden.*"[9]

Perhaps some people have kept journals of the jokes that have emerged during all these years. That would be worthwhile because their chronology is revealing.

There is also an act of stylistic discourtesy that comes to light in phrases like "*Nichts weniger als*" [nothing less than] or "*ne pas ignorer*" [do not ignore]. They are like snarls woven into the weft of prose and left up to the reader to disentangle. Toxic little fish berries of irony.[10]

PARIS, 14 MARCH 1943

In the afternoon I visited Marcel Jouhandeau, who lives in a little house on Rue du Commandant Marchand. It is one of tiny nooks in Paris that I've grown so fond of over the years. We sat together in his diminutive garden with his wife and Marie Laurencin. Although the garden is barely wider than a hand towel, it produces masses of flowers. The woman reminds me of those masks one comes upon in old wine-producing villages.[11] They fascinate us less by their facial expressions than by the rigidity that these wooden and brightly painted faces project.

We took a tour through the apartment consisting of one room on each of three floors (except for its little kitchen). Downstairs there is a small salon; in the middle, the bedroom; and on the top floor, almost like the observatory in a planetarium, a library that has been set up as a living space.

The walls of the bedroom are painted black and decorated with gold ornamentation to complement the scarlet lacquered Chinese furniture. The sight of these silent chambers was oppressive, yet Jouhandeau enjoys spending time and working here in the early hours when his wife is asleep. It was lovely to hear him tell how the birds gradually awaken and the way their songs echo and answer each other.

Heller joined us later, and we went to sit in the library. Jouhandeau showed us his manuscripts—he gave me one as a present—as well as his books on medicinal herbs, and his collections of photographs. One folder of images of his wife also contained nude photographs of her from her days as a dancer. Yet that did not surprise me because I knew from his books that, in the summertime especially, she liked to go about the apartment unclothed. And in this state, she dealt with tradesmen, workmen, or the gasman.

Conversations. One concerned Madame Jouhandeau's grandfather, a postman who worked in his vineyard at four in the morning before delivering the mail. "Working in this vineyard was his prayer." He considered wine the universal medicine and even administered it to children when they were ill.

We then talked about snakes because a friend of theirs once brought a dozen to the house. The creatures dispersed throughout the apartment and would turn up months later under the carpets. One of them had the habit of winding its way up the base of a standing lamp in the evening; it then coiled itself around the middle of the lampshade, the warmest spot.

Once again my impression of the Parisian streets, houses, buildings, and dwellings was confirmed: they are the archives of a substance interwoven by ancient life, filled to the brim with bits of evidence with all sorts of memories.

Sickbed visit to Florence in the evening. She injured her foot in Céline's house. She said that, despite his substantial income, this author always suffers from penury because he donates everything to the streetwalkers who come to him when they are sick.

If all buildings were to be destroyed, language would remain intact as an enchanted castle with towers and turrets and ancient vaults and passageways that nobody will ever completely explore. There in the shafts, oubliettes, and caverns we will be able to tarry and abandon ourselves to this world.

Finished reading the *Contes Magiques*. I took great pleasure in this sentence from the book: "Here on earth only human beings of exalted spirit are capable of great love, because they alone do not sacrifice the idea to external stimuli."

PARIS, 17 MARCH 1943

Concerning my text "The Worker."[12] The description is precise, yet it resembles a finely etched medal lacking a reverse side. A second section would have to describe the subordination of those dynamic principles I described as a static sequence of greater status. When the house has been furnished, the mechanics and the electricians leave. But who will be the head of the house?

Who knows whether I'm ever going to find the time to work on this while I'm here, yet Friedrich Georg was able to make significant progress in this area with his *Illusionen der Technik* [*Illusions of Technology*]. This shows that we are truly brothers, always united in spirit.

Blood and spirit. The connection between the two has often been claimed, insofar as blood corpuscles and serum also show a spiritual correlation. Here we must differentiate between material and spiritual layers—a dual game of the worlds of images and thoughts. Yet in life both are closely allied, and only rarely are they separate from each other. Images are carried off by the torrent of thought.

Correspondingly, we can differentiate between a prose that is like serum and one that is like corpuscles. There are grades of embellishment through images ending with Hamann's hieroglyphic style. There are also curious interpenetrations, as in the case of Lichtenberg. Here we are dealing with an imagistic style refracted by the intellect—a kind of mortification. To stay with the analogy, you could say that the two elements have separated from one another and then been artificially recombined. Irony must always be preceded by such a rupture.

PARIS, 20 MARCH 1943

Had a conversation about executions with the president[13] at midday. In his role as chief prosecutor, he has seen a great number of these. Regarding types of executioners: For the most part, horse butchers apply for the profession. Those among them who still use the axe show a certain artistic pride in comparison with guillotine operators—theirs is the consciousness of custom handwork.

At the first execution under Kniébolo: The executioner, who had taken off his tailcoat for the beheading, gave his report in his shirtsleeves, top hat askew upon his head, carrying in his left hand the axe dripping with blood. Raising his right arm for the German salute,[14] he said, "Execution accomplished."

The neuroanatomists, who want to embalm the skull and its contents when it is still as fresh as possible, lie in wait for the blow like vultures. Once at the execution of a man who had strung himself up in his cell, but had been cut down while still alive, they were visible in droves at the foot of the scaffold. It is claimed that precisely after this kind of suicide attempt, a certain kind of mental illness sets in later in life, and that this inclination shows up early in changes to the brain.

In the afternoon visited a church in Saint-Gervais, one I had never seen before. The narrow streets that encircle it preserve a bit of the Middle Ages. The irreplaceable quality of such buildings: with each one, part of the root system is destroyed. Visited the chapel of Saint Philomela, a saint I had not heard of before. There I saw a collection of hearts from which flames erupted as if from little round flasks; some were copper, others bronze, a few were gold. This seemed to be a good place to ponder the turn of events of the year that had begun in the Caucasus.

On 29 March, 1918, a projectile from the German shelling of Paris[15] penetrated the vault of this church, killing numerous worshippers assembled here for a Good Friday service. A special chapel is dedicated to their memory with windows showing a speech banner bearing the inscription, *"Hodie mecum eritis in paradiso"* [Today you shall be with me in paradise].

Afterward I went to the quais to look at books. This is always a particularly satisfying hour, an oasis in time. There I purchased *Le Procès du Sr. Édouard Coleman, Gentilhomme, pour avoir conspirer la Mort du Roy de la Grande Bretagne* [*The Trial of Sir Edward Coleman, Gentleman, Who Conspired to Kill the King of Great Britain*] (Hamburg, 1679).

I heard from Florence that Jouhandeau had said after my visit to him that I was *"difficile à developper"* [difficult to draw out]. That assessment could come from a photographer of the psyche.

MOISSON, 21 MARCH 1943

Departure to Moisson, where I have been ordered to take a training course. From the railroad station in Bonnières, we marched along the Seine valley, and on our left on the far side, saw a towering chain of chalk cliffs. In front of them stood the fortress and chateau of La Roche-Guyon and also a solitary belltower built over the vault of the cave church of Haute-Isle.

I am living under the roof of an old priest named Le Zaïre, who spent his life as a Jesuit building churches in China and has devoted the rest of his days to this undesirable parish on poor soil. His looks are pleasant in a childlike way, even though he's blind in one eye. I conversed with him about topography and found him to be of the opinion that it is not worthwhile to travel far, since we always encounter the same formations wherever we go—just a few different patterns that are the basis for everything.

This opinion comes from one who has insulated himself, someone who loves life on the other side of the prism to the point where he can say that it isn't worth looking at the spectrum because its frequencies are already contained in sunlight. Yet you have to respond that the frequencies also give human eyes the ability to see colors—in itself a precious gift.

The discussion reminded me of one of my early doubts: whether we lose a pleasure when we retreat into our unique self—a pleasure that only time and variety can provide. And I wondered whether or not this concealed the very reason for our existence, namely that God requires individuation. I often had this feeling when observing insects and sea creatures and all of life's astonishing miracles. The pain is great at the thought that one day we take our leave of all this.

By contrast, it must be said that when we revert, we shall regain organs that we do not know about, although they are located and prefigured within us, such as the lungs of the child that the mother carries in her womb. Our physical eyes will wither just like our umbilical cords; we shall be equipped with new vision. And just as we see colors *here* in refraction, *there* we see their essence with greater enjoyment in the undivided light.

Had a conversation this evening about the East and also about cannibalism. It has been claimed that people have been observed enjoying testicles. This is supposedly not explained by hunger alone. Captured partisans have apparently been found to carry these among their rations to trade for things like cigarettes.

When it comes to such bestial—or even demonic—traits from our basest motivations, I always think of Baader and his theory. Purely economic doctrines must necessarily lead to cannibalism.

MOISSON, 23 MARCH 1943

New pleasures I have experienced here: the sight of cherry blossoms as they produce a miraculous awakening from their dormancy—like a butterfly spreading its wings as it creeps out of its dark chrysalis. This new glory heightens the barren soil of the fields and the gray walls of the houses: they are animated by a delicate chromatic veil. This pink blossom is more frugal than the white, but brings more blossoms when they bud on the bare branch, making a deeper impression upon one's mood. The gentle curtain signifies that the year has begun its magic show.

Then to the morning fire on the hearth. In the cold room the night before, I stacked up the pile of wood consisting of dry vines and oak bark and then I set these alight in the morning a half hour before getting out of bed. The sight of the open fire giving warmth and light is a cheerful beginning to the day's activities.

MOISSON, 26 MARCH 1943

Had field duty in the morning on the dry heath. It was covered with pale gray and green lichen, with a sparse growth of birch and conifer. Once again we confront things we have lived through, and we overcome them. It is a spiral: if these experiences are not meaningless, they become the material for higher conquests. This is how World Wars I and II strike me. It is said that in death the chronicle of our life will pass before our eyes. Then coincidence will be sanctified by necessity. A more exalted seal will leave its stamp upon it once the sealing wax has melted in the pain.

Incredibly hot today on this heath with its stands of conifers. In the light of noon, a creature whirred past me in the air that I did not recognize: It moved its glassy wings in a blaze of pale pink and opal light and trailed two long, beautifully curved horns behind it like trains or pennants. Then I realized that it was the male long-horned beetle I was seeing in flight for the first time. Such lightning-fast impressions hold immense happiness, and we sense the secret workings of nature. The insect appears in its authentic guise, in its magical dances, and in the costume given it by nature. This is one of the most intense pleasures that consciousness can grant us: We penetrate the depths of life's dream and coexist with its creatures. It is as if a small spark ignited in us the intense and uncomplicated desire that infuses them.

In the afternoon, I took a second excursion to Haute-Isle and La Roche-Guyon with Münchhausen and Baumgart. This landscape—with its steep and frequently hollowed-out chalk cliffs that follow the river's course like organ pipes towering above it—contains an element that makes us feel it has been settled by human beings since the dawn of time. The chronology is evident in La Roche-Guyon. Here in the white ivy-covered cliffs, you see the dark entrances to deep, branching caverns. Some of these still serve as storehouses and stables. Close by them come the bulky fortifications from the Norman period, and finally in the foreground, there stands the proud chateau with its towers built over the course of gentler centuries. Yet beneath all this lie the deep cellars where the spirit of antiquity hovers; the caves with their bands of flint are still preserved, perhaps containing treasures with gold and weapons, along with bodies of the slain and giant ancestors that may lie with dragons in many a secret, collapsed corridor. You can even sense this magical presence out in the open air.

Paris, 27 March 1943

Return journey to Paris in the evening after having sat by the fire in the morning making various entries in my journal. Piles of birthday mail were already awaiting me at the Raphael. I first read the letters from acquaintances and from my readership, then those from intimate friends, and finally those from closest family members, particularly Perpetua and Friedrich Georg.

Perpetua describes her dreams. She cast a net in order to catch a fish, but instead she tugged at it with great effort and finally pulled up an anchor with these words incised on it: "Persian Divan 12.4.98, Rimbaud to his last friends." She scrubbed off the patina and realized that the anchor was made of pure gold.

We are allowed to assign rank to our nearest and dearest. Our position on firm ground, at the right place, becomes evident. Likewise, the faithlessness of our pupils, friends, and lovers reproaches us. Their suicides even more so. That is evidence of shaky foundations. When misfortune befalls us, as it did Socrates, one last symposium must still be possible.

Paris, 28 March 1943

At Valentiner's. He brought me a letter from Berlin from Carl Schmitt containing a dream image that he had jotted down for me in the early morning hours.

He also included a quotation from Oetinger's *Das Geheimnis von Salz* [*The Secret of Salt* (1770)]: "Have the salt of peace within you, or you shall be cured with salt of another kind."

That reminded me of an image of freezing and thawing.

PARIS, 29 MARCH 1943

Because the clocks were turned forward one hour during the night, I vaulted into a new year of life in a single leap. Waking up from a dream, I scribbled something down on a piece of paper that I found when I got up:

Evas Plazenta. Der Mad(t) reporen-Stock.

[Eve's placenta . . .][16]

The insight, if I remember correctly, was something like this: The physical umbilical cord is severed, but the metaphysical one remains intact. This context gives rise to a second, invisible family tree deep in the flow of life. We are forever united through its veins and participate in a communion with every person who ever lived, with all generations, and hosts of dead souls. We are interwoven with them by an aura that returns in dream imagery. We know more about each other than anyone realizes.

We can multiply by two different means—by budding or by copulation. In the second sense, it is the father who begets us; in the first, we descend solely from our mothers, with whom we have a permanent connection. In this sense, there is but one single birth- and death-day for the whole human race.

Of course, the mystery also has a paternal pole, in that a spiritual act lies at the heart of every insemination, and this association is expressed most purely in the pro-creation of the absolute human being. Thus the human being corresponds not only to the masculine but also to the feminine aspect of its origins, to its greatest potential.

Incidentally, this dual origin can be intuited from the parables. These may be divided into those where the material aspect predominate, and others where the spiritual origin predominates: Humans speak as here lilies, as mustard seeds, and grains of wheat. They also speak as the heirs of heaven and of the Son of Man.

Speidel telephoned me from Kharkov at nine o'clock and from that immense distance was the first to congratulate me. The day passed cheerfully and pleasantly. In the evening went with Heller and Valentiner to visit Florence; this is also the first anniversary of our acquaintance. We picked up the conversation we had been having about death where we had left off last time.

PARIS, 30 MARCH 1943

In the evening, visit to First Lieutenant von Münchhausen, whom I had gotten to know during our training in Moisson. Like the Kleists and Arnims or the Keyserlings in the East, his bearing makes it evident that he comes from one of our intellectual dynasties. There I also met a doctor, a Russian émigré named Professor Salmanoff.

Fireside chat about patients and doctors. In Salmanoff, I discovered the first doctor with broader knowledge since Celsus, who treated me in Norway for a while, and Weizsäcker, who visited me briefly in Überlingen. I would gladly have trusted him to take care of me. He proceeds from the whole, and in doing so, from our age taken in its entirety, calling it "sick." He claims that it is just as difficult for the individual who lives in these times to be healthy as it is for a drop of water to be motionless in a stormy sea. He considers the tendency to convulsions and cramps to be a particular bane of our age. "Death comes gratis." That means you must earn your health through the common effort exerted by the patient and the physician. In the patient, sickness often begins as a moral disorder that then spreads to the organs. If the patient does not show himself willing to be healed at this moral stage, the physician must refuse treatment; he would only be taking a fee he had not earned.

Salmanoff is seventy-two years old. He has studied and treated people in almost every country in Europe and in several war zones. He left his career as a university professor in academic medicine at a ripe old age to combine his expertise with clinical practice. Lenin had been one of his patients, and he claimed that the reason for Lenin's death had been ennui. His essential talent lay in the art of conspiracy and the creation of small revolutionary cells, but once he had reached the highest level and attained absolute authority, he found himself in the position of a chess master who cannot find a partner, or an exceptional civil servant who is pensioned off early.

Salmanoff's fee took the form of being allowed to hand Lenin a small note with the names of prisoners who were then released. Lenin also arranged for his passport, thus making it possible for him to emigrate with his family.

Salmanoff does not think the Russians can be defeated, but he believes they will emerge from the war changed and cleansed. The invasion would have succeeded, he claims, if it had been supported by higher morale. Furthermore, he predicts an alliance between Russia and Germany after an interval of a few years.

Paris, 31 March 1943

During the midday break, visited the Musée de l'Homme, an institution where I have always marveled at the dual nature of rational intellectuality and sorcery. I see it as a finely engraved medal made of ancient, dark, radioactive metal. Accordingly, the mind is exposed to a dual influence of systematically organized intelligence and the invisible aura of its accumulated magical essence.

In the evening played chess with Baumgart in the Raphael. Afterward had a discussion with him and Weniger, who had served in the artillery with me in Monchy in 1915. He is visiting the troops, giving lectures and sounding out the officer corps in late-night conversations. He says that there is a movement afoot among the more important generals that is reminiscent of a passage in the Gospel of Matthew: "Art thou he that should come, or do we look for another?"

PARIS, 1 APRIL 1943

Visited Florence for lunch, where I also saw Giraudoux and Madame Bousquet. She gave me a letter by Thornton Wilder for my autograph collection.

Letters. It's odd that I write such cursory letters to the women I am closest to and pay so little attention to style. Possibly the result of the feeling that letters are almost superfluous in this case. We exist in the physical world.

On the other hand, I always make an effort when I am writing to Friedrich Georg or Carl Schmitt and two or three others. The effort is like that of the chess player who adapts to his partner.

PARIS, 3 APRIL 1943

In the afternoon, I went to a Turkish café on Rue Lauriston where I met Banine, a Muslim woman from the southern Caucasus whose novel *Nami* I recently finished. I noticed passages in her book that reminded me of [T. E.] Lawrence, as well as a similar recklessness about the body and its violation. It is odd how people can distance themselves from the body, from its muscles, nerves, ligaments, as though it were an instrument made up of keys and strings. In that state one listens like a stranger to the melody played by fate. This talent always carries the danger of sustaining injury.

PARIS, 3 APRIL 1943

Visited Salmanoff in the afternoon during his office hours when he sees patients in a small room completely crammed with books. While he was interviewing me, I studied their titles, which won my trust. Thorough physical examination. He found the small growth that is a vestige of my lung wound. Diagnosis and instructions are simple; he said that I would be feeling like myself in three months' time. *Speramos* [let us hope].

Incidentally, he differs from my good old Celsus in that he uses medications, if only moderately. Even the best doctors have a bit of the charlatan about them. I could deduce a pattern of their interaction with their patients. That's how it is with these prophet types: They ask a question that magnifies their reputation, whether the answer is yes or no. If the answer is yes, then it was a serious deliberation being pursued; if the answer is no, they resort to divination: "You see, that's just what I was thinking."

As a result, I am a bit disgruntled. This relates to the hyperacute sense of observation with which I am cursed, the way others have an especially keen sense of smell. I detect the shady moves that are endemic to humans all too clearly. In periods of weakness and sickness, this increases. There are times when I have seen through the doctors at my bedside as though I had X-ray vision.

The good stylist. He really wanted to write: "I acted correctly," but inserted "incorrectly" instead because that fit the sentence better.

PARIS, 4 APRIL 1943

Sunday. As I was leaving the Raphael after eating, the air-raid sirens began, accompanied by artillery fire. From the roof, I saw a high wall of smoke hovering on the horizon though the bombers had already departed. Attacks like this last barely more than a minute.

Then, because the Métro is out of commission, walked to Georges Poupet on Rue Garancière. It was a beautifully mild blue spring day. Groups of Parisians were promenading together under the green chestnut trees of the Champs-Élysées, while out in the suburbs hundreds were foundering in blood. I stood there for a long time in front of the most beautiful group of magnolias I had ever seen. One of them bloomed blinding white, the second gentle pink, and the third crimson. Spring throbbed in the air with that magic felt once each year as vibrations of the cosmic energy of love.

At Poupet's I met the Mégrets, a married couple. Discussions about war and peace, about rising prices, about Hercule and the anarchists of 1890, for just now I am studying the trial of Ravachol.[17] Mégret told an anecdote about Bakunin who was riding in a carriage one day when he passed a building being torn down. He leapt out, took off his coat, grabbed a pickaxe, and joined the work. Such men dance the grotesque opening number for the world of destruction as they lead the red masque before the eyes of the alarmed citizens.

Paid a brief visit to the Church of Saint-Sulpice. There I examined Delacroix's frescoes; their colors have suffered. Also admired Marie Antoinette's dainty pipe organ, remembering that Gluck and Mozart had once touched its keys. In the chancel, two elderly women were singing a Latin text; an old man sang along with them as he accompanied them on the harmonium. Lovely voices rose from the exhausted bodies and shriveled throats that showed the working of subcutaneous sinew and gristle. The sounds that emanated from these mouths surrounded by wrinkles were testimony to the timeless melodies possible even on brittle instruments. Beneath these arches—as in the Church of Saint Michael in Munich—rational theology and intellectual cosmogony hold sway. As so often happens in such places, I began to reflect on the plan of creation and the spiritual structure of the world. Who can tell what role such a church plays in human history?

Despite the lateness of the hour, I found a guide to take me via the narrow winding staircase described by Huysmans in *Là-Bas* [*Down There*] to the taller of the two towers. From here the view of the surrounding cityscape is perhaps the most beautifully comprehensive. The sun had just set and the Luxembourg Gardens blazed with riotous greens amid the silver-gray stone walls.

It can always be said in favor of human beings that no matter how deeply they founder in their pursuits and passions, they have been capable of such achievements. By the same token, we marvel at the artistic, burnished shells produced by a mollusk's secretion; these still continue to glisten on the seashore long after the creatures that inhabited them have disappeared. They bear witness to a third power beyond life and death.

PARIS, 5 APRIL 1943

By noon today the death toll had exceeded two hundred. A few bombs hit the racecourse at Longchamp when it was crowded with people. As Sunday strollers emerged from the depths of the Métro, they ran into a crowd of panting, injured people with their clothing in tatters. Some were clutching their heads or an arm; one mother held a bleeding child to her breast. One direct hit to a bridge swept many pedestrians into the Seine. Their corpses are now being fished out of the water.

At the same moment, on the other edge of the little forest, a cheerful group of people in their finery was promenading and enjoying the trees, the blossoms, and the mild spring air. That is the Janus head of these times.

PARIS, 10 APRIL 1943

I was on the Place des Ternes when the air-raid alarm sounded. Conversation near the little flower stand on the traffic circle while people rushed passed us toward the shelters. Rhetorical figures—during the most spirited part of our conversation, fire-bursts from falling bombs lit up the air. Walked through empty streets to the Étoile while trails from white, red, and green tracer shots were shooting over the forest, where they exploded high above us like sparks from a blacksmith's forge. That was a symbol of life's course—like the path in *The Magic Flute*.

PARIS, 11 APRIL 1943

Human encounters and separations. When a separation is imminent, there are days when the exhausted relationship intensifies once more and crystallizes to the point where it reaches its purest, fundamental form. And yet it is precisely such days that inevitably confirm the end. In the same way, clear days often follow uncertain weather until one morning heralds particular clarity, when every mountain and valley shows itself again in its full glory just preceding the sudden drop in temperature.

I was standing in the bathroom this morning thinking about these things, just as I had before my trip to Russia, when I knocked over a glass and broke it.

Good prose is like wine and continues to live and develop. It may contain sentences that are not yet true, but a hidden life raises them to the level of truths.

Fresh prose is usually still a bit unrefined, but it develops a patina over the years. I often notice this in old letters.

Discussion with Hattingen at lunch about clocks and hourglasses. The trickling of the sand in the hourglass weaves the unmechanized time of destiny. This is the time to which we are attuned in the rustling of the forest, the crackling of the fire, the surge of the breakers, the eddies of falling snowflakes.

Later, even though the light was fading, I went to the Bois de Boulogne briefly near the Porte Dauphine. I saw boys playing there who were between seven and nine years old; their faces and gestures seemed remarkably expressive. Individuation comes out earlier here and shows itself with more pronounced features. Yet you get the feeling that in most cases, starting around age sixteen, their spring has lost its bloom. The Latin type crosses that borderline too early, the line that marks his final stage, whereas the Germanic type usually never reaches it. For this reason, commingling is beneficial; two deficiencies combine to create an advantage.

I rested at the foot of an elm tree surrounded by a profusion of pale violet nettles. A bumblebee was visiting the blossoms, and while it hovered over the calyxes, displaying its velvet brown band and gently curved abdomen, its extended proboscis pointed like a stiff black probe. The insect's forehead bore a golden-yellow blaze of pollen formed by countless points of contact. It was remarkable to watch the moment it plunged into the flower. Once inside, the tiny insect gripped the long throat with both forelegs and pulled it over its proboscis like a sheath, almost the way a Mardi Gras clown puts on an artificial nose.

Had tea at Valentiner's, where I met Heller, Eschmann, Rantzau, and the Doctoresse. Discussions about Washington Irving, Eckermann, and Prince Schwarzenberg, who is said to have instigated the collection of a huge, still uncatalogued body of material in Vienna relating to European secret societies.

Paris, 12 April 1943

Current reading: *Carthage Punique* [*Punic Carthage*] by Lapeyre and Pellegrin. The conquest of this city is rich in anecdotes befitting this phenomenal event. After the Romans had breached the walls, those citizens who were determined to fight to the death carried on their defense from the highest temple in the city. Among them were Hasdrubal with his family and other noble Carthaginians. And by their sides another nine hundred Roman defectors who expected no mercy.

During the night before the decisive attack, Hasdrubal secretly leaves his people to look for Scipio. In his hand, he bears an olive branch. The next morning Scipio parades him in front of the temple and displays him to the defenders to demoralize them. They, however, after venting an endless stream of abuse and invective against their disloyal general, set the building on fire and throw themselves into the flames.

It is said that, as the fire was being laid, Hasdrubal's wife donned her finest raiment in one of the innermost chambers of the temple. Then, in all her finery, she came to the rampart with her children and addressed Scipio first. She wished him happiness on his life's journey, saying she was leaving him without anger because he had acted in accordance with the laws of war. Thereupon she cursed her husband in the name of the city, its gods, herself, and her children, and then turned her back on him forever. Then she strangled her children and threw them into the flames, finally throwing herself into the fire as well.

In such circumstances, people achieve greatness in the way that individual vessels are filled to the brim with symbolic content. At the moment of its destruction, Carthage itself makes its entrance onto the flaming stage in the person of this woman approaching the altar prepared for her ultimate sacrifice. Inspired with a formidable, sacred power, she utters blessings and curses. The place, the circumstances, and the human being—all is prepared, and everything secondary fades away. The ancient sacrifice to Baal, the incineration of children, is reenacted here for the last time, performed in order to save the city and now consummated so that it may live forever. The mother sacrifices herself so that the vine may burn with its fruit.

PARIS, 13 APRIL 1943

Carthage Punique. In that age, contact among states was more malleable and the powers of treaties more binding. When Hannibal and Philipp of Macedon signed their famous treaty, the gods—notably the gods of war—were present, tangibly represented by the priests of their cult.

After the destruction of the city, the site was cursed. It was sown with salt as a sign of malediction. Thus salt here symbolizes barrenness. Otherwise, it symbolizes the mind, and so we find both negative and positive poles associated with an object, as is true everywhere in symbolism. This applies particularly to colors: yellow for both the nobility and the rabble; red for both authority and insurrection; blue for both the supernatural and nothingness. This division is surely accompanied by differences of purity, as Goethe notes about yellow in his treatise on color theory.[18] We may thus imagine the salt of malediction as coarse and impure, in contrast to the Attic salt used to preserve food or to season dishes at the table of the intelligentsia.

Kubin mailed me another of his hieroglyphic texts from Zwickledt; I plan to decipher this when I can meditate on it at leisure. Grüninger reports the arrival from Stalingrad of copies of the last letters of Lieutenant Colonel Crome. It appears that people show a powerful reversion to Christianity when they are facing a lost cause.

PARIS, 14 APRIL 1943

Visit from Hohly, the painter. He brought me greetings from Cellaris's wife and reported that he was mentally very active, despite his long imprisonment and poor physical health.[19] Let us hope that he will see daylight again. The conversation reminded me again of that terrible day when I had driven to Berlin and telephoned Cellaris's lawyer. There, in the metropolis, I held out as much hope for assurance as I would for a drink in the desert. Standing in the telephone booth, I had the impression that Potsdamer Platz was glowing.

In the evening attended the premier of Cocteau's *Renaud et Armide* in the Comédie Française. I noted that I clearly recalled the two powerful moments in the play that I had noticed when it was read aloud on Rue de Verneuil: Armida's magical song and Olivier's prayer. A talent like Cocteau's lets us observe the extent to which our age claws at him, and how much the subject matter must resist that. His miraculous ability waxes and wanes corresponding to the level on which he is focusing his talent. At its most rarified, it becomes a tightrope dance or buffoonery.

I noticed many familiar faces in the audience. Among them, Charmille.

PARIS, 15 APRIL 1943

Conversation with Rademacher in the morning about the military situation. He is placing his hope in Cellaris and Tauroggen.[20]

Visited Salmanoff in the evening, who said, "if the German intelligentsia had understood the Russian intelligentsia as well as the Russians understood the Germans, it never would have come to war."

We spoke of the mass grave at Katyn, where thousands of Polish officers who were Russian prisoners of war have apparently been discovered. Salmanoff thinks the whole thing is propaganda.

"But how would the corpses have gotten there?"

"You know, nowadays corpses don't need tickets."

Conversation about Aksakov, Berdyaev, and a Russian author named Rozanov. Salmanoff has obtained a book of his for me.

Made my way home through the Bois de Boulogne. The half-moon stood high above the new foliage. Despite the populous city nearby, complete silence reigned. That produced a half-pleasing, half-terrifying effect, like that of being onstage just before a difficult production.

PARIS, 16 APRIL 1943

Had a substantive dream about Kniébolo in the early morning hours, in which events were linked to my parental home. For some reason that I have forgotten, people were expecting him. They were making all sorts of arrangements, while I escaped into distant rooms so as not to run into him. When I finally appeared again, he had been and gone. I heard details about the visit, in particular, that my father had embraced him. When I awoke, this fact struck me in particular, and it made me recall the sinister vision that Benno Ziegler had related.[21]

In discussions about the atrocities of our age the question often comes up about where those demonic powers come from, the persecutors and murderers—people nobody had otherwise ever seen or imagined. Yet they were always a potential presence, as reality now shows. Their novelty lies in their visibility, in their having been turned loose and allowed to harm other human beings. Our shared guilt led to this release: By robbing ourselves of our social bonds, we unleashed something subterranean. We must not complain when this wickedness also touches us individually.

PARIS, 17 APRIL 1943

Visited Parc de Bagatelle in the afternoon. The intense heat of these days concentrates the flowering like a symphony: Myriad tulips blazed on the lawns and on the islands in the little lake. Flora seemed to outdo herself in many of the blossoms, like the violet-blue and silky gray clusters of the wisteria, light as feathers yet heavy in beauty. These hung down on the walls; the whole effect produced a magical display like fairytale gardens.

I always find this enticing, a promise of endless splendors, like a ray of light from treasure vaults glimmering through doors just briefly opened. Transience dwells in the withering, and yet these floral miracles are symbols of a life that never wilts. From it comes the beguiling charm that awakens their hues and aromas as they shoot sparks into the heart.

I also saw my old friend the golden orfe,[22] whose back glistened in the green water of the grottoes. It has been waiting here silently while I was on the move in Russia.

Thoughts about perversions—wondering whether the source could be an aversion that existed between father and mother. In that case, they would have to predominate in countries and social strata where marriages of convenience are prevalent. By the same token, they ought to be prevalent among the cold-blooded races and not vice versa, as is commonly thought. Hatred and aversion for the opposite sex are passed down through procreation. That is basically it; other things come later. Naturally, selection takes place, as nature gives preference to the fruits of sensual copulation. Perhaps, however, individuals are compensated with intelligence, since brilliant types are often the fruits of late conception, like Baudelaire. The bizarre way in which father Shandy[23] winds the clock also comes to mind.

These connections have hardly been researched, and they elude the scope of science. I would have to penetrate the secret histories of entire families, entire clans.

I could counter this thesis by objecting that there are rural regions where marriages of convenience have been common since time immemorial. In these places, individuation has evolved less in the meantime; any healthy person is acceptable to another one. Furthermore, in particular areas, degeneration can reach the level of that in the big cities; it is simply more covert. Perhaps the symptoms are different as well. Sodomy is probably more prevalent in the countryside than in the city.

Incidentally, that which we view as aberrant can definitely be associated with a more profound view of the world. The reason for this is precisely that this view is less subject to the pressure, the veil of our species. This is generally observable among homosexuals, who judge by intellect. They are, therefore, always useful to intellectuals, quite apart from the fact that they are entertaining to have around.

The Dreyfus trial is a piece of clandestine history. In other words, it is generally invisible, the sort of thing that is otherwise submerged in the labyrinths beneath political structures. When reading about this affair, I have the feeling of trespassing upon the taboo. It is like getting close to the mummy of Tutankhamun, with its dense layers of matter. As a result, the casual approach with which young historians like Frank treat such material is frightening.

Career choice. I would like to be a star pilot.[24]

Concerning self-education. Even if we are born with infirmities, we can rise to remarkable levels of health. The same is true in the realm of knowledge. Through study you can liberate yourself from the influence of bad teachers and from the prejudices of your age. In a completely corrupted situation even the most modest progress in morality is much more difficult. Here is where things come down to fundamentals.

When an unbeliever—let's say in an atheist state—demands that a believer swear an oath, that is tantamount to the action of a corrupt banker who expects the other players in the game to lay real gold on the table.

In an atheist political system there is only one sort of oath that is valid, and that is perjury. Everything else is sacrilege. On the other hand, one may swear an oath to a Turk and exchange oaths with him. That is an exchange without chicanery.

Finished reading the Old Testament last night with the Book of the Prophet Malachi. I had started this project in Paris on 3 September 1941. Tomorrow I plan to begin with the Apocrypha.

I have also have begun *Esseulement* [*Solitude*] by Rozanov. I immediately sensed here that that Salmonoff had steered me toward a mind that would trigger thoughts in me, if not actually inspire them.

PARIS, 18 APRIL 1943

Had tea with Marie-Louise Bousquet on Place du Palais-Bourbon; the house stands out for the Roman severity of its architecture. These old apartments filled with inherited objects have adapted themselves to human beings and their nature over the course of decades and centuries—like garments that, after long wear, caress the body with each fold. These are shells in the sense of a higher zoology. Here I also met Heller, Poupet, Giraudoux, and Madame Ollivier de Prévaux, a great-granddaughter of Liszt. Madame Bousquet—whom I always treat with the same caution that a chemist exercises when handling questionable compounds— showed me the small, square, wood-paneled library. There I examined manuscripts, dedications, and beautiful bindings. Some of the books were bound in textured leather; touching them doubles the pleasure of reading. The bindings stamped in gold leaf displayed a color palette from a violet so deep that it approaches black, and then to its lighter shades. The patterns in dark golden-brown were often dotted with gold or embellished flame shapes.

Made my way back in the evening across the Champs-Élysées. It was a magnificent sunny day. I was also pleased with myself, and note this only because it is something I can say so seldom. Finished reading Rozanov's *Esseulement*, one of the rare moments in which authorship and independent thought have succeeded in our age. Considering such acquaintances, I always think it seems as if one of those bare patches on the ceiling that encloses our space had been filled in with paint. Rozanov's relationship to the Old Testament is remarkable; for example, he uses the word "seed" in precisely the same sense. This word, when applied to humans as a symbol of their essence, has always distressed me slightly. I've always felt a certain opposition toward it, like Hebbel's toward the word "rib," which he scratched out in his Bible. Ancient taboos are probably at work here: the spermatic character of the Old Testament in general, in contrast to the pneumatic of the Gospels.

After 1918, Rozanov died in a monastery, where he is said to have starved to death. He remarked of the Revolution that it would fail because it offered nothing to men's dreams. It is this that will destroy its structures. I find it so appealing that his hurried notations came to him as a sort of plasmatic motion of the spirit in moments of contemplation—when he was sorting his coin collection or sunning himself on the sand after his bath.

PARIS, 19 APRIL 1943

Neuhaus, who is a great devotee of flowers, had the sensible idea of getting out of the office with me for an hour and visiting the Botanical Garden of Auteuil, where the azaleas are in bloom. A large cool-house was filled with thousands of azalea bushes so that it resembled a hall with brightly woven carpeting and multicolored walls. It seems impossible that a greater profusion or a greater exuberance of such a delicate palette could ever be assembled in one place. Yet I don't count myself among the friends of the azalea; I find its hues unmetaphysical, for they display only one-dimensional colors. Perhaps that explains their popularity. They speak only to the eye and lack that drop of *arcanum arcanorum supra coeleste* [heavenly mystery of mysteries] in the pure essence of their tincture. This explains their lack of fragrance.

We also visited the gloxinias and *calceolaria* [lady's slipper, or slipperwort]. The *calceolaria* constitute living cushions on which variety achieves its greatest range, for among the millions of individuals there are no two flowers that are completely identical. The varieties with dark purple and yellow stripes are the most beautiful; in order to appreciate the deep interior of these calyxes that brim with life, you would have to be able to transmogrify into a bumblebee. This remark, which I addressed to Neuhaus, seemed to amuse our driver, who kept us company, and I guessed the reason.

Only a few orchids were in bloom, but we strolled through the cultivars since Neuhaus is a breeder. A green and purple striped lady's slipper caught my eye thanks to the dark spots on its upper lip; each wing whimsically sprouted three or four tiny, spiky hairs. It made me think of the smile of a long-lost girlfriend who had a dark mole.

It's important that the gardeners remain invisible in gardens like this so that we may see only their oeuvre. By the same token, tracks that we leave in the sand need to be erased immediately by a phantom hand. That's the only way we can fully appreciate plants and their language. Their essence could be summarized in the motto, *Praesens sed invisibilis* [present but invisible].

The prototype for all gardens is the enchanted garden, and the prototype for all enchanted gardens is the Garden of Paradise. Horticulture, like all modest professions, has sacred origins.

I finished reading the Book of Judith in the Bible; it is one of those pieces in the style of Herodotus. The description of Holofernes leads us into one of the state rooms of the Tower of Babel where the curtain of his bed is encrusted with precious stones. Preceding the night that Judith spends in his tent, Holofernes exchanges oriental compliments with her. The lip of the chalice is dusted with sugar; at the bottom lies deadly poison.

Though she was ready to do so, she was spared having to submit to Holofernes. In this book, I sense the power of beauty, which is stronger than armies. Then the triumphal song over the severed head of Holofernes. In my work on higher zoology, I want to describe the primeval figure that is the model for this; it will be in a chapter on triumphal dances following the one about *Schwärmen*.[25]

"Judith and Charlotte Corday: a Comparison"; "Judith and Joan of Arc as National Heroines." Two topics for advanced school students, but in order to do justice to the material, they must have already eaten from the Tree of Knowledge.

PARIS, 20 APRIL 1943

Spent a Mauritanian interlude with Banine at midday. It is her custom to have coffee in her bed, which she does not enjoy leaving any more than a hermit crab its shell. The windows of her studio look out at the tall water tower on Rue Copernic. Just outside these, a tall *Paulownia* [princess tree] still lacks its leaves but is in flower. The long, light purple, funnel-shaped blossoms into whose Cupid's-bow shaped openings the bees descend, stand out markedly yet subtly against the pale blue of the spring sky.

Conversation about the southern type, especially Ligurians and Gascons. Then about law and mysticism in religion. In mosques, the presence of the law is apparently obvious. I believe this is also true for synagogues. Finally, we spoke of expressions for fear and their nuances in different languages.

Visited Rademacher in the evening. He returns to Paris now and then and lives on Rue François Ier. There, for a few minutes, I also saw Alfred Toepfer, who has come back from Spain and is about to depart for Hannover. I asked him to look around for a little house on the heath for me near Thansen.[26] Political discussions, then reminiscences about Cellaris and the old days of the nationalist movement. The clandestine meeting in Eichhof in 1929 remains especially memorable. The history of these years with their thinkers, their activists, martyrs, and extras has not yet been written. In those days, we lived in the yolk of the Leviathan's egg. The Munich version[27]—the shallowest of them all—has now succeeded, and it has done so in the shoddiest possible way. My letters and papers from those years mention a host of people; people like Niekisch, Hielscher, Ernst von Salomon, Kreitz, and the recently deceased Albrecht Erich Günter. All were men of great perception. The other players have been murdered, emigrated, are demoralized, or have high-ranking positions in the army, the intelligence branch, and the Party. But those who are still alive will continue to enjoy discussing those days; people lived with a strong devotion to the idea. This is the way I imagine Robespierre in Arras.

Making progress with my Bible reading and have begun The Book of Wisdom [of Solomon]. Death has very different significance depending on whether it strikes the foolish man or the wise man. To the one it brings destruction; the other is purified and tested like gold in the furnace. His death is illusory: "And having been a little chastised, they shall be greatly rewarded" (3:5).

These words reminded me of the Léon Bloy's nice observation, according to which death is less significant than we imagine—perhaps no more so than dusting off a piece of furniture.

PARIS, 21 APRIL 1943

At midday, I had a visit from an old fellow from Lower Saxony, Colonel Schaer. Discussed the situation. Still no olive branch. His debriefing included a description of the shooting of Jews that was horrifying. He got this from another colonel, I think it was Tippelskirch, who had sent his army there to find out what was going on.

Horror grips me when I hear such accounts, and I am crushed by the sensation of overwhelming danger. I mean this in the general sense, and would not be amazed if the planet were to fly apart into fragments, whether from a collision with a comet or from an explosion. I really have the feeling that these people are probing the planet, and the fact that they choose the Jews as their primary victims cannot be a coincidence. Their highest-ranking executioners have a kind of uncanny clairvoyance that is not the product of intelligence but of demonic inspiration. At every crossroads, they will find the direction that leads to greater destruction.

Apparently, these shootings are going to stop because they have moved to a system of gassing their victims.

Visited Gruel at midday. On the way I again broke off one of the fresh leaves from the fig tree growing by the Church of the Assumption. This tree's annual budding has given me joy for three years now. It is among my favorite trees in this city. The second is the old pollarded acacia in the garden of the Palace of the Legion of Honor. Perhaps the third addition is the *Paulownia* in Banine's garden.

PARIS, 22 APRIL 1943

Breakfast with the Morands; Countess Palffy, Céline, Benoist-Méchin also there. The conversation tended toward ominous anecdotes. Benoist-Méchin told how his car had skidded on some ice, and he had crushed a woman against a tree as she was walking with her husband. He took the couple into his car to drive them to the field hospital and during the journey heard the man sobbing and groaning more than the woman.

"I hope you are not hurt too?"

"No, but a pelvic fracture—that means at least three months in the hospital—what an expense. And what's more, who's going to cook for me all that time?"

The examination revealed that it was luckily only internal lesions but that the healing would still take eight weeks. After that time, the minister visited the woman to inquire about her health, and he found her wearing mourning. Her husband had died of some gastric complications in the meantime. When he tried to express his condolences, she responded: "Oh please stop it. You don't know what joy you have brought me."

We talked about the wives of prisoners of war as well. Just as the Trojan War has become the mythical model of every historical war, the tragedy of returning soldiers and the figure of Clytemnestra constantly recur. A woman who hears that her husband is to be released from prison camp sends him a little parcel of delicacies as a love token. In the meantime, the man returns earlier than expected and discovers not only his wife but also her lover and two children. In the prisoner of war camp in Germany, comrades divide the contents of the parcel and four of them die after consuming the butter she had laced with arsenic.

On this subject, Céline recounted anecdotes from his own medical practice, which seems to be studded with an array of gruesome cases. Incidentally, that he is a Breton explains my first impression that had led me to consign him to the Stone

Age. He is just about to go visit the mass grave at Katyn, now being exploited as propaganda. It stands to reason that such places attract him.

Benoist-Méchin walked with me on my way home. He is consumed by a demonic agitation. We carried on a conversation that has been repeated endlessly since the dawn of time: which type of display of power provides greater satisfaction, the practical, political form or the invisible, spiritual one?

In the evening I read Cocteau's essay about the death of Marcel Proust, given to me by Marie-Louise Bousquet. It contains a sentence that graphically demonstrates the vast silence to which the dead descend: "*Il y régnait ce silence qui est au silence ce que les ténèbres sont à l'encre.*" [There reigns the silence that is to silence what darkness is to ink.]

I could not help thinking of Thomas Wolfe's terrifying description of a corpse in the New York subway.

PARIS, 23 APRIL 1943

Good Friday. Visit from Eschmann this morning, who has come from Valéry. Discussion about dreams. Our conversation touched on things I thought it best not to pursue. It nonetheless gave me insights, as if I were looking at myself in a crystal clear mirror. By the way, even the clearest mirrors are hazy—they possess a dream dimension. We enter into them, and they capture our aura.

In the afternoon went to Quai Voltaire via Rue du Faubourg Saint-Honoré. I tend to be late here; hourglass time controls this route. I made my way to Saint-Philippe-du-Roule. The white chestnut blossoms with their tiny traces of red had fallen and now lay on the pavement in the courtyard like a frame of ivory and other precious materials. This gave a ceremonial quality to my entrance. Visited the chapel first, where a crucifix was on display. Then the church thronged with women. There I heard a good Passiontide sermon. Great symbols renew themselves each day, like the one showing human beings choosing the murderer Barabbas over the Prince of Light.

Visited Valentiner. Both brothers were there, as well as Eschmann and Marie-Louise. Discussion about Jouhandeau's *Nouvelles Chroniques Maritales*, the game of chess, insects, Valéry. Then visited the Doctoresse in the company of Schlumberger. We had not seen each other since 1938.

PARIS, 24 APRIL 1943

Conference with Colonel Schaer in the morning. I asked him once more whether I had remembered correctly that Tippelskirch had personally heard or seen details of the butchery he had told me about. He confirmed that for me. At times, these things oppress me like a nightmare, a diabolical dream. But it is necessary to view the evidence with the eyes of a physician and not to shrink from it. The general public insulates itself from such revelations.

Some thoughts about the column stinkhorn mushrooms I examined yesterday in Saint-Roule. Despite their vigorous appearance, they are actually just dead bits—nonspace within space. By the same token, we too are just corpses in the flow of life. Not until death breaks us open do we gain life.

In the evening I read *Titanen* [*Titans*][28] sent to me today by Friedrich Georg, then fell into a deep sleep as if induced by some mysterious narcotic.

PARIS, 25 APRIL 1943

Went to the Bois in the afternoon. Strolled from Porte Dauphine as far as Auteuil. Various types of *Balanini* [acorn beetle] on the bushes; the creatures reminded me of my dream in Voroshilovsk.[29] Then I wandered through unknown streets until I suddenly found myself in front of a large building on Quai Louis-Blériot; we once had a birthday party there for the little milliner on its seventh floor. Continued along the Boulevard Exelmans. There the Métro emerges as an elevated train; the enormous arches have a certain classical, ancient Roman feeling—something decisive about them that differs from our architecture. People would live more agreeably in cities built on such a model. You encounter the *Paulownia*, the imperial tree, everywhere. It enhances this city as the exquisite gray of the buildings cloaks itself felicitously in its purple veils. Its trunks have an intrinsically stately architectural form: they resemble ceremonial candelabra flickering with gentle flames. What the flame tree is to Rio, the *Paulownia* is to Paris. This comparison could also include the women.

Visited Valentiner; there I also saw the sculptor Gebhardt, whose mother is in danger since his aunt disappeared without a trace. On the staircase, I met Princess Bariatinski, who, along with Count Metternich, is caring for him. Metternich has given him asylum under the wing of the commander-in-chief. Walked back through the Tuileries; again, more *Paulownia*, and Judas trees too. Their blossoms shone like bunches of coral-colored grapes. A toothless old woman wearing thick makeup had carried two chairs into the bushes and waved invitingly at me with a grotesque smile. It was dusk, and this was a dreary sight.

Back at the Raphael continued reading *Titanen*. I stride through the chapters as if through the ancient construction site of the world. I imagine the coming of the gods to be something like an arrival from other planets bathed in joyous radiance. While I was reading, I could occasionally picture Friedrich Georg smiling gently as he inclined his head slightly to examine pictures or flowers on our walks together.

PARIS, 27 APRIL 1943

At the Morands' for lunch, where I also met Abel Bonnard. I had them show me the picture of the Mexican goddess of the dead that Eschmann had told me about and which Madame Morand keeps hidden in the half-light behind a screen in her large salon. It shows a cruel, fearsome idol of gray stone with numerous victims bleeding to death before it. Pictures like this are infinitely more intense, infinitely more real than any photograph.

Discussion about the situation, then about Gide, whom Bonnard called "*le vieux Voltaire de la pédérastie*" [the old Voltaire of pederasty]. He went on to say that any literary movements, such as the ones that have formed around Gide, Barrès, Maurras, and [Stefan] George, would soon consume themselves. He finds something inherently sterile in them resembling the rustling of barren wheat fields beneath the rays of an artificial star. By the time the sun sets, it has all passed and no fruit remains, for it is all nothing more than pure emotion.

Bonnard also accused Léon Bloy of having believed in a miracle that had been performed for his benefit—a quality I rather like. He also spoke of Galliffet and about Rochefort, whom he had known personally. He said that the latter left the impression of a short photographer.

Talked about the Russians, who today are as overestimated as they were under-estimated two years ago. In reality, they are more powerful than anyone thinks. It could be, however, that this power is not to be feared. This applies, incidentally, to any true, any creative power.

The conversation engaged my general interest because Abel Bonnard embod-ies a kind of positivistic intellectuality now almost defunct. For this reason the somewhat muted, solarian character of his attributes are apparent; these have something both childlike and senescent about them in their sullenness. I sense that there are epicenters of this kind of thinking. To be sure, such conversations, like those with my own father, resemble time spent waiting in anterooms. Yet they reveal more than conversations with our visionaries and mystics.

Paris, 28 April 1943

Sent a letter to Friedrich Georg about his *Titans*. Also wrote about dreams in which our father appeared to us. My brother had written to me that he had seen him with me in a garden and noticed particularly that our father was wearing a new suit.

At the Raphael in the evening with the Leipzig publisher Volckmar-Frentzel, Leo, and Grewe, the expert in international law from Berlin. From him, I gleaned details about the agonizing death of A. E. Günther.

Continued my reading in the Wisdom of Solomon. The seventh chapter may be seen as a counterpart to the Song of Songs, but on a more significant level. What was sensual desire there is spiritual here. There exists a spiritual lust. It remains inac-cessible to those who spend their days only in the antechambers of the true life. Its glories are closed to them. Yet, "And great pleasure it is to have her friendship" (8:18).

Wisdom is here exalted as the highest independent human intelligence; it is the Holy Ghost that fills the cosmos with his universal presence. Even the boldest ways of the human mind lead not one step closer to it. Only when man purifies himself, when he makes an altar of his own breast, then wisdom enters into him unnoticed. Thus everyone may participate in the highest wisdom. It is cosmic, whereas intel-ligence is an earthly, perhaps a merely brutish power. We are more intelligent in our atoms than in our brains.

It is remarkable that the Sayings of Solomon incorporated the most extreme skepticism into Holy Writ. Whereas this book, so pervaded by a divine economy, is placed among the Apocrypha.

PARIS, 30 APRIL 1943

The mail brought a letter from Hélène Morand about *The Worker*. In it she calls the art of life the art of forcing other people to work while one enjoys oneself.

"The famous saying of Talleyrand '*n'a pas connu la douceur de vivre*' [never knew the pleasure of life]"[30] applied only to a tiny elite, which was not even particularly appealing. We all would have found the salons of Madame du Deffand or Madame Geoffrin stifling. These people had neither heart, nor wits, nor imagination and were ripe for death. What's more, they all died quite nicely. It is just a pity that Talleyrand was able to crawl away from danger—"on his belly."

I am struck by the tough political flair of this woman, as well as the fascination and horror she arouses. There is some magic art in all this—especially a fiery will—which, in its brilliant light, calls forth the idols upon the roofs of alien temples licked by flames. I used to feel this too in response to Cellaris. The real danger is not that people are playing with cards that decide the fates of thousands and their happiness. Rather, danger dwells in the decisions of individuals—in the way they stretch out their hands. That can reveal the demonic realm. Every one of us knows the moment of resolve when we silence all within us in order to take this leap or to reach out. I have experienced this moment, albeit much more intensely—and this silence, though infinitely more profoundly: experienced it during particular encounters along my way. Demonic natures are accordingly more frightening when they are mute than when they speak in the midst of activity.

Then I read a new issue of *Zeitgeschichte* [*Contemporary History*] edited by Traugott and Meinhart Sild. I don't take much pleasure in the fact that these essays draw their support from *The Worker*. A comment by one of the contributors is at least correct when he says this book offers only a floor plan without suggesting what sort of architectural structures could possibly be built upon it.

Sleep has its different intensities, and resting its various levels. They resemble the gear ratios of wheels that turn around a center point that is itself still. Minutes of the deepest sleep can thus be more restorative than nights of dozing.

LE MANS, 1 MAY 1943

Took a trip to Le Mans with Baumgart and Fräulein Lampe, a young art historian, in order to visit the painter Nay. We had spent the better part of the previous night at one of the little get-togethers given by the commander-in-chief. A professor was there who is said to be one of the most important specialists on diabetes. I am consistently amazed by the gravity with which I hear sentences like the following nowadays: "To date there have been twenty-two hormones identified that are secreted by the pituitary gland."

No matter how far this mentality advances, its progress remains merely one of refinement. Insights spiral heavenward, as on the exterior of a top hat, whereas truth fills its interior. Diseases must naturally increase. The most important hormone is the one that cannot be identified.

Weniger was among the dinner guests; he has just returned from Germany, where he heard an epigram that isn't bad:

Der siegreichen Partei die dankbare Wehrmacht

[To the victorious Party (from) the grateful Wehrmacht][31]

—an inscription on a future monument commemorating this Second World War. At moments like this, the commander-in-chief has a charming quality about him, the smile of a fairytale king dispensing gifts to children.

In the morning I departed from Montparnasse. It was the day when lilies of the valley were being offered for sale everywhere in large bunches. They reminded me of Renée. I am still filled with pain when I recall gardens I never entered. It was raining, but the land was in full bloom. Among the trees I was particularly taken with the hawthorn. I find its chalky pigmentation especially appealing, somewhere between pale and dark pink. Wild hyacinth fills areas of the woods, flowers that one simply does not see in Germany. Their deep dark-blue blossoms were especially showy along a slope where they blazed in the middle of a stand of green and yellow spurge.

Nay picked us up from the train in Le Mans. Since he is serving as a corporal here, we met in his studio after lunch. A Monsieur de Thérouanne, whose hobby is sculpture, has made it available to him. Looking at Nay's images, I had the impression of a laboratory where Promethean creativity is expressed in solid form. But I did not reach a verdict, because these are works that require frequent and long examination. Discussion about theory, about which Nay, like most good painters, has something to say. Carl Schmitt has even inspired him with his notions of space. I thought he used a particularly fitting expression that described his work at the point when the canvas "gained tension." At such moments, it seemed to him as though the image were greatly expanding. This happens in prose as well, where a sentence, a paragraph, gains particular tension, more specifically, torsion. This is comparable to the moment when a woman whom you have long considered with indifference or simply as a friend, suddenly gains erotic significance. At that moment everything changes completely.

We then went to Morin, the antiquarian bookseller, who showed us his books and some magnificent early prints.

Paris, 2 May 1943

Pouring rain. The three of us went out to L'Épeau to eat in spite of it. Afterward, visited Morin where we also met Nay. Monsieur Morin showed us his collections: pictures (among them one by Deveria), furniture, coins, Chinoiserie, and the like. His collection represents a distillation, a melting down and recombination as the result of culling, sifting, selecting, and trading accumulated items. In this sense, it was a potent essence, representing the consolidated content of two, three rooms.

I stood with Monsieur Morin in the studio of his only son, who had recently been sent to work in Germany, specifically to Hannover. The father told me a good deal about him, how for example, as a child he already treated books with respect and would rather spend time with them than out of doors or playing sports. *"C'est un homme de cabinet"* [he's an indoor man]. When he mentioned that he had set his son up in a small secondhand bookshop on Rue du Cherche-Midi, I immediately knew that he could be none other than the man who recently sold me the book *De Tintinnabulis [On Bells]* by Magius.[32] The father confirmed this, and even said that his son had recounted the conversation to him that he and I had had during the transaction. Because this encounter seemed extraordinary to me, I wrote down the address and made a note to look in on him on my next furlough.

Then we went back to the books. I was able to acquire a good supply of old paper, mostly from the eighteenth century. It was partially bound in large, barely used ledgers of the sort I had seen in Picasso's flat, and that I could use as herbaria.

Walked to the cathedral through the upper part of town, where the streets still retain their Gothic character. The cathedral has a narrow, exceptionally high choir that is particularly impressive. The plan of the building hits the viewer squarely with its startling skeletal austerity. Much coming disaster lurks in this bravado as it proclaims its goal so openly to the initiate.

At the end, we returned to Nay for a second look at the pictures. They bear the stamp of primitivism coupled with awareness, and with that, they represent the true mark of our age. The colors are loosely related, sometimes in a way that symbolizes their dynamic value. Consequently, the arm raised in action is painted blood red.

We then returned to Paris, arriving at nine o'clock.

PARIS, 3 MAY 1943

At Valentiner's place at noon; he is leaving for Aix today. His garret on Quai Voltaire plays a role in my life similar to the one played earlier by the round table in the George V. I gave him an introduction to Médin.

Carlo Schmid came by in the afternoon. Discussion about the situation. The approaching fiasco in Tunis will bring political changes in its wake, especially in Italy.[33] They are supposedly building huge batteries of rocket launchers on the Channel coast. The rockets, fueled by liquid air, will be able to hit London. Kniébolo has always overestimated novelties of this sort.

PARIS, 4 MAY 1943

There were letters from Banine and Morin in my French mail. Morin has a good archivist's handwriting. In the afternoon, I visited Weinstock and took him a copy of *The Titans* to take along on his trip. Went to the Ritz in the evening with Carlo Schmid. He told me, among other things, the grotesque story of one of his colleagues, a sixty-year-old lawyer from the military administration in Lille who was the head of the passport office. When girls or women applied for passports, it was this man's habit to order them to come to his apartment, where the same conversation always ensued before he would hand over the document:

"My child, before you receive your passport first you will have to cry."

"But why do I have to cry? I don't understand!"

"You'll see soon enough."

With these words, he placed his victim with great ceremony upon a sofa, quickly lifted her skirts and meted out robust blows upon her backside with a cane.

This bizarre compulsion was repeated, because in a majority of the cases, the concerned parties had no recourse for lodging a complaint until finally the military tribunal addressed the issue.

The hero of this scandal was until recently the head of an office of Jewish affairs in Berlin and a contributor to *Der Stürmer*,[34] where he had published articles about the sexual offenses of Jews. These things correspond like mirror images. You have to seek the culprit hiding in your own bushes.

Then we talked about Kniébolo. Many people, even his opponents, concede a certain diabolical greatness to him. This could only be elemental, infernal, without any personal stature or dignity, such as one observes in a Byron or Napoleon. Carlo Schmid said on this topic that Germans lack an instinct for physiognomy. Anyone who looks like that, so that neither painter nor photographer can create a face for him—anyone who treats his mother tongue with such indifference—anyone who collects such a swarm of losers around him . . . but still, the enigmas here are unfathomable.

PARIS, 5 MAY 1943

So many *Paulownia* on Place d'Italie—it's a walk among magical candelabra that are burning delicate aromatic oil. Experiencing this again called to mind my dear father, with all his severity and flaws. How death glorifies the memory of the dead. More and more, I distance myself from the opinion that people, deeds, and events irrevocably retain their form for all eternity at the moment when they enter the hereafter and continue to exist in that form. On the contrary, that point in time constantly changes eternity, which, back then, was still in the future. At this point, time is a totality, and just as all that has gone before affects the future, the present also changes the past. Thus there are things that at the time were not yet truth; we, however, *make* them true. Furthermore, books change in the same way that fruits or wines mature in the cellar. Other things decay quickly, become ciphers. Never existed, colorless, insipid.

This conceals one of the many meanings that justify the cult of ancestor-worship. When we live as complete human beings, we exalt our forefathers in the same way that the fruit exalts the tree. You see this in the fathers of great individuals as they emerge from the anonymity of the past as if bathed in a nimbus of light.

Past and future are mirrors, and the present flickers between them, incomprehensible to our eyes. In death, however, the perspectives change: the mirrors begin to dissolve and the present emerges with ever-greater purity until, at the moment of death, it merges with eternity.

The divine life is everlasting present. And life exists only where divinity is present.

Unpleasant, embarrassing thoughts, impure words or oaths surface in our soliloquies when we brood. These are infallible signs that something inside us is amiss—just as when smoke mingles with the flames of unseasoned wood on the fire. Things like vehemence and intemperance directed against others—often symptoms of nights spent boozing, and worse.

Went to see the president at midday; called on him in his room at the end of a long, winding corridor in the Raphael. Conversation about the loss and acquisition of belongings—they accrue to us over the years as we mature. In our youth, we are like the restless hunter who frightens his quarry. Once we gain tranquility, we perceive the eagerness of the game to run into our traps.

Went to a little restaurant on Rue de la Pompe in the evening. It seems much easier for women to move from friendship to love than vice versa. I sense this in marriages that continue as friendship—yet they are forever a grave of extinguished mysteries.

Bodies are vessels. The meaning of life is to fortify them with ever more precious essences, with unguents for eternity. If this happens completely, whether the receptacle breaks or not is irrelevant. This is the meaning contained in a maxim in the Wisdom of Solomon, that the death of the wise man is only illusory.

Read further in the Apocrypha. The "wisdom" dwindles when it merges into the historical portion. One reads this with a diminished sense of expectation, rather like Spinoza's proofs, which follow from his theses.

The path through the Red Sea left behind a trauma in Israel; it was one of the decisive ruptures never to be forgotten. Miracles are the material that life feeds on. The sea is red, and it is also the Reed Sea. These are symbols for the life cycle, dominated by the code of the fishes: this teaches that one eats the other. It is the greatest of miracles that we are not devoured by this sea. What once happened in the past offers hope in all future persecutions.

Tobias, an uplifting story and pleasant to read. It gives delightful insights into ancient pastoral life during the phase when it clashes with historical powers and is threatened by them. I started with Jesus Sirach. If I recall correctly, Luther calls this a good domestic manual, but from the outset it offers great insights.

Concerning style. The use of the noun is in all instances stronger than verbal forms. "They sat down to eat" is weaker than "They sat down at the table," or "they sat down to the meal." "He regrets what was done" is weaker than "he regrets the deed." This is the difference between movement and concreteness.

PARIS, 6 MAY 1943

I got a phone call from the Doctoresse asking me to come to Ladurée during the midday break. I visited a bookseller on Rue de Castiglione beforehand where I bought a few nice volumes, such as the collection of Grothius's source material concerning the Goths. Also found the *Mémoires sur Vénus* [*Memorials of Venus*] by Larcher, who covers all the names, rituals, and sculptures of this goddess. I bought this for Friedrich Georg, despite his prejudice against any French research on mythology.

The Doctoresse told me that the police had entered her apartment in the morning and had asked her, among other things, about her circle of acquaintances. Judging from details in her account, I could tell this was a simple case of denunciation. I liked the way she dealt with these visitors when they identified themselves as police: "Thank you," she said, "I can already see that."

PARIS, 7 MAY 1943

Went to the Eastman [Dental] Clinic. I usually spend a little time on Place d'Italie watching the performance of a man approximately fifty years old. He is a gray-haired giant in tights who earns his daily bread by lifting weights and dumbbells and performing similar feats. He personifies something good-humored, gentle, and animal like in human form. He collects his money in a funnel.

I like to take the Métro in this direction because it emerges above ground in a number of places. The building façades seem abandoned and sun-bleached, yet they have a cheerful aspect. The sight of them awakens a primeval little lizard's soul in me. Behind the silence of their sun-bathed walls, I see people resting idly in their rooms, dreaming, or indulging in amorous play. I travel past a gallery of intimate still lifes—past tables set with sliced melon and glasses filmed with condensation; past a woman in a red dressing gown cutting the pages of a novel; past a naked man with a full beard sitting comfortably in an easy chair and dreaming of sublime things; past a couple sharing an orange after their caresses.

Anyone who thinks in concepts and not in images perpetrates the same brutality toward language as someone who sees only social categories and not human beings.

The path to God in our age is inordinately long, as if man had lost his way in the endless expanses that are the product of his own ingenuity. Even the most modest advance is therefore a great achievement. God must be imagined anew.

Given this condition, man is essentially capable only of negativity: He can purify the vessel that he embodies. That will suit him well, for new luster brings increased exhilaration. Yet even the greatest rule he can impose upon himself culminates in atheism, where no god dwells, a place more terrifying than if it had been abandoned by God. Then one day, years later, it may happen that God answers—it could be that He does so slowly, through the antennae of the spirit; or He may reveal Himself in a lightning bolt. We sent a signal to a heavenly body, and it turns out to be inhabited.

This reveals one of the great beauties of Goethe's *Faust*, namely the description of the lifelong, undaunted striving for exalted worlds and, ultimately, for access to their laws.

Conversation in the Majestic with Dr. Göpel about Max Beckmann, whom he occasionally sees in Holland and who asked Göpel to remember him to me. Painting in the period of Romanticism transcended the limits of literature and today dares to attempt feats reserved for music. Beckmann has a powerful, idiosyncratic line. His energy is convincing even where it is brutal: the statement "*Auch hier sind Götter*" [Here too are gods][35] proclaims a certain brilliance. One could imagine an archaic hybrid combining European and American elements: Mycenae and Mexico.

Dr. Göpel also told an anecdote about a count he had visited on the coast of Normandy, a man whose family had lived there for a thousand years.

"Over the course of this time, my family has gone through three castles here."— What a good way to put it, since houses are to dynasties what garments are to individuals.

Clemens Podewils joined us later, bringing me greetings from Speidel in Russia. Spent time with Weniger in the Raphael in the evening. Discussion about George and Schuler's *Blutleuchte* [*Blood Beacon*], and also the terrific book Klages has written about it.[36] Weniger knows almost every one of any importance in Germany, and his knowledge even extends to their genealogical connections. In this day and age such people are especially important because fundamental changes of the political-intellectual climate have occurred but not filtered down into the general consciousness. They are like the individual strands picked up by knitting needles and worked into one fabric. We find that they usually lead peripatetic lives, often getting submerged in discussions, conversations, and banter so that later on history barely records their names.

There was a letter from Friedrich Georg in the mail. He concurs with my suggestion to suppress the introduction to the *Titans*.

PARIS, 8 MAY 1943

Heller and I visited Henri Thomas in Saint-Germain in the afternoon. He lives in an old apartment opposite the château with the salamander decorations. We also met Madame Thomas and two literary friends. I was again amazed at the intellectual precision in these sorts of encounters; what a contrast to similar ones with young Germans, who display their fundamentally anarchic character. They lack higher-level small talk.

In Thomas, personally, I notice the peculiar juxtaposition of mental presence and absence. Talking to him is like having a conversation with someone who lingers far away in distant dreamscapes, and then comes out with surprising and pointed rejoinders. Perhaps both are connected; he "imports" answers. One could say of him, quoting Prince de Ligne, "*j'aime les gens distraits; c'est une marque qu'ils ont des idées*" [I like inattentive people; it is a sign that they have ideas].

Discussion about Pascal, Rimbaud, Léon Bloy, then about the progress of the European revolution. Also talked about Gide, who is staying in Tunis these days. Walked back across the Seine. On the banks the willows gleamed a powerful, almost black green. This river valley is an altar to Aphrodite nourished by ideal moisture conditions.

Visited Florence in the evening; she has just returned from Nice. The usual crowd was there. She talked about Frank J. Gould, who, after reading *Falaises de Marbre* [*On the Marble Cliffs*] said, "it goes from dreams to reality," which for an American billionaire is not a bad review.

After Jouhandeau had been drinking a while, he began to regale us with stories from his marriage, which we found amusing—of course, for the wrong reasons.

He told about a time when Elise was once setting the breakfast table and making a scene about something. He kicked the tray she was holding right out of her hands. The move was done with such perfectly aimed, high-wire accuracy that all the crockery was scattered in pieces across the floor.

PARIS, 10 MAY 1943

Visited the antiquarian bookshop of Dussarp on Rue du Mont-Thabor. There I purchased Balthasar Bekker's *Verzauberte Welt* [*Enchanted World*], a book I have been coveting for a long time. In it I even found the author's inscription in each of the four octavo volumes printed in Amsterdam in 1694.

Thought: I, too, now belong to the untold millions who have contributed to the life's blood of this city, to its thoughts and feelings that are absorbed by the sea of stone and over the course of the centuries, mysteriously transmuted and fashioned into a coral reef of destiny. When I consider that I passed by the Church of Saint-Roch, where César Birotteau[37] was wounded, and passed the corner of Rue des Prouvaires, where the beautiful stocking-seller Baret[38] took Casanova's measurements in the back of the shop—and that those are but two tiny facts in an ocean of fantastical and real events—then I am overcome by a sort of joyful melancholy, of painful desire. I am glad to be part of human life.

The dark afterglow of past life stimulates memory through aromas, odors. In the narrow alleys around the Bastille, I always pick up a little "*essence de Verlaine*" [whiff of Verlaine]. Shadows do the same. By the same token, Méryon is the great draftsman and portrayer of the city.

Visited Salmanoff in the afternoon. He gave me a book by Berdyaev, who is one of his patients. Discussed the fall of Tunis and the political situation in general. He repeated his prophecy about an impending alliance between Russia and Germany. That assumes the collapse of the dictatorship there as well.

Then, talk about illnesses: "sickness unmasks man; it exposes both his good and bad sides more clearly."

He compared Schopenhauer's idea about "what one perceives" to the leaves of an artichoke: there are situations that peel back the human foliage, and reveal "what a man is" in all its glory or triviality.

PARIS, 11 MAY 1943

In the evening I spoke with General Geyer in the Ritz; he was a colleague of Ludendorff in World War I. We talked about the situation, which has become more critical since the fall of Tunis. Then, about the relationship between Ludendorff and Hindenburg, which to me has always illustrated the difference between will and character. After 1918, all Ludendorff had to do was to keep his head down in order to gain everything, but he was incapable of that. He is a case study of all the strengths and weaknesses within the Prussian General Staff, which after the departure of Moltke Senior, focused more single-mindedly on pure dynamism. Herein lies the reason why the General Staff was and remains incapable of resisting

Kniébolo. Minds like this can only implement, only organize, whereas something more, something fundamentally organic, is the prerequisite for resistance.

This organic quality is present in Hindenburg. When Grüner heard that Hindenburg had become Reich president, he said, "at least the old gentleman is never going to do anything stupid." In saying that, he was surely correct. If anything was going to oppose what the future held, it was never going to be the forces of democracy, which had only increased the intensity. Hindenburg's capitulation was unavoidable; it was not a function of his advanced age—that was more or less symbolic. The organic quality that he possessed was particularly related to wood. The "iron Hindenburg" was a wooden, nail-studded Hindenburg. The aura of inherited power certainly surrounds this old gentleman—in contrast to Kniébolo's intrinsically disastrous charisma.

As a young officer I was, of course, for Ludendorff. A contributing factor was a remark the old gentleman once made about me that I found irritating: "it is dangerous for one so young to be decorated with the highest honor." Back then I considered it pedantic, but today I know that it was right. He had seen this confirmed by the fates of many a comrade from 1864, 1866, and 1870.

PARIS, 12 MAY 1943

Discussion with the Doctoresse, who phoned me because her husband had been arrested in Vichy, and what's more, on the very day after she had received that visit here in Paris. Because such abductions are carried out under the aegis of Kniébolo's "Night and Fog Decree"[39]—which means without stating a reason or revealing a place of custody—we first have to find out where they have taken him. I'm glad she relies on me.

PARIS, 13 MAY 1943

Went to Chapon Fin at Porte Maillot in the evening with Dr. Göpel, Sommer, and Heller. Talked about pictures and the magic captured by their artistic content. After the banker Oppenheim had purchased the *White Roses* by van Gogh, he stared at this picture for two hours before going to the meeting where he acquired a majority of stocks in the National Bank—which turned out to be his best business transaction. Viewed this way, the ownership of paintings also possesses a power both magical and real.

Conversation with the owner of the restaurant, who served our meal elaborately. In doing so, he came out with a saying significant to his profession: "*je peux vivre partout où j'ais quarante copains*" [I can live anywhere as long as I have forty companions].

Back in my room, I pondered the tragic side of the people I have encountered here. This restaurateur is an example. His neighbors call him "*le Boche de la Porte Maillot*" [The Kraut of Porte Maillot]. He brims with a passion for all things military and has developed a childlike fondness for Germans. He feels a kinship with our martial, comradely spirit. For me, it was touching to see his fruitless attempts to square this astrological affinity with the contrast based on blood and soil.

Paris, 15 May 1943

About style: Schopenhauer's injunction not to insert relative clauses into the main clause, but rather to let each phrase unfold independently, is absolutely right—especially so when it refers to the clear and logical flow of thoughts in sequence. The presentation of images, on the other hand, and our appreciation of them, may be enhanced by the insertion of the relative clause. Suspense grows and is propelled forward, as if the current in the sentence had shot a spark across the interruption.

We apply such techniques for quite a while before we begin to think about them. In this we are like the peasant who one day suddenly discovers to his amazement that he has been speaking prose.

Read further in Jesus Sirach. The description of the moon, the sun, and the rainbow in Chapter 43 is beautiful. Nearby, in that context, there appears the thought that every detail of creation is good: Evil provides perspective because it appears over the course of time when God then finally puts it to his use. The example of the scorpion is cited. That demonstrates that poisons emerge only temporarily, as in a chemical reaction, during the production of an arcane elixir, where they then function in wisdom's greater plan.

One such sentence, of which there are many in Sirach, can form the foundation for philosophical propositions and moral codes, or for visions like those of Jakob Böhme. In this sense, the Bible is surely the book of books, seed and raw material for all texts. It has brought forth literatures and will continue to do so.

In all its worldly experience, in all its accumulated common sense, Jesus Sirach also contains the bounty of the Orient: "Yet have I more to say, which I have thought upon, and I am full of thoughts as the moon at the full" (38:12).

The Jewish people must return to this, their great literature, and surely the terrible persecution that they now suffer leads them back to it. The Jew, whose cleverness so often makes him disagreeable, becomes a friend and teacher when he speaks as a sage.

Hannover, 19 May 1943

Departure for Kirchhorst from the Gare du Nord. Preceded by a restless night. While my gear was being brought down, I scribbled a line to the president on behalf of the Doctoresse's husband. The prison where he is being held has now been located.

Late arrival in Hannover where I was greeted by air-raid sirens. I took my place in an air-raid cellar and there continued my reading—a story about the unfortunate spring lobster fishermen who were abandoned on the island of Saint-Paul and suffered a lingering death from scurvy.[40] Their fate lets us glimpse the secrets of the most isolated islands as well as the secrets of our bureaucracies. The company that wanted to exploit these cliffs teeming with spring lobsters went bankrupt, and the representatives that they had sent disappeared from contemporary consciousness along with their bankruptcy assets.

After the all-clear signal, I rested for several hours in Hotel Mussmann, where I was shown to a room already occupied by a sleeping guest.

KIRCHHORST, 20 MAY 1943

As I was dressing in the morning, I had a brief conversation with my roommate. He told me that he had commanded a punishment detail in Norway. In that capacity, he had been required to inform a twenty-year-old volunteer who had been sentenced to death that just before his execution, his appeal had been rejected. That had affected him so powerfully that he had been crippled by convulsions, which had now become chronic.

I listened to this long drawn-out story while I was shaving, and I asked him a series of questions while he was still lying in bed, a thick-set man of approximately fifty-eight years of age. He had an amiable face and answered my questions eagerly. I was in a hurry and not all that curious, which gave our exchange an oddly businesslike quality.

I then took the bus the rest of the way. Perpetua showed me the garden, which was in fine shape. It looked more verdant and lush, and at the same time, strangely unfamiliar, like those oases that we speed past on the train, but whose glimpses nonetheless awaken in us a longing to retreat into a shady sanctuary. Here I saw my wish fulfilled. Among the plants, I greeted the *Eremurus* [foxtail lilies] that I had entrusted to the earth before departing for Russia. It had produced four tall stems that had a silver sheen in the snowy green shadows.

Went to the quarry with Alexander where we sunbathed. The veronica: Although I've known this flower since my earliest childhood, it was as if I had seen it today for the first time, with its blue centers whose gray pupils are surrounded by the darkly striated enamel of the iris. It seems that blue things have made a stronger impression on me lately.

KIRCHHORST, 23 MAY 1943

Dreamed of being burdened with the corpse of a murdered man without being able to find a place to conceal it. This was connected to the terrible fear that this dream must be of ancient origin and generally widespread. Cain is certainly one of our great progenitors.

The age of the Book of Genesis is reflected in the fact that it contains great dream figures that reappear in us by night. Perhaps every night. This shows that it is among the sources, the primeval testimony of human history. In addition to the dream of the curse of Cain, other Genesis figures include that of the snake and the dream of being naked and exposed to view in public places.

What will man have been when the final bargain is made about the history of this planet earth? Something sinister and unknown surrounds this being, about whom Psalm 90 sings its terrible song of fate. There have actually been only three figures on the same level with this anonymous one, who lives in all of us: Adam, Christ, Oedipus.

In a world where everything is of consequence, art must cease to exist, for it presupposes differentiation, selection. By extension, if there were no weeds, but merely fruit alone, that would spell the end of horticulture.

The great trajectory of the spirit thus transcends art. The philosopher's stone stands at the culmination of a series of distillations that lead with ever-greater purity toward an absolute, undiluted state. Whoever possesses the stone no longer needs chemical analysis.

We can think of this relationship as traversing a series of gardens where each surpasses the one before it. In each succeeding one, the colors and forms become richer and more luminous. Abundance necessarily reaches its limits at the point when it can no longer be enhanced. Then qualitative changes appear, which both simplify and conceptualize.

In this way, the colors gradually become brighter, then as translucent as gems as they lose their tint and ultimately transmute into colorless clarity. The forms increase into ever-higher and simpler relationships, recapitulating the forms of crystals, circles, and orbs, ultimately eliminating the tension between periphery and center. At the same time, the demarcated areas and differences merge as fruit and blossom, light and shadow are transformed into higher entities. We emerge from this abundance into its source as we enter the glass-walled treasury rooms. Related to this are those crystal tubes in the pictures of Hieronymus Bosch that carry the symbolic meaning of transcendence.

We can already grasp the first beads on this rosary in our daily life—then we must cross over by leaving our bodies behind.

In Paradise—the first and last of these gardens, the divine garden—highest unity prevails: good and evil, life and death are not yet differentiated. Animals do not slaughter each other; they still rest in the hand of the Creator both in their primeval and their spiritually sacrosanct forms. It is the role of the serpent to instruct us in these differences. Then heaven and earth, father and mother, are sundered.

The two great sects that can be traced through the whole history of human thought and knowledge have their origins in this garden. One of these recalls the unity and views the world synoptically, whereas the other works analytically. When times are good, we know where truth originates, in whatever field or area it may appear.

Accusatory precision.[41]

Atome + Hamannsches H = Athome = At home.[42]

KIRCHHORST, 26 MAY 1943

In the early morning, the stationmaster of Burgdorf announced the arrival of Princess Li-Ping. We sent our stout maid, Hanne, out to receive her. In order to protect the little lady from wind and weather, she held her against her substantial bosom. The little creature is beige in color with head, tail, and legs all smoky as if tinged with Chinese ink. She accepted no more than a little piece of tuna fish, but that lustily. Despite her tiny size, this little Siamese sat opposite our three Persian females with arched back, commanding respect with her bristling tail and a hiss like a snake. After sleeping in my bed for a little, she then followed me into the garden like a puppy and jumped onto my lap when I sat down. She displays features of her delicate breeding, her lissome Oriental form reminiscent of bamboo, silk, and opium.

I long ago lost any sense of the Darwinian logic that I used to apply to the coloration of such creatures. Nowadays, it seems to me that she must have been produced by a spontaneous act, as if with brush and ink from a paint box. A little animal like Li-Ping looks as if she had her paws, ears, and the end of her tail dipped in black. Black masks and dark extremities, like the tips of a crab's pincers, naturally suggest creatures that seek shelter in caves, but mask and cave coincide at points that defy analysis.

Darwin's theory is true in the way perspectives are true: they are alignments. Masses of incidental material come into play here, and these can be explained by the role of time—all those millions of years. Amplification lets us glimpse creation.

There was a letter from Friedrich Georg in the mail; we had been waiting for it. In it he devotes some commentary to the word *übrigens* [incidentally]. True, we should pay closer attention to such particles, especially if one has a penchant for them. First of all, they must be necessary, and following that, they need to fit the situation that they are meant to suggest accurately. From this point of view, frequent dissection of sentences that we have written is advisable.

Then there was also a letter from the president, who promises to intervene on behalf of the prisoner. I am now experiencing the friendship of fifty-year-olds as a source of good-natured productivity.

KIRCHHORST, 27 MAY 1943

Mother and Friedrich Georg have arrived. Took a walk via Fillekuhle to the little pond, while Friedrich Georg told stories about the less familiar years in our father's life—for example, the time he spent in London. Perpetua: "When I saw him lying there in his coffin I had the feeling that the nineteenth century now bids us farewell." That is right, for he embodied it quite distinctly, almost too acutely, and I am grateful that Friedrich Georg is collecting memories of him.

In the last war, when we saw each other again, we used to talk about those who had been wounded and killed in action. In this war, we add to those names the ones who have been abducted and murdered.

KIRCHHORST, 30 MAY 1943

Received a visit from Charles Morin, my Parisian antiquarian bookseller. I showed him the books and papers I had purchased from his father in Le Mans. Took a walk with him, Friedrich Georg, and Alexander on the moor where the mullein was in bloom. Its brown cushion throbbed with a lovely warmth.

In my conversations with young French people, I am amazed by their absolute solidarity. This makes the discussion relaxed; the four walls of the room are always there. By contrast, the character Vult from the *Flegeljahre*[43] feels at home in a house that lacks a front wall, which makes it possible for him to enjoy the freedom of nature with its mountains and flowering meadows. The intellectual connections between the Germans and the French could render the contrast between Shakespeare and Molière irrelevant.

Concerning Friedrich Georg's *Titans* and the possible philological objections that have been raised, for example, that sources like the tragedies of Sophocles were not cited. You could counter this by saying that the author is cognizant of the sources and that he generates texts but not the commentary on them. A further word about our methodology in general, about the difference between the recombinative and the logical result: The great laws of correspondence are less dependent upon their era than the laws of causality and are thus better suited to describe the relationship between gods and man. A third work devoted to the heroes is planned. It will cover works about mythology.

KIRCHHORST, 3 JUNE 1943

Mother and brother have departed. I accompanied them to the railroad station in Hannover, which is looking more and more desolate. Who knows what will happen before we see each other again? There is only one maxim, namely that we must befriend death.

When I was with Friedrich Georg, I got the impression that he has entered that stage of life when a man achieves full consciousness of the powers given to him.

The jasmine is blooming in the garden, and this is the first year I have liked its scent. So it goes with many things that are highly prized: in order to take them seriously, we must first break out of that zone where we thought of them as decorations, as literary subjects.

There are people in our lives who take on the role of magnifying glasses, or better said, lenses that warp or coarsen and in doing so, damage us. Such types embody our urges, our passions, perhaps even our secret vices, which are increased by their company. On the other hand, they lack our virtues. Many people attach themselves to their heroes as if to cheap mirrors that distort. Writers frequently employ such characters, often in the person of a servant, for they cast the main characters in a more critical light. An example is Falstaff, who is surrounded by lowly drinking cronies, sensual associates who lack spiritual vigor. They, in their turn, live off his credit.

Such company is sent to test us, to stimulate self-reflection. These characters praise the cheap and gaudy materials of our intellectual and emotional equipment, and we then develop in this direction. It is usually not our own insight that separates us, but some ignominious adventure to which their fellowship has led us. At that point, we bid farewell to our evil spirit.

KIRCHHORST, 4 JUNE 1943

In the afternoon, I spent time in the garden, now in full bloom. I pruned the grape vines and because my time was limited, I did so earlier than experts would have advised. Two small tasks came up that needed attention. One was to preserve those vines that offer some leafy shade to Perpetua's room, and then I had to preserve a robin's nest that was positioned beneath the library window.

The vine stock uses its woody growth of years past to grip more tightly than with those tendrils that are just sprouting. This is a good example for the role of moribund organs in nature's plan. Dead material continues to function and not just historically but also today.

The dead but still functional material (like this wood)—is no mere tool, but pulsates with the echoes of life. It is at work in substances like coal, oil, wax, chalk, wool, horn, ivory. This relationship is mirrored in human economy. Humans feed on that which soon decays, but then they are surrounded by a further layer of matter that resonates with life. Man clothes himself in linen undergarments, in woolen and silken apparel; he lives in a wooden house surrounded by wooden furniture by the light of wax candles or oil lamps. The trappings of temporal life—bed, cradle, table, coffin, wagon, and boat—and then his nobler instruments: the violin, paintbrush, pen, oil painting—all this envelops him like an aura of living matter. His urge to break free from this shell that life has constructed for his protection and bestowed upon mortals, however, has been obvious for a long time. He desires to use his intellectual powers to weave himself an artificial garment. Unforeseen dangers will be the consequence. He will stand before the sun like someone devoid of our atmosphere exposed to cosmic rays.

If our love is to bear fruit, we must prune the *Phalaenopsis* orchid back to one node.

The resistance of the Jews in the Warsaw Ghetto seems to have ended with their annihilation. Here, for the first time, they fought as if against Titus[44] or during the persecutions of the Crusades. As always in such encounters, several hundred Germans apparently joined their cause.

KIRCHHORST, 7 JUNE 1943

Current reading: Have gone back to Lichtenberg again, that rare example of a German who recognizes limits. It seems that the Germanic race always has something weighty tying it down, a kind of shackle, so that we don't escape and get lost in the atmosphere. With the English, that can be the fetters of the sea; in the case of [Theodor] Fontane, the admixture of blood from the West.[45] For Lichtenberg, it's the hunchback he bears.

The German is like certain kinds of wine that are most enjoyable when blended.

Read further in *Naufrage de la Médus* [*Shipwreck of the Medusa*] by Corréard and Savigny (Paris, 1818). The instructive aspect of these shipwrecks—and I have studied quite a few recently—is that they depict doomsday scenarios in miniature.

KIRCHHORST, 16 JUNE 1943

Last day of my furlough—perhaps the last one I'll get in this war? After breakfast, a walk in the garden and in the cemetery. There on the graves, magnificent examples of freshly blooming fire lilies. The flower exudes remarkable power, incandescent as it blazes amidst the lush plants in the dappled shade of the bushes. There it glows like a lamp radiating sensuality onto the hidden abundance of life. Our capacity is comparable to the tent that Peri Banu gave to her prince in *One Thousand and One Nights*: When folded, it fits into a nutshell, and when unfolded, it offers shelter to entire armies. This indicates its origin in an unexpanded world.

There are moments when we have direct recourse to this capacity, as for example when we extend our hand to take leave from a visitor after an important conversation. In that moment of silence, we seek to convey more than all the words that preceded our parting. After weighing the pros and cons of a plan, it also happens that we finally listen to our inner self without any thought or intention. Then we feel either encouraged or pressured to change.

The relationship between youth and age is not linear across time, but rather qualitative and periodic. There have already been several times in my life when I was older than I am today, most especially when I was roughly thirty years old. I also see this in photographs of me. There are periods when we are "finished." These can be followed by periods of relaxing, which are so important for creative people. Certainly Eros often brings renewed youth. New growth can be promoted by pain, sickness, or losses in the same way that the tree's new foliage crowns what the gardener has pruned.

A creative person's strength relies, generally speaking, on his vegetative state, whereas the strength of the active man draws on his animal volition. No matter how old the tree grows to be, it is young again in each of its new buds. Sleep, dreams, games, relaxation, and wine are also part and parcel of this.

Current reading: Faulkner's *Pylon*, a book I am rereading after many years because it describes the abstract hell of the world of technology with such precision. I also picked up the tale of *Captain Raggad, the Mountain Splitter* again, which Cazotte included in his continuation of *One Thousand and One Nights*. Reading this is always such a pleasure. This man Raggad is the prototype of the braggart and petty tyrant who undermines himself through his own boundless avarice carried to extreme. His extraordinary gluttony can barely be satisfied, yet "the fear he instills in everyone keeps any help at bay." He intimidates people with his arsenal of technology, yet that breaks down of its own accord. He is destined to be victorious without ever enjoying the victory.

ON THE TRAIN, 17 JUNE 1943

Departed from Hannover in the afternoon as I have so often; Perpetua brought me to the station. Tight embraces—I do not know what can happen in the coming days, but I know the human being I am leaving behind.

Journey through the burned-out cities of western Germany, which form a line like a dark chain, and the thought again occurs—this is how things look in people's heads. That impression was intensified from my conversations with other travelers. Their response to this ruined cityscape expressed itself in the wish to see the carnage expanded. They hoped to see London soon in the same condition and muttered rumors about immense artillery batteries that are supposedly being built along the Channel coast to target that city.

PARIS, 18 JUNE 1943

Arrived in Paris around nine o'clock. Right away, I received a report from the president about the prisoner's fate, which is uncertain.

The mail brought a letter from Friedrich Georg. He is coming to the end of his stay in Leisnig and plans to travel to Überlingen. The employment bureau there has got their hooks into him for a job as a typist. The authority of these secretaries and policemen leads to grotesque developments. Minds like this would scrape the paint off a Titian to make themselves a pair of canvas slippers.

Grüninger continues to send letters and journal entries written by soldiers killed at Stalingrad. The noncommissioned officer Nüssle—a man I knew—was killed near Kursk on 11 February. During the past two winters, there have been decisive confrontations in the East and engagements in the desert after we had already reached the absolute nadir. Once broken like this, the spirit takes on child-like, touching traits that are apparent in the monologues from Nüssle. Clutching a hand grenade to his breast, he staggered across the snow-covered street as the fire from pursuing tanks blazed all around him in the darkness. "Dear God, You know that if I pull the pin now, this grenade is not meant for me."

PARIS, 19 JUNE 1943

Went to Rumplemeyer's [Café] in the afternoon to inquire about the prisoner, who seems to be doing better than the information from the president implied. Purchased the new monograph about James Ensor in a bookshop on Rue de Rivoli. Then off to Auteuil to visit Salmanoff, who was satisfied with my earthly form.

"There are two clinical methods. One is cosmetic, the other, hygienic. I used the latter with you."

Salmanoff said that the contest will be over in the month of October. Consideration of morale: This is insignificant no matter how low it may sink. The despairing masses are like zeroes who will, of course, become extremely important as soon as somebody new makes them feel significant.

It's remarkable that the handwriting of gastronomes is almost always vertical.

Kniébolo's, on the other hand, tends downward more strongly than any I have ever seen. It represents the *nihilum nigrum* [little black spot] in the divine pharmacopoeia. He certainly has no appreciation of good food.

PARIS, 22 JUNE 1943

Hohly, the painter, paid me a visit and brought me one of his woodcuts. Discussion about Cellaris, whose conduct is viewed as exemplary. It demonstrates how rare true resistance is on this earth. As early as 1926, he had already founded a journal with this name—*Resistance*. It seems that shortly before his arrest, he had a premonition of things to come. His aged mother, who was dying at the time, would call out in her death throes, "Ernst, Ernst, it is so terrible the way they persecute you." Later, in Blankenburg, Dr. Strünkmann sank into a trancelike state during a conversation. It lasted for a couple of seconds. Turning quite pale, he said, clairvoyantly, "Cellaris—I shall never see you again—terrible things loom in your future." All this contrasts starkly with Cellaris's very sober and worldly character. This much is certain: This man could have been a significant force in German history. He would have channeled the stream in a direction that would have permitted a unification of power and mind, which are currently divided. He could have done so well enough to bring incomparably greater stability and security. Of course, the demagogues promised all this more cheaply, while also recognizing how dangerous he was. It is certain that under his aegis war with Russia would have been avoided, perhaps even war in general. Nor would it ever have come to these atrocities perpetrated against the Jews, which enrage the cosmos against us.

PARIS, 23 JUNE 1943

Visited Florence at noon. She showed me paintings that she has ordered to decorate her place. Among them are a portrait of Lord Melville by Romney, a Goya, a Jordaens, a few primitives—in short, a small gallery. I was impressed by the way she picked the pictures up off the floor so matter-of-factly, like a person used to handling burdens heavier than human strength can bear.

Breakfast, then coffee in my "little office." Discussion about Faulkner's *Pylon* and Irving's *Sketchbook*.

Took a walk in the Bois in the evening. At the foot of a mighty oak, I spotted a male stag beetle, one of the variety whose antlers have atrophied to a simple pair of pincers. Back in Mardorf, that forsaken hamlet in the Steinhuder Meer region, I used to catch huge specimens of this insect in the ancient oak forests, and I have always hoped I would find this small type. Now I was seeing it here sitting on a root, its ruddy carapace glistening in the late sun, emerging from a long-cherished dream. Such a sight always reminds me of how immensely wonderful animal display is, and that these creatures are just as much part of us as the rose petals are of the calyx. This is the stuff of our life, our primeval strength is here reflected in the faceted mirror.

As is always the case when we eavesdrop on private worlds, other unbidden insights emerge. I stumbled upon couples in the woods, out in the mild evening weather, in every stage of amorous embrace. Over the years, the undergrowth of round bushes has been hollowed out like green globes or lanterns, into bowers. Into these, courting couples had carried the yellow chairs that the city places all around the woods in large numbers. One could spy on the sexes there in silent embrace as the shadows fell. I passed by sculptural compositions like this: The man sitting on the chair stroked his lover's thighs slowly upward with both hands as she stood before him, and when his hand reached her hips, pulled up her light spring dress. In this manner the thirsty reveler grips the lovely belly of the amphora and lifts the vessel to his mouth.

In this struggle, I stand on the side of letters and against numbers.

PARIS, 25 JUNE 1943

In the morning, Dr. Göpel came by and told me of his visit to the house where van Gogh died. There he had a conversation with the son of the doctor who had treated van Gogh. He mentioned his name—I think it was Dr. Gachet. Göpel said that in such cases a milieu that is emotionally understated more readily prevents the catastrophe. Thus it was only right for Hölderlin to go and live with a master carpenter. Gachet was remarkably reticent: "No one can know what someone may write in fifty years about our conversation." That is surely true but cannot be changed. Our words are stones we throw, and we cannot know whom they may hit behind that wall of years. And that is especially true in the context of great solitary figures, who act as lamps in the darkness of our amnesia.

Then had a conversation with Colonel Schaer about Kirchhorst, where his sister used to reside in the parsonage in front of us. The so-called Security Service here seems to have allied itself with French criminals in order to extort rich Frenchmen. Their tactic is apparently to forge a photograph showing the victim keeping company with Freemasons.

Schaer also said that the last attack on western Germany cost sixteen thousand lives in a single night. The images are becoming apocalyptic; people are seeing fire raining down from heaven. This is actually an incendiary compound of rubber and phosphorus that is inextinguishable and inescapable as it engulfs all forms of life. There are stories of mothers who have been seen flinging their children into rivers. This hideous escalation of atrocities has produced a kind of nightmare. People are expecting unimaginable retribution and the enemy's use of more potent horrors that await them. They cling to the hope of new weapons, yet all the while, they are in a condition where only new thoughts, new feelings are imperative.

Now, letters. After a considerable interruption, I thought I would soon receive a letter from Feuerblume again, but I then noticed that it was not from her but rather in her mother's handwriting. She informs me of the death of her daughter, who died in Paris! I knew that this city was her goal—and so she reached it after all, yet this time without first having heard the word "tosdo" in a dream: "*so Tod!*" [Thus death.][46] This girl, from whom I first received that curious letter in Bourges, the Capua[47] of 1940, looms as a romantic figure in my life. There was a time when in my mind she would take me by the hand and show me her garden with its castle topped by the weathervane bearing the inscription, "Do as you wish."[48] We saw each other a few times; over the years, she sent me hundreds of letters. This blossoming, this intellectual development, as if in a hothouse, presented a drama that could have been very fulfilling for someone less preoccupied. To me it all seemed excessive, but today I can see its significance. I think I'll also find it in the stacks of hastily written papers: In these times of collapse, she was looking for a sincere reader, a good chronicler. In that I hope I will not have disappointed her.

Then there was a letter from Zwickledt from that old sorcerer Kubin, whose astrological scratchings are becoming ever more illegible, yet at the same time more logical. These are the true letters, ideograms drawing our eyes into surreal vortices. In one passage, I thought I had grasped it: "—and yet, at the end of the day, nothing more than the astral theater, which our soul produces by itself—me!"

Evening. It has become an almost daily habit to take a solitary walk in the Bois. Here, for the first time, I saw the little woodpecker, the smallest of its family, and noticed how its behavior was just like that in the fine description that Naumann provided for it. I related this to Heinrich von Stülpnagel, who always appreciates such communiqués.

Perhaps I should start collecting material for an account of the historical era when my consciousness first awakened, that is to say, between 1900 and the end of this war. I could use my own story for it, as well as what I have seen and heard about other people. Of course, it would not be much more than notes, because I don't have the free time to do more, and furthermore, I am still much too young for it.

Finished reading the Book of Baruch. The last chapter of this book is significant for its detailed description of magic cults and idolatry. It counts among those portions of holy writ allied with that of the world of Herodotus.

Paris, 26 June 1943

Visited Gruel. My time there and our conversation about types of leather and bindings always give me the feeling of the late flowering of craftsmanship. What a delight it would be to live in cities populated solely by such fellows. Perhaps Tamerlane created something like that when he captured the artists, the masters from all lands, like colorful birds for his birdcages.

Then stopped by the little Church of Saint-Roch. There on the steps, I am reminded of César Biroteau[49] every time. Here, too, I find that tiny Parisian symbol, the ammonite [fossil whorl snail], scattered throughout the stone.

On the quays, among the books; just reading the countless titles alone is instructive. Interrupted again when the sirens sounded, which happens frequently, but the Parisians don't let that disturb them as they go about their business.

Thought about my grammar as I strolled. I have to go deeper into the vowel sounds. The written word has created a connection between language and the eye that is too strong—the original relationship is between language and the ear. Language is *lingua*—it is tongue, and when written, it assumes the presence of an especially strong listener in the mind. *Orare* [pray] and *adorare* [worship]—the activity here designated is the same, yet the prefix points to the divine presence. What an enormous difference between *o—a* and *a—o—a*.

Current reading: Guégan, *Le Cuisinier Français* [*The French Cook* (Paris, 1934)].

"*Couper en morceaux la langouste vivante et faites-la revenir à rouge vif dans un poêlon de terre avec un quart de beurre très frais.*" [Cut a living lobster into pieces and let it turn bright red again in a crockery cooking pot with a quart of fresh butter.]

Paris, 29 June 1943

Clemens Podewils told me about Maillol, whom he visited in Banyuls. He is now over eighty and lives there as a sculptor and sage. Every third thing he says is supposedly, "*a quoi ça sert?*" [what good is that?]. Then about Li-Ping. The peculiar thing about Siamese cats is that they are more devoted to people than the house they live in. In this, they combine the attributes of cats and dogs.

Felt flushed with fever in the evening; took a long bath and pored over the new beetle catalogue from Reitter in Troppau. I am now studying the arid Latinisms as if they were musical notation, but instead of music, colors keep coming to mind. The great lack of merchandise and the excess of insects are producing a boom in the market for dried specimens. This is one of the unusual consequences of our economic situation. Whereas the principal branches of our economy are withering on the tree, the most remote twigs are thriving. Sometime I'd like to speak with an economist about this, someone who has an overview of the field and insight into the fiction of currency. There is a lot to be learned here, as is especially true in times when the disintegration of those obscure inner workings of the social machine are revealed. We can discern things the way children examine the insides of their broken toys.

We humans—our amorous encounters, our struggles about fidelity, about attraction. Their significance is greater than we know, yet we perceive them in our suffering, our passion. The issue is which rooms we shall share in that absolute state beyond the realm of death; it depends on what heights we shall attain together. This explains the terror that can come over us when we are between two women—these are matters of salvation.

Vokale: Pokale?[50] The vowel is carried by the consonant; it captures the inexpressible in the same way that the fruit holds the kernel and the kernel the seed.

PARIS, 30 JUNE 1943

Direct hits from bombs have struck the Cologne Cathedral. As I read in the newspaper, its "smoke-blackened walls are said to be a beacon of vengeance for the German people." Is that supposed to mean that we intend (to the extent that we can) to set Westminster ablaze?

PARIS, 2 JULY 1943

Had a number of different visits in the course of the morning. One was from a military chaplain named Mons, who brought me greetings; another from a ballistics expert named Kraus, who is friends with Brother Physicus;[51] and another from Valentiner, who is back in his studio for a few days. Noncommissioned officer Kretzschmar also brought me a copy of his Schiller biography.

I heard from the ballistics expert that Cellaris is now in the gravest danger. They have begun to "clear" the prison where he is being held, but at the first attempt to take him, the director, the chaplain, and the guards are all said to have stood in front of him. The protection that these people can give the infirm, defenseless victim is for the moment only minimal. The son of this same Cellaris is, incidentally, posted to the Russian front.

Paris, 3 July 1943

In Cologne, divine services are being held outdoors in front of the smoking rubble of the churches. This is one of those details that can't be invented. I predicted it long before the outbreak of this war.

Many of the letters I receive take on an ominous, eschatological tone, like cries from the deepest regions of the vortex, that place that gives us a glimpse of rock bottom.

Perpetua, on 30 June: "As far as you are concerned, I feel certain that you will escape the great maelstrom unscathed. Never abandon your trust in your true destiny."

In Edgar Allan Poe's tale about the maelstrom, we possess one of those great visions that foretold our catastrophe in the most vivid way. We have now sunk into that region of the whirlpool where the dark mathematics of the alliances can be gauged in all their grim proportions; at the same time, all is more simplified and more terrifying. The noblest gesture instantly produces paralysis.

Paris, 4 July 1943

There is a collection of records from military tribunals circulating around here for our edification. Among them I find the following verdicts:

Without being threatened himself, an officer guns down several Russian prisoners and at the hearing explains the deed by declaring that his brother had been murdered by partisans. He is sentenced to two years in prison. When the verdict is presented to Kniébolo, he countermands it and orders the officer acquitted with the justification that, when fighting beasts, it is impossible to keep a cool head.

During a traffic jam, another officer is negligent in not leaving his vehicle to intervene with the other drivers, as prescribed by orders. He is sentenced to two years in prison and a demotion.

From such a contrast, we can see what is considered excusable and what is considered criminal in a world of chauffeurs. Of course the issue is not, as I had long believed, merely one of moral color-blindness; that applies only to the masses. In their innermost inclinations, minds like Kniébolo's are bent on the most comprehensive homicide possible. They seem to belong to a world of corpses that they want to populate—they find the stench of the slain pleasant.

Finished reading Fridtjof Mohr, *Weites Land Afrika* [*The Expanse of Africa* (Berlin 1940)]. Such books provide the same sort of pleasure as good films, but they also leave behind the same dissatisfaction. The way they record colors or the motion of forms has a mechanical quality. Images flash past, as though through the windows of a moving car that accelerates in some places and slows down in others. With this style of factual description, literature reaches a level that really everyone, or at least the majority, can attain—just as the great majority can take photographs.

I've gradually changed my mind about this, namely that this kind of technical realism is preferable to impressionism. Yet their close chronological succession is inevitable.

An annoying stylistic aspect of this translation from the Norwegian is the especially frequent use of the construction *als* [when; as] with the present tense.

"When I reach the peak of the hill I espy an antelope at the edge of the forest." The "when" always indicates past time; with this conjunction, one more or less applies the first brushstrokes to a canvas of the past. Regarding the succession, the demarcation, and intersection of time levels: In general, innate logic persists in language, no matter how many forms of verbs have passed out of use or become rare. Over time, we have developed a series of methods and tools that can help us preserve the temporal aspect and the architectonics of the description without succumbing to the demand that Schopenhauer makes in his annotations: that we artificially preserve archaic verb forms.

PARIS, 5 JULY 1943

Benno Ziegler has arrived; I haven't seen him for almost a year. We discussed his publishing house, which—against all the odds of current practice—has been converted into a private commercial venture. He had to conduct all the necessary negotiations and business deals with the utmost tact. In these days of automatism, it is always refreshing to see someone swimming diagonally across, not to say against, the current.

We got down to the situation at hand. Two different wars are coming into focus with ever-greater clarity: one being waged in the West, the other in the East. This corresponds to an ideological distinction. The best that Kniébolo can offer the German people today is that the war will last indefinitely. Ziegler observed that the young Clémenceau, if I'm not mistaken, heard from Gambetta: "Do not rely on the generals. They are cowards."

Troubled sleep. In the early morning hours, I started thinking, as I often do, about various writers, among them Léon Bloy. I saw an image of him in a small house in the suburbs, where he was sitting at his desk. Along the garden path, the blossoming chestnut trees could be seen through the open window, and there was an angel dressed in the blue uniform of a postman.

PARIS, 6 JULY 1943

Visited Florence's apartment, where there was plenty of good conversation rich in anecdotes. I liked the story that Giraudoux told about a grateful prisoner who was rescued from the guillotine by a certain lawyer, Dupont, from Lyon. The man was deported to Cayenne.[52] Once there, he wished to send a present to his attorney. Because, however, he owned nothing, all he had was what nature provided, and, furthermore, as a prisoner, he was not allowed to send packages. One day a ship landed in Marseille with a cargo of parrots. Among them was one that was heard to cry out, "*Je vais chez Maître Dupont à Lyon.*" [I am going to Master Dupont in Lyon.]

PARIS, 8 JULY 1943

After breakfast, I read Psalm 90. In it the mayfly[53] achieved its most powerful and tragic hymn.

Found a letter from Grüninger in the mail. He inquires whether or not I wish to come to the East on a particular mission that General Speidel has for me concerning the fate of the soldiers of Stalingrad. This confirms my experience that once we have come in contact with a country, we continue to feel drawn to it. In this case, I had not even tossed a coin into the Pshish, which is otherwise my habit along riverine borders. When will they all take effect—those copper coins I tossed into the Aegean on Rhodes or dropped into the Atlantic at Rio? Perhaps in death—when we inhabit all the regions of the seas and stars and are at home everywhere.

Visited Dr. Epting in the evening. There I also saw Marcel Déat and his wife. We talked about the third part of the journal by Fabre-Luce, which was published thanks to cleverly avoiding the censors and now seems to be causing considerable outrage. I get the impression that a story involving the police will follow.

Déat, whom I met for the first time, has certain traits that I have noticed in different people, but which I cannot quite define. I am talking about severely moral processes that become discernible in a person's physiognomy, notably in the skin. These traits sometimes give it a parchment quality and, at other times, a hard-edged aspect, but in any case, a coarsened character. Striving for power at any price toughens a man and also makes him vulnerable to demonic urges. One can sense this aura; it became especially clear to me when he drove me home in his car after the evening ended. Without even having seen the two brawny gentlemen, who had been invisible all evening but were now sitting beside the driver, I would have sensed that our journey was not completely innocent. Danger loses its appeal in bad company.

"Youth" is one of those fetish words that constantly crops up in conversation with minds like this: "*Les jeunes*" is pronounced with the sort of emphasis that used to be reserved for "the Pope." For what it's worth, it is insignificant whether youth is actually on their side or not. It is more a matter of the combination of their ardor and minimal judgment—a combination that the troublemakers recognize as a resource that can be used to their benefit.

Current reading: the great glossary in medieval Latin by Du Cange, which I bought in three folios for a song. Here one skims along through the cosmos of a bygone literature. Afterward, I browsed a bit in Schopenhauer for the first time in years. In his pages, I found confirmation for many an experience I've had recently: "If only I could dispel the illusion that the spawn of toads and adders are creatures like me, I would be a lot better off."

All right, fine. But on the other hand, you always have to say to yourself, when confronted with the lowest of the animals: "This is you!"

This is my eternally dual role: to perceive both antagonism and affinity at the same time. This limits my participation in actions where I recognize patterns of injustice. It also makes me aware that the demise of a lesser creature is accompanied by some justification. As a result, I see things more clearly than is sometimes advantageous for an individual, unless he is writing history in retrospect.

Paris, 9 July 1943

Said my goodbyes to Benno Ziegler at Le Caneton. He brought me the news that Fabre-Luce had been arrested this morning. We talked about the last days of

A. E. Günther, who fought for breath for a long time before he died. His last word to his brother: " . . . and all this while fully conscious." This applies to the suffering of the twentieth century in general.

At ten o'clock, I strolled back via Boulevard Poissonnière. Every time I do so, I'm reminded of the con artist who accosted me there so many years ago. It was typical that I immediately saw through the situation, but I nonetheless let myself be clumsily duped by him and his accomplices, who appeared so obviously "by chance." In sum, I played along with them against my better judgment.

Today I read in the Army Regulations Journal that General Rupp had been killed, that small melancholy convivial division commander I knew in the Caucasus. Reports of the deaths of my friends are increasing, as are those of the destruction of their houses in the bombings.

PARIS, 10 JULY 1943

I fasted. I feel that in the long run the artificial life of this city is not good for me. This morning briefly in Saint-Pierre Charron, my little church with the toads where I again found the gate of death open.[54]

The battle that has been raging in the center of the eastern front offers a new spectacle of unusual ferocity for this region. The forces have equalized, and with that there is no more mobility; the fire is reaching a crescendo.

Went back to the little streets around Boulevard Poissonnière in the afternoon, where I delved into the dust of the past. In the pleasant bookshop of Poursin on Rue Montmartre, it was a joy to peruse books. There I purchased a series on the *Abeille* [*Bee*] quite advantageously. The first volume had a dedication in an old man's handwriting from the entomologist Régimbart.

In the evening had a discussion with Schery, the Viennese musician, about rhythm and melody, representation and coloration, consonants and vowels.

This day is notable for the British landing in Sicily. This first contact with Europe has had repercussions; we are at a higher level of alert.

Current reading: *Les Bagnes.*[55] The book contains the assertion that when the prisoners of *bagnos* are executed, even the most violent and fearsome man embraces the priest who has escorted him. The presence of the clergyman here represents the human being *per se*, which does not mean the representative of humanity as opposed to the Eternal, but rather symbolic man, the one who on our behalf has raised his voice in Psalm 90. As such, he has the role of witness in a matter that transcends crime or punishment.

Words: For *terasser*, meaning "knock down, throw to the ground," we lack a verb of similar precision. In general, verbs derived from nouns are stronger. In them movement is intensified by the material quality that is the royal prerogative of the noun. By the same token, *fourmiller* [teem, tingle] is more evocative than *wimmeln* [swarm, teem]; *pivoter* is more plastic than *schwenken* [swivel]; and *barbieren* is preferable to *rasieren* [shave].

Conversely, those nouns derived from verb forms are weaker. "Dying" is thus weaker than "death;" "wound" is more forceful than "cut."

PARIS, 11 JULY 1943

Continued my fasting regimen. Was in the city on many streets and squares in the middle of the day. I was aimless, a man in the crowd, which had an idle Sunday air about it. Brief visit to Notre Dame de Lorette. There I noticed a row of votive candles that were made of glass and not of the customary wax. A pointed electric bulb formed the flame. These were placed on tables with slots where people inserted money, and these then produced the electric circuit that lighted the candle for a shorter or longer period, depending on the denomination of the coin. I watched women play this devotional vending machine, for that awful word is the only one that does justice to the process.

This church preserves a door to the cell that once confined one of their priests, the Abbé Sabatier. He was imprisoned behind it before the mob murdered him in 1871.[56]

Afterward, I visited Valentiner, who is returning to Aix today. On the quai, I saw two old hourglasses, which were unfortunately very expensive.

Scant news from Sicily. The landing is successful. We shall have to wait and see whether it will advance beyond the formation of bridgeheads. The results of this fighting will let us predict the general outcome. The island is once more reverting to its ancient role of the pointer on the scale between two continents, just as in the days of the Punic Wars.

PARIS, 13 JULY 1943

Restless, nervous night, triggered by air-raid sirens. Then I dreamed about snakes, particularly about dark, black ones that devoured the bright, colorful ones. I seldom get a feeling of terror from these creatures, which are so central to our dreams—for the most part, they seem to be showing me their side of life, their fluid, swift, flexible character stated so beautifully by Friedrich Georg:

Und wie der Natter Bauch
Der silbern glänzet
Wenn schnell sie fliegt, so floh
Der Bach umkränzet.

[And as the adder's belly / Glistens silver, / When quickly it flees, thus fled / The festooned brook.]

The primal force of these creatures lies in the fact that they embody life *and* death, as well as good *and* evil. At the same moment that man acquired the knowledge of good and evil from the serpent, he acquired death. The sight of a snake is thus an experience filled with incomparable dread for each of us—almost stronger than the sight of sexual organs, with which there is also a connection.

The commander-in-chief communicated to me through Colonel Kossmann that, for the moment, I cannot travel to Russia. I am sorry about that, because I would have liked to clear my head, and I could do with Caesar's remedy of those long marches.

The mail included a letter from First Lieutenant Güllich. He writes that his regimental staff on the eastern front is reading the *Marble Cliffs*: "At night, once the pressure of the battle and the appalling experiences of the day had subsided, we went to our tents, where, in the *Marble Cliffs*, we read about what we had actually experienced."

At noon I encountered the young captain who had covered me with his coat in Kiev. It is always remarkable how the different pieces, the different landscapes, of our existence interweave and coalesce. We hold the power to create patterns within us, and I can say that everything we experience is like those pictures in a tapestry that have been wrought from a single thread.

In the evening, visited Count Biéville de Noyant, who lives on Rue des Saints-Pères in a large house that is decorated with extraordinary care. Such dwellings, of which Paris—and especially the Left Bank—boasts a large number, are secret repositories of ancient cultural material radiating extraordinary power. Of course, at the same time, objects can gain the upper hand—things whose only function seems to be to radiate an aura but which have lost their utility and that gives a haunted aspect to any visit there. The thought came to me when I saw an old chess set with exquisite figures that graced a table but was for the eyes alone.

There I met the critic Thierry Maulnier, Mlle. Tassencourt, and Admiral Ceillier, who is a man of considerable substance, as are most Navy men in this terrestrial nation. It is his opinion that art in France is much less individualized than in Germany, which explains the lack or absence of geniuses but the abundance of talents. That is also the reason, he said, that the creative urge is more collective: its greatest feat, its most significant work of art, is the city of Paris.

We conversed about Marshal Lyautey, André Gide, Hércule, Janin, Malraux, and others. Later the talk turned to the fighting in Sicily and the prospects for a German-French rapprochement. All this makes it clear to me how far outside our national state I already stand. Such conversations remind me of Lichtenberg, who sometimes would play the atheist just for the sake of practice, or of General Jomini on the battlefield, who tried to think for the enemy's General Staff. Today people are fighting under the old banners for a new world; they still believe they are back where they began. Yet this is not a moment to try to be too clever, for the self-delusion that guides them is necessary for their actions and it belongs to the greater apparatus.

The German position is favorable, as will be revealed if we should be defeated. At that point all secondary advantages will disappear, leaving only the primary ones, like that of our location. It will then be clear, as Rivière said so well, that the Germans are not a people of "either-or" but rather of "not only, but also." As a result, two paths will open to them rather than today's single one that has brought this deadlock upon them. In this scenario, it will depend on them whether the twentieth century world looks to the East or West, or whether synthesis is possible.

Paris, 15 July 1943

Style. In phrases such as "I would like to hear your views about it" and the like, language reaches erroneously from the domain of one of the senses into a different one. This sort of thing usually happens when people thoughtlessly accept clichés. When it is the product of vitality, however, such a change of imagery can cause the expression to take on synaesthetic proportions.

Paris, 16 July 1943

Went to the Ministry of the Navy in the morning for a briefing on the situation. Topic: the *Penicion Aktion*, meaning the deployment of all available canal barges to the South to be used there as small shipping vessels to supply the troops in Sicily. The superiority of the English in the air and on the seas makes it impossible to deploy large freighters. That says enough about the situation.

Paris, 17 July 1943

At lunch with the president, brief discussion about our prisoner just between the two of us.

Coffee at Banine's. It was such a potent Turkish brew that I had an accelerated heartbeat all afternoon. She gave me Bunyan's *Pilgrim's Progress* and *Brave New World* by Huxley, which she had bought for me. We spoke at first about harems, then about Schopenhauer, and about Professor Salmanoff, and finally about the domain of the senses within the realm of language, a subject that I find myself turning to frequently these days. She told me that in Russian one says, "I hear an odor."

For the expression, "He fixed his eyes on an object," the Turk says, "He sewed them to it." I asked her to do a little bit of word hunting for me; I need assistants for my plan. For a title I could choose *Metagrammar* or *Metagrammatical Excursions*.

It was extremely hot on the way home; the intense heat brought street life to a standstill. Through a shop window, I observed the interior of a small antiquarian bookshop on Rue Lauriston. There among the ancient furniture, pictures, glass objects, books, and rarities, sat the shop girl—a beautiful young woman wearing a hat decorated with feathers—asleep in an embroidered easy chair. There was something magnetic about her sleep: neither her chest nor her nostrils moved. And so I gazed into an enchanted chamber where all the contents seemed precious, but even the sleeper herself had been transformed into an automaton.

The afternoon in general seemed bewitched, as when I entered the German bookstore, where it seemed that all the salesgirls collectively defied me. Things like that have happened to me only rarely in my life. As if in a dream, I climbed the steps that led up into other rooms without worrying whether or not the public had access to them. And I entered a room where magazines lay on a table. I thumbed through them and wrote a few marginal notes beside political images that caught my eye. Then I turned and went back into the shop, where the cohort of salesgirls scrutinized me with great deliberation. I heard one of them ask, "What was he doing up there?"

Browsed in the *Dictionnaire de la Langue Verte. Argots Parisiennes Comparés* by Delvau [*Dictionary of the Green Language; a Comparison of Parisian Argots* (Paris, 1867)]. There I found Breda Street defined as a Parisian Cythera[57] inhabited by a population of women for over twenty years, "*Dont les moeurs laissent à désirer—mais ne laissent pas longtemps desirer*" [Whose morals leave something to be desired—though desire is not long deferred].

A *Bismarcker* was a double hit in billiard players' jargon. The word first appeared in May 1866.

Donner cinq et quatre, to deal five and four [fingers], designates one of those slaps with the hand that is given first from the right and then from the left with the open hand, and then in the other direction, with the back of the same hand. With the second swipe, the thumb is not used. If this slap is given twice, one says *donner dix-huit*, to give someone eighteen.

PARIS, 18 JULY 1943

A sleepless night, after reading the first stations in Bunyan's *Pilgrim's Progress*. Banine's coffee had a lasting aftereffect. I turned on the light again around midnight and wrote down the following notes while sitting up in bed:

I notice that I harbor a special dislike for people who make insupportable assertions, and yet they apply all their energy in an attempt to persuade me. Brazen insolence or flippancy—of propaganda, for example—has something that I initially take seriously. I have trouble believing that nothing more than pure wishful thinking backs up such arguments.

Years later when the facts speak for themselves, I often feel the sting all the more sharply. I realize that I have been made a fool of by true pimps, by wicked rent boys of the regime in power. They had dressed up their whore to resemble truth.

Then there is the fact that they lack any sense of intellectual shame. The only blush they know is the one that results from a slap in the face. That means that they will always put their whoremongering to new uses, even for men and authorities for whom one has some respect and considers honest. That is especially galling to hear when these villains praise truth out of sheer opportunism.

I sense that my love of truth almost makes me an absolutist. I can break the moral code, act irresponsibly toward my neighbor—but I cannot deviate from what I recognize as authentic and true. In this respect, I am like a youth who might agree to marry an old lady—yet that wedding night sees no consummation, aphrodisiacs notwithstanding. The involuntary muscles of my mind will not perform their duty here. For me, truth is like a woman whose embraces condemn me to impotence in the arms of another. She alone embodies freedom and, hence, happiness.

Thus it happens that my access to theology comes via insight. I first have to prove to myself that God exists before I can believe in Him. This means that I must return to Him along the same path on which I left Him. Before I can dare to cross the river of time and reach the other shore with my whole self and without reservation, spiritual bridgeheads and subtle reconnaissance must precede me. Grace would certainly be preferable, but that is not appropriate to the situation, nor to my condition. That stands to reason; I sense that it is my work—these arches that anchor me to earth. Every one of these braces the interplay of doubt from the ground up and keeps me anchored. Thus, through my work, I can guide some people to that good shore. Another man may be able to fly, or lead those who trust him by the hand across the waters. Yet it seems that the eons do not give birth to such types.

When it comes to our theology, this has to be utterly modest and appropriate to our species, which is so devoid of fundamental vitality. For anyone who can see such vitality, our faith has long since lived more powerfully in biology, chemistry, physics, paleontology, than in the churches. In a similar fashion, philosophy has become splintered into specialized disciplines. These are naturally dead ends. The disciplines must again be purged of theology as well as of philosophical influences. This must happen for their own sake so that mere *weltanschauung* may again become science. The theological and philosophical elements have to be precipitated out, like gold and silver; as gold, theology then lends currency and value to the sciences. It also reins them in, for it is obvious where unbridled knowledge leads. Like Phaeton's chariot, it sets the world aflame and has made us and our *imagos* into Moors, Negroes, and cannibals.

Additional notes:

After a strenuous hunt for insects in the mountainous forests of Brazil, I work through my trophies back on the ship at night. It happened that I once made a mistake by one day as I completed the labels showing time and place of discovery. I wrote something like 14 December 1936 instead of the 15th. Although it in no way changed anything, I then rewrote those hundreds of entries.

My conversation is often halting because I weigh each sentence before uttering it, anticipating any doubts or objections it could elicit. This puts me at a disadvantage with conversational partners who blurt their opinions.

When conversations end in agreement, the results are often a sort of congeniality and emotional accord. Even in my own family circle, even in response to Friedrich Georg, I am aware that I tend not to let this mood last long, but rather I seem to steer away from this port either by introducing a new, as yet untested, argument, or by making some ironic comment. This trait makes me unbearable on all committees and in meetings where people need to reach consensus, and that applies essentially to all group sessions, conspiracies, and political assemblies. This can be especially embarrassing when I am the object of the group's attention. I have always preferred moderate, critical respect or substantiated recognition to admiration. I have always mistrusted admiration. Incidentally, the same applies when I read reviews of my books; an elucidation of the material or a reasoned rejection is more comforting than praise. I am ashamed of this, but also unjustified censure—perhaps out of personal or willful bad temper—offends me and gnaws at me. On the other hand, I appreciate criticism that presents me with good rationales. Then I don't feel I have the obligation to enter into debate. After all, why should my adversary not be right? A critique that gets to the heart of the matter is not to be taken personally. It is like that prayer I can hear beside me when I am at the altar. It does not matter whether *I* am right.

This last sentence reveals the reason why I did not become a mathematician like my Brother Physicus. The precision of applied logic does not hold ultimate gratification. When something is right—right in the highest sense—it must not be demonstrable, it must be debatable. We mortals must strive for it in configurations that are accessible but not absolutely attainable. This then leads to areas where imponderable rather than quantifiable concepts honor the master and produce the artistic urge.

Here it is especially the service to, and with, the word that enthralls me—that subtlest of efforts that takes the word to the dividing line that separates it from the ineffable.

This also contains a longing for the correct dimensions according to which the universe was created, and which the reader should see through the word as through a window.

Went to the Jardin d'Acclimatation in the afternoon. There I watched the color palette unfold from deep blue lapis lazuli, green-gold, and bronze-gold shades as the male of a particularly splendid species of peacock produced his display. A foam of green and gold fringe encircled the extravagant plumage. The voluptuous nature of this bird lies in that exquisite parade as he fans out his allures. When he has reached the climactic point of his display, he escalates it with a shivering gesture that produces a delicate, spasmodic rattle and clattering of his feathers, as if under an electric frisson, as though he were shaking his tough, hornlike spears in their quiver. This gesture expresses blissful trembling, while at the same time producing the reflexive, bellicose pose of ardor.

Afterward, went to Parc de Bagatelle, where *Lilium henryi* [tiger lilies] were in bloom. I also saw the golden orfe again. The weather was very warm.

Finished reading Maurice Alhoy, *Les Bagnes* (Paris, 1845), an illustrated edition. The old *bagnos* tended to treat criminals more like criminals and did not apply concepts from other disciplines. As a result, the criminals led a harder life, but one that was also closer to nature and more robust than in our prisons today. In all conventional theories of rehabilitation, all institutions of social hygiene include a special kind of ostracism, a special brutality.

True misery is profound, substantive, and by the same token wickedness is part of its essence, its inner nature. We must not dismiss this puritanically. The beasts can be locked up behind bars, but once they are there, they cannot be allowed to get used to cauliflower; a diet of meat must be placed before them. We can concede that the French lack this puritanical urge to improve others, such as we observe among the English, Americans, Swiss, and many Germans. In their colonies, on their ships, and in their prisons, things run more naturally. The Frenchman often leaves well enough alone, and that is always pleasant. The French are accused of a flawed approach to hygiene, which is relevant here. Yet despite that, living, sleeping, and eating are all better among the French than in regions that are overly disinfected.

One curiosity struck me, namely that only a few years before 1845 in the *bagno* of Brest, the wastewater from the latrines was diverted to the prisoner in charge of the laundry. He would wash the shirts in urine, which presumably possesses an inherent cleansing property; there is probably an extensive ethnographic history of its use. In general the book is a good contribution to the study of the predatory, bestial side of human beings—but also of their better side, such as a well-developed good nature and a persistent noble instinct. The *bagnos* were to some extent criminal states, and upon examination, you get the impression that if the world were inhabited solely by criminals, then the law would evolve to prevent it from ever ending. By the way, a history of penal colonies confirms this premise.

PARIS, 20 JULY 1943

Visited Florence at midday. Cocteau said that he had been present during the proceedings against a young man accused of stealing books. Among these was a rare edition of Verlaine, and the judge asked: "Did you know the price of this book?"

Whereupon the accused answered: "I did not know its price, but I knew its value."

Books by Cocteau were also among the stolen volumes, and the judge asked a further question: "What would you say if someone stole a book from you that you had written?"

"That would make me proud."

Conversation that included Jouhandeau about various types of *curiosa*. He was familiar with the narcissistic performance of the peacock, which had so enthralled me on Sunday afternoon. This phenomenon is apparently audible only when the weather is dry. The cleansing action of urine, as described in the book about the *bagnos*, probably relates to its ammonia content. Throughout the Orient, nursing mothers are said to savor a tiny amount of the infant's urine, which is thought to be beneficial for their milk.

Cocteau claimed that a fakir in India had set his handkerchief on fire from a distance of twenty paces, and that in emergencies, the English there rely on telepathic transmissions of messages by the natives, because this is faster than the radio.

Shops that outfit hunters apparently carry whistles of such high pitch that they are inaudible to us and the game, but which dogs can hear from far away.

Florence had large vases full of very beautiful larkspur, *pied d'alouette*. Certain strains produce metallic hues rarely seen in blossoms, such as an enchanting blue-green and blue-violet. The blue blossom seems to be drenched in fiery green or violet ink that has dried with a reflective sheen. These flowers, like the monk's hood, should be bred for their blue alone—their best feature.

In the office in the afternoon: the president. Then met with Erich Müller, who published the book about the *Schwarze Front* [*Black Front*][58] when he was younger. He is now a corporal in an anti-aircraft unit in Saint-Cloud. We discussed Cellaris and his imprisonment.

PARIS, 25 JULY 1943

How does it happen that I find myself more uninhibited, less ceremonious, more nonchalant and carefree, and less cautious with intelligent and very intelligent people? They have a tonic effect on me. There must be something like "all men of science are brothers" behind this. In the rapport of the back-and-forth, the free and easy exchange of views, I find something fraternal, as if we were *en famille*. By the same token, I find an intelligent adversary less dangerous.

When I encounter fools, on the other hand, minds that acknowledge platitudes and live by them, people who are hell-bent on the empty, superficial hierarchy of the world, then I become uncertain, awkward; I commit *faux pas* and talk nonsense.

In such situations, I lack the ability to dissemble. As soon as I interact with a visitor, Perpetua always knows what we are in for. "For whosoever has, to him shall be given."[59]—this is also my maxim.

"*Das war die Lage in der ich stand.*" [That was the situation in which I stood.]

A pattern for countless errors that are permissible when speaking, but incorrect when writing.

Cependant [meanwhile, however] has, like our corresponding *indessen* [meanwhile, however], a temporal as well as a contradictory sense. This points to one of the connections between grammar and logic: when perceived, two simultaneous events are mutually exclusive.

PARIS, 26 JULY 1943

Visits in the morning: one from Major von Uslar and one from First Lieutenant Kutscher who arrived from Holland. He brought me a letter from Heinrich von Trott, whose earlier odd, nocturnal visit to the vineyard house in Überlingen became part of my concept for the *Marble Cliffs*.

Spent the evening with Alfred Toepfer in the garden of the officers' quarters on Rue du Faubourg Saint-Honoré. We started out talking about Cellaris, and then went to the park and found a secluded bench where we could sit. Toepfer spoke to me the way many have in recent years: "You must now prepare an appeal to the youth of Europe."

I told him that back in the winter of 1941–1942, I had already begun to make notes on this very topic, but had then consigned them to the flames. I thought about it later in the Raphael.

"Peace / Peace an Address to the Youth of Europe / An Address to the Youth of the World."

PARIS, 27 JULY 1943

Began working on the *Appeal*, which I have divided into thirteen sections; that took me half an hour. It is imperative that I keep this simple and clear and avoid clichés.

PARIS, 28 JULY 1943

Continued working on the *Appeal*. Sketch and draft of the first paragraph, a sort of introduction that presents me with certain difficulties because it has to set the general emotional tone. I am not writing the way I first began—cryptically—but rather in plain language.

In writing the word *Jugend* [youth], I became aware of the solemn euphony of the first syllable, parallel to words like *Jubel, Jung, Jul, iucundus, iuvenis, iungere, coniungere.* [rejoicing, young, Yule, acceptable, young, to join, to connect], as well as in many cries of greeting, and names of divinities: the ancient festival *Juturnalia* [Roman goddess of wells and springs, Juturna].

Went to the Wagram in the evening with Ministerial Director Eckelmann, Colonel Kräwel, Count Schulenburg, the president of Silesia. Kräwel, who recently sat across from Kniébolo for twenty minutes, described his eyes as "flickering"— eyes that look through people and belong to a mind that is quickly veering toward catastrophe. I discussed my *Appeal* with Schulenburg, who wondered whether I would not do better by going to Wehrmacht headquarters in Berlin. It does not seem, however, that I would enjoy the protection there that the commander-in-chief guarantees me here. Keitel warned Speidel about me long ago.

Popularity is a sickness that threatens to become all the more chronic the later in life it afflicts the patients.

PARIS, 29 JULY 1943

Piles of mail. Friedrich Georg answers my question about the whirring sound made by peacocks by citing a passage in one of his own poems that refers to these animals.

Er schlägt sein Rad auf
Und bringt die starken
Federn zum Schwirren,
Dass sie wie Stäbe
Von Gittern erklirren.

[He opens up his wheel / and makes his powerful / feathers whirr, / so that they rattle / like bars of a cage.]

My brother also paid a call on Pastor Horion at my behest. He has been living in Überlingen since his collections were destroyed by fire in Düsseldorf. Since January, he has contributed a further 1,400 species of beetles. Unfortunately, Goecke's house also burned, but he was able to save his collections. News of fresh horrors in Hamburg and Hannover reaches us. We hear that in the phosphorus attacks, the asphalt bursts into flame, causing anyone who is fleeing to sink into it and be incinerated. We have reached Sodom. Perpetua writes that gas masks are quickly being distributed to the populace. A citizen of Bourges informs me that a lot of people are reading and discussing the translation of *Gärten und Straßen* [*Gardens and Streets*].[60]

Finished reading Huxley's *Brave New World*. One can see from this book that all utopias essentially describe the author's own age. They are versions of our life that project our own issues into a space with meticulous acuity, a space called the future. Since future and hope are essentially related, utopias are generally optimistic. This case, however, is one of a pessimistic utopia.

I found the following significant: a group of five tall skyscrapers illuminates the night far and wide, like a hand that raises its fingers in praise of God. None of the civilized atheists who live in these buildings is aware of this. Only a wild man from the jungle, who has ended up in this landscape, understands it.

PARIS, 30 JULY 1943

News from Perpetua has finally arrived. The raid on Hannover happened at midday while she was working in the garden. Our child was frightened and recited a long prayer. The city center was demolished: the Opera House, the Leine Castle, the Market Church with most of the narrow old streets and their Renaissance and baroque houses—all were destroyed. It is still unclear how the parents-in-law have fared.

It has never been clearer to me than when I was reading these lines that cities are dreams. This makes them so easy to erase when dawn breaks, yet within us they take on a life of extraordinary depth and indestructibility. With this, as with so many other experiences of our times, I have the sensation that I am watching a beautifully painted cloth hanging in front of a stage as it goes up in flames while revealing the invincible depth behind this trembling curtain.

Strange as it may sound, loss also incorporates a feeling of deep joy. It is the foretaste of that joy that will surprise us at moment of our final temporal loss—the loss of life.

Visited Potard in the middle of the day; he has still heard nothing about the fate of his wife.[61] The *lemures* on Avenue Foch supposedly call these deportations "*Meerschaumaktion*" [Operation Sea Foam]. The complete uncertainty that the family suffers is specified by Kniébolo's Night and Fog decree.[62] Such concepts are preparations for a grotesque language of thugs and demons—borrowings from the details of Hieronymus Bosch.

"The people who have done this are no friends of Germany," said good old Potard, and with that he is probably right.

PARIS, 1 AUGUST 1943

On Saturday and Sunday went with the commander-in-chief to Vaux-les-Cernay, where it was pleasant during this heat wave.

On the lake and in its dense reed beds where I studied flora and fauna with Weniger. We were sweltering in the tropical heat, which adds such atmosphere to swamp excursions. We talked about people, for whom Weniger has a particularly good memory; his head is an encyclopedia of names. We also discussed Hannover and the Guelphs, whom I have decided to mention in my *Appeal*.[63] My political core is like a clock with cog wheels that work against each other: I am a Guelph, a Prussian, a *Gross-Deutscher*,[64] a European, and a citizen of the world all at once.

Yet, when I look at the face of the clock, I could imagine a noon when all these identities coincide.

In the evening we had discussions about botany, which the commander-in-chief finds fascinating. The description of *Hottonia palustris* [water violet]—sketched for me by Lottner, head of the customs office—has stimulated the desire to study this plant someday in its aquatic habitat. What is more, I have never seen bog myrtle.

Wille [the will] and *Wollen* [volition]: In the second word, we hear a more moral and logical nuance—that is one of the examples of the power of O. This increases in the repeated assonance of *Wohlwollen* [good will], whereas *Wohlwillen*[65] produces dissonance.

Pondre [to lay, put down]. By contrast, we lack a powerful noun like *la ponte*, at best translated as "egg laying." This shows how linguistic designations of everyday facts are more or less hastily stitched together.

Tailler un crayon [to prune, clip, sharpen a pencil]; by contrast, our *den Bleistift spitzen* [to taper the pencil to a point] is more precise and apt.

Paris, 2 August 1943

In the mail I found a narrative from Alexander—his child's eye view of the bombardment of the city.

In the afternoon, like every Monday, lesson with Madame Bouet. We worked on prepositions. It is odd that with cities whose names begin with vowels, the old form with *en* has been retained only for Avignon. Could it be because this city was once a state in itself? I think that even Daudet was amused at this "*en Avignon*." In the ancient mind-palace of language such details are like remnants of earlier architectures barely discernible behind the plaster.

At the door Madame Bouet said, "I prayed that Kirchhorst would not be hit."

Aquatic plants in Cernay that gleam dark green on the lake bottom. They resemble dream vegetation and the still water is their sleep. When we remember details of a dream by day it is like seeing a blossom, a tiny leaf, or a tendril on the surface of that water. We reach for it and pull the dark labyrinthine growth up into the light.

Paris, 3 August 1943

Letters are taking on an apocalyptic quality, the likes of which have not been seen since the Thirty Years' War. In such situations, it seems as if the people's afflicted reason had lost any sense of earthly reality. It gets swept up into a cosmic vortex that reveals a new world of visions of doom, prophecies, and extrasensory appearances. It surprises me, incidentally, that no flaming omen has appeared in the heavens, the way it otherwise does in such times of transition. Perhaps we could designate Halley's Comet as a harbinger of the fiery cataclysm.

Continued working on the *Appeal* and began, as well as ended, the second chapter today: "suffering must bear fruit for all."

PARIS, 4 AUGUST 1943

Had breakfast with Florence Gould. People are saying that in recent days the air raids on Hamburg have cost two hundred thousand people their lives, which surely is grossly exaggerated.[66]

Florence has returned from Nice and reports that the news of Mussolini's resignation was announced there at midnight. The troops were burning him in effigy even before the sun had risen. Although I have basically always known this, it still amazes me how ingloriously, how insignificantly, a dictatorship built upon terror simply evaporates into nothing.

Heller told me with great joy that Fabre-Luce's prison sentence has been reduced thanks to the information about him that I had provided to the commander-in-chief. He will also appear before a proper court.

PARIS, 5 AUGUST 1943

As often happens in dreams, I was at some fair or carnival grounds. I crossed it with a small elephant that I sometimes rode and sometimes led by draping my left arm around its neck. Among the images I still recall is the open field where enclosures were being built for wild animals. It was a cold, foggy morning, and in order to protect the animals, keepers were shoveling great loads of iron—pieces like chain links and brown magnets. These had all been heated to high temperature so that the activity illuminated the mists with vivid, shimmering light.

I gave this system of heating but a cursory glance; it was a technique familiar to me in all its detail. They were using a material that, unlike coal, did not have to be burned, but emanated radioactive warmth.

Finished reading Washington Irving's *Sketch Book*, one of those works of great literature that I have neglected for too long. In it I found pieces that spoke to me powerfully and others that were instructive, such as the one entitled "John Bull," which contained a description of the English character. I copied out some excerpts of this for my own *Appeal*.

Boethius is mentioned in a section where James I of Scotland is named—a monarch who spent long years of his youth as a prisoner at Windsor Castle. It is certainly true that reading his works in moments of despair is particularly comforting. I experienced that myself in the thatched hut on the *Westwall*.[67]

I have also found a nice comment about certain arrivistes: "they attribute the modesty of others to their own exalted positions."

PARIS, 6 AUGUST 1943

In the morning, I worked more on the *Appeal*, particularly on the third chapter. There I have to clarify the point that the seed from which the war will bear fruit is sacrifice—not only of the soldiers but also the workers and the innocent victims. I must not forget the sacrifice of those who were senelessly and savagely massacred. The construction of the new world will rest upon them in particular, as it once did upon those children immured in the bridge buttresses.

Stylistic considerations: "*stärker verblassen*" [to become more intensely pale] annoys me, and rightly so. I always have to try harder to use language with appropriate imagery, language that has fallen prey to a leveling of logic. In general, I have to go back to the images, of which the *logos* [word] is merely the emanation, the sheen. Language is the oldest, most honorable edifice that remains to us—our history and prehistory express themselves in it, with all their most nuanced expressions of life.

During the noonday break, I paid another visit to the Musée de l'Homme [Museum of Mankind]. Who is more macabre, the savage who with artistic care tans, dyes, and decorates the skulls of slain enemies with colorful incisions and fills their eye sockets with mussel shells and bits of mother of pearl; or is it the European who collects these skulls and displays them in glass cases?

Once again it has become crystal clear to me how material like stone is incredibly enhanced when worked by hand. The extent to which it is inhabited, imbued with soul, is physically palpable. All ancient artisanship lets you feel its magic. This hardly exists anymore, except in far-flung Chinese provinces or on the remotest of islands, and then only if there is a painter who still knows what color is, and a writer who knows what language is.

Incidentally, in the Musée de l'Homme, I have a powerful urge to touch things—something I've never felt when I'm in other collections. It is also nice that one can frequently encounter boys between twelve and sixteen years old.

Went to the Coq Hardi in the evening with Neuhaus and his brother-in-law, von Schewen. Spoke about diplomats from the period before World War I, men like Kiderlen-Wächter, Rosen, Holstein, and Bülow—all of whom Schewen worked with closely.

The slightest moves are significant here, as if it were the opening of a cosmic chess game.

In Germany, the sect with the slogan "enjoy the war, because peace will be terrible" is growing. In general, in all conversations about the way things are going, I notice that there are two kinds of people: One kind believes that if the war is lost, they will no longer be able to carry on, while the other type can easily imagine it. Perhaps both of them are right.

Paris, 7 August 1943

Worked more on the *Appeal* and began the fourth chapter, which is supposed to develop some observations about sacrifice. My plan is to contrast four strata that are becoming more and more promising. The first involves the sacrifice of active participants, including soldiers and workers of both sexes. Then there are those who simply suffer, including victims of persecution and murder. And, finally, there is the sacrifice of mothers, in which all these categories coalesce, as if in a vessel of pain.

Street studies in the afternoon behind the Panthéon. On Rue Mouffetard and its side streets—an area that has retained something of the bustle of the overpopulated prerevolutionary quarter of the eighteenth century. There I found mint for sale, which put me in mind of the curious night in the Moorish quarter of Casablanca. Markets are always rich in associations; they are a dreamland and a child's paradise. Once more I was overcome by a strong feeling of joy, of gratitude that this, the city of cities, has survived the catastrophe unscathed. How amazing it would be if she could be spared, if like an ark, heavily laden to the gunwales with ancient treasure, she should reach a safe harbor after the flood has receded and be preserved for centuries to come.

PARIS, 10 AUGUST 1943

Lunch with Florence in her apartment, where I spoke with Chief Engineer Vogel about our aircraft production. A few months ago, he had predicted that the stepped-up building program of night fighters would begin to curtail air raids on our cities right about now. But what about the fact that the squadrons of bombers now appear in broad daylight? We also spoke of phosphorus as a weapon. It seems that we actually possessed this material when we enjoyed air superiority, but we waived that option. That would be to our credit, and in light of Kniébolo's character, bizarre enough. The load of phosphorus is carried in large earthenware containers and makes an extremely dangerous cargo for the pilot. A single piece of shrapnel is enough to blow his aircraft into an inescapable ball of flame.

Visited Jouhandeau in the evening on that peaceful little street, the Rue du Commandant Marchand, on the edge of the Bois. At first I visited with his wife alone—Elise, the woman he has made famous in so many of his novels. She is like a woman possessed. Her character is strong—much too strong for this day and age. Jouhandeau likes to compare his lady of the house with a stone, whether it be the boulder of Sisyphus or the cliff where he is doomed to eternal failure. We conversed for a while, and during our chat, she came up with the concept of the *dégénéré supérieur* [superior degenerate], which can be applied to most contemporary French writers: our physicality and morality have already entered their decadent phase, whereas the mind distinguishes itself through its power and lofty maturity. She went on to say that the clockwork is too weak for the powerful mainspring that drives it, and that explains the essence of indecency and perversions.

Around ten o'clock, Jouhandeau arrived and accompanied me on a walk through the streets around the Étoile. There in the west a glassy green sky glowed with the cold light that announces sunset. It was wreathed in the lustrous amethyst and grayish-violet hues of night. "*Voilà un autre Arc de Triomphe*" [Look! Another Arc de Triomphe], said Jouhandeau. We also passed the spot where I once made the acquaintance of Madame L., a brash act to test Morris's technique. I consider him as one of my mentors in the ways of wickedness. When we walk through the labyrinth of cities, the bygone hours live again, as if the buildings and streets were awakening and taking on color in the kaleidoscope of memory. Jouhandeau agreed with me and said that he consecrated certain squares and streets to the memory of particular friends. We walked along Avenue de Wagram, which he called a curious island in the otherwise very dignified 16th Arrondissement. Here the cafés illuminated in red, the courtesans, and the hotels that rent rooms by the hour—all seemed like an inflamed artery in its maze of streets.

PARIS, 11 AUGUST 1943

Throughout the night the anti-aircraft fire pounded away at the high-altitude planes returning from the destruction of Nürnberg. In the morning, the commander-in-chief summoned me and presented me with a beautiful botanical volume. I then received a visit from First Lieutenant Sommer who had been in Hamburg. He told me of seeing a procession of gray-haired children there, little elderly people aged by a single night of phosphorus.

I finished the fourth section of my *Appeal*; getting it on paper is slow progress. Its two parts could be called Principles and Applications. The first is meant to describe the reason for the sacrifice and, the second, the new order that can be built upon that. In the first part, it is difficult to resist succumbing to pity, and so I expect my pen will move faster in the second part.

Played two games of chess with Baumgart in the evening. Krause was in Hamburg during the bombardment and reported that he saw twenty charred corpses leaning close together across the wall of a bridge there, as if they were lying on a grill. On this spot people covered in phosphorus had tried to save themselves by leaping into the water, but they were carbonized before they could do so. He told of a woman who was seen carrying an incinerated corpse of a child in each arm. Krause, who carries a bullet deep in his heart muscle, passed a house where phosphorus was dripping from the low roof. He heard screams but was unable to help—this conjures up a scene from the *Inferno* or some horrific dream.

PARIS, 13 AUGUST 1943

These days I sometimes rise twenty minutes earlier in order to read some Schiller with my morning coffee, specifically the little edition that Kretzschmar edited and recently gave me.

Reading this book put me in mind of one of my old plans to produce a volume of "Worldly Edification." In it I'd like to collect a series of short pieces that, on the one hand, show how religion produces art, and on the other, how art produces religion. It would be a compilation of the highest expressions of the human spirit in accordance with the nature of eternity. Natural man attains this state thanks to his innate goodness; so does the religious man, by rising to the heights through his utterances that possess validity as they transcend the fragmentation of faith and all dogmatic traditions. A few reproductions of works of art could also be included in this reader. In my extensive reading, I have always felt the need for a vade mecum of this sort.

Schiller's "Three Words" and Goethe's "*Urworte Orphisch*"[68] introduce a juxtaposition of the ideal and the empirical mind. It will always remain a thing of wonder that two luminaries of such magnitude should come together in a provincial princely capital, which in itself was otherwise not exactly devoid of great lights.

Nowadays the space of a hundred million worlds cannot produce anyone to hold a candle to them.

The vaunted conversation about the *Urpflanze*[69] is significant, as is the mention of astrology in the correspondence on *Wallenstein*[70] in light of the distinction just touched upon.

The mail included an almost illegible letter from Tronier Funder, who, it seems, had to leave Berlin in a hurry. There was also a review of *Gardens and Streets* by Adolf Saager from the journal *Büchereiblatt* [*Library Journal*] from 19 July 1943. In his piece I read, among other things: "The naïveté of this anti-rationalist writer proves itself to be advantageous during the reality of a military campaign. To be sure, he conducts himself correctly, even humanely, but despite his delicacy of feeling, he gets chummy with all sorts of Frenchmen as if nothing had happened."

PARIS, 15 AUGUST 1943

Returned from Le Mans, where I spent Saturday and Sunday with Baumgart and Fräulein Lampe.

Visited Nay's studio. He gave me a drawing: A pair of lovers in the middle of a tropical park bursting with flowers. A gigantic moon has risen above their stalks and fronds; a watchman stands in the background with a single large red eye painted on his forehead.

There I met Monsieur de Thérouanne again, a man whose intellectuality can be nurtured only by a life of pure leisure. It makes me think that the garment of intellect is old and comfortable; its every fold fits the body of the wearer like a second skin. Herein lies the superiority over all differences of class, fortune, nationality, faith—even of the intellect itself—a superiority achieved not by a leveling or generalizing tendency but through the advancement and growth of aristocracy and gentility. Aristocracy can become so significant that it bestows childlike traits and exemplifies in its bearer those ancient times when men were brothers. When it comes to powers of discrimination the simplest remains the most elegant. Adam is our highest prince. Every noble line traces itself back to him.

Nay belongs to the sort of obsessive workers the likes of which I've often met among artists; he even paints during the short midday break that his duties allow him. Now and then, Thérouanne comes to the studio and by way of communication, lies on the sofa and reads a book.

Although Nay is a very busy corporal, he feels quite at home in Le Mans with his duties. This shows that the state hardly pampers artists. No police barge into his studio here to finger his brushes and see if they have been used. Just as everything about Kniébolo is symbolic, so too is his profession as a house painter. The revenge for Sadowa is complete.[71]

Went to the Catholic military service on Sunday morning by happy coincidence. In this way, I got to enjoy a good, brief sermon about Mary as the eternal mother. Afterward walked along the Huine, a smooth, flat stream the color of clay. The heart-shaped leaves of the water lettuce spread across its surface while countless fisherman performed their cultic rites of relaxation. Large covered boats are moored beside the banks, where they serve as public laundries.

Then I visited the cemetery, where there was a good deal of brisk activity, for it was the Feast of the Assumption, and the dead participate in the festivities. In the midst of the grave monuments, a modest obelisk proclaimed the last resting place of Levasseur de la Sarthe, which gives him the unusual title of an "Ex-Conventionnel."[72] When I saw it, I wondered whether later, perhaps in thirty years or so, someone may have himself buried as an "Ex-Nazi." Who would ever care to predict the subterfuges and aberrations of the human mind?

At the Morins' for lunch; the meal went on until around five o'clock. The lady of the house made everyone happy with delicacies like a *paté* of mushrooms, eggs, and beef marrow, the so-called *amourette*. The wines included a Burgundy that M. Morin had bottled in his son's birth year and is meant to accompany him in his life's celebrations like a melody that becomes lovelier and gentler, for the inside of the bottle had become coated with tannins over the course of the years. Downstairs in the shop, we inspected the books; there I purchased a copy of the Vulgate Bible, which I have long wished to have by me, especially in this beautiful Paris edition of 1664, a famous printing but with microscopic typeface.

During the trip back, we were surprised by the spectacle of a lunar eclipse. Because the point of greatest darkness happened during the twilight, the white edge of the crescent moon took on a brighter hue as it progressed, eventually turning a brilliant gold.

My reading during the train trip: Charles Benoist, *Le Prince de Bismarck; Psychologie de l'Homme Fort* [*Prince Bismarck; the Psychology of the Strong Man* (Paris: Didier, 1900)]. The only thing I found significant was the enjoyment of a certain *déja vu* while reading, because when I was growing up, decades of my father's table talk had acquainted me with all the details of Bismarck's life.

Afterward I browsed in *Spleen de Paris*, specifically the edition that Charmille gave me last year as a present. The epilogue—

Je t'aime ô capitale infâme! Courtisanes
Et bandits tels souvent vous offrez des plaisirs
Que ne comprennent pas les vulgaires profanes.

[I love thee, oh ignoble capital! Courtesans / And low-lifes too, for you often offer pleasures / That the vulgar herd cannot understand.]

—captures the intellectual pleasure in ordinary things, their variety, which you experience like someone who has entered the confines of a zoo. This also explains the pleasure one derives from Petronius.

The *Appeal* can only appear when the time is right, and no one can foretell when that will be. Should it be finished sooner, then I shall keep going over it like a gardener, until its hour has come.

PARIS, 16 AUGUST 1943

In my dream, I was inspecting a newly perfected machine that could spin fabric from air. When it rotated slowly, you could see a kind of loose cotton coming out of its nozzles and congealing; when it sped up, shirt fabric and linen. At full speed, it spat out ropes of thick wool. In each case, different gases were assimilated. I observed this whole notion of spinning with air with a certain admiration, although I found it simultaneously repugnant.

In the morning about three hundred aircraft flew over the city; I watched the anti-aircraft fire from the flat roof of the Majestic. These flyovers offer us one of the great spectacles; they convey the expanse of this titanic power. I could not pick out details, but some shells seem to have hit their marks, because over Montmartre a parachute could be seen floating to earth.

PARIS, 17 AUGUST 1943

The bombardment of Hamburg constitutes the first event of this sort in Europe that defies population statistics. The registry offices are unable to report how many people have lost their lives. The victims died like fish or grasshoppers, outside of history in that primordial zone where there is no accounting.

Style. The repetition of certain prepositions in German—as in *"das reicht nicht an mich heran"* [that does not touch me, that does not affect me] of *"er trat aus dem Walde heraus"* [he emerged from (out of) the forest]—does not bother me as much as it used to. These imply an intensification or affirmation. You just have to use them sparingly.

In the evening had a discussion with Weniger and Schnath about insider secrets regarding Hannover; the destruction of our old hometown inspired the conversation. The bathhouse attendant Schrader, the mask-carver Gross, and my grandfather, the teacher of boys—all came up, along with other characters.

Behind the Waterloo column, a dark lane led to the Masch, where the soldiers from the Bult barracks would say goodnight to their girlfriends before curfew. It was also a place where drunks wandered around and people got up to all kinds of mischief and dirty goings-on. For this reason people called it Köttelgang [Turd Alley]. After the revolution of 1918 made Leinert mayor (a capable man, incidentally), you could read the following words on a fence: "Leinert Street, formerly Köttelgang."

Example of a Lower Saxon joke.

PARIS, 21 AUGUST 1943

With Jouhandeau in the evening, a man who has many an aspect of the medieval monk, specifically of the visionary type. His intellectuality is striking for its exquisite flights of fancy; any lighter and he would take wing. There's a demonic side to this, too, of course.

Discussion about the dangers of the Bois, which recently came home to me especially vividly as I was walking alone in the dark. The paths and bushes were full of dubious characters. The fact that many of them had been called up to work in Germany and have deserted their residences means that the number of people living outside the law is substantially increasing, and this promotes criminality. The significant and assorted threats to personal freedom attract myriad recruits to the ranks of these crooks. Years ago I predicted this without yet knowing any specifics.

Rue du Commandant Marchand runs close to the Bois. Jouhandeau described hearing frequent pistol shots there; that was followed recently by a fearful wailing for the dead. Elise went into the street to see if she could help; that is impressive in itself. She is like the soldier, attracted by cannon fire, like one of those natures whose energies are not released unless danger is present. Women like her can inspire popular uprisings. Incidentally, I have observed that Germanophilia—naturally with the exception of those venal types—appears right in that segment of the populace where intrinsic strength is still alive. This is the same covert undercurrent that shows up in Germany as Russophilia. The authorities who are allied with the West oppose them. New structures will emerge from this conflicting polarity that is playing out in the center.

Regarding the dead. Jouhandeau's mother died an old woman. At the moment of death, her face became transfigured, as if by an inner explosion. She took on the appearance of a twenty-year-old girl. Then she seemed to age again, and kept the face of a forty-year-old until her burial. We discussed modern idiocy, especially as it relates to death, and our blindness to the mighty powers that are right beside us. Then we spoke about Léon Bloy.

In a night during the year 1941, the wife of one of Jouhandeau's acquaintances was preparing to give birth. Her husband rushed out of the house to inform the midwife. It was after curfew, and a French patrol stopped him and took him into the station. There he explained his situation. The midwife was told and the husband held in custody until the morning in order to corroborate the truth of his assertions. In the meantime, news of an assassination had been circulating. Hostages were rounded up, and this man was executed among others who had violated the curfew. The story tells a greater truth, thereby reminding me of one of those wicked tales from *A Thousand and One Nights*.

Mauritanian stories:[73]

1. The Porphyry Cliffs. Description of the city excavated by Braquemart as the primeval seat of power.
2. The Path of Masirah. Fortunio's search for the mine of precious stones and his adventures on this journey.
3. The God of the Cities. Meant to transcend the *Übermensch* [superman] since the highest concept of humanity has been both brutalized and deified. That is one of the goals of modernity and its science, which carries magical features beneath its mask of rationality; ossification in the Tower of Babel.

The first fifty years of our century. Progress, the world of machines, science, technology, war—all elements of a pre- and postheroic world of titans. How everything glowing, everything elemental, becomes dangerous. In order to describe this range, perhaps in the novel, you would have to begin with a figure who embraces this indistinctly but with great enthusiasm—a sort of Werther of the twentieth century. Rimbeau perhaps. This demonic character must be juxtaposed with another figure, one with a sense of higher purpose, someone not merely conservative, but stunningly effective, a Grand Master of the Tower of Babel.

Paris, 24 August 1943

I was sitting at a table with my father and a few acquaintances; it was the moment when the waiter approached us to present the bill. I was surprised that he became so expansive about details concerning the wine and its purchase price. In the course of the conversation, he even pulled up a chair and sat down. A remark of my father's made me realize that it was the innkeeper who was talking with us. His speech and body language were appropriate to his station, but they did not belong to that of a waiter.

When I awoke I asked myself, as Lichtenberg does, about the conciseness and dramatic nature of events like these. Why were the facts not revealed from the beginning when there was never any doubt until a casual remark was made? Does the dreamer perhaps actively direct this scene in order to heighten the suspense? Or is he an actor in a play that dwarfs him in significance?

Both are correct inasmuch as we appear as characters in our dreams and, at the same time, are parts of the universe. In this second category, we are inhabited by a higher intelligence that we marvel at when the waking state has jolted us back into our individuality. In our sleep, we are like statues with thinking brains and, what's more, we are connected with all our molecules to a cosmic current of thought. We submerge ourselves in the waters of pre- and postmortal intelligence.

Was Lichtenberg too clever to grasp this duality? I would like to talk to him about it in any case, for I find his question more productive than many an answer has been.

Finished reading *Cashel Byron's Profession*[74] by Bernard Shaw, a book that I relished despite all its Victorian dust. Such rather old-fashioned works teach us to see what things first fall prey to the passage of time. I note the following, which is but one of the countless aphorisms sprinkled throughout: "Rational madness is the worst, because it possesses weapons against reason."

Also read a short biography of the painter Pierre Bonnard recommended to me by Madame Cardot. The anecdotes told about him include one that struck a particular chord with me: the proclivity to begin working again on old pictures, even if he had sold them long ago. He felt it was a shame that they had been separated from their state of finished perfection by the passage of time. Consequently, he would lurk in museum galleries until the guard had disappeared then quickly produce a tiny palette and paintbrush in order to add some highlights to one of his own paintings.

Such behavior throws light on all kinds of associations, among them the intellectual property of the painter, which is less well defined than that of a writer. The painter relies much more on the medium, which is why the Greeks correctly placed him lower in the hierarchy than the philosopher, the poet, and the bard.

Today I remembered one of the thoughts about philosophy I had as a child, but one that wasn't bad for someone who was only a boy: "The 'actual' chicken is naked, just as we see it hanging in the poultry dealer's shop. Then what do the feathers have to do with anything? They're just there as a suit to provide warmth."

By extension, I should have been able to conclude that man's "actual" form consists basically of the skeleton or the flayed muscle tissue or the nervous system with brain and spinal column. Today I actually still feel a bit like an explorer when I glance through atlases of anatomy. But at the same time, I see things from the other perspective, in that I comprehend the various systems that constitute our body, that appear as patterns, as projections into the expanse of space. Their reality exists solely in their relationship to the whole, the unexpanded instance, and without them, they become as ridiculous and meaningless as a plucked chicken.

Trees, incidentally, are the best images of development from insubstantial form. Their actual point of vegetation cannot be located in space any more than we can see the pivot point on the axle of a wheel. This relates to the complex and radiciform character typical of many of our organs. By the same token, the brain resembles a bifoliate cotyledon that has attached itself in the body to the main and tendril roots of its spinal column. This would imply that it is not in itself the fruit, but rather the preliminary fructifying substance.

At quarter-to-six a massive phalanx of aircraft flew over the city at low altitude, framed by little brownish-purple clouds of anti-aircraft smoke. Undeterred, the planes lumbered along down Avenue Kléber toward the Étoile. These spectacles are titanic events being played out above large cities. Here the astounding power of collective toil emerges from anonymity and acquires visible contours. This also gives them a certain exhilarating quality.

The attack was targeting the airfield at Villacoublay where it destroyed twelve hangars and twenty-one bombers as it ploughed up the runways. Additionally, many farms in the nearby villages were destroyed and many inhabitants killed. Near a patch of woods, they found a cyclist with his bicycle who had been hurled there from a great distance by the blast of one explosion.

PARIS, 25 AUGUST 1943

Went grouse shooting in the afternoon in Les-Essarts-les-Roi. Autumn has now begun its invisible intrusion into summer, like a crystal forming at the bottom of a chemical solution. It perfumes the day's first breath and puts its fecund stamp upon the landscape as it fills out the ripening fruits, making them robust.

I never got off a single shot because I got distracted by *subtiles* at the edge of a pool. Hunting for them is much more thrilling. Here I encountered *Yola bicarinata* [water beetle], a Western European organism whose structure occupied me in the evening as I consulted Guignot's beautiful volume on the water beetles of France.

It was late when I made my way up to the president's room. He has just returned from Cologne, and he described the way people congregate in bombed-out ruins of the cellars of the Rhenish wine taverns. An intense feeling of warm conviviality prevails there. The drinkers often sing the old Karneval[75] songs. A special favorite is "*Ja, das sind Sächelchen*" [Yes, those are nice little things].

This is reminiscent of Edgar Allan Poe's tale, "The Masque of the Red Death." Along with Defoe, author of *A Journal of the Plague Year*, he should be considered one of the writers for our age.

PARIS, 26 AUGUST 1943

Worked a little more on my *Appeal*. I had set it aside during the heat wave, noting as I did so how little gets done by dint of willpower alone. The artistic muse is part of our vegetative, not our animal nature. This makes it more susceptible to weather conditions. What is more, this cannot be trained or forced into submission. Authentic writing cannot be coerced.

Went to Maxim's with Neuhaus and his brother-in-law, von Schewen. I find in him, as in most old conservatives, the error of overestimating the new regime. Such people fail to recognize that its superiority rests on the fact that their people will work for lower wages by observing the rules of convention, law, and propriety when it suits them. That's their way of double-dealing, which always leaves them with one last resort. Thus they end a chess game with a truncheon blow or conclude a pension contract by murdering all the pensioners. These tactics have shock value, but only for a while. It is precisely such mental gymnasts who turn sheepish when you respond to them in their own language, the only thing they understand. The conservatives are also capable of this when they actually reflect seriously enough and when they connect with their native soil, as you can see in cases like Sulla, and even in Bismarck. It often seems to me as if certain turning points in history are repeated only to elicit and unlock this reaction as an answer from the our primeval ancestors—as the rain brings forth the bud. With that, of course, innocence is lost; the monarchy is restored after the Fall of Man.

PARIS, 27 AUGUST 1943

Coffee at Banine's. The art of getting along with people lies in keeping the same pleasant middle distance over the course of time without becoming estranged, without becoming close, and without a change of quality. Compatible relationships depend on this desirable midpoint between centrifugal and centripetal forces. As in the universe, equilibrium depends on repetition, not change. This is so in the most pleasant relationships, marriages, and friendships.

This evening I had a long conversation with Weniger in the Raphael about our countryman Löns and that particular form of *décadence* that he has in common with several Nordic and English writers. In recent decades, the Germanic type has been undermined by a curious *morbidezza* [softness, delicacy]. Recognizing this is the key to a whole host of things and peoples. For example, it exerts a powerful influence on *Art Nouveau*, which nowadays is seen to be narrowly formalist and lacking in intellectuality. One particular decade is almost completely dominated by this style. This became clear to me when I was in the officers' mess of the Seventy-Third Regiment in Hannover, where portraits of the old officers since Waterloo hung on the walls, and I noticed a curious loosening of form in the artistic style that prevailed since the turn of the century. In this connection, the Germanic type needs a Jewish mentor, figures like his Marx, Freud, or Bergson, whom he naively adores and eventually strives to emulate like Oedipus. You have to know this in order to comprehend anti-Semitism as a typical symptom of the *Belle Époque*.

In bed I started reading Huxley's *Point Counter Point*. Even temperatures below freezing are fascinating if they plummet low enough. You get this impression from certain novels of the rococo, and it's just possible that by the same token, Huxley will also enjoy posthumous recognition. At such temperatures, the flesh and erotic encounters lose their luster, and their physical dimension comes to the fore. In general, Huxley—the precise observer and analyst—delivers the scientific scaffolding of our era. Nowadays, good style presupposes a background in the natural sciences, as it once did theology.

Paris, 28 August 1943

As so often in the early morning, as so often in life, I was talking about books with my father and suddenly noticed that I had been misinterpreting our relationship for a long time. The error lay in the fact that it was I, not my father, who had died. "Correct, he dies in me; then it cannot be otherwise than that I have died in him."

Then I tried to recall the particulars surrounding my death, but had trouble finding a point of reference. It was as if this were nothing but a brief journey, a mere change of place that we soon forget. But then the scene of the final moment suddenly welled up in my memory with all its details.

It was in a large railroad station with many small waiting rooms; in one of these a group of travelers was standing in front of a door. We could have been seven or nine, perhaps even twelve in number. We were dressed simply, like workers out for a Sunday excursion. The men were in coarse blue drill, the women in overalls of brown corduroy. As a badge, we all wore pins showing one of those yellow butterflies whose wings reveal shades of blue when they move. I noticed that not a single one of us carried any luggage, no suitcase—not even the small briefcase that workers carry so often.

After we had been standing in the throng of the waiting room for a while, the door opened and a clergyman hurried in. He was a short, gaunt man in a dark cassock, and he bustled around us, as pastors typically do in large, poorly funded congregations where their duties are constantly being interrupted by baptisms, burials, or a quick confession. These are pastors from the suburbs.

The priest squeezed our hands and led us through long, poorly lit passageways and up and down flights of stairs into the interior of the railroad station. I thought that perhaps we were being diverted to a suburban train for a short outing to see some miraculous statue or to a monastery where a visiting bishop was preaching.

Still, as we strode along, I felt waves of ever-increasing anxiety sweeping over me; finally, after struggling as though in a dark dream, I grasped the situation I was in. The people with whom I was being guided through these subterranean corridors were a group that had made a pact to die together. Feeling that they needed purification, they wanted to cast off their bodies like old garments. Such groups had become common since the world has fallen into disorder. They were constituted according to the method of death that their members had chosen. In our case, it was a shower of phosphorus that awaited us. Hence, ours was a small group.

How I had longed for this great purgation. My theological studies, no less than my metaphysical insights; my stoic and spiritual tendencies; my innate desire for a final act of daring and the luxury of sublime curiosity; the teachings of Nigromontanus,[76] the longing for Dorothea, and the lofty warriors who had gone before me—all of this had come together to strengthen my resolve and remove all obstacles. And now, in this narrow dark passageway, I was quite unexpectedly gripped by hideous fear.

"How good," I thought, "that you at least left your luggage behind and can fold your hands." I immediately started to cling to prayer like someone hanging from a terrifying precipice clutching at the end of the only protruding root. I recited the Lord's Prayer fervently, with true ferocity, and repeated it as soon as it was ended. There was neither comfort nor benefit nor a single thought in any of this, but only a wild, final instinct, a primal awareness like that of the drowning man struggling for air, or the man parched with thirst craving water, or the child crying for its mother. In those moments, when a wave of relief brought respite, I thought, "Oh you magnificent prayer, you incalculable treasure, no invention on earth can equal you."

Our path through this labyrinth finally came to an end, and we were led into a space lit from above and furnished like a music hall. The clergyman disappeared into a small sacristy and returned wearing a choir robe of white silk and over it a stole covered with colored gems. In the meantime, we had mounted a sort of platform, or balustrade, and from high up, I could see that it was constructed of the lid of a huge piano. The priest sat down at this instrument and struck the keys. We all started to sing the tune he played, and with the music that filled my every fiber, there came an outpouring of immense happiness—new courage, which was stronger than any mental or physical elation can ever impart. My joy increased and became so intense that I woke up. And strange to say, this was one of those dreams you would prefer not to wake up from.

PARIS, 29 AUGUST 1943

Sunday afternoon, and I spent it browsing a bit in my book of fairy tales—by that I mean in the *Musée de l'Homme*. There I saw Miss Baartmann again, the Hottentot Venus.[77] There is always a jostling crowd of half-amused, half-shocked visitors around her. She died around 1816 in Paris at the age of thirty-eight and wasn't exactly stuffed, but instead, a plaster mold was cast that reproduced every intimate detail of her body, which deviates from every physical norm. You can also see her skeleton right beside her.

Had a thought as I was observing the observers: I wonder whether invisible and extremely menacing life-forms exist for which you are museum exhibits and collectible objects?

Then went to the Maritime Exhibition on display for several weeks in the lower galleries of the museum. There were not only many ship models, weapons, nautical instruments, hourglasses, and documents but also paintings. These included various views of harbor and coastal sites by Joseph Vernet. One of these pictures, a panorama of the Gulf of Bandol, is brought to life by a depiction of a tuna catch in the foreground. The fishing boats where the butchering is in full swing are surrounded by luxurious vessels while an elegant audience gawks at the blood bath from their decks. Among the whitecaps and the coarse nets, a throng of half-naked lads grapples with the oddly stiff fishes, each one as big as a man. They are tugging at them with hooks they have thrust into their gills—or, wrapping their arms around them, they slice their throats with long knives. Murderous children with their toys. The city folk are fascinated by the slaughter; the women cover their eyes or, half-fainting, stretch out their arms in defense against the onslaught of images, while the gentlemen support them by putting their arms around their chests. We see that tuna fishing is a drama drenched in red, which Abbé Cetti's beautiful description shows.

A sinking ship painted by Gudin around 1828[78] brought the violence of such an event home to me for the first time. This catastrophe is condensed in an amazingly concentrated welter of images. A first impression of the painting is enough to produce a weak light-headed feeling in the viewer. We see a huge ship in a terrifying, turbulent sea, occluded by dark clouds and curtains of rain. The ship is poised almost vertically on its bow as the huge roiling current sucks it into the deep as if it were but a log or chunk of wood. Its broad stern rises out of this vortex, where you can just make out the word "Kent" and a portion of the ship's side, where smoke and flame belch from the portholes. A crowd of people huddle together on this slab of wood partially obscured by red flames, yellow smoke, and white spray. A few have separated themselves from this knot of people and have either thrown themselves into the waves or clambered down the rope ladders. A woman holding a child dangles from a pulley over the churning chasm in an attempt to reach one of the boats. It is astonishing that anyone can still think of saving himself in such horrific turmoil. And yet we can make out a figure in a tall hat among a group of people at the top; his arms gesture with authority as he seems to be giving orders. The wreck is surrounded by overcrowded boats fighting against the waves. In one, we see an approaching swimmer being fended off with the blade of an oar. In the midst of the white swirling sea spray, the waters have calmed into a sleek green surface of narcotic power. There we see people clutching at debris and others who have already drowned and are floating in the deep like sleepers, their bodies colorfully clad and still visible, yet already embedded in the limpid green-aquamarine. A pretty red bandanna shimmers from below.

In the evening visited Morand, who has been made ambassador to Bucharest. Autumn is coming; the swallows are flying away.

PARIS, 30 AUGUST 1943

In one spot on the staircase at the Majestic they have put a fresh, soft, brightly colored piece into the old worn-out runner. I notice myself climbing the steps more slowly at that point, just noting the relationship between pain and time.

Carl Schmitt writes that his beautiful Berlin house lies in ruins. He mentions that all he could rescue of his property were the paintings by Nay and Gilles. And this preference is appropriate, for works of art are magical furnishings, part of the more important possessions, equal to images of the *lares* and *penates*.[79]

PARIS, 30 AUGUST 1943

Dinner with Abel Bonnard on Rue de Talleyrand. Conversed about ocean voyages, flying fish, and *Argonauta argo* [greater argonaut; pelagic octopus], the last of the ammonites, which only surfaces when the sea is absolutely still in order to display its exquisite shell like a splendid ship drifting as it feeds. Then we talked about the picture in the Maritime Exhibition by Gudin, and I described it in detail. Bonnard added that, for his preliminary studies of shipwreck panoramas, this painter would smash lovely old sailing ship models from the eighteenth century with a club in order to reduce them to the condition he desired.

Why does such a clever, clear-headed man like Bonnard get involved in these areas of politics? As I watched him, I thought of Casanova's statement about a minister's actions, which surely have an appeal he himself is unaware of but which affect all who hold such posts. By the twentieth century, all that is left is probably the work and the kicks from the *demos*,[80] that donkey they have to contend with sooner or later. Shady business is perpetually on the increase.

PARIS, 1 SEPTEMBER 1943

More and more often I find that I have to enter two symbols in my address book, namely † for dead, and ☺ for bombed out.

On this subject, I received a letter from Dr. Otte in Hamburg saying that on 30 July the entire fish market and his pharmacy were destroyed along with all his inherited property from his great-grandfather's generation and also the rooms where he kept his Kubin archive. He had opened an emergency pharmacy in a cigar store: "I'll never leave Hamburg. I'll live here or perish."

Dinner with the president in the evening. He told me about concentration camps[81] in the Rhineland from the year 1933, including many a detail from this world of butchery. I am aggrieved to feel such things beginning to influence my relationship, if not to my Fatherland, then to the German people.

PARIS, 4 SEPTEMBER 1943

Yesterday, at the beginning of the fifth year of this war, deep melancholy. Went to bed early. I am worried about my health again, yet this troubles me less since I have begun to formulate an idea about it. My growth reminds me of a rhizome that lies dormant underground, where it often almost withers, yet occasionally as the years go by, when spiritually motivated, it brings forth green shoots, blossoms, and fruits.

Kept going in Huxley, whose arid chill makes reading difficult. In one passage that I found noteworthy, he explains that the influence of the seasons—that rhythmically recurrent order in life—is diminished as civilization advances. An example would be Sicily, where the birthrate in January is twice that of August. This makes sense; periodicity diminishes over the course of time. This is a kind of attrition, abrasion, caused by rotation. At the same time, the difference between normal days and holidays disappears; every day is a fun fair in the city. There are echoes of an earlier moral code that varied with the months. In the region around Lake Constance, married couples take it for granted that during the pre-Lenten carnival season they will treat each other with special tenderness. The disappearance of periodicity is but one aspect of the process—the other is that its loss brings a gain in rhythm. The range of the oscillations lessens but the number increases. Finally, our machine age emerges. The rhythm of the machine is frenzied, but it lacks periodicity. Its oscillations are incalculable but uniform; its vibrations are consistent. The machine is a symbol; its economy of motion is merely an optical illusion—it is just a kind of prayer wheel.

I began to feel better as I slept. I saw myself in a garden where I was saying farewell to Perpetua and our child. I had been digging there and my shovel opened a small hole in the earth, where I saw a dark snake napping. As we said goodbye, I mentioned this to Perpetua for fear that the child might get bitten by the creature while playing. Consequently, I turned around to kill it, but now I found that the garden harbored lots of snakes—knots of them were sunning themselves on the tiles of a derelict gazebo. There I saw dark red and blue ones, and others that were yellow, black and red, or marbled in black and ivory. When I started to fling them across the terrace with a stick, a bunch of them rose up and clung to me. I recognized that they were benign and was barely scared at all when I saw our little boy beside me. He had followed me unnoticed. He picked them up by their midsections and carried them out into the garden as though it were all a jolly game. The dream cheered me up and I awoke invigorated.

This morning it was announced that the English had landed on the southwest tip of Apulia. Yesterday's sorties over the city targeted the central areas for the first time. Among them, streets that I love like Rue de Rennes and Rue Saint-Placide. Two bombs also fell on Rue du Cherche-Midi—one very close to Morin's bookshop, which I immediately phoned, and another right across from where the Doctoresse lives.

Went to the Latin Quarter in the afternoon, primarily to meet a reader of mine named Leleu whom I did not know. He had requested a private meeting via pneumatic post. He turned out to be a traveling cloth salesman from Lyon who received me in a tiny room of a rundown hotel. Once I had sat down on the only chair and he settled onto the bed, we got deeply engrossed in conversation about the situation, during which he expressed strong but vague Communist proclivities. That reminded me of the years when I too would try to use logic like scissors to cut life into paper flowers. How much precious time we squander in these ways.

Afterward visited Morin. On the way, I inspected the damage on Rue du Cherche-Midi. The lovely soft stone from which the city is built had already been heaped into great white piles in front of the buildings that had been hit. Curtains and bed linens hung from the empty windows, and in places a solitary flowerpot stood on the windowsill. The bolts from the blue affected small merchants and many of the simple people who lived above their shops among the nooks and crannies of the ancient apartments. I also entered the Doctoresse's apartment, which I had someone unlock for me, as she is traveling. I wanted to see if everything was in order. As in almost all the other houses, windowpanes had fallen out of their frames, but otherwise nothing had been damaged.

While I was attending to these errands, another lone aircraft circled the center of the city, surrounded by bursts of smoke. No alarm was sounded, and the busy pedestrians carried on undisturbed.

The greatest theft that Kniébolo has perpetrated on the nation is the theft of law—that is to say, he has robbed the Germans of the possibility of having legal rights or feeling that they have any legal recourse in response to the tribulation that is inflicted upon them, or that threatens them. To be sure, the people *per se* have made themselves complicit by their acclamation—that was the terrible, alarming undercurrent audible beneath the cheering orgies of jubilation. Heraclitus got to the core of the matter when he said, "the tongues of demagogues are as sharp as the butcher's knife."

Paris, 5 September 1943

Poor health again. What is more, I am losing weight visibly. I see two causes for this: on the one hand, the sedentary life of the metropolis is always harmful after a while, and on the other, my mental activity is like a lamp burning too much fuel. I made the decision to adopt the only course of action that promises success: long walks. And so I began with the route from the Étoile past the waterfall toward Suresnes and from there along the banks of the Seine across the bridge at Neuilly back to the Étoile.

Brief *subtile* hunt on the shore of the pond in Suresnes. The plants on the large ever-expanding rubbish dump—a paradise for nightshade. I looked for jimson weed in vain, but there in an open field I found *Nicandra* [nightshade] for the first time, the poison berry from Peru. It clustered in lush, thick bushes climbing on the south slope of a rubbish dump; from its branches, there hung the five-pointed star shaped, yellow and darkly flecked calyxes as well as its green lanterns. I have never seen it so vigorous, even in garden soil. Like so many of the nightshades, these do not require cultivation because they thrive best in rubble and on the slag heaps of society.

Crowds of fishermen along the Quai Galliéni; one had just caught a common rudd the length of a man's little finger, which he was carefully reeling in across the surface of the water, saying gently, "*Viens mon coco*" [come, my darling]. Across the silted water kingfishers whirred away with their wonderfully delicate, plangent tones. Rested in a small church among the outlying districts. It was in a state of rural dilapidation. In a rundown barracks on the Quai National, there was a plaque to the memory of the composer Vincenzo Bellini who had died there on 23 September 1835. As I read this, thoughts came to me about the sacrifices made by creative people and their roles as outsiders in this world. There were also groups of anglers here hunkering either in boats or on stones along the shore as they conjured tiny silverfish out of the water. The sight of a fisherman is exhilarating—he has mastered the art of idly extending time, of relaxing, and that makes him the antithesis of the technician.

Impatiens noli tangere—jewel weed—yellow balsam, or touch-me-not. When I would take walks in the woods with women, I always found that they responded to the tactile appeal of this plant: "*Oh, ça bande*" [oh, it stretches]. This casting of seed represents tumescence and high energy, the trigger-happy, buoyant, procreative force. In greenhouses, I have seen tropical species almost larger than life. I would like to plant these in my ideal garden along the borders that will surround the joyous herms of Priapus[82]—these and several other mischievous little plants as well.

I do not contradict myself—that is a contemporary prejudice. Rather, I move through various layers of the truth. Of these the one that is uppermost at the time dominates the others. In these higher strata, when viewed objectively, truth becomes simpler; this is similar to the way—when viewed subjectively—concepts are subordinated at the higher levels of thought. When viewed outside any temporal frame of reference, this truth is like a branching root system sending out everstronger shoots and then, where light penetrates, converging into a single bud. That will be—at least this is my hope—at the moment of death.

Read more in Huxley. There is much theoretical thinking and purely constructive thought process in his style. In individual passages, his mind condenses images of substantive power like grains of gold in the alluvial deposit. An example is the observation that struck me today: that human economy forces us to exploit life, like those coal deposits that are remnants of prehistoric forests, or oil fields, and guano coasts, and the like. At such sites, train and shipping lines converge, and swarms of newcomers then settle. When viewed from the perspective of a distant astronomer, over the passage of time, such a spectacle looks like the activity of a swarm of flies that has picked up the scent of a huge cadaver.

The author goes deeper into such imagery, reaching levels where the superiority of our century's thought can be found—superior when compared with that of its predecessor. This is a difference of light, which no longer appears as pure vibration but as something corpuscular as well.

PARIS, 6 SEPTEMBER 1943

Worked more on my *Appeal*. I notice in this work a kind of exertion that is difficult to describe, a sentence seems clear to me—I could write it down. Yet getting it on paper is preceded by an inner struggle. It is as if this audacious act needed a drop of special essential oil that is hard to come by. Still it is extraordinary that the written word usually fits the greater plan. Nonetheless, I still have the impression that what I have written has mutated since surviving the strain of that exertion.

Read further in Huxley. Then had a long dream about a stay in a farmhouse where I was a guest, but the only feature I could remember in the morning was that I had entered a room. On its door there was a sign that read *astuce.* "Aha," I thought, as I awoke, "that must have been a sort of formal living room because *astuce* means 'arrogance.' " As I look it up in the dictionary just now, I see that this word is translated as "guile," "shiftiness." And that applied to the situation.

Paris, 7 September 1943

I repeated my woods and water circuit in the company of Jouhandeau, who told me that the onslaught of images and thoughts kept him so busy that he was working almost around the clock. In fact, I did find him writing busily, engrossed in his notes, sitting on a bench at our rendezvous point at the Étoile. I get the impression that the massive calamity plaguing the nations has released mental energies that affect our subtle perceptions in ever-increasing waves, in stronger pulsations. Our heads are like the tops of towers during a storm when they are circled by pigeons and jackdaws. Legions of minds are seeking a place of refuge.

I showed Jouhandeau the plants on the mound of rubble and learned from him the name for mullein: *Le Bon Henri.*

Paris, 9 September 1943

Italy's unconditional surrender was announced this morning. While I was still studying the large map of the Mediterranean, the alarm sirens sounded again, and I went over to the Raphael. There I finished my reading of the Apocrypha and with that of the Old Testament, begun two years ago on 3 September 1941. I have now read the entire Bible and plan to reread the New Testament, this time making use of the Vulgate and the Septuagint as I do so.

These books relate to each other in a marvelous way. They present the history of man, first as God's creation, and then as God's Son. The open, incomplete quality of the book seems to require a Third Testament: *after* the resurrection, beyond the transfiguration. This is actually intimated in the last section of the Bible in the Book of Revelation. One might interpret the supreme enterprise of western art as an attempt to create this testament; it filters through its great works. Yet one could also say that each and every one of us is the author of the Third Testament; life is a manuscript and from it is formed the higher reality of the text in the invisible space after death.

Stepping over to the window, I saw two bomber squadrons flying over the city in low V-formations while the anti-aircraft guns pounded away.

The beautiful passage at the beginning of the texts about Esther, where the letter of Artaxerxes begins. It is addressed to the 127 princes and their ministers between India and the land of the Moors [Ethiopia] who are all his subjects. Yet his words form the introduction to an execution order. That is a pattern still in force today.

Visited Jouhandeau in the evening. We examined poems from the sixteenth and seventeenth centuries—such as the sonnet by Mellin de Saint-Gellais, with its graceful refrain "*Il n'y a pas*" [there aren't (isn't) any], which ties all the loose ends together in the final verse. It reminded me of the beautiful *Trost*-Aria [aria of comfort] by Johann Christian Günther, where the word *endlich* [finally] repeats in a similar fashion.

Endlich blüht die Aloe,
Endlich trägt der Palmbaum Früchte
Endlich, endlich kommt einmal.

[Finally the aloe blooms, / The palm tree finally bears its fruit, / Finally, finally comes one day.]

The dying words of Saint-Gellais are, incidentally, noteworthy. The doctors were holding a conference at his bedside, arguing about his sickness and how it was to be treated. After listening to them disagreeing, he turned to them and said: "*Messieurs, je vais vous mettre d'accord.*" [Gentlemen, I am going to make you agree], and turning to the wall, he passed away.

Read further in Huxley. The prose resembles a net of finely spun glass filaments that occasionally catches a few lovely fish. These alone stick in our memory.

PARIS, 10 SEPTEMBER 1943

A night full of dreams, but only fragments stayed with me. For example, in order to characterize a bad painter, I said, "when he couldn't sell his paintings, he accepted unemployment compensation."

When I woke up, I thought about those years of my journals that I had burned along with early works and poems. To be sure, my thoughts were flawed and often naïve, but over the course of the years one tempers self-criticism. We must gain distance from our early work and change in order to see it more fairly and impartially. This bond resembles that of fathers who disapprove of their sons, and for no other reason than that they are so similar, while at the same time they have good relationships with their grandchildren. At the time back in the spring of 1933 even Perpetua regretted my *auto-da-fé* after our house had been searched. I believe they were looking for letters in my possession from the old anarchist Mühsam. He had a childlike attraction for me before he was so brutally murdered. He was one of the best and most good-natured people I have ever met.

Affiliation and human contact on this earth must always remain very important. I note this in the pain caused by those connections we have neglected; it is pain that stings forever. This applies in part to the little dark *Tentyria* [beetle] on the parched cow path near Casablanca, where a stunted fig tree stood. How frustrating that I did not grab the little creature. Then there are especially those amorous relations—all the missed opportunities, the neglected rendezvous. Something has to be lost here that transcends the physical sphere, when in our role as hunters we do not "get off a shot." We did not make the most of our talents. I am sure that is part of the great equation, if only to a small degree.

Thought: when we do make connections, perhaps a light goes on in unknown rooms.

I have gotten ahead of myself on the subject of the perception of historical realities, which is to say that I am aware of them somewhat in advance of the event. This is not beneficial for my daily life because it leads me into conflict with the powers that be. Nor do I see any metaphysical advantage; what difference does it make whether my insight refers to current conditions or later developments? I am striving for a spiritual union with the moment in all its timeless intensity, because that alone, not permanence, is the symbol of eternity.

Visited Florence in the evening. Jouhandeau was there as well. He had spent a sleepless night because he is said to be on an execution list. When he talked about these worries, there was something about him that reminded me of a little boy who had just been apprehended by a policeman.

PARIS, 11 SEPTEMBER 1943

The mail brought a letter from Carl Schmitt, one of those rare minds capable of viewing the situation impartially. He wrote concerning Bruno Bauer's book *Russland und das Germanentum* [*Russia and the Germanic Concept*].

"The situation was already perfectly obvious to Tocqueville in 1835. The conclusion of the second volume of his *Démocratie en Amérique* remains the foremost document of the '*Decline of the West*'."[83] Then concerning *Benito Cereno*[84] and reference to it in Fabre-Luce, which I inspired. "*Du reste* [as for the rest]: *Ecclesiastes, 10:1*."[85]

Perpetua, who enjoyed my dream about the snakes, writes in her daily letter: "I too feel that you derive your necessary energy from this solitary point and that you will return to complete your task here."

These years involve the risk that there is no escape on the horizon. No star shines through the desolate night. This is our situation in astrological and metaphysical terms; the wars, civil wars, and weapons of destruction appear as secondary, as mere contemporary décor. We have the responsibility of transcending this world of destruction, which can never succeed on the historical stage.

Visited the National Archive in the afternoon, where Schnath showed me a series of records in which German and French history converge. Throughout the centuries, particularly in the papal chanceries, a high culture flourished on parchment. When patronage was bestowed, a seal was attached to a silken ribbon; otherwise, it was attached to one of hemp. The monks, whose task it was to affix the seals, had to be illiterate—*fratres barbati*—so as to preserve secrecy. The skins of unborn lambs produced especially fine parchment.

Toured the stacks, which contain sustenance for generations of archivists and bookworms to come. The National Archive is deposited in rooms at the Hôtel de Soubise, one of the municipal buildings of the old Marais quarter, where you can see that the nobility was powerful and unconstrained when it was built.

Took a zigzag route from Rue du Temple through the old quarters to the Bastille. The street names included many I found delightful, such as Rue du Roi Doré and Rue du Petit Musc.[86] I bought some grapes and offered some to children who were sitting in their doorways. Almost everyone refused the offer or gazed at me with suspicion. People are not used to being given things. Went to the bookdealers on the quais, where I picked up a few pictures of tropical birds.

Read further in Huxley. There I came across the remark: "Every experience has an essential connection to the peculiar nature of the human being affected by it." I share this view. In a murder case, it is not by chance that we appear as the murderer, the murder victim, witness, policeman, or as the judge. Nor does sociology contradict this view; on the contrary, it affirms it. Our milieu is a distinctive mark of our species, like the form and color of mussel and snail shells in the mollusk world. Just as there are a lot of *petits gris* [edible snails], there are also a lot of proletarians.

Hence the extraordinary significance of work for our inner life. We do not only shape our fate but also our world.

K has the consistency of the *Kürbis* [squash, pumpkin]: when you poke it with your finger, first it is hard, then soft, then hollow.

P, on the other hand, is like the *Pfirsich* [peach]: first comes the flesh of the fruit, then the hard pit, which in turn, encloses the mild seed.

Paris, 12 September 1943

At noon, I visited the sculptor Gebhardt on Rue Jean Ferrandi. Conversation about the chaos in Italy, where this war is forcing new and outlandish blossoms. The two great aspects of war and civil war are explosively combined here; we simultaneously glimpse scenes unknown since the Renaissance.

Then discussion about France. Here, too, hatred is constantly on the increase, but as in standing waters, it is more covert. Many people are now getting miniature coffins in the mail.[87] It is also Kniébolo's role to discredit good ideas by carrying them aloft on his shield. For example, the friendship between these two countries, for which there is so much evidence.

I returned via Saint-Sulpice; I stepped into the church for a while, where I noticed details like the two huge seashells that serve as holy water fonts. Their fluted edges were trimmed with a metal border, their mother-of-pearl luster was the color of honey opal. They rested upon pedestals of white marble; one was decorated with marine vegetation and a large ocean crab. The other was ornamented with an octopus. The spirit of water pervaded everything.

While I stood there in front of a mediocre painting of the Judas kiss, the thought came to me: The sword that Saint Peter draws must have been something that he usually wore. Did Christ then permit him to carry it? Or did he wrest it from Malchus before striking him with it?

Paris, 13 September 1943

In the morning, the news arrived that Mussolini has been freed by German paratroopers. No mention of his location or of the circumstances. The war is becoming more and more graphic. If things in Italy keep on like this for a long time, they will lead to far-reaching exterminations, as in Spain. Mankind is in dire straits.

Telephone call with Schnath concerning Count Dejean and the possibility of gaining access to the files on him. I would like to include a series of essays among my shorter works. These will be expressions of gratitude and tributes to men and books that have helped me in life.

Horst has just told me that General Speidel's beautiful house in Mannheim has been destroyed. Right afterward a courier who had just arrived from Russia handed me letters from Speidel and Grüninger, in addition to a detailed report about the Battle of Belgorod. Grüninger says that we cannot count on champions on white horses to march through the Brandenburg Gate; for that matter, it is uncertain how much longer the Brandenburg Gate will remain standing, and furthermore, the color white is becoming extinct. Correct, but the higher counteroffensive against red will take place on the blue field.[88]

Read further in Huxley, where I found the following nice observation: "You should never name an evil you feel attracted to, for in doing so you present fate with a model it can use to fashion events."

This describes the process that people designate as a "calling," which millions of people surrender to nowadays. To give your imagination free rein, or lose yourself in details of a disastrous future—that is, in a word, fear. Fear destroys the delicate, protective layer of salvation and security within us. This is particularly alarming under conditions where we have lost the knowledge of how we can reinforce and preserve this layer, especially the knowledge of prayer, which has largely been forgotten.

PARIS, 14 SEPTEMBER 1943

Telephone call with Marcel Jouhandeau. "*Je vous conseille de lire la correspondence de Cicéron—c'est le plus actuel.*" [I advise you to read the correspondence of Cicero—it's most timely.] Yes, one always comes back to it. Wieland wrote almost the same thing after Jena and Auerstedt.[89]

PARIS, 15 SEPTEMBER 1943

Low fever during the night. Dreams in which I crossed lush wetlands on the lookout for insects. I picked a few off a tall chickweed or water dropwort—delicate, metallic species. To my astonishment, I saw that they were *Buprestidae* [jewel beetles].

"A truly remarkable find—their shape adapts them for a dry, sunny environment: water and marshland are quite alien to them."

Then a deeper voice answered.

"But these are transitional creatures that have established themselves in this alien environment. These species have adjusted to moisture along with the fennel, yet the fennel's height lets it tower upward seeking sunlight. Just think of Prometheus."

Actually, then, nothing is more intelligible than the exception—there is a direct correlation between the exception and the explanation. Like light, the rule is inexplicable, invisible, and illuminates only when striking objects that resist it. Thus we say correctly that the exception proves the rule—we could even say that it renders the rule discernible.

Herein lies the intellectual appeal of zoology, in the study of those prismatic deviations that register invisible life in infinite variations. When I was a boy I was delighted when my father would reveal such secrets to me. All these details compose the arabesques in the design of the great mystery, of the invisible philosopher's stone, which is the object of our striving. One day the design will evaporate, and the stone will suddenly catch the light.

Visited the Doctoresse in the middle of the day. Then walked through different quarters and streets of the city with a brief rest in the Church of Saint-Séverin, where both the exterior and interior move me deeply. Here the Gothic has not remained mere architecture. Its incandescence has lasted.

I was eating alone in my room in the Raphael when the air-raid sirens sounded at approximately twenty minutes to eight. The sound of intense cannon barrage soon erupted; I hurried up to the roof. The scene presented a display that was both terrifying and magnificent to my eyes. Two great squadrons were flying in wedge formation over the center of the city from northwest to southeast. They had apparently already dropped their payloads, for broad swathes of smoke clouds towered to the heavens from the direction they had come. The sight was ominous, but the mind immediately grasped that in that area hundreds, perhaps thousands, of people were now suffocating, burning, and bleeding to death.

In front of this leaden curtain lay the city in the golden twilight. The rays of the setting sun glinted on the underside of the aircraft; their fuselages contrasted with the blue sky like silverfish. The tailfins in particular focused and reflected the rays as they shone like beacons.

These squadrons moved in formation like flights of cranes, shimmering at low altitude over the cityscape while groups of little white and dark clouds accompanied them. I watched the points of fire—focused and tiny as pinheads—gradually melt and spread out into burning orbs. Occasionally, a flaming plane would drift slowly downward like a golden fireball without leaving a trail of smoke. One of them plummeted in darkness, spinning to the ground like an autumn leaf, leaving only a trace of white smoke behind. Yet another was torn apart as it plunged, leaving a huge wing hovering in the air. Something of considerable size, sepia-brown, gathered speed as it fell—most likely a man attached to a smoldering parachute.

Despite these direct hits, the offensive maintained its course without deviating to the right or left, and this straight trajectory conveyed an impression of terrifying power. On top of this came the deep drone of the motors, filling the air and chasing the swarms of frightened pigeons in circles around the Arc de Triomphe. The spectacle bore the stamp of those two great attributes of our life and our world: strictly ordered discipline and visceral release. It embodied both great beauty and demonic power. I lost track of everything for a few moments as my consciousness dissolved into the scene, into the sense of the catastrophe, but also into the meaning that lies at its heart.

Vast fires from furnaces emerged on the horizon and blazed even more blindingly once darkness fell. Throughout the night flashes from the explosions streaked the sky.

Read further in Huxley, whose lack of structure is tiresome. His is a case of an anarchist with conservative memories who opposes nihilism. In this situation, he ought to employ more imagery and fewer concepts. As it is, he seldom exploits the real strength of his talent.

The image that he uses to describe the impersonal and tangled nature of sexual relationships is good: a knot of serpents, their heads lifted up into the air, while below their bodies are entwined in chaotic turmoil.

Film, radio—the whole array of technology—is perhaps meant to lead us to a better knowledge of ourselves: knowledge of what we are *not*.

PARIS, 17 SEPTEMBER 1943

The mail brought a contribution to my Hamann miscellany, sent by Donders, the dean of the cathedral in Münster: "*I. G. Hamann, eine Festrede gehalten am 27. Januar 1916 in der Aula der westfälischen Wilhelms-Universität zu Münster von Julius Smend*" [I. G. Hamann, an Oration by Julius Smend held on 27 January 1916 in the auditorium of the Wilhelms University in Münster (Westphalia)].

Hamann, after Herder a "man of the Old Covenant"—that is the hieroglyphic quality that I refer to as a pre-Herodotus, pre-Heraclitus character. Just as Weimar had Goethe and Schiller, Königsberg had Hamann and Kant.

Kant speaks of Hamann's "divine language of observant reason."

As an author, you also have to learn from painters—especially when it comes to matters of "overpainting," meaning applying new and more subtle improvements to the rough text.

Finished reading Huxley in the evening. One of the mistakes he makes is not taking his fictional characters seriously, much less so than Dostoevsky, and just a bit less than Gide.

PARIS, 18 SEPTEMBER 1943

Walked the woods and water circuit with the Doctoresse. Among the diverse species of nightshade blooming along this path, I discovered a luxuriant, grass-green jimson weed proliferating, bearing blossoms and fruit on an embankment of the Seine opposite the little country church of Nôtre Dame de la Pitié.

Finished reading: Jean Desbordes, *Le vrai Visage du Marquis de Sade* (Paris, 1939) [*The True Face of the Marquis de Sade*]. It is remarkable how this name is maligned and associated with disgrace more than almost any other. This is understandable given the immense influence of the pen and the mind: a life of disgrace would be long forgotten were it not for disgraceful writers.

When names enter a language to become concepts and create categories, it is seldom a result of accomplishments. Among the great men of action and princes, only Caesar lights the way. Of course you can say that something is Alexandrine, Frederician, Napoleonic—but a certain special individuality is always inherent in the word. Caesarean conjures up a Caesar, a Czar, a Kaiser; here the word has become independent of the name.

Cases in which a name becomes attached to a doctrine, like Calvinism, Darwinism, or Malthusianism, et cetera, are much more common. Such words are numerous, arbitrary, and usually short-lived.

At the highest level, we find names that unite doctrine and exemplar: Buddhism and Christianity. The situation among Christians is unique, where (at least in our language) each one bears the name of the founder: "*Ich bin ein Christ.*" [I am a Christian.] Here "Christ" substitutes for human being, thereby revealing the dignity and mystery of this doctrine echoed in designations like "*Mensch*" [man], "*des Menschen Sohn*" [son of man], and "*Gottes Sohn*" [son of God].

PARIS, 19 SEPTEMBER 1943

In the morning, I worked in the Majestic finishing the first section of the *Appeal*. It is entitled "The Sacrifice." While browsing in Spinoza, I chanced upon an epigraph for this section in Proposition 44 of the *Ethics*: "Hatred, when completely conquered by love, is transformed into love, and love is then stronger than if hatred had not preceded it."

PARIS, 20 SEPTEMBER 1943

Began the second section of the *Appeal*, "The Fruit."

My reading matter: A. Chavan and M. Monotoccio, *Fossiles Classiques* (Paris, 1938) [*Classic Fossils*]. From this book, I have learned that my little spiral snails are called *Cerithium tuberculosum*. The large one that I found in the bomb crater near Montmirail is called *Campanile giganteum*. Both were first described by Lamarck.

PARIS, 23 SEPTEMBER 1943

Reports came this morning of a new intense bombardment of Hannover; I am waiting for more detailed news.

In the afternoon, I went with Baumgart to Bernasconi, who is binding the *Catalogus Coleopterorum* [*Catalogue of Coleoptera*] for me. The way back took us through the gardens of the Trocadéro; there on the lawn were large, brick-red dahlias and multibloom asters: purple stars with yellow centers. Around this time of year, they are surrounded by honey-brown maggot flies; Admiral butterflies perched on them with outspread wings. The bright, pure, vivid red of this insect's bands blends with images of quiet parks and gardens in my memory, places dreaming in the sun when autumn has begun to cast its chill upon the shadows.

Then came the air-raid sirens while I was engaged in political discussions with the president in his room. The German armies on the eastern front are in retreat, while the English and Americans are clawing their way forward in Italy, while their air forces are leveling the cities of the Reich.

Sometimes it seems to me as if, with all this misery that surrounds us, the laws of mirroring are in force. The universe encircles us like a great mirror, and we must first illuminate ourselves before the horizon can brighten.

The swimmers struggle slowly toward the coast against the tides. Only a few will reach it, only a few will get as far as the surf. At that point, we shall see who will prevail against the most powerful wave.

In the evening was with Heller and Dr. Göpel in the Chapon Fin. Conversation with the host, who is remarkable for clearly exhibiting all the traits of Mars in the descendant. The powerful physique is crowned by a head with dark hair and a very low hairline. His cheekbones are prominent, eyes restive, peering; and he is constantly bustling around. The disparity between intention and intelligence can be seen in the kind of torment obvious in his language when he struggles to get his ideas out. Our entertainment is a noisy congeniality among comrades. A sort of elective affinity has led him to befriend the Germans, whose martial nature appeals to him and provides him with activity and employment. For some time now, he has often been harassed and followed, and he has already been sent a small coffin.

As we were leaving, the sirens sounded the alarm and squadrons flew over the city. Our man now showed himself to be in his element. In his German helmet, his coat, and equipped with a flashlight, he roamed the dark square accompanied by a large German shepherd; with his whistle he signaled pedestrians and stopped cars. People like him are trusty servants, the odd-job men in this world of fire. It must be said that they are not without virtues and courage; just as they display a dog's merits and flaws, by the same token they always have dogs nearby. Even Kniébolo displays descendant aspects of Mars, yet at the same time, different planets like Jupiter govern him with his aura of disaster. He had all the attributes to introduce an era of strife; an instrument of wrath, he has opened Pandora's box. When I compare the legitimate claims of our Fatherland with what has occurred at his hands, I am overcome with infinite sadness.

PARIS, 24 SEPTEMBER 1943

Visit from Pastor B. who often comes to read me poems. Discussion about the situation, for which he sees only one way out, namely the deployment of the new weapon. Everywhere in Germany people are whispering miraculous claims about this, abetted by covert manipulation from the Propaganda Ministry. They think that the destruction of most, or even all, of the English population is possible. At the same time, they are convinced (and not without justification) that similar wishes exist on the other side, and not just among the Russians but also the English. The massive attacks that employ phosphorus, like the one on Hamburg, are seen as a concrete evidence of this. Thus the charred desolation brings forth hopes and dreams directed at the extermination of large nations. The example of a clergyman is significant for the degree to which people have become bound together in this crimson jungle. Not only is he in the grip of this madness, but he sees extermination as the only salvation. They can be seen disappearing step by step into darkness and spiritual death like the children of Hameln vanishing into the mountain.[90]

Finished reading Maurice Pillet, *Thèbes, Palais et Nécropoles* [*Thebes: Palaces and Necropolises*] (Paris, 1930). It contains a photograph of the sarcophagus of Tutankhamun with his golden mask and jewels. As I read this, it became clear to me once again how our urge to archive and store relics corresponds in a minor way to the Egyptian cult of the dead. Mummified culture is to us what the mummified human form was to them, and their metaphysical fears are our historical ones. The worry that dominates us is that our magical expression could be lost in the stream of time; that is the fear that motivates us. Peace in the womb of the pyramids and in the solitude of those cliff chambers surrounded by works of art, texts, utensils, divine images, jewelry, and rich grave goods—this is meant for more sublime types of permanence.

PARIS, 26 SEPTEMBER 1943

At breakfast I started my second reading of the New Testament. Compared Matthew 5:3 to the texts in the Nestle edition.[91] "Blessed are the poor in spirit [*geistig arm*] . . . " I had always remembered this passage as "geistlich" [spiritual, sacred]. The discrepancy does not arise with *spiritu* or τῳ πνευματι. Without doubt, both are meant—on the one hand, *geistlich*, in the sense of learned, scholarly, like the Pharisees; and on the other, *geistig*, insofar as this superior ability promotes doubt, thereby making the path to salvation invisible. Both are captured in the word *einfältig* [simple; simpleminded]. "Blessed are the foolish." This word contains both worldly weakness and metaphysical superiority, even the mustard seed is foolish [*einfältig*]. A large number of these comparisons involve man's naïve powers, those virtues from his dreams and childhood. Then Matthew 6:23, the dreadful words: "If therefore the light that is in thee be darkness, how great is that darkness!" I also find a positive association in this passage: darkness is an immense force. Our eyes separate and compartmentalize a bit of this when we split and refine that profound essence of darkness—the sense of touch—thereby refining and weakening it. The sexual act reminds us of the significance of tactile experience.

Perhaps when we have reduced our numbers by 90 percent, like the mutineers of Pitcairn Island,[92] we, too, shall return to Scripture as law.

PARIS, 28 SEPTEMBER 1943

The reports again mention a fierce air strike on Hannover last night. Thus the days pass over us like the teeth of a saw.

Finished reading Erdmannsdörffer's *Mirabeau*, one of the best historical character studies I have ever come across. The author was in his late sixties. It radiates the gentle clarity of age, and in doing so, shows us the finest change that the mind can experience in its autumnal years: the inclination toward simplicity.

On my desk I found a four-leaf clover. It was floating in a vase—a present from an unknown hand. Books arrived as well, such as *Plaisir des Météors* [*The Pleasure of Meteors*] by Marie Gevers, an author unknown to me. The mail also included

Friedrich Georg's *Wanderungen auf Rhodos* [*Hikes on Rhodes*] and the *Briefe aus Mondello* [*Letters from Mondello*]. During the noonday break, I immersed myself along with him in our walks along the Mediterranean.

PARIS, 29 SEPTEMBER 1943

Still aboard this slave ship for no reason. In my next incarnation, I shall return to earth as a school of flying fish. That way I'll be able to subdivide myself.

A night of dreams. In a room where I was a guest I found a guestbook bound in red leather on the night table. Among the many names, that of my good old father stood out.

Went to Rue Raymond-Poincaré in the afternoon. There I bought a present for Perpetua from Schneider: Lizst's piano transcription of Berlioz's *Symphonie Fantastique*. Strange melodies for Kirchhorst.

The queues in front of the public offices and the shops are getting longer. When I pass by them in uniform, I am the object of glances filled with contempt—contempt that nurtures murderous intentions. I can read in their faces that it would be perfectly marvelous if I just dissolved into thin air and evaporated like a dream. Multitudes of people in all countries are feverishly awaiting the moment when it will be their turn to shed blood. Yet that is precisely what we must avoid.

PARIS, 30 SEPTEMBER 1943

Autumn weather, damp and gray. The pale foliage on the trees blends into the fog. Violetta, a half-forgotten friend, appeared to me in my dream. In the meantime she had learned to fly—or rather something more like hovering. She was appearing in a circus act wearing a short blue skirt that billowed around her pink thighs like a parachute. We, her old friends from Berlin, met her in a church where she was supposed to take communion. Standing up in the gallery we were whispering *doubles entendres* jokingly to each other the way we used to do about this "sailor's sweetheart." But we also sensed the particular gamble involved here; below us she crossed the red tiles to the center aisle toward the altar. We were horrified when a trapdoor suddenly opened in front of her with a thunderclap, revealing a yawning chasm to our gaze. A dizzy feeling made us turn away. But then, when we finally dared to look down again, we could make out a second, altar, which looked tiny because it was at the bottom of the crypt. It was encircled by a ring of golden objects. In the middle we could see Violetta standing. She had floated down like a butterfly.

In the afternoon went to *Salon d'Automne*, Avenue de Tokio, to see the pictures by Braque, whom I plan to visit on Monday. I found them powerful, both in form and color, and painted with more emotion than those of Picasso. For me they embody the moment when we emerge from nihilism and the ideas for new compositions converge for us. Accordingly, curved lines replace splintered ones. A deep blue color is particularly effective, as is a rich blue, then a deep violet coalescing with a soft velvet brown.

The exhibition offered a varied assortment of works. One had the impression that painters, like artists in general, are continuing to work obsessively during the catastrophe, like ants in their half-destroyed colony. Perhaps that is a superficial view, and it may be that beneath the great destruction deep veins remain unscathed. I, too, certainly depend on these.

I found viewing the pictures to be a challenge; an accumulation of artwork has the effect of a magical assault. If we develop an intimacy with individual ones, or even take them home and domesticate them, then their vitality inhabits us.

PARIS, 2 OCTOBER 1943

Depression, which always makes me lose weight.

Over breakfast continued reading the Gospel of Matthew. The story with the stater,[93] which the disciples will find in the belly of a fish, is surely a later, magical addendum, and contradicts the uncomplicated character that aims at salvation, not at mystification—which characterizes the other miracles. Chapter 4, verse 14 attests to the conviction that individuals are resurrected on earth. John, Elijah, and Jeremiah are mentioned. Perhaps this belief derives from the prophets. This passage, like so many others, seems to retain the small, ordinary coin of discourse, whereas it is usually the gold pieces that are bequeathed to us.

The mail brought a letter from First Lieutenant Häussler from the Kuban bridgehead. He writes to me saying that Dr. Fuchs, who was our host when we were in Shaumyan, was killed in action.

Made the woods and water circuit with the Doctoresse in the afternoon. The trees by the pond in Suresnes reflected their delicate crimson, dun, and deep golden brown hues in the clear water, with its margin of pale green plants and algae. Visited Parc de Bagatelle briefly, where I searched in vain for the large golden orphe. Still, I was compensated by being able to watch a water lettuce unfold its delicate spiked hyacinth blossom. The leaves where insects had inscribed their hieroglyphic trails had already been touched by autumn and enclosed the miraculous blossom in a heart-shaped form, like a circle of lacquer seals.

In the evening browsed in an issue of *Crapouillot*[94] about the French press with the feeling that I was deep inside the labyrinths of the *cloaca maxima*.[95] Freedom of the press in the political and social arena is what the freedom of the will is in the metaphysical—one of those problems that always arises and can never be solved.

PARIS, 3 OCTOBER 1943

In the morning I read further in the Gospel of Matthew. In 18:7 I read: "It must needs be that offences come; but woe to that man by whom the offence cometh."

There in a nutshell we have the distinction between predestination and free will, and certainly this passage was one of those that nourished Boethius.

Ich bin einfältig gewesen und ich werde mich wieder einfalten.[96] [I was foolish, and I shall make myself foolish again.]

PARIS, 4 OCTOBER 1943

Visited Braque in the afternoon with Jouhandeau. He owns a small, warm south-facing studio not far from Parc Montsoris.

We were received by a powerfully built man of middle height wearing a blue linen jacket and brown corduroy trousers. Comfortable leather slippers, soft wool socks, and a continually lit pipe magnified the effect of easygoing activity in his casual company. His face was expressive, determined, and his hair thick and white; the eyes of blue enamel and unusually prominent like the lenses of extrapowerful magnifying glasses.

The walls were richly hung with paintings. I particularly liked the image of a black table; its surface reflected the vessels and glasses standing on it in a way that etherealized rather than simplified them. On the easel, inherited from his father, stood a still life he had begun. The paint was laid on in thick layers of impasto and dripped down like colorful stalactites.

We conversed about connections between Impressionist painting and military camouflage, which Braque said *he* had invented, being the first to produce art in which the destruction of form was achieved with color.

Braque rejects the presence of any prototypes and models, thus painting solely from memory, endowing his pictures with their deeper dream reality. Expanding on this, he recounted that recently he had included a lobster in one of his pictures without knowing how many legs the animal has. Later, when he was dining and he saw one, he was able to confirm that he had gotten the number exactly right. He related this to Aristotle's notion of a particular numerical correspondence that applies to every species.

As always, when I encounter productive people, I asked Braque how he experienced the aging process. He said that the pleasant thing about it was that it put him in a position where he no longer had to make choices. I interpret that to mean that in old age life becomes more essential and less accidental; the path becomes a single track.

He added: "One also has to reach the point when creativity no longer comes from here but from here." In saying this he pointed first to his forehead, then to his belly. The order of his gestures surprised me, because it is generally assumed that work is a self-conscious activity—even in cases where practice, routine, and experience simplify it. We consciously abbreviate creative processes. Nonetheless, it made sense to me with regard to his own evolution, evident in his turn from cubism to more profound realism. There is also a progress toward naiveté. In the realm of the mind there are mountain climbers and mountain dwellers; the first follow the paternal inclination and the second, the maternal. One group gains greater heights and increasing clarity; the others are like the hero in Hoffmann's tale of the mine at Falun, whose hero penetrates the earth through ever-deeper shafts toward that place where slumbering, fecund ideas reveal themselves to the mind in crystalline beauty. This is the true difference between the Apollonian and Dionysian. The greatest artists possess both of these energies, a double portion.

They are like the Andes, whose absolute elevation is divided in half to our sight by the ocean's surface. Yet their domain spans the sphere of the condor's wings down to the measureless reaches of the ocean's depths.

In Braque and Picasso, I have met two great painters of our age. The impression that each made was equally powerful, yet different in details. Beneath his intellectuality, Picasso appeared as a powerful magician, while Braque embodied a radiant geniality. The difference between their studios projects this as well; Picasso's has a particularly Spanish touch.

In Braque's studio, I was struck by the number of small objects—masks, vases, glasses, idols, shells, and the like. I had the impression that these are less models in the traditional sense than talismans, rather like magnets for attracting dream material. This accumulated and, again, radiating matter might come into play when one purchases one of Braque's pictures. One of the objects was a large butterfly adorned with dark blue spots. Braque caught this in his garden, where he has a *Paulownia* growing. He believes that the insect arrived here from Japan along with the tree.

To the Ritz in the evening, where Schulenburg and I were alone together. We mulled over the situation and my related *Appeal for Peace*, which I outlined for him. The time may have come for me to move to Berlin. I of course mentioned that Keitel already views my presence here with suspicion and that, on the other hand, Heinrich von Stülpnagel under orders from Speidel, has not given me permission.

PARIS, 5 OCTOBER 1943

In the mail I found the first letter from Perpetua about the night of September 28 in Kirchhorst. Bombs hit the meadows near the house. The terror seems to reach its crescendo when the Christmas trees[97] light up the sky—these clusters of lights announce a mass bombardment. The little seven-year-old daughter of a neighbor was taken to the mental hospital the next morning. The future of our children makes me think—what fruits can this spring bear? The high and low temperatures will etch bizarre patterns into the butterfly wings of these little souls.

PARIS, 6 OCTOBER 1943

Took a stroll in the evening with Husser, whom I had arranged to meet at the Tomb of the Unknown Soldier. He told me his life story as we walked along the Bois to the Porte Maillot, and from there back across Place des Ternes. Husser's misfortune is that he is the son of a Jewish father while at the same time a passionate German soldier and warrior at Douaumont.[98] Under the prevailing circumstances, that was hard to reconcile. As a result, he turns up here like a man who has lost his shadow—anonymous, living under a pseudonym with a new identity and new passport from a deceased Alsatian. He lives in a cheap hotel in Billancourt and has just come back from the coast where he was a shepherd for a Breton nationalist on Hielscher's recommendation. Incidentally, Hielscher himself will probably be coming through Paris soon because he wants to send Bretons to Ireland.

I took along mail for Husser's wife and plan to send her parcels too. The problem is that neither she as their receiver, nor her husband as sender, nor I as go-between, can ever be exposed.

In the Raphael pondered the petty viciousness that no future historian will ever record, such as the behavior of the old regimental groups who at first tried to protect their members like Husser, but then betrayed him to the *demos* once things became dangerous. A similar case is the reason that Friedrich Georg and I, along with others, resigned from the Veterans' Association of the Seventy-Third Regiment. In my plan of the "House," I should include a room where the corrupt assembly of knights delivers up their wards under pressure from the mob rioting outside. The combination of false dignity, fear, and empty bonhomie—I saw them all on the mask of President Bünger when he interrogated the undesirable witnesses in the trial of the Reichstag fire.[99] Pontius Pilate is the prototype here. The accused is then set free, knowing full well into whose hands he will fall on the steps of the courthouse. The same fate could befall me if the commander-in-chief ever has to leave the Majestic. Except then the handwashing ritual might be made to smell sweeter: "My dear Herr J., Here your talents do not reach a wide enough circle. For that reason you are being 'reassigned.' " Then comes the farewell celebration where one puts a good face on things and lifting the glass for the parting toast. These are details present in Shakespeare that put any professional historian to shame.

PARIS, 10 OCTOBER 1943

This morning in bed I finished the Book of Matthew. Then had my Sunday breakfast, which thanks to the good offices of the president, is always very satisfying. Thought: Even though I live for the most part surrounded by the trappings of comfort in this Second World War, I am in greater peril than when I was at the Battle of the Somme or in Flanders. It also seems to me that out of a hundred old veterans, hardly any one of them is able to bear up under the new atrocities that arise when we move from that stage of heroism into one of demonic possession.

Matthew 25: The main subject of this chapter is that in his lifetime man can acquire eternal value. He can collect oil for the lamp that burns forever. With his inherited portion, his talents, he can secure eternal riches. This transcendent power—to earn interest from time—is actually an extraordinary miracle, worth studying in one hundred thousand monasteries and countless hermits' cells: time, the wine press, and the world, its fruit. It is not for nothing that so many images refer to wine and to the work of the vintner in the mountains, for the evolution of the wine up to that moment when it is drunk and transformed into spirit, provides us with a powerful symbol of life.

We live in order to realize ourselves. This realization makes death meaningless—man has converted his personal effects into gold, which everywhere and irrespective of borders, retains its value. Thus the pronouncement of Solomon that death is merely imaginary for the just: "As gold in the furnace hath he tried them and received them as a burnt offering."[100]

Thus, we can attain a state where we never lose value when we are exchanged.

PARIS, 11 OCTOBER 1943

Great plans of destruction can only succeed when they parallel changes in the world of morality. Man must continue to sink in value, must become metaphysically indifferent, before the transition to mass extermination as we are experiencing it today becomes total annihilation. Just as our entire situation was predicted by Scripture, so too was this specific one—and not just in the description of the Flood but also in that of the destruction of Sodom. With that God says explicitly that He wishes to spare the city as long as ten just men can still be found there. This is also a symbol of the immense responsibility of the individual in our age. One can guarantee the security of untold millions.

PARIS, 14 OCTOBER 1943

Climbed down into an open grave onto the coffin of my grandfather, the teacher of boys. That morning I looked up *tombeau* [tomb] in a book of dream imagery, where I found it defined as *longévité* [longevity]. This is one of those shallow explanations typical of these books. To step down into the grave of an ancestor more likely means that one seeks advice under duress, advice that an individual cannot give himself.

The mail brought a letter from a young soldier, Klaus Meinert, who wrote me once before about my little piece on vowels. This time he tells me of his discoveries about the symbolic content of the *antiqua majuscules*:[101]

A is meant to embody breadth and height. The symbol [XX, see p. 170, German original] expresses this most simply. Two distant points meet at the zenith.

E is the sound of the void, of abstract thought, of the mathematical world. Three uniform parallels [XX, see p. 170, German original] connected by a vertical express this.

I, the erotic sign, expresses the lingam, blood kinship, love, and passion.

O represents the light-sound, the embodiment of the sun and of the eye.

U, or as our forebears wrote it *V*, is the earth sound as it delves into the depths. It also becomes clear that it is in opposition to *A*.

I was pleased by this work because it shows insight. I also thought about the conditions under which he wrote it—on maneuvers, on sentry duty, in his bivouac. Young people clutch at the intellectual elements of life as if at a constellation observed from a doomed outpost. How rarely do they find support in this, their finest instinct.

Horst was sitting beside me at the table when he got the news that his aged father had been killed in the attack on Münster. Uncanny circumstances surrounded this event. The bombings continue to multiply. The damage caused on the night of 9–10 October in Hannover is extensive; hundreds of thousands of people are said to be homeless. Still no news from Perpetua!

In the afternoon had a conversation with a Captain Aretz, who once visited me in Goslar when he was a student. We talked a long time about the situation. He

said that I would not recognize the mental state of twenty- to thirty-year-old people, who believe only what the newspapers print because they have never learned
anything else. He seemed to think that was advantageous, considering the inflex-
ible attitude of the authorities. But the opposite is actually true. It would be enough
simply to change what gets printed in the newspapers.

PARIS, 16 OCTOBER 1943

Gave some thought to technology and what we have lost because of it. As a product
of the purely masculine intellect, it is like a predator whose overwhelming menace
mankind has not immediately recognized. We have foolishly raised this animal in
close quarters with ourselves, only to discover that it cannot be domesticated. It is
striking that its first application—namely in the form of the locomotive—brought
good results. The railroad under complete or partial state control, and subject to
highly regulated discipline, has made it possible for countless families to make
their modest, decent livings in the past hundred years. Generally speaking, a railroad employee is a contented person. The engineers, civil servants, and workers
in this area enjoy the benefits of soldiers, and only a few of their disadvantages.
We would be better off if we had structured the industry of automated mills in the
same way, as a constructive development from the very start. Of course, something particular always pertained to the railroad, namely its geographical presence, which continued to expand across large areas. The railroad has the ability
to connect a great number of lives that are only partially beholden to technology
while the rest belongs to organic life. This would describe the simple, healthy quality of life of track inspectors and crossing guards. From the very beginning, every
one of the technical professions should have been given a plot of land, if only a
garden, for every life is dependent on the earth—that all-nourishing force that
alone offers us protection in times of crisis.

Technology resembles a construction project built upon ground that has been
inadequately analyzed. In a hundred years, it has grown so massively that changes
on the great blueprint in general have become inordinately complex. This applies
especially to those countries that have seen the highest rates of development. Russia's advantage stems from this, and now becomes obvious when explained by its
two essential causes: The country had no technological prehistory, and it possessed
sufficient territory. To be sure, it also went through an immense upheaval, destroying property and life, but the reason for this lay outside the planners' intentions.

There could be *one* positive aspect to the great destruction of our Fatherland,
in that this will provide a new beginning for these things that seem inevitable.
These upheavals will create conditions that will far exceed Bakunin's most audacious dreams.

Finished reading the first volume of the *Causes Célèbres*, published in Amsterdam
in 1772 by M. Richet, former attorney in parliament. In the descriptions of the
trial brought against Brinvilliers, I found the sentence, "*Les grands crimes loin de
se soupçonner, ne s'imaginent même pas*" [Great crimes, far from being suspected,

are unimaginable]. That is quite right and stems from the fact that crime increases at the same rate that it rises from the level of bestiality and acquires intellect. The clues also disappear to the same degree as its animal origins fall away. The greatest crimes depend on combinations that are superior to the law in points of logic. Crime also shifts from the deed to a state of being, reaching levels where it exists as an abstract spirit of evil in pure cognition. Finally, interest itself wanes and evil is done for evil's sake. Evil is celebrated. Then there is also the face that the question "*cui bono?*" [who benefits?] no longer provides a guiding principle—it is only *one* force in the universe that it benefits.

In the evening Bogo[102] came to the Raphael with Husser. In our age so lacking in original talent, Bogo is one of those acquaintances I have been devoting the most thought to, and yet have been the least successful in forming an opinion about. I used to think that the history of our age would record him as one of its exaggeratedly witty, yet least known, figures. Yet today I believe that he will deliver more. Many, perhaps most, intellectual young people who grew up in Germany after the Great War were influenced by him or were his disciples. I could usually tell that they had been affected by the encounter.

He arrived from Brittany after previously visiting Poland and Sweden. As was his quirky habit, he began to prepare for our discussion by unpacking various objects, such as a series of carved pipes with a tobacco pouch and pipe cleaners. He also produced a little cap of black velvet for his bald head. While doing so, he watched me with his crafty, quizzical gaze—one that was also agreeable—like that of a man who was expecting certain revelations, but at the same time, kept amusing things hidden. I had the impression that he chose his pipe according to the progress of the conversation.

I asked him about a few acquaintances, like Gerd von Tevenar who had recently died, and I learned that Bogo had buried him. Von Aretz, on the other hand, who visited me yesterday, said, "I officiated at his wedding." This confirmed a suspicion I have had for a long time, namely that he had founded a church. Now he's studying dogma and has made great progress in the area of liturgy. He showed me a series of hymns and a festival cycle, "The Pagan Year." It coordinates the gods, festivals, colors, fauna, foods, stones, and plants. In this I read that the *Lichtweih* [Festival of Lights] is to be celebrated on 2 February. This holiday is sacred to Berchta,[103] whose attribute is the spindle, whose animal is the bear, and whose flower is the snowdrop. Her colors are rusty red and snow white; the mistletoe is considered the gift to give on her day. The celebratory food consumed is herring with dumplings. The accompanying drink is punch, and the pastry is a flat waffle cake. The entry for Fasnacht,[104] a holiday honoring Freya,[105] calls for tongue, champagne, and crullers.

Discussed the situation. He held the opinion that, since the Biedenhorns[106] had not succeeded in blowing Kniébolo sky-high, this was the task of certain particular circles. He implied that under specific circumstances he felt obliged to prepare and organize—almost like the Old Man of the Mountain[107] who sends his young people into the palaces. The underlying problem in our contemporary politics, as he sees it, may be stated as: how do you penetrate the inner circle for five minutes with weapons? When I had finished listening to him expound on the details, Kniébolo's situation became clear to me: these days he is surrounded and deified by his huntsmen.

I thought I noticed a fundamental change in Bogo—a change that seems characteristic of the entire elite echelon. To be specific, he rushes into metaphysical areas with rationalist ardor. I noticed this about Spengler, and it is an auspicious omen. In brief, the nineteenth century was a rational one, whereas the twentieth century is sectarian. Kniébolo feeds on this—hence the complete inability of the liberal intelligentsia even to perceive where he stands on matters.

Then, concerning Bogo's travels. Many a secret here. I was especially appalled by details he reported from the ghetto of Lodz, or as they are now calling it, Litzmannstadt. He contrived to gain entrance there under a pretext that allowed him to consult with the overseer of the Jewish community, a former Austrian first lieutenant. A hundred and twenty thousand Jews live there crammed together in a small space where they work for the arms industry. They have constructed one of the largest plants in the East. In this way, they are just able to scrape by, because they are essential labor. At the same time, new deported Jews pour in from the occupied countries. To dispose of these people, crematoria have been built not far from the ghettoes. They take the victims there in vehicles that are supposed to be an invention of Chief Nihilist Heydrich. The exhaust fumes are piped into the interior so that they become death chambers.

Apparently, there is also a second butchering method that consists of leading naked victims to a large steel plate through which an electric charge is passed. Then the bodies are burned. They moved to this method when it turned out that the SS soldiers who were ordered to deliver the pistol shots to the back of the head were developing psychological ailments and finally refused to carry out their orders. These crematoria need only a small staff; it's a sort of fiendish gang of masters and their lackeys who carry out this work. Here, then, is where those masses of Jews are being sent who are being "resettled" from Europe. This is the landscape that reveals Kniébolo's nature most clearly, and which not even Dostoevsky could have predicted.

The ones destined for the crematoria must be picked by the ghetto overseer. After conferring extensively with the rabbis, he chooses the old people and the sick children. Many of the old and infirm are said to volunteer, and thus such horrific negotiations always reveal the honor of the persecuted.

The ghetto of Litzmannstadt is enclosed. In other, smaller cities there are some that consist only of a few streets where Jews live. Jewish police, who have the task of seizing victims, are said to have picked up German and Polish pedestrians who were walking through the ghetto and handed them over, and nothing was ever heard from them again. This claim is made particularly by Volga Germans[108] who are waiting for confirmation of their land allotments. Of course, they protested to these executioners that they weren't Jews, but the only response they got was, "That's what everybody here says."

No children are conceived in the ghetto except by the most pious sect, the Chassidim.

The name Litzmannstadt makes it explicit how Kniébolo distributes honors. He has linked the name of this general, who can claim military victories, for all times with a charnel house. It has been clear to me from the beginning that his commendations were to be feared the most, and I said, quoting Friedrich Georg:

Ruhm nicht bringt es, eure Schlachten
Mitzuschlagen.
Eure Siege sind verächtlich
Wie die Niederlagen.

[To fight your battles with you brings no honor. / Your victories are as despicable / As defeats.]

PARIS, 17 OCTOBER 1943
Went to the reopened Théâtre de Poche, Boulevard de Montparnasse. Schlumberger invited the Doctoresse and me to see his play *Césaire*. Strindberg's *The Tempest* was also performed. This space heightened the ghostly aspect of the performance. It was done in costumes from the end of the last century, which had been dug out of old clothes cupboards; even a telephone (which would have been quite a novelty on the stage of that era) was in period style.

Afterward over tea the Doctoresse said, "The works of great artists are identifiable by their mathematical character: The problems are divisible and everything tallies. There is no remainder left over."

This assessment is on the right track, but it describes only one of the two sides of productivity. The other side produces striking results precisely because they do *not* add up—there is always an indivisible remainder. That's the difference between Molière and Shakespeare, between Kant and Hamann, between logic and language, between light and darkness.

Of course, there are always a few minds that are both indivisible and divisible. Pascal and E. A. Poe, and, in ancient times, Saint Paul—all of these belong to this category. At the point where language as blind power pours into the luminescence of thought, palaces gleam in polished darkness.

PARIS, 18 OCTOBER 1943
Visited Florence in the middle of the day. The colors of all the bottles and glasses continue to delight me, treasures found in ancient graves. Their blue is deeper and more exquisite than that of the butterfly's wing in the mountainous forests of Brazil.

Marie-Louise Bousquet told of a woman who traveled to one of the bombed-out cities on the coast to look for her husband, who had not returned from a trip. She asked at the town hall, but his name was not among the lists of victims. Walking out into the marketplace, she saw a group of coffins on some wagons. Each one had a small peg that held a card with the name of the deceased. Her husband's name immediately caught her eye, and what's more, just at the moment when the wagon began to move toward the cemetery. And so she walked behind the coffin in her traveling clothes—in one of those lightning transformations of scenes familiar only from dreams. Life becomes more surreal.

PARIS, 19 OCTOBER 1943

Another report of a terrible attack on Hannover last night. I'm trying in vain to get through to speak to Perpetua. The lines are down. By now the city seems to have been utterly destroyed.

In the afternoon, paid a call on the art dealer Etienne Bignou who, in response to my request, brought a painting by the customs agent [Henri] Rousseau out of his bank vault. The painting had been missing for a long time. Rousseau called this large work from 1894 *War* and gave it the epigraph, "Gruesomely she passes, leaving despair, tears, and ruins in her wake."

The colors are striking at first glance: clouds unfolding before a blue sky like large pink blossoms, and in front of these, a black and pale gray tree with tropical leaves hanging from its branches. The Angel of Discord gallops across a battle-field on a black, sightless steed. He wears a feathered smock. In his right hand he brandishes a sword and, in his left, a torch trailing a dark cloud of smoke that belches sparks. The terrain beneath this terrifying flying celestial visitor is strewn with naked or barely clothed corpses; ravens are making a meal of them. Rousseau gave his own face to the corpse in the foreground, which is the only one mea-gerly clothed in patched trousers. Another in the background, whose liver is being devoured by a raven, has the face of his wife's first husband.

Baumgart informed me that this painting had been rediscovered. In it I see one of the great visions of our time. It also conveys a concept behind painting's essen-tials, in contrast to a kaleidoscopic choice of possible subjects. Just as the canvases of the early Impressionists conformed to the old daguerreotype process, this painting approximates a snapshot. A kind of frightening spell, a sort of decorative brutality, stands in stark contrast to the fundamental power of its content. We can contem-plate in peace and quiet that which is otherwise beyond our ken, be it because of the demon's stealth or its terrible speed. You can see that around this time things had become incredibly dangerous. Then there is the Mexican element. Thirty years before, Galliffet had returned from that country. Without a doubt, a source of our world of terror derives from those tropical seeds that developed on European soil.

Among the various qualities of the painting, the childlike aspect is notable: purity in fairytale horror like the novel by Emily Brontë.

PARIS, 20 OCTOBER 1943

News from Perpetua has finally arrived. The terrifying attack of 10 October that destroyed large sections of Hannover just strafed Kirchhorst. From the parsonage, she watched as the phosphorus poured down on the city like molten silver. On the afternoon of 11 October, she forced her way through smoking ruins to her parents' house. It was the only one within a large perimeter that was spared, but incendiary bombs had blasted into the rooms. She found her parents exhausted and with eyes swollen from fighting fires. Her little niece, Victoria, had acted especially bravely. And so we see in such moments that it is precisely the weak who find strength no one thought them capable of.

PARIS, 23 OCTOBER 1943

Capriccio tenebroso [dark fantasy]. Image of a dead Eurasian jay with its rosy-gray breast plumage and its black, white, and patterned pinion feathers. There he lies, already half-sunken into the loose earth; beneath it there toils a swarm of grave-diggers. Its body disappears in jerks and spasms into the dark soil. Soon only the light blue tip of a wing is visible. It is covered by a clutch of tiny yellow eggs. This, too, disappears as the maggots crawl their way out of the eggs and glide down off it.

When crime becomes illness, execution becomes an operation.

PARIS, 24 OCTOBER 1943

A letter from Perpetua concerning the terrible night of 19 October finally puts my mind at ease. Kirchhorst was hit. Farmyards and buildings were burned down. High explosive and incendiary bombs as well as phosphorus canisters fell around the parsonage while the inhabitants lay on the floor of the hallway. Then there came an incredible noise, as if the good old building were collapsing, and Perpetua rushed out into the garden with our little boy. There they both pressed themselves against the arbor vitae.

This year I lost not just my father but also my native city. I also hear threatening news from Leisnig and Munich. In World War I, I was alone and free; I am going through this second one with all my loved ones and all my belongings. Yet there were moments in World War I when I dreamed of the second one; just as on the advance through France in 1940, I was less frightened by images of the present than by the anticipation of future worlds of destruction that I inferred in that deserted region.

In the afternoon, I visited Klaus Valentiner who has come over from Aix. He brought me greetings from Médan, whose fellow countrymen had sent two coffins and a death sentence to his house. His crime is believing that friendship between Germany and France is possible.

Ahlmann, Valentiner's uncle, whom I got to know through the Magister, and a general were all invited to dinner at Carl Schmitt's. Together they went looking for Kaiserswertherstrasse in Dahlem [Berlin]. When they arrived, they found the house in ruins, yet more by way of an experiment, they pushed the doorbell at the garden door. In response, Frau Duschka appeared from one of the cellar rooms. She was wearing a black velvet dress and announced to them formally that she was unfortunately forced to cancel dinner. This quality does her credit.

Valentiner also told a terrible story from Aix. An SS company is stationed there, from which a young soldier went AWOL and fled to Spain. The desertion succeeded, but he was extradited. The company commander ordered him brought in chains before the troops in formation, where he executed him personally with a machine gun. The action must have produced a horrifying effect; many of the young soldiers fainted and fell to the ground.

This violation is barely believable when we keep in mind that the commander is still always the father of his men. Of course, it applies to conditions dominated by raw force alone, thus placing the highest authority in the hands of the hangman.

Visited the Luxembourg Gardens during a drizzle. There the magnificent canna lily was in bloom, gaudy red with fiery yellow edges around the large oval, where in wartime people now grow cabbages and tomatoes.

PARIS, 25 OCTOBER 1943

Visited Florence at noon. She described details about decorating a castle in Normandy that she had bought years ago, but she couldn't recall its name.

Marie Laurencin also at the table. I conversed with her about the customs agent Rousseau. She had known him when she was a young girl at a time when he gave painting and violin lessons; she praised his mellifluous speech. She found listening to him was much more enjoyable than watching him paint. She sat for him as he painted her portrait; it depicted her with huge girth, although she was a slender girl. When she pointed this out to him, he said, "*c'est pour vous fair plus important*" [It's to make you more important]. Such a Paleolithic concept.

PARIS, 26 OCTOBER 1943

Was present at a meal where Socrates was also invited. He was a small man, thin, with short hair, a gaunt, intelligent face; he wore a gray, well-cut suit.

"It is so comforting that such a man is still alive," I said to myself, and reacted as if I had just discovered that Burckhardt or Delacroix were still alive.

I chatted about this with one of my table companions, who poured liquid butter onto white bread toast for me. He was a Scandinavian critic who also knew my friend Birgit and heartily recommended an epic she had sent him. I remember some of the verses he quoted to me. They began: "*Morus mehr Tänzer als Heimer—*" [Morus, more dancer than Heimer—].

He called this beginning "outstanding," yet I understood intuitively that he was using the word in both its laudatory and its restrictive sense, since "outstanding" establishes a relationship to the generic, which cannot be said of the absolute.

Dreams bring me hope for the future, give me security. This applies especially to the one in which I survived Kniébolo and his gang at the height of their power on a ship crossing to Rhodes. "*Tout ce que arrive est adorable*" [Everything that happens is adorable] is one of the best expressions Bloy has ever come up with.

As I woke up, I recognized a new harmony. I refer to the sort where a delicate green and a delicate yellow unite in lines and bands that can be called the harmony of the rushes. In gazebos at the water's edge, in bungalows, in pavilions, and chicken coops, on bamboo bridges, on the binding of the works of Turgenev and Walt Whitman—that's where it would belong.

Worked further on the *Appeal*. I have started the chapter about nihilism and at the same time am also recopying sections.

PARIS, 27 OCTOBER 1943

In her letter of 21 October, Perpetua writes about the children from Berlin that we are sheltering. One of them, a poor little thing only six years old, said to her: "Auntie, the bees are so afraid of me that they wiggle."

Then there is the faith that the little boy has in the strong mother who keeps danger at bay. Such are the things we would never experience in times of safety.

PARIS, 28 OCTOBER 1943

Cramer von Laue visited me in the afternoon. He is one of those readers who was introduced to my works as a child and has grown up with them. In the meantime, he has been promoted to captain and his left cheek bears a scar gashed by a bullet wound, which becomes him.

Discussion about the situation and especially the question as to what extent the individual must feel responsibility for Kniébolo's crimes. For me it is a pleasure to see how young people who have learned from me can get right to the point. The fate of Germany is hopeless if a new chivalric order does not emerge from its youth, and especially from among its workers.

Cramer drew my attention to a book by Walter Schubart published in Switzerland and called *Europa und die Seele des Ostens* [*Europe and the Soul of the East*]. He summarized passages from it, and I hope that I can track it down, even though there aren't more than a few copies in circulation.

PARIS, 29 OCTOBER 1943

Visited Bernasconi, Avenue de Lowendal. There I picked up both volumes of the *Catologus Coleopterorum* in the sturdy bindings he had made for me. Then via Rue d'Estrées and Rue de Babylone to the Doctoresse, who had been ordered to appear at Gestapo headquarters that morning in the matter of her husband, who is still languishing in prison. Since such a summons always involves the danger of new accusations, my call was like visiting a convalescent.

Back on the ancient streets again, I was in such a good mood. I walked along under their spell as if in a state of exquisite intoxication.

PARIS, 30 OCTOBER 1943

Horst had just returned from Münster, and the funeral of his old father, who had been killed by a bomb. He brought me greetings from Donders, the dean of the cathedral. Donders lost his beautiful library of over twenty thousand books in the great fire.

"A good thing that I gave the Hamann to Ernst Jünger," he told Horst.

The huge fires change the consciousness of property more than all the old tomes that have been written about it since the beginning of the world. That is the *Révolution sans phrases* [revolution without mincing words].

"The six nectar vineyard." *Pariser Zeitung* [*Paris Newspaper*] from today. A nice typographical error.[109]

From Benoist-Méchin's work on the history of the German army, I have just learned that Kniébolo's driver had the apocalyptic surname "Schreck" [fear, horror].

VAUX-LES-CERNAY, 31 OCTOBER 1943

Have been in Vaux since yesterday afternoon as a guest of the commander-in-chief. Our usual discussions by the great fireplace in the evenings. The general said that in the Ukraine henchmen of Sauckel[110] had announced that from now on the Easter festival would be celebrated according to the ancient rite. They then surrounded the churches and from the crowds pouring out of the service they abducted anyone they considered useful.

Went to the woods on Sunday morning to hunt for *subtiles*. Found a lovely *Coccinellidae* [ladybug] that landed on a reed in the sunshine. Its pale yellow carapace was dotted with white spots—a balance that only works when nature mixes the colors.

Two large hornets with lemon yellow abdomens tattooed with mahogany stripes were drinking deeply at a trickle of oak sap. Sometimes they would touch each other with their mandibles, almost billing and cooing as they tried to lap up the last bits of sap from each other's head and thorax. Their gestures looked like a tender embrace, and attraction must motivate such antics, for one of the sources of tenderness is grooming. This explains the licking of newborns that is performed not only by most mammals but also by the Eskimos. Stroking and arranging the feathers with the beak is similar. These are sources of affection, captured in its essence by Rimbaud's beautiful poem, "*Chercheuses de Poux*" ["The Lice Pickers"].

Then I found the *Bovista* fungi [puffballs] that populate the edges of the peaceful autumnal paths in their guise as yellowish-brown pods with their top third already decomposing. When they reach ripeness, a fontanelle forms on their crests that releases a cloud of dust spores. These are structures that transform themselves completely into seed and fertility, leaving only thin parchment shells behind as individual remnants. One could even see these as mortars that bombard us with life. Seen in this light, they wouldn't make bad grave decorations or appropriate designs on the coats of arms of philanthropists.

PARIS, 1 NOVEMBER 1943

Beginning of November. Slept poorly. In my dream, I was wandering through the destroyed city of Hannover because it had occurred to me that in my worry about my wife and children I had completely forgotten my grandmother and her little apartment on Krausenstrasse.

PARIS, 5 NOVEMBER 1943

Visited the Didiers in the evening. Hendrik de Man, the former Belgian prime minister, was there; he gave me a printed though unpublished copy of his text on peace.

We conversed about Leipzig, where he had lived before World War I, where he was on the staff of the Social Democratic *Volkszeitung* [People's Newspaper]. I am consistently astounded by the generic traits of these old Socialists, who were considered revolutionaries back in their day. They were basically a new class of ruling elite who elbowed their way upward in all the countries experiencing the birth pangs of a worker's state. The transformation from civil servant to functionary—or to use Carl Schmitt's phrase, from legitimacy to legality—resembles the transition from hieratic to demotic writing systems. You can read it in their faces. MacDonald in England and Winnig in Germany are types of this sort.

PARIS, 8 NOVEMBER 1943

Had breakfast with Florence. While I was there, Heller told me about a doppelganger I have who supposedly resembles me down to every detail of gesture, voice, and handwriting. In such a case, there has to be some blood kinship.

To Marie-Louise [Heller] who cannot remember dates.

"Marie-Louise, you are certain you can't remember your husband's birthday anymore?"

"Yes, but on the other hand I can never forget his death day."

This retort is apt, for in death that person is permanently linked to us—as I now feel about my father.

Kniébolo's speeches are like bankruptcy hearings; in order to stall for time, the insolvent person promises to pay his creditors fantastic profits.

I think that people still underestimate his monstrous quality.

PARIS, 9 NOVEMBER 1943

Today I finished the draft of my *Appeal*. I am curious to think what the fate of this work will be. Léon Bloy might perhaps praise the fact that it is directed "against everybody." For me, it is just a good sign that I was able to write it at all.

PARIS, 10 NOVEMBER 1943

In the afternoon conversation with Schnath, who is off to Hannover. His archive too was largely destroyed by the flames, along with the indices, with the result that the remaining inventory of his files has been transformed into an impenetrable mass of paper. We talked about storing his treasures in potash mines. The environment there is so dry that the bindings become brittle. Salt crystals also form on all surfaces, and these attract water. The pain that archivists feel as a result of the fires is especially acute.

In the evening visited a small publisher on Rue Boissonade named Haumont; the man is obsessed with a mania for typography. I talked with him and Heller about Prince de Ligne, whose works he is printing. Dr. Göpel then joined us and brought me Huebner's book on Hieronymus Bosch. We went to Les Vikings and dined with a poet named Berry, who has written an epic poem over six thousand verses long about the Garonne River. He quoted one of them between two swallows of wine. It went like this:

Mourir n'est rien, il faut cesser de boire.

[Dying is nothing, you have to stop drinking.]

He was a jovial fellow in other ways as well. In honor of the only woman in our party—one who had come with Haumont—he proposed to pen a dialogue in which one of her breasts engages in a competition with the other. I found the idea unsuited to a subject made far more appealing by symmetry than difference.

Paris, 13 November 1943

In the morning, I received a visit from one of my readers, Frau von Oertzen, director of the Nursing Branch of the Red Cross. We exchanged those secret signs that people use nowadays to recognize each other. We talked about the trips she takes to every war zone and to all the occupied territories. Then about the Old and New Testaments. She said that if she could carry only two books with her, one would have to be the Bible. And what about the other one? In my case that would probably be *One Thousand and One Nights*. In other words, two works of Orientalia.

In the afternoon went with Marie-Louise to visit Marie Laurencin, who owns a studio on the top floor of a house on Rue Savorgnan de Brazza; the place is like a doll's house or the garden of the good fairy from an old children's story. Her favorite color predominates inside: bright green mixed with a touch of pink. We looked at illustrated books of fairytales, especially those published in the second half of the last century in Munich.

I learned that the F's[111] are showing Bolshevist tendencies in Bucharest. That's a bad sign for Kniébolo. His biceps are losing their charm.

Paris, 14 November 1943

Visited Versailles with the Doctoresse in the afternoon to stroll in the rain through the long deserted *allées*. It was almost dark when we returned to the city from the Trianon. No painter will ever be able to capture the colors that one could merely sense in the fog—the night was bathed in a trace of yellow, red umber, as though colorful sea creatures were retreating into their shells and revealing their mysterious glory as they disappeared.

Paris, 15 November 1943

Breakfast with Florence. Cocteau called a writer whose prose uses platitudes meaningfully, a "flatfish of the deep sea"—"*une limand des grandes profondeurs.*"

In the afternoon Husser sneaked in to see me like Peter Schlemihl.[112] He brought me a copy of the *History of the Spanish Conspiracy Against Venice*.

Discussed the situation: when doing so, I always take the phone off the hook. During our talk, he mentioned a quotation from Voltaire's *History of Charles XII* that says how difficult it is to destroy completely anyone fighting a coalition of powerful adversaries. Yes, but first he will be thoroughly thrashed.

Then talked about the Catholic clergy. Husser said he thought that they express nihilism in their disputations against science.

PARIS, 16 NOVEMBER 1943

Received a visit from Morin in the afternoon. He told me about his father's death and asked me for help settling his affairs. I was again amazed at the skill that young Frenchmen have in putting things in order. He focuses on the crux, whereas the young German gets distracted by his own interests outside the plan and soon loses concentration. His development is more fundamentally chaotic and to a great extent includes an element of unpredictability. It always comes down to the difference between Molière and Shakespeare that occurs to me with such comparisons, and with it comes the thought of whether or not a higher humanity would be possible atop these two pillars—an embodiment of a new order formed from opposing energies of centrifugal force and gravitation.

At the German Institute in the evening; the sculptor Breker was there with his Greek wife. In addition, Frau Abetz, Abel Bonnard, and Drieu la Rochelle, with whom I exchanged shots in 1915. That was at Le Godat, the town where Hermann Löns was killed in action. Drieu also recalled the bell that struck the hours there; we each heard it. Also present were the pens for hire, characters you wouldn't want to touch with a pair of fire tongs. The whole thing seethes in a stew of self-interest, hatred, and fear. And some already bear the stigma of gruesome death on their foreheads. I am reaching the stage where the sight of these nihilists is becoming physically unbearable.

PARIS, 18 NOVEMBER 1943

Discussion with Bargatzky, to whom I gave a copy of my *Appeal*. We talked about the possibility of a clandestine publication *rebus sic stantibus* [things being what they are]. This made me think of Aumont and also of a translation by Henri Thomas that Heller is about to begin.

In the afternoon, Ziegler arrived from Hamburg and reported on the massive air raids. Where sections of the city are in flames, the people suffocate either from lack of air or because carbon dioxide pours into the cellars. Such details make the death toll more comprehensible. An enormous cloud of ash transformed day into night, just as Pliny recounts in his description of the destruction of Pompeii. It was so dark that when Ziegler tried to write to his wife in the middle of the day he had to light a candle.

The great focal points. Prophets radiate toward them, apostles emanate from them.

PARIS, 20 NOVEMBER 1943

Cramer von Laue brought me another book by Schubart. It places Napoleon, Nietzsche, and Dostoevsky in a triptych as the three main figures of the nineteenth century; as such, the great man of action is flanked on one side by the bad thief and, on the other, by the good one.

Cramer also had some information about the life of the author. It seems that before the outbreak of war he traveled to Riga to visit his wife, and there he was abducted after the Russians invaded. After that he was never heard from again. For this reason alone, his books are quite significant because they explore the Germans' second option: our alliance with the East. It was thus no coincidence that I discovered quotations from my own *Worker* in his book—the book that represents my most radical swerve toward the collectivist extreme.

On the Train, 24 November 1943

Traveling to Kirchhorst. I'm reading *A Midsummer Night's Dream*. Right there in the first scene of the fourth act, Oberon says to Titania:

Titania, music call; and strike more dead
Than common sleep of all these five the sense. (IV.i.82–83)

Sleep, in other words, has different aspects. One can also say that it possesses different dimensions, one being the duration, the other, the depth, which knows other regions than that of pure recovery. When viewed mechanistically, sleep is the simple opposite of the waking state, but the depth one can reach in sleep depends on the strengths of the different components that fuse to create it. To these belong prophecy, warning, healing, contact with the spirits of the dead. In these depths, refreshment can be extraordinary—for example, there is a kind of slumber we can sink into for a few minutes and waken from as if reborn. Illness ends with a healing sleep that flushes the remnants of the malady out of us like a bath. Throughout the ages, the healing arts have always tried to grasp this affinity. Greek culture did so especially beautifully in the temples of Aesculapius where the divinity would prophesy remedies to the dreamers in the sleeping quarters. Where those aspects of Mesmerism have proven tenable, they relate to this state of deeper sleep. Nowadays we are quite alienated from all this; in our cities sleep never achieves those deep layers where the great reward beckons, and it is horrifying to think that perhaps death loses its potency for the same reason.

Porta Westfalica.[113] When arriving from the West, I always greet it as a port of entry leading to the narrower Lower Saxon homeland. These are sacred signs; they remain standing. As I sat at the window pondering, I thought about placing my own gravestone in this region.

Kirchhorst, 26 November 1943

At my desk in the upstairs room where many unopened packets of books are stacked along the walls. Piles of Oriental carpets, rescued and brought to us by friends from the city, are also in storage here. In the entryway stand the pieces of getaway luggage, ready and packed as if this were a waiting room. The garden is overgrown; prisoners built a shelter in it. The beds and the paths are green with quickweed. On the moor and in the fields lie phosphorus canisters dropped by the bombers, along with leaflets and clumps of silver paper. At night the English fly over the house by the hundreds, while the anti-aircraft fire blazes away and shrapnel clatters down onto the roof tiles. The building seems to be losing its mooring; we relate to it in a way familiar only to inhabitants of river islands. It's as though it had transformed itself into a ship. I only hope that it does not founder in the storm, but will reach port with its precious cargo.

In the library I am organizing piles of letters and manuscripts into folders. Later, at the microscope, where I study the water beetles I caught on the moor with Alexander. The cushions of floating mosses that flourish in the brown waters of the peat ditches conceal species of the far North that I can now compare with their western varieties that I have brought with me from the streams and ponds of the Paris basin. I take such a magical pleasure in observing such structural variation. From the tiniest details of the runes of creation we can discern differences in habitats with the sort of precision that only music can otherwise achieve. I look at the scientists of the nineteenth century as though they were typesetters who may have known their fonts, but knew nothing of the wonderful texts they worked on. This accounts for part of their greatness, which, by the way, will eventually be acknowledged.

The proximity of destruction gives new pleasure to the pursuit of these delicate objects—a new perception of their impermanence.

Local business. Perpetua visited the Grethes' little boy, who was attacked and nearly killed by a ram. He was playing with his brother near a pasture when the animal knocked him down, probably because he was wearing a red jacket. Every time he tried to get up, the ram grew wilder, crushed both his clavicles, and butted his head, which swelled until he was unrecognizable. His little brother ran to the village to get help. He could hear the little boy trying to calm his horned attacker as he tried to get up, saying, "ram, I'm a good boy."

A fireman who was on duty during the big attack on Hannover saw an old man running toward him down a street that was in flames. At that the very moment a tall building façade buckled and came down. It crashed down over the old man, but as soon as the dust had cleared, he could be seen standing there, unharmed. There he stood, to the amazement of the firemen, framed by a window opening like a gap in a net.

Kirchhorst, 27 November 1943

Afternoon in Hannover, which I found transformed into a heap of rubble. The places where I had lived as a child, as a schoolboy, as a young officer—all had been leveled. I stood for a long time in front of the house on Krausenstrasse, where my grandmother lived for more than twenty years and where I had kept her company countless times. A few brick walls still stood, and in my memory, I reconstructed the kitchen, the little guestroom, the parlor, and the cozy living room where my mother raised flowers on the windowsills. In a single night, tens of thousands of such dwellings, with their auras of active lives, were destroyed like nests swept to the ground by a storm.

Ernstel and I visited the house on Ifflandstrasse where my grandfather died. Just after we had walked a few paces past it, a building collapsed. Walking in this wasteland is a risk.

The tops of the church steeples were burned down, leaving their stumps towering in the air like open crowns blackened by smoke. I was glad to find that the Beginen Tower on the Hohes Ufer[114] had survived. The very old structures are stronger than the Gothic ones.

There was bustling activity in the midst of the rubble. The pushing and shoving of the gray masses reminded me of scenes I had seen in Rostov and other Russian cities. The East is advancing.

This sight oppressed me, but the pain was less than what I had felt long before the war at my own mental premonition of the firestorm. I also sensed it in Paris in 1937. A catastrophe was bound to come; it chose war as its best medium. Yet even without it, the civil war would have accomplished its work, just as it did in Spain—or simply a comet bringing fire from heaven, an earthquake. The cities were ripe for it and dry as tinder. And man was eager to commit arson. What had to come could be guessed once he set fire to the churches in Russia, the synagogues in Germany, and let his own kind rot in penal colonies without recourse to law or justice. Things have reached the point where they now cry out to high heaven.

KIRCHHORST, 6 DECEMBER 1943

On the Old Horst Moor. Because it was frozen, I was able to take paths among the birch groves normally trodden only by deer.

I am reading the back issues of *Zeitschrift für wissenschaftliche Insektenbiologie* [*Journal of Scientific Entomology*], alternating with the *Jewish War* by Flavius Josephus. I came across the passage again that describes the beginnings of the unrest in Jerusalem under Cumanus (II.12). While the Jews gathered to celebrate the feast of unleavened bread, the Romans placed a cohort above the columned hall in the temple to monitor the crowd. One of these soldiers lifted his cloak, turned his backside to the Jews, and bent over contemptuously "producing a lewd sound unbecoming for someone of his station." That ignited the conflict that would cost ten thousand lives, making it possible to refer to the most catastrophic fart in the history of the world.

Of course, this example clarifies the immediate cause, or provocation, but not the actual cause. The philosophical significance of the provocation has not been fully appreciated. It can be seen as containing a powerful attack on the law of causation. In a certain sense, every provocation unleashes unintended consequences. In commerce, we are like customers writing checks; we know nothing of the bank and its reserves.

Like all physical processes, the provocation only becomes truly interesting in the world of morality. A child plays with matches and a populous city is reduced to ashes. The question is whether or not the one who caused the event under such circumstances did not play a more significant role than is generally assumed. Here I am thinking of Kniébolo—I sometimes have the impression that the world spirit[115] has chosen him in a subtle way. "In his most subtle moves he places his less important pieces to the fore." Even the firing pin that ignites the charge with minimal energy has its particular form. *One Thousand and One Nights* provides a description of the intrigues of a wicked woman who is finally drowned in the Nile. The corpse washes up on land at Alexandria, where it causes an outbreak of pestilence. Fifty thousand people die as a result.

KIRCHHORST, 9 DECEMBER 1943

Read further in Flavius Josephus. In addition to the historical narrative, he also gives a series of general scenes of the highest quality. Among these are the descriptions of Roman military force and the city of Jerusalem. He is the source of invaluable insights.

It is curious how little Jewish culture is associated to this author, despite the fact that he was a priest and leader of his people. The Jewish element seems more difficult to cast off than other cultures, but in those rare cases where the rejection succeeds, the human quality is especially enhanced.

KIRCHHORST, 10 DECEMBER 1943

Visit in the evening from Cramer von Laue, who came by bicycle and brought me the book by Schubart. Conversation about the tremendous destruction in Berlin he witnessed and about the creation of a new kind of proletariat emerging under the cover of these events. I let him look at my essay about peace.

KIRCHHORST, 14 DECEMBER 1943

I spent the morning examining Persian insects I acquired from Reitter. Bodo von Bodemeyer brought these back from the Orient thirty years ago.

Reading matter: A. W. Thomas, *Das Elisabeth Linné-Phänomen* [*The Elisabeth Linné Phenomenon*]. The work examines the flashes displayed by certain flowers at twilight—a phenomenon that has interested, not to say disturbed, me for a while.[116]

In addition: Veressayev's *Erlebnisse* [*Memoirs of a Physician*]. These are memoirs from the Russo-Japanese War that record the beginning of disinterested and mechanical butchery—though that had actually begun before, during the Crimean War.

Read further in Flavius Josephus; I was struck by a passage at the end of the fifth book, where the author writes that, had Jerusalem not been destroyed by the Romans, it would have been swallowed by the earth and covered by a flood, or consumed by fire from heaven like Sodom. I keep coming upon thoughts here that concern me greatly today and will probably always recur when catastrophes happen. Illness becomes irrelevant as the hour of death approaches. Death puts on masks when he detects its presence.

The remarkable passage in book seven also stood out, where he writes about voluntary self-immolation in India. Fire supposedly has the property "to separate the soul from the body in its purest possible form." Fire functions here as a cleansing element. For this reason it is used as a means to extract the substance from the tough flesh. The same applies to the burning of heretics, such as when the spirit is entangled with the material world as it once was with *luxuria* [lust] in the days of Sodom.

The mail brought a letter from Carl Schmitt in which he discusses the disparity between protection and obedience that has shown up among the populace in the cellars during the bombing raids. Of all the minds I have ever met, Carl Schmitt is the one who defines things best. As a classically trained legal scholar, he wears the laurels, and his position is necessarily precarious when the *demos* exchanges one costume for another. With the rise of illegitimate powers, a vacuum is left in place of the top jurist, and the attempt to fill it could cost him his reputation. These are the adversities of his profession. In this respect, performers have it best nowadays; a world-famous actor will survive any upheaval without effort. To paraphrase an observation from Bacon, one could say that to survive the world of today, one should have neither too little of the actor nor too much of the honest man.

As is his wont, Carl Schmitt closes his letter with a Bible passage, Isaiah 14:17.

KIRCHHORST, 17 DECEMBER 1943

Browsed in the journals of the brothers Goncourt. The changes that affect a reader during this war are remarkable. One feels that huge numbers of books will not cross those customs barriers of the mind that he erects. These represent worlds of loss that go almost unnoticed. This is how moths do damage in locked cupboards. We pick up a book and notice it has lost its appeal like a lover thought about longingly whose beauty has not survived certain crises, certain adventures. Ennui will cull the collections more harshly than any censor, than any book ban. Yet it is predictable that this will be advantageous for books of the highest quality, especially the Bible.

In the entry of 16 May 1889, I found a good dream of Léon Daudet. Charcot appeared to him carrying a copy of Pascal's *Pensées*. At the same time, he showed him the cells that these thoughts had inhabited in the great man's brain. They looked like a dried honeycomb.

Nearby there is a reference to the obelisk on the Place de la Concorde. The sight of this has often reminded me of a magical pointer—in this context, it calls forth memories "of the pink color of champagne sorbet." Such an image evokes the *morbidezza* [softness, delicacy] that is disintegrating the stone.

Edmond de Goncourt mentions conversations with Octave Mirbeau while, for his part, he has a connection to Sacha Guitry, with whom I have talked many times. These are bridges that connect the dead with the living across intermediary links. I often think of the erotic chain of events: Two men can have embraced one and the same woman. One of them was born in the eighteenth century before the French Revolution, whereas the other died in the twentieth century after the World War.

ON THE TRAIN, 20 DECEMBER 1943

Departure from Kirchhorst in warm wind and gentle showers. Loehning sent his car for me. Because I missed my train, I wandered through the sorrowful ruins and in the midst of all the rubble. I recalled the evenings in Advent 1914 and even 1913, when a happy crowd laden with presents filled the streets. What a throng there was on Packhofstrasse, now transformed into two walls of rubble. My good mother used to take me along, and there she would buy me little meat pies in the morning, and in the afternoons, nut tortes.

Now the faces have changed; not only are they more tired, careworn, and sickly but also uglier in the moral sense. I notice this especially in waiting rooms where you get the feeling of sitting in a cage surrounded by animals. But isn't it our own loneliness, our own loss, that creates this impression? Such waiting rooms emphasize the immense distance that separates us from our goal.

Then I went to Königswortherstrasse after I had visited the old cemetery on Langen Laube with its curious grave monuments. The house on the Leine River, where we lived in 1905, was undamaged. There I recalled the gloomy moods that often used to come over me on my way to school, a great feeling of isolation. In those days, I was tormented by worry about what would become of me if my mother died, as well as the feeling that I was so different from what people expected of me. Now, as I walked through the devastated streets, this long-forgotten mood returned, as if I had remembered earlier fears in some bad dream.

The rainbow in the haze that hovers over thundering cataracts—is this mist created from tears or the essence that gives birth to the pearl? It doesn't matter; one senses the miraculous bridge that leads from annihilation.

PARIS, 21 DECEMBER 1943

When I picked up the French mail waiting for me in the Raphael, I found a letter from Jean Leleu about Léon Bloy, whose works people have recommended to me. He is struck by the "inhumanity" of this author. He brings the accusation that his Catholicism often stops being Christian. That is correct; Bloy, like many other Romance-language writers, could be accused of the "Spanish" variation that leads to a peculiar callousness and ultimately turns into ruthlessness. On the other hand, we have the Germanic variant, always striving toward dissolution into fundamental principles. The Grand Inquisitor and Angelus Silesius.[117]

Current reading: Horst Lange, *Das Irrlicht* [*Will-o'-the-Wisp*], a story that Kubin illustrated and sent me from Zwickledt. From his very first novel, I noticed this author's perfect mastery of the swamp world, with all its fauna and flora, and its roiling life. Here in the desert of our literature there appears someone who shows command of his symbolism. He belongs to that sinister group of eastern writers that may someday be viewed as a school—here I am thinking of names like Barlach, Kubin, Trakl, Kafka, and others. These eastern portrayers of decadence are more profound than their western counterparts; they penetrate the surface of society, reaching its fundamental connections to the point of apocalyptic visions.

Trakl is experienced in the dark secrets of decay, Kubin in the worlds of dust and mold, and Kafka in surreal demonic realms, as Horst Lange is in the moors, where the powers of destruction hold sway, where they breed. Kubin, who has known this writer for a long time, once predicted to me that bad times lay ahead for him.

PARIS, 22 DECEMBER 1943

Celebrated Christmas at the home of Vogel, the aircraft engineer. There I made the acquaintance of an Italian pianist named Benvenuti, who traces his genealogy back to the Donati family and shares a line of common ancestry with Dante. His face had a curious similarity to the well-known head of Dante, which was magnified alarmingly when Florence wrapped a red shawl around his head, giving his face a masklike quality.

PARIS, 25 DECEMBER 1943

Among the bad news that has reached me is that of the death of the young Münchhausen son. I had just gotten to know him this past spring. His manners and his intellectual style had something of the eighteenth century about them. Salmanoff also liked those qualities in him. It often seems that our preparations for the future involve a negative selection process: people, buildings, feelings—all are being pruned just as the gardener prunes the branches in a park. We are heading for a "truncated" society.

Read further in Luke, finished chapter 22 today. Here Christ accuses his adversaries of attacking him by night, although he may be found in the temple every day: "When I was daily with you in the temple, ye stretched forth no hands against me: but this is your hour, and the power of darkness" (22:53). This is also the motto for the acts of terror in our own time, committed in horrific darkness behind facades built to the taste of the *demos*.

PARIS, 28 DECEMBER 1943

Walked my woods and water circuit alone through dense fog and balmy air. I paused on the riverbank at Suresnes at a spot where a drain muddies the waters of the Seine. There I watched a group of half a dozen fishermen. They were baiting their hooks with red maggots and flipping little silver fish with steel blue scales, about the size of sardines, out of the water.

Evening at the president's with Leo, Schery, and Merz. Discussed the situation. The German ordnance has now been worn so thin that it won't withstand the challenges that the new year will present here in the West.

In my *Historia in Nuce* [*History in a Nutshell*], I ought to include a chapter on the "Germanic Wars," where I would explain that the same mistakes are always being repeated. There are secrets here that other tribes will never comprehend, such as the enchantment of Attila's hall.[118] Was he the one who conjured up Kniébolo? Otherwise, how else can we explain this penchant, this brilliance, for avoiding victory when it has been placed in our hands?

PARIS, 28 DECEMBER 1943

Dreamed of Li-Ping, who was wailing for me. When I picked her up, I found her to be heavier, and now she also had a white coat: as I lifted her, I was also picking up the tomcat Jacko, who was inside her.

That is typical of dreams—there we can encounter a woman who combines traits of the mother, sister, or wife. In these hazy states, we enter the world of archetypes, which can be seen as generic images. This brings me to the thought that the genera in zoology are archetypes of the species. Like its primeval image, the genus does not exist in the everyday world, nor in the visible world. It appears only in the species, not by itself. In dreams we see things that are otherwise invisible.

When Schiller and Goethe discuss the *Urpflanze* [archetypal plant],[119] the difference between its day and night aspects also arises.

"To fight against [*gegen*] the enemy" and "to fight with [*mit*] the enemy"—two synonyms characteristic of the Germanic people. One fights *with* him, namely about something that belongs to either both or neither of them. Therefore, it isn't actually *about* victory.

Shakespeare sensed the secret that Rivière surmised as well when he assigned to the Germans not the label "either-or" but "both-and." Eckhard states the mystical version of this.

Perpetua writes that now her brother has been killed in action, too. Fate caught up with him on the Dnieper on 4 November during a reconnaissance mission. I had grown closer to him over these past years. From him, I borrowed traits for my character Biedenhorn, including his maxim:

Ihr Mannen, macht das Armbein krumm,
De Wille kum geiht um.

[You fellows, bend your elbows, / the welcome cup is passed around.] [120]

Without ever giving a thought to its causes, of course he welcomed this war as a license for brawling and boozing. The ancient spirit of Lower Saxony shone through his everyday exterior. He came from one of the indigenous families that goes back to pre-Guelph times. He was someone who devoted his life to camaraderie, and that is where he thrived. Unreliable in many ways, here he was worth his weight in gold. Once when I was standing beside him in the garden near the tomatoes, I noticed that, although he was coarse, he was capable of great tenderness. I am saddened by his loss.

He fell behind the Russian lines. His comrades couldn't retrieve his body. He had gone alone because he considered the situation too dangerous.

PARIS, 29 DECEMBER 1943

With Jouhandeau in the afternoon. Conversation about his new book, *Oncle Henri*. Then we talked about my current reading matter, the novel by his contemporary, Alain-Fournier, *Le Grand Meaulnes* [*Meaulnes the Great*], published in 1913. We told each other our dreams, and Jouhandeau recounted how he had visited a doctor because of a painful infection he had developed in his index finger. The doctor split the finger open in the midsection, exposing a red lump like a bud. From this, a geranium of great beauty opened, which Jouhandeau carried carefully, with his hand stretched in front of him, from that day on.

At his place, I again saw the chick that he has raised as a surrogate for the brood hen; he fed it at the breakfast table and warmed it in his bed. It had now grown into a large white rooster with a red comb that let people stroke it, embrace it, and take it onto their laps. It would even crow if encouraged.

During the night, I thought I was standing in our garden in Kirchhorst. Out on the street, small trucks raced past. They were loaded with blocks of iron, huge cubes of white-hot steel, waves of heat radiating from them. The drivers tore past at full speed so as to distribute the heat backward. It was futile because their clothing and bodies caught fire as they shot by. Their screams of pain could be heard dying away in the distance.

At the edge of the garden, there stood a sign with ideograms on it that read, "Whoever rides upon a tiger's back can never dismount again." In front of this message, someone had placed a special sign like a musical clef: "western transfiguration."

PARIS, 31 DECEMBER 1943

Massive squadrons flew over the city in the morning. As usual, I moved over to the Majestic, into the president's room. It is our habit to celebrate these interruptions by making coffee and having breakfast there. We could hear the anti-aircraft batteries hard at work. Then the building began to shake from the exploding bombs as they brought devastation to the outlying precincts.

By evening over two hundred and fifty dead had been accounted for. More than twenty workers died in a shelter that took a direct hit. I heard that a woman who was trying to dig down into the rubble had called out her husband's name. He had been doing an errand that had kept him from the disaster area and ran up out of the crowd. In moments like this, people embrace each other with great intensity, as after the Resurrection—with the power of the spirit.

Visited Dr. Salmanoff in the afternoon, who was sad about Münchhausen's death when I found him. Discussed the situation. Salmanoff believes that an English and American landing may be expected in the coming weeks. There is much to support this, but on the other hand, there is the consideration of what advantage such an undertaking would bring to England, even if it should succeed. The longer and more thoroughly Germany and Russia continue to grind each other down, the greater England's power grows. It is now in the position of a banker who profits from the sum total of all the losses. An attack would lead one to conclude that Russia's strength is already greater than we suspect.

Furthermore, Salmanoff held the view that Russia's hegemony in Europe is yet to come, and that we can count on internal political changes in that country and strong ties to Germany. Bolshevism was just a first phase; in the second, the Orthodox Church will rise again. Pillars of the new order will be the farmers in alliance with the victorious generals. People will not turn in their weapons again. A necessary consequence of victory will also be the control of the Balkans and possession of the Bosporus.

In this context, he touched on the peculiar nature of Russian colonization with the small farmer as its hero. With a piece of bread and a handful of onions in his pocket, far from the theater of world history, he will fan out over rivers, through primeval forests, and the icy steppes of three continents. Of course there is immense power here.

Concerning war reparations. These can only consist of a workforce, as prescribed by the era of the worker. Yet we will see degrees here ranging from slave labor to reparations contractually agreed upon, including the free cooperation of all those forces that once raged against each other. This is how I saw it in my *Appeal*. Yet perhaps hatred, which is always nourished by baser motives, makes this a utopia. By contrast, I never want to forget that a higher path—that of the spirit—leads to new worlds. We humans stand on that threshold. Like the rainbow, we shall arise from the ruins.

Of all the cathedrals only one remains—that built by the dome of our folded hands. In that alone lies our security.

1944

PARIS, 2 JANUARY 1944

The year that has just passed, 1943, which I greeted in the Caucasus, has produced all that I feared. But it has not brought the end of the war, which many had predicted would happen by the autumn.

I began the new year by walking my circuit and retreating from my usual routine, enjoying a two-day siesta, conversations, reading, strong coffee, fruits, and wine.

During this time, when I was reading Hölderlin, I came upon the letter to Bellarmin, so full of terrible truths about the Germans.[121] How accurate his observation is that in this country the superior man lives like Odysseus, taunted by worthless usurpers in his own palace as a beggar. Another one also has such a ring of truth to it: "servility is on the increase and with it, coarseness of mind."

Finished reading Alain-Fournier, *Le Grand Meaulnes* [*Meaulnes the Great*]. This is one of the dry branches that stretches from Romanticism into the twentieth century. We can see how the transport of sap to the treetop becomes more difficult from decade to decade.

To end my circuit, took a long labyrinthine stroll through the crooked streets and byways of the Latin Quarter and the curious alleys around Rue Mouffetard back to the Raphael, where I slipped in by the back stairs.

PARIS, 3 JANUARY 1944

I tried to visit the grave of Verlaine during the midday break but accidentally blundered into the cemetery of Clichy instead of Batignolles. At one of the walls, I encountered the gravestone of one Julien Abondance, who walked upon our earth from 1850 to 1917. Well, now I know where all the abundance has gone.

PARIS, 4 JANUARY 1944

Air-raid alarms in force since this morning. They are almost a regular occurrence. I use the time to examine the *Altar of the Last Judgment* by Hieronymus Bosch in the book by Baldass. Dr. Göpel gave me this recent publication as a present. These paintings are puzzle pictures of horror that continue to reveal new and frightening details.

Bosch differs from all other painters by virtue of his literal vision, which Baldass calls his prophetic character. The prophecy consists of the deeper truths that reflect and reproduce the ages of man—as the details of the world of technology do today. One can actually discern the shapes of fighter bombers and submarines on these panels, and one of them—I think it is the *Garden of Earthly Delights*[122]—contains E. A. Poe's macabre pendulum, one of the great symbols of the throbbing world of death. Bosch is the visionary of an eon, as Poe was of a saeculum. How apposite is the image of the naked man: in order to propel weird machines he runs like a squirrel, on a spike-studded wheel. The fact that Moors appear among the hosts of the blessed conceals a truth that, had it been spoken aloud, would have sent the painter to the stake.

Visited Verlaine's grave in the Batignolles Cemetery. It bore a simple stone structure, like thousands of others one finds in Parisian graveyards. Among the names engraved on the monument was his:

Paul Verlaine

Poète

A cross of blue paper violets covered this inscription, yet at the foot of the grave, there was a green bouquet from which I picked a small leaf. Not every poet still has fresh flowers on his grave after fifty years.

At the head of one of the death notices that I have received in the last few days:

"Your pathway is in the ocean, your roads in great waters, and your footsteps are unknown."

"Eternal joy will be upon their heads."

These two sayings contain a good contrast between the mysteries of earthly power and the clarity of heavenly power. Both are in us, which is why I take particular note of these words for the chapter "Head and Foot" in the work I am planning about the relationship between language and physique. In it I want to examine human growth as the symbolic key to cosmic structure.

Paris, 7 January 1944

The mail brought a letter from Carl Schmitt about the *vis verborum* [power of words] in which he quotes the Arabs Avicenna and Averroes, the Italian humanist Valla, Bismarck, and E. A. Poe. He calls Bismarck's "*In verbis simus faciles*" [let us be easygoing about words],[123] an extreme case of the "Head Forester mentality."[124] In the middle of the day, I waited for Madame Noël in the Majestic. She was working in Hamburg where her husband was blown to pieces before her eyes by an aerial bomb and her belongings consumed by flames. In addition, she is being persecuted as a "*collaboratrice*" [collaborator]. Because I was able to do a few things for her, she brought me a bouquet of flowers.

Paris, 9 January 1944

The first anniversary of the death of my dear father is approaching.

This morning I read further in the Gospel of John. "He must increase, but I must decrease" (3:30) is one of the greatest passages where the meaning of the words is not fully expressed. The Latin is better: "*Illum oportet crescere, me autem minui.*" *Autem* is one of the mildest of the *conjunctio adversativa* [adversative, or contrasting, conjunctions][125] and reveals not only a contradiction but also an association: immortal man will triumph, but at the same time, mortal man will lose.

Then I read John 4:50, which was thoroughly appropriate for this commemorative day: "thy son liveth." Pondered this. The Master is speaking to the unbelievers, which makes these momentous words inadequate. In order to convince their dull wits, he must make visible the truth of the corporeal revelation: the *corpse* must be resurrected. People thus expect cheap tricks from him in all things—including an earthly kingdom. The Prince of Light must cloak his words and deeds in shadows so that men's eyes can sense their true power. Even his miracles are parables.

Then finished reading "The Garden Party" in the stories of Katherine Mansfield, a New Zealand writer who died young. In it she gives a lovely description of her country by moonlight: the shadows resemble bars of a bronze gate. I am familiar with this feeling of fear of the moon's shadow and of its magical spell. It becomes considerably heightened when it occurs in an erotic encounter.

Finally, browsed in a portfolio of pictures of Oriental antiquities in the Louvre, especially Assyrian and Phoenician examples. One, the sarcophagus of Eshmunazar, was amusing despite its venerable age. The king of Sidon is clothed in the Egyptian funerary style, with all its provincial naiveté.

Following our conversation, Hielscher sends me excerpts from the journals of Leonardo along with some prophecies. One passage says this about human beings: "In their boundless conceit, they even want to fly to heaven, but the heavy weight of their limbs will keep them earthbound. Nothing will remain on the earth nor in the water that they will not hunt down, root out, or destroy. Nor will anything be spared that they can take from one land and haul into another. Their bodies will serve as tombs and entranceways for all living things they have killed."

My Berlin publisher finally informs me that the entire stock of my books was destroyed in the attack on Leipzig. A further stockpile burned in Hamburg, according to what Ziegler writes me. This relieves me of many a worry.

Went to the Madeleine in the afternoon because I needed a space where I could think about my father. There I sat beside the memorial plaque for the priest Deguerry, who died in the prison of La Roquette on 24 May 1871 *"pour la foi et la justice"* [for the faith and for justice]. Happy is the man who succeeds in this without becoming too much of a slave to fear.

Following that, my adventure with the leper on Rue Saint-Honoré.

PARIS, 11 JANUARY 1944

In a dream I saw Leisnig carpeted with bombs. Apartment houses were collapsing on distant hills, and facades of buildings were crumbling. I crossed over the market square and saw my father wearing a white coat and standing at the front door of a house. It was his old laboratory coat that was now in the service of higher research. Soldiers prevented me from entering by engaging me in conversation, but we waved to each other nonetheless.

Visit from Hotop, who as a physical type eludes the usual categories of classification. In India, he would be immediately recognizable as belonging to that particular caste whose lot it is to serve at table, in the kitchen, and in the baths, and generally attend to the pleasures inside the palaces. Theirs are natures that have a highly developed sense of touch and have also been granted a special sympathy with fear and pleasure. Here we find the most subtle connoisseurs of materials that can be evaluated by touching, tasting, or smelling. They are experts with cloth, with exquisite varieties of leather, perfumes, pearls, gemstones, woods, furniture, and refined cuisine, as well as with female slaves and all things from the world of the senses. Anyone who reads the Kama Sutra lingers in their milieu.

Their knowledge makes them invaluable to princes and great lords, for they are people who can discern rare objects, organize festivities, act as procurers, and *maîtres de plaisir* [masters of ceremonies]. In our country you, can find them among the ranks of the gastronomes, the manufacturers of luxury goods, the chefs of great restaurants. And it will always turn out that they have a particularly tactile sense; this is the capital they live off in the spheres of luxury and *luxuria* [lust]. But in every case, it is soon obvious that their efforts derive from a humble station. For them to establish themselves in elevated circles, these must consist of intellectuals or aristocrats, which explains why they rarely appear independently, but rather only in entourages. Tailors are not the ones flattered most by clothing, nor barbers by hairstyles.

Conversation about perfumes and how they are made. In order to concoct a scent for a client, the specialists in the large perfume houses do not inquire about hair color, but rather they request a piece of underwear that she has worn.

Current reading: *L'Equipage de la Nuit* [*Night Shift*] by Salvador Reyès, the Chilean consul, whom the Doctoresse introduced me to. Reyès takes as his models English-speaking authors who found their voices around the turn of the century—writers like Kipling, Stevenson, and Joseph Conrad, whose works can be described in three words: romantic, puritanical, global.

One of the images from this prose that I was particularly struck by was a description of stars that appear in the sky on a stormy night—gleaming as though they had been polished by the clouds. Although meteorologically far-fetched, this is poetically powerful. Among his sentences I find, "*C'est l'amour des femmes qui forme le charactère de l'homme*" [It is the love of women that forms a man's character]. Correct, yet they shape us as the sculptor his marble: by removing parts of us.

PARIS, 16 JANUARY 1944

Read further in the Gospel of John. There is the verse 8:58, "before Abraham was, I am." By contrast, going in the other direction chronologically: "Heaven and earth shall pass away, but my words shall not pass away" (Matthew 24:35). Christ recognizes that he is the Eternal Man, and as such, he describes Himself as being of divine origin as the son of God. He will outlast the cosmos, a creation of the spirit.

Here man speaks as the eternal being, in contrast to the mortal point of view, that of the mayfly in Psalm 90. The difference between the language of Christ and that of Moses is the same as that between the prose of the baptized and that of the circumcised. Light and cosmic forces unite with the earthly.

Nihilism and anarchy. Distinguishing between the two is as difficult as differentiating between eels and snakes, but nonetheless it is essential for recognizing the game that is at stake. A relationship to order is critical here—the anarchist lacks this, but it defines the nihilist. This makes nihilism more difficult to discern; it is better disguised. A good indicator is the bond to the father: the anarchist hates him, while the nihilist despises him. Hence the examples of Henri Brulard in contrast to Pyotr Stepanovich.[126] Then we have the differences in attitudes toward the mother and particularly to the earth, which the anarchist seeks to transform into primeval forest and the nihilist, into desert. An examination would have to begin by clarifying the theological position. This will train the eye to see the figures behind the canvas, hidden behind the scenes in modern painting. This would be especially useful to our martial youth. A young person necessarily goes through an anarchist phase, during which time he can easily fall prey to the power of pure destruction.

PARIS, 17 JANUARY 1944

Read further in the Gospel of John. In chapter 10, verse 34, Christ responds to doubts about his divine origin by referring to Psalm 82. There we read about the human race: "I have said, ye are gods; and all of you are children of the most High" (Psalm 82:6). In the next two verses, he goes on to interpret this in relation to himself.

Passages like these are important for exegesis in the twentieth century, which must be able to counter every objection of the conscious mind, and in doing so, differ from all earlier exegeses.

What is the difference between the miracles and the parables? The parables refer to the absolute, whereas the miracles confirm the parables in time and space, that is, in the realm of episodic experience. The parables are accorded a higher status, since they are spiritual expressions, whereas miracles are material expressions.

Finished reading Silvio Pellico, *My Prisons*. These memoirs from 1833 create a textbook case of classical prose, to which the Italians have direct and undiluted access through these significant character types. The sentences and thoughts are presented with an instinctive knowledge of proportion. It is always obvious which is the main and which the subordinate clause; which are the main ideas and which the secondary. This has a stimulating and edifying effect, like walking among palaces and statues.

Conversation with Doctor Schnath, the archivist from Hannover. He has just returned from Lower Saxony and brought me a remarkable observation. If one were to get used to living in the destroyed cities, and afterward in the others that were spared—places like Hildesheim, Goslar, or Halberstadt—it would feel like living in a world turned into a museum or an opera set. This sense shows more clearly than the destruction itself that we have shed the old reality and the historical consciousness we were born with.

In the evening, visit to the Schnitzlers on Rue des Marronniers. Bourdin was there, the former correspondent for the *Frankfurter Zeitung*, and Naval Lieutenant von Tirpitz, the son of the admiral. He told us that among his father's files from the period before World War I, he had found a lot of letters from prominent German and English Jews. They all called the possibility of a war between these two empires a huge disaster. Even if one posits purely commercial interests, these are more plausible than the opposite assumption.

Paris, 18 January 1944

Breakfast at Drouant's with Abel Bonnard, Heller, and Colonel Alerme at the round table of the Académie Goncourt. Bonnard poked fun at the sort of speakers who prepare their speeches so well that they sound improvised. They even imitate apparently spontaneous asides as these occur to them, and then they learn these by heart. He called this a particular mutation of the confidence game.

"But what if someone lacks the gift of improvisation?"

"Then he should read from his notes. Even great orators like Mirabeau did that."

About Poincaré: He not only memorized his speeches but prepared different versions predicting the mood he was going to encounter in the audience. In readying an address he was to give before the Assembly during a period of tension with Italy, he memorized a gentle, a medium, and a harsh version. Because the mood in the chamber was angry, he presented the third option.

About Abel Bonnard's automobile accident; it left him unconscious for three hours. When I asked him for details:

"It was night, deepest night."

"And do you think that it will be just that way after death?"

"I am certain of it."

When he said that, he looked at me sadly, like someone who had revealed a terrible secret to a friend.

Colonel Alerme, who was the head of Clémenceau's cabinet during World War
I and served in the Sahara as a young officer, told us about his life among the
Tuaregs. Their good breeding was not only obvious from their facial features but
also in the nobility of their behavior. This is to be expected whenever race is the
topic. Our modern experts are numismatists who prize only the impression, but
not the metal from which the coin is minted. They are illiterates who think that the
mere form of the letters is important, because they lack any knowledge of the texts.

Following that, there was conversation about riding camels. The noblest of
these beasts loses its vigor when taken out of the heart of the desert and led to
oases. I am noting a few details for my own *Path of Masirah*.

PARIS, 20 JANUARY 1944

Visited Florence. During the meal, Jouhandeau told us that near the Place du Palais-Bourbon he had entered an antiquarian bookshop where a statue of an Indian
god was displayed for sale because of its miracle-working properties. The bookdealer takes advantage of this by charging a fee from the stenographers when their
appeals for winning lottery tickets are answered. Jouhandeau watched an older
gentleman perform his devotions in the shop, which involved touching the image
with his right hand while reverently removing his hat with his left. Things like this
do not surprise me; we will be seeing more such marvels.

Dr. Göpel visited me in the afternoon and Friedrich Hielscher in the evening;
he and I had been together in the Raphael. The conversation eventually turned
to that remarkable evening in Stralau[127] in the winter of 1929 that began with the
big euphonium and the burning of furniture, when Bogo and Edmond [Schultz]
shook hands over the glowing embers.

PARIS, 22 JANUARY 1944

Walked the woods and water circuit with the Doctoresse. There are minds we
communicate with in particularly harmonious ways, not according to their degree
but to their kind. Our relations are not ruled by tension but by rapport. The conversation is beneficial, relaxing, pleasing; it proceeds like clockwork, the wheels all
functioning in unison. This is intellectual eros that softens any edge.

The Doctoresse called my manner of thinking that of a chemist, whereas
Paul works like a mason. She's right about the fact that I do not proceed along
physical principles with a close correlation between cause and effect, but rather
atomistically by osmosis and filtration of the smallest particles of thoughts.
A logically correct sentence is insignificant to me if isn't right at the level of
its vowels. Hence the feeling of being active—not with consciously discrete
thought processes—but perpetually, by day and night (especially during the
night), like an hourglass. This makes it difficult to appreciate what I'm up to, or
even fathom it structurally. Yet the change is radical; it is at the molecular level.
This explains why I know people who couldn't help becoming my friends, even
through dreams.

Eros has a particular connection to symmetry—something suggested by its symbols: the bow of Cupid, the mirror of Venus, and her birth from the shell. Plato's *Symposium* has the two sexes originating from a division, a separation. Two is the number of symmetry: the couple. It tries to cancel itself out in the whole, in union. This produces hermaphroditic forms in the insect world. On the right and left sides of the axis of symmetry. Sexual organs will always be symmetrical, as we see most beautifully in flowers. What is the link between symmetrical and asymmetrical design in creatures, and can we conclude anything from them about the plan behind their structures? I want to concentrate on these questions in my project about the connection between language and physique.

In addition to the existence of the physical complementary color, there is also a spiritual one. Just as green and red are part of white, higher entities are polarized in intellectual couples—as is the universe into blue and red.

The great struggles of our age take place beneath the surface: that is where the contest between the technician and the artist occurs. We have good weapons for this, such as Friedrich Georg's *Titans*, which I received today from [the publisher] Vittorio Klostermann.

PARIS, 24 JANUARY 1944

It is always a good feeling to hear a doctor talk about matters of health with hearty optimism. Doctor Besançon does so in his book *Les Jours de l'Homme* [*The Days of Man*], which the Doctoresse recently inscribed to me. Besançon is a pupil of Hufeland and, like him and his work, *Macrobiotik*[128] (and my paternal friend Parow), he estimates the human life span at 140 years. Like many older doctors, he is a cynic, but he possesses healthy common sense and a good empirical foundation.

I note the following from among his popular maxims:

"Death is a creditor. Now and then we have to pay him an installment to extend the terms of our loan."

"Health is perpetual procreation."

"Surprise attack, fool's attack." ("*Tour de force, tour de fou.*")

"To cure down to the root is to cure to death."

It is striking that, as rules for general health, he scorns the drinking of water, frequent baths, vegetarian fare, and athletic activity, especially when undertaken after age forty.

He maintains that water is impure, especially because it is not "isotonic." He prefers good wine, sweetened tea and coffee, and fruit juices to it. Infinitely more people, he claims, have died from water than from wine.

"We digest with our legs."

There is only one way to cleanse the pores, and that is through the cleansing power of sweat. Toweling oneself off in front of an open window followed by a rubdown with strong alcohol is preferable to frequent baths.

Fur coats are not recommended; when you remove them, a mantle of ice falls down onto the shoulders. Woolen undergarments are preferable.

In one's later years, it is good to spend a day in bed now and then.

It is good to heat the bedroom with an open-hearth fire of dry wood, especially during those critical periods of chill that attend the changes of seasons. Central heating, on the other hand, has the effect of poison.

"*Le bordeaux se pisse, le bourgogne se gratte.*" [Bordeaux makes you piss; burgundy makes you itch.]

The book is profusely sprinkled with erotic curiosities. For example, when he was in his late eighties, Marshal Richelieu married a sixteen-year-old girl and lived another eight years in marital happiness. The marshal's widow seems to have inherited longevity from him, for one evening she astonished Napoleon III with the sentence:

"Sire, as King Louis XIV once said to my husband . . ."

Whales must live to extreme old age—all indications point to this. Someone found the point of a Norman harpoon from the ninth century inside the body of one of these beasts.

PARIS, 29 JANUARY 1944

Finished reading the Gospel of John. In the last chapter, when the resurrected Christ appears at the Sea of Galilee: "And none of the disciples dared ask him, Who art thou? knowing that it was the Lord" (21:12).

When confronted by the miraculous, man falls into a state of rigidity where the power of words fails. Yet it is from here that the Word has its origin—language is freed from those who were dumb.

This corresponds to the opening of the gospel: "In the beginning was the Word, and the Word was with God, and the Word was God" (John 1:1). For the divine Word to reach mankind and become language, it must be revealed—then it becomes audible, divisible, becoming words the way colorless light reveals the rainbow when it is split. The phenomenon is described with the precision of a physical process in the Acts of the Apostles, 2:2–4. After the roaring of a mighty wind, there appeared "cloven tongues like as of fire, and it sat upon each of them," granting the Apostles the gift of tongues. Such language lets them go out among "all" peoples, for there is something inherently indivisible, something pre-Babylonian about the nature of this Word.

My reading these days: Robert Burnand, *L'Attentat de Fieschi* (Paris, 1930) [*The Assassination Attempt by Fieschi*].

The study of assassination attempts is worthwhile because it is one of those unknowns in the historical equation. This applies only superficially, for upon closer inspection, they reveal a great deal. In the person of the assassin, even in cases of insanity, we can see the individual only against the background of ethnic tensions, political opposition, or minority identity. In addition, the assassin's attempt must succeed. The individual of historical importance has his own aura, his superior necessity, a power that repels those fateful shots. Napoleon's statement applies here: As long as he was under the spell of his mission, no power on earth could bring him down, whereas after he had fulfilled his mandate, a speck of dust would suffice. But how do we fit Caesar and Henri IV into this paradigm?

Assassinations often function as stimulants: They are responses to certain fundamental tendencies of the moment. One such is the failed attempt upon Lenin's life. It is a sign of sloppy thinking to imagine that we can discern the representatives by their physical appearance. We lop off the buds on twigs so that they may blossom all the more vigorously.

In Fieschi's case, madness—the self-destructive urge—is obvious behind such an act. This is the reverse side of the historical fabric that he is part of. Outside Louis Philippe rides past in the sunshine with his dazzling retinue, while Fieschi in his small, shrouded room where a fire burns, sets the fuse to his hellish machine resembling a pipe organ made of rifle barrels. Some of them explode, mutilating his hands and ripping open his skull, while on the street forty people heave in their own blood, among them Marshal Mortier. Such natures are agents of discord. Yet, we have to ask whether it is the diabolical machine or Fieschi that is exploding here. They restored his health with great difficulty and then decapitated him. Today he stands among the Church fathers in the catacombs of anarchy.

The chapter headings include one that delights me with its precision: "*Le roi monta à cheval à neuf heures*" [The king mounted his horse at nine o'clock]. In this simple sentence, the words appear in order of their importance; there is not one too few nor too many. The translation weakens it and would go like this: "*Der König stieg um neun Uhr zu Pferd*" [Literally: The king mounted at nine o'clock his horse]. Here the words deviate from their optimal order; in terms of logic, phonetics, and syntax, their connection is looser.

Also read Marcel Fouquier, *Jours Heureux d'Autrefois* (Paris, 1941) [*Happy Days of Yesteryear*]. This description of Parisian society from 1885 to 1935 is like a cake full of raisins in the form of wonderful quotations. Among them is an observation by the Duchess de la Trémoille: "Gullibility is spreading in inverse proportion to the disappearance of religion."

La Rochefoucauld: "We find it more difficult to conceal those feelings we have than to affect feelings that we do not have."

Nego [I disagree]—I think the second is more difficult. This difference of evaluation touched on one of the significant contrasts between the Romance and the Germanic peoples.

PARIS, 2 FEBRUARY 1944

About language. A bottle of wine, a spoonful of soup, a cartload of coal—in such expressions our language emphasizes the content of containers through word placement—in contrast to soupspoon and wine bottles. The Frenchman, on the other hand, uses a special ending to designate the contents: *assiettée* [plateful], *cuillerée* [spoonful], *gorgée* [swallow, throatful], *charrettée* [cartload]. Nice how the accented "e" at the end designates "the contents" of the vessel. One could also say that it acquires an exaggerated feminine quality equivalent to pregnancy.

PARIS, 7 FEBRUARY 1944

In bed with influenza. Visit from the president, who had heard from the commander-in-chief about the evening he spent with Baumgart and me. He said I was
like a powerful motor, hard to start up but then suddenly revving in high gear.

We are distressed about Speidel; he and his army are surrounded in Russia. There
is talk of General von Seydlitz appealing to him over Russian radio transmitters.

About language. *Wort* [word] in our language has two plural forms. The dictionaries generally state that *Wörter* is used for words without reference to any
context, whereas one uses *Worte* for words that are [syntactically] connected. The
definition is blurry; I tend to think that in the plural, the meaning splits into a
grammatical-physical branch and a metaphysical one. *Worte* contain indivisible
material. A similar effect is produced in other nouns by different articles, such as
in *der* versus *das Verdienst* [earnings *versus* merit].

PARIS, 12 FEBRUARY 1944

Got out of bed, but I still feel the influenza deep in my bones. Around midnight
I received a call from Ronneberger, the Wehrmacht pastor. In my fever I saw a
waiter enter the room and heard him say, "*Capitaine, un appel téléphonique à
longue distance*" [Captain, a long-distance telephone call]. At first I wanted to stay
in bed, but I thought I picked up the word "Wilhelmshaven," and it suddenly went
through my mind that Ernstel was stationed on the coast as part of the Naval Auxiliary Personnel. "There may have been a gunnery accident." That got me up in a
hurry. Downstairs I heard, to my relief, of the arrest of a group of high school students; their leaders were a boy named Siedler and a comrade of his. They have both
been detained in Wilhelmshaven for a few weeks and, as far as I can understand,
sentences of six and nine months have already been handed down. The reason
given was supposedly candid conversations about the situation. Our boy feigned
reticence and divulged nothing, although such action is only to his credit, it also
seems that none of his superiors considered it necessary to inform me. Instead, the
children were spied on for months in order to "collect material," after which they
were delivered into the claws of the state authorities.

It is preferable to receive such news when we are not in total control of our faculties.

PARIS, 13 FEBRUARY 1944

Spent the morning with long-distance calls to Hannover and Wilhelmshaven.
Professor Erik Wolf phoned me in the afternoon; he is staying with Valentiner
and involved me in a conversation about the *Buprestidae* [jewel beetles] of the
Kaiserstuhl region. I couldn't follow it all with the kind of attention that this subject would otherwise elicit from me.

PARIS, 15 FEBRUARY 1944

Because I found the boss in Wilhelmshaven to be a reasonable man, I was able
to do some good on the case. It also looks as though his admiral, Scheuerlen, is

not one of the really black ones.[129] Through General Loehning, the commander of Hannover, I was able to contact Perpetua so she could pay our boy a visit right away. At first the difficulty was a technical one, as it was so hard to get through by telephone. This finally succeeded thanks to the efforts of Corporal Kretzschmar, who works in the communications office.

Current reading: *Lieder aus der Silberdistelklause* [*Songs from the Silver Thistle Refuge*], sent to me by Friedrich Georg in manuscript. It is curious how his hand becomes lighter and freer to the degree that destruction advances all around us. Something mysterious lies behind the world of fire—the system of spiritual configurations that the sea of flame occasionally penetrates.

Then in the evening hours I picked up Saint-Simon again for the first time in a long while. I felt I had never appreciated the elegance of certain phrases so deeply, especially as they bring nuance to the descriptions of characters and their social positions. We also mature as readers.

Paris, 16 February 1944

Visit from Dr. Göpel, who is back from Nice and brought me an hourglass. Judging from the shape, it could date from the fifteenth or sixteenth century. Its age has given the glass an opalescent sheen so that the reddish dust trickles down behind a veil woven by time. It is gratifying to have this piece, since I find the sight of mechanical clocks ever more unpleasant, especially when I am conversing, reading, or meditating and studying. One doesn't want to calibrate such activities down to the minute—better to let the sand run in a little glass. Hourglass time is different, more intimately linked to life. No hour strikes and no hand jumps forward. Here is time that still passes, trickles, drizzles away—relaxed, erratic time.

In the evening, a Special Forces officer lectured us about the methods for interrogating and hoodwinking English and American flyers in order to get intelligence out of them. The technical side of these procedures is repugnant; our grandfathers would have considered it beneath their dignity ever to ask prisoners even a simple question of this kind. Today humans have become peculiar raw material for other humans—material to be used as a resource for work, information, et cetera. This is a condition that can only be called higher-level cannibalism. People don't exactly fall into the hands of cannibals, although that can happen, but they are prey to the methods of the psychologists, chemists, racial thinkers, so-called doctors, and others who would exploit them. They work in the same way as those weird demons on the large panels by Bosch. With their instruments, they dismember the naked human victims they have abducted. I note this remark from the details: "that smokers are much more talkative than non-smokers."

Paris, 18 February 1944

Got another phone call from Wilhelmshaven, where in the meantime Perpetua has used all her powers to gain access to the jail. On Tuesday, I'll make the journey to Kirchhorst and Berlin on behalf of our boy. The commander-in-chief, whom I had

Weniger inform, said, "This is one of the cases where you're allowed to request a furlough from your general."

Thus, we repay the debts of our fathers, and for this reason, childlessness in our hives has produced drones—unless metaphysical fecundity flourishes instead of natural reproduction. That would mean that individuals—whether clerics, donors, or breeders—join the ranks of the *patres* [fathers].

In the afternoon, there was noise in the corridor in front of my office in the Majestic. An Air Force corporal had encountered a woman who apparently had been deceiving and causing harm to soldiers for quite a while. He immediately grabbed her arm, and, as both parties shouted at each other, began to kick her. I watched this unseemly display as the man, who was out of control, stared at the woman with blazing eyes while she faced him like a ferret confronting a snake. Had them both arrested.

The incredible weakness—even self-destructiveness—is extraordinary when we give in to hatred to that extent.

Read further in Saint-Simon. There is something modern about the sensibility of this prince; the court is described like a large molecule in organic chemistry. The social relationships, the gradations of people's status, down to the most delicate nuances—by contrast, much younger observers like Stendhal come across as dolts. It is indicative of Saint-Simon that he knows his task and responsibilities; it is an attitude encompassing historical pain, the knowledge of one who inhabits the city of brass.[130]

Continued reading in Paul's Letter to the Corinthians. The parables of Christ all pertain to man's relationship to God, whereas Paul's letters focus on the relationship of human beings to one another and the idealized life within the community. That is the decline we always encounter in the history of the riches of the earth—abundance must decrease when it is passed from founder to custodian. This applies equally to princes and art. Thus a contraction in subject matter produces an increase in details, even in the relation between Bosch and Breughel.

Much from the Old Testament recurs in the New Testament in the form of heightened mirror images, and so for me the magnificent thirteenth chapter of Paul's First Letter to the Corinthians seems to correspond to the Song of Solomon. It contains wonderful sentences like this: "But when that which is perfect is come then that which is in part shall be done away" (13:10).

Verse 12 is also significant: "We now see through a mirror in a dark word, but then face to face" (13:12).[131]

By translating *enigma* with "*dunkles Wort* [dark word] the text loses that element from Plato's theory of forms that graces his text in the Greek. One would have to ponder such passages for days on end.

Words. *Wabe* [honeycomb] from *Weben* [to weave]—it is the swaddling clothes [of the bees]. The resonance between *Wachs* [wax] and *Waffel* [wafer] can hardly be attributed to chance.

KIRCHHORST, 29 FEBRUARY 1944

I was in Berlin working on Ernstel's case; I returned on Friday. First I wanted to get in to see Dönitz, even went out to his base of operations, but I was expressly warned about him. It would only aggravate the situation and result in a more severe verdict. In general, I noticed that the Navy people had the tendency to brush me off with unruffled courtesy; this is especially obvious to anyone from a "white" staff like Stülpnagel's.[132] I was there on an awkward mission that they wanted as little to do with as possible. I found myself directed to people who deal with such things professionally, men like the Naval judge Kranzberger. In the office of his deputy, Dr. Siedler, I was given access to the verdict, where I read a few more charges that made the case more serious. Our boy is charged with saying that, if the Germans wanted to arrange favorable peace terms, they would have to string up Kniébolo. Of the sixteen comrades named as witnesses, it was of course only one of them—the spy—who heard him say it. Yet the court accepts it as a proven fact. Furthermore, it is stated that, "during the proceeding he showed no remorse," which suits me better. The people that we deal with in a matter like this give an accurate picture of the black and white strands from which our political fabric is spun.

The consequences of the desecration of such great cities cannot yet be assessed. It seems extraordinary that at first glance traffic seems to be increasing amidst the ruins, yet it is logical that its static counterpart, the dwellings, have been reduced in number. The roads and trains are filled to bursting. Seeing the capitol again in its new condition was less alienating than I had expected, and that reminded me that for a long time now I have had no faith in the stability of the city. Right after World War I and during the inflation, it looked as if it was beginning to deteriorate; in my mind, this period is filled with memories of a dream city. Then, after the so-called seizure of power, pickaxes were everywhere; whole streets were reduced to rubble. Ultimately, shops were looted, synagogues set afire, without such crimes ever being brought before a judge. The land stayed blood-soaked. An ecstasy raged for all red, explosive things.

Yet we must also see the destruction from the inside, like the stripping away of old skin. That creates bafflement; numbness is the consequence. America is conquering the places of ancient culture—I mean that aspect of America that has been more evident in modern Berliners with each advancing year.

I lived with Carl Schmitt, who had moved into a little villa in Schlachtensee after his house in Dahlem had been destroyed. We enjoyed a good red wine in the evening as we talked about the situation. He compared it to that of the Anabaptists during the siege: two days before Münster was captured, Bockelson promised his followers paradise.[133]

Together we read the conclusion of Volume II of Tocqueville's *Démocratie en Amérique* [*Democracy in America*]. Amazing insights are to be found there. In the light of this perspective, our historical drama becomes small and distinct, and its players, straightforward and focused. These are writers who uphold our faith in the sensibility that lurks behind this apparently amorphous activity.

Talked more about Bruno Bauer, whose posthumous papers were bought up by the Bolsheviks before this war and sent to Moscow. Friends like Carl Schmitt are irreplaceable merely by the fact that they relieve me of the immense effort of examining them.

The next day, I left for Kirchhorst around noon.

KIRCHHORST, 1 MARCH 1944

March has begun and is bound to be a month of momentous events. I am studying what Bruno Bauer wrote about Philo, Strauss, and Renan, which Carl Schmitt handed me for my travel reading. It makes me want to study Philo more closely. The great destruction of libraries will make the hunt for books more difficult and may create a situation over the coming decades similar to the period that preceded printing. People will probably even copy books by hand. As we can read in Grimmelshausen, the fact that certain areas like Switzerland will have been spared, is again going to be a great blessing.

Life is perpetual procreation—during its course we seek to reunite with father and mother. That is our true mission, and our conflicts and triumphs derive from it. This is followed by new birth.

The way that father and mother alternate and combine within us is beautifully demonstrated graphologically. For this reason alone, collections of letters are significant—so that we may study the forces that influence our character over the course of years and decades, as well as how they are integrated.

KIRCHHORST, 2 MARCH 1944

Breakfast in bed. As I ate, I read Samuel Pepys and had a leisurely conversation with Perpetua about arranging our household in the coming time of peace. Of course, the question remains whether we shall ever reach that shore.

Read further in Bruno Bauer. His remarks about Renan's landscape descriptions, reminiscent of opera sets, are good: actually, they remind one of landscapes by Millet. Philo urges us to practice and cultivate sensuality, for without this, the world of the senses is incomprehensible, thus leaving the "antechamber of philosophy sealed."

Snow showers, yet the warm March sun broke through the clouds. I let its rays pour over me at the open window as I read Grabbe's critical reviews. His pronouncements about the correspondence of Goethe and Schiller are noteworthy for their impertinence. More successful is the threat he aims at Betttina: "If the authoress carries it any further, then she shall not be treated like a lady, but rather like an author."

What Grabbe says in his play *Gothland*, applies to him:

—*Der Mensch*
Trägt Adler in dem Haupte
Und steckt mit seinen Füßen in dem Kote.

[—Man / Carries eagles in his head, / His feet placed squarely in the dung.]
In this way, each of us coins his own heraldic motto.

Textual criticism of the nineteenth and twentieth centuries offers no more insights into the Bible than Darwinism does into the animal world. Both methods are projections onto the chronological plane—just as here the *logos* is subsumed into temporality, the same applies to species. The word becomes divisible; the image of the animal becomes but a passing phase, an impression.

By contrast, Luther's statement applies: "The Word they shall allow to stand." Both the Bible and the animal world are revelations, and therein lies their immense allegorical power.

KIRCHHORST, 3 MARCH 1944
In the morning, I enjoyed a letter from Ernstel, who thank God is allowed reading matter in his cell.

The weather was stormy, the sky covered by huge, blindingly white cloudbanks. Just after eleven o'clock several squadrons flew over the house; they were encircled by numerous little fire bursts that stood out sharply against the bright patches. The aircraft also left white vapor trails behind as they made their gentle curves, like skaters on blue ice.

Read further in Gide's *Journal*, which wore me out. Every diary is of course a reflection of the author; but it mustn't produce a result like this. His wonderful sense of justice, however, is significant. He has an ear that can calibrate the words and sentences of his prose with the precision of a jeweler's scale, but this too is merely an endowment, a result of this profoundly derived origin; it lends its bearer prominence beyond the borders of his own country.

Later began reading *Journal d'un Interprète en Chine* [*Journal of an Interpreter in China*] by Count d'Hérisson, which I came across in my library. When writing such descriptions of distant countries and important events, it's an advantage when the author does not possess too much expertise. In order to describe Goethe, for example, a second Goethe would be less suitable than Eckermann.[134]

ON THE TRAIN, 4–5 MARCH 1944
Departure from Kirchhorst. During the morning, I went through my old journals from Rhodes and Brazil but could not make up my mind whether to take one of them along to Paris.

Again, as so often when I have parted from Perpetua, I had the feeling that there will be huge changes before we see each other again. At the moment when we were saying goodbye, General Loehning's driver, who had come to pick me up, delivered the news that Wilhelmshaven had been badly bombed. Our distress was great when we thought of the flimsy barracks where our boy is being held prisoner.

On the train, I had a conversation with a doctor with the rank of colonel about childhood memories of Hannover from 1905. "Before 1914"—the awareness of this date is going to become as meaningful as "before 1789" once was. Then we talked about Russia and the Russians, whose language my interlocutor seemed to speak fluently. One of the proverbs he quoted sounded especially pertinent: "A fish rots from the head down."

With great delays along the tracks we passed through cities on alert, like Cologne, where a bomb had just hit the slaughterhouse, mutilating sixty people.

Thought about this and that in my semi-waking state. Perpetua's penetrating comment on Weininger came back to me: "He must have committed suicide in the autumn." In this regard, she possesses judgment and because she is not impressed by elaborate scholarly methodology. She sees through it as if it didn't even exist, in order to evaluate its proponents. In contrast to her, keen intellects sometimes resemble ostriches: when they stick their heads into their theories, speculations, and utopias, they are burrowing into crystallized sand and unwittingly make themselves figures of fun in her eyes.

After passing San Miguel, I took pleasure again in the sight of the first flying fish. I perceived a school of them flying past on the starboard side. I was hyper-aware of this—down to the drops of water that dripped like pearls from their fins. Yet this was a mental construct. The creatures seemed to be made of mother-of-pearl, nearly transparent. I thought this apparition was an optical illusion, especially because I had been expecting such an image. Then I saw a second school appear before the bow, and others corroborated this. The two images captured both ideal and empirical reality—the reality of the dream and everyday reality. My imagination worked incomparably harder to produce the first image, which shone forth more wondrously. Were those really fish that glowed in the opalescent light, or just the sunbeams flickering on the waves that affected my inner being? The question seems almost trivial. At times I have had the same experience with animals—as though I have invented them, but then they were familiar to me. The mythical aspect takes precedence over the historical.

At two in the afternoon, the train rolled into the Nordbahnhof [North Station].

PARIS, 7 MARCH 1944

Continued reading in the First Letter of Paul to the Corinthians. There I find verse 15:22: "For as in Adam all die, even so in Christ shall all be made alive."

Appreciating the difference between natural and supernatural man is like discovering a higher chemistry. Christ is the agent who makes mankind capable of metaphysical bonding. Humans have possessed the innate possibility since the very beginning. Thus the sacrifice does not create them anew, but rather "releases" meaning, translates them to a higher level of activity. This has always been the power of matter.

I leave the house in the morning, and as I descend the stairs, I remember that I have forgotten my keys. I return to put them in my pocket and a minute later am back out on the street again. In so doing I encounter different people, different experiences. I meet an old friend whom I haven't seen in twenty years; a flower shop is just opening up, where I spot an unfamiliar species; I step on an orange rind that a pedestrian in front of me has dropped; I fall and sprain my arm. And so that lost minute is like the smallest turn of a screw on an artillery piece calibrated to hit a distant target. Truly an aspect that has often frightened me—especially in this time of malicious clashes on my way through a world fraught with danger.

I have to comfort myself by saying that, although the number of coincidences is infinite and unpredictable, in every combination, they probably lead to the same result. When measured by this result, rather by than its individual moments, the sum of a life produces a fixed quantity, namely the image of fate that we are destined for, and which—when viewed temporally—seems to be made of a series of accidental events. When viewed metaphysically, such points do not exist in the course of our life, any more than they do in the flight path of an arrow.

Then we have great minds like Boethius, who provide a theological resolution to this labyrinth. As long as we follow our destiny, chance is powerless; we are guided by our trust in Providence. If we lose this virtue, chance is set free and attacks us like armies of microbes. Hence, the regulatory function of prayer, as an apotropaic force. Chance remains crystallized, calculable.

Certain aspects of nihilism resolve everything into coincidence. Modern man's ridiculous fear of microbes belongs among these. This is particularly prevalent in the most benighted regions and is on the same level as the witch and demon craze of the fifteenth and sixteenth centuries. This also applies to many abstractions in modern physics, which as *scienza nuova* [new science] releases powers of randomness that can be controlled only by the queen of the sciences: theology. Hence, it is so important that our best minds devote themselves to its study, which is in decline. There is no place for half measures. The close connection between science and faith—so characteristic of our age—makes it desirable that anyone who would become a master, *magister*, in this area, must first pass his journeyman's test in specific disciplines. The most advanced should have an overview of the whole; that provides the evidence for their authority.

This solution would put great areas of controversy to rest. For example, the dispute about secular versus religious education. The precondition is that the state gets involved in a completely different way. The liberal national state is completely incapable of this. Given the way things may stand tomorrow in Russia and in Europe, there is hope of realizing the spiritual worlds we are trying to create. Then that nightmare will subside, which today robs so many of their desire to live: the hollow feeling of being without purpose in the midst of extermination, where they are victims of pure chance. People will also comprehend what happened during these years in Russia, in Italy, in Spain, and in Germany, for there are depths of suffering that will remain forever meaningless if they prove fruitless. And in this lies the immense responsibility of the survivors.

PARIS, 9 MARCH 1944

Visited Florence at midday. There I saw Dr. Vernes, the great expert and syphilis specialist. We discussed patients' payments to doctors, which he said he considered as immaterial as the method of payment for the fire brigade during a blaze. It's curious how in our day and age notions of sickness have become distinct from the individual—here, too, ownership gets lost. In fact, both the capitalist and the

Bolshevist systems arrive at the same results. That was apparent to me in Norway. Vernes invited me to visit his laboratory on Tuesday.

Conversation with Jouhandeau, who recommended that I read Michelangelo's correspondence with his father. Supposedly it contains important advice about health and how to lead one's life.

PARIS, 11 MARCH 1944

My text *The Worker* and Friedrich Georg's *Illusion of Technology* are like positive and negative prints of a photograph. Their simultaneity of methods suggests a new objectivity, although a narrow mind will merely find contradiction in them.

Thought while at the Métro station Concorde: how much longer will I continue to follow these tunnels and tubes dreamed up by technological brains around the turn of the century?

Illnesses of this sort can only be cured by amputating the head. This is from La Roquette.[135]

The Christian in the twentieth century has more in common with the first-rate physicist, chemist, and biologist than with the Christian of the nineteenth.

Books in name only, but actually just psychological machines to manipulate people. The reader enters a chamber and gets a dose of cosmic radiation. After reading the book, he becomes someone else. Reading, too, is now different—it is accompanied by the awareness of danger.

PARIS, 13 MARCH 1944

The mail included a letter from Speidel, which was also a confidential report on the breakout battle of Uman,[136] which he had commanded. It is a document of human struggle, human suffering, human courage, that one can only read with the deepest respect. The operation was preceded by the decision to burn the vehicles and leave 1,500 casualties with their doctors and medics to meet their fate. This will improve the situation and straighten out a lot of things.

PARIS, 14 MARCH 1944

Visited Dr. Vernes's institute in the afternoon. I started out with him in the laboratory, where I had a long discussion with a white-bearded cancer researcher, an affable man who produced genealogies of vulnerable families. Members who had been spared by the scourge were designated by white circles, whereas victims showed up on their branches as dark spots. The pattern resembled a page of musical notes and made me think of the mighty symphony of fate lying sealed and impenetrable within it.

"Here you see the uncle of this woman who had cancer of the nose; he had a predisposition to the disease, which never presented itself in his case." In doing so, he gestured toward a fetus in a jar of alcohol.

I also saw pictures of two aged sisters, twins who developed breast cancer simultaneously at age ninety-two. Such a demonstration made it clear that our modern science provides more data about piety than any earlier one.

I then went with Vernes into his dispensary, where the doctors were checking in the swarm of three hundred syphilitics. They were channeled to the examination cubicles, where women were seen to pull their skirts up and their underpants down to get injections in the buttocks. At the same time, other doctors in white coats were giving patients Salvarsan[137] in the veins of their arms or drawing blood samples. At the end of this row of booths stood a cot where a nurse was attending to an old man; he had collapsed in reaction to an injection that was too strong.

The whole thing resembled a huge machine that the patients fall into only to be directed to one or the other course of treatment dreamed up by the brain of Dr. Vernes according to how they respond. He is the inventor of a purely mathematical medical treatment and is thus the polar opposite of Dr. Parow, who treated me in Norway. Of course, their patients are also very different: Parow devoted his attention to independent individuals, while Vernes's task is to treat the anonymous population of the metropolis. This makes illness something else again; one person sees the individual corpus of the sickness, while the other sees its mycelium.[138] In Vernes's patients things other than the individual are the most important factor—things like statistical curves and sociological indicators. Parow, on the other hand, rarely mentioned syphilis; such labels were mere abstractions for him. He considered every patient to be unique.

During the night, I had dreams of worlds that had advanced along the same lines as our own. I was standing at a desk inside a gigantic airplane and observing the pilot, who sat at a second table as we took off. He was distracted and several times almost grazed mountain ridges as we flew over them. Only the utter composure with which I watched and spoke to him prevented disaster.

PARIS, 15 MARCH 1944
The progress of the years is like the motion of a centrifuge. It spins and precipitates an extract of minds that have greater range, thus creating a small body of European and world talent.

PARIS, 17 MARCH 1944
I cannot shake this influenza. It turned chronic when I interrupted my healing sleep. Was with Heller and Velut in a restaurant on the Champs-Élysées at noon. We sat there in the warm sun on the first day of spring and toasted each other with red wine. Velut is engaged in translating *The Worker*. We talked about the word *style*, which he plans to use as the equivalent of German *gestalt* [shape, form]. That alone suggests the difficulty of the enterprise. Precise empirical intelligence.

PARIS 23, MARCH 1944
My influenza is gradually abating; the cough is going away and my temperature is back to normal. I can tell this by the fact that the telephone receiver is dry after I have made a call.

The mail brought a letter from Kubin in which he writes about his drawings for the edition of *Myrdun* that Bruno Ziegler is planning.

Yesterday I finished the draft of my Sicilian journal from 1929. I have entitled this "The Golden Shell." The text became significantly longer during the writing. Brief notes from travel journals expand like tea blossoms when I'm revising. They provide scaffolding for memory.

Read further in Paul. His Letter to the Colossians contains the lovely passage in 2:17: "Which are a shadow of things to come." This sentence includes the sublime flowering of Greek wisdom. We too are shadows cast by our own body. One day it will emerge.

PARIS, 24 MARCH 1944

Visited Banine for coffee again after a long absence. The lovely *Paulownia* in her garden is still in in its winter dormancy. On my way home, I passed the antiquarian bookseller, whom I once noticed snoozing among her rarities. I would enter her shop if I saw an item in the window that gave me an excuse to do so—but there hasn't been any bait with sufficient appeal for quite a while.

Pondered further the nature of symmetry and its relationship to necessity. Perhaps we need to start with atoms and move from them to molecules and then to crystals. What is the relationship of symmetry to sex, and why is symmetry a particular feature of plants and especially of their sexual organs? In addition, there is the symmetry among nerves and structures of the brain as those vessels that give form to the mind. And then again, all symmetry can never be more than secondary. Tibetans avoid it when they construct their buildings for fear of attracting demons.

PARIS, 25 MARCH 1944

I began revising the text of my essay on peace.

The mail brought a letter from Rehm signed "Your unforgettable Rehm." He describes his escapades in the East, including his two wounds. Earlier, in 1941, he broke his arm on a dark staircase in Magdeburg during an air-raid alarm, and then last autumn, he was hit by a piece of shrapnel. A little while ago he also injured his wrist. I finally recall a similar injury that he had on the same arm on the *Westwall* [Siegfried Line]. It sometimes seems that astrologers point to a well-founded relationship when they see in our horoscopes that particular organs or areas of the body are at special risk. There are other explanations for this, such as our inborn dancer's rhythm, which always makes us commit the same *faux pas*. But for all this, the horoscope provides the best key.

PARIS, 27 MARCH 1944

Read further in Paul. There, in the Second Letter to the Thessalonians (2:11): "And for this cause God shall send them strong delusion, that they should believe a lie."

Yesterday, Sunday, went to Saint-Rémy-les-Chevreuses with the Doctoresse; after I recommended her to Vernes, she is now working for him. Breakfast in the restaurant de l'Yvette. How lovely it would be here in peacetime. It was the warmest, sunniest day we have had for a long time, yet the trees and bushes blazed in the sunshine without any hint of green. View from the slopes across the expansive landscape, where a couple of solitary English or American pilots were performing their Sunday afternoon flight routines.

My reading these days: Smith, *Les Moeurs curieuses des Chinois* [*Chinese Characteristics* (1894)]. Contains good observations. In addition, Lord Byron's *Letters and Journals*, and the poems of Omar Khayyam: red tulips spouting from the soft earth of a graveyard.

Continued going over the *Appeal*. It is true that many of my views have changed, especially my assessment of the war and of Christianity and its permanence. But you never know when working down in these old mine shafts whether you are going to hit a seam. You also have to view the structure, which resembles an hourglass: When the grains of sand approach the point of their greatest volume, of the greatest friction, their movement is different from when they have passed that point. The first phase is governed by the law of convergence, of the choke point, of total mobilization; the second is subject to their final position and dispersion. And yet they are one and the same atoms spinning and producing the shape.

Lieutenant Colonel von Hofacker paid me a visit in the evening, and when he entered, he took the telephone receiver off the hook. He is one the figures in our circle, whom the staff has designated with a particular name. They call him "*L'Aviateur*" [The Pilot], while Neuhaus is called "*Il Commandante*" [The Commandant], and I am "*La Croix Bleue*" [The Blue Cross].[139]

Although he had removed the telephone receiver, he did not seem at ease in my office, where we have dealt with so many issues. He invited me to accompany him out onto Avenue Kléber for a heart-to-heart talk. As we walked back and forth between the Trocadéro and the Étoile, he informed me of details from reports by his confidants who work for the General Staff at the highest echelons of the SS leadership. People there view the circle around Stülpnagel with deep suspicion. Hofacker told me that Pastor Damrath and I are looked upon as opaque and suspect. He thus thinks it advisable that I leave the city for a while and go to the South of France, perhaps Marseille. He is prepared to suggest this to the commander-in-chief. All I could say in response was that I would await a decision.

Following this we discussed the situation, and he listed a series of names beginning with von Goerdler. His name has been mentioned for years in all sorts of contexts, especially if one knows Popitz and Jessen. It is impossible that Schinderhannes [Himmler] and Grandgoschier [Goebbels] are not informed of this, especially if one thinks of the Mexican characters disguised as generals who eavesdrop in the Raphael and the Majestic.

Hofacker believes that the Fatherland is now in extreme danger and that catastrophe can no longer be avoided, but can probably be mitigated and modified, because the collapse in the East is a more terrible threat than that in the West and will surely be compounded by extermination on the grandest scale. Consequently, we shall have to negotiate in the West, namely *before* there is an invasion.

In Lisbon, they are already making preparations. This is all predicated on the removal of Kniébolo, who has to be blown to pieces. The best opportunity would be during a conference at his headquarters. Hofacker gave names of people in his inner circle.

As in other similar circumstances, I expressed my skepticism here—the objection that fills me with mistrust at the prospect of an assassination. He contradicted me: "If we don't prevent the fellow from getting to the microphone, it will take him five minutes to turn the people around again."

"You will just have to be more forceful at the microphone. As long as you lack that power, they won't be brought over to your side by assassination. I think one could create a situation that would make it possible simply to arrest him. If Stülpnagel wants—and there's no doubt of this—Rundstedt must go along with the plan. That will put the Western radio transmitters into your hands."

We then went back and forth as I had done with Schulenburg, Bogo, and others. Nothing says more for the extraordinary aura that Kniébolo creates around himself than the extent to which his strongest opponents depend upon him. The big match will be played out between the voting *demos* and the remnants of the aristocracy. If Kniébolo falls, the hydra will grow a new head.

PARIS, 29 MARCH 1944

Birthday. The president arranged a little table with candles in my room. Valentiner, who had come over from Chantilly, was among the well-wishers. Read further in Paul, where I found this good maxim in the section for today: "And if a man also strive for masteries, yet is he not crowned, except he strive lawfully" (II Timothy, 2:5). Went to the Pavillon d'Arménonville at noon. The air was already filled with tiny insects. Their shiny buzzing in March has always seemed especially festive and mysterious, as if they let us glimpse a new area of sensation, a new dimension.

To Florence in the evening. This is the third time I have celebrated my birthday with her, and as we were sitting around the table, the air-raid sirens sounded, just as they had the first time. The mood was gloomy following numerous arrests in the city. Jouhandeau said that in his hometown young people were killing each other "*pour des nuances*" [over trivia].

"*Gegen Demokraten helfen nur Soldaten.*" [Only soldiers are any use against democrats.] That may have been right in 1848, but it's not even true anymore in Prussia. Given the primitive condition we're in, we should rather follow the adage that you can only fight fire with fire. Democracies regulate themselves on a global scale. For this reason, the only thing left is civil war.

If, however, the warrior caste thinks it can benefit from this, it is deceived. The best minds on the General Staff were not only against the occupation of the Rhineland and adjacent territories but also against compulsory rearmament in general. The commander-in-chief told me some details of this that every later historian will declare to be implausible. The situation could be described as a paradox: the warrior caste certainly wants to support war but in its archaic form. Nowadays it is waged by technicians.

This is an area that includes the attacks of the new rulers against the ancient concept of military honor and the remnants of chivalry. When I studied the documents, I was often astonished by Kniébolo's intransigence in minor differences (to put it diplomatically), for example, in the dispute over the heads of a handful of innocent people. We will never grasp this if we cannot see through his desire to destroy the *nomos* [law, customs], which guides him infallibly. This can be expressed impartially: He wants to create a new standard. And because there is still so much about this new *Reich* that is medieval, it involves a steep decline.

When viewed politically, man is almost always a *mixtum compositum* [hodge-podge]. Time and place exert huge demands upon him.

In this sense, when seen from the ancestral and feudal perspective, I am a Guelph, whereas my concept of the state is Prussian.[140] At the same time, I belong to the German nation and my education makes me a European, not to say a citizen of the world. In periods of conflict like this one, the internal gears seem to grind against each other, and it is hard for an observer to tell how the hands are set. Were we to be granted the good fortune to be guided by higher powers, these gears would turn in harmony. Then our sacrifices would make sense. Thus we are obligated to strive for the greater good, not for our own benefit, but for reasons of our mortuary practices.

PARIS, 2 APRIL 1944

Farewell breakfast for Volckmar-Frentzel. The Leipzig publisher is returning to his old profession, since his books, machinery, and buildings have all been destroyed in the bombings. While I was there I spoke with Damrath, the pastor of the *Garnisonkirche* [Garrison Church] in Potsdam. The commander-in-chief has decided to send Hofacker there so that Damrath wouldn't have to do without our company. Damrath also quoted the motto he had inscribed on his great bell in Potsdam. He had chosen a passage from the letters of Friedrich Wilhelm I to Leopold von Dessau: "Were I only to till the land without making Christians of the people, then nothing at all would help me. He who is not devoted to God will not be devoted to me, a man."

A quotation from Léon Bloy could be placed beside that: "*Il n'y a plus de serviteurs dans une société qui ne reconnaît plus Dieu pour maître.*" [A society that has ceased to recognize God as its master no longer has servants.]

Departed for Kirchhorst in the evening, where I will spend several days of furlough to work on Ernstel's case. I am also hoping to see him in Wilhelmshaven, where he's in jail while his case is still undecided. But he must gain his freedom before the catastrophe.

ON THE TRAIN, 3 APRIL 1944

Huge delays are holding up the train; these are caused by the daily attacks on the lines and stations. My reading: the *Journals* of Byron and *Les Moeurs curieuses des Chinois*.

Two young officers from the tank corps sitting by the window; one of them stands out by virtue of his fine features, yet for the last hour they have been talking about murders. One of them and his comrades wanted to do away with a civilian suspected of spying by throwing him into a lake. The other man expressed the opinion that after every time one of our troops is murdered, fifty Frenchmen should be lined up against the wall: "That will put a stop to it."

I ask myself how this cannibalistic attitude, this utter malice, this lack of empathy for other beings could have spread so quickly, and how we can explain this rapid and general degeneration. It is quite possible that such lads are untouched by any shred of Christian morality. Yet one should still be able to expect them to have a feeling in their blood for chivalric life and the military code, or even for ancient Germanic decency and sense of right. In principle they aren't that bad, and during their short lives, they are willing to make sacrifices worthy of our admiration. We can only wish that the words "above reproach" might be added to their unassailable motto, "without fear." The second has value only in conjunction with the first.

Sitting opposite me was a first lieutenant, a paratrooper, with a book. He turns the pages silently, pausing now and then to raise his head and stare into space, like someone in contemplation. Then he continues his reading, smiling suddenly when he comes upon an entertaining passage. "The Reader"—a huge topic and an important emblem of intellectual humanity.

In Aachen in the afternoon, and then via Cologne through the succession of burned-out western German cities. It is horrible how quickly we grow accustomed to this sight.

"By the blessing of the upright the city is exalted: but it is overthrown by the mouth of the wicked" (Proverbs 11:11). A word of wisdom for future cornerstones, for new city gates.

KIRCHHORST, 4 APRIL 1944
Organized notes and books and browsed a bit in Byron's *Don Juan*.

My compatriots from Lower Saxony. Today I found evidence in the *Hildesheim Chronicle* of that unshakable calm that is one of their finest intrinsic traits. On 1 August 1524 fire broke out in the Neustadt area of Hannover, destroying a huge number of houses and ultimately spreading to the top of the Pulverturm [Gunpowder Magazine]. The lead roof began to melt and drip down the walls. Master Builder Oldekopp was directing the firefighting efforts from atop the tower; beside him stood his son, Johannes. After the father had tried various ways to get him to leave his post, he said, "even one of us here is one too many—don't you know that we probably have twenty tons of gunpowder under our feet?"[141] Only then did the younger Oldekopp leave his station.

KIRCHHORST, 5 APRIL 1944
Went to the Oldhorst Moor with Alexander to examine the anthill I discovered last winter. It's always gratifying to accomplish such a goal—another knot tied in the net of life. The tiny creatures were very active; among their guests I found one

unfamiliar to me: *Myrmecoxenus subterraneus* [darkling beetle], which Chevrolat, erstwhile tax official in Paris, described in 1835.

Along our way, we stepped into a shed because American bombers were being fired on overhead; on the way home we got soaked. Conversation about Don Quixote's adventures with the fulling mills and the fairy Peri Banu from *One Thousand and One Nights*.

The lilies are poking their heads up in the garden and the *Eremurus* proclaims its presence with six hardy shoots. Everywhere on the overgrown lawn the crocuses that I planted with Friedrich Georg before the war are blazing—pure golden yellow, deep blue, white on an amethyst ground that sends out veins to embrace the calyx like clasps on a silver goblet. These vivid hues are cheering: the brilliance of the first flush. With these little brown bulbs I planted treasure here, which, like a fairytale hoard, sometimes makes its way to the surface. The plant kingdom contains an entire system of metaphysics that becomes discernible in the annual garden cycle.

The golden pollen deposited on the blue ground of the calyx by bumblebees.

Spent the evening browsing in my old journals, which Perpetua had packed away in a special suitcase. I see that I have always had to wait a few years before I look at notebooks like this again. Over time certain passages wither on the vine, while others continue to mature.

Also read in Origen's *Exhortation to Martyrdom*. There in paragraph 46 one reads the warning not to call upon God with names other than those that are proper to him—such as not calling him something like Jupiter. Particular sounds and syllables could act like whirlwinds and attract other gods with those names. Noted this for my piece about vowels.

KIRCHHORST, 7 APRIL 1944

Out on the meadow in the afternoon where, in the company of Alexander, I dug wild acacia from the soil. While we worked, two American squadrons flew over in broad daylight. They ran into massive anti-aircraft fire over the city, and not long afterward, we saw one of the planes return with a stream of smoke coming from its right wing. Massive anti-aircraft fire followed it out of the cauldron and went silent once its fate became clear. Above us the plane plunged downward in a curve as three parachutes dropped clear of it. Without a pilot, it now made a constantly widening spiral. We thought it was going to crash near the house, but it floated toward the woods at Lohne, where a dark copper-colored sea of flames billowed up right after it disappeared. This then turned into a wall of smoke. Who could have imagined such drama in our quiet village?

After the famous void of the battlefield, we enter a theater of war encompassing operations that are visible for miles around. As a result, hundreds of thousands, perhaps millions, of spectators participate in the great aerial battles.

Read further in *Don Juan*. In the third canto, beginning at verse 61, there is a prototype of a sumptuous banquet where sensuality and intelligence compete.

KIRCHHORST, 9 APRIL 1944

Reflected on the immense numbers of books lost to the bombings. Old books are going to be rare; to reprint them will require intelligent planning. It would be possible to blaze a trail through utterly ruined terrain by reconstituting the classics in theology, world literature, philosophy, and other individual disciplines through a series of good editions. Then we could move down the ladder to include third- and fourth-rate authors, and then include the outliers, and produce these subdivisions in smaller print runs. This would bring certain advantages, such as forcing people's minds to engage with essentials.

Of course, it will be difficult to replace the journals, but perhaps they can be reconstructed from various library holdings. The collective nature of our existence will greatly promote library culture in general.

KIRCHHORST, 13 APRIL 1944

Have returned from the coast, where I had traveled with Perpetua to work on Ernstel's case. We departed on Easter Monday. Even Easter Sunday brought numerous sorties with *Vollalarm* [general alarm] or "Vollala," as three-year-old Peter, the little evacuee child staying with us here says. As we were leaving, I again noticed the blue calyxes of the crocuses in the garden; their deep background color showed a saffron dusting left by the bees. Those are hearty provisions for a journey.

There are many reasons why traveling is so difficult at the moment, but the planes cause the most trouble. We went through Oldenburg an hour after it had been attacked, and when we got out in Wilhelmshaven, we were greeted by the wail of sirens. We had met two officers on the train. One of whom, Emmel (an adjutant of the commandant) had already visited Ernstel in his cell on his own initiative. We did not let the alarm hold us up, but went right to the hotel. Once we had eaten there, we went to look for Dean Ronneberger in his half-demolished apartment.

The next morning a new alarm sounded while we were waiting for the streetcar in front of our hotel. We decided to walk along the streets that were quickly becoming less and less crowded, laden down with our parcels for Ernstel. We finally stepped into one of the air-raid bunker towers. Here you have the feeling of stumbling into a particular section of the Inferno that Dante missed on his progress. The interior of such a tower is like the cavity inside a snail's shell. A gently sloping walkway spirals around a central axis; countless benches hug the walls. Large segments of the population huddle here to await whatever might come. The snail shell was filled with human plasma, exuding a feeling of stifling dread. As I walked up the spiral path, I examined the exhausted faces dozing there. The populace in cities like this spends a significant part of its days and nights crouching in these joyless towers. As in all such facilities, here you find the dreamlike vegetative state intimately combined with mechanical activity. I could hear the humming of fans as well as a voice that intermittently called out, "Conserve oxygen!"

After we had looked this spiral over and sensed that it was more distressing there than the thought of being hit by a bomb, we went outside and found a place to sit in a neglected garden amidst the rubble. There was still a little bit of shooting, but then the sirens announced the all clear.

In the detention center. A sergeant led our boy into the room where we were waiting. He looked pale and weakened. His chin protruded and showed little wrinkles. His eyes were sunken and had lost their childlike vigor; they communicated premature experience. Yet his bearing was good, both modest and strong. Seeing him sitting there in front of me in his short sailor's jacket, I was reminded of how much he had longed for military laurels when he was a child, and how all his thoughts and energies focused on battlefield glory. He wanted to prove himself worthy of his father and was thus drawn to the most dangerous assignments. "You've acquitted yourself well, my boy," I thought to myself, "and it's a good thing that I understand that as a father." This war that is being waged among nations represents just the crude backdrop—the struggle involves more dangerous trophies. And I realized it was a good thing that I had come to this modest cell wearing the high order of World War I. We truly knew a kind of glory no longer accessible to these boys, and for that reason, their achievement is all the greater.

The next day we traveled on to Cuxhaven to visit Admiral Scheuerlen, commander-in-chief of the coastal defenses of the German Bight[142] and presiding judge in Ernstel's case. We discovered him to be an exceptional person. When one is involved in a case like this, it is possible to observe both of the actual points of contention in the greater process. Whether the man one meets is a human being or a machine is revealed in the first sentence he utters.

Kirchhorst, 17 April 1944
This was my last day of furlough, and I picked up some peas for Ernstel and planted my good wishes for him along with them. Today I plant the seeds without knowing who will harvest their fruits.

Cut some chervil in the garden. This little herb is to soup what woodruff is to wine. It grows in abundance under the old lime tree, and Alexander helped me pick it. I kept a nervous watch in case he picked hemlock by accident. This led us to a conversation about the cup that Socrates drank—his first introduction to the subject.

I brought back seeds in bulk from France. They have different shapes and coloration, and we'll just have to see how they take here.

On the Train, 18 April 1944
During the night, I was in Japan, where I acted boorishly toward strangers and strange things. I thought the rack used to display a shop's merchandise was a stairway and started to climb it. This caused some damage. The Japanese regarded me with apprehension that mixed courtesy with disgust.

Afterward, in a room where I found men and women on a sofa intoxicated with ether. One of them staggered toward me lifting a heavy jug, ready to strike out. Because I could see that he was drunk and would miss his mark, I tried not to move, "Otherwise he is going to hit me by mistake."

In the afternoon, Loehning sent a car to drive me to the station, where I boarded the train to Paris in a deluge of shrapnel.

On vowels. A new version of this essay would include the suggestions that the sound gradations of words are not arbitrary: When we perceive new things, several words usually suggest themselves to name them. The spirit of language will choose the most fitting of these and establish it as usage. In doing so, it will give precedence to the sequence of sounds rather than to logical meaning. For this reason, the word *Auto* is more powerful than *Kraftwagen* [car, vehicle].

PARIS, 21 APRIL 1944

Massive sorties last night, defensive fire, bombs hit the 18th Arrondissement and Saint-Denis. In the morning, I discovered the residents of the Raphael gathered for the first time in the air-raid shelter. A sort of lethargy kept me in bed. We hear that hundreds were killed.

Visited the Schnitzlers at midday; they are leaving tonight.

PARIS, 22 APRIL 1944

Current reading: the journal of First Lieutenant Salewski, who describes his days in the cauldron of Uman. Horst Grüninger sent me the manuscript. I also discussed it with Speidel, who has been given a command under Rommel; yesterday I saw him for the first time in a long while. Salewski's description is straightforward and objective. It has the coldness of molten metal that has hardened to a mirror finish, rather like the air around an abandoned outpost. I found familiar trains of thought, but they seemed to have sprung from seeds that had drifted over the garden wall onto sand and grown there under extremely austere conditions. All this is edifying because the cauldron is the purest expression of our situation; that was obvious to me before this war began. It was prefigured by signs such as the fate of the Jews.

Visited Heller in the afternoon, where I looked at the picture Dr. Göpel had given me for my birthday. On the way, I found the Place des Invalides cordoned off. In its center, a battery of heavy anti-aircraft guns had been constructed, surrounded by stacks of ammunition and small pointed tents for the troops. There was something ominous about this sight, especially the presence of tents in the middle of such a huge city, which was beginning to look like a deserted wilderness.

My place is at the bridgehead that crosses a dark river. My existence on this projecting arch becomes more untenable every day as its collapse becomes more imminent—unless its mirror image stretches across to meet it from the other side to complete and perfect it. But the other shore is blanketed in dense fog, and only sporadically can lights and sounds be vaguely discerned in the darkness. That is our theological, psychological, and political situation.

PARIS, 23 APRIL 1944

Excursion into the Trois Vallées.[143] In order to get a sense of the people's resilience, you have to see the rural populace—people who live on the country roads, not just the grand boulevards.

Dans les forêts lointains
On entend le coucou.

[In the distant forests / One hears the cuckoo's call.]

PARIS, 29 APRIL 1944

I spent last evening and a large part of the night in the company of the commander-in-chief, who brought Colonel Ahrends, Baumgart, and the mathematics
professor Walther with him to my *malepartus* [fox's den]. The general's love of
mathematics led to a conversation about prime numbers and then turned naturally to military and political topics via questions of ballistics and rocket experiments, which are planned for the near future. After Walther had said goodbye—he
was passing through and wanted to make the night train—I spent a while alone
with the general. He gave me a description of the situation, in particular of Rundstedt's character. It is due to him that we have not had any clarification or transpar-
ency in the West by now.

Anyone who knows Stülpnagel, Popitz, and Jessen—or even Schulenburg and
Hofacker—has a picture of the *Fronde*.[144] One can see that the moral element—not
the political—is ready to make its move. It is the weaker part of the operation,
meaning that the situation could take a turn for the better if a Sulla were to appear,
or maybe just a simple *Volksgeneral* [people's general].

Concerning mirrors and the curious change they encourage in human facial
expressions. When our glance wanders and sees conversational partners in the
mirror, completely new traits are revealed. Their ancestors could have looked out
from them in the same way, or intellectual substance is revealed that was otherwise concealed. This has an especially strong effect when the surface of the mirror
seems to move or undulate. That happened yesterday when smoke wafted upward
from cigars placed on a sideboard. Mirrors reveal things. Consider the changes on
the faces of the dead; we see them in light that emanates from a dark looking glass.

In the morning two Flemings, Klaes and Willems, paid me a visit. We discussed
Germany and France; they understand the reciprocal relationship between the two
countries more clearly from their position *à cheval* [on horseback]. Talked about
the situation, the Mauritanians, the two literatures, especially about Léautaud,
whose *Passe-Temps* [*Pastime, Hobby*] I am reading just now.

For many years now I have noticed that my ability to speak depends on the
intellectual acuity of my listeners. It's as though the wheel of the conversation were
rolling over a surface that is more or less smooth, meaning with more or less ease.
Yet it is odd, that during a first encounter with strangers, I don't need to wait for
them to say anything—probably because that person possesses a spiritual aura, a
trace of intellectuality.

PARIS, 30 APRIL 1944

First visit to Speidel, who now has a command under Rommel and is probably
the man with the clearest overview of the situation on the western front. His

headquarters are located out in La Roche-Guyon, a castle belonging to the La Rochefoucauld family. I spoke briefly with the duke and duchess while there, in particular about my stay in Montmirail.

The landscape around La Roche-Guyon, with its huge caves and cliffs rising from the Seine valley like organ pipes, has a labyrinthine and mysterious quality. It seems the perfect base for historical exploits, which is precisely what has happened throughout the various periods since the Normans and earlier. The place attracts history and colors it with the hues of its own fabric.

The slopes were crowned with anti-aircraft gun emplacements, and a tank unit was stationed in the valley for the personal protection of the commander-in-chief as well as for political considerations. In these regions, the prodigious efforts of war take on the air of greater ease. We are closer to the center around which the terrible weight of the wheel turns. I want to stay with this image in the technological sphere, in the system of coordinates that applies to the wielding of power with more or less mental states in Mauritania.[145] There is a certain exhilaration about this, such as Sulla must have experienced when he laid siege to Athens.

Paris, 1 May 1944

Lily-of-the-Valley Day. Speidel sent someone to collect my manuscript of the *Appeal* for Rommel, who wants to read it. I parted with it unwillingly.

Breakfast with Drouant and Abel Bonnard. I continue to admire the order and precision of his thought processes. His Voltaire-like and yet feline intellectuality, deftly reaches out to people and things, twists them playfully, and draws blood when it scratches. I used the opportunity to inform him that Léautaud—perhaps the last of the classic writers—lives in miserable circumstances on the outskirts of the city, almost without support and quite aged. Bonnard listened eagerly and asked me for more information. Léautaud is, of course, a cynic who is happy living among his cats, content in his easy chair. Visitors run the risk of being treated uncivilly by him. Add to this the calamitous political situation offering such bleak prospects for all human activity.

Back in Vincennes again in the company of the Doctoresse. We sunned ourselves a bit on the lawn by the path that goes around the fort. Half-naked soldiers were joking around on the ramparts as they looked down on the Parisians in their Sunday best. Like Roman legionnaires they gazed down from the citadel upon their conquered city.

In the woods, thousands of *Scilla* [Siberian squill] were in bloom. The gray-green streams were teeming with tadpoles; some already sported tiny back legs. What could be the reason for the second pair of legs' developing at different times? After all, they depend on each other. The old school will suggest the metamorphosis of the ventral fins—but that is just what makes the prospect wondrous. We see the demiurge arranging its designs in the stuff of life. Barefoot children were fishing for the little creatures and barricading them in small pools enclosed by mud walls.

Then back at the fort, just at the moment when two American squadrons flew over and a gun opened fire from the ramparts. Images of death and terror permeate everyday life and its pleasures in the most surreal way—like coral reefs that reveal the tentacles and jaws of monsters in their colorful shadows.

PARIS, 2 MAY 1944

On the Pont de Neuilly at midday; from its height, I gazed down into the water for quite a while. There, near the low river bank a big school of tiny fish was swirling around. The mass contracted and expanded like a breathing organism before seeming to condense around the center. From where I stood, the process was difficult to discern because the backs of these fry barely contrasted with the shade of the water. At moments, however, the anonymous throng flashed like silver lightning as it made a sparkling circle. This happened when one of the creatures occasionally shot upward through the collective excitation, making an ascending maneuver like a little ship gyrating on the water. At the water's surface, this fish then exposed its pale flank to the noonday sun.

Watched a long time as the silver specks glimmered from out of the dark mass and then submerged again after performing their spasmodic figures. What signals are these, and for whose eyes are they conceived?

Kept watching. Here in this simplest of images was a revelation of fame in our day. Each of its constituent parts was discernible: the congregation of the anonymous masses; their throbbing rhythm; their energy, which is then discharged at a higher level toward an individual who steps forward and is swept into the limelight. In the same way, heroes shine as solitary fighters among the horde of warriors and stand out from drab armies. By the same token, a soloist in a striking costume stands out more distinctly from other dancers as voices of the great singers resound in concert over the voices in the choirs.

How profound, how simple, is that the life force within us that focuses our senses, makes our hearts beat faster—the cradle of the deep sea, memories of fins, wings, dragons' forms, the sundials and astrolabes of the universe, the great dreamland and kingdom of childhood of our genesis. And above us, bridges of marble, high as rainbows. When viewed from them, the whole drama makes sense.

PARIS, 3 MAY 1944

During the midday break visited the dog cemetery located on one of the small islands in the Seine near the Porte Lavallois. At the entrance stands a monument to the Saint Bernard, Barry, who saved the lives of over forty hikers lost in the snow. He stands in stark contrast to Becerillo,[46] the huge attack dog who mauled and killed hundreds of naked Indians. Man, with all his virtues and vices, is reflected in the animals he breeds. The place reminded me of days from my childhood and those play cemeteries where we used to inter insects and little birds.

Read more in the Letter to the Hebrews. Here the tribe of the Jews brings forth superior blossoms from the pure wood without any grafting. It's very good to read between the lines about the sublimation of sacrifice.

A progressive comparison might look like this:

Cain / Abraham / Christ : Abel / Isaac / Jesus

This is the sequence of priests and of sacrificial offerings. Each of these pairs reveals a new condition in society, law, and religion.

PARIS, 4 MAY 1944

Visited Florence; there I met Dr. Vernes and Jouhandeau; Léautaud was also present, wearing a suit in the style of 1910 and a long, narrow necktie he had tied into a bow like a shoelace. As an author he has walked a straight line, avoiding romantic debility, uttering far less dross than all of his other colleagues I have observed so far.

Conversation about the *Mercure de France*, then about language and style. Léautaud hates imagery, similes, and digressions. He believes an author must express what he means with absolute precision and economy. He should also not waste his time worrying about rhythm and polishing. "*J'aime plutôt une repetition qu'une préciosité.*" [I would sooner have repetition than preciosity.] If one wants to say that it's raining, then one should write: "It is raining." In response to Paulhan's objection that this sort of writing could be delegated to an employee: "*Alors, vivent les employés.*" [Then long live the employees.]

It is his view that we can express anything we wish in words, provided we have absolute mastery of language, which prevents the slightest diminution between what is meant and what is said. Of course this only applies among non-metaphysicians. They are the only ones he recognizes.

What especially fascinates him is the sight of a human being who knows absolutely and unequivocally what he wants, for that is much rarer than one imagines nowadays.

His response to my remark that Victor Hugo was one of those authors I've been neglecting for too long, he said, "*Vous pouvez continuer.*" [You can continue.]

PARIS, 5 MAY 1944

Regarding the symbolism of the sea. If a young married couple wants the child they are expecting to be a girl, then it is the custom for a mother in the Turenne region to wear a necklace of fossilized mussel shells. This would be an addendum to the fine essay by Mircea Eliade that I read in *Zalmoxis*.[147]

Style: "Queen Hortense retreated to this place after sitting on a throne and bearing the brunt of all the shame." From the translation of Chateaubriand's *Mémoires d'Outre-Tombe* [*Memoirs from Beyond the Grave*].

Reading such a sentence is as disastrous as jumping out of a vehicle against the direction of traffic.

PARIS, 7 MAY 1944

At the pond in Suresnes in the evening to observe the life in the blossoming maple trees. As is now the norm, squadrons flew over the city's outskirts, which had already sustained varying degrees of damage. These noises and images are part of the fabric of daily life.

The Judas tree and the particular tint it lends to the palette of spring. Its pink hue verges on coral red and is bolder than that of the peach blossom, the pink hawthorn, and the chestnut trees. It is also more carnal.

PARIS, 8 MAY 1944

Dreams last night about trilobites that I purchased in the institute of Rinne, the Leipzig mineralogist. I bought them from a catalogue and took the incomplete ones as casts, which were molded with extraordinary care, partly of pure gold and partly of red shellac. Like all my paleontological dreams, this one was particularly concise. In the morning Clemens Podewils paid me a visit. He had accompanied Rommel on one of the inspection tours that he has been carrying out along the Atlantic coast. There is something classical in his attempt to see as many soldiers as possible before the action. The marshal is preparing his defense of the shore: "Our adversary must be destroyed on the water." This is in keeping with his calling up the reserves.

The landing is on everyone's mind; the German Command as well as the French believe that it will happen in the next few days. But what advantages could this bring to the English? They are like bankers who derive certain profit from the vagaries of the war in the East. Why should they abandon this highly lucrative role? American wishes notwithstanding, there could be many reasons: Russia could become too strong or too weak. Russia could threaten to negotiate. The existence of Kniébolo militates against this: As long as he is in power, he serves as the glue in any coalition against Germany. He is the sort of person who, in Goethe's words, "stirs up the universe against himself."

The situation for Germany is not desperate yet—but how disgusting it is to watch the drama.

PARIS, 10 MAY 1944

Nighttime bombing raids and fierce defensive fire. Agents had predicted four in the morning as the beginning of the invasion.

Finished reading *Passe-Temps* by Léautaud. Writers can be as different as fish, birds, and insects are from one another. What we want to see and enjoy in their work is the secure mastery of their medium. This is true in Léautaud's case. Among the French, Chamfort is like him, as Lichtenberg is among the Germans. I note the following quotation: "*Être grave dans sa jeunesse, cela se paie souvent par une nouvelle jeunesse dans l'âge mûr.*" [Seriousness in youth often leads to new youthfulness in mature adulthood.]

Coming from Rousseau, we can learn from him how confessions may be served up without sauce. In doing so, you expose yourself to the danger of cynicism. For that, the book is a treasure trove. Furthermore, in a Russian combat manual, *Partisan's Handbook*, third edition of 1942, in the chapter on "Reconnaissance," we read the sentence "Enemy corpses must be *camouflaged*"—a clever euphemism for "buried."

PARIS, 12 MAY 1944

Boring conference on Avenue Van-Dyck. But I had the good fortune that there was a huge horse chestnut tree outside the windows in full bloom. In the noonday radiance, I saw this tree for the first time. Its blossoms seemed to lose color in poor light; then they take on a dull brownish flesh tone. But in full sunlight, their bright coral red hue now stands out against the blue sky. Yet even in the shade, they stand there so vividly, set against the green foliage as though fashioned from rose wax. Later, when they wilt, the petals fall so thickly that they form a deep dark red-colored ring around the trunk. Stripped of its petal dress, the tree produces yet one more lovely sight.

The subject focused on our implementation of battalions from the Caucasus. Major Reese and I have been put in charge of these troops under the command of the military commandant. A tedious and unpleasant business, but thank God General von Niedermayer's Eastern experts are responsible for the technical side. The general has enlisted huge numbers from among prisoners of war. When these men are kept in occupied territory, all kinds of abuses occur, and these are then, naturally, on our heads. In the Métro, the Parisians now gaze in astonishment at Mongols in German uniform. Yellow tribes of ants are being absorbed. Guarding them calls for particular expertise. In addition to the informers whose identity is known to the units, there are others that the boss consults only in secret, and they are monitored by a third party. Organizational systems like this fall outside our usual norms; they would be impossible if we did not have despotic powers. As a result, new types are showing up among the officers. Niedermayer himself is extremely remarkable. During the World War, he fomented riots in Persia or Afghanistan; I recall Stapel characterizing him as a German Lawrence.[148] In the Caucasus, I saw pictures of him standing among hundreds of Asians. He combines expertise in geographical, ethnographic, and strategic knowledge and affinities.

PARIS, 13 MAY 1944

In the afternoon, went with Horst and Podewils to visit General Speidel in La Roche-Guyon. We ate together and then took a walk through the park and drank a bottle of wine in the most ancient part of the castle, beneath the Norman parapets.

In the coming action (the signs of which are growing more and more obvious), Speidel will be the decisive mind on the German side. It is good to see that he does not share the manners of other chiefs on the General Staff, whom one sees retreating to their rooms late at night with thick folders full of documents. In his vicinity tranquility tends to be the norm, producing that dead calm appropriate for the axle of the great wheel, the eye of the cyclone. I observe him while he sits at his desk admiring a flower, or making an observation about the Seine Valley, which we can see below us with its meadows and trees in bloom. The telephone rings; he lifts the receiver and puts it back after making a quick decision:

"A tank division is not a trucking company; requisition one of those."

"What? The Führer cannot judge that."

In the village the wisteria is in bloom, as well as the white stars of clematis, lilac, the golden rain tree; the first roses, more luxuriant than ever. Enjoying their colors and aromas, we strolled along the garden borders. Speidel quotes the verse from Platen:

Wer die Schönheit angeschaut mit Augen—
[Whoever has gazed on beauty . . .][149]

And then makes one of those utterances that befits a field marshal who is supposed to have oracular powers: "By autumn the war in Europe will be over."

PARIS, 15 MAY 1944

Read further in the Book of Revelation. This contains one of the greatest insights of the unmediated perception of the construction of the cosmos. Along with it, strange currents appear—such as those that are beginning to break down the rigid symbolism of the ancient Orient. Butterflies with wings bearing eye-spot-patterns emerge from their Egyptian, Babylonian pupal state to return to the splendid glories of their origins. That feature still introduces confusion to the selection today, as if we were witnessing the most exalted transformations. Here one senses the tremendous bifurcations—not a decisive battle, no rise or fall of empires—just one that places display at the center. Above kings and their deeds, there stands the prophet.

Only those marked with God's seal upon their brows shall escape the great destruction that has been foretold.

I read in this journal during the afternoon. In light of the precarious situation, I had given Hanne Menzel portions of the text to copy, and in the entry from 10 January 1942, I found that I recorded I had seen my dear, departed father in a dream. It is still strange that he died exactly one year later, namely during the night of 10 January 1943. At that hour I saw him in spirit, that is to say, when I was awake. I saw his eyes in the night sky gazing at me more meaningfully and with greater radiance than ever during my lifetime.

In the evening at the Didiers'. There I met Hendrik de Man again; he showed me the passage in his *Après Coup* [*Afterwards*] where he described our previous encounter.

PARIS, 17 MAY 1944

Visited Florence. Abbé Georget, her *aumônier* [chaplain], was also there. Talked about the Celts and about Brittany, where he is from. Is there still anything Celtic

in us? Just as fragments of old buildings are incorporated into castles, elements
of lost races are intertwined with the modern nations. Forgotten foster-mothers
approach our beds in dreams.

Georget was the confessor to the daughter of Léon Bloys. When he recounted
details about this author he mentioned *"Entrepreneur de Démolitions"* [Demoli-
tion Contractor],[150] which Bloys had printed on his calling card. This is a nihilistic
quirk similar to Nietzsche's "Philosophizing with a Hammer" and more. Yet the
assessment of nihilism lacks detachment—it must reflect the surroundings the
nihilist encounters. And the dubiousness of its values, which he embodies both
in his person and his actions, becomes evident. He thus becomes an annoyance;
even more irritating is the drama of those minds that cannot perceive changes in
the weather, like a drop in atmospheric pressure that precedes the typhoon. They
seek to stone the prophets.

In the city the shortages of electricity, light, and gas are getting worse. We are
living in the midst of a new kind of siege. The attack does not target factories
and warehouses as much as it does the arteries of energy and traffic. This is in
keeping with a war among workers. Assaults reinforce the effects of the huge
bombardments.

The situation calls to mind that of 1939 when people talked about war until it
finally came. It's been like that with the invasion, which perhaps neither of the parties sincerely desires. Yet this is precisely where the stroke of fate will be revealed.

Through all this, you can still see beautiful women on the streets in their new
hats, styled rather like tall turbans. This is the couture of the Tower of Babel.

PARIS, 19 MAY 1944

Current reading: "Essay on the Destruction of Hamburg" by Alexander Friedrich—an account sent to me in manuscript. You get the feeling that these cities
are like Bologna bottles:[151] internal tension makes their structure so delicate that a
jolt is enough to make them crumble. It is curious that so many people seem to be
gripped by a new sense of freedom that follows the complete destruction of their
property. Friedrich Georg predicted this, even at the spiritual level:

Das Wissen, das ich mir erworben,
Ist dürrer Zunder,
Kommt, Flammen, und Verzehrt, Verschlingt
Den ganzen Plunder.

[The knowledge that I have acquired / Is dry tinder / Come, flames, and engulf,
devour / All this old rubbish.]

Property is not considered suspect only by outside observers but also by the
disinherited themselves; it is even thought burdensome. Possessions require the
strength to possess—nowadays who wants to keep up a castle, be surrounded
by servants, or collect masses of objects? The nearness of the world of carnage is

relevant here. Anyone who has ever seen a metropolis hit by a meteor and go up in flames will look at his house and his furniture with new eyes. Perhaps we will see the day when people offer each other their property as presents.

Capriccios—like the ones Kubin predicted as early as 1909 in his novel *The Other Side*. There, herds of cattle that had broken out of their pens on the edge of town came trotting down the burning streets. The animals entered the city, while humans spent their nights in the forests.

In one of the houses that was in flames, a little shop clerk was sitting between the cowering inhabitants of the building who were all prevented from fleeing by the exploding bombs. Suddenly a man of Herculean strength forces his way in to take her to safety. He grabs her around the hips and drags her outside. He carries her across a plank into a room not yet engulfed in fire, while behind them the house collapses. By the light of this pyre the man sees that he has not rescued his wife at all, but a woman he does not know.

Friedrich ends his essay with the reflection that it is a lovely thought for Goethe to let his Faust regain consciousness "*in anmuthiger Gegend*" [in a pleasant region].

PARIS, 20 MAY 1944

Jean Charet, the polar explorer: "above the polar circle there are no Frenchmen, no Germans, or Englishmen anymore—there are only men." The yearning for the north and south poles in the nineteenth and twentieth centuries is analogous to the search for the philosopher's stone: They are magical sites, endpoints that create a planetary consciousness. They are also seminal poles, fructified by the eyes of their discoverers. The nations of the Old World are changed by these new dimensions. The polar circle is the absolute state where no differentiated energies can exist except the primal force. Compare that to the narrow view of Schubart, who envisaged eternally separate heavens and homelands for the nations. That's one of the passages I read that harmed me; it also contradicts Germanic sensibility. For our fathers, the enemies that had just hacked each other to pieces entered the gates of eternity as shades, arm in arm, and proceeded to Glasor,[152] the grove with the golden leaves, where they were united at the banquet table.

Visited Madame Didier on the Boulevard des Invalides. Because there was no fresh clay to be had, she sculpted my head from the material formerly used in her bust of Montherlant. That is a detail that would have amused Omar Khayyam.

In the Tuileries. The field poppies were in full bloom. I thought in passing how well the name fits the essence of this plant.[153] It connotes both the garish, snappy quality of the color and also the fragility of the petals, which are destroyed by a breath of air. This applies to all authentic words—they are woven from a combination of meanings, from ever-changing material. For that reason alone, I do not share the avoidance of imagery shown by such authors as Marmontel and Léautaud, nor do I share the developmental perspective of etymology. Writing or speaking a word sounds a bell that sets the air vibrating within its range.

PARIS, 23 MAY 1944

In the afternoon, the death sentence that had been handed down *in absentia* for General von Seidlitz was announced. It seems that his activity fills Kniébolo with worry. Maybe the Russians have a general on their side to match our Niedermayer. As this was happening, an oath of allegiance to Kniébolo from the field marshals in the Wehrmacht was proclaimed; it used the familiar clichés. I think it was Gambetta who asked, "Have you ever seen a general who is courageous?" Every little journalist, every working woman, is capable of greater courage. The selection process is based on the ability to keep your mouth shut and follow orders; then add senility to these qualities. Maybe that still works in monarchies.

Visited Madame Didier in the evening; her portrait bust of me is coming along. During the process, I had a feeling of Promethean emergence into being, like a demiurge. It is an uncanny sensation, especially the kneading, stroking motion that conjures the material into form. Artists are closest to the great creative energies of the world. It is *their* symbols deposited in the graves and rubble of the earth that bear witness to life that once pulsed with vitality.

PARIS, 25 MAY 1944

Visit from Wepler, who is passing through. We spoke together about the death of Feuerblume.[154] The older and the younger friend of one deceased. Her death brings us closer.

PARIS, 26 MAY 1944

Departed very early for Sissonne. I had not been in this place since 1917. In Laon I found the area around the railroad station destroyed by recent bombing, but the cathedral and upper part of the town were almost unscathed. Those cities and paths, so central to our destiny—the ones we keep returning to—what form does our transformation inscribe itself upon the earth? Perhaps that of garlands and blossoms of some miraculous kind.

We had work to do on the parade ground because irregularities had emerged in one of the battalions from the Caucasus. For the trip, we used a vehicle that burned wood gas from a stove mounted in the rear. We had to stop and stoke it occasionally with more wood, which we did under dense cover to elude the dive-bombers. The burned-out vehicles by the side of the road made us all the more wary. The machine guns that we now hold between our knees when we take such trips are evidence that things are less pleasant.

I must change my rules of conduct; my moral relations with my fellow man have become too strained. That's how it stands with the battalion commander, who stated that he would have the first deserter who was caught brought before the company where he would "dispatch" him with his own hands. When I hear such hostility, I get sick to my stomach. I have to reach a plane from which I can view things the way a doctor examines patients, as if these were creatures like fish in a coral reef or insects on a meadow. It's especially obvious that these things apply to the lower ranks. My disgust still betrays weakness and too great an identification with the "red world."[155] We have to see through the logic of violence and beware of euphemism in the style of Millet or Renan. We also have to guard against the disgraceful role of those citizens who moralize about people who have made terrible bargains while looking down from the safety of their own roofs. Anyone not swallowed up by the conflict should thank God, but that does not give him license to judge.

This occupied my thoughts as I stood beside Reese while he addressed the foreign soldiers. They stood around us in an open square formation wearing German uniforms with badges of their ethnicity emblazoned on their sleeves—things like a mosque with two minarets encircled by the words *"Biz alla Bilen, Turkestan."* Reese spoke slowly and in short sentences, which were translated by an interpreter.

Our position in the center of this quadrangle seemed bizarre, as if we were on a chess board planning intelligent moves, including ones involving ethnographic finesse.

We ate with the German officers, who gave the impression of being composed half of technicians and half mercenary leaders—the eighteenth and twentieth centuries merge into pseudo-forms that are difficult to classify. Wherever theory flakes off, it reveals pure force underneath. There is no military tribunal; the commanders have the power of life and death. On the other hand, they have to count on being murdered along with their officers should their troops desert in the night.

In Boncourt we then drank a mug of vodka with the Russian company commander, while the Turkomans and Armenians joined together around us in a wide circle. They huddled on the ground for hours, singing their droning chants. Every now and then dancers would leap into the circle and exert themselves either individually or in pairs to the point of exhaustion.

In the occasional hiatus, I was able to slip away for a brief half hour to go hunting for *subtiles*. In doing so, I came upon the blue-green *Drypta dentata* [ground beetle] in the wild for the first time; it is a creature of exquisite elegance. The Italian Rossi, who was a doctor in Pisa, first named it in 1790.

Paris, 27 May 1944

Air-raid sirens, planes overhead. From the roof of the Raphael, I watched two enormous detonation clouds billow upward in the region of Saint-Germain while the high-altitude formations cleared off. They were targeting the river bridges. The method and sequence of the tactics aimed at our supply lines imply a subtle mind. When the second raid came at sunset, I was holding a glass of burgundy with strawberries floating in it. The city, with its red towers and domes, was a place of stupendous beauty, like a calyx that they fly over to accomplish their deadly act of pollination. The whole thing was theater—pure power affirmed and magnified by suffering.[156]

Paris, 28 May 1944

Pentecost Sunday. I finished reading the Apocalypse after breakfast and with that, my first complete reading of the Bible begun on 3 September 1941. Previously I had read only portions, including the New Testament. Commendable is what I would call this effort, especially since it was the result of my own decision, and I prevailed despite some opposition. My upbringing ran in the contrary direction. Since my early youth my thinking had been directed by my father's rigorous realism and positivism, and every important teacher I had abetted his endeavors. The religion teachers were for the most part boring; some of them gave me the impression that they were embarrassed by the material. Holle, the brightest among them, encouraged insights by explaining the appearance of Christ on the water as an optical illusion. He said that that region was well known for its ground fog. My more intelligent classmates and the books I loved all took the same line. It was necessary to have gone through this period, and its vestiges will always stay with me—particularly the need for logical evidence, by which I mean bearing witness to truth rather than relying on confirmation, and the immediacy of reason, which must always light our way. Such goals must remain before us. This sets me apart from the romantics and lights my journeys through this world of the living and the netherworld in my spaceship, which lets me dive, swim, fly as I speed through realms of fire and dreamscapes, accompanied by instrumentation that is the product of science.

PARIS, 29 MAY 1944

Excursion to the Trois Vallées. A glaring, hot day. How beautiful it was in the silent thicket beneath the leafy bushes with the bright cloudless sky overhead: pure presence. "*Verweile doch—*" [Tarry a while . . .].[157]

The wisteria and the way its woody, winding vines curve around the bars of the garden fence. A single glance reveals to the eye the chemical substance they have been depositing there for decades.

The emerald wasp *Chrysis* against a gray wall—its iridescent, silky green thorax and garish raspberry-red abdomen. A tiny creature like this seems to collect the rays of the sun like the focal point of a magnifying glass. It lives cloaked in finely woven embers.

The tree frogs and the sound of scythes being sharpened that makes them break into their choral song.

"*Der wollte auf der Geige reiten*" [He wanted to ride on the fiddle]—an expression meant to describe an arrogant person.

With the president in the evening. Here in France, fifty thousand people have died by aerial bombs during these Pentecost holidays. One reason is that a crowded train on its way to the Maisons-Laffitte racetrack was hit.

The president told me about a corporal, who is eager to serve on firing squads. He generally aims at the heart, but if he does not like the man to be executed, then he aims for the head, causing it to shatter. It is a subhuman trait to want to disfigure, to want to rob another person of his face.

I wonder which ones he aims at in this way. Probably the prisoners who come closest to the concept of human being—those who are successful, kind, or well-bred.

"Soldiers, aim for the heart, spare the face," shouted Murat when he stepped up to the wall.

Incidentally, the day before yesterday, a twenty-six-year-old captain was executed, the son of a shipowner from Stettin. The reason given was that he said he wished a bomb would hit headquarters. A Frenchman from the region of La Val reported him.

Paris, 30 May 1944

Visited Madame Didier in the afternoon. Conversation with her nephew, a child of five who was very nice. The little boy had recently been taken along to mass for the first time, where he saw the distribution of the sacrament. When asked what the priest had done: "*Il a distribué des vitamins à tout le monde*" [He handed out vitamins to everyone].

Vaux-les-Cernay, 31 May 1944

With the commander-in-chief in Vaux. Despite the stifling heat, we lit a fire to freshen the air. In addition to the general, Professors Krüger, Weniger, and Baumgart sat around the fire.

Generals are mostly energetic and stupid, which means they have a kind of active and calculating intelligence that any one of the best telephone operators possesses, and yet the masses pay mindless homage to them. Or they are educated, which diminishes the brutality that is part of their craft. There is always a flaw somewhere, either in their willpower or their sense of control. Very rarely is there a union of energy and education, as in the likes of Caesar and Sulla, or as we saw in our own age in Scharnhorst and Prince Eugene. For this reason, generals are mostly stooges for hire.

Then there is Heinrich von Stülpnagel who is called "the blond Stülpnagel" to distinguish him from other generals in this old military dynasty. He exhibits princely qualities befitting his proconsular station. These include his appreciation of peace and quiet, of leisure, and of the society of a small intellectual circle. All this contrasts with the workings that are otherwise found in the higher echelons of the staff. His aristocratic character tends to judge people by their minds. His life suggests that of a scientist, particularly in the way he acquired his comprehensive erudition during long periods of convalescence. He seeks out mathematicians and philosophers, and on the subject of history, he is fascinated with ancient Byzantium. Yet, one may say that as a strategist he was a good leader; as a statesman a good negotiator; and as a politician someone who never lost sight of our situation. All this makes it understandable that he has been an opponent of Kniébolo since the very beginning. Yet I notice clearly from one of his repeated gestures that he is tired: With his left hand he tends to rub his back, as if supporting it or keeping his posture erect. At the same time his face bears a worried expression.

Discussion about the Stoics and their premise: "In certain situations leaving one's life is the duty of the capable man." It looks as though the general carries on a private correspondence with his wife in which they discuss this and other topics of ethics.

Started reading Herman Menge's translation of the New Testament, which Pastor Damrath gave me as a present.

Browsed some more in Georges Migot's *Essais pour une Esthétique Générale* [*Essays Toward a General Esthetic*], a small volume where I noticed several observations about symmetry. This is a topic I have been thinking about more often over the past months. The author attributes to the Egyptians a tendency to asymmetry and cites their preference for heads in profile as evidence. Mirror imagery in art corresponds to repetition in music. The need for symmetry is apparently a subordinate trait. This means it applies more readily to the form than the content, like those related parts in painting where the size of the canvas, the frame, and in some cases, even the subject matter could correlate with each other but not the actual execution. Incidentally, the marginal notations are not especially precise. Symmetry is an immense topic. When I have the leisure time, I'd like to try to work my way into it via two paths—specifically, studying the relationship to free will and to the erotic sphere. An examination of insects and a description of a hermaphrodite butterflies gave me the idea.

PARIS, 31 MAY 1944

Before returning, I swam in the lake and then went hunting for *subtiles*. This spring I have again fallen prey to this passion.

Had breakfast with Madame Didier. She put the final touches on the head and then wrapped it in damp cloths to store it in the cellar, since she is traveling to the mountains to visit Hendrik de Man.

Concerning the style of engineers: *Entscheidung* [decision, determination] becomes *Entscheid* [decree, decision], which means first, that it turns it crudely into a masculine noun, and second, that the meaning is shifted from a connotation of deep consideration to the superficial, willful present.

PARIS, 1 JUNE 1944

Visited Florence at noon. After we had eaten, had a brief conversation with Jules Sauerwein, who had arrived from Lisbon. We discussed the possibility of peace and what form it could take.

In the evening had a discussion with the president and a Captain Uckel about Stalingrad. It seems that teams of cameramen from a propaganda unit were filming until the final hours. The films fell into the hands of the Russians and are supposedly being shown as part of Swedish newsreels. A portion of the grim events takes place in a tractor factory where General Strecker blew himself up along with his staff. You can see their preparations and watch the camera teams, who are not on the staff, leave the building before the huge explosion. This urge to record the final moments has something robotic about it and expresses a kind of technological reflex, like those twitching frogs' legs in Galvani's experiment.[158] There is a scientific aspect to this as well. These are not monuments like those we leave to posterity or build to gods, be they only in the form of a cross hastily tied from willow twigs—these are, rather, documents by mortals for mortals, and mortals alone. How terrifying and real is the Eternal Return in its most lugubrious form: Again and again, this dying in an icy region is monotonously repeated. It is demonically conjured up without refinement, without splendor, and without solace. Where is the glory in any of this?

The captain [Uckel] thought the films should have been destroyed—but to what end? These are just reports from workers to other workers.

Then, concerning photography in general. On this subject, the president talked about a scene he had personally witnessed in Dreesen's Hotel near Godesberg. As Kniébolo was coming down the steps, he was greeted in the foyer by a little girl, who approached him to present a bouquet. He leaned down to receive this and to touch the child on her cheek, and at the same time turned his head a bit to the side, calling out sharply, "Photograph!"

PARIS, 6 JUNE 1944

With Speidel last evening at La Roche-Guyon. The journey was complicated by the destruction of the Seine bridges. We drove back around midnight. Consequently, at headquarters, we missed the first reports of the landing by an hour. By morning, Paris had heard about it and been stunned by the news—especially Rommel, who was absent from La Roche-Guyon yesterday because he had driven to Germany for his wife's birthday. That is merely one false note in the overture to this huge battle. The first troops that parachuted in were captured after midnight. Countless fleets and eleven thousand aircraft were deployed in the operation.

There is no doubt that this is the beginning of the great offensive that will make this a historic day. I was still surprised, precisely because so much had been predicted about it. Why now and why here? People will be talking about these questions well into the distant future.

Current reading: *The History of Saint Louis* by Joinville. I recently visited Husser in his apartment on Rue Saint-Placide, where he gave me an excerpt from the work to take home. In some scenes, such as the one of the landing of the Crusaders at Damietta, one sees humanity in the greatest glory it can achieve. Materialistic historiography only grasps things it can see. It does not recognize the variety that gives the fabric its color and pattern. This helps define our task: to rediscover the diversity of driving forces. This demands a more powerful objectivity than the positivistic approach.

PARIS, 7 JUNE 1944

Took a walk with the president in the evening. Two heavy tanks had halted on the Boulevard de l'Amiral-Bruix on their way to the front. The young soldiers were perched on their steel behemoths in the waning sunlight of the day in that kind of elation tinged with melancholy that I remember so well. They radiated a tangible aura of the imminence of death, the glory of hearts ready to embrace immolation.

Watched the way the machines retreated, disappeared with all their technological intricacy and grew simpler and more comprehensible as they did so, like the shield and lance that the hoplite[159] leans against. And the way the lads sat on top of their tanks, warily eating and drinking with each other like betrothed people just before the ceremony, as if partaking of a spiritual meal.

PARIS, 8 JUNE 1944

As we were eating, Florence left the table to take a telephone call. When she returned she said: "*La Bourse reprend. On ne joue pas la paix.*" [The stock market has rebounded. You don't bet on peace.]

It seems that money has the subtlest feelers and when bankers assess the situation, they do so more meticulously and with greater precision than generals.

In the afternoon, I received a visit from Dr. Kraus, the ballistics expert. Conversation about my Brother Physicus and his work on suspension bridges and prime numbers. Then we talked about Cellaris, who is still in prison but for whom the hour of freedom will soon toll, as it also will for many thousands of his fellow sufferers.

We then talked about the so-called new weapon and the attempts to launch it. Kraus told me that a recent launch had taken an unexpected trajectory and landed on the Danish island of Bornholm. What's more, this rocket was not only a dud, but by evening, the English had already photographed it. They were able to study its electromagnetic guidance system and immediately set up a power station with huge defensive capability in the southern part of their country.

The rumors surrounding this weapon make it possible to study destruction as the polar opposite of eros. Both possess a certain commonality, like positive and negative electrical charges. The whispers everywhere are very like the ones you hear that surround a lewd joke: no one is supposed to talk about it. At the same time, Kniébolo hopes that rumors he has carefully nurtured will circulate. The whole matter is highly nihilistic and stinks of the charnel house.

PARIS, 11 JUNE 1944

Back again on the Route de l'Impératrice on my way from Saint-Cloud to Versailles. I sunbathed again among the chestnut bushes in the little clearing. Each time I do this I think: this could be the last.

PARIS, 12 JUNE 1944

Visit to Husser in his apartment on Rue Saint-Placide where I want to store files, perhaps even seek shelter here for a few days. This is the base to my left in the Latin Quarter. The Doctoresse holds the center spot, and the secondhand bookseller Morin has the one on my right. Better than gold are those friends we have made.

I am reducing my luggage to a bare minimum. Kniébolo and his gang are predicting a swift victory. Just like the Anabaptist prince.[160] What figures the rabble follow, and how universal the *ochlos* [mob] has become.

PARIS, 17 JUNE 1944

Yesterday and the day before I again sensed the incubus, a weird constriction of the diaphragm that I was finally able to get rid of last night. Was there a danger that threatened me personally or others? I felt I had fended it off.

The army report states that the so-called *Vergeltungswaffe* [Reprisal Weapon][161] has been launched. At the same time, the propaganda in the French factories describes the large areas of London have been reduced to rubble. The masses are gripped by a wave of jubilation. These flying bombs are said to produce a bright flash just before detonation and are one of the last ploys in this morass of destruction. If they had any utility as weapons and not merely as propaganda, they would be deployed at the site of the beachhead. One thing about this is quite genuine: the will to transform the living world into a wasteland and there achieve the victory of death. Nowadays anyone who expresses doubt in "reprisal" and "destruction" commits a sacrilege.

In the morning, Lieutenant Trott zu Solz entered my room; he is company commander of an Indian regiment—someone I haven't seen since that fateful night in Überlingen.[162] Once again he comes to me under portentous circumstances. Discussed the situation, particularly about General von Seidlitz, and then about the way Prussians have been victimized by the Party.

PARIS, 22 JUNE 1944

With Florence at midday. Heller was there; he had returned from Berlin and on the way his train was strafed. He told me that just after the landing Merline had submitted an urgent request for papers to the embassy and has already fled to Germany. I still find it curious how very much people who callously demand the heads of millions are afraid for their own paltry lives. The two things must be linked.

In the evening, there were sorties overhead and shrapnel rained into the courtyard of the Majestic. In the course of the bombardment, huge reserves of fuel and oil were hit, producing a thin cloud rising up to darken the heavens like the pine tree of Pliny the Younger.[163] A huge bomber crashed near the Gare de l'Est [railroad station].

For the word *Kettenglied* [chain link] the French language has a special one: *chaînon*. Our south German (probably archaic) *Schäkel* comes from the same root. The chain maker is *le chaînetier*, for which we say *Kettler*, which is preserved as a surname.

The building on the corner of Rue du Regard opposite the military prison on Rue du Cherche-Midi. Every time I pass it, I think of Pearl, Kubin's dream city.

PARIS, 24 JUNE 1944

Visited Speidel in La Roche-Guyon in the evening. The destruction of the Seine bridges means that we could only get there via detours. At one point, we even had to get out of the vehicle because planes were swooping around overhead.

Walk in the park after we had eaten. Speidel told us details of his visit to Kniébolo, whom he had debriefed a few days ago in Soissons. He said that Kniébolo had aged, was stooped over, and that his conversation jumped around distractedly. For breakfast he devoured a huge amount of rice, drank different colored medicines from three different liqueur glasses, and also swallowed pills. He held a set of colored pencils between his fingers, using them occasionally to draw lines on the map. He expressed his displeasure that the English and Americans had been able to land at all, but did not go into details like the enemies' air superiority. He has only a vague idea about the next step in the process and seems to hope—and perhaps even believe—that a providential man of destiny who has often rescued him from desperate situations, might appear again. In this connection he twice cited the Seven Years' War.[164] He also believes that there is discord among his opponents and that they are all on the brink of revolution. He is announcing the release of new weapons for the autumn, particularly armor-piercing shells, and then he falls into a *rage du nombre* [obsession with numbers] when he starts talking about industrial "output." He also spoke of the "hell hounds," those flying bombs, one of which had taken an especially comical course and landed near his headquarters when he was present, which triggered a hasty exit.

I also talked with Admiral Ruge about details of the landing. It seems to be true that during that decisive night not a single German patrol boat had put out to sea "because of the heavy swell." The English landed at low tide when all the underwater defenses were exposed and visible on the beach. The defensive system of obstacles for low tide had been planned but not yet deployed.

Colonel von Tempelhof spoke of the death of General Marcks whose brother, a lieutenant colonel, asked about the hour of death, because on the death day a picture had fallen off the wall at eleven o'clock. In fact, the general was hit at a quarter-to-eleven, and he died when the hour struck.

On the way back, our driver lost control of the vehicle and spun off the road into a blackberry bush at high speed. Its branches absorbed the impact like gentle springs.

Current reading: Hendrik de Man, *Après Coup* [*Afterwards*]. A nice rule comes at the very beginning of the memoirs, "that one must always aim higher than one's goal." In this book, I also found the description of our encounter at the Didiers'.

PARIS, 27 JUNE 1944

Street fighting in Cherbourg. Perpetua has written to me that on the morning of 15 June bombs fells near the house. One of them landed in the little swimming hole belonging to the Lohnes, blowing hundreds of carp and whitefish into the air.

PARIS, 1 JULY 1944

In accordance with my policy that you can never revise work too often, I'm looking through my *Appeal*.

A new dream vision: friendly, auspicious; it was the deacon. Such encounters leave me feeling that they belong to our clan and keep returning as part of my own cast of characters.

A few days ago, following this, in great caverns that disappeared deep into the earth in serpentine tunnels, behind a barbed wire barrier that I had crossed. There stood the Head Forester, wearing a light hunting jacket, as an apparition of intensely concentrated power. He stood on the landing of the steps "entering," and even though I carried a weapon, I recognized that it was futile to use such toys here. His aura paralyzed my hand.

On style. Tenses may be indicated, but we can also add nuance by temporal auxiliaries. Instead of saying *"ich werde das tun"* [I shall do that], we have *"dann tue ich das"* [then I'll do that], or *"Morgen tue ich das"* [I'm doing that tomorrow].

This involves a slight loss of logic and also a bit of pedantry. I'm making progress in Menge's Bible translation, which renders *"Klopfet an, so wird euch aufgetan"* [Knock and it is opened unto you], as *"Klopfet an, so wird euch aufgetan werden"* [Knock and it will be opened unto you]. That is schoolboy sophistry.

My reading these days: General J. Perré, *Minerve sous les Armes* [*Minerva Armed for Battle*], an essay about intelligence and military strategy that I, as the censor, read in manuscript form. This contained a remark of Marshal Joffre about the art of command at the highest level: *"Ne rien faire; tout faire faire; ne rien laisser faire"* [Do nothing; have others do everything; leave nothing to others].

Very true; a divine streak must be present in a military leader: Caesar-like divinity. His aura is more important than his directives.

Later browsed in a *Guide Officiel des Voyages Aériens* [*Official Guide to Air Travel*] from 1930 that contains a quotation about aeronautics on every page. It is filled with platitudes:

"L'aviation constituera un des facteurs les plus importants de la civilisation." [Aviation will constitute one of the most important factors of civilization.] Louis Bréguet.

"Il n'ya plus de Pyrénées—surtout en avion." [There are no more Pyrenees—especially in an airplane.] Albert I, king of Belgium.

"L'air deviendra le véritable élément d'union entre les hommes de tous les pays." [Air will become the element that truly unites men of all countries.] General de Goys.

"L'aviateur conquérant du ciel es l'incarnation véritable du surhomme." [The conquering aviator in the sky is the true incarnation of the superman.] Adolph Brisson.

And so it goes on for pages. Old Leonardo saw things a bit more clearly.

PARIS, 3 JULY 1944

Colonel Schaer visited me in the Majestic in the morning. Since we last saw each other, he has commanded a regiment in the East, where he was sentenced to eleven months in prison because, in the heat of the moment, he did not keep his opinions under wraps. In general, the arrests and executions of officers are on the increase.

Schaer also showed me the photograph of a charnel house in the vicinity of Nikopol—a horrifying picture that one of his people was able to take during their retreat. He did so covertly, for these are taboo places of the most hideous kind. Seeing it moved me to make a correction in my own text about peace.

PARIS, 6 JULY 1944

Visited Florence. Léautaud was there and he recommended that I read Jules Vallès. He very delicately offered me his help in case the Germans here in the city should encounter difficulties.

There are two ways to transcend differences among nations: through reason and through religion. Léautaud has achieved the first goal. Yet, even in his case, one can see that the more nationalism disappears from one's consciousness, the more powerfully it is expressed in his personality.

Paris, 13 July 1944

The Russians are closing in on East Prussia. The Americans, on Florence, while the battle at the site of the landing rages on with heavy losses. The leadership is trying to promote hope in new and unknown weapons because they are incapable of new ideas. The complete lack of judgment shown by the masses as they permit themselves to be deceived into a state of euphoria remains remarkable.

Paris, 14 July 1944

I visited Monsieur Groult on Avenue Foch with Baumgart and Fräulein Lampe. After you cross through the courtyard, his house reminds you of Aladdin's enchanted castle or Ali Baba's treasure cave. Gardens with fountains and pools of water where swans and exotic ducks paddle on the surface, pergolas with statues and reflecting surfaces, Pompeiian galleries, terraces with parrots and ringneck doves are protected from view by high trellises covered with ivy and wild grapevines.

The Goncourts amassed their collections with the advice of Groult's father, and these surpass the disbelieving accounts that Balzac delights in. They unite well over a hundred paintings and drawings by Fragonard and more by Turner than can be found in the British Isles. The formidable galleries are lined with one masterpiece after another. What is more, over a thousand of the best pieces have already been distributed to distant châteaux. The collections are barely known; a catalogue has never been published. Furthermore, only friends or people brought by friends are allowed to enter these rooms.

We spoke with the owner about the unparalleled treasures and about their security as well as their value. He considers best to leave these things in Paris. Transporting them could damage them, and they could also be shelled in the process. Furthermore, the fate of all other places in France is almost less certain than that of this city, which—one hopes—like Rome will be protected by its aura. During the air attacks, falling shrapnel sometimes breaks panes in the skylights. If that ever happens during wet weather, rain pours into the rooms, causing damage. We examined a pastel by Watteau with damaged velour and discolored by little green spots, as if mold were growing on it. The damage had affected this picture in an unusual way, less in a purely mechanical way than by distorting its features, rather like illness in a human being. The portrait of Dorian Gray changed along similar lines.

The coal shortage is a nuisance. The household requires a staff of more than twenty.

On the subject of value, Herr Groult maintained that this consideration did not exist for him, for he was never going to part with any of the pictures. Hence the question was irrelevant. How oppressive ownership has become, especially in this inferno. To shoulder a responsibility like this nowadays demands the courage of a swimmer who is laden with gold, like the soldiers of Cortez in that Sad Night.[165]

Current reading: Léon Bloy, *Méditations d'un Solitaire* [*Meditations of a Solitary Man*]. The book was written in 1916 under conditions similar to today's and reflects all the author's virtues and vices—even his shockingly powerful hatred, which can vie with Kniébolo's own. Yet I find reading this to be not only entertaining but also downright bracing. It contains a true Arcanum aimed at our age and its debilities. When he lifts himself from his foul debasement to such heights, this Christian puts on an exceptional show, and the tops of his towers achieve rarified heights. This must be linked to the death wish that he often expresses with such power: desire to embody the philosopher's stone emerges from base, dark, seething turmoil as it strives for lofty sublimation.

PARIS, 16 JULY 1944

In the afternoon at La Roche-Guyon to see Speidel, who hosted us in his small study in the oldest part of the chateau below the Norman parapets. He had to make frequent phone calls. Kniébolo, who fears a new landing, wants to take command of two tank battalions after having made a personal assessment; he wants to give orders that differ from what the situation requires. Conversations included the topic of how much more time the Germans are going to take before they get this carnival huckster off their backs. Fate has started his countdown. This made me think of an expression of my father's: "A terrible misfortune has to happen before anything changes." And yet the general seemed to be in good spirits because he observed, "the essay on peace will soon be appearing."

I then drove with Podewils and Horst to Giverny. We called on Monet's daughter-in-law, who gave us the key to his garden. At the waterlily pond with its weeping willows, black poplars, bamboo borders, and half-derelict Chinese wooden bridges—there is magic in this place. Every wet pastureland contains these shallow pools filled with green water, edged with rushes and irises. Yet none seems more succulent, more suggestive, more colorful. A piece of nature like thousands of others made all the more distinguished by intellectual and creative vitality. Nineteenth-century science is also at home on this island, from which the artist took his astonishing colors as if from a retort, heated by the fire of the sun and cooled with water. Like our eyes, each little pool catches a universe of light. In the large studio in front of the waterlily cycle that Monet began working on when he was seventy-five. Here we can observe the creative rhythm of crystallization and dissolution that brings a spectacular convergence with the blue void and with Rimbaud's primeval azure slime. On one of the great panels a bundle of blue waterlilies takes shape at the edge of the pure wavering radiance like a tangle of tangible beams of light. Another picture shows only the sky with clouds reflected in the water in a way that makes one dizzy. The eye senses the daring nature of this gesture as well as the powerful visual achievement of the sublime disintegration and its agonies amid the cascading light. The final canvas in the series has been vandalized by knife gashes.

PARIS, 21 JULY 1944

Yesterday news spread of the assassination attempt. I found out details from the president when I returned from Saint-Cloud toward evening. This aggravates our extremely precarious situation. The plotter is said to be a certain Count Stauffenberg. I had already heard the name from Hofacker. This would confirm my opinion that at pivotal points the old aristocracy comes to the fore. Everything predicts that this act will generate appalling reprisals. It is getting more and more difficult to continue the masquerade. This led me to an exchange of words with a comrade this morning who called the event an "outrageous disgrace." And yet I've been convinced for a long time that assassinations change little and improve nothing. I implied as much in a description of Sunmyra in *The Marble Cliffs*.

By the afternoon, the news had circulated among the insiders that the commander-in-chief had been relieved of his duties and ordered to Berlin. As soon as the news came from the Bendlerstrasse,[166] he had all the SS and the intelligence officers arrested and then had to free them again after he had reported to Kluge in La Roche-Guyon and there was no longer any doubt that the assassination had failed. "Had the huge snake in a sack and then let it out again," as the president put it in a state of high agitation when we were consulting behind closed doors. The dry businesslike nature of the act is astonishing—the basis for his arrest was a simple phone call to the commander of Greater Paris. He was probably concerned that no more heads should roll than absolutely necessary, but that makes no difference to authorities like these. On top of that there was the completely incompetent Colonel von Linstow as chief of staff—a man with stomach problems who had been clued in shortly beforehand and was invaluable for his technical abilities; now he is seen slinking around the Raphael like a ghost before he disappears. If only my old NCO Kossmann were still in charge; at least he would have done what is expected of an officer on the General Staff, namely, verified the reliability of the reports. In addition there is Rommel's accident on 17 July,[167] which removed the only pillar that could have provided meaningful support for such an effort.

By contrast, the terrible activity of the *Volkspartei*[168] has hardly wavered in the wake of this offensive. Yes, it has been instructive. One does not heal the body during the crisis, neither in whole nor in part. Even if the operation were to succeed, today we would have instead of one pustule a dozen, with hanging judges holding court in every village, street, and house. We are undergoing a test that is justified and necessary; there is no reversing this machinery.

PARIS, 22 JULY 1944

Telephone call from General Loehning from Hannover reporting that everything in Kirchhorst is fine. His jokes surprised me, for without doubt all conversations are monitored. Immediately afterward, I got the terrible news from Neuhaus that yesterday on the way to Berlin, Heinrich von Stülpnagel had put his own pistol to his head. He is still alive, but he has lost his sight. That must have happened at the same hour for which he had invited me to his table for a philosophical discussion.

I was moved by the fact that during all the commotion, he actually canceled the meal. That is typical of his character.

Oh, how the victims are dying here, and especially in the smallest circles of the last chivalric men, of those freethinkers—the very people who are superior to the others, whose feelings and thoughts are but petty emotions. And yet these sacrifices are nonetheless important because they create an inner space and prevent the nation as a whole from falling into the horrifying depths of fate.

PARIS, 23 JULY 1944

I heard that the first question the general asked when he woke up blind was about the facilities at the hospital. He wanted to know whether the senior physician found everything satisfactory. He is already being isolated by attendants who are also guards; he is a prisoner.

I thought about our conversation by the fireplace in Vaux about Stoic philosophy and that the gate of death is always open to man, and that given this reality, decisive action is possible. These are frightening lessons.

PARIS, 24 JULY 1944

Visited General von Niedermayer in the afternoon, who vaguely reminds me of the Oriental scholar Hammer-Purgstall—I mean in the way that the Eastern ethos, the Asiatic spirit, can inhabit a person—his ideas, his deeds, even to the point of affecting his exterior.

In the army, the so-called German salute has been introduced as a sign that they have lost the contest.[169] This is one of the recent formalities to make people submit *sub jugo* [under the yoke] several times a day. This can also be seen as the progress of mechanization.

The Americans are in Pisa, the Russians in Lemberg [Lviv] and Lublin.

At the table we discussed Laval and his superstitions, including the one involving the white necktie he wears. He also always carries a copper two *sous* coin with him and steers clear of negotiations if he has forgotten it. He is convinced of his luck, of his guiding star, and took it as a particularly good omen that he had been born with a caul. At his birth, this lay upon his head, which popular superstition sees as an auspicious portent. Well, we shall see.

PARIS, 26 JULY 1944

At Vogel's in the evening. We talked about the details of the assassination attempt, which Vogel had been informed about. The effect of such actions is beyond calculation; usually very different forces are unleashed than what the perpetrator expected. They exert influence less in the direction than in the rhythm of historical events: the process is either accelerated or inhibited. An example of the first kind happened in response to an attempt on Lenin's life, whereas Fieschi's attack on Louis Phillippe retarded the progress of the democratic cause. Generally speaking, we can observe that an assassination attempt, if not actually abetting the cause of its target, at least propels it violently forward.

PARIS, 30 JULY 1944

A peculiar mechanism of history is that the flaws of the German are being exposed as the wheel of fortune carries him downward. He is now feeling the experience of the Jew: being a *skandalon* [stumbling block, offense]. Whenever the conversation would turn to this topic, Valeriu Marcu used to say that the vanquished are plague carriers.

Panic is spreading through the Raphael. Types are turning up who can't be called superiors in the old sense of the word. Instead they are commissars, and they are utterly destroying the last bonds that have remained intact since the days of Friedrich Wilhelm I.

My final breakfast with the Doctoresse. My way back takes me along Rue de Varenne, where as usual I am enchanted by the tall entryways typical of the old palaces of the Faubourg Saint-Germain. They were built to permit wagons piled high with hay access to the stables. A cloudburst drove me indoors for a short visit to the Musée Rodin, which would not have otherwise attracted me. *The Waves of Sea and Love.*[170] Future archaeologists may find these images right below the layer containing tanks and aerial bombs. People will then ask what could link the two so closely, and they will propose clever hypotheses.

PARIS, 31 JULY 1944

Max Valentiner arrived from Lyons. In the South, the pure ethos of the *lemures* seems to be spreading. For instance, he told about a woman who had already been in prison there for four months. Two henchmen of the Secret Service were discussing what to do with her since she showed little interest in the matter they had arrested her for. "We could shoot her too. Then we'd be rid of her."

PARIS, 1 AUGUST 1944

Visited Dr. Epting in the evening. He told me that Médan had been murdered in Aix. Now he, too, has fallen victim to the hatred that increases every day. His only crime was that he considered friendship between our two peoples possible. Expressing this sentiment, he once embraced me in 1930 when I met him in Aix for the first and only time in my life. We had each commanded combat patrols in World War I.

I have his last letter before me. It is from 15 July, where he writes, "If I am to die then I would rather it be in my house, or at least in my own city than somewhere by the roadside in a muddy ditch. That is more dignified and also less trouble."

He then added, *"Je tiens à vous dire que c'est l'amitié admirative que vous m'avez inspirée qui m'a rapproché de mes anciens adversaires de 1914/18."* [I must tell you that you have inspired in me admiration and friendship that have reconciled me to my former adversaries of 1914/18.]

I now see that these were meant deliberately as parting words—as was his prayer, which Claus Valentiner told me about: that God might prevent any young Frenchman from bringing guilt upon his head by shedding his blood. In these past weeks, I've become acquainted with bitterness that debases the best people.

In World War I, my friends were killed by bullets—in this second war, that is the privilege of the lucky ones. The others are rotting in prisons, must take their own lives, or die by the executioner's hand. They are denied the bullet.

PARIS, 5 AUGUST 1944

The Americans have reached Rennes, Mayenne, Laval, and have cut off Brittany. I am making my farewell visits; this evening I was with Salmanoff. Even my barber, who has been cutting my hair for years, seemed to have the feeling that he was performing his office for the last time. His farewell reflected the mentality of his class and of his sympathy for me: "*J'espère que les chose s'arrangeront.*" [I hope things will work out.]

PARIS, 8 AUGUST 1944

Stood outside the portal of Sacré Coeur to cast a last glance over the great city. I watched the stones quiver in the hot sun, as if in expectation of new historical embraces. Cities are feminine and only smile on the victor.

PARIS, 10 AUGUST 1944

Visited Florence at noon. This may be our final Thursday.

Walked back through the heat on Rue Copernic. There I purchased a little notebook of the kind I used to use when I was a journalist in more stirring times. As I walked out of the shop I ran into Marcel Arland, whom I became aware of in the last weeks after reading his novel. I respect his courage, which at times approaches hubris. We shook hands.

> *J'aime les raisins glacés*
> *Par ce qu'ils n'ont pas de goût,*
> *J'aime les camélias*
> *Parce qu'ils n'ont pas d'odeur.*
> *Et j'aime les hommes riches*
> *Par ce qui'ils n'ont pas de coeur.*

[I love candied grapes / Because they have no taste, / I love camellias / Because they have no fragrance / And I love rich men / Because they have no heart.]

The verses suggested the notion of including dandyism as one of the precursors of nihilism in my treatise.

PARIS, 13 AUGUST 1944

Farewell visits in the afternoon; last times together. Walk with Charmille along the banks of the Seine. Every great watershed is expressed in countless private goodbyes.

4

KIRCHHORST DIARIES

EN ROUTE, 14 AUGUST 1944

Left in haste when it got dark. I straightened up my room, placed a bouquet of flowers on the table, and distributed tips. Unfortunately, I left some irreplaceable letters behind in a cupboard drawer.

SAINT-DIÉ, 15 AUGUST 1944

Journey via Sézanne, Saint-Dizier, Toul, Nancy, to Saint-Dié in Lothringen [Lorraine]. The roads shimmered in the late summer light; fighter-bombers patrolled overhead. We drove past numerous burning vehicles. Others had already been reduced to white dust.

SAINT-DIÉ, 17 AUGUST 1944

Stayed in a garrison that was called Witzleben Barracks just a few days ago, but which has now been stripped of this name.[1] During the night, vivid dreams in extremely sharp outline, just like looking through a telescope the wrong way around so that not only the shapes but also the colors were intensified. I was standing on a marble staircase with snakes slithering up the steps.

With Klaebisch in Hotel Moderne in the evening. He had brought along a comrade who debriefed us on the progress of our withdrawal from Paris. Kniébolo's strict order to blow up the bridges over the Seine and leave a trail of devastation behind had not been carried out. It appears that among those courageous souls who resisted this desecration, friend Speidel was at the forefront right beside Choltitz.

SAINT-DIÉ, 18 AUGUST 1944

Arrival of the president yesterday evening; Neuhaus and Humm accompanied him. The president inspected my room once more; he found it tidy and in good order. Our farewell from the staff of the Raphael was cordial, even emotional.

In the afternoon had a swim in the Meurthe. Its surface was glassy, but with clear ripples that carried curling strands of pale green aquatic plants. Had a view of the round-topped foothills of the Vosges.

Current reading: Maurice de La Fuye's *Louis XVI*. Given the events of our day and age, this king's reputation gains as much as Napoleon's loses. Such reversals are evidence of the degree to which historiography depends upon the historical process itself. In some obscure way, all clocks that have run down seem to be connected to the great clock of fate.

The destruction of the Old World begins to manifest itself with the French Revolution, or rather with the Renaissance, and corresponds to the dying of organic fibers, of nerves and arteries. Once the process is complete, men of violence appear; they attach artificial threads and string to the corpse and manipulate it in a more intense and also more grotesque political game. They themselves embody this character of jumping jacks—a quality that is shrill, blatant, and often frightening. Modern nation-states tend toward weakness. They can only prosper where some legacy is available. When that is consumed, the hunger becomes unbearable, and, like Saturn, they devour their own children. It is thus out of pure self-preservation that we might contemplate other systems of organization than those established in 1789.

SAINT-DIÉ, 20 AUGUST 1944

Took a walk with the president to the large cemetery up the hill. As usual when I have such opportunities, I note a few inscriptions for my journal. Among these were the following from a small oval bronze plaque:

Ici repose Paul Rotsart, Bon de Mertaing.[2]
Né à Bruges (Belgique). Mort loin de sa
Famille pour ses idées trop liberals.

1835–1885

[Here rests Paul Rotsart, Baron de Mertaing. / Born in Bruges (Belgium). Dead far from his / Family for his too liberal ideas. / 1835–1885.]

When I ponder such a short life span, I sometimes get the feeling that I am understanding the fate of an anonymous person more deeply than any biography can convey. The details melt away.

Saint-Dié, 21 August 1944

Read further in *Louis XVI*. Certain sections, like the flight to Varennes, move me so powerfully that I have to alternate my reading with chapters from Dauzat's *Géographie linguistique*.

De La Fuye notes that the flight to Varennes is remarkable for a host of symbolic references and cites examples of these. There is nothing astonishing about this, for the more significant an event, the more meaningful its details will be. In moments of earth-shaking consequence, the core of symbolic connections is revealed. Golgotha thus becomes the hill of the world; the cross, the fate of man; Christ becomes mankind.

Went swimming in the Meurthe in stormy weather. There I joined some boys in a hunt; they were turning over rocks in the current and using forked spears to impale fish hiding underneath. The finger-length creatures were marbled (or rather, flecked) with green and strung on a line in great numbers "*pour faire la friture*" [for frying]. This process was delightful for that small-scale economy Goethe appreciated so much, in contrast to the greater one.

In the evening read further in *Géographie linguistique*, from which I took a few notes for my work about language and physique. The question of literature has been bothering me since this orgy of fire began. We shall learn to appreciate the fact that countries like Switzerland have been spared. Incidentally I consider the Swiss support of the reestablishment of intellectual and cultural standards to be their contribution to the incredible advantage of neutrality. This is no longer a given, because it is not the balance of power, but rather the fate of the world at stake. In this respect, the preservation of Switzerland is a particularly happy outcome, and not just for the neutral nations, but for everyone else as well. Something of the riches of the past survives here.

Saint-Dié, 22 August 1944

New arrivals, including Lämpchen,[3] who took a walk with me along the Meurthe, and Toepfer, who was still in Paris on Saturday evening, the day before yesterday. Our troops had established defensive positions[4] around the Majestic and around the Ministry of the Navy. Rifle shots could be heard on the island [Île de la Cité], on the Place de la Concorde, and in the outer suburbs. On many streets people were already displaying the *tricoleur* [flag] from their windows.

Saint-Dié, 23 August 1944

The Americans have entered Paris. Went to the Meurthe again in the afternoon. The tops of the Vosges mountain range and their dark cliffs have a calming effect and convey a sense of earthly stability.

While sunbathing, I thought about the consonant clusters *cl, kl*, as well as *schl*—perhaps sounds the lips make in imitation of something closing. For example, *clef, claves, χλεἴξ, klappe, clapier, claustrum, clandestine, Schlinge, Schluss*.[5] Here we have connections that transcend time. Modern etymology with its derivations persists in the same empiricism as Darwinism in zoology.

Walked in the darkness through the forbidden gardens.

SAINT-DIÉ, 24 AUGUST 1944

Toepfer came by in the afternoon and took part of my *Appeal* with him to Hamburg for Ziegler. I am carrying a further portion of the essay among my portable files. The third section stayed behind in Paris, while the fourth is concealed beneath the false bottom of an insect display case in Kirchhorst.

In the evening went to the hunting lodge in the forest with the president and Lämpchen, who drove us.

I have come to understand diversity and its various systems—such as that found among insects. The appeal lies in their visual display embedded by those hundred thousand facets of *natura naturata* in the core of the *natura naturans.*[6] The beams of light are those of an inverted prism. They dazzle the eye primarily by reflecting the colors of the spectrum. In the realm of variegated color, our sense of wonder predominates; in white light, by contrast, we respond with joyous and apprehensive dread. The mind descends into the treasure grottoes where the great *sigillum* [seal] resides, the prototype for all subsequent creation.

And then, the workshops. When I look down from the cliffs into the coral gardens into the activity of the colorful creatures at the life source—how superior are such images to all destruction of individuals, to all selfish enmities. I have gained magnificent insights, and I am overcome by a feeling of gratitude when I consider that I may still have many a year of such visions before me.

SAINT-DIÉ, 28 AUGUST 1944

Life is like a stalk of bamboo that forms recurrent nodes, thereby achieving height and strength. Similarly, now and again we encounter forces when purely chronological progress, the aging process, becomes concentrated in a meaningful way. These are birthdays in a higher sense, stages of maturation and not mere aging. When we die, we close the circle of life again before the fecundity of eternity.

SAINT-DIÉ, 29 AUGUST 1944

A group of soldiers is billeted at a farm. When chickens are stolen, straw is confiscated without a receipt, or further excesses take place, someone or other among them will recognize the illegality and try to prevent it. It might be the farmer's son who is looking out for his father's property. When the order came to arrest hostages, I observed among the upper echelons, such as those of the commander-in-chief, that members of the staff were deeply affected and suffered as if the act cut to the core of their consciences. On the other hand, a primitive person follows the maxim, "anything my group does is good," and unfortunately, it seems that this primitive behavior is increasing unchecked and with it, the bestial character of politics.

What can one advise a man, especially a simple man, to do in order to extricate himself from the conformity that is constantly being produced by technology? Only prayer. Here even the lowest human being has a vantage point that makes him part of the whole and not just a cog in the machinery. Extraordinary benefit surges from this source as well as self-mastery. This applies beyond the bounds of any theology. In situations that can cause the cleverest of us to fail and the bravest of us to look for avenues of escape, we occasionally see someone who quietly recognizes the right thing to do and does good. You can be sure that is a man who prays.

Saint-Dié, 30 August 1944

In the afternoon with the president on La Roche Saint-Martin, one of the nearby peaks marked by a cliff of red sandstone. From its summit, we had a panoramic view across the green meadows and the dark rounded hilltops of the Vosges region.

Saint-Dié, 1 September 1944

In the evening, read the book by Filon about Empress Eugénie. All the while rifle shots echoed from the nearby Kempberg [mountain]; now it is in the hands of the Maquis.[7] Began preparations for defending the cottage where Sergeant Schröter and I were sharing quarters. It was like remembering an ancient, half-forgotten craft.

In a dream, I was walking through a magnificent city. It was far more elegant than all the others I have known, chiefly because ancient Chinese and European designs merged there. I saw the street of grave monuments, the marketplace, the tall buildings of red granite.

As usual when I take such strolls, I also collected a few beetles in my ether flask. When I emptied it to examine my booty, I noticed two or three creatures I did not recall picking up. Among them was an almost transparent carnelian red *Anoxia* [dung beetle]. Upon awakening, however, I recalled that a few nights ago, in a different dream, I had thrown it into the flask, and was astonished that it seemed as if it were something intruding into this world in such a strangely concrete way.

I'll make the journey to Hannover tomorrow; the military commander's staff is disbanding.

Saint-Dié, 2 September 1944

Cavalry Captain Adler has just returned from a conference at headquarters. Himmler gave a speech there, too. His message was that one had to be tough. He told about a junior officer who had deserted and been returned to his battalion busy drilling in the barracks courtyard. The matter moved quickly and a verdict was reached. The man was forced to dig his own grave and then shot. The earth was thrown on top of him and stamped down. Then the drilling continued as if nothing had happened.

This is one of the most gruesome acts I have ever heard of in this world of butchery.

Colmar, 3 September 1944

In Colmar by evening. A splendid rainbow shimmered over its houses. I spent the night in the room of a doctor in a cot covered with black oilcloth where he examined his patients. When I opened the window another rainbow hung there in the heavy atmosphere, magically connecting the Vosges with the Black Forest.

KIRCHHORST, 4 SEPTEMBER 1944

Early morning arrival in Hannover, where I was able to get a few hours of sleep. I then reported to General Loehning and, on my way, noticed to my amazement the green vegetation that was already covering the ruins. Grasses and plants had sprung up on the masonry rubble in the city center.

Kirchhorst. Was welcomed home. New refugees in the house. The garden gone to seed. Fences in disrepair. The hallways are overflowing with suitcases and crates.

The walnut tree I planted in 1940 is bearing its first fruit.

KIRCHHORST, 7 SEPTEMBER 1944

New housing for refugees in the village—this time they are Dutch, people who no longer felt safe in their own country. The persecutions will be called by other names, but they won't stop.

In the afternoon Dr. Göpel arrived. He was on his way from Amsterdam to Dresden. He reported that Drieu La Rochelle had shot himself in Paris. It seems to be a law that people who support intercultural friendship out of noble motives must fall, while the crass profiteers get away with everything. They say Montherlant is being harassed. He was still caught up in the notion that chivalrous friendship is possible; now he is being disabused of that idea by louts.

KIRCHHORST, 9 SEPTEMBER 1944

Visit from Ziegler, with whom I discussed printing my *Appeal*. He always carries it with him in his briefcase. I heard from him that Benoist Méchin had been shot by terrorists in Paris.

KIRCHHORST, 16 SEPTEMBER 1944

Endless squadrons overhead. Misburg, their main target nearby, was hit again and huge oil reserves have been burning off beyond the moor beneath the clouds of leaden smoke. Since 1940, the sounds of the night have become significantly more ominous; the impression of impending catastrophe is growing.

I have been placed on furlough with the reserve command staff and am awaiting the final stage of the process. This, too, is extraordinarily dangerous; it is how the *lemures* commit a great number of murders that are identified by the postmortem conditions of the corpses. They are carrying out a kind of anticipatory revenge that has already claimed the former Communist leader, Thälmann, and the Social Democrat Breitscheit as victims. If they were more intelligent, one could quote Seneca to them, "No matter how many you may kill, your successors will not be among them." One can only hope that they don't have much longer to wait. Apparently, a huge number of the aristocrats in Pomerania have already been assassinated.

KIRCHHORST, 17 SEPTEMBER 1944

Out on the moor with Alexander and Ernstel, whom I found still weakened after his incarceration. He has reported to an armored unit, but I get the impression that he is not yet up to the rigors of the training. I am especially pleased that he does not harbor any resentment.

As I watched him sitting exhausted, at the edge of the woods, it became clear to me what a terrifying situation we are in. Compared to this, the acrid odor of the burnt-out cities is paltry.

Kirchhorst, 18 September 1944

My current reading includes *L'Ile de Ceylan et ses Curiosités Naturelles* [*The Island of Ceylon and Its Natural Curiosities*] by Octave Sachot (Paris, 1863). The work has a nice excerpt about daily activity in the tropics from the book by Sir James Emerson Tennent. I've been on the lookout for this volume for a while.

Visit in the afternoon from Gustav Schenk. Years ago I corresponded with him about the spotted arum [jack-in-the-pulpit]. Discussed the hallucinogenic peyote cactus, and then the three-day fast he is preparing for. Much reminded me of my years following World War I, when I was always keeping an eye out for those extra tickets to the spiritual heights. It is, of course, better to choose the portals that are open to everyone.

Discussed the situation. Our Fatherland is like a poor man whose just cause has been usurped by a crooked lawyer.

Kirchhorst, 21 September 1944

Worked a little bit on the "Path of Masirah." I began by inventing the names and writing the introduction.

Beobachten [observe, watch] and *Betrachten* [look at, view, regard]—here we have a subtle difference between concrete and abstract seeing: *Ich betrachte den Zeiger der Uhr* [I am looking at the hand of the clock] but *Ich beobachte seinen Lauf* [I observe its movement].

In the morning, I looked for Banville's *Odes Funambulesques*, which was brought to my attention thanks to a remark of Verlaine's. Although I searched carefully in the library and the study, I was unable to find the book, so I thought I had lost it. But then I found it among my signed copies, because it bears a dedication from the author to Elisabeth Autement.

It's a nice image: after believing we have lost something, we then find it in a more distinguished form.

Kirchhorst, 2 October 1944

Current reading: the Greek myths in the version by Schwab. Despite several shortcomings, it has enjoyable qualities in its description of the ancient pagan world. Schwab captures the clear, still, crystalline depths of its domain, where the spiritual conceptions and births take place before and outside of history. The origin precedes the beginning.

Yesterday evening I read in the second volume as far as the beautiful passage where Agamemnon is compared to Odysseus. There we read that, when standing, the Shepherd of the People[8] was the taller of the two men, while Odysseus was taller when they were seated.

After a short sleep, I was awakened by the noise of an intense barrage. Perpetua got up and dressed our little son while I watched the spectacle standing at the window in my dressing gown. We could hear the roar of myriad engines and watched as shells soared high into the sky—no bigger than the sparks that spew from burning steel in the forge. Then beyond the moor, at Anderten, red flames erupted. A long, shrill whistle immediately followed; now all attention, all fear, seemed focused on a red arrow falling out of the sky to earth. I stepped back, and immediately felt a fiery punch that shook the house to its foundation. We hurried downstairs to reach the garden and found the door jammed shut by the shockwaves, but panes of glass from its windows lay shattered in the hallway. The exit facing the meadow was still unobstructed. We carried the children outside through it, while shrapnel hissed down through the treetops. Down in the air-raid shelter, we waited for the bombardment to end.

A blockbuster bomb had fallen onto the field halfway between Kirchhorst and Stelle. It damaged the Cohrs's farm primarily and ripped off roofs for some distance around. In our house, a crack goes from the cellar down into the ground below; the stairwell sags, and the roof shows signs of damage.

The mail brought a letter from Ruth Speidel. She reports that the general has been arrested. With him, the last participant at the historical conference of La Roche-Guyon has been caught, and all the rest are dead.

KIRCHHORST, 4 OCTOBER 1944

I am removing the tomato plants in the glaring autumn sun, while the admiral butterflies flutter around. The blade glides through the succulent stalks; my hands become impregnated with the tangy aroma. When I wash them, the rinse water flows dark green.

The search for mushrooms on the cow paths. From a distance, we can make our way toward these bright gleaming clusters. The most beautiful ones are like eggs, completely closed. But the others are exquisite, too—the pink-ribbed gills that smell faintly of anise and are visible through their torn membranes. They are grasped on the stalk with the whole hand like the clapper of a bell and then pulled out gently, letting their firm, waxy skin cool the fingers.

Turned to the task of putting my hunting books in order.[9] Today, I entered the locations where I found *Dromius meridionalis* [ground beetle]. It was mostly underneath chestnut husks in Parisian cemeteries, for example, not far from Verlaine's grave at Batignolles. Others came from the bark of the large sycamores that line the banks near the bridge of Puteaux. The beautiful work of Jeannel gives me to understand that this is a variety dispersed particularly around the Atlantic. In addition to Great Britain and Ireland, he lists among their habitats São Miguel and Terceira in the Azores. In fact one of my own specimens is labeled: "Ponta Delgada, São Miguel, 26 October 1936." There was a blue carapace sunning itself on the silvery-gray bark of a felled laurel tree. This shows that within my own extensive hunting grounds, I am not unacquainted with the territory from the North Cape to the oases of the Sahara, and from the islands of the Yellow Sea to the Hesperides. Despite the inhospitable nature of our times, I am still looking forward to further wonderful campaigns in this region.

KIRCHHORST, 6 OCTOBER 1944

On the moor. The golden crowns of the woods gleam in the distance accentuated by blue shadows. The autumn sun produces an abundance of blue. The same applies to the spirit. Autumn brings out metaphysics and also melancholy.

I need a lot of sleep, long nights. The brain is like the liver of Prometheus: plucked from his body by the eagle, it must regenerate in darkness.

Fruits of my reading: *Arbeiten über morphologische und taxonomische Entomologie* [*Essays on Morphological and Taxonomic Entomology*].

Here I find mentioned an article on the honeybee in ancient India, published in 1886 by Professor Ferdinand Karsch, and what is more, under the pseudonym "Canus."

A similar pseudonym was the one used by J. Ch. F. Haug, who signed himself "Hophthalmos."

After a period of great fasting, the German was led to the mountaintop by Kniébolo and shown dominion over the world. It did not take much urging before he was worshipping his tempter.

KIRCHHORST, 11 OCTOBER 1944

Dreamed about my father last night. We were playing chess in two different rooms; I was in the outer room, but we could see each other through a sliding door that gradually opened as the game progressed.

Afterward, was standing before a building that held memories for me. At first it seemed to be the demolished and then reconstructed house of my grandmother. Then it was the one belonging to Florence on Avenue de Malakoff; then it was on Rue du Cherche-Midi. That is the tremendous thing about dreams: they echo the archetypes—here, the one of "the lost house." In light of such imagery, individual experience becomes indistinct. Only the deeper sorrow remains intact. Something similar happens at dusk when individual traits are blurred and general ones become more distinct. At the threshold of that night of death, we will finally recognize the identity of such experiences and the illusion of the world of numbers. There exists but one number, just as there is but one human being. Eros strains to reach him.

KIRCHHORST, 12 OCTOBER 1944

Dreamed about my father again last night. We were together on a stairway; he was bringing me wine from the cellar to drink on my journey. Then I was back in Paris.

Air-raid sirens in the morning, just the way they gradually wear down the populations in the cities.

Schenk encouraged me to assemble a collection of seed specimens from plants. The result would not just be a formidable archive of tangible objects, but one that also included their powers, poisons, medicinal, and hallucinogenic properties. Fields of flowers, forests, and flower gardens also would be concentrated in that vial.

Worked further on "The Path of Masirah." Working in a new area may be too different, too strenuous for this day and age. I am now using an ink that flows blue from my pen but turns a deep, dark color overnight. This feature clearly differentiates the new work; I can now see the freshly plowed furrows in the field.

KIRCHHORST, 15 OCTOBER 1944

Squadrons overhead during the night. A great fire blazed over toward Braunschweig. Low-flying aircraft circled the region at breakfast. The house shook under the bombardment.

KIRCHHORST, 18 OCTOBER 1944

Worked more on "The Path of Masirah" despite the huge hardships these days. It's strange how difficult it is to come up with names for characters in such stories, even though we have the whole alphabet at our disposal. It's no less strange that they can seldom be changed once the text has been developed past the beginning. The characters that bear them have then achieved their own life, their own reality.

The use of the past perfect tense over the course of long paragraphs makes a text wooden. It is preferable to use the imperfect [simple past] at the cost of grammatical precision and just let the past perfect be audible on occasion. The reader then remains in the temporal dimension of the narrative. Style permits carelessness, but not outright mistakes.

Went to the Oldhorst Moor with Ernstel in the afternoon. The pale pink plant with waxy blossoms that I collected for my moor herbarium turned out to be bog rosemary. At eight o'clock in the evening as I sat at my microscope, warnings of enemy aircraft came through. The planes themselves followed shortly thereafter. We could see red and green Christmas trees[10] over the city where the southern section was being transformed into a boiling cauldron of explosions. A farm in Neuwarmbüchen went up in flames.

Kniébolo's radio appeal for the formation of *Volkssturm* [civil defense; home guard] battalions makes it easier to institute new policies of annihilation that are directed against the populace as a whole. All his ideas turn out to be experiments that are then applied to the Germans on a large scale. I am thinking of the bombing of the synagogues, the destruction of the Jews, the bombardment of London, the flying bombs, et cetera. He demonstrates primarily that such deeds are imaginable and possible; he destroys all safeguards and gives the masses a chance to show their approval. The frenetic acclaim that accompanied his rise to power was essentially the approval of self-destruction, a deeply nihilistic act. My horror stems from the fact that, from the start, I could sense the terrifying cheering for the Pied Piper. Of course, Kniébolo is a European phenomenon as well. Germany's central location will always make it the place where such things appear first and most distinctly.

KIRCHHORST, 20 OCTOBER 1944
I heard from Army High Command that my discharge has gone through. People in Berlin even seem to have been in a hurry to get rid of me by this method. Now I can work here a little bit, as if I were on a sinking ship or in a city under siege, where one presents the wave offering[11] before deserted altars. A good thing that the whole publishing business is collapsing. That makes my work more meaningful and more futile. By the same token, we might engrave chalices to offer to the sun and then cast them into the sea.

In the city, I discovered that the attack that happened the day before yesterday took many lives. Most were crushed by the crowds in front of the bunker doors. Some bunkers have flights of steps leading down; some individuals jump over the railing onto the people crowded together below. When they land, they break people's cervical vertebrae. Harry witnessed one of these entrances to the inferno; the wailing and moaning from the dark shaft penetrated far and wide through the night.

Afterward went with Schenk to the studio of Grethe Jürgens, where we chatted about plant life on the moors and the small islands.

Return trip via Bothfeld. I visited the cemetery and, among the graves noticed that of W., a man with whom my father went to court over land disputes. Now both are lying in the same earth and returning to it. What is left to us from this life if we do not accumulate worth that can be exchanged for gold at the tollgate to death's realm, to be exchanged for eternity?

In my dream I was dining with the commander-in-chief in the evening, and while doing so I thought, "So the reports of his death were wrong." But I could see the pale scar of the pistol shot on his temple.

KIRCHHORST, 25 OCTOBER 1944
In the afternoon, I took Ernstel to the station in Burgdorf. He is still debilitated from his time in prison; his feet are also still sore from the marching. Yet he didn't want his comrades, who are ready to head out, to leave without him. We embraced each other in the small chilly passageway that leads to the platform.

KIRCHHORST, 27 OCTOBER 1944
In Bothfeld for my discharge from military service. Since the war has now become ubiquitous, it hardly changes anything. On the way, I found a fragment of a horseshoe.

KIRCHHORST, 28 OCTOBER 1944
Current reading: Léon Bloy again, this time his diaries, followed by *Sueur de Sang* [*Sweating Blood*], containing a description of his (probably largely invented) adventures as one of the *Francs-tireurs*[12] during the winter of 1870–1871. This

foreshadows the current situation with the partisans and *maquisards*. In recounting the deeds he ascribes to the Germans, hardly any atrocity is omitted. But among the actions of his own heroes, Bloy praises the bludgeoning of adversaries with machetes and bottles, burnings with petroleum, desecration of corpses, and more. This reaches the level of the horrors of Tantalus.[13] Bloy is like a tree rooted deep in a swamp yet producing sublime blossoms at its top. My own relationship to him—repellent in so many ways—makes me recognize the degree that my own work has purged me of national hatred.

Myth and science. One interprets the world, the other explains it. When Palinurus[14] falls asleep at the helm, a god touches his eyelids. A chemist attributes this phenomenon to the accumulation of lactic acid in the tissues. Alchemy offers a strange intermediate notion—experimentally scientific while in theory mythological.

Friedrich Georg is right when he says that the Titanic world is closer to the technical than to the Olympian world. The Titans sought refuge and shelter from Hephaestus, the only god one could call a technician. The scene is superbly described when they pitch in eagerly in his workshop to forge the weapons of Aeneas.

Seen in mythical terms, the sinking of the *Titanic* after it struck an iceberg corresponds to the Tower of Babel in the Pentateuch. The ship is a Tower of Babel *en pleine vitesse* [at full speed]. Not only is the name symbolic, but so are almost all the details. Baal, the Golden Calf, famous gems and mummies of the pharaohs—it's all there.

KIRCHHORST, 30 OCTOBER 1944

Went to Celle, where I had things to do. The spirit of the first settlers lingers on in the abandoned farms along the way. Back then royal favor was dispensed to everyone. When that disappears in human beings, we experience periods like the one we have today. Loss of sovereignty precedes an assault upon dignity.

Read further in Léon Bloy. The effect he has derives from the fact that he represents the human being per se in all his infamy but also in all his glory.

Through my bedroom window, I gaze out into the morning fog, where the leaves of the grapevine are turning pale yellow at my windowsill. Their tips are turning red, as if dipped in blood. The life of plants and their cycle ensures the reality that is threatened with dissolution by demonic powers. The adversaries of the Head Forester[15] are gardeners and botanists.

When the blockbuster bomb fell, the walls of the house seemed to be rendered transparent, as if only the organic shell of beams and rafters might hold up.

Went to the cemetery, where since time immemorial indigenous families have lain: the Ebelings, the Grethes, the Lahmanns, the Rehbocks, the Schüddekopfs.

The act of dying must produce a significant gesture, perhaps one of genius. Whenever I receive death announcements, I consistently notice that a kind of emotion grips me and I feel astonished disbelief. It is as though the departed had passed a difficult examination and achieved something I had not believed him capable of. At that moment, the contours of his life are instantly transformed in the most wonderful way.

Thought about Lessing and his poem dedicated to the dead baboon:

Hier liegt er nun, der kleine, liebe Pavian,
Der uns so manches nachgethan!
Ich wette, was er itzt gethan
Thun wir ihm alle nach, dem lieben Pavian.

[Now here he lies, the little, sweet baboon, / Who imitated us so well! / I'll bet that what he did, we'll soon / Imitate ourselves, that sweet baboon.]

KIRCHHORST, 1 NOVEMBER 1944

First day of November. The fighting continues in Holland, in Alsace, in East Prussia, in Poland, in Hungary, in Czechoslovakia, in Greece, the Balkans, and Italy. Tremendous escalation of the air war concentrating on Germany.

We hear that Holland seeks restitution for those parts of its land that were flooded by annexing German territory. Old mistakes seem to get repeated while the world—instead of learning from the emergence of Kniébolo—seems indebted to him as its example.

Concerning prayer. It possesses a conductive power, in the sense of a superior mechanism that dissipates and depletes fear. In ages when the practice is lost, large indigestible masses of feral dread build up in populations. In the same proportion, our freedom of will and powers of resistance diminish; the appeal of demonic powers becomes more compelling, and its imperatives more terrible.

Prayer clears the air. In this sense, the sound of bells represents collective prayer, the unmediated prayer of the church. This has been replaced by the wail of sirens, some of which are even mounted on the church towers.

KIRCHHORST, 2 NOVEMBER 1944

Current reading: The tome by Volhard about cannibalism that Schenk brought me contains a wealth of material. The conclusions are less exhaustive; it's also difficult to judge the ramifications of such a phenomenon. It is presented here like the "behavior of fishes"—meaning that they devour each other—and then it becomes incorporated into higher culture.

There are significant individual myths dispersed across our planet suggesting that superior sacrifices triumphed over cannibalism. In the South Seas, on the evening before a festival, the son of a king meets a slave wrapped in crimson robes and asks him where he's going. The man answers that he is on his way to the royal palace; he has been designated as the ritual meal. In reply, the king's son promises to save him, goes to the palace in his place, and lets himself be wrapped in palm leaves. When he is served before the king in this manner, the wrapping is opened, revealing to the king his son rather than his slave. This sight rouses and moves the father so much that he forbids the slaughter of human beings forever after. Here we perceive an echo of the highest theme of the human race.

For Indo-European peoples, a dreadful taboo must have been associated with human flesh since ancient times. This is suggested by our own folktales. The curse of Tantalus can also be traced back to a meal. The power of the prohibition can be gauged by the fact that even this war, which was instigated for the basest reasons, has hardly made a dent in it. This is surely noteworthy when we realize who the perpetrators are. Any rationalist economy, no less than any consistent racial doctrine, must essentially lead to cannibalism.

The theory of these matters is, incidentally, best worked out by the Anglo-Saxons, men like Swift. In Huxley's *Brave New World* the corpses are exploited for their phosphorus content and their economic viability.

KIRCHHORST, 3 NOVEMBER 1944

In the mail, a letter from Ina Speidel, the general's daughter. She writes that Horst was also arrested on 29 October. Our old circle of the Knights of Saint George[16] and our cohort from the Hotel Raphael have been drastically winnowed. Some have been hanged, poisoned, imprisoned; others have been dispersed and surrounded by thugs.

The German language still possesses country lanes, whereas French runs on tracks. As a consequence, conventional nonindividual elements are on the increase [in German]. We need a liaison officer.[17]

Rivarol's observation seems apt here: "if vowels and consonants were to attract each like magnetic substances, according to the laws of nature, then language would resemble the universe, unified and immutable."

Visit from Hanne Wickenberg in the afternoon; she was recently surprised by a daylight raid on Hannover when she was in the old part of the city. She described the scenes that took place in the air-raid bunkers. The bombs screamed down nearby. Dust and smoke got in through a small window and made all the faces indistinguishable. The space was filled with sighs, screams, and groans; women fainted. People tied cloths over the children's faces because they would vomit from fear. One woman was about to give birth:

"A doctor, quickly, a doctor. It's starting to burn. It's burning."

Other voices responded:

"Where is the fire? For heaven's sake, where?"

By the end, not one of the people inside was able to stand up any longer. They lay there quaking, foaming at the mouth, stretched out on the floor. Even sturdy Hanne said: "I was worn out when it was all over."[18]

KIRCHHORST, 4 NOVEMBER 1944

Massive detachment of aircraft overhead around noon, during which everyone in the house gathered in our little air-raid shelter. First came a squadron of forty planes, which took heavy anti-aircraft fire. Two were seen to have smoke trails; one made a hairpin turn in flames and disappeared in a white cloud that showered debris.

Huge numbers of bombs followed, glistening silvery white in the sunshine. The anti-aircraft fire surged to full force and occasionally the air was filled with the whistling of incoming bombs. I watched the events from our garden but entered the shelter during the worst parts. Just after the planes passed—the wind was from the west—thick clouds blowing over from the city obscured the view.

The roar of the squadrons darkening the sky is so strong that it drowns out the defensive fire and even the detonation of the bombs themselves. It is like standing under a bell filled with a buzzing swarm of metallic bees. The incredible energy of our age—otherwise diffused far and wide—emerges from its abstract potential and becomes perceptible to our senses. The impression of the squadrons lumbering on undeterred even when planes are exploding in their midst, is mightier than the detonation of the bombs themselves. We see the will to destroy, even at the cost of one's own destruction. This is a demonic trait.

I was pleased with little Alexander and his courage—astonishing when we think about the monstrous weapons of destruction confronting such a tiny heart: "Now I really am having heart palpitations," when the bombs screamed past and (as we later discovered) hit near the autobahn.

In the evening, there was a further attack with countless Christmas trees. Below them it was like a great array of gleaming white Christmas presents all spread out. Fires also tinged the horizon with red. A new anti-aircraft battery has been put in place at the edge of the moor woodland. Whenever it fires a shell, the house is jolted to its foundation.

When the alert sounds, the children are hustled into their little coats and, as soon as the droning of the aircraft or the noise of the first rounds reaches us, they are led to the shelter. Only thirteen-year-old Edmund Schultz remains out in the garden taking risks. His Aunt Fritzi stays in the house and occasionally looks out, remarkably unconcerned. I'm glad to see that a fearless soul stays indoors. As for me, I go indoors now and then to see that things are under control. At those moments, it's strange to observe how the demonic powers deplete our communal spirit, especially our basic stability. I have the feeling of moving through the staterooms of a ship, particularly when I glimpse the illuminated dial of the radio. Aside from the red glow of the stove, this is the only light that penetrates the darkness of this strictly enforced blackout. The genderless voice of an announcer reports the maneuvers of the squadron up to the moment when they "are entering the city limits with bombardment to follow immediately." I sometimes listen to other stations; many places on our planet are broadcasting dance music; others present scholarly lectures. Radio London transmits news and comforting words and reminds its listeners at the end to switch to a different frequency. In between come the rolling echoes of the detonations.

KIRCHHORST, 5 NOVEMBER 1944

After eating went to church, where several panes of glass in the lovely rose window over the altar have been shattered.

General Loehning came for coffee accompanied by Schenk and Diels, who has particular insight into the political underworld—especially knowledge of the origins of the *Staatspolizei* [State Police], which he in fact founded.[19] From him,

I heard details about horrifying suffering inflicted on friends and acquaintances before they were executed. Schulenburg, for example, was (like his coconspirators) addressed as "*Schurke* [scoundrel] Schulenburg" or "*Verbrecher* [criminal] Schulenburg" by the president of the People's Court.[20] At one point, when this hangman type accidentally addressed him as "*Graf* [Count] Schulenburg," he corrected himself with a bow; "Excuse me: *Schurke* Schulenburg, if you please." A trait that brought him vividly to my mind.

Diels also mentioned Röpke, *Die Gesellschaftskrisis der Gegenwart* [*The Social Crisis of Our Time*], a book that is apparently being widely read abroad. This is something Diels seems intimately familiar with; the general said that he had been observed with one of the chiefs of the Secret Service at a Turkish airport.

KIRCHHORST, 6 NOVEMBER 1944

Took a walk in the afternoon to Moormühle and Schillerslage as far as the boulder with the horseshoe. Had a look there at the animals that had fallen into the holes dug along the road as shelter from dive-bombers.

As I walked, I thought about the cursory style of contemporary thinkers, the way they pronounce judgment on ideas and symbols that people have been working on and creating for millennia. In doing so, they are unaware of their own place in the universe, and of that little bit of destructive work allocated to them by the world spirit. But what is it, other than foam that sprays its fleeting whitecaps over the solid ancient cliffs? We can already feel the incipient tug of the undertow.

It's also wonderful to watch the drama of the old liberals, Dadaists, and free-thinkers, as they begin to moralize at the end of a life devoted completely to the destruction of the old guard and the undermining of order. Dostoevsky, who knew this whole aquarium from the bottom up, depicted it in the mollusk form of Stepan Trofimovich.[21] His sons are encouraged to scorn anything that had formerly been considered fundamental. Finally, it is said of the all-too-eager master: "Well, old boy, you've blathered on long enough. Now it's time to boil you down for soap." Then the wailing starts. Once the conservatives have also been bumped off, the chaos is over. And so in *The Demons* the matter rests with the German governor (Lemke, I think), who is not up to the task. Lemke's situation is remarkably similar to that of the old Hindenburg. Add to this the young conservatives who first support the *demos*[22] because they sense its new elemental power, and then fall into the traces and are dragged to their deaths. In this chaos, only the nihilist retains his fearsome power, and anyone who thinks he can mount a counteroffensive must have learned how to do so from him.

KIRCHHORST, 9 NOVEMBER 1944

Air-raid sirens at midnight, and right afterward while we were dressing the children, four bombs hit with a roar. The same thing happened at half past three this morning. After the all-clear signal, the shells with time-delay fuses exploded. Rain poured down on the garden, and from the old Hanoverian city center, the red glow of detonations flamed up through the steamy air.

During the alarm, even during the raid and the defensive fire, a certain order prevails. But once the first bombs begin to whistle, everyone—more or less dressed—piles into the shelter. Even then, the children are led by the hand; our concern focuses especially on them.

KIRCHHORST, 10 NOVEMBER 1944

In the mail a card from Ernstel who is on his way to Italy as a *Panzergrenadier* [infantryman in a heavy-armor division]. In addition a letter from Ruth Speidel, from which we can see, to our great joy, that the general is still alive. I have thought about him, as well as Ernstel, every evening and every morning.

A raid just now—it is nine o'clock in the evening—which reddened the rain-soaked western sky with fires and powerful explosions. A bomb also fell in the area; the shockwave smashed a windowpane in my study that was already cracked, as well as the transom over the front door.

Current reading: *Grundzüge einer Ökologie der chinesischen Reptilien* [*General Outline of an Ecology of Chinese Reptiles*] by Mell. In certain sea snakes with paddle-shaped tails, only one ovary functions, while the other produces immature eggs. This prevents interference with the creature's swimming while gravid. It also safeguards the fully developed capacity to search for food during this period, when nourishment is most crucial. In some species, the gums seem to be adapted for the absorption of oxygen and are thus capable of breathing. During long dives, these substitute for lungs, like oxygen canisters aboard submarines. There is one of the strangest cases ever attested in which snakes attack human beings: A Chinese woman on an island near Hong Kong was busy cutting grass. She laid her little child on the earth where it was devoured by a python that darted from the bushes. It was impossible to get help. Of course, infants left unguarded are prey to attacks from almost all animals, right down to the ants.

Here too I find the opinion (as I did recently in Sachot's book about Ceylon) that certain people in regions where snakes proliferate possess a distinct ability to handle the creatures. A particular affinity exists in such places. I assume that, when seized by its captors, the snake perceives a sort of neutrality or even sympathy, rather like the touch of one of its own species.

The book is good because of its underlying passion for the observation of animals, the *frisson* of the magical and totemic encounter, without which all zoology becomes merely an arid summary of data.

In this context, I again pondered Darwinism. His main weakness lies in his lack of metaphysics. This finds its expression in the methodology, in that only one of the forms of observation—namely time—predominates.

By contrast, we have to see that animals have a relationship to their environment and to each other that resembles a bundle that is intricately knotted and intertwined. Their abundance requires less a chronological than a synoptic approach. The immense simultaneity—the parallel coexistence—becomes broken up by Darwinism into a succession: the bundle uncoils into a roll. This diminishes the grandeur of creation, the miracle of the genesis, as it emerges at a single stroke or in mighty cycles and eons, such as in the seven days of Moses, or in Hesiod's hierarchy of the cosmos, or in Chinese natural philosophy.

From a theological perspective, Lamarck's views are more significant. But it was, however, predictable that the more mechanistic theory would carry the day. After a certain point in time, selection takes place based on the greatest capacity for destruction.

KIRCHHORST, 11 NOVEMBER 1944

After writing last night's entry, I read Goethe's [comedy] *Die Mitschuldigen* [*Partners in Crime*, 1787]. The work skillfully captures the milieu of a small inn, yet the ending is abrupt, and it is annoying that Sophie remains under the control of the wicked Söller. On the other hand, one could argue that the title announces the moral of the tale.

After midnight—it had turned into a clear, starry night—then came a second attack with countless aircraft. One of them, pinned like an insect by the beams of the searchlights, was pitching from side to side from the impacts of the shells that zigzagged around it like little red stars shooting off an anvil. The presence of the children made the events more intense, more human, than anything familiar to me from the bunkers of World War I. Perpetua holds our little boy on her lap, bends over him completely, almost embracing him with her shoulders so that no harm can come to him that would not first touch her. This is Niobe's posture when confronting Apollo's arrow.[23]

Then fell asleep and dreamed of animals. I was engrossed in the observation of birds in an ornithological cabinet, particularly a large, speckled hawfinch. I was surprised that the bird's mottled coloration also extended to its beak, and pondered the reasons for this. Then there was a Javanese magpie that looks just like ours. "What makes this Javanese?"—I see, like some birds-of-paradise, it had a clump of red plumage under its open display of tail feathers.

KIRCHHORST, 12 NOVEMBER 1944

The air-raid alarms sometimes yank us out of deep sleep. When this happens, I am again made aware that there are unknown regions of dreams, nethermost depths of the sea where no ray of light penetrates. Just as the organisms that respond to light and sun are accidentally caught down there in the net, the plasma of the deep dream state also changes in response to the consciousness of the moment. Only a few scales get stuck in the twine of the net. We descend into unfathomable, eyeless depths, down into the placenta of imagery.

KIRCHHORST, 14 NOVEMBER 1944

Had an uninterrupted night. Read Goethe's [play] *Natürliche Tochter* [*The Natural Daughter*, 1803], a coldly artificial display of fireworks. It is like a creation still in its preliminary, Promethean phase. It is precisely the high level of its workmanlike quality that speaks for its ingenuity.

Then read still unpublished biographies of Planck and Laue sent to me by Keiper, the Berlin bookseller. I want to pass these along to Brother Physicus. At these highest levels of insight into the physical world, the relationship to the environment becomes streamlined, instinctual—the visual, mathematical, oscillating, crystallographic sensibility suffuses the body like a fluid. Science cannot direct us to other areas than those concealed deeply within ourselves. Whatever telescopes and microscopes may discover someday—*we* have known it forever in our innermost being. We arduously retrieve fragments of palaces buried within us.

Yesterday's mail brought a letter from Gerhard Günther, and included excerpts from the diaries of his son, who was killed in action in the mountains of the Southern Carpathian range. These included, in addition to prayers, meditations, and quotations, notations to my own works, which he read with great attention.

The prefigured image. Our science strives toward this. It is a mosaic pieced together on a background with a predetermined pattern. The more of these little pieces that are "laid out," the narrower the choices become for the remaining pieces. At the start, you can work in any field or area. By the end, each location is defined.

Free will seems to be diminished in the process, yet it must be viewed as essential to the whole. Powerful decisions determined the greater process, which seems to become more and more automatic toward the finish. We are engaged in fitting the capstones into vaults and domes—stones that hermits envisioned and planned in their theological meditations. Free will is, of course, greater in *Homo magnus* than in the individual, yet the individual also has a share in it. In his undivided state, in the decision about good and evil, the individual is still in command today. Just appeal to his sense of sovereign mastery and you will see miracles.

Went to the dentist in Burgdorf in the afternoon and read Eckermann in the waiting room.[24] There I found a mention of the *Pastoralia* of the Sophist Longus and immediately felt the desire to own the work. In light of the difficulties involved in acquiring books, this won't be the case for the time being. At the same time, I recalled the banks of the Seine between the bridges and their rich fishing grounds.

Later, while he was drilling, the dentist whispered political news in my ear.

KIRCHHORST, 15 NOVEMBER 1944

The first snowfall of the year.

Many people in Germany today may feel as I do—people whose knowledge of infamy has produced disgust at their participation in the collective, in anticipation that future bodies of authority will just be branches from the same trunk. Even now, after such powerful portents of what is to come, the delusion of the numberless legions of the rabble surpasses all imagination and all moderation.

KIRCHHORST, 18 NOVEMBER 1944

Nights without bombing raids, partially due to the November weather. On the other hand, the English and Americans need their strategic squadrons for their autumn offensive on the western Rhineland.

I am reading Stifter. His *Bunte Steine* [*Colored Stones*, 1853] has been standing untouched on my bookshelf for a long time because his circle of admirers is so unappealing. Lovely chapels filled with the smell of cheap incense.

I wonder whether the propensity for establishing total states corresponds to musicality. In any case, it's obvious that three musical nations in particular have emerged: the Germans, Russians, and Italians. Within musicality, a shift to the coarser elements probably occurs—a shift from melody to rhythm. This development culminates in monotony.

KIRCHHORST, 19 NOVEMBER 1944

Last night there was a raid and distant heavy bombardments. A Christmas tree spread out over Hannover like a red star of misery. Powerful tremors followed.

Read further in *Colored Stones*: "Granite," "Limestone," "Tourmaline," and "Rock Crystal." Saving one's first ascent of particular peaks among the literary mountain ranges for one's later years has its merits.

Stifter is the Hesiod of the moderns, someone who still understands the *nomos*[25] of the earth. It is wonderful how old Austria looms large, like a great work of art that we will be able to appreciate again once the last Napoleonic structures have disappeared. An ancient mountain forest where the topsoil of happiness is formed. By contrast, anguish is produced here where we are.

I can recall talking with readers of Stifter who thought his suicide incompatible with his work and life. But we should pay attention to those pedantic and overly scrupulous traits in his nature. These can easily develop into hypochondria. This shows up both in grammatical and narrative structures and points to a delicate, fragile constitution—at least in intellectual terms:

"The children wore broad straw hats; they had clothes with sleeves from which their arms protruded."

KIRCHHORST, 22 NOVEMBER 1944

Intensified bombing raids and attacks as they become more clever and malicious. The oil tanks in Misburg were burned out again. The ranks and columns of aircraft appear by day like white hydras snaking their way through the ocean of air. Fighter planes cut through the space above them with the speed of bullets.

Read further in Stifter, whose prose is infused with elements of the old Austrian chancery style. You get used to catchwords like "idem," "ditto," "the former," and "the latter" and other peculiarities that you even begin to appreciate.

Dreams last night. I was being shown plants, among them a tropical specimen as tall as heather bearing numerous dark cherries. "Also has the virtue that nobody knows they are edible."

Then I was standing at the edge of a pool facing someone else and playing a sort of chess game with him. Yet we had no chess pieces but were operating with mental constructs. In this way, we produced armadas on the surface of the water for our own sea battles, yet their strength lay not in their fighting ability but in their beauty. Strange creatures surfaced to chase or grab one another; it was a contest that revealed the treasures of the deep.

"In infinity every point is the center." I came up with this axiom this morning while I was digging in the flowerbeds. It would affirm that infinity does not possess quantitative, but rather qualitative metaphysical authority. One can imagine a circle, a sphere, extending to an extreme degree without increasing the number of midpoints even by one. That remains the one and only central point. For every point to become the center, a process would have to occur that would require something beyond the realm of our sensory perception—a mysterious folding of space, probably to its irreducible form.

Like every mathematical or physical fact, this relationship also has a moral implication. As a metaphysical being, every human is the center of the universe and, as such, cannot be dislodged from this position even by the most distant galaxies. The vertiginous expanses of space fall away at the moment of death, yielding to reality.

The impression called forth in us by immeasurable distance is close to animal fear; it is how we reflect the world of illusion.

The encounter. The aura of the great hunt and also of magical practices predominates here. There is enchantment that is like the approach of very timid animals; we also find the realization of dreams that we used to doubt. These call forth a mixture of skeptical wonder, fear, and delight, even great tenderness. Repetition disperses these in favor of a feeling of splendid security.

Judar the fisherman. When he enters the subterranean regions to seek the ring of highest power, he meets a series of phantoms he must vanquish. At last he finds his own mother. So even here is the knowledge, as Boethius terms it, that defeated earth grants us the stars.

World conquest by men like Caesar or Alexander has to be understood symbolically. Purple is the symbol of victory, and the ivory scepter the symbol of the victor. The one betokens matriarchal lineage, the other, the patriarchal. Gold is the apotheosis of purple; it represents the concentration of earthly power.

KIRCHHORST, 23 NOVEMBER 1944

In some unnamed metropolis, I was living in one of the many furnished rooms at my disposal in my dream life. Pons entered and took a seat on an easy chair so he could tell me about a love affair. He added that he was going to get married tomorrow. Upon awakening I thought; "look at that, the woman he described is better suited to him (given all the circumstances of their acquaintance) than the one he chose in reality."

This is the way people can enter our dreams: not only in their historical guise but also in a way that embodies their potential. In our dream images we understand both their empirical and also their explicit character.

After having set aside the "Path of Masirah" several weeks ago, I am starting to revise my journal from Rhodes. The times are not conducive to such works. In the "Path of Masirah," I wish to depict a survey of morality in historical, geographical, and physical scenes. The world of the spirit must shine through the natural one but also put its stamp on it like sealing wax.

KIRCHHORST, 24 NOVEMBER 1944

Not a history, but a *synopsis* of philosophy presenting the philosopher's stone with its facets polished by the guiding spirits of different ages and peoples.

Conversation with Alexander on how to keep a journal. I corresponded about this same topic with a Sergeant Müller, who sent me his own entries.

Going through my travel journals makes it clear how much they have been shaped by topical themes. The age we live in affects their content the way fermentation and aging affect wine in the depths of the cellar. Eventually, it must be carefully rebottled and have the yeasts poured off. At Florence's apartment, I once had a long talk with Léautaud about this. He disapproves of this practice and declares that the word in its first version is inviolable and sacrosanct. That rule cannot be implemented in my case for technical reasons, because I intersperse much associative material as a sort of seal of memory. The best depiction of first impressions is the fruit of repeated exertion and intense rewriting.

KIRCHHORST, 26 NOVEMBER 1944

Sunday morning. After hard rain over the past few days, dry weather and clear skies. Since we experienced two raids during the night, I put the Rhodes journals aside in order to organize *Elateridae* [click beetles]. Looking at them reminded me of walks in the woods of Saint-Cloud.

Then the report came through that massive bomber squadrons were getting nearer. I put on my coat to go into the garden, from which I could see a large number of aircraft crossing northern airspace. Then over five hundred planes approached from the direction of Celle in staggered formations of about forty planes each. After leaving jagged bands of white smoke signals over the southern part of the sky, they swung around in formation toward Misburg and dropped their payloads. We could hear the roaring and screaming noise drown out the antiaircraft fire. Powerful explosions shook the earth far and wide. The attackers came in at low altitude below the little clouds of our defensive positions.

Two or three squadrons swerved straight toward the house, and opened their bomb bay doors above it in order to drop their payloads, as far as I could estimate, somewhere near Bothfeld. The defensive fire was stronger than before. The lead aircraft sustained a direct hit, and a long, pale red blazing flame trailed out behind it before it crashed nearby. The smoke clouds of the impact soon surrounded our house. It looked as though one of the aircraft parts, a large silver wing with an engine hanging from it, was spinning slowly and would crash onto us, yet it corkscrewed off toward the schoolteacher's house making a hissing noise, disappearing behind it. Two parachutes also drifted over the garden; one was so low that the man hanging on it was as close as someone you'd meet on the street. Suddenly the air was thick with scraps and shavings, as if the airplane had been shredded into black confetti. The pageant was powerfully intoxicating; it staggered all reason. There comes a point in such events when one's own safety starts to become secondary: the vivid elements become so intensified that they leave no room for reflective thought, not even for fear.

Kirchhorst, 27 November 1944

Without light, without water, without electricity since the power plant in Ahlten was hit. They say that six hundred planes flew over us with their white loops and trails. They looked like swarms of microbes romping about in an immense blue drop of water.

The wing came down in a nearby field; the aircraft hit the ground just behind Bothfeld and burned out. Near Grosshorst, they found a head and a hand. Two more shattered corpses were lying nearby; you could see that the parachutes had become tangled in each other and as a result failed to open.

One of the pilots landed in Stelle. We heard that an inhabitant of the village—none other than a Dutch refugee—went after him and hit him a couple of times with an axe. His neighbor, Rehbock, a soldier on furlough, was passing in his farm cart, got the wounded man out of his clutches and, in danger of his own life, brought him to safety.

Kirchhorst, 28 November 1944

The two Americans whose parachutes had become entangled were buried in the little cemetery today. General Loehning came by in the afternoon. He had heard the rumor that had been circulating for weeks that I had been captured or shot.

The task of the author is not to achieve absolute, but optimal precision. This is justified by the difference between logic and language. It is thus a prerequisite of good style that an author must be satisfied with the optimal expression. To seek the absolute leads him in the wrong direction.

Words are a mosaic; that is to say that cracks exist between them. When viewed logically, these are spaces. On the other hand, they reveal the earthly realm below for deeper speculation.

Kirchhorst, 29 November 1944

Perpetua dreamed she was having one of her eye teeth pulled.

Toward noon countless squadrons appeared under dense cloud cover and dropped their payloads. A gigantic carousel seemed to be revolving above our village, raining down steel as it turned. This fell in a circle around Kirchhorst, in Stelle, near Lohne, where from our garden I could watch thirty bombs explode. They hit Buchholz causing great damage, as well as in Misburg, where the corpses of fifty Women's Auxiliary personnel were pulled out of the rubble.

The mail brought a telegram from Countess Podewils. Her husband writes from England—a happy report in the midst of so much dismal news.

In my dream, I paid a visit to my father and also found him, yet both of the columns at the entrance to his house had grown so closely together that it took great effort to force myself in between them.

KIRCHHORST, 2 DECEMBER 1944

Doing nighttime guard duty, which has been instituted here in our village because of the airplanes. The farmers are deep sleepers and usually don't wake up until the bombs start falling. Luckily I had my neighbor Lahmann as my partner—a man with some brains in his head. Time is compressed by the presence of an intelligent or pleasant person. This noticeable effect goes so far that in intellectual or erotic encounters, time can completely lose its meaning. Pain, on the other hand, and mental dullness draw it out interminably. Anyone who wishes to comprehend the true power of death as the destroyer of time must come to terms with this thought. Death brings something that nothing else can.

Visit from Kohlberg in the morning; conversed with him about Löns and writers from Lower Saxony in general. Our dry soil is extremely unsuitable for the production of artistic types. "*Frisia non cantat.*" [Frisia (*i.e.*, Holland) does not sing].[26]

Went to Burgdorf in the afternoon to pick up the Rhode Island Reds [poultry], a present from Hanne Menzel from Silesia.

KIRCHHORST, 4 DECEMBER 1944

Current reading: Origen's *On Prayer*, in addition the diaries of Léon Bloy.

Bloy is eminently human in the way he is at home among sordid things: excrement, stench, aspects of hatred; and, yet at the same time, he recognizes the highest invisible law. That makes reading him distressing. Long passages can seem like festering splinters lodged under the skin. Yet I may say that I have exerted myself as a reader, and done so under challenging conditions. One cannot shrink from slights and insults. Only then can one sift the grains of gold from the froth.

Perhaps I shall include Bloy in the series of writers I am planning to cover in a study, just as an act of intellectual gratitude. I have been collecting material for such documentation for a long time. It will examine those people, books, and things that I have chanced upon along my way, people who have given me so much.

In the morning Ernstel's favorite cat, the beautiful Persian named Hexe, was found dead in a nearby field. She was already stiff, and we assume she had eaten poison. She was the daughter of the old cat, Kissa, who spent many years in our house, and the mother of the young Kissa, who brings me such joy. In addition to her, the large white broad-headed angora tomcat Jacko and the Siamese princess Li-Ping still keep us company.

KIRCHHORST, 5 DECEMBER 1944

Air-raid sentry duty last night with my neighbor Lahmann while we discussed the way things are going and broke open a bottle of vermouth. The fire in Grosshorst, the blockbuster bomb near Stelle, those Sunday and Tuesday mornings last week that will forever be inscribed in the history of the village, and even grandchildren will tell their grandchildren about such matters—if they even still exist.

Dense bomber formations in the morning but no bombs dropped. I sensed that and just kept on turning the soil in the garden in Spartan fashion "in the shade."

Kept reading in *Mon Journal* by Léon Bloy. There you can encounter passages, as I did this morning, like the following:

"Colding in Denmark. 8 April 1900. Palm Sunday. Terrible weather. Today is the birthday of stupid King Christian [IX], and it is a holiday all over Denmark. His reprehensible son-in-law, the Prince of Wales, has arrived in Copenhagen after escaping an assassination attempt at the Parisian Gare du Nord. A young Belgian fired at this pig but missed. It is better just to stab them. That is more reliable and is better for the sausage!"

It takes either incredible impertinence or manic confidence in one's own judgment to write and even publish (Paris, 1904) such things. In truth, a decadent sense of security accumulated in the person of this Edward to an unrivalled extent. As a memorial to him, Paris preserves a device, a sort of orthopedic chair he had built to accommodate his fat paunch with the greatest possible comfort during intercourse. Travelers are shown this in one of the big *lupinares* [brothels] as a curiosity, and Morris,[27] who seems to have thought it one of the wonders of the modern world, urged me to go see it. Although I otherwise do not avoid erotic curiosities, I could not bring myself to do so—the thoroughly mechanical and soullessly comfortable aspect of the concept is just too awful. Such machines would be at home in the great pictures by Hieronymus Bosch.

As I write this, I am watching several dogfights taking place in the gaps of blue sky in the area between my study and Isernhagen. These dramas are perhaps—no, certainly—connected magically and causally to the fact that there were monarchs like this Edward, Leopold of Belgium, and even Wilhelm II. They are not the final duels of western chivalry.

Through the keyhole I watched the new chickens I'm still keeping in the coop. The rooster stands majestically at the feed trough, summons a few hens and pecks others away. After their meal, one of them approaches him, perhaps his favorite, stretches up on her toes and touches him, pecking very gently at his pink wattles and his comb while the rooster struts. This is courtly.

KIRCHHORST, 7 DECEMBER 1944

The garden is coming along. Here they say of fertilizer that has been exposed to air too long that it "burns out." That is graphic.

Concerning the distribution of intelligence. It matches the particular properties of the organisms, for it works logically only in combination with them. The duck, the frog, the pelican, the lily—each possesses a particular intelligence that matches its predisposition. And so they get by. Too much or too little would be equally detrimental.

The towering intelligence of human beings seems to transcend this proportional requirement. At the same time, the surplus can be explained as relegated to invisible organs. When these metaphysical organs are no longer stimulated, when they atrophy, a disruption of the balance appears of the sort we are now experiencing: large amounts of intelligence are freed up to be applied to annihilation.

In addition: Intellectual training of the artisan has reached the level that surpasses organic needs. This releases immense amounts of energy in society, with destructive results. There are two ways to counteract this—either reduction of spiritualization or the creation of new entities, and these can only be invisible ones. This is one of the reasons I am motivated to augment my book about the worker with a theological section.

Of all Weininger's hypotheses, the one stating that few benefits can be seen in maternal love has generated the most powerful outrage. By the same token, one cannot say he is wrong when we look at the robin, the cat, the pelican with her brood. There is no differentiation in the animal world. The devotion of animals is just as wonderful as that of human beings. Qualities to be venerated lie in a realm beyond and presume an advance over the sexual, even over all temporal connections. Our consciousness of the final unity of matter that transcends any accidental contact: affinity in eternity.

KIRCHHORST, 8 DECEMBER 1944

The mail brought the long-awaited letter from Ernstel, who is camped in a town in northern Italy. I'm glad he has ended up on this front. He writes that he is reading *The Charterhouse of Parma* in a French edition. In the afternoon, Hanne Wickenberg came by, as she does every Friday. We talked about the female Air Force Auxiliary personnel who were killed last week in the big attack on Misburg. They were found without any signs of external injury, lying close beside one another in the communications trenches. They died when their lungs ruptured. Because the air pressure of the shockwave had stripped off all clothes and underwear from their bodies, they were completely naked. A farmer who helped bury them was quite overcome by this horrible indignity: "All such big, beautiful girls, and heavy as lead."

KIRCHHORST, 10 DECEMBER 1944

Went to church and afterward visited the grave of the two Americans. Aside from a few flowers, it is decorated solely by their helmets.

Melancholy. Today metaphysical need is particularly worth our attention because our upbringing is aimed primarily at destroying, at eradicating the best in us. Yet perhaps quite new and unknown prospects reveal themselves as well, as they can to the climber who has ascended the mountain peak across a rock face that was thought to be unconquerable. We must fasten ourselves to the cliff with our own blood.

Arras. I wonder if it has been noticed that this is the town that gave birth to two regicides, namely Damiens and Robespierre. I assume so. By way of redress, two peace treaties have also been signed there.

In 1493 when Arras fell to the Austrians, they carved this verse above one of the gates:

Quand les Français prendront Arras,
Les souris mangeront les chats.

[When the French capture Arras, / The mice will eat the cats.]

In 1640, when the French captured the city, however, they chiseled the "p" off the inscription.[28]

This is an example of a retort that has a more concise and also wittier effect than the initial insolent challenge. I noticed this about the propaganda in France as well. The huge posters showing a French worker standing at a machine in Germany and showing all the signs of contentment is an example of this. By contrast, the nocturnal counterpropaganda was limited to a simple nose ring drawn in chalk on the poster figure.

KIRCHHORST, 11 DECEMBER 1944

Fortifications are hastily being built near the village. The goal is to set up two dozen anti-aircraft emplacements. This is going to draw heavier attacks closer to us, not to mention the chaos from the planes they will shoot down.

Raid and bombardment in the evening. Advent: a green Christmas tree hung in the air. A heavy bomb flew over the town with a hellish roar, only to detonate in the distance, perhaps over by the autobahn. The shockwave tore all the windows open and ripped off our blackout material.

Aboard sinking ships and floating wrecks. First the supplies are rationed, then the planks begin to loosen, and the struggle for places begins. Finally, the sinking amidst debris, corpses, and sharks.

Burckhardt was right when he expressed his fear of a "rapid decay." He suspected something shady.

I am reading the *Thankless Beggar* by Léon Bloy, in which a poor man in disguise left behind a great wealth of consolation.

Words. *Désobligeant* (disagreeable, unpleasant) is generally translated as "discourteous," which is actually a sort of inverted expression, since it describes the condition that discourtesy creates in another person.

KIRCHHORST, 13 DECEMBER 1944

Dreams about examinations. This kind of fright is too precise, too narrowly confined to be the result of memory alone. By contrast, why do impressions that are so much more powerful, like those of battle, return so seldom and so vaguely?

The test-taking dream must be connected with death; it conceals a warning that life's tasks, its allotted time, are not yet completed. The final school examination, as my father used to tell me, reappears regularly as an apparition of terror.

"Oh God, I'll soon turn fifty, and have been to university and I still haven't done my final exams."

This is the dream of the foolish virgins,[29] of the wicked husbandmen,[30] and of the man who buried his talents.[31] The feeling that one will never pass the test is a horrible one, and it's marvelous to awaken from this of all dreams.

In another dream, I was counting money when Friedrich Georg was present. The popular interpretation of this has it that one will encounter hardship to be surmounted. Such explanations are, by the way, usually inadequate, even though they derive partially from experience or from insight into the secret nature of matter. Primers of dream imagery treat symbolism like translation, like dictionaries, by offering subordinated lists, as Huysmans does in his novel *The Cathedral*.

Léon Bloy's nice comment about the occultists of this type occurs to me. In order to conjure evil, they need rituals, books of magic, and forays into the strangest and most esoteric regions, while at the same time, they completely miss the obvious Satanism of their grocer living on the next street corner.

It's a rare thing when our mail doesn't bring bad news. Our little postmistress approaches in the morning like a bird swooping through the garden, spreading tidings of disaster. Today, she brought the information that Edmond, whose sister and children are living with us, is missing in action, but it is probable that he's been taken prisoner.

Friedrich Georg writes that, during the raid that destroyed the beautiful old city of Freiburg in twenty minutes, his book, *The Illusions of Technology*, which was being stored in a warehouse before publication, also went up in flames. It almost seems as if technology wanted to suppress the book. Twice now, the cast type has been melted in Hamburg after it was set.

KIRCHHORST, 14 DECEMBER 1944

I helped dig up a huge termite nest. It took a lot of work. Cranes were employed for the excavations, which were as big as a significant gravel pit. Deep in the middle of the steep yellow slope, the dark spherical structure glowed. Hosts of termites marched out in military formation. Among them I saw *Termitophiles* and *Symbiotes* like the many-legged wood louse with its black leathery carapace as it scrabbled away. My participation was that of an expert, a connoisseur of such political systems.

Construction of the batteries at the edge of the moor. The first families are leaving town. Mutterings precede the impending catastrophe, of the sort Defoe so ably describes in his book about the plague in London, or Hebbel in his [drama] *Judith*. It is the little details that produce panic. For example, here, word is going around that people should "remove the pictures from the walls."

Went to the doctor in Burgdorf in the morning. I am overcome by a strange feeling of embarrassment when people ask me about the books I write. This is probably due to my difficulty in expressing in words the meaning of the things I do. Seen from an absolute perspective, it is insignificant that I am even writing at all—I could achieve as much by different means, for example, by meditation. Books are shavings, detritus of existence. A clandestine quality, related to the erotic, ultimately informs this feeling. On the one hand, you can present your children in public, but on the other, you don't expound on the details of their procreation.

Rested in the little Beinhorn Woods, which is one of my spiritual haunts, something like the Place des Ternes in Paris. It was here that I decided to undertake a second complete reading of the Bible, in particular Luther's translation with scholarly apparatus. I am hoping that these different readings will make the network of passages meaningful to me, and that in the course of time, I shall develop an exegesis for my personal use.

While I was tidying my files, I came upon a review of the *Marble Cliffs* by Näf that appeared years ago in a Swiss newspaper. When a neutral critic, who can be in no doubt about the situation in Germany, connects the content of the book with our political conditions, then carelessness, if not malice, must be at work. He criticized my style for starting a sentence with the particle "so" on almost every page, while pointing out that one of the greatest masters of language, Mallarmé, struck the word from his dictionary. For me that is not authoritative. It is important in my attitude toward life as a relationship to something higher, and a power that proves discernible in objects and their context.

Back to my tendency to introduce sentences with conjunctions and particles. It is not from the sentence per se that we can expect the words to acquire a necessary relationship to one another. It helps when the connection among the sentences is explicit: the logical sequence, the contradiction, the symmetry, the amplification, the introduction of an unexpected viewpoint. Introductory words accomplish this. They resemble clefs that announce tonal value, or the mood of the movement to follow. Words may live in sentences, but sentences, by contrast, live in a broader context.

I consider it the duty of the author to ponder these things; that is the least bit of technical tidiness that can be expected of him. The only objection worth responding to here would be: Is not language too worthy of our veneration to be approached with such techniques? Don't they tend to damage the dark and unconscious aspects that dwell in it too easily?

By contrast, one could expound further: language itself is not worthy of veneration, but rather the inexpressible alone is. It is not churches that are to be venerated, but rather the invisible quality of what dwells within them. The author approaches this with words without ever attaining it. His goal lies beyond language and can never be contained by it. With words, he invokes silence. Words are his tool, and it is to be expected that he keep this tool in good repair by constantly staying in practice with it. He must not let a syllable pass that does not satisfy him, but he must also never imagine that he possesses mastery. He must always be dissatisfied with himself. He also must get used to the fact that he will surely provoke displeasure.

KIRCHHORST, 15 DECEMBER 1944

Very threatening raids in the morning and evening; bombs fell not far from here.

In the afternoon received a visit from Cramer von Laue, who was wounded for a second time in Italy and is walking on crutches. Conversation about the assassination attempt, and in particular, Kniébolo's health, which they say has declined markedly. His distress at not having recognized his enemy, that he hadn't perceived him, seems to have overshadowed all other considerations. That would correlate with details [General] Kleist told me in Stavropol and is also the reason why I always avoided a meeting with him. It is said that he has introduced a new instrument, a kind of garrote, for exterminating his opponents. The charnel house, this our reality.

The mail brought a letter from Ernstel, who is anticipating his first military encounter. In addition, *The Illusions of Technology* by Friedrich Georg, which he has given a new title: *The Perfection of Technology*. He sent me one of the few author's copies that had been distributed before the great fire in Freiburg.

And unto Adam he said, "Because thou hast hearkened unto the voice of thy wife, and hast eaten of the tree, of which I commanded thee, saying, Thou shalt not eat of it: cursed is the ground for thy sake; in sorrow shalt thou eat of it all the days of thy life" (Genesis 3:17).

The passage corresponds to the sentence in Hesiod describing how the gods reduced man's crops, for previously the work of a single day was sufficient to provide for an entire year.

True profusion, Edenic abundance, exists outside the realm of time. There lies the landscape of great, immediate harvests such as myth describes and Genesis illustrates. Nor does death exist there. In the lovers' embrace, we have retained a small spark of the great light of the world of creation—we fly beyond time as though shot from a crossbow. In myth, this primeval power is halted by the victory of Kronos. Kronos, who mutilates the primeval father with his diamond sickle, makes the race of gods incapable of further procreation. The role of Gaia is allied to that of the serpent.

Then Genesis, 3 and 24. The expulsion from Paradise happens less as punishment than as a means to prevent man from reaching for the Tree of Life and living forever. This is why the cherubim, with their slashing swords drawn, block the approach to the Tree of Life.

What does this mean? Man in a state of sin, and at the same time immortal, would become a demon of immense power. Should he then want to approach the Tree of Life, he will be cut down by the steel of the Angel of Death and, as a creature of earth, laid low before the gates. Yet he returns to eternity in his other form, as God's breath.

KIRCHHORST, 16 DECEMBER 1944

In the afternoon went into Hannover; it has been burning since yesterday morning. The streets were covered with debris and shrapnel, also with vehicles and streetcars that had been hit. They were crowded with people rushing everywhere as in a Chinese catastrophe. I saw a woman walk past me; tears glistened as they fell from her face like rain. I also saw people carrying on their shoulders lovely old pieces of furniture covered by a layer of plaster dust. An elegant gentleman, gray at the temples, was pushing a cart on which there stood a small rococo cabinet.

Went to the address of my parents-in-law on Stephansplatz. Windows and doors had been recently blown in again when a cluster of bombs devastated the area. Anyone located in the fan-shaped target area of this kind of bombing pattern hears the rumbling growing frighteningly louder and changing to a whistling sound just before impact. It does not seem to be true, as is often claimed, that you can't hear the bomb that is targeting you. A heavy layer of mortar dust filled the space in which the people in the houses waited for the end as they lay on the ground. I had someone show me the cellar: a bare, white-washed corridor where seven chairs stood as if in a waiting room. This is what modern torture chambers look like.

Returned through the streets as night fell. I was repeating a portion of my way to school from the year 1906—but not going past illuminated, well-stocked shop windows as in the old days, but instead past ruins of Piranesian bleakness. From the cellars came the red glow of the winter coal supplies. There were still crowds of people. Now and then, they would pass by a house where fire was still flickering on the walls and ceilings inside—but no one paid any attention.

KIRCHHORST, 18 DECEMBER 1944

In a subterranean department store the rooms had been built deep into the cliffs. Among them was a butcher's stall carved from a vein of white-streaked red marble. It was very clean. The scraps were rinsed away by a mountain torrent that gushed down out of the chasms.

Back in Hannover in the afternoon where clouds of steam still rise from the ruins. I saw men and women sorting through the debris and pulling objects from it. Furniture lined the pavement as it began to rain. It is strangely affecting to see that the streets are perfectly clean and meticulously swept. Such a surviving trait of orderliness could be taken in different ways. I found it half repugnant and half admirable.

Mixed in with the bomb payloads are some with time-release fuses that don't explode for hours, or sometimes even days. *Est modus in rebus* [moderation in all things]—in the context of the world of aerial bombing, this embodies a comic element. The comedy may be magnified: for last year's attack on Berlin on Christmas Eve, the fuses were timed to go off at the hour when presents were being exchanged.

Visited Grethe Jürgens in her studio. Today, people visit others they know, not to see how they're doing but to see whether they still exist.

KIRCHHORST, 19 DECEMBER 1944

Continued reading in Genesis. Lamech, who boasts to his wives Adah and Zillah that he has slain a man for wounding him and a boy for bruising him, says that he shall be avenged, not seven times like Cain, but seventy-seven times. It is a stroke of genius on Herder's part to connect mankind's earliest song of triumph with the invention of the sword that had been referred to in a passage shortly before. Lamech is the father of Tubalcain, the first master of all mining and ironwork who thus has tremendous superiority.

Lamech is one of the Titans, a superman of Cainite culture, which we must imagine as possessing primeval fecundity as well as a dark splendor. Human sacrifice is part of their rituals. Their corruption (Genesis 6:2) reaches an extreme.

Cainite culture is the antediluvian model of pure power. In this regard, places like Sodom, Gomorrah, Babylon, and Dahomey are its later offshoots. The great fratricidal ritual sites on this earth are Cainite, like the Mexican *teocallis*,[32] the Roman Circus, the barbaric dungeons of machine civilizations. Cainite are also red flags, whatever symbols they may display; Cainite are the death's head units of Kniébolo; Cainite is a battleship that flaunts the name Marat,[33] who was one of the greatest butchers of humanity.

Cainite women are described as extraordinarily beautiful. "*Dans l'état de chute, la beauté est un monstre*" [In its fallen state, beauty is a monster] (Léon Bloy).

KIRCHHORST, 21 DECEMBER 1944
Dreams are froth—from eternity.[34]

KIRCHHORST, 23 DECEMBER 1944
Continued reading in Genesis. I am reading Delitzsch's *Commentar über die Genesis* (1860) [*A New Commentary on Genesis* (1888)] and Goldberg's *Maimonides. Kritik der jüdischen Glaubenslehre* [*Maimonides: Critique of Jewish Doctrine*, 1935] at the same time. Goldberg touches on themes that have engaged me for a long time, such as the relationship of Judaism to the twentieth century. In this context, Weininger's suicide is like the loss of a military leader in a skirmish at a far-flung outpost. The Jew is eternal—this means he has an answer for every century. I am beginning to change my view that the twentieth century has been so unfavorable toward him. I believe the second half will bring surprises in this connection. It is precisely this terrible victimization that suggests this.

Shared human attributes are becoming more nationalized and differentiated as written culture evolves. Adam is the father of the human race. Abraham, the father of the Semitic peoples; Isaac, the father of Jews and Edomites; Jacob, the father of Israel.

Jacob may not be the greatest, but he is the most remarkable of the patriarchs. His person embodies a series of important decisions. His deception in gaining the blessing of the firstborn from his father finds its analogue in the preference of the Chosen People versus all others. His time spent in the house of Laban is the first Jewish exile, and Esau, the first anti-Semite.

The ancient gods still stand before us with their magical presence, perhaps even in competition. The abduction of Laban's idols represents a robbery of the *nomos*.

They are stolen by Rachel and concealed from the pursuing Laban by a taboo act. Rachel conceals them under her and makes herself untouchable by claiming that she is menstruating. Later they are buried at the foot of an oak tree near Sichem, along with the women's brooches. Perhaps this is the same oak under which Abimelech is later exalted as king (Judges 9:6).

Jacob's nocturnal wrestling with the Lord. Two general thoughts on this:

Man must not let himself be vanquished cheaply: God must force it upon him. Man will be tempted to let himself be thrown down before he is thoroughly subdued, completely subjugated by the High Power. This is a particular danger of our time, when human beings are threatened en masse and dragged innocent to execution.

Furthermore, the struggle takes place at night because, ever since his fall, man cannot endure looking upon the face of God. It is not until morning that he recognizes Him and receives a blessing from Him. Here night is human life, during which the arm of the invisible God often makes itself violently felt; dawn, when His face appears, represents death.

We must allow our rationalist nature to be overcome. This wrestling match is taking place today. God is prosecuting our case.

KIRCHHORST, 28 DECEMBER 1944

Pure activity rises only to the level of anecdote, but not to historical reality. In this connection, it is correct that Columbus is seen as the discoverer of America and not the Icelanders, who made landfall there long before him. In order to produce historical reality and productivity, we need to hit the target intentionally, not by accident. There must be a spiritual dimension here. This is the only way to transcend hazard and blind chance.

The powerful echo of lovemaking—a trembling answer from the innermost marrow of life.

KIRCHHORST, 29 DECEMBER 1944

There is frost on the garden, but we have beautiful sunshine. When I look at the bare beech tree streaming with light, I get a feeling of secret joy: "Summer is resting in the cupboard."

I've begun to read about the quite topical subject of shipwrecks, starting with Raynal *Les Naufragés* (1870) [*Wrecked on a Reef* (1874)]. The book describes the Robinsinade of the author and his four companions after a shipwreck in the Auckland Islands south of New Zealand. The stranded survivors lived on the flesh of the plentiful sea lions there, as well as fish, mussels, albatross eggs, and wild berries. This gives the author the opportunity to mention a tree covered by tasty flaming-red berries, which might lend itself to planting and grafting in our gardens. The climate is raw; for weeks, storms howl around the rugged cliffs where the Pacific Ocean surf breaks. A woods stunted by the winds grows on a patch of turf. Colorful birds swoop through this thicket. Among them is a little gray parrot with a bright red breast that breeds in caves.

The little community is active, at first building a tent from the sails they have salvaged. This is soon followed by a hut and a workshop with a forge and carpentry shop, where they build a seaworthy boat over the course of twenty months. They are able to accomplish a crossing to Stewart Island on the southern tip of New Zealand with this craft in July 1865. The author is straightforward, clear, filled with common sense. He mentions Bible reading and group prayer as beneficial to communal life. On the other hand, he also mentions fermented drink and card playing as dangers. Consequently, they burn their cards and destroy their still after a fight.

A translation of this book would be worthwhile. I made a few excerpts for the book on islands that my brother Wolfgang, the geographer, is planning.

Kirchhorst, 30 December 1944

In the morning I received a visit from a reader named Rosenkranz. Penchant for botany, combined with knowledge of modern pharmacology and toxicology. We sat near the stove, talking about mescaline. He told me of a blind man, whose appetite for color had driven him to write to him, hoping for a visual hallucination. We then discussed the different ways of preparing opium cakes in China, India, Persia, and Turkey. The poppy capsules have to be scored on sunny days, for only in the presence of light does the bitter milk coagulate and develop the narcotic power that forms its inner luminescence. We also talked about an obsolete drug, *lactuacarium*, that derives from the thickened sap of wild lettuce. Fields of this plant were supposedly cultivated in Zell on the Moselle River. In former times, doctors equated its effect to opium.

Kirchhorst, 31 December 1944

The last day of the year. In the morning went to church, which was not just falling apart on the outside but also losing its charisma within. Nonetheless, it is still the best place to honor the dead and those who have been taken from us by fire, as well as our own fate.

Then had breakfast with Hanne Menzel, and Perpetua. An air-raid alarm put an end to this; it wasn't long before squadrons appeared overhead in the brilliant blue sky while earth lay below under a blinding white blanket of snow. The new gun emplacements in Stelle began to fire. Soon the dome of the sky was flecked with little clouds. Waves of aircraft struggled through these from the direction of Grossburgwedel heading toward Misburg, where huge clouds of smoke soon billowed up. The two vapor trails that clung to the motors like short beards left an impression of concentrated power, of the intensified vortex in the wake of their energy. Above them, the fighters swirled like spirochetes dangling from an extended thread, making their wide circles and spirals; we could hear the planes' own guns in combat. One of them crashed in smoke and flames over in the direction of Bothfeld. Sometimes I stood at the window; others, in the meadow in order to commit each and every impression to memory, like someone busily taking a series of photographs.

1945

KIRCHHORST, 1 JANUARY 1945

Spent New Year's Eve with Perpetua, Hanne Menzel, Fritzi Schultz, and Hilde Schoor. A speech by Kniébolo launched the new year, a speech manacled by the spirit of hatred and Cainite vision. This descent into ever-darker regions is horrifying—it is a meteoric plunge from the sphere of salvation. Destruction must inevitably grow from these chasms and fire spew forth from them.

New Year's meditation: We are approaching the innermost vortex of the maelstrom, almost certain death. I must prepare myself, steel myself inwardly to step across into the other, shining side of existence, and not as a captive under duress, but with inner affirmation and calm anticipation at that dark gate. My baggage, my treasures, I shall have to leave behind without regret. After all, they are valuable only to the extent that they have an intrinsic connection to the other side. The mass of manuscripts, the work of my mature years—I must become accustomed to the thought of seeing them go up in flames. Then all that will remain will not be what I thought and wrote for human beings: the core of authorship. This will be held in abeyance for the long trek beyond the realm of time. The same applies to the people and things I will be leaving behind. The real and divine aspect of my connection to them is the plane on which I loved them. The most fervent embrace is only the symbol, the metaphor for this inseparability. There we shall be united in the eternal womb, and our eye will no longer be sensitive to light, because it will exist in light itself forever.

The new year began with blue skies and sunshine. But soon enough, these skies were swarming with squadrons performing complex maneuvers while coming under heavy shelling. We could see some of the shots that hung in the air as incendiary puffs. Our house was right on their straight flight path—the formations seemed to chart their deadly course above us. Somewhere near Schillerslage, one of the jagged smoke signals was released and trailed downward from above almost to the earth. In the intervals, there came the terrible drumroll of the barrage, giving the impression that it creates zones of destruction everywhere, places where life can no longer exist. The target must be the town of Dollbergen, an oil transport point.

Aircraft also overhead in the evening, with red Christmas trees.

Léon Bloy, *Lamentation de l'Epée* [*Lamentation of the Sword*], which appeared in October 1890 in *La Plume* [*The Pen*]. The sword expresses its disgust with modern man who is no longer worthy to bear the weapon. It threatens to transform itself into its ancient form, into that of the sword of flame that will eradicate the whole human race.

Motto for a blackout curtain: "*S'ils on éteint le jour, qui'ils soient éclairés de la foudre*" (Michelet).

[If they have extinguished the day, let them be illuminated by the lightning bolt.]

One can certainly say, "God's hand," but not "God's fist."

KIRCHHORST, 4 JANUARY 1945

Current reading: Baader, who is difficult for me. As with everything in the tradition of Böhme, individual images really stand out, such as when he speaks of the advantage of mechanical prayer. He compares devotion arrived at by this method to the pressure applied by the cabinetmaker who forces two warped boards together until the glue has joined them.

I would like to say that, through mechanical prayer, a vacuum, a lacuna arises in the causality of one's daily routine that invites higher influence. In our modern age, this makes our decision to adhere to a credo less pointless than one might imagine, even if the inner calling is absent. Actually, it gives one the best opening moves in the metaphysical match. It is up to God to follow with a counter move. On this, see Matthew 7:7–11.

The passage is also revealing because it contrasts the fish as the goal and the gift of prayer with the earthbound creature, the serpent. Christ never comes up with such imagery by chance. Instead, He reaches deep into the foundations of the world order.

KIRCHHORST, 5 JANUARY 1945

Went to Burgdorf in the morning because of the Civil Defense Unit I am supposed to take over. Our situation is such that desperation is its only positive aspect. This directs intelligent people to seek shelter in their inner and authentic fortresses. Rescue is now possible only if intervention comes from a different dimension.

In the afternoon, I took Hanne Menzel to the station. Thick formations of aircraft overhead in the evening. In the air-raid shelter. From our attic window I watch the city seethe under the bombardment. The yellow umbrellas of fire from the formation bombing[35] rose over the moor.

As I sit here in the quiet room that is under strict blackout conditions, the monotonous voice of the radio announcer again issues from the instrument.

"Numerous aircraft are approaching the district capital from the region of Steinhuder Meer. Air defensive action is urgently required."

My God, who could have thought of such scenes in 1911? It eclipses any science fiction novel.

At ten o'clock a new, even heavier incendiary attack. The explosions were so powerful that objects inside the house fell over.

Read further in Leviticus. Anyone who sees merely hygienic intentions behind the ritual commands of the old lawmakers is like someone who interprets the streets and squares of a metropolis simply in terms of airflow management. That is also correct, but only up to a point. The issue here is not one's physical hygiene, but rather one's optimal conduct, including the hygienic optimum—the condition of sanctity that exalts and elevates one's natural state of health. As a holy thing this even approaches immortality—see those passages where Moses's face is "radiant" and thus unbearable to human eyes.

In this context, see Walter F. Otto, *Dionysos*, a work that is part of my reading these days. The introduction contains good insight into our theological situation:

"The basic character of ritual acts does not derive from the fact that those who first performed them wished to invoke something they yearned for, but from the fact that they already possessed what they yearned for: nearness to their God."

It can be assumed that the Israelites tried to expunge any residual traces of the Egyptians during their exodus. A tangible example of this is the stoning of the son of Shelomith (Leviticus 24:10–16).

KIRCHHORST, 6 JANUARY 1945

Friend Speidel sent word from Freudenstadt that he is out of prison. His letter, dated Christmas Eve, was one of those rare pieces of happy news. I have thought of him every day with great intensity. On the other hand, still no word from Ernstel. That millions of people long to receive letters is a mark of this nightmarish world.

Was in the city in the afternoon. The ruins are new and have been harder hit; the thrashing has been followed by the scorpion's sting. The southern part of the city was burning. Coal cellars were aglow and roofs were collapsing in showers of sparks in the houses on Podbielskistrasse and on Alte Celler Heerstrasse, where I used to ride my bicycle. Nobody notices the fires anymore; they are just part of the scene. On the corners the homeless were packing up their salvaged possessions in bedsheets. I saw a woman come out the door of a house holding a chamber pot in her hand; little more than a fragment was still attached to its handle. Huge craters surrounded the railroad station, where the equestrian statue of King Ernst August still stood in front of the bare, empty halls. Two entrances of the great air-raid bunker where twenty-six thousand people had sought shelter, had been buried in debris. The ventilation system worked only sporadically, making the trapped crowd start to tear their clothes from their bodies and scream for air in the first stages of suffocation. God protect us from mousetraps of this sort.

Burned-out trains stood on the platforms; the pedestrian passage facing the Central Post Office had been hit by a dud that lay on the pavement.

My father-in-law's apartment on Stephansplatz was the reason I had undertaken this mission, and I could see that it was still standing. The building's air-raid shelter had withstood several direct hits without collapsing. Between the first and the second raid, men had left the shelter to visit their homes, and returned to their wives with the sentence, "The house is gone."

KIRCHHORST, 7 JANUARY 1945

Tristitia [sadness]. Dreamed about Cellaris before awakening. I also think of him daily—what I would give if he could only glimpse the light of day again and be spiritually and physically free—if only his health has not been broken forever.

There is a lonely hut deep in the moor between Colshorn and Stelle. From it a soldier fires Christmas trees into the air during night raids in imitation of the target area markers used by the lead planes of the English squadrons. Yesterday Alexander called this a "lightning rod"—a superb comparison for a child.

Started reading the first volume of the *History of Shipwrecks* by Deperthes (Paris: Third Year of the Republic). First, his account of the winter spent by Barent and his crew in 1596–1597 on Novaya Zemlya. Fights with polar bears, which were truly threatening given the explorers' very deficient guns. They conjure up images of encounters between humans and large prehistoric animals. There is a description of the toxicity of the polar bear's liver; consumption of it is followed by almost lethal illness and a peeling of the skin. To counteract scurvy, people eat *Cochlearia* [scurvy grass]; it can even heal acute stages within two days. Another excellent cure is "low-growing prunelle" [blackthorn, sloeberries]. I assume that this is a variety of cloudberry.

KIRCHHORST, 8 JANUARY 1945

Read more about shipwrecks. Eight English sailors, whale fishermen who in 1630 became separated from their ship, the *Salutation*, were forced to spend the winter in Greenland. They set themselves up in a hut that had been used for boiling whale oil. Here they lived mainly on the cracklings left over in heaps where the blubber had been cooked down. They also caught foxes in traps constructed from whalebones. The sun disappeared on 14 October and was not visible again until 3 February. Their vessel returned on 28 May 1631.

This account comes from one of the eight sailors, a man named Pelham. When I read such names, I sometimes think of the wish that Friedrich Georg once expressed during one of our nocturnal conversations: He wished for an index to the catacombs in which could be found the name of every human being who had ever walked this earth, including a short description of his fate. Who knows whether or not something like this exists? When viewed as an absolute, however, it might be no more powerful than a sheet of hieroglyphics on which the temporal notations resemble each other and record a curriculum vitae of human beings. In the same way, the millions of books that have ever been written can be reduced to twenty-four letters.

We have heard that Langenhagen was destroyed in yesterday's raid. Corpses from the village were thrown through the air as far away as the distant autobahn. A few bombs also hit nearby in the parish of Altwarmbüchen.

Still no letter from Ernstel.

KIRCHHORST, 9 JANUARY 1945

Anniversary of the death of my dear father, a date that I always commemorate.

Continued reading about shipwrecks. Winter encampment of the English captain Thomas James on Charlton Island in Hudson's Bay. Scurvy causes the teeth to fall out and the gums to swell. In order to grow fresh vegetables, they plant peas in a covered space. Consuming melted snow causes illness, and so they dig a well that yields water, which they find to be "as mild and nourishing as milk." They return after many fatalities and much privation. The description of such suffering had such a chilling effect on the English that they refrained from any further Arctic exploration for thirty years.

Then there is the Robinsonade about seven sailors who were put ashore by the Dutch Greenland Company on the island of Saint Mauritius on 26 August 1633 with their own permission so that they could observe the course of an

Arctic winter. Scurvy soon sapped their strength, while they suffered under cold so severe that it froze the brandy in its casks, cracked the stones, and made the sea steam like a laundry room. They died one after another, keeping up their journal entries until 30 April 1634. On 4 July, the whaling fleet returned and found the corpses in their beds. One was holding the bread and cheese he had eaten shortly before he died; another had a prayer book in his hand and a box of salve to apply to his gums.

Concerning synchronicity. During these instances of solitary suffering, Wallenstein was murdered in Eger as the Thirty Years' War played out in different parts of the planet. Such thoughts always touch me particularly deeply. They point to the sun's great, all-seeing eye and to the great heart of the world.

KIRCHHORST, 10 JANUARY 1945

Raids in the evening with intense bombardment, after several vicious "dog stars"[36] had been set off over the city. I stayed with Frau Schoor, whose bad influenza made it impossible for her to go to the air-raid shelter.

Read further about shipwrecks. Among other winter survival narratives, the one experienced by Bering is mentioned. His ship, the *Saint Peter*, foundered on 5 November 1741 on the coast of the Kamchatka Peninsula. Before the vessel was wrecked, the men were already suffering from scurvy. Many died when they were lifted out of the musty ship's hold into the open air—it was too powerful, too debilitating for the faltering life force. Bering died as well and was buried on the island named for him. Among his officers was a doctor, a naturalist named Steller. Their food source was the abundant sea life along that coast, especially the sea cow (which has since become extinct) that was named for Steller.[37] Two stranded whales were greeted with great joy; the men used the frozen cadavers as meat larders. Using their natural Russian talent for working with wood, they finished a new craft that was forty feet long on 10 August 1742. In this they were able to return to Siberia. Steller's presence gives the expedition an intellectual, academic aspect, and puts the ever-recurring scenes of dazed suffering during this winter in a more illustrious light.

KIRCHHORST, 12 JANUARY 1945

Ernstel is dead, killed in action, my good child. Dead since 29 November of last year! We received the news yesterday on 11 January 1945, just after seven o'clock in the evening.

KIRCHHORST, 13 JANUARY 1945

The dear boy met his death on 29 November 1944; he was eighteen years old. He was felled by a shot to the head during a reconnaissance patrol in the Apuan Alps in central Italy and, according to his comrades, died immediately. They could not take him along, but went back for his body later with an armored vehicle. He was given his final resting place in the cemetery of Turigliano near Carrara.

Such a good lad. Ever since childhood, he strove to emulate his father. Now he has done so on his first try, and truly surpassed him.

Today I went up into the little attic room that I had vacated for him, and which is still filled with his aura. Entered quietly, as if it were a sacred place. Found there among his papers a little journal that began with the epigraph: "He advances farthest, who does not know where he is going."

KIRCHHORST, 14 JANUARY 1945

Anguish is like rain that runs off in torrents and is only gradually absorbed by the earth. The mind cannot grasp it all at once. We have now entered the true, the only community of this war—entered its secret brotherhood.

I cannot stop thinking about Ernstel. So much about his life is a riddle that is hard to solve. What does it mean that during the same year he was able to free himself from the grip of tyranny? That was such a propitious sign; all the benevolent powers seemed to be working together, as if secretly in league with each other. Perhaps he was meant to bear witness before his death and prove himself in the true cause of which so few people are capable.

KIRCHHORST, 15 JANUARY 1945

Sleep does me good, but as soon as I awaken, the pain starts up again. I ask myself how it is possible that we thought about the boy every day for all those weeks without ever even hearing an echo of the truth. Of course, there is always the notation that I made in the pages of this journal on 29 November 1944, on the day of his death, perhaps even in the hour of his death.[38] At the time I was thinking of the widespread popular superstition, yet it is strange that in all my attempts to interpret Perpetua's dream, the closest possibility was the furthest from my mind.

We stand like cliffs in the silent surf of eternity.

KIRCHHORST, 16 JANUARY 1945

Memorial service for Ernstel. Superintendent Spannuth held it in the library. The boy's picture stood on the table between sprigs of fir and two candles. The conclusion of Psalm 73 and Ernstel's confirmation motto (Luke, 9:62) were chosen as texts: "And Jesus said unto him, no man having put his hand to the plow and looking back, is fit for the kingdom of God."

Present were: the family, the refugees living under our roof, and our two neighbors, Lahmann and Colshorn.

The death of a son introduces one of those dates—one of those watersheds—into my life. The things, the thoughts, the deeds before and after are now different.

KIRCHHORST, 17 JANUARY 1945

Went to Burgdorf. Had vivid thoughts of Ernstel near Beinhorn. When we were there last December the two of us walked through the woods in the fog and discussed death. He said, "At times I'm so curious that I can hardly wait for it."

KIRCHHORST, 20 JANUARY 1945

The *lemures* try to intrude into a death like this, as if they could appropriate it. A case in point is the company commander who sent me the message that Ernstel had died "for the Führer." What is more, he was well acquainted with the boy's record. After that there was the functionary who had the task of bringing me the message "in a dignified manner" (as stipulated in his printed instructions)—horrendous. Yes, that's all part of our reality, and it dawned on me early that one emotion is the only appropriate response: grief.

It is the tragedy of the best people that *ethos* and *polis* do not coincide in reality. Yet, like parallel lines, they cross in infinity.

KIRCHHORST, 23 JANUARY 1945

While I have frequent and meaningful dreams about my dead father, things regarding my son are opaque. There is something about his death that seems unsolved, unreconciled, unsettled. Last night Perpetua had the first clear dream about him. She was in a hospital and met him in the corridor; he was startled to see her. He was already very weak, and died in her arms. She could hear his dying sweat *splash* onto the floor.

The Russians have entered East Prussia and Silesia. New efforts to halt this breakthrough while the butchering continues in the West. The energy, resilience of people's wills remains astonishing. Of course, this quality only shows itself as we are heading downhill—its only trait and accomplishment being mindlessness and decline. This is no longer war, which is why Clausewitz warned that politics must never be allowed to reach this state.

According to reports, the Tannenberg memorial[39] has been blown up and Hindenburg's body taken to safety. "Der Alte" ["The Old Man"] finds no peace in his grave, but then he was the gatekeeper, the man who held the door for Kniébolo. At first he thought he could oppose the man and then exploit him, but Kniébolo turned out to be the more cunning.

KIRCHHORST, 24 JANUARY 1945

A night rich in dreams. I found myself in exotic climes, surrounded by brightly colored birds. Inside my coat on my left, I clutched a white dove and on my right, a dark bat. Both creatures—I cherished the dark one more—would occasionally take flight and then return to me as if to their nests. The dream image was comforting and lovely.

These days I often look at pictures of Ernstel with new ideas about photography. No photograph can compete with a good painting in that sphere where art reigns supreme and where ideas and consciousness hold sway. Yet photography has a different, darker quality—the photograph is basically a shadow image. It records something of a person's substance, of his aura; it is a replica of him. In this sense, it is related to script. We leaf through old letters and photos to jog our memories. At such times, wine is beneficial.

KIRCHHORST, 26 JANUARY 1945

Two weeks have now passed since I got the news. Starting to work again. I finished the manuscript of my Rhodes journals, and all that is left is to make a clean copy. I often have the impression of writing on paper that is already beginning to be scorched by the flame.

Read further about shipwrecks. In the course of my reading, I had some good thoughts of a general nature. For example, a ship represents order, the state, the status quo; a shipwreck loosens the planks and, with them, all cohesion, so that human relationships sink to their most basic level. They become more physical, bestial, or cannibalistic. Those amputated hands that are consistently mentioned demonstrate the physics of this dynamic. The lifeboats can only take a certain number of people; anyone else who clutches at their sides threatens to sink them in the deep. Because there is *modus in rebus* [a limit in all things], the crew will defend itself with oars, knives, and axes against any fatal overloading. This occasionally proceeds under a veneer of order, such as in 1786 when the Portuguese admiral's ship *Saint James* foundered on a group of cliffs in East Africa. In this case, the crew of the overfilled lifeboat chose a leader with absolute power, namely a half-blooded Indian from a noble tribe. All this man had to do was point his finger at the weakest person, who was then immediately thrown overboard. Under such circumstances, it is typical that power always seeks the point of least resistance. And so whenever it happens that cannibals attack, they agree on the cabin boy—according to Bontekoe's account.

The leaders who emerge from the crew in such cases, or who impose themselves on the crew, could be called "black captains"; they act as pirates in the way they manage the crime and the violence. When the *Batavia* was wrecked on a desert island off the coast of New Holland [Australia], power was handed over to a ringleader named Cornelis, who had everyone killed who did not accede to his plans. He divided the booty, including five women who had been among the passengers. He kept one for himself and designated another, an ambassador's daughter, for his lieutenant. The others were given to the crew for their general use.

Shipwrecks pose the question of whether any higher order than that of the state exists. For order alone can save us, and we have seen this in the case of those sailors who settled on Pitcairn.[40] At such moments, every crew stands at the crossroads.

The evacuation of East Prussia and Silesia brings us pictures hitherto unknown in European history. This reminds me of the destruction of Jerusalem. The persecution of the Jews has aspects of which the blind perpetrators know nothing. As such, it negates the New Testament and promotes Abrahamic law.

KIRCHHORST, 27 JANUARY 1945

The punishing cold continues. We hear that many of the children who fled from the Eastern provinces have frozen to death along the country roads and in open freight cars. Scores are now being settled, and the innocents are paying the terrible price. Went into the forest in the afternoon with old Herr Kerner to mark trees, since our coal supply is running low. We were also on the moor, where there is still a small stand of birches. The axe revealed the heartwood in its gleaming brilliance. As I was writing down the numbers, I saw my father, the man who purchased this forest, as if on the surface of a mirror. Wood is a wonderful, honorable material.

On the way home, I conversed with the old fellow. I noticed that a certain sense of homespun ease—familiar in many a Lower Saxon farmer—comes with a brazen heart. These are characters who even in their own family circles would walk right over corpses. He described a scene from his youth when he was both half-drunk and pretending to be drunk, and he eavesdropped on his wife with a friend. His wait for the *fait accompli* came to nothing.

KIRCHHORST, 28 JANUARY 1945

In church for the memorial service for Ernstel. Tomorrow it will be two months since the boy was killed. For me, he will always be one of those I carry with me in the sanctuary of my heart. *Omnia mea mecum porto* [all that is mine I carry with me]—the proverb is more apt than ever.

KIRCHHORST, 29 JANUARY 1945

Read more about shipwrecks. The crew of a Portuguese cutter that ran aground on a sandbank on the Calamian Islands in 1688 suffered a strange fate. In the first half of the year, the survivors lived on this desolate patch by eating sea tortoises that would come on land to lay their eggs. During the second half they lived off the flesh and the eggs of gannets, large sea birds that build their nests in the sand. These two creatures alternated as food sources. They were marooned there for six years until the birds stayed away. The shipwrecked men, whose number had dwindled to sixteen, then set to work constructing a boat, or rather, a type of chest out of driftwood and caulked with a mixture of birds' feathers, sand, and the fat of tortoises. This was stitched together with the strong sinews of the tortoises. A sail was stitched from the birds' skins. With this craft they were able to reach a port in Southern China, and from there they were taken by missionaries to Macao.

KIRCHHORST, 2 FEBRUARY 1945

Read in the memoirs of Count de Viel-Castel; Friedrich Georg and I had talked about this work years ago. Unpleasant view of the world that sees only the dark side of human beings and their scandalous behavior. Of course, there was no lack of profiteering during the Second Empire. All the preconditions for the catastrophe we are now wallowing in were well established back then. I am often amazed that a war like the one of 1870–1871 could have ended so favorably—I mean for both sides—without worsening. Bismarck himself sensed this and was happy when the peace terms were finally ratified.

KIRCHHORST, 6 FEBRUARY 1945

Most of our mail relates to Ernstel's death, but today it also brought a card from Carl Schmitt:

Ernestus non reliquit nos sed antecessit. Cum sciam omnia perdere et Dei sententia qui mutat corda hominum et fata populorum, rerum exitum patienter expecto.

[Ernstel has not left us but only preceded us. Since I know that all things die, and that the will of God alters the hearts of men and the fates of nations, I await patiently my departure from life.]

Name of sender: *Volkssturmmann* [Civil Defense Man] Schmitt, Albrechtsteerofen. The card upset me; it made me clearly aware of the abrupt shift that has cast millions of people these days into utter catastrophe, into mud and fire. Just as individual moments attach themselves to such ideas, the red silk easy chair surfaced in my memory. That was where I had sat so often in his apartment in Steglitz to discuss the course of the world late into the night over good wine.

Since Ernstel's death, I have forgotten to record the raids and bombardments, although there has been no shortage of them in the interim. As I write this morning, the air is filled with activity. Am also worried about Brother Physicus. The last I heard, he was in Schneidemühl, which is surrounded.

Browsed in Chamfort again. What can be said of Rivarol is also true of him: There is a particular kind of clarity that can be attributed to disinfection [of prose style]. Yet this also incorporates a new freedom and to see it *in statu nascendi* [emerging] is a great pleasure. For a century, witty writers drew on him.

The following anecdote amused me once again: The Regent did not wish to be recognized at a masked ball. "I can remedy that," said Abbé Dubois, and during the ball proceeded to dole out kicks to his backside. Finally the Regent said, "Abbé, you disguise me too well."

To split firewood, *aufklöben*.[41]

KIRCHHORST, 7 FEBRUARY 1945

Finished my reading about shipwrecks. The material should be organized into a systematic treatise.

Cannibalism. After the *Betsey* went down off the coast of Dutch Guyana in 1756, the helmsman, a man named Williams who was the strongest of the nearly starved survivors, showed his "generosity" by offering his comrades a piece of his hindquarters to help them cling to life with his blood.

The crew of the American ship *Peggy* was reduced to butchery in 1665 when she became impossible to steer while sailing from the Azores to New York and had to spend months as a plaything of the waves.[42] Once the ship's cat had been devoured as the last of their provisions, the crew decided to extend the lives of the survivors by killing one of their own. Against the will of the captain, who lay ill in his cabin, lots were drawn and a Negro slave on board was chosen. This suggests that the unfortunate man had been chosen in advance and that the lottery was merely a sham. He was slain at once.

The body kept them alive for over two weeks. Then they had to settle upon a second victim, and this time the captain was in charge of drawing lots out of concern that it would otherwise take place without him. He wrote the names on small pieces of paper, threw these into a hat and shook it. The crew watched these preparations in silence, their faces pale and mouths quivering, their fright visibly etched on every feature. A man drew the piece of paper; the captain opened it and read the name: David Flat. The crew gave in to the captain's request to postpone his slaughter until the eleventh hour of the next morning. At ten o'clock, when a large fire was already blazing and the cauldron in place on it, a sail came into view. It was the *Susanne* whose captain re-victualed the ship and took her in tow.

A detail reminds me of one of Joseph Conrad's novels. An English ship, the *Fattysalam*, a troop transport vessel, sprang a leak in 1761 off the Coromandel Coast. It was so serious that it seemed inevitable the ship would sink in no time. Before the crew found out about the disaster, the captain and the officers secretly boarded the dinghy that was in tow and abandoned ship. From their safe distance, they watched as panic broke out aboard the *Fattysalam*. But soon the signal was given that the damage had been repaired. The captain was in favor of returning to the ship but was cautioned against it by his officers. Shortly thereafter, they saw the ship go down. The signal had just been an attempt to coax the dinghy back.

The collection is rich in similar examples of rational bestiality. The study of shipwrecks gives us a key to our age. The sinking of the *Titanic* is its most portentous omen.

An example of Wilhelmine baroque style: "It is in my opinion subject to no doubt at all . . . "

This example from *Bürgermeister Mönckeberg, Briefe* [*Mayor Monckeberg, Letters*] (Stuttgart, 1918). On the same page, he uses *unbedingter* [more absolute] as a comparative.

KIRCHHORST, 11 FEBRUARY 1945
During the church service, the gun emplacements in Stelle were booming— a spotter plane circled low over the village, probably to take photographs. Since the Misburg oil works have been operational again, we've had to expect new raids close by. In Burgdorf a low-flying aircraft strafed a passenger train. Twenty fatalities.

KIRCHHORST, 12 FEBRUARY 1945
Letters still come every day regarding Ernstel's death, and with them, many a comforting word. Today, for example, the thought that our life presupposes another side; the effort [to see it] is too great for our physical existence.

Verses from Friedrich Georg that reminded me of Ernstel's childhood in Goslar and Überlingen.

Auf Ernstels Tod
Die Winde fragen nach dem Gespielen:
"Wo bist du?" Und das Echo kehrt wieder.
Der Frühling kommt nun, bald kommt der Frühling.
"Wo bist du, Ernstel? Kommst du nicht wieder?"

Der Harz will grünen. Und auf den Wiesen
In dichten Hecken tönen die Lieder.
Die Amsel ruft dich aus den Gebüschen:
"Wo bist du, Erstel? Kommst du nicht wieder?"

Er ruht nun. Ach, ihr ruft ihn vergebens
An kühlen Wassern und in den Hainen.
Ihm ward ein früher Friede beschieden.
Wir aber blieben, ihn zu beweinen.

[On Ernstel's Death / The winds are asking for their playmate: / "Where are you?" And the echo comes back. / Spring is now coming, soon spring will arrive. / "Where are you, Ernstel? Won't you return?" // The Harz [region] is about to erupt in green. And on the meadows / The songs resound in the dense hedges. / The blackbird calls you from the thicket: / "Where are you Ernstel? Won't you return?" // He is at peace now. Oh, you call him in vain / At the cool waters and in the groves. / To him was granted an early peace. / But we stayed behind to mourn him.]

Despite his youth, he left behind a definite impression, was also loved by many. Today the photo of his grave arrived from Carrara. Thus, every day brings an echo of him.

Ziegler writes to me from Hamburg that by special order of the Grandgoschier [Goebbels], the press will print no mention of my fiftieth birthday. That happens to be the only honor that I prize.

KIRCHHORST, 14 FEBRUARY 1945

Restless night. The English have adopted a strategy of demoralization by sending a single aircraft to circle over the landscape and just drop a bomb now and then to keep tensions high.

During the day, one air-raid alert follows the next. We hear that Dresden has been heavily hit. With that, the last untouched city was probably reduced to rubble. Apparently hundreds of thousands of incendiary bombs were dropped, and countless refugees died in the open spaces.

I worked in the garden. Yesterday, I got an early glimpse of the red shoot of a peony. Turned over the compost underneath the large elm. The way that all things there decay and return to earth has something instructive and comforting about it.

Read in the small dual language edition of Heraclitus that Carl Schmitt gave me on 23 March 1933. Also read in Louis Réau's monograph on Houdon, who has interested me ever since I saw his bust of Voltaire in the foyer of the Comédie Française.[43] This sculptor of the rococo period achieves an extraordinary degree of physiognomic truth. One feels that here the inner truth of the age itself finds its expression: namely its mathematical-musical core. A chisel of Mozartian precision. A comparative study on him and Anton Graff would be instructive.

Heraclitus: "Sleepers are active participants in the events of the world."

Their successes were the worst thing for the Germans—in any reckless match, a victory at the outset is most dangerous. That is the bait, the barbed hook that ensnares greed. Winning also seduces the player into showing his cards. He removes the mask.

After the victory over France, the middle classes were convinced that everything was fine. They no longer heard the voices of the unfortunates and their *De Profundis*.[44]

Incidentally, the Western powers are entering a similar phase. Success is making them ruthless. Just as their weapons become superior, their broadcasts also change from praising justice to threatening vengeance. The language of reason is displaced by violence. The willingness to make peace stands under the sign of Libra, the scales: one of the pans rises as the other falls. That has remained unchanged since the time of Brennus.

Who will stand by us after these spectacles have finished? Not the ones we shared our pleasures with at the banquet table, but rather those who shared the pain with us. This applies to the friends, the women, and to the relationships among us Germans in general. We are now finding a new, firmer ground for our commonality.

KIRCHHORST, 15 FEBRUARY 1945

At my desk in the morning while the anti-aircraft guns fired and dense formations roared over the house. The windowpanes, the doors, the glasses in the cupboards, the pictures on the walls dance and shake like a ship on rough seas.

In the afternoon, I took Alexander along on my subterranean studies in order to train his eye a bit. We dug up a mole's burrow and a nest of wood ants, and also visited a rabbit warren. The wood ants' nest was located in the heart of a dead fir tree; its chambers, passages, and galleries followed the tree's grain and had created recesses by leaving paper-thin walls that had perforated the wooden block like a honeycomb. The bleached-out structure possessed a certain delicate stability, so that if a hand were to grab a piece of it, one would have to strain in order to break it into dry fragments. The sight of all this made me think of the great story about my adventures with the ants, which I used when I was fifteen years old to keep my brothers and sisters spellbound until late at night. If this kind of innocence in storytelling were ever to come back to me, it would overflow like the contents of a *krater*.

Read further in the Old Testament. Deborah's song of victory (Judges, 5): that terrible, joyous celebration over steaming blood. Verses 28–30, ironic enjoyment at the pain of Sisera's mother, who waits for her son in an anguished state, still unaware that he will not return, because a nail has been driven through his skull. Abimelech also appears as a man of unbelievable violence in this book.

Mountainous areas are generally regarded as places of refuge, strongholds of freedom, where the collapsing national character survives. Here we find the opposite: The Israelites penetrate the mountains and cannot establish themselves on the plains, the home to peoples who possess "chariots of iron." Perhaps the rule is that mountains are favorable to the weaker but more determined power.

KIRCHHORST, 16 FEBRUARY 1945

A beautiful day. The tall hazel bush by my study has adorned itself overnight with woolly, greenish-yellow ribbons of blooms. The terrible destruction continues; in addition to Dresden, Vienna has also been heavily bombed. One gets the feeling that these are blows aimed at a cadaver. It seems that the cup of agony is not yet full.

Worked more in the garden and at my desk. Thought: whether this activity resembles that of those insects that we sometimes find along footpaths, their heads continuing to eat and their antennae moving, while their bodies have been stepped on.

This is only one side of the process; the other is allegorical, sacramental. One sows one's seed without expectation of ever reaping a harvest. Such activity is either completely senseless or transcendental. Which of the two: it lies in our hands to determine that.

Discourse at the garden gate:

I: "Things are lively in the air today."

Neighbor: "Yes, they say Osnabrück and Chemnitz have been destroyed."

But I was talking about the mosquitoes that were buzzing around for the first time.

KIRCHHORST, 22 FEBRUARY 1945

Manfred [Schwarz] was here for a few days of furlough and departed today. He was recently made commander of a tank unit and is wearing the Iron Cross. Nor does he lack for wounds: His left hand is crippled, the arm shattered by an explosion and rendered useless. During all this time of ferment, his thoughts have become clearer in a horrible distillation. These are the youths I have watched grow up over the years.

I was pleased by the way he judged the situation and showed him my essay on peace, making him one of its very few readers. We discussed it and later also talked about the books by Schubart and Tocqueville, as well as about Russia in particular.

We live in a state of nearly constant air-raid alerts. I was out on the Winkelwiese [meadow], partly to supervise the felling of trees and partly to do a little hunting for *subtiles*. While I was there, dense formations of aircraft overhead. Shrapnel whistled down; a dud struck some marshy terrain with huge force.

KIRCHHORST, 23 FEBRUARY 1945

In the garden in the afternoon, still breaking up the soil, when I dug out a mandrake root. It had a slender twisted waist and hermaphroditic gender, a female that was also male. In flowers, the structure that people are more apt to take for a masculine than a feminine feature is formed similarly. I view this as a conundrum with sometimes the one and sometimes the other characteristic predominating.

KIRCHHORST, 24 FEBRUARY 1945

Formations overhead while I worked on revising my Brazilian journal. They put down three "carpets."[45] From the window, I again watched black smoke clouds rise over Misburg but heard later that a dummy factory had been set on fire. Burgdorf was hit; church and parsonage are destroyed. It is now the turn of the small towns, those last abodes of the old times. Swarms of low-flying aircraft accompany the squadrons in order to "go for the villages."

During the day there is, incidentally, less incentive to head for the air-raid shelter. That says something about the role our imagination plays during these attacks.

KIRCHHORST, 26 FEBRUARY 1945

Two Russians who cut wood for us told Perpetua in the kitchen that after three years of captivity, this was the first time that they had been fed inside a house they worked for. That is more troubling than the cruelty itself. Of course, Rozanov was already seeing things like this in Russia after World War I. This is generalized suffering.

An age that possesses such understanding of the physics of energy transfer has lost contact with the immense power contained in the offer of a little piece of bread.

Read further in the Old Testament. Anyone who wants to shape policy, like Kniébolo, should avoid lazy slogans and use the language of Nahash the Ammonite (I Samuel, 11:2).

Saul and Samuel, the first emperor and the first Pope.

Thought about Carus.[46] I wish him a beautiful physique and a great intellect. On this point: the first is always there to vouch for us. The second we must reveal ourselves: presence of mind. This explains the preference of Aphrodite over Athena; the Judgment of Paris incorporates astrological justice. Eventually, of course, the more intellectual power triumphs, and therefore Troy had to be destroyed

KIRCHHORST, 27 FEBRUARY 1945

Pondered the naming of colors, always a vague and uncertain venture. Take *weinrot* [wine red]—red wine has dozens of shades. It would seem that the some spirit of speech bases the connections on vowel sounds. Hence the visual impression is stimulated less by comparisons than by direct experience.

It is inherent in the sound that *purpurn* [purple] must glow more darkly than *scharlachrot* [scarlet]. *Bordeaux* is brighter then *Burgunderrot* [Burgundy red]—and not just in view of the substances being compared, but also "synaesthetically," meaning by sound magic. Without an instinctive control of these laws, good style is not possible.

The word is that Überlingen has been bombed, that magnificent old city. I am worried about Friedrich Georg.

We hear that Poland is to be compensated for those territories it will have to cede to Russia by being given Upper Silesia and East Prussia. This means that the other side does not plan to do things any better than Kniébolo would have. Human blindness to everything that has shown us the fiery omens for years fills me with horror.

Current reading: have picked up Huysmans's *Là Bas* [*The Damned*] after many years. This book exerted particular influence on me after World War I, awakened an inclination toward expressionist Catholicism, which was then suppressed. Certain texts work like vaccinations.

Also reading *Pitcairn, the Island, the People, and the Pastor* by Rev. Thomas Boyles Murray (London, 1860) as a follow-up to my reading about shipwrecks. A passage about the Fiji Islanders asserts: "Their horrible habit of feeding on human flesh is the more remarkable, as they exceed their neighbors in talent and ingenuity," as one of those not infrequent indications that cannibalism and higher culture are not mutually exclusive. I first became aware of this when reading Stucken's *Die Weissen Götter* [*The Great White Gods* (1934)].

KIRCHHORST, 3 MARCH 1945

In the afternoon was at the fence that borders the churchyard; its stones and inscribed marble slabs peer over it. I have fallen behind with my digging, partly because of the general situation and also because of Ernstel's death. This morning after snowstorms alternated with dense bomber formations, the sun broke through around the edges of the white cloud banks now and again. There was already warmth in the earth; I ran my fingers through it to pull out the roots of weeds among the currant bushes. In the loose, previously cultivated soil, my hand grabs hold of the still-hidden plants and gently pulls them out like creatures of the sea caught in a net. Under the thin covering things are sprouting vigorously, such as the nettles that shoot their green splendor from the yellowed root crown in a star pattern. This is true power, more real than a thousand airplanes.

The voice we use to attract animals or to drive them away differs depending on the species. The chicken, the dog, the cat, the sparrow, the horse, the snake—we have different calls for each one, special sounds and special melodies. Here we speak in tongues with the language of the Life Spirit that pours both over us and them.

KIRCHHORST, 5 MARCH 1945

Planted fava beans on the final recommended date. The flat seeds are large, plump, copper colored, like two-*Pfennig* pieces; I press them—not without pleasure—into the soft soil. When they are young, they produce an admittedly northern, but delicious, dish with chopped celery and mild bacon. Surely Hamann must have feasted on this. In Sicily, I once saw a smaller version; it was sweeter and served like sugar peas.

The early morning arrival of the donkeys and carts loaded with vegetables in southern cities is part of some of the most powerful memories of my life. For example, I recall the hour when I watched from a Neapolitan balcony as loads of onions, leeks, and fennel swayed in bright green and white bundles. They were accompanied by symphonies, as if whole populations of birds were chirping. These are images, like public offerings, that revive and strengthen us.

KIRCHHORST, 7 MARCH 1945

There was a letter from Hanna in the mail today. She writes from Leisnig that the news of Ernstel's death was the fanfare announcing the entire calamity that has overtaken us. For weeks there has been no word from my two younger brothers, the geographer in Schneidemühl or the physicist in Crossen.

She also writes: "Of course, we can cross goodness and humanity off our agendas—but that makes the waves of hatred tremendously powerful."

Read in the Bible, the passage on the building of the Temple and its dedication (I Kings, 6:7). The aversion to the use of iron for ritual purposes and sacred services is strange. Even the stones are dressed at distant locations, so that no sound of iron is heard during construction. Ore, on the other hand, is used copiously. This aversion is mysterious; it implies conservative as well as moral attributes. Iron is also a Cainite metal, and the foundation of superhuman power.

By contrast, it makes me ponder how little opposition was raised to the introduction of electricity into our churches. Every religious rite has the incorruptible Levite sense for the purity of sacrificial material and sacrificial instruments. Of course, this sense must not, as in Huysmans, derive from a feeling of nausea.

KIRCHHORST, 9 MARCH 1945

Concerning style. I have an aversion to the appearance of any kind of numbers in a text—the only exception being the notation of dates and textual references. This essentially stems from the fact that every concept that is predetermined and remote from perception is repugnant to me. Numbers are among these, with the exception of the dates of years, for they have substance: 1757, 1911, 1914 are quantities one can visualize. For me, it goes against the grain to write 300 horses, 256 dead, 100 Christmas trees. We don't want to view things through the lens of statistics.

In this context, I should mention my horror of the decimal system in any non-secular text. To me, in prose, words like centimeter, kilometer, kilogram sound like the sounds of iron during the construction of the Temple. In trying to avoid them we come back to the concepts: a foot, an ell, a span, a brace, a stone's throw, an hour on foot—these are natural quantities.

The same applies to fashionable notions and topical expressions; these are primarily generated by politics, technology, and social interaction. They are the short-lived recombinations of linguistic material, and an intellect may be gauged by the extent to which it succumbs to them. Abbreviations belong in this category as well. Expressions formed this way should either be avoided or stated in their original words, which means writing them out.

Rivarol. I began with the translation of his *Thoughts and Maxims*. Perhaps today our language is finally achieving the same fluent consistency so that it, too, can be poured into such molds. That is naturally contingent upon a loss of potential energy.

I was again charmed by: "*Un livre qu'on soutient est un livre qui tombe*" [A book one defends is a book that falls]. The perfection of this utterance lies in the congruence, the absolute correspondence of its physical and intellectual quality. This balance embodies the hallmark of exquisite prose in general.

Death has now drawn so close that people take it into account in their trivial decisions—like whether or not to have another tooth filled.

Read further in the Book of Kings. The third chapter of the second book provides insights into the terrible splendor of the magic world. The king of the Moabites is besieged by a league of allied empires massed before his city. Under this duress, he gathers seven hundred swordsmen to attack the person of the King of Edom in the Asiatic way that Xenophon describes in detail. After this desperate action has failed, he slaughters his firstborn son on the city wall with his own hand for a burnt offering. No superior power is equal to this terrible incantation. It even exceeded Jehovah's support: "Then he took his eldest son that should have reigned in his stead and offered him for a burnt offering upon the wall. And there was great indignation against Israel: and they departed from him and returned to their own land" (II Kings 3:27).

I am sometimes overwhelmed by the unimaginable reality of these events—how much more real they are than Darwin's theory or Bohr's model of the atom. But then I think, perhaps it is precisely in this unreality, in this realm of the absolute fantastic, in this late Gothic spirituality of our world, that its actual merit lies.

KIRCHHORST, 13 MARCH 1945

Elijah. Elisha. The miracles of these men of God are the models, counterparts, for Christian ones. Their earlier magical aspects later become charismatic. Power also serves wickedness, lets children be torn apart by bears, or brings leprosy upon the head of the unfaithful servant.

The similarity is nonetheless evident. Among the Disciples there are thus some who see the resurrected Elijah in Christ. Peter, however, stresses the difference: "Thou art the son of God."

There are passages in the New Testament where the charismatic miracle does not completely separate from its counterpart, the magical. Take, for example, the anecdote about the coin found in the gullet of the fish.

KIRCHHORST, 14 MARCH 1945

Perpetua's birthday. New refugees have joined our household. We increasingly resemble a lifeboat in the vicinity of sinking ships. Perpetua shows herself equal to the throngs—her resources seem to increase as she distributes them. Something is always left over. From that I recognize the authentic relationship to abundance, to fecundity.

Piles of mail. Friedrich Georg calms me with one of his restorative letters, but nonetheless, he confirms that Überlingen has been bombed. At the very time of this peril, he was visiting Ziegler, the philosopher. I recognize in his report traits that are his alone: "People were killed and buildings destroyed. All around, the air was heavy with the scent of red cedars, cypresses, trees of life, firs, and other conifers, whose branches and foliage had been shorn off and crushed by the shrapnel."

From Leisnig I also hear that Brother Physicus has written to me. That takes a further load off my mind.

Rosenkranz, who provides me with an ample supply of literature, sends a manuscript from the posthumous papers of Georg Trakl. I shall send this on to

Friedrich Georg. I found nothing new here, for Trakl's poetry is like a dream kaleidoscope viewed through the wrong end. In the moonlight behind the frosted glass, monotonous configurations of a few—but no less authentic—stones repeat.

KIRCHHORST, 15 MARCH 1945

Went to the dentist in Burgdorf in the afternoon. My prognosis does not seem completely unfavorable.

Magnificent spring weather. At the edge of the patch of woods near Beinhorn, I thought about Ernstel as usual, and the fact that he will never see earthly meadows and flowers again. His death brings new experience to my life—that of a wound that will not heal.

On spring days like this, the air is thick with swarms of the red *Aphodius* [dung beetle]. Its wing covers still have a reddish sheen, not the dirty, rusty brown tinge of later months. I watched legions of them buzzing around today and countless others that had been crushed flat by feet or wheels covered the country road. Such a mass hatching in this previously deserted space always makes me reflect on the question of the archetype that propagates itself with such enormous power in these myriads. The phenomenon resembles that red curtain, the red cloud that encircles an invisible pole. Ernstel's curiosity was focused on this in these fields when he once told me that he could hardly wait for death, as if it were some mysterious ceremony.

Incidentally, contact with the archetype is inherent in every conception—transubstantiation, from which flesh springs. Novalis:

Sie wissen nicht,
Dass du es bist,
Der des zarten Mädchens
Busen umschwebt
Und zum Himmel den Schoss macht.

[They do not know, / That it is you, / Who hovers over the / Gentle maiden's bosom / And makes the womb a heaven.]

Formations of planes flew over the area during my whole excursion. They gleamed silver as they lumbered away like titanic war chariots overhead. Still, I could sense spring in such power, so that even this cheered me. Potent life everywhere.

I read Kipling in the waiting room. His later dandyism combines with a good knowledge of all those aspects of morality and amorality that are necessary for dominance. Good alloy: from his Germanic forebears comes the wide-ranging, broad territorial consciousness of power; his Latin blood endows him with a formal and social component; and then—possibly absorbed from ancient Celts—a further metaphysical bonus, a kind of second sight into the mysteries of the world and its peoples, archipelagoes, and landscapes.

In terms of the common mold, the Germans have assimilated less felicitously, yet among them, there is greater probability that a solitaire, a Koh-i-Noor, can emerge from the slag of the melting pot.

Went to the garden center on my way back. Bleeding Heart, in spikes of most delicate jade tipped with gleaming reddish jasper—one of my favorite flowers—had already broken through the prepared soil along the borders. The power of the Earth Spirit in such organisms is enchanting, extraordinary. These are organs at the womb of our good little mother: the old Earth, who is still the youngest of red-skirted lasses. How desirable then, that our whole body should finally merge with hers at the end of this great pageant.

In the evening as I write these journal entries, one of the heaviest attacks on Misburg is taking place. Reconnaissance planes first laid down a veritable avenue of orange-yellow flares. The bombardment followed immediately.

KIRCHHORST, 18 MARCH 1945

I was a racecar driver arriving home with a huge trophy in my arms. I called to my wife to set the table in the garden because we were expecting guests:

"Put the trophy on the table too, and all the prizes from the cabinets along with it. You can also take some of the ribbons and the other award stuff off the walls."

Was exhausted and, during all of this, had the manners of the arrogant champion completely addicted to the applause of the masses.

As usual, when I awoke, this intrusion into my habits and into the nature of a completely foreign, not to say contrary, existence, was disturbing.

Finished reading *À Rebours* [*Against the Grain*]. In theological terms, Huysmans's merits do not extend beyond the late Romantic impulse. Aesthetic, but not moral, disgust also forces him to seek refuge in the old fortresses. Léon Bloy, who incidentally is mentioned in *À Rebours*, is in this sense, incomparably more vibrant. Still, Huysmans has exerted significant influence, especially when he fished in the lagoons and backwaters where no one else's net reaches. The primary spark for revelations that acknowledge no gradations of health often springs from unhealthy circumstances and neurotic influences. At this moment, the most delicate glasses in the sideboard are starting to vibrate as the squadrons approach.

In areas of style, the same applies to the palette he uses to decorate his prose. In this outrageous adulteration and fraying of colors, in these esoteric festivals of the retina, *décadence* celebrates its triumphs and awakens sixteenth and thirty-second notes of a new sensibility. The mania to discern and describe the last ray of light at the margins of the invisible produces prose that sometimes reminds one of de Sade and owes him an obvious debt. How different is this scale to that of a Memling; his conjures the pure spectrum of the rainbow with its clear, gemlike colors.

And yet the degeneration of high style can be commendable, for there can no more be a hierarchy of primitivism and *décadence* in pure literature than in morality and immorality. There is only perception and object, eye and light, author and the world, and optimal expression will always be the victim between them.

KIRCHHORST, 19 MARCH 1945

Back in Burgdorf. The weather was somewhat cooler, which explains why I spotted only a few lone red specimens of *Aphodius*. They were no longer spinning gossamer strands in the air. In my mind, I sometimes like to let the legions of *Coprophagi* [beetles] pass in review. They are the most harmless of guilds in this motley world, and they do not even take nourishment from vegetation, except when cleaning up its digested remains. They lead a holy sort of life; the scarab has even been canonized. Their horns, antlers, and growths are extraordinary; these can be found in many animal species that also rely on vegetation for their nourishment. But they are not so much weapons as they are heraldic crests symbolizing the strength of wood and root. Finally, there are those magnificently colored types—true gems. I can recall once on Rhodes when I was on the edge of a meadow and touched a little piece of donkey manure with my foot; it crumbled into half a dozen gleaming emeralds. There was the green *Onitis* [scarab beetle] feasting away. This is the true alchemy of the Great Mother, as she creates diamonds from dung and distills golden life from decay.

While driving, pondered political systems in which progressive and conservative forces must be congruent—the only systems that offer anything better to hope for. To this end, the historical consolidation of parcels of land over great areas under the Empire should promote variety while at the same time stabilizing the land by letting it occasionally lie fallow. The growing independence and freedom of these organic areas must submit more rigorously to the integration of technology. The ultimate expression of this is the World State as a *machina machinarum* [engine of engines]. Fatherland and Motherland. The New Order must resemble logical clockwork, where the main wheel of centralization drives the smaller gears of decentralization. The significant innovation here is that the conservative powers will no longer function as restraints, but rather as a driving force.

The extension of suffrage could be further expanded if one were also to include children in addition to women, children who would then be represented by their fathers during elections. This would embody both a greater liberality and stability, a barrier to the influence of radical, purely intellectual, or literary impulses, to which a married man is less likely succumb. The *patres* will have to come to the fore again. Rural areas would also gain influence against the popular parties so frantically active in the big cities.

Furthermore, abstentions could also be mobilized by counting them as votes for the incumbent government, because it may be logically assumed that a voter who is too lazy to make it to the polls is not dissatisfied with prevailing conditions. The nonvoters represent a passive element of value.

Speeches in our parliaments would have to be read aloud, as in Mirabeau's age. That would lend weight to the arguments and reduce the amount of empty rhetoric. The unalterable—not the intellectual—composition of the people should also be mirrored in the parliaments. Insofar as practice comes into its own at the expense of theory, the influence of unpredictable figures is also kept in check.

I am reading Petronius in Heinse's pleasant translation. Of all the characters that appear in the novel, that of Trimalchio is the most convincing. He is one of those great hits of world literature and has all their unmistakable attributes: validity for every age and every place. When and wherever speculation thrives under diminished authority, figures like Trimalchio will emerge, as they most probably will after this war. Just as Homer described the *topos* of the returning hero, Petronius described the *topos* of the war profiteer. This is his great achievement. He is the author of a *species nova* [new species] of a "good" sort.

KIRCHHORST, 20 MARCH 1945

This morning Alexander, who is in bed with a cold, showed me a fairytale he had written. In it, five apprentices were transformed into frogs.

Perpetua, Hanne Wickenberg, and I were at the table together around noon because it was laundry day. I told a few witticisms in a mood that Hanne described with the Lower Saxon adjective *wählig*, a word that connotes a kind of relaxed comfort with an added dash of the erotic.

Later in the garden, attending to the business of weeds. Because their roots and shoots are so fragile, they have to be pulled out more carefully than a Guinea worm,[47] so that they don't tear.

During the night, Kniébolo appeared to me again; I was setting up a room for him to be used for a conference with the English. The result was the proclamation of the gas war. I realized that whatever was going to happen, it meant profit for him, for he had attained a level of nihilism that excluded him from the participants. For him every single death, no matter on which side, signified profit. I thought to myself: "yes, that's why you also had all those hostages shot; now you'll get back interest a thousandfold at the expense of the innocent."

And finally this: "soon you will have achieved almost everything you have craved from the outset."

All this was in a tone of almost noncommittal disgust, for my roof had been shot to pieces, and I was annoyed that it was raining on my South American insects. This, of course, made them soft and flexible; it even seemed to me as if life had returned to them.

KIRCHHORST, 21 MARCH 1945

When a March evening arrives after one of the first warm days, an amazingly pungent vapor rises from the plowed furrows that were fertilized a few weeks earlier. Its elements comprise highly concentrated animal fumes underscored by decay and combined with pulsing fecundity from the ferment of life in its legions of microbes. This is a smell in which melancholy and high spirits merge—enough to make you go weak in the knees. This is the radical estrus of the Earth and her womb, of the *terra cruda nuda* [raw naked earth]—the source of every flower's scent. Health and vital energy also dwell in it, and the ancient doctors were not wrong when they prescribed sleeping in stables to cure wasting diseases.

KIRCHHORST, 24 MARCH 1945

Snowdrops and crocus are wilting, but for all that, the thimbleweed, violets, and yellow narcissus are starting to bloom.

I am reading Johann Christian Günther's poems in a beautiful old Breslau edition I have had among my books for a long time. This is hearty fare, sort of a ginseng root of the baroque. They include observations like the following:

Und damit lag zugleich ihr Haupt in meinem Schoss.
Der Zephir riss vor Neid den halben Busen bloss,
Wo Philomen sogleich, so weit sie ihm erlaubte,
Der Schönheit Rosenknopf mit sanften Fingern schraubte.

[And suddenly her head lay in my lap. / And Zephyr out of envy, her breast did half reveal, / where Philomen at once, as far as she allowed him, / With gentle fingers stroked her beauty's rosy bud.]

"*J'espère que les chose s'arrangeront.*" [I hope things will work out.][48]

Parting words of my Parisian barber last August. Even if not quite right for this situation, nonetheless well meant and, when taken in the right spirit, an example of the best of French rationality.

KIRCHHORST, 25 MARCH 1945

Radiant Sunday morning until huge bomber formations appeared and hit an oil or rubber depot in Hannover, producing fire clouds that obscured the sky like an eclipse of the sun.

Letters that come to us from regions farther to the West carry warnings about the low-flying aircraft. When they appear, children in particular are threatened.

Novalis writes in his *Hymns to the Night*:

Die Lieb ist frei gegeben
Und keine Trennung mehr
Es wogt das volle Leben
Wie ein unendlich Meer—

[Love is given freely / And there is no more separation / Life surges in its fullness / Like an infinite sea—]

With the elimination of the subdivisions of lands, earthly conflicts will decline. Separation and jealousy. Note here the superior answer Jesus gives to the question asked by the Sadducees about whom the woman who had known many men would be reunited with after death.[49] We advance to the highest spiritual component of love. All earthly contact is a mere metaphor of this.

Cum enim a mortuis ressurexerint, neque nubent, neque nubentur, sed sunt sicut angeli in caelis (Mark 12:25).

[For when they shall rise from the dead, they neither marry, nor are given in marriage; but are as the angels which are in heaven . . .]

KIRCHHORST, 28 MARCH 1945

English and American troops are positioned in Limburg, Giessen, Aschaffenburg, and in the outer precincts of Frankfurt.

Squadrons overhead in the morning, during which I worked partly in the garden and partly at my desk, thinking all the while that with each of the resounding booms that follow the screaming of the bombs, dozens and perhaps hundreds of people have been annihilated. And this is going on in a terrain of pure horror that lacks any mountain peak where one could receive the *absolutio in articulo mortis* [absolution at the moment of death].

We have to keep in mind that this carnage elicits satisfaction in the world. The situation of the German is now like what the Jews experienced inside Germany. Yet it is still better than seeing the Germans with their illegitimate power. Now one can share their misery.

KIRCHHORST, 29 MARCH 1945

Fiftieth birthday. This is the midpoint of life, when it is measured with the scale rather than the yardstick. Yet in this century, it is also an advanced age, considering the long, dangerous climb, especially of someone who never shirked his duties and was always put into harm's way in both great wars—in the first one, into the frenzy of the war of attrition, and in the second, into the dark perils of the demonic world.

This new year of life began with a solitary nighttime vigil, during which I permitted myself a small ceremony using the following readings:

1. The 73rd Psalm
2. Goethe, *Urworte: Orphisch* ["Primal Words"]
3. Droste-Hülshoff, "*Gründonnerstag*" ["Maundy Thursday"]
4. Johann Christian Günther, "*Trost-Aria*" ["Aria of Comfort"]

The poem by Droste-Hülshoff recaptures one of the ancient, secret hurdles in my life and, at the same time, utters a powerful exhortation to modesty. In that respect, it fits this double occasion of birthday and Maundy Thursday well.

The *Trost-Aria* also has wonderful passages like these:

Endlich blüht die Aloe,
Endlich trägt der Palmbaum Früchte;
Endlich schwindet Furcht und Weh;
Endlich wird der Schmerz zunichte;
Endlich sieht man Freudenthal,
Endlich, endlich kommt einmal.

[Finally the aloe is in bloom, / Finally the palm tree bears its fruit; / Finally vanish fear and pain; / Finally agony is abolished; / Finally we see the vale of joy, / Finally, finally, come all of you.]

Rosenkranz visited in the afternoon. Together we planted a butterfly bush in the garden in order to attract that insect. Later General Loehning joined us; yesterday, he lost his apartment and all his property in Hannover, yet nowadays, such things are no more disturbing than it used to be to move from one house to another. Perpetua set a bounteous table and had not only wine but a bottle of champagne, so we feasted merrily.

KIRCHHORST, 1 APRIL 1945

Americans in Brilon and Paderborn. Out on the streets there is a sort of surge of unrest, of fever, which is typical when a front is advancing. The farmers are beginning to bury their silver and provisions, and are preparing to go off into the moor. Behind the village, defensive ditches are being dug. Should a firefight erupt between the large gun emplacements at Stelle and tanks approaching along their route of advance toward Celle—as is planned—then all these villages and farms that survived the Thirty Years' War are doomed. I paced through the house and its rooms, especially my study and the library.

Ernstel. When someone in a family dies, it can seem as if a forward scout has been sent ahead at the approach of great danger. For wisdom prevails there, but we do not know the situation.

Began reading Evelyn Henry Wood, *Vom Seekadetten zum Feldmarschall* [*From Midshipman to Field Marshal* (1906)], specifically to learn about the English fleet, one of the great institutions and formative establishments of our world, like the Jesuit order, the Prussian General Staff, or the city of Paris.

The book begins with the siege of Sebastopol. Wood takes part as a midshipman in a battery landed from the *HMS Queen*. During these last years, I have come upon different descriptions of this episode in the course of my reading, such as Tolstoy's and Galliffet's. It's no coincidence that the truly grave and painful side of modern warfare (those aspects that will cause him suffering) come up early and powerfully in all encounters that have to do with Russia. One can already sense this in 1812 and also at the Battle of the Nations at Leipzig [1813]. The Russian element comes clearly to the fore. The Crimean War and the Russo-Japanese War predict all the horrors of subsequent wars of attrition, and by now, our eyes have seen unspeakable hells like those of Stalingrad or the Second Sebastopol. When Spengler warned against any incursion into Russia because of its size, he was right, as we have seen in the meantime. Any such invasion justified on metaphysical grounds is even more spurious because one approaches one of the great repositories of hardship, a Titan, a genius in the stamina of suffering. Within that sphere of influence, one will learn to know agony in a way that surpasses imagination.

And yet it seems to me as though the Germans may have learned something there. I sense this occasionally in conversations with soldiers returning from the cauldron battles.

In the afternoon went with Fritz Meyer to the Oldhorst Moor to survey the land. The second bloom of the year is beginning to die back in the garden. I got particular joy from a carpet of yellow narcissus, violets, and bush anemones. The intensity of two complementary colors is enhanced by adding white. It seems to radiate a concealed harmony of the whole and its parts. Perhaps the play of colors is revealing the same truth that the Pythagorean theorem does for geometry.

KIRCHHORST, 3 APRIL 1945

Before the storm. In the afternoon had a visit from General Loehning and Diels, who has been released from prison. Diels brought his wife, Göring's sister, who divorced him.[50] Diels was in a good mood; Loehning had stuck him into the uniform of a Luftwaffe corporal. Later a junior officer appeared carrying a letter from Manfred Schwarz asking that this courier should be given a copy of my essay on peace, so that Manfred could take it with him to southern Germany. So it seems that the essay is beginning to have some effect independent of its author.

At the same time, I had the leaders of the *Volkssturm* [Civil Defense] in my library so that I could issue orders to them. During the past weeks, I haven't gotten around to recording the details, which are gripping and very complex. The *Volkssturm* was founded by the Party; its orders come from Burgdorf. But it also relies on cooperation with the mayors, rural leaders, the *Arbeitsdienst*,[51] and the military units. This brings a host of delicate contacts into play. The approaching catastrophe exposes the conditions more blatantly. I gather from radio reports that many local authorities are inclined to order a few minor executions as they make their exits. This creates respect and makes it easier to flee. One would not like to abet their efforts and make their departure any easier—especially not at one's own risk.

The *Volkssturm* leaders are farmers; in this landscape, the old Guelph traditions are the ultimate political reality. We talked through a plan to construct tank barriers. When we broke up, confused and dazed, someone said, "The farms must be kept intact." That, of course, is not up to us alone, but I had the impression that every man agreed in his heart.

KIRCHHORST, 4 APRIL 1945

I dreamed about Ernstel for the first time, at least at that deep stratum where memory resides. He died, and I embraced him. I heard his last words, which expressed the hope that we would see each other again.

In addition to him (he was wearing a dark blue sailor's uniform), I also dreamed of Pfaffendorf, my comrade from World War I. His character had changed without sacrificing any of his style. He had become a notary in a medium-size city and gave a banquet for me where a lot of strange and, to some extent, intimidated guests were present. Upon awaking, I realized that he must have been in Kassel, which fell yesterday after a brief but violent struggle.

In the morning, I received a visit from the *Feldmeister*[52] of the large gun battery, who wanted to know how I was planning to assemble the *Volkssturm* when the tanks approached. Because I keep my own counsel on such matters, I told him that I was still awaiting orders and weapons. He then revealed to me his intention to "level" the P.O.W. camps, as he put it, with his long-range guns.

Since one should try to rebut madmen whenever possible in their own terms, I answered him that doing so would only achieve the opposite of his intentions—namely that blowing up the camps with the first rounds would disperse the inmates (already driven to extremes) across the whole country. Then I had to put my cards on the table and tell him that I would resist that with force and appeal to the people. Here, I got to know a person who combines obtuse intelligence with brutality, as is so common in our world. The characters of those types who influence broad historical events are composed of the following ingredients: one quarter each of technical intelligence, stupidity, bonhomie, and brutality—that is the mixture one must know in order to comprehend the contradictions of our age.

In the afternoon, collated a copy of my "Essay on Peace" with the junior officer. In the evening, he left with two copies after I had written a brief foreword. I am dedicating the work to my dear Ernstel.

KIRCHHORST, 5 APRIL 1945

The English are still at the Weser River, but they will cross it in a few days. The *Gauleiter*[53] of Hannover has circulated a bloodthirsty appeal calling for a fight to the last man, but Loehning knew that he was already taking measures to save his own skin. The farmers are burying objects, stowing some in their cellars, and destroying others.

The increased traffic on the streets means that all sorts of acquaintances drop by. Today it was a Lieutenant Wollny, who is on his way to the Weser. He brought me news from Niekisch. It seems that plans are in place for the "liquidation" of all prison inmates. Niekisch succeeded in getting a letter to his wife in which he wrote that this was probably the logical conclusion to his fate. All his prophecies, especially the ones in his work *Hitler, ein deutsches Verhängnis* [*Hitler, a German Disaster*], have come to pass. His wife still cherishes the hope that this will not end in slaughter. I always think about his fate with a particularly bitter feeling.

KIRCHHORST, 6 APRIL 1945

I saw a huge oak that was festooned like a Christmas tree with swordfishes longer than a man. The color of the creatures turning on their silken fishing lines shimmered from deep nacreous blue to all the hues of the rainbow. From a distance, I saw the bauble at which Neptune, Diana, and Helios were all at work, and I could also hear its music box sound.

English armored point units have now crossed the Weser and are said to be at Elze. The *Volkssturm* was mobilized and is supposed to be guarding the anti-tank barriers. This meant that I had to drive to Burgdorf to get information.

The roads were already crowded with refugees streaming eastward. Burgdorf was throbbing with excitement. Baskets and household items were being hauled down into cellars. I spoke with the *Volkssturm* leaders and the *Kreisleiter*;[54] their vital spirits seem to have been drained from them. Orders were handed down detailing our resistance, especially with respect to firing on tanks, yet these were fairly pro forma because in the next rooms, people were already packing up. I briefly expressed my objections to any rape of prisoners and discovered no intention to do so.

The farmers of Lower Saxony are beginning to act rationally now that their properties are at stake. Of course, it is still very dangerous to express any desire to hold onto them, and many a mayor who tried to do so has been stood up against the wall. Still, I think I've done my best to support the old estates. It was to my credit during all this that no one thought me cowardly.

In two or three days, our parish will see foreign troops. This pageant has not been repeated since the Napoleonic Wars, if we discount 1866[55] for the moment. During this transition period, I miss Ernstel terribly.

KIRCHHORST, 7 APRIL 1945

A sunny morning after a cool night. Long columns of prisoners are still marching to the East. Low-flying aircraft are scouring the road; we can hear the rolling salvos of their guns. Farther forward they seem to have found a target: A pack of horses comes galloping back with flowing manes and empty saddles. Now and then prisoners come in to seek cover. As a result, the barn is overflowing with a troop of Russians that dived into a pile of carrots. Perpetua passes out slices of bread to them. Then there are the Poles. I ask one of them if he wants to march as far as the eastern border:

"Oh no, not for a year. First Russian must go."

Signs of new conflicts are already emerging.

Right after dinner, the voice of the radio announcer comes on:

"The tanks are continuing their advance toward the Northeast and are now threatening the district capital."

The road becoming devoid of travelers. You can see farmers driving their wagons into the moor; their white and red featherbeds catch the eye from a great distance. Even our neighbor Lahmann has hitched up his team—"for the horses' sake"—as he himself wants to go out into the field to plant potatoes.

In the afternoon, I "rammed" some radishes [into the soil], slept, and finished reading Wood, while refugees looked in on us occasionally. Because I undertook yesterday's trip in the rain, now I unfortunately have a bad cold. I am noting this less on account of my discomfort than because circumstances like these require extremely keen powers of observation.

Otherwise, conditions are not unpleasant. Party orders, food rationing cards, police regulations—have lost all authority. The radio station in Hannover has terminated its broadcasts. Those voices that for years used to wallow in false pathos fall silent in the hour of danger just when the populace urgently needs updates about the situation. Not even air-raid sirens sound anymore.

KIRCHHORST, 8 APRIL 1945

Peaceful night. I had taken quinine, which relieved the flu somewhat. I read a few of Turgenev's hunting stories beforehand. I have admired these greatly for a long time, even though I am bothered by the detail of the extravagant Parisian gun that he carries in these forests.

My dear father's birthday. He was so eager to know how this war would end and what the new world that it brought would look like. But surely he did find out—

I am thinking here of the nice observation by Léon Bloy that at the moment of death a spirit experiences history tangibly.

The English are said to be near Pattensen, Braunschweig, and even on the coast. Refugees are still fleeing the city.

In the afternoon, violent explosions in the area; there were immense black clouds around Winsen an der Aller. By contrast it's very pleasant that around here the pressure that came along with the twelve years of Party rule—pressure that I could feel even during the campaign in France—has gone up in smoke.

Artillery shelling in the evening, probably over near Herrenhausen, accompanied by illuminated target locators.

KIRCHHORST, 9 APRIL 1945

Took quinine again. During the night, the road was crowded with soldiers flooding back in disarray. A young junior officer came inside, and Perpetua outfitted him with a hat and raincoat.

Dr. Mercier returned from the Weser this morning. I presented him with a carbon copy of my essay on peace.

All day long, fierce artillery shelling could be heard here and there across our wide moor and marshland. You get the feeling that the Americans have seeped into this landscape as if it were a piece of blotting paper.

By the afternoon, rumors circulate that we are surrounded. In the evening, not far away, we hear pistol and rifle shots.

KIRCHHORST, 10 APRIL 1945

Restless night. After dawn, the artillery battery near Stelle opens fire in the thick fog in rapid, crackling salvos right past our house. Its inhabitants, more or less dressed, rush out into the garden and seek the shelter. I am writing this in my study amid new salvos that make the house reverberate like an anvil under the blacksmith's hammer blows.

Later the sun breaks through. In the afternoon, two American armored cars from Neuwarmbüchen drive into the village, take four anti-aircraft gunners prisoner, and turn around again. We also hear that other tanks have shown up in Schillerslage, in Oldhorst, and in other towns. The gun emplacement at Stelle continues to pepper the outskirts of town with anti-tank shells as it keeps up the shelling. We can still hear them hammering away in the first half of the night and watch their tracer rounds fly over the house toward Grossburgwedel. Later, intense exchanges of fire in the woods around Colshorn.

KIRCHHORST, 11 APRIL 1945

We are awakened at dawn by the rumbling of tanks. The Stelle artillery emplacement does not open fire. We hear that its crew has scattered during the night after using their last shells to blow up their own guns; their *Feldmeister*, who wanted to escape in civilian clothes, has committed suicide. That was the man who had plans to level the prison camps. Now his body is lying in the firehouse.

At nine o'clock, a powerful, ever-increasing grinding sound announces the approach of the American tanks. The road is deserted. In the morning light, through bleary eyes, it looks even bleaker and more airless. As so often in life, I am the last man in the district who has the authority to give orders. Yesterday, I issued the only order in this connection: to guard the tank barrier, then open it as soon as the point unit comes into view.

As always in such situations, unforeseen things happen, as I learn from observers. The barrier is located at a piece of land, the "Lannewehrbusch," of the old *Landwehr*[56]—a patch of forest that my father once purchased. Two strangers show up there armed with grenade launchers and take up positions at the edge of the forest. They are spotted and cause the forward unit to halt during the considerable time it takes to send riflemen forward, who disarm and capture them.

Then a solitary hiker appears and remains standing on a forest path not far from the barrier. At the moment when the first gray tank with its five-pointed star appears, he releases the safety catch on his pistol and shoots himself in the head.

I stand at the window and look out over the bare garden and across the high road. The grinding rumble is getting nearer. Then, like a mirage, a gray tank with its gleaming white star glides slowly past. Following it in close formation come armored vehicles—myriads of them pass by for hours and hours. Small aircraft hover overhead. The pageant makes an impression of highly coordinated effort in its military and mechanical uniformity—as if a procession of dolls were rolling past, a parade of dangerous toys. At times, the order to halt spreads through the column. Then we can see the marionettes bend forward and then again backward when they start up again—as if jerked on their strings. As often happens when the eye becomes fixed on particular details, I notice especially the radio antennae that sway above the tanks and their escort vehicles: they give me the impression of an enchanted fishing expedition, perhaps out to catch the Leviathan.

Seamlessly, slowly, yet irresistibly, the flood of men and steel surges past. The quantities of explosives transported by such an army column endow it with a terrifying mystique. And, as in 1940 on the roads approaching Soissons, I sense the incursion of a mighty superpower into a completely crushed region. And the feeling of sadness that gripped me then returns as well. A good thing that Ernstel cannot see this; it would have hurt him too much. Recovery from such a defeat will not be the same as after Jena or Sedan.[57] This portends a change in the lives of populations; not only must countless human beings die, but much of everything that used to motivate our deepest being perishes in this transition.

We are capable of recognizing necessity, even of understanding and desiring and loving it as well—and yet at the same of being overcome with intense anguish. One must know this in order to comprehend our age and its people. What are birth pangs or the pain of death in light of this drama? Perhaps they are identical, just as sunset is simultaneously sunrise for new worlds.

"Defeated earth grants us the stars."[58] This aphorism is coming true in a spatial, spiritual, and otherworldly sense. Supreme effort implies a supreme, though as yet unknown, goal.

NOTES

Foreword

I wish to express my deep gratitude to Jennifer Crewe and Marielle Poss of Columbia University Press for their expert guidance and hard work on this book. Roland Knappe of the Klett Verlag was also very helpful. Eliah Bures, Joana von de Loecht, and Heath Pearson all read earlier versions of my introduction and made necessary corrections and expert suggestions for improvement. Finally, my thanks to the talented translators of these journals, who have performed a deep and welcome service to scholarship and world literature by making Jünger's Second World War journals available to all readers in the wider English-speaking world. —Eliot Neaman

1. Ernst Jünger, *First Paris Journal*, Paris, 18 August 1942.

2. Of the many reliable biographies, see most recently Thomas Amos, *Ernst Jünger* (Hamburg: Rowohlt, 2011); Allan Mitchell, *The Devil's Captain: Ernst Jünger in Nazi Paris, 1941–1944* (New York: Berghahn, 2011); Heimo Schwilk, *Ernst Jünger: Ein Jarhundertleben* (Munich: Piper, 2007); Helmuth Kiesel, *Ernst Jünger: die Biographie* (Munich: Siedler, 2007); Steffen Martus, *Ernst Jünger* (Stuttgart: Metzler, 2001). Also important from the 1990s are Paul Noack, *Ernst Jünger: eine Biographie* (Berlin: Fest, 1998); Thomas R. Nevin, *Ernst Jünger and Germany: Into the Abyss* (Durham, NC: Duke University Press, 1996); Martin Meyer, *Ernst Jünger* (Munich: Hanser, 1990). Of earlier biographies, see Gerhard Loose, *Ernst Jünger, Gestalt und Werk* (Frankfurt: Klostermann, 1957).

3. See Walter Z. Laqueur, *Young Germany: A History of the German Youth Movement* (London: Routledge & Kegan Paul, 1962), 66–73.

4. Carl Schmitt, *The Crisis of Parliamentary Democracy*, trans. Ellen Kennedy (Cambridge, MA: MIT Press, 1985).

5. See the latest edition: Armin Mohler and Karlheinz Weissmann, *Die konservative Revolution in Deutschland 1918–1932* (Graz: Ares Verlag, 2005). Jünger's journalistic writings of the period have been collected and annotated by Sven Olaf Berggötz, ed. *Ernst Jünger: Politische Publizistik 1919 bis 1933* (Stuttgart: Klett-Cotta, 2001).

6. Ernst Niekisch, *Gewagtes Leben, 1889–1945*, 2nd ed. (Cologne: Wissenschaft und Politik, 1980).

7. See Marcus Paul Bullock, *The Violent Eye: Ernst Jünger's Visions and Revisions on the European Right* (Detroit: Wayne State University Press, 1992), 180–84.

8. Ernst Jünger, *The Adventurous Heart: Figures and Capricios*, trans. Thomas Friese (Candor, NY: Telos Press, 2012).

9. See Karl Heinz Bohrer, *Ästhetik des Schreckens: die pessimistische Romantik und Ernst Jüngers Frühwerk* (Hamburg: Ullstein, 1983).

10. Schwilk, *Ernst Jünger: Ein Jarhundertleben*, 320–21.

11. Ernst Jünger, "Über Nationalismus und Judenfrage," *Süddeutsche Monatshefte* 12 (September 1930): 843–45.

12. On recent debates about Jünger and his brother Friedrich Georg's complicated relationship to Jews and Judaism, see Thomas Bantle, Alexander Pschera, and Detlev Schöttker (Eds.), *Jünger Debatte Band 1: Ernst Jünger and das Judetum* (Frankfurt: Klostermann, 2017).

13. Interview with Ernst Jünger in *L'Express*, 11–17 January 1971, 105.

14. Thilo von Throta, "Das endlose dialektische Gespräch," *Völkischer Beobachter*, 22 October 1932.

15. Noack, *Ernst Jünger*, 126.

16. Elliot Yale Neaman, *A Dubious Past: Ernst Jünger and the Politics of Literature After Nazism* (Berkeley: University of California Press, 1999), 104.

17. Inge Jens, *Dichter zwischen rechts und links* (Munich: Pieper, 1971), 33–35.

18. Ernst Jünger, "Auf den Marmorklippen," *Sämtliche Werke*, 18 vols. (Stuttgart: Klett-Cotta, 1978–2003), 15:265.

19. "It was horrible to hear what [General Alfred] Jodl reported about Kniébolo's [i.e., Hitler's] objectives" (Jünger, *First Paris Journal*, 8 February 1942). See also 6 April 1942 and many other entries.

20. On Jünger's relationship to La Rochelle, see Julien Hervier, *Deux individus contre l'Histoire: Pierre Drieu La Rochelle et Ernst Jünger* (Paris: Klincksieck, 1978).

21. "At the German Institute this afternoon. Among those there was Merline. Tall, rawboned, strong, a bit ungainly, but lively during the discussion—or more accurately, during his monologue" (Jünger, *First Paris Journal*, 7 December 1941). The German Institute was headed by Karl Epting, an anti-Semitic and anti-French novelist. The Nazis hoped to use the Institute to undermine French culture and indoctrinate the French with German culture and language along National Socialist lines. The Institute was not collaborationist because the goal was to prepare the French for their diminution to an agrarian state and submission to the German yoke. Jünger did not share those goals in the least, but he had a soft spot for Catholic French writers.

22. David M. Halperin, *What Do Gay Men Want? An Essay on Sex, Risk, and Subjectivity* (Ann Arbor: University of Michigan Press, 2007), 71.

23. Florence Gould had various pseudonyms; see Mitchell, *The Devil's Captain*, 82–84.

24. See Neaman, *A Dubious Past*, 143–44.

25. Nevin, *Ernst Jünger and Germany*, 169.

26. See Horst Mühleisen, "Im Bauch des Leviathan: Ernst Jünger, Paris und der militärische Widerstand," in *Aufstand des Gewissens*, ed. Thomas Vogel (Hamburg: Mittler, 2000), 454. In the correspondence between Gershom Sholem and Jünger, the latter inquires

whether Jünger had tried to help Walter Benjamin be released from a French internment camp. After so many years he couldn't remember, but it is possible, he responds. See Ernst Jünger and Gershom Scholem, "Briefwechsel 1975–1981" *Sinn und Form* 61 (2009): 293–302. See also Scholem's letter of 17 May 1982.

27. Ernst Jünger, *Notes from the Caucasus*, Kutais, 31 December 1942.

28. Jünger, *First Paris Journal*, Paris, 7 June 1942.

29. Ernst Jünger, *Second Paris Journal*, Paris, 22 June 1943.

30. Jünger, *Notes from the Caucasus*, Rostov, 22 November 1942.

31. Schwilk tracks down all various female relationships in *Ernst Jünger: Ein Jarhundertleben*, 373–405.

32. See Mitchell, *The Devil's Captain*. Jünger finally ended the relationship sometime between 1946 and 1947. The correspondence between Jünger and Sophie Ravoux is held by the German Literature Archive at Marbach.

33. Jünger, *Second Paris Journal*, Paris, 6 March 1943.

34. Jünger, *Second Paris Journal*, Paris, 27 May 1944.

35. See Tobias Wimbauer, "Kelche sind Körper: Der Hintergrund der Erdbeeren in Burgunder-Szene," *Ernst Jünger in Paris: Ernst Jünger, Sophie Ravoux, die Burgunderszene und eine Hinrichtung* (Hagen-Berchum: Eisenhut Verlag, 2011), 9–75. Another possibility is that Jünger did witness a bombing raid but simply wrote down the wrong date in the journal. He often wrote diary entries at later dates than the events described and constantly reworked the texts.

36. See Jünger, *Second Paris Journal*, Paris, 28 May 1944, upon the completion of his reading of the *Apocalypse*.

37. Neaman, *A Dubious Past*, 122–26.

38. See André Rousseaux, "Ernst Jünger a Paris," *Le Figaro littéraire*, 13 October 1951.

39. Schwilk fills in the details Jünger leaves out in the journals in *Ernst Jünger: Ein Jarhundertleben*, 415–419.

40. Jünger, *Second Paris Journal*, Paris, 21 July 1944.

41. Richard J. Evans, *The Third Reich at War* (New York: Penguin, 2008), 640.

42. His pseudonym in the journals is "Bogo."

43. Schwilk, *Ernst Jünger: Ein Jarhundertleben*, 436.

44. See especially Jünger, *Second Paris Journal*, Paris, 29 January 1944 and 21 July 1944. After World War I, General Ludendorff and other officers spread the theory that communists and Jews had conspired to rob the German army of victory in the last months of the war—had "stabbed the nation in the back."

45. Ernst Jünger, *Kirchhorst Diaries*, Kirchhorst, 7 September 1944.

46. Jünger, *Second Paris Journal*, Kirchhorst, 13 April 1944.

47. Wolf Jobst Siedler, *Ein Leben wird besichtigt: in der Welt der Eltern* (Munich: Siedler Verlag, 2000), 334. Ernstel's body was later exhumed and returned to Jünger's last domicile at Wilflingen, which provided evidence of the supposition that he had been executed.

48. Jünger, *Kirchhorst Diaries*, Kirchhorst, 14 January 1945.

49. Jünger, *Kirchhorst Diaries*, Kirchhorst, 29 March 1945.

50. Jünger, *Kirchhorst Diaries*, Kirchhorst, 11 April 1945.

51. See Neaman, *A Dubious Past*, chap. 7.

52. See Gerhard Nebel, *Ernst Jünger: Abenteuer des Geistes* (Wuppertal: Marées Verlag, 1949). Nebel is mentioned thirteen times in the war journals and was a trusted confidante. See Jünger, *First Paris Journal*, Paris, 11 October 1941, in which Jünger discusses with Nebel "the matter of the safe."

53. See Georg Simmel, *Philosophische Kultur: Über das Abenteuer, die Geschlechter und die Krise der Moderne* (Berlin: Wagenbach, 1983), 14.

54. See the introduction by Eliah Bures and Elliot Neaman in Jünger, *The Adventurous Heart*, xiii–lii.

55. Ernst Jünger, *Sämtliche Werke*, 9:83.

56. See, for example, his descriptions from the Jardin d'Acclimatation, a park on the northern edge of the Bois de Boulogne, which until 1931 exhibited foreign peoples, mainly Africans, in a kind of "human zoo," but by the time Jünger visited only animals were on display (Jünger, *First Paris Journal*, Paris, 16 September 1942).

57. Jünger, *Notes from the Caucasus*, Voroshilovsk, 26 November 1942.

58. See Ernst Jünger, "Sicilian Letter to the Man in the Moon," in Jünger, *The Adventurous Heart*, 121–130.

59. Jünger, "Sicilian Letter," 130.

60. I borrow here the term "*Unschuld des Werdens*" (innocence of becoming) from the title given by Alfred Bäumler to a collection of some of Nietzsche's unpublished works. See *Die Unschuld des Werdens: Der Nachlass, ausgewählt und geordnet von Alfred Baeumler* (Leipzig: Kröner, 1931). Although Bäumler was a prominent advocate of aligning Nietzsche's philosophy with National Socialism, the phrase cogently captures an essential characteristic of Nietzsche's attempt to reverse early modern pessimism, as well as Jünger's notion of *Heiterkeit* (a combination of serenity and cheerfulness). Jünger of course breaks with Nietzsche by embracing multiple levels of reality below the surface of visual perception, a notion that Nietzsche scoffed at as a Platonic illusion. See Jünger, *First Paris Journal*, Paris, 7 January 1942 and 10 March 1942.

61. Jünger, *First Paris Journal*, Paris, 8 October 1942.

62. Günter Figal and Heimo Schwilk, *Die Magie der Heiterket: Ernst Jünger zum Hundertsten* (Stuttgart: Klett-Cotta, 1995).

63. Figal and Schwilk, *Die Magie der Heiterket*, 7.

64. I am indebted to Eliah Bures for this observation.

65. Richard Herzinger in this context coined the phrase "*Übermoderne*," a deeper version of postmodernity. See "Werden wir alle Jünger?" *Kursbuch* 122 (December 1995): 93–117.

1. First Paris Journal

1. E. J. applies to Wagner categories from Nietzsche, which include a caricature of the composer as sorcerer.

2. Nietzsche *contra* Wagner (published 1895) refers to a critical essay written by Nietzsche that collects earlier passages from his writings focused particularly on Wagner's religion. It promoted a major aesthetic debate about music and the role of the composer.

3. *Quai*: public path along a waterway; a wharf or bank where ships' cargo is unloaded.

4. Member of the female *Wehrmacht* auxiliary.

5. The *Arc de Triomphe* stands at the center of this junction of twelve avenues that form a star (*étoile*) pattern, hence the "Square of the Star." In 1970 the square was officially renamed Place Charles de Gaulle. E. J. usually refers to this spot simply as the *Étoile*.

6. Perpetua: E. J.'s pseudonym for his wife, Grethe. See Glossary of Proper Names for pseudonyms and nicknames.

7. Knacker's yard: a slaughterhouse for old or injured horses.

8. *Subtiles*: *Cryptopleurum subtile*, the brown mushroom beetle, a collecting passion of E. J. who was an accomplished amateur entomologist. In 1967, he published a book on his beetle collecting forays with the punning title, *Subtile Jagden* [*Subtile Hunts*].

9. Mme. Richardet's aunt.

10. Reference to a work by the Roman satirist Decimus Junius Juvenal that mentions a satirical book (possibly two, now lost) by Caesar answering eulogies on Cato—the so-called Anticato or Anticatones. The implication is to a gesture indicating a man's penis as big or as long as these works, which would have been written on papyrus rolls.

11. Reference to the explosion of the hydrogen-filled passenger airship *Hindenburg* in Lakehurst, New Jersey, in 1937.

12. Kniébolo: E. J.'s pseudonym for Hitler, an invented name that echoes *diavolo* (devil).

13. A reference to Thomas Mann's novel *Lotte in Weimar* [*The Beloved Returns*, 1939].

14. Quotation from Ambrosius Theodosius Macrobius, fifth-century Roman writer.

15. This luxury hotel on Avenue Kléber served as headquarters of the German military command in occupied France.

16. Sea Lion (Ger. *Seelöwe*), code name for the plan to invade Great Britain.

17. Des Esseintes: character in Huysmans's *Against the Grain*.

18. In May 1941, Rudolf Hess astonished the world with his flight to Scotland, where he hoped to be granted an audience with King George VI and sue for peace with Germany. He was imprisoned and later tried in Nuremberg.

19. Duk-Duk dancers: males of the Tolai people of Papua New Guinea invoke the male spirit *duk duk* in their ritual dances with elaborate masks and costumes.

20. Quotation from Friedrich Nietzsche's *Twilight of the Idols* (1888).

21. *Chypre* (French for Cyprus): a perfume developed in 1917 by François Coty from Mediterranean ingredients.

22. *Recte: Fumeurs d'Opium*, 1896 [*Smokers of Opium*].

23. Jünger was quartered in the luxury hotel Raphael on Avenue Portugais, quite close to the Hotel Majestic.

24. Rastignac: character in the novels of Honoré de Balzac.

25. *Lemures*: vengeful spirits in Roman mythology. E. J. uses the term to refer euphemistically to the executioners and butchers of the NS regime. His source is Goethe's *Faust* where the *Lemuren* serve Mephistopheles as gravediggers. This translation retains the Latin form.

26. On 21 August, a German naval cadet was assassinated in Paris, which ignited a string of assassinations of German military officers in France. French hostages were taken in reprisal and many were executed. Despite Hitler's directive to execute 100 hostages for every German killed, General Otto von Stülpnagel resisted the order, which he thought would only fuel French resistance.

27. Ernstel, affectionate diminutive of Ernst, E. J.'s elder son. See Glossary of Proper Names.

28. Reference to E. J.'s novel, *Auf den Marmorklippen* [*On the Marble Cliffs*]. As soon as the work was published in 1939, it was considered a *roman à clef* in both Nazi and anti-Nazi circles and made enemies for E. J. within the regime.

29. Stavrogin: character in Dostoevsky's novel *Demons* (1872).

30. Pyotr Stepanovich Verkhovensky: character in Dostoevsky's *Demons*.

31. Friedrich Georg Jünger, E. J.'s younger brother.

32. Prose piece by E. J., which appeared in the collection *Das Abenteuerliche Herz* (1938).

33. Sancho Panza: character in Cervantes's *Don Quixote* (1605).

34. Reference to Burckhardt's influential work, *The Civilization of the Renaissance in Italy* (German original, 1860).

35. Imagism: reference to literary movement of the early twentieth century that emphasized the precision of concrete pictorial symbols.

36. Gerhardt Nebel's two-page essay, "Auf dem Fliegerhorst" ["On the Military Airbase"], appeared in the *Neue Rundschau* (October 1941) and compared fighter airplanes to insects. This was interpreted as a criticism of the Luftwaffe and led to his demotion.

37. Reference to flamboyant Reichsmarschall Hermann Göring, who loved to hunt and often appeared in elaborate hunting garb. E. J.'s fictional character of the Head Forester appears in *Auf den Marmorklippen* [*On the Marble Cliffs*, 1939].

38. Manfred, Graf [Count] von Keyserling.

39. Cauldron: refers to the German *Kesselschlacht* or cauldron-battle, a military maneuver involving encirclement, in which an enemy is surrounded, as if in a soup kettle.

40. Conditions in the bone mills of the Industrial Revolution were particularly noxious. Friedrich Engels's *The Condition of the Working Class in England* (1844) describes the plight of workers in Manchester, England.

41. E. J. refers to Joseph Conrad's *An Outcast of the Islands* (1896) in English.

42. Cheka: Russian secret police.

43. For E. J., the Greek *demos* (common people) connotes mob, rabble.

44. Line from Friedrich Hölderlin's poem "An Zimmern" (1812).

45. Creed: refers to the phrase in the Nicene Creed, "and was crucified also for us under Pontius Pilate."

46. Köppelsbleek: The old Germanic name E. J. gives to the equivalent of a concentration camp in *On the Marble Cliffs*. That place has all the attributes of a gothic horror tale, including a torture chamber where a dwarf flays and dismembers corpses.

47. E. J. coins the euphemism *Schinderhütte* for concentration camp to evoke a shack where victims are tortured. Meanings of *schinden* include "to flay," "to skin," "to overwork," "to mistreat." This translation uses "charnel house" for the concept.

48. *Ad patres*, "to my fathers," that is, die.

49. Reference to Francisco Goya's *Desastros de la Guerra* (*Disasters of War*), a series of prints depicting gruesome scenes from the Peninsular War (1808–1814).

50. Cousin of Otto, the former commander-in-chief.

51. Reference to apocalyptic visions of violent social disruption in Grillparzer's tragedy *Ein Bruderzwist in Habsburg* (1848) [*Family Strife in Habsburg*].

52. E. J. refers to the folk superstition that one should always have money in one's pocket upon hearing the first cry of the cuckoo, for then one's pockets will always have money.

53. Affectionate nickname for Frederick the Great, King of Prussia (1740–1786).

54. Reference to Goethe's last words.

55. E. J.'s own *Gärten und Strassen* [*Gardens and Streets*] had recently appeared in French.

56. Parc de Bagatelle is an arboretum on the grounds of Chateau Bagatelle in the Bois de Boulogne in the western suburbs of Paris. E. J. often refers to this favorite spot simply as Bagatelle.

57. *Chouans*: refers to members of the Royalist uprising against the French Revolution.

58. Lines from the poem "Patmos" by Friedrich Hölderlin (1770–1843).

59. From *Fleurs du Mal*: *Amis de la science et de la volupté / Ils cherchent le silence et l'horreur des ténèbres; / L'Erèbe les eût pris pour ses coursiers funèbres, /S'ils pouvaient au servage incliner leur fierté*. "Friends of learning and sensual pleasure / They seek the silence and the horror of darkness; / Erebus would have used them as his gloomy steeds / If their pride had let them stoop to bondage" (William Aggeler, trans., *The Flowers of Evil* [Fresno, California, 1954]).

60. Presumably for astrological implications.

61. See *First Paris Journal*, Kirchhorst, 18 May 1942.

62. *Sédan*: French defeat in the Franco-Prussian War (1870). After his superiors had surrendered, General Wimpffen negotiated the French capitulation of eighty-two thousand troops.

63. Reference to a 1926 German film, *Die Strasse des Vergessens* [*The Street of Forgetting*].

64. Reference to Hamlet's thought that he "could be bounded in a nutshell" and still count himself a king of infinite space.

65. Biedenhorn: character in E. J.'s novel, *On the Marble Cliffs*.

66. OC: "Organization Consul," an ultra-nationalist paramilitary group during the Weimar Republic.

67. *Landsknecht*: fifteenth- and sixteenth-century German mercenary soldiers connoting toughness and raw strength.

68. Battle of the Teutoburg Forest: 9 CE, in which Germanic tribes under Arminius [Hermann] defeated three Roman legions led by Publius Quinctilius Varus.

69. Figure of the worker: refers to an essay by E. J. entitled *Der Arbeiter* [*The Worker*] (1932).

70. *Septembriseurs* carried out widespread murders of prisoners during the French Revolution (September 1792), as called for by Marat.

71. E. J. refers to Robert Dodsley, *The Oeconomy of Human Life* (1750), which was a collection of moral observations attributed to ancient Indian authors and an anonymous translator.

72. Peter Schlemihl: refers to the novella by Adelbert von Chamisso, *Peter Schlemihls wundersame Geschichte* (1814) [*Peter Schlemihl's Wondrous Story*] in which the protagonist sells his shadow to the devil and leads a life of fear and concealment ever after.

73. *Thebais*: also *Thebaid*, a Latin epic poem by Publius Statius (45–95 CE) that includes a vision of the underworld.

74. See entry for Paris, 28 June 1942, in which E. J. refers to a book with the same description, which suggests an occasionally erratic chronology of personal material.

75. Reference to a publication by E. J., *Myrdun. Briefe aus Norwegen* [*Myrdun. Letters from Norway*] (Oslo, 1943), a special soldiers' edition produced by the German Military Command in Norway to be distributed to the troops.

76. Veil of Maya: in Indian philosophy this concept signifies the world as illusion and appearance.

77. Reference to Alfred Rosenberg, Der *Mythus des zwanzigsten Jahrhunderts* [*The Myth of the Twentieth Century*], an ideologically biased history of the human race based on fallacious theories of biological determinism.

78. Reference to the murder-suicide of the writer Heinrich von Kleist (1777–1811) and his friend Henriette Vogel. He suffered from depression, and she was terminally ill.

79. Alcor and Mizar are double stars in the handle of Ursa Major and together are called the "horse and rider."

80. Reference to the asylum granted Martin Luther in Wartburg Castle in 1521 by Frederick the Wise, Elector of Saxony. Here he translated the New Testament from Greek into German.

2. Notes from the Caucasus

1. E. J. reproduces the local dialect of Lower Saxony.

2. Reference to Johannes von Popitz.

3. Reference to Hans Otto Jünger, E. J.'s brother, a physicist.

4. Region in northern Poland, formerly East Prussia.

5. Boyen Fortress: nineteenth-century military fortification in the Masurian Lake district of northeastern Poland.

6. Stalino: city in eastern Ukraine, known as Donetsk since 1961.

7. Kuban steppe: region in southern Russia around the Kuban River.

8. GPU: State Political Directorate, the Russian state security organization.

9. Kleist's rank as *Generaloberst*, literally, general colonel, corresponds roughly to the rank of four-star or brigadier general in the U.S. military.

10. Taurus Mountain range in Turkey near the Taurus River.

11. Cauldron: for this concept, see note to entry in *First Paris Journal*, Paris, 2 March 1942.

12. Polyphemus: Cyclops in Homer's *Odyssey*, whom Odysseus slays to save himself and his men.

13. The term Siamese for conjoined twins derives from Chang and Eng Bunker (1811–1874), Thai-American brothers who gained fame in P. T. Barnum's Circus.

14. See *First Paris Journal*, Kirchhorst, 18 May 1942, for the source of this plot.

15. Reference to Alfred Kubin's surrealist novel, *Die andere Seite* [*The Other Side*, 1909].

16. Small, hardy horses originating in Poland, used by indigenous troops allied with the Germans.

17. Goethe's *West-östlicher Diwan* (1819) is a collection of poetry (Persian *diwan*) inspired by the poet Hafez.

18. Acts of the Apostles, chap. 10.

19. *Wandsbecker Bote* [*The Wandsbeck Messenger*] is the title of the main body of work by Matthias Claudius (1740–1815).

20. Meister Anton: character in drama by Christian Friedrich Hebbel (1813–1863), *Maria Magdalena* (premier 1846).

21. Pshish, a tributary of the Kuban River in the Stavropol region, North Caucasus.

22. Swabian emigrants: German emigration to Russian territories dates back to the sixteenth century; by the nineteenth century, there were five separate colonies of German speakers in the Caucasus.

23. Kulaks were a class of peasant successful enough to own property and hire labor. They were exterminated by Stalin in the 1930s.

24. S-mine: shrapnel mine, a class of bounding mines known as the Bouncing Betty.

25. German, *Stalinorgel* [Stalin Organs], military slang for the *Katyusha* [multiple rocket launchers].

26. Reference to the siege of Sevastopol (1854–1855) in the Crimean War. The city was again besieged in the Russo-Japanese War (1904–1901), which ended in defeat for Russia.

27. Verdun, the Somme, and Flanders: places of intense fighting and heavy casualties in World War I.

28. Persian Wars: the Graeco-Persian Wars of the fifth century BC; Greece was victorious.

29. Rostov-on-Don was occupied by the Germans from November 1941 to February 1943.

30. The title of this war novel, *Der Wehrwolf* (1910), contains a pun that evokes the words for "defense" and "wolf." It is usually translated into English as *War Wolf*.

31. *Nomos*: Greek for "law" or "custom," relating to problems of political authority and the rights of citizens.

32. *Ecstasis* (Greek), to be or to stand outside oneself; a condition of rapture.

33. Jünger adds a humorous tone by recording the driver's local Swabian (south German) dialect.

34. *Limes* (Latin), reference to the fortified borders of the Roman Empire.

35. See *First Paris Journal*, Paris, 28 July 1942.

36. On E. J.'s euphemism for concentration camp (*Schinderhütte*), see *First Paris Journal*, Paris, 6 March 1942.

37. Raskolnikov: the fictional protagonist in Dostoyevsky's *Crime and Punishment*.

38. *Fieseler Storch* [stork], a small, maneuverable airplane for personnel transport.

39. Eichhof meeting: In 1929, E. J. participated in a meeting of nationalist leaders and journalists at the Eichhof near Mönchen-Gladbach. He recalled his contacts with conservative political circles and nationalist writers with frustration, considering this period a missed opportunity to fuel a conservative revolution in Germany. See Helmuth Kiesel, *Ernst Jünger: Die Biographie* (Munich: Siedler Verlag, 2007).

40. *Der deutsche Gruss*, a salute that appropriated the outstretched arm of the Italian Fascists accompanied by the words "Heil Hitler." At first its use was a declaration of one's personal ideology, but after the plot against Hitler in July 1944, this salute was imposed on the military as a show of loyalty.

41. Electrophorus: an electrostatic generator.

42. Residential section of Berlin.

43. Reference to Friedrich Georg Jünger's work, *Perfektion der Technik* (1946) [*The Perfection of Technology*], which was originally to have been entitled *Illusionen der Technik* [*The Illusions of Technology*]. It is a pessimistic critique of contemporary notions of progress.

44. Axel is the hero of Villiers de L'Isle-Adam's novel of the same name.

45. Reference to E. J.'s *Sizilischer Brief an den Mann im Mond* (1930) [*Sicilian Letter to the Man in the Moon*].

46. Original: "*Wem Gott ein Amt gibt, dem gibt er auch den Verstand dazu.*" A popular saying.

3. SECOND PARIS JOURNAL

1. In ancient Rome, (nonmilitary) tribunes swore their allegiance to the *plebs*, from whom they derived power.

2. From a poem by Goethe in his cycle "Wilhelm Tischbeins Idyllen" ["Wilhelm Tischbein's Idylls"], philosophical meditations on art.

3. The year 1918 marked the German surrender and the end of World War I; the imminent German defeat at Stalingrad was now widely evident.

4. In 1763, the Peace of Paris ended the Seven Years' War; Prussia retained Silesia.

5. Frederick II ("the Great"), King of Prussia.

6. *Schwärmen*: the root meaning of the verb includes "to swarm, or flock together"; in common usage, it means to dream about, fancy, or be enthusiastic about, and even more strongly, to have a passion for something.

7. Martin Luther apparently coined this word to designate fanatics, zealots.

8. *Das Käthchen von Heilbronn* (1808) is a historical drama; "*Über das Marionettentheater*" ["On the Puppet Theater" (1810)] explores the aesthetic problem of natural grace and self-reflection.

9. "Butter rations will rise when the portraits of the Führer are unframed," or when the cream is skimmed off the Führer portraits." The joke lies in the pun on the word *entrahmen*, meaning both to remove a picture from its frame [*Rahmen*] and "to skim off the cream [*Rahm*]."

10. The image refers to the poisonous fish berry, or Indian berry (*Kokkelskörner* [*Anamirta cocculus*]).

11. Reference to carved masks worn by vintners' guilds during pre-Lenten Carnival processions.

12. Reference to E. J.'s own book *Der Arbeiter. Herrschaft und Gestalt* (1932) [*The Worker. Dominance and Form*].

13. Reference to Max Hattingen.

14. See *Notes from the Caucasus*, Kirchhorst, 21 January 1943.

15. The Shelling of Paris [*Paris-Geschütz*] was a long-distance artillery offensive using the huge new weaponry made by the Krupp firm. Between 12 March and 8 August 1918, Paris was hit by approximately eight hundred shells.

16. E. J.'s recollection of words he perceived in dreams bears little resemblance to standard communication and thus must be accepted as a highly personal linguistic recombination.

17. In 1892, the anarchist Ravachol was sentenced to death for murders and a bombing he committed.

18. Goethe's *Theory of Colors* [*Zur Farbenlehre*, 1810] describes the perception of the color spectrum, rather than its physical properties.

19. Cellaris, E. J.'s pseudonym for Ernst Niekisch, was jailed for anti-Nazi resistance in 1937 and, because he was arrested and tried by the police and not by the Gestapo, was sent to a civil prison and not to a concentration camp. He survived the war.

20. The Convention of Tauroggen, 30 December 1812, was an armistice between the Prussian troops and the Russian army that permitted the Russians to pursue Napoleon's retreating forces.

21. See *First Paris Journal*, Paris, 26 June 1941.

22. See *First Paris Journal*, Paris, 12 August 1942.

23. Reference to Lawrence Sterne, *The Life and Opinions of Tristram Shandy* (1759).

24. E. J.'s word *Sternpilot* could also correspond to the modern word "astronaut," but that would obscure the possibility of a pilot who flies a star.

25. For this concept, see note to entry of 1 March 1943.

26. E. J.'s original spelling "Tanzen" recorded incorrectly from memory Alfred C. Toepfer's estate in Lower Saxony called the "Thansen Hof."

27. Munich version: refers to the National Socialist ideology, which was closely associated with the city of Munich where Party headquarters was located.

28. *Die Titanen*, poem by Friedrich Georg Jünger, published 1944.

29. See *Notes from the Caucasus*, Voroshilovsk, 7 December 1942.

30. The entire quotation asserts that "One who did not live before 1789 never knew the pleasure of life."

31. The dark irony of this phrase is revealed by juxtaposing its terms: soldiers would expect, "To the victorious Wehrmacht from a grateful Party."

32. See *First Paris Journal*, Paris, 22 October 1942.

33. Tunis fell to the western allies on 12 May 1943. The defeat brought the end to Axis resistance in Africa and the capture of more than 230,000 German prisoners of war.

34. *Der Stürmer*: the National Socialist tabloid newspaper known for its virulent propaganda and coarse anti-Semitic and anti-Socialist caricatures.

35. A quotation from Gotthold Ephraim Lessing's drama about tolerance, *Nathan der Weise* [*Nathan the Wise*] (1779).

36. This discussion included topics such as the symbolist poet Stefan George and a man who influenced him, the neo-pagan Alfred Schuler, a member of a politically conservative, occult circle, the Blood Beacon, of which the philosopher Ludwig Klages was also a member. Klages wrote a book about George's poetry in 1902.

37. *César Birotteau* (1837), character in a novel of the same name by Honoré de Balzac.

38. Madame Baret, shopkeeper's wife with whom Casanova had an affair.

39. Hitler's so-called Night and Fog Decree (*Nacht-und-Nebel Erlass*) of 7 December 1941 stipulated that opponents of the regime be arrested and then vanish without a trace. No questions would be answered about a prisoner's whereabouts. The measure imposed a new level of intimidation on the populace.

40. This event from 1928–1930 refers to the book by Daniel Floch: *Les Oubliés de Saint-Paul* on Île Saint-Paul [*The Forgotten Ones on Saint Paul Island*]. The story is of the island in the Indian Ocean where seven workers in the lobster cannery were left to guard the installation, and only three were rescued two years later.

41. Reference to the accusatory principle, a style of interrogation used in legal proceedings.

42. E. J. engages here in linguistic mysticism, a subject he had explored in *In Praise of Vowels* (1934). In this, as in so many speculative passages in his journals, he teases meaning out of word associations. The reference to "Hamann's H" does not mean the first letter of the philosopher's name but rather, in Hamann's philosophy, a silent phonetic sign that connotes secret things—a symbol of the spiritual content of words. E. J. is here attempting to convey the spiritual world that letters embody everywhere (in atoms, in our world, at home.)

43. Walt and Vult are twin brothers in Jean Paul's novel, *Flegeljahre* [*Adolescent Years*] (1804).

44. Roman emperor who destroyed Jerusalem in 70 CE and sacked the temple.

45. Theodor Fontane, the great novelist of realism in the nineteenth century, descended from Huguenots who emigrated from France to Protestant Prussia in the seventeenth century.

46. See *Notes from the Caucasus*, Kirchhorst, 22 January 1943.

47. Capua: a city in Italy 25 kilometers north of Naples, synonymous with brutality in many European minds because of the Roman gladiatorial training center there.

48. Here E. J. quotes a famous adage found in Montaigne and Rabelais: "*Fais ce que voudras*" [Do as you wish].

49. *César Biroteau* (1837): novel by Honoré de Balzac.

50. E. J. here infers hidden meanings from language. *Vokale* means vowels; *Pokale* means chalices, goblets.

51. Reference to Hans Otto Jünger, E. J.'s brother, a physicist.

52. Cayenne: the French penal colony known as Devil's Island.

53. The mayfly's brief life span of a single day provides the metaphor for humans in the sight of God.

54. E. J. seems to misidentify this church. Whereas there is no church named Saint-Pierre Charron, he might mean Saint-Pierre de Chaillot, although that is not a small building. The "gate of death" [*Todestor*], in addition to its metaphorical association, is also the portal to the crypt.

55. The book is later identified as Maurice Alhoy, *Les Bagnes* (Paris, 1845). *Bagnes* (*bagnos*) were prisons where inmates were subjected to hard labor.

56. Abbé Sabatier was one of several clerics murdered by mobs during the Paris Commune in May 1871.

57. Cythera: Greek island off the Peloponnesus, said to be the birthplace of Aphrodite and, thus, the isle of love.

58. *Schwarze Front*: a splinter party during the Weimar Republic formed in 1930 by Otto Strasser after he was expelled from the NSDAP. The group, which opposed the National Socialists and desired a rapprochement with the Soviet Union, was dissolved after a few months.

59. Gospel of Luke 12:48.

60. E. J.'s *Gärten und Strassen. Aus den Tagebüchern von 1939 und 1940* (1942) [*Gardens and Streets. Excerpts from the Journals, 1939–1940*] was published in French in 1942.

61. See *First Paris Journal*, Paris, 28 July 1942.

62. See note to *Second Paris Journal*, Paris, 12 May 1943.

63. Guelph (Ger. *Welf*): a German princely family and European dynasty; they were dukes of Saxony and rivals to the House of Hohenstaufen for the imperial crown.

64. *Gross-Deutscher*: literally, "greater German," an adherent of the nineteenth-century policy in support of the unification of all German states, including Austria.

65. Not an actual word.

66. The final raid on Hamburg during so-called Operation Gomorrah took place on 3 August, killing approximately forty-three thousand people and injuring thirty-seven thousand more. A million civilians were forced to flee. Hamburg experienced sixty-nine more air raids during the war.

67. *Westwall*: series of fortifications built between 1938 and 1940 along the western frontier between the Netherlands and Switzerland, called the Siegfried Line by the Allies.

68. Schiller's poem "*Drei Worte des Glaubens*" ["Three Words of Faith"] names "free," "virtue," and "God" as watchwords at the core of human values. Goethe's "Urworte. Orphisch" ["Primal Words"] is a cycle of five short poems on metaphysical and mythological questions of human life.

69. *Urpflanze*: the archetypal plant, reference to Goethe's theory of a basic, hypothetical botanical form from which other plants descend.

70. *Wallenstein*: drama by Friedrich Schiller.

71. Sadowa: "Revenge for Sadowa" was a slogan heard in Austria after the Prussian defeat of the Austrian forces at Konigggrätz (Czech, Sadowa) on 3 July 1866, during the Austro-Prussian War.

72. Levasseur was the deputy representing Sarthe at the National Convention from 1792 to 1795.

73. Allusion to E. J.'s own novel, *On the Marble Cliffs* (1939). There the Mauritanians seek a nihilistic despotism founded on the theory of the superman that represents a negation of Western values.

74. George Bernard Shaw's fourth novel, published in 1882.

75. Pre-Lenten season known in some places as *Mardi Gras*, is called *Karneval* in the area of the Rhineland.

76. Nigromontanus: a fictional character of E. J.'s private mythology who first appears in *Das abenteuerliche Herz* (1938). He interprets the world as a conundrum that reveals its mysteries to fine-tuned vision capable of perceiving simultaneous incongruities.

77. Hottentot Venus: reference is to Sara "Saartjie" Baartmann (c. 1790–1815), a woman of the Khoikhoi tribe, whose effigy and skeleton were exhibited in nineteenth-century Europe for her physical anomalies. In 2002, her remains were returned to her hometown in South Africa.

78. E. J. views "Fire on the Kent," which was first exhibited in 1827. This ship of the British East India Company burned in the Bay of Biscay on 1 March 1825. Eighty-one people on board died, while five hundred and fifty survivors were rescued by the *Cambria*.

79. *Lares* and *penates* were Roman household gods, frequently represented in house altars or wall paintings.

80. See note to *First Paris Journal*, Paris, 22 February 1942.

81. In this passage, E. J. avoids his customary euphemism, *Schinderhütte*—in these journals translated as "charnel house"—and uses "concentration camp."

82. Priapus: a Greek god of fertility whose symbol was the phallus.

83. *Decline of the West*: the reference is to Oswald Spengler's two-volume *Untergang des Abendlandes*, published in 1918 (vol. 1) and 1923 (vol. 2), an influential work that contributed the cultural pessimism of the 1920s and 1930s.

84. *Benito Cereno* (1855): novella by Herman Melville.

85. Ecclesiastes, 10:1: "Dead flies cause the ointment of the apothecary to send forth a stinking savour: so doth a little folly him that is in reputation for wisdom and honor."

86. Rue du Roi Doré, literally Street of the Golden King, got its name from a street sign showing Louis XIII; Rue du Petit Musc, from "Put-y-Musse," designated a street habituated by prostitutes.

87. The French Resistance sent miniature coffins to compatriots they identified as collaborators.

88. E. J. here resorts to the metaphysics of his symbolic color system to interpret and predict historical events. In this scheme, the color white represents political opposition to the regime; red, his favorite color, represents the elemental life force in nature as well as violence and revolutionary extremism; blue, on the other hand, while it is a color of calm nature, water, and air, also represents the rational and, by extension, the forces of reasoned conservatism. See Gisbert Kranz, *Ernst Jüngers symbolische Weltschau* (Düsseldorf: Pädagogischer Verlag Schwann, 1968), 105–22.

89. At the two simultaneous battles of Jena and Auerstedt on 14 October 1806 near the river Saale, the armies of Napoleon encountered those of Frederick William III of Prussia. Napoleon's forces prevailed over the Prussians.

90. Pied Piper of Hamelin.

91. E. J. uses the edition with critical apparatus edited by Eberhard Nestle of the *Novum Testamentum Graece* (1898).

92. Pitcairn Island. In 1790, mutineers from *HMS Bounty* settled on Pitcairn Island. After discord and hardship, several of them eventually turned to scripture, using the ship's Bible as their guide.

93. Stater: a silver coin mentioned in Matthew 17:27: "go to the sea, cast a hook, and take up the first fish that comes up. When you have opened its mouth, you will find a stater coin. Take that, and give it to them for me and you."

94. *Le Crapouillot*: outspoken French satirical political magazine (originally for the military) published from 1915 to 1996.

95. *Cloaca maxima*: the main sewer of ancient Rome.

96. E. J.'s wordplay produces the neologism *einfalten*—a back-formation from the adjective *einfältig* (foolish, simpleminded)—suggesting the activity of becoming "one-fold" or monodimensional.

97. The popular name (*Christbaum, Tannenbaum*) for incendiary flares dropped by parachute. These produced colored fire to mark a target area.

98. Military fort at Verdun.

99. On 27 February 1933, an arsonist set fire to the *Reichstag* [Parliament Building] in Berlin.

100. Wisdom of Solomon 3:6 (Apocrypha).

101. Capital letters in the typeface Antiqua that resemble hand lettering.

102. Pseudonym for Friedrich Hielscher.

103. Berchta: a female goddess from the tradition of alpine paganism. She appears during the twelve days of Christmas and oversees spinning.

104. Fasnacht: carnival.

105. Freya (Freyja): a goddess in Germanic mythology associated with fertility, love, beauty, and gold.

106. Biedenhorn refers to Jünger's fictional character in *On the Marble Cliffs*, a corrupt leader of mercenaries.

107. Reference to Rashid ad-Din Sinan, called "The Old Man of the Mountain," a leader of the sect of Ismaelite assassins in Syria at the time of the Third Crusade.

108. Volga Germans designates ethnic Germans (including Moravians and Mennonites) who in the eighteenth century were recruited to colonize areas along the Volga River in Russia where they kept their language and culture.

109. *Pariser Zeitung* [*Paris Newspaper*]: German language daily newspaper (1941–1944); the typo "nectar" [nectar] should read "hektar" [hectare].

110. Sauckel moved 5 million people from the Occupied Territories to work in Germany's munitions industry. His methods for rounding up this labor force were infamously brutal.

111. Reference to Paul and Hélène Morand.

112. Peter Schlemiel: see note to *First Paris Journal*, Paris, 10 September 1942.

113. Latin, "Gate to Westphalia," referring in this case to a gorge, also called the Westphalian Gap, in the district of North Rhine-Westphalia.

114. Beginen Tower: a fourteenth-century defensive tower, part of the original city wall, on the bank [*Ufer*] of the Leine River.

115. The world spirit: E. J. invokes Hegel's concept of history, which is dominated by the deeds of important men.

116. The Elisabeth Linné phenomenon: at the age of nineteen, Elisabeth von Linné (daughter of the naturalist) wrote an article describing the flash of light in nasturtiums (Indian cress) at dusk; later research revealed it to be an optical anomaly.

117. Angelus Silesius was born to Protestant parents but converted to Catholicism when he was twenty-nine. He strove to persuade Protestants to return to the Catholic faith. His epigrammatic, mystical poetry, and hymn texts aimed to encourage devotion.

118. Attila's hall: refers to the Middle High German epic *Das Nibelungenlied*, in which the king's hall is the site of a bloodbath

119. Urpflanze: see note to *Second Paris Journal*, Paris, 13 August 1943.

120. Quotation from the drinking song "Und als der Herr von Rodenstein "by Viktor von Scheffel (c. 1856).

121. Bellarmin: refers to Friedrich Hölderlin's epistolary novel *Hyperion oder Der Eremit in Griechenland [Hyperion or The Hermit in Greece]*, published in 1797 (vol. 1) and 1799 (vol. 2). One letter that Hyperion writes from Greece to his friend Bellarmin contains a particularly severe criticism of Germany and the Germans.

122. Bosch's triptych (1490–1510), one of his best-known works, hangs in the Prado Museum (Madrid).

123. "Let us be easygoing about words"; Bismarck reputedly used this phrase to mean it did not matter whether the navy was called Prussian or North German.

124. Reference to E. J.'s *On the Marble Cliffs*.

125. Adversative conjunctions such as "but, yet, however" introduce contrast or opposition.

126. The first name refers to Stendhal's novel, *The Life of Henri Brulard*; Pyotr Stepanovich Verkhovensky is a character in Dostoevsky's novel *The Demons*.

127. Stralau is a section of Berlin. E. J. lived there on Stralauer Allee in 1928.

128. *Makrobiotik oder die Kunst das Menschliche Leben zu Verlängern* (Jena, 1797), [*Macrobiotics or the Art of Extending Human Life*].

129. The colloquial designation *schwarz* ["black"] describes committed zealots who support the regime. By contrast, see *Second Paris Journal*, Kirchhorst, 29 February 1944.

130. Reference to *One Thousand and One Nights*.

131. "For now we see through a glass darkly, but then face to face."

132. "White": military colloquialism, connoting a skeptical, potentially subversive attitude toward the regime.

133. Jan Bockelson (1509–1536), "John of Leiden": Anabaptist leader of the Münster Rebellion.

134. Johann Peter Eckermann was Goethe's secretary and biographer.

135. La Grande Roquette: dungeon in Paris where those condemned to death were incarcerated.

136. A breakout battle [*Ausbruchsschlacht*] is a military maneuver to escape encirclement.

137. The compound Salvarsan (arsphenamine) was introduced in 1911 as the first effective treatment for syphilis.

138. Mycelium: the vegetative part of a fungus made of long, branching, threadlike tubes.

139. Reference to the blue-enameled cross, badge of the order *Pour le Mérit* [*For Merit*], the highest German military honor. E. J. earned this decoration in September 1918 for his valor in combat during World War I.

140. See note to *Second Paris Journal*, Paris, 1 August 1943.

141. E. J. cites the original Low German dialect: "Unser *Ein* is hire to vele. Westu nicht, dat wi wol twintig tonnen pulvers under den voten hebben?"

142. Bight: a nautical term for bay. The German Bight is the southeastern bight of the North Sea, bounded by Denmark and The Netherlands.

143. *Les Trois Vallées* [the Three Valleys] is a region of the Savoie in the South of France near the Italian border.

144. *Fronde* (French, "sling"): a political faction in France opposed to the policies of Cardinal Mazarin; metaphorically, any violent political opposition.

145. Whereas the two brothers in *The Marble Cliffs* belong to the old Order of the Mauritanians, E. J. also sometimes uses the reference to allude to his own earlier activity as a political activist with nationalist leanings.

146. Becerillo: a particularly vicious dog of the conquistadors (sixteenth century).

147. Reference to E. J.'s earlier reading, see *Notes from the Caucasus*, Berlin, 15 November 1942.

148. Reference to T. E. Lawrence, "of Arabia."

149. The first line of Platen's poem, "Tristan" (1825). It continues: "is at the mercy of death."

150. Phrase from the title of Bloy's book, *Propos d'un Entrepreneur de Démolitions* (1884) [*Remarks of a Demolition Contractor*].

151. Bologna bottle, also called Bologna phial: a container strong enough on its outside to hammer a nail, while a small scratch on its interior causes it to shatter; often used in physics demonstrations and magic tricks.

152. Reference to Glasir, a tree or grove in Norse mythology that bears golden red leaves beside the gates of Valhalla.

153. Reference to the German designation. The first element of the word (*klatsch*) means clap, snap.

154. See *Second Paris Journal*, Paris, 25 June 1943.

155. This image evokes "Nature, red in tooth and claw" (Tennyson) and is E. J.'s metaphor for the Darwinian struggle for existence.

156. E. J. admitted that he sometimes conflates experiences. It has been determined that the last bombing raid on Paris ended on 27 May 1944 at 13.45. By the evening then, the roof of the Raphael was indeed a safe place, and there were no squadrons overhead that evening. See Tobias Wimbauer, "Kelche sind Körper. Der Hintergrund der 'Erdbeeren in Burgunder'–Szene," in *Anarch im Widerspruch. Neue Beiträge zu Werk und Leben der Brüder Ernst und Friedrich Georg Jünger*, 2nd ed. (Hagen-Berchum: Eisenhut Verlag, 2010), 25–76.

157. Fragment of a famous line in Goethe's *Faust* in which Faust addresses the moment, saying, "Tarry a while, thou art so fair."

158. Luigi Galvani, professor of anatomy at the University of Bologna after 1775, induced muscular contractions by attaching electrodes to laboratory specimens.

159. Hoplite: armed Greek warrior.

160. Reference to Jan Bockelson. See entry of *Second Paris Journal*, Kirchhorst, 29 February 1944.

161. The so-called V-weapons (V-1 and V-2) were long-range artillery rockets used against cities, particularly London in 1944–1945.

162. See *First Paris Journal*, Paris, 23 February 1942.

163. Reference to Pliny the Younger's eyewitness account of the eruption of Mount Vesuvius in 79 CE.

164. 1756–1763, a war fought across the globe by all the major powers.

165. Reference to *La Noche Triste* on 30 June 1520 when the conquistadors were expelled from the Mexican capital at Tenochtitlan.

166. Bendlerstrasse: address of the German ministry of war in Berlin.

167. Although Berlin issued a report of Rommel's supposed automobile accident in Normandy, the field marshal actually sustained severe wounds and a concussion from a fighter attack.

168. Here, the NSDAP (National Socialist Party).

169. See *Notes from the Caucasus*, Kirchhorst, 21 January 1943. E. J.'s comment acknowledges the subservience of the army to the Party.

170. Reference to the drama *Des Meeres und der Liebe Wellen* (1831) by the Austrian playwright Franz Grillparzer treating the mythological story of Hero and Leander. E. J. could have been reminded of these tragic lovers by Rodin's sculpture of Cupid and Psyche.

4. KIRCHHORST DIARIES

1. Field Marshal Erwin von Witzleben was executed after the 20 July 1944 bomb plot on Hitler's life.

2. E. J. copied Rotsart's title incorrectly. It should read "de Hertaing."

3. Lämpchen. Nickname for Ursula Lampe, art historian.

4. E. J. refers to such bases as *Igelstellungen*, "hedgehog positions."

5. Key, key, valve, rabbit hutch, cloister (prison, enclosure), clandestine, noose (snare), conclusion (end).

6. *Natura naturans*, "nature naturing," that is, expressing its own self-generating activity, which is the infinite essence of God; *Natura naturata*, "nature natured," that is, all created things, the products of God's attributes.

7. Maquis: armed resistance groups who hid in rural areas of occupied France.

8. One Homeric epithet for Agamemnon is "shepherd of the people."

9. Hunting books: E. J.'s catalogues of beetles he has collected.

10. See note to *Second Paris Journal*, Paris, 5 October 1943.

11. The wave offering [Ger. *Webopfer*] derives its name from the Old Testament ritual in which the priests held up the offering and waved it back and forth before the altar.

12. *Francs-tireurs*, literally "free shooters," a term for irregular military units during the Franco-Prussian War (1870–1871); sometimes applied generally to guerrilla fighters.

13. Tantalus: a son of Zeus and thus immortal who was punished for his crime of stealing the food of the gods and giving it to mortals. He was made to stand in water forever

receding before he could drink, beneath a fruit tree with branches that moved beyond his grasp before he could eat.

14. Palinurus, helmsman of Aeneas, was overcome by the god of sleep and fell overboard.

15. For Head Forester, see note to *First Paris Journal*, Paris, 1 February 1942.

16. Reference to the group of friends who met regularly in Paris the Hotel George V.

17. In his elliptical way, E. J. here expresses regret at what he perceives as the collectivization, that is, politicization, of language by the primitive ideological jargon of National Socialism. The function of the liaison officer would be to act as interpreter.

18. E. J. quotes her dialect: *"Ek was fertig, as es to Enne was."*

19. In 1933, Göring appointed Diels to head the new political branch of *Geheime Staatspolizei*, or *Gestapo* [Secret State Police]. Caught in the power struggle between Göring and Himmler, Diels was dismissed in 1934. When working in Hannover, he had refused to round up Jews, but he escaped punishment thanks to Göring's protection.

20. The so-called People's Court [*Volksgerichtshof*] was established by Hitler in 1934 to enforce the agenda of the NS party without regard for due legal process. The judge-president E. J. alludes to is Roland Freisler (1893–1945).

21. Stepan Trofimovich is a character is Dostoevsky's novel, *The Demons* (1872).

22. See note to *Second Paris Journal*, Paris, 1 September 1943.

23. Apollo and Artemis killed Niobe's children because she boasted that, as the mother of so many children, she was thus the equal of Leto.

24. Johan Peter Eckermann, *Conversations with Goethe* (1836; 1848).

25. See *Notes from the Caucasus*, 23 December 1942.

26. Popular saying attributed (probably falsely) to Tacitus.

27. See *First Paris Journal*, Paris, 5 July 1941.

28. Thereby changing *prendront* (will capture) to *rendront* (give up, return).

29. See Gospel of Matthew, 25:7. In this parable, the five wise virgins went out to meet the bridegroom with oil in their lamps, while the lamps of the foolish virgins had gone out.

30. Wicked husbandman, *recte:* husbandmen or tenants. See Gospel of Matthew 21:33–46; Mark 12:1–12; Luke 20:9–19.

31. Gospel of Matthew 25:14–30, parable of the servant who buried his master's talents (unit of currency), rather than increase his fortune through commerce.

32. *Teocalli*: the Aztec pyramid, on top of which is the temple where human sacrifice was performed.

33. Marat: The Russian battleship *Petropavlovsk* was renamed *Marat* in 1921 by the Soviets after the radical journalist and politician of the French revolutionary.

34. E. J. glosses a German proverb about the nature of dreams: *"Träume sind Schäume* [Dreams are foam, froth].

35. E. J. refers to payloads (*Kettenwurf*) dropped from aircraft flying in wedge formations, called the *Keil* (wedge) or *Kette* (chain).

36. E. J.'s word *Hundssterne* evokes Sirius in the constellation Canis Major, the brightest star visible in the night sky of the northern hemisphere and is thus an appropriate metaphor for aerial flares.

37. Steller's Sea Cow (*Hydrodamilas gigas*).

38. On 29 November 1944, Gretha Jünger, Ernst's mother, dreamed of having an eyetooth pulled.

39. The Tannenberg Memorial commemorated the German soldiers who died at the second battle of Tannenberg (1914). The coffin of Paul von Hindenburg, who had commanded the German troops, was placed here in 1934.

40. Pitcairn: In 1790, the mutineers from the *HMS Bounty*, together with other Polynesians, settled these islands in the south Pacific.

41. Reference to a regional verb for splitting that means literally "to split something apart or rive open a log."

42. E. J. cites in translation the words of the Roman poet Lucretius (first century BCE), *ludibrium pelagis* (plaything of the waves).

43. Houdon; see *First Paris Journal*, Paris, 9 March 1942 and 14 March 1942.

44. *De Profundis*, see Psalm 130: *De profundis clamavi ad te, Domine* [From the depths, I have cried out to you, O Lord].

45. The strategy of carpet-bombing, or saturation bombing, was used by both sides in Europe. The goal was to inflict maximum destruction within a specific target area.

46. Carus is E. J.'s imaginary son. See *First Paris Journal*, Paris, 18 January 1942.

47. Guinea worm: parasite ingested by drinking water infested with water fleas.

48. See *Second Paris Journal*, Paris, 5 August 1944.

49. Gospel of Luke 20:27–36.

50. Diels was actually married to Hermann Göring's cousin.

51. *Reichsarbeitsdienst* [RAD]: The official state labor organization established during the Weimar Republic, originally to counter unemployment, and adapted and expanded after 1933.

52. *Feldmeister*: a rank equivalent to lieutenant in the *Reichsarbeitsdienst (RAD)*.

53. *Gauleiter*: a district leader, *Gau* being an old Frankish term used to designate Nazi Party administrative regions.

54. *Kreisleiter*: county leader(s), a Nazi Party administrative rank.

55. 1866: Reference to the Austro-Prussian War or Seven Weeks' War between the German Confederation lead by the Austrian Empire versus Prussia. The war resulted in Prussian dominance over the German states.

56. " 'Lannewehrbusch' of the old *Landwehr*": this patch of forest takes its local name from the *Landwehr*, the old territorial militia before World War I.

57. Jena (1806) was a major victory of Napoleon over the Prussian armies; at Sedan (1870), the decisive victory in the Franco-Prussian War, the Germans defeated the French and were thus able to march on to Paris.

58. E. J. cites Boëthius, The *Consolation of Philosophy*, as he had earlier on 22 November 1944, but now he has just witnessed a procession of white stars on the armored vehicles of the invaders and, refusing to see this as a symbol of defeat, he reads it as one of hope.

GLOSSARY OF PROPER NAMES

The entries in this glossary are drawn from the following index to Jünger's original German journals: Tobias Wimbauer, *Personenregister der Tagebücher Ernst Jüngers* (Schnellroda: Edition Antaios, 2003), revised and expanded edition. Emendations and corrections have been made where necessary.

A

Abetz, Suzanne (d. 1958), née de Bruycker, married to Otto Abetz, secretary

Abt, captain, World War II

Abt, war comrade of Friedrich Georg Jünger

Adler, Cavalry captain [*Rittmeister*], General Staff, Paris, World War II

Ahasver (c. 486–465 BCE), Xerxes, king, symbolic figure for the Wandering Jew

Ahlmann, Wilhelm (1895–1944), banker, uncle of Klaus Valentiner

Ahrends, see *Arendts, Wilhelm*

Aksakov, Sergey Timofeyevich (1791–1859), Russian writer

Alain-Fournier, Henri-Albin (1886–1914), French author

Albert I (1875–1934), king of Belgium

Alerme, Marie Marcel Etienne Michel (1878–1949), French colonel, head of Clémenceau's cabinet during World War I

Alexander, see *Jünger, Alexander Carl*

Alexander the Great (356–323 B. C. E.), king of Macedonia

Alhoy, Philadelphe Maurice (1802–1856), French author

Alighieri, Dante (1265–1321), Italian poet

Andois, lieutenant colonel, World War II

Andreyev, Daniel Leonidovich (1906–1959), Russian writer, son of L. N. Andreyev

Andreyev, Leonid Nikolayevich (1871–1919), Russian writer

Andromeda, see *Geyr von Schweppenburg, Sophia Reichsfreiin [Baroness] von*

Andronikos I, Komnenos (1122–1185),
Byzantine emperor

Angelis, Maximilian de (1889–1974),
general, World War II, in command of
the Forty-Sixth Army Corps

Annunzio, Gabriele d' (1863–1938), Italian
writer

Antinous (c. 110–130 CE), favorite of the
Roman Emperor Hadrian

Antoinette, Marie (1755–1793), queen of
France

Aphrodite, Greek goddess of love

Apollo, Phoebus, Greek god of the sun

Arendts, Wilhelm (b. 1883), colonel on
General Staff in France, World War II

Aretz, Heinrich von, captain, World War
II, member of the resistance group F.
Hielscher

Arland, Marcel (1899–1986), French author

Arletty (1898–1992), *recte* Léonie Bathiat,
French film actress

Armance, E. J.'s pseudonym for Florence
Gould

Armand, unidentified acquaintance of E. J.,
Paris (1942)

Arnim, Bettina von (1785–1859), German
writer

Arnim, von, noble family, originally from
Brandenburg

Artaxerxes, Persian king

Arthur (c. 500 BCE), legendary British
king

Asclepius, Greek god of healing

Athena, Greek goddess of wisdom,
daughter of Zeus

Attila (c. 450 CE), king of the Huns,
character in the Middle High German
epic *Das Nibelungenlied*

Assadoulaeff, Umm-El-Banine
(1905–1992), French writer of
Azerbaijani descent

Aubrincourt, d' (seventeenth century),
recte François Calvi

Autement, Elisabeth, unidentified

Averroes, Ibn Ruschd abu el-Walid
Muhammad (1126–1198), Arabic
philosopher

Avicenna, Ibn Sina Abu Ali el-Husain
(980–1037), Arabic doctor and
philosopher

B

Baader, Franz Xaver von (1765–1841),
German Catholic philosopher,
theologian, and engineer

Baartmann, Sara "Saartjie" (c. 1790–1815),
the "Hottentot Venus" in the Musée de
l'Homme

Baeumler, Alfred (1887–1968), writer,
philosopher, teacher, see *Kastor*

Bakunin, Mikhail (1814–1876), Russian
revolutionary, leading anarchist

Baldass, Ludwig (1887–1963), Austrian art
historian

Baluze, Étienne (1630–1718), librarian of
the Bibliotheca Colbertina

Balzac, Honoré de (1799–1850), French
author

Banine see *Assadoulaeff*

Bannier, Jean, bookseller, Paris

Banville, Théodore de (1823–1891),
French poet

Barabbas, murderer, New Testament

Bargatzky, Walter (1910–1998), president of
the German Red Cross, on the General
Staff in Paris, World War II

Bariatinski, princess

Barlach, Ernst (1870–1938), German
sculptor, graphic artist, and dramatist

Barrès, Maurice (1862–1923), French author

Bashkirtseff, Marie (1860–1884), French
painter

Baudelaire, Charles (1821–1867), French
poet

Bauer, Bruno (1809–1882), Protestant
theologian

Baumgart, Fritz Erwin (1902–1983), art
historian, ordnance officer stationed in
Paris, World War II

Beckmann, Max (1884–1950), German
graphic artist and painter

Begbie, Harold (1871–1929), English writer
and journalist

Bellini, Vincenzo (1801–1835), Italian
composer

Bekker, Balthazar (1634–1698), Dutch
theologian

Benningsen, Rudolf von (1824–1902),
politician

Benoist, Charles (1861–1936), French
journalist and politician

Benoist-Méchin, Jacques de (1901–1983), French writer and politician

Benvenuti, Italian pianist

Bérard, Chistian Jacques (1902–1949), French painter

Berdyaev, Nikolai Alexandrovich (1874–1948), Russian philosopher

Bergmann, Gustav von (1878–1955), physician

Bergson, Henri (1859–1941), French philosopher

Berlioz, Louis Hector (1803–1869), French composer

Bernanos, Georges (1888–1948), French writer

Bernasconi, Parisian bookbinder

Berry, André (1902–1986), French poet

Bertram, Ferdinand (1894–1960), doctor

Besançon, Jean Julien (1862–1952), French doctor and writer

Best, Werner (1903–1989), administrative head, General Staff, Paris; "Beust"

Bettina, see *Arnim, Bettina von*

Betz, Maurice (1898–1946), French translator

Beust, see *Best, Werner*

Bias (sixth century BCE), Greek statesman, one of the Seven Sages of Greece

Biéville de Noyant, count, Paris

Bignou, Etienne (d. 1950/51), art dealer in Paris

Bismarck, Otto von (1815–1898), chancellor of the German Empire

Bloy, Jean Baptiste, French official, father of Léon Bloy

Bloy, Léon Marie (1846–1917), French writer

Blum, J., Dr., unidentified

Bodemeyer, Bodo Eduard Wilhelm Leopold von (1883–1929), entomologist and traveler

Boëthius, Anicius Manlius (c. 480–524), Roman statesman and philosopher

Bogo, *recte* Friedrich Hielscher

Böhme, Jacob (1575–1624), German philosopher and mystic

Boineburg-Lengsfeld, Hans Freiherr von (1889–1980), lieutenant general, commander of Greater Paris

Boissière, Jean Stanislas Jules (1863–1897), French journalist and writer

Bokelson, Jan (1509–1536), Johann von Leyden, Anabaptist leader

Bon, Henri (1844–1894), French missionary, martyr, and botanist

Bonnard, Abel (1883–1968), French writer and politician

Bonnard, Pierre (1867–1947), French painter and graphic artist

Bonaparte, Napoléon (1769–1821), emperor of France

Bontekoe, Willem Ysbrandsz (1587–1647[?]), ship's captain

Bosch, Hieronymus (1450–1516), Netherlandish painter

Boudot-Lamotte, Madeleine, Gallimard's secretary, wife of Horst Wiemer

Bouet, Madame, E. J.'s French tutor in Paris

Boulanger, Georges E. J. M. (1837–1891), French general and politician

Bourdin, Paul, correspondent for the *Frankfurter Zeitung*

Bourget, Paul (1852–1935), French writer

Bousquet, Marie-Louise, unidentified; "Masketta"

Bouyer, Frédéric Marie (b. 1822), French explorer, ship's captain

Braque, Georges (1882–1963), French painter

Bréguet, Louis Charles (1880–1955), French automobile and aircraft mechanic

Breitbach, Joseph (1903–1980), writer; "José"

Breker, Arno (1900–1991), sculptor

Brennus (fourth century BCE), chieftain of the Gauls

Brinon, Fernand de (1885–1947), ambassador, French diplomat, head of the *Comité France-Allemagne* in Paris

Brinon, Lisette de, née Franck, wife of Fernand de Brinon

Brinvilliers, Marie Madeleine marquise de (1630–1676), French poisoner

Brisson, Adolphe (1860–1925), French journalist

Brock, Erich (1889–1976), Swiss philosopher and literary historian

Brockes, Barthold Heinrich (1680–1747), German writer of the early Enlightenment

Brontë, Emily Jane (1818–1848), English writer

Brother Physicus, see *Jünger, Hans Otto*

Browne, Thomas (1605–1681), English theologian and writer

Brueghel, Pieter (1520/25–1569), Netherlandish painter; "The Elder"

Brueghel, Pieter (1564–1638), Netherlandish painter; "The Younger"

Bruno von Querfurt (c. 977–1009), missionary bishop and martyr

Büchner, Georg (1813–1837), German author and dramatist

Bülow, Bernhard Fürst von (1849–1929), German chancellor

Bünger, Wilhelm (1870–1937), jurist, presiding judge at the trial following the Reichstag fire (February 1933)

Buonarotti, Michelangelo (1475–1564), Italian painter and sculptor

Bunyan, John (1628–1688), itinerant English pastor, preacher, and author

Burckhardt, Carl Jacob Christoph (1818–1897), Swiss historian

Burnand, Robert Eugène (1882–1953), French historian

Byron, George Gordon Noel, Lord (1788–1824), English poet

C

Caesar, Julius (100–44 BCE), Roman emperor

Caillaux, Henriette (1894–1943), née Clarétie, married to Joseph Caillaux, murderer of Calmette

Caillot, Jacques (1592–1635), French graphic artist

Calmette, Gaston (1858–1914), French journalist

Calvet unidentified, Paris

Calvin, John (1509–1564), French theologian and religious reformer

Cange, Charles du Fresne Du (1610–1688), French lexicographer and orientalist

Capoceda, Giulio (1630–1701), *recte* Gregorio Leti, Italian writer

Cardot, Jeanne, *recte* J. Cohen, bookseller, Paris

Cargouët, comtesse de

Carus, E. J.'s imaginary son

Casanova, Giacomo Giovanni chevalier de Seingalt (1725–1798), Venetian writer and adventurer

Cazotte, Jacques (1719–1792), French general and author

Ceillier, Raymond, French admiral

Céline, Louis-Ferdinand (1894–1961), *recte* Louis Destouches, French writer and physician; "Merline"

Cellaris, *recte* Ernst Niekisch

Celsus, pseudonym for Parow, Johann Heinrich

Cervantes Saavedra, Miguel de (1547–1616), Spanish author

Cetti, Francesco (Abbé) (1726–1728), Italian zoologist and mathematician, author of a natural history of Sardinia

Chamfort (1741–1794), *recte* Nicholas-Sébastien Roch, French writer and aphorist

Chamisso, Adelbert von (1781–1838), German writer

Charcot, Jean Martin (1825–1893), French neurologist

Charet, Jean, probably Jean-Baptiste Charcot (1867–1936), French Antarctic explorer

Charlemagne (742–814), king of the Franks, Holy Roman emperor

Charles II, the Bald (823–877), West Frankish king, Holy Roman emperor

Charmille, *recte* Sophie Ravoux

Chateaubriand, François René viconte de (1768–1848), French writer

Chavan, André, French paleontologist

Cherubini, Luigi (1760–1842), Italian composer

Chevrolat, Louis Alexandre Auguste (1799–1884), French tax official and entomologist

Chirico, Giorgio de (1888–1978), Italian painter

Choltitz, Dietrich von (1894–1966), general, last commander of German troops in Paris; sometimes hailed as savior of Paris for his role in preventing its destruction

Chopin, Frédéric (1810–1849), Polish composer and pianist

Chrysippos (c. 280–205 BCE), Greek philosopher

Churchill, Winston Leonard Spencer (1874–1965), English statesman

Cicero, Marcus Tullius (106–43 BCE), Roman orator

Clausewitz, Carl von (1780–1831), Prussian general and military theorist

Clémenceau, Georges Benjamin (1841–1929), French statesman

Closais, des, unidentified

Coburg-Gotha, Prince of, aviator, World War II

Cocteau, Jean (1889–1963), French writer

Colbert, Jean Baptiste (1619–1683), French statesman

Coleman, Edward (1636–1678), courtier under Charles II of England, executed under false accusations on charges of conspiracy to murder the king

Colshorn, Frau, neighbor in Kirchhorst

Conrad, Joseph (1857–1924), *recte* Teodor Jozef Korzeniowski, English novelist

Copernicus, Nicholas (1473–1543), astronomer

Cortés, Hernando (1485–1587), Spanish conquistador

Cramer von Laue, Constantin (1906–1991), captain, personal advisor to Adenauer; later in the German Ministry of Justice

Cranach, Lucas (1472–1553), painter and graphic artist

Crébillon, Claude Prosper Jolyot de (1674–1762), French writer

Crisenoy, Baron de [bookplate], noble French family

Crome, Hans (1900–1997), major on General Staff, Paris, World War II

Cuchet, Gasper Joseph (d. 1779), French publisher

Cumanus, Ventidus (c. 50 BCE), Roman procurator in Judea

D

D., unidentified

Damiens, Robert François (1714–1757), French assassin

Damrath, Rudolf, Protestant military chaplain, pastor of the garrison church, Potsdam

Dancart, E. J.'s pseudonym for Ravoux, Paul

Dancart, Mme., E. J.'s pseudonym for Ravoux, Sophie

Darwin, Charles Robert (1809–1882), English naturalist

Daudet, Alphonse (1840–1897), French author

Daudet, Léon (1867–1942), French journalist and author

Daumier, Honoré (1808–1879), French artist and sculptor

Déat, Hélène, married to Marcel Déat

Déat, Marcel (1894–1955), French politician

Debussy, Claude-Archille (1862–1918), French composer

Deffand, Marie marquise du (1697–1780)

Defoe, Daniel (1660–1731), English politician and author

Deguerry, Gaspard (1797–1871), French priest

Dejean, Pierre François Auguste comte de (1780–1845), French soldier and entomologist

Delacroix, Eugène (1798–1863), French graphic artist and painter

Delitzsch, Franz (1813–1890), Protestant theologian

Delius, see *Diels, Rudolf*

Delvau, Alfred (1825–1867), French historian and writer

Deperthes, Jean Louis Hubert Simon (1730–1792), French writer and lawyer

Desbordes, Jean (1906–1944), French writer

Devéria, Eugène François Marie Joseph (1805–1865), French painter

Dezaïre, Joseph, Jesuit priest, former missionary in China, resident of Moisson, French philosopher and writer; "Le Zaïre"

Didier, Edouard (b. 1895), Belgian-French publisher

Didier, Lucienne (b. 1902), née Bauwens, married to Edourd Didier, French sculptor

Didot, French publishing family founded
by François Didot (1689–1757/59)

Diels, Rudolf (1900–1957), Gestapo leader;
pseudonym "Delius"

Dietloff, captain, managed an estate in the
Caucasus

Dietrichsdorf, Major

Dix, sergeant

Doctoresse, *recte* Sophie Ravoux

Don Capisco, E. J.'s pseudonym for
Schmitt, Carl

Donati, noble Florentine family

Donders, Adolf (1877–1944), dean of the
cathedral, Münster (Germany)

Dönitz, Karl (1891–1980), grand
admiral, Navy; Hitler's successor as
Reich president

Donoso Cortés, Juan Francisco Maria de la
Salud (1809–1853), Spanish politician

Donoso, unidentified friend of Armand,
Paris

Dorothea, E. J.'s dream character

Dostoevsky, Fyodor Michaelovitch
(1821–1881), Russian author

Doyle, Arthur Conan (1859–1930), English
author

Drescher, unidentified

Drescher, Maggi, sculptress

Drieu La Rochelle, Pierre (1893–1945),
French writer

Droste-Hülshoff, Annette von (1797–1848),
German poet

Du Bos, Charles (1882–1939), French writer

Ducasse, Isidore, see *Lautréamont*

Dumas, Alexandre, Sr. (1802–1870), French
author

Dumont-d'Urville, Jules Sébastian César
(1790–1842), navigator and Arctic
explorer

Dussarp, bookseller, Paris

E

Eckart, Meister (1260–1329), mystic and
theologian

Eckelmann, Hermann, administrative chief
of the Commandant of Paris

Eckermann, Johann Peter (1792–1854),
German writer, Goethe's private
secretary and biographer

Eliade, Mircea (1907–1986), Romanian
writer and scholar of religion; editor of
Zalmoxis

Emmel, officer, World War II

Ensor, James (1860–1949), Belgian
painter

Epting, Karl (1905–1979), head of the
German Institute in Paris, scholar of
French culture

Erdmannsdörffer, Bernhard (1833–1901),
historian

Ernstel, see *Jünger, Ernst*

Eschmann, Ernst Wilhelm (1904–1987),
German writer, sociologist, and
playwright

Eshmunazar (d. c. 525 BCE), Phoenician
king of Sidon

Eugene, Franz (1663–1736), prince of
Savoy-Carignan, French-Austrian field
marshal and statesman

F

Fabre-Luce, Alfred (1899–1983), French
author

Falkenhausen, Alexander von (1978–1966),
lieutenant general, military commander
of Belgium, World War II

Faulkner, William (1897–1963), American
novelist

Federici, Federico, Italian translator

Feltesse, Emil (b. 1881), French illustrator
and engraver

Feuerblume, see *Neumann, Marliese*

Feydeau, Ernest-Aimé (1821–1873), French
dramatist

Fieschi, Joseph (1790–1836), Italian
assassin, attacked King Louis Philippe

Filon, Pierre Marie Augustin (1841–1916),
French pedagogue and writer

Fischer, Ernst Hugo (1897–1975),
philosopher; "Magister"

Flaubert, Gustave (1821–1880), French
novelist

Fontane, Theodor (1819–1898), German
writer

Fouquier, Marcel Michel Louis (1866–1961),
French author

France, Anatole (1844–1924), *recte*
Jacques-Anatole Thibault, French writer

Frank, Walter (1905–1945), German
historian

Freud, Sigmund (1856–1939), Austrian
neurologist, founder of psychoanalysis

Freyhold, Rudi von, unidentified

Friedrich, Alexander, unidentified, author

Friedrich II (The Great), (1712–1786), king
of Prussia

Friedrich Wilhelm I (1688–1740), king of
Prussia; "The Soldier Kin"

Friedrich Wilhelm III (1770–1849), king of
Prussia

Friedrich Wilhelm IV (1795–1861), king of
Prussia

Fritsch, Werner Freiherr von (188–1939),
lieutenant general, commander-in-chief
of the Army

Fuchs (d. 1943, killed in action), military
doctor

Fuchs, Hermann (b. 1896), librarian

Funder, Tronier, unidentified, Berlin

G

Gachet, Paul Ferdinand (1828–1909), van
Gogh's doctor, sculptor and painter

Gachet, Paul Louis (1873–1962), son of the
Paul Ferdinand Gachet

Galliffet, Gaston Alexandre Auguste
marquis de (1830–1909), French general

Gallimard, Gaston (1881–1975), French
publisher

Galvani, Luigi (1737–1798), Italian
naturalist and doctor

Gambetta, Léon (1838–1882), French
statesman, prime minister

Gautier, Théophile (1811–1872), French poet

Gebhardt, Hans, probably Hans-Berndt
(1915–1995), sculptor

Gentz, Friedrich von (1764–1832),
journalist

Geoffrin, Marie-Thérèse (1699–1777),
unidentified

Goerdler, Carl Friedrich 1884–1945),
politician in the Resistance

George, Stefan (1868–1933), German poet

Georget, French priest

Gerhard, unidentified

Gerlach, Erwin (1894–1957), colonel,
quartermaster

Germaine, unidentified

Gerschell, André, French photographer

Gerson, Jean de (1363–1429), *recte* Jean
Charlier, French theologian

Gerstberger, Karl (1892–1955),
composer; "G"

Gevers, Marie (1883–1975), Belgian writer

Geyer, Hermann (1882–1946), German
general, World War I and World War II

Geyr von Schweppenburg, Sophia
Reichsfreiin [Baroness] von
(1916–1978), "Andromeda"

Gide, André (1869–1951), French writer

Gilles, Werner (1894–1961), painter and
graphic artist

Giono, Jean (1895–1970), French writer

Giraud, Henri Honoré (1879–1949), French
general

Giraudoux, Jean (1882–1944), French
author

Goldberg, Oskar (1885–1953), philosopher
and mystic

Goebbels, Joseph (1897–1945), N.S.
politician, minister of propaganda;
"Grandgoschier"

Goecke, Hans (1892–1963), entomologist

Georget, French abbé, Paris

Goethe, Johann Wolfgang von (1749–1832),
German author and poet

Gogh, Vincent van (1853–1890), Dutch
painter

Gogol, Herbert (d. 1942, killed in action),
private

Gogol, Nikolai (1809–1852), Russian writer

Goncourt, Edmond Louis de (1822–1896),
French writer

Goncourt, Jules Alfred de (1830–1870),
French writer, brother of Edmond

Gondroxon, Saint-Michel, "Richardet"

Gonod, antiquarian bookseller in Paris

Göpel, Erhard (1906–1966), art historian

Gould, Florence (1895–1983), née Lacaze,
wife of Frank J. Gould; "Lady Orpington," "Armance," and "Mme. Scrittore"

Gould, Frank J. (1877–1956), philanthropist,
businessman, son of financier Jay Gould

Goya y Lucientes, Francisco de
(1746–1828), Spanish painter and
graphic artist

Goys de Mezeyrac, Louis Marie Joseph
(1876–1967), French general

Grabbe, Christian Dietrich (1801–1836),
German writer

Graff, Anton (1736–1813), painter

Grandgoschier, E. J.'s pseudonym for
Goebbels, Joseph

Grävenitz, von (d.1963), doctor in
Voroshilovsk

Grethe, neighboring family in Kirchhorst

Grewe, Wilhelm G. (1911–2000), legal
scholar and diplomat

Grillparzer, Franz (1791–1872), Austrian
dramatist

Grimm, Friedrich Melchior Baron von
(1723–1807), diplomat and writer

Grimmelshausen, Johann Jacob Christoffel
von (1622–1676), German writer

Groener, Wilhelm (1876–1939), General,
politician, statesman

Gros-Meunier, *recte* Jacques de
Benoist-Méchin

Gross, mask-carver, Hannover

Grotius, Hugo (1583–1645), *recte* Huigh
de Groot, Dutch legal scholar and
statesman

Groult, art collector, Paris

Gruel, Léon, bookbinder in Paris

Grunert, Christian (b. 1900), poet and
gardener

Grüninger, Horst (b. 1900), first lieutenant

Grüninger, Maggi, married to Horst
Grüninger, sculptor

Gubernatis, Angelo de (1840–1913),
professor of Sanskrit and mythology in
Florence

Gudin, Théodore (1802–1880), French
painter of maritime scenes

Guénon, René (1886–1950), French author,
metaphysician, theologian

Guérin, Maurice de (1810–1839), French
poet

Guiche, Armand de Gramont
Comte de (1638–1673), French
nobleman-adventurer

Guitry, Sacha Alexandre-Pierre Georges
(1885–1957), French writer and actor

Güllich, Hans, first lieutenant,
World War II

Günther, Albrecht Erich (1893–1942),
journalist and translator

Günther, Gerhard (1889–1976), writer and
brother of A. E. Günther

Günther, Johann Christian (1695–1723),
German poet

H

Hach, professor, director of the Plague
Institute in Voroshilovsk, Stavropol
Research Institute for Plague Control

Hamann, Johann Georg (1730–1788),
German philosopher

Hammer-Purgstall, Joseph Freiherr
(Baron) von (1744–1856), Austrian
scholar of oriental studies, translator,
diplomat

Hannibal (c. 247–183 BCE), Carthaginian
general

Hansjakob, Heinrich (1837–1916), writer

Harry, unidentified

Hasdrubal [the Boetharch] (second
century BCE), general of Punic forces
in the Third Punic War (c. 146 BC)

Hattingen, Max (d. 1958), captain, district
attorney, General Staff in Paris, head of
the Department for Prisoners of War

Hauff, Wilhelm (1802–1827), German
author

Haug, Johann Christoph Friedrich
(1761–1829), writer; pseudonym
"Hophthalmos"

Haumont, Jacques Paul Louis (1899–1975),
French publisher

Häussler (Häußler), first lieutenant; World
War II

Hebbel, Christian Friedrich (1813–1863),
dramatist

Heinse, Johann Jakob Wilhelm
(1746–1803), German writer

Heinsheimer, Friedrich (Fritz)
(1897–1958), painter; pseudonym
"Fernand Husser"

Heller, Gerhard (1909–1982), translator

Heller, Marie-Louise, née Knüppel, wife of
Gerhard Heller (b. 1914)

Heraclitus (c. 544–483 BCE), Greek
philosopher

Hércule, unidentified, Paris

Herder, Johann Gottfried von (1744–1803), German philosopher and theologian

Hérisson d'Irisson, Maurice conte d' (1839–193), French officer, linguist, and traveler

Herodotus (c. 484–425 BCE), Greek historian

Hess, Rudolf (1894–1987), National Socialist politician and Hitler's representative

Heydrich, Reinhard Tristan Eugen (1904–1942), chief of Reich Security Head Office and protector of Bohemia and Moravia

Hielscher, Friedrich (1902–1990), writer, journalist

Himmler, Heinrich (1900–1945), National Socialist Politician, Reichsführer SS; E. J.'s pseudonym "Schinderhannes"

Hindenburg, Paul von (1847–1934), field marshal and Reich president

Hitler, Adolf (1889–1945), politician and dictator; E. J.'s pseudonym "Kniébolo"

Hofacker, Caesar von (1896–1944), lieutenant colonel, co-conspirator in the 20 July 1944 plot against Hitler

Hoffmann, Ernst Theodor Wilhelm (Amadeus) (1776–1822), German author, dramatist, and music critic

Hohly, Richard (1902–1995), German painter

Hölderlin, Johann Christian Friedrich (1770–1843), German poet

Höll, Werner (1898–1984), captain, artist

Holle, E. J.'s school principal and teacher

Holofernes, Old Testament, Nebuchadnezzar's general

Holstein, Friedrich von (1827–1909), German diplomat

Homer (eighth century BCE), Greek epic poet

Horion, Adolf (1888–1977), pastor and entomologist, monsignor

Horst (d. 1943), father of Max Horst

Horst, Max (b. 1903), administrator on the General Staff, Paris, World War II

Houdon, Jean Antoine (1741–1828), French sculptor

Houssaye, J. G. (nineteenth century), French writer and traveler

Huebner, Friedrich Markus (1886–1964), translator

Hufeland, Christoph Wilhelm (1762–1836), physician

Hughes, Richard (1900–1976), English novelist

Hugo, Victor (1802–1885), French novelist

Humm, Albert (d. 1945), soldier

Husser, Fernand, see *Heinsheimer, Friedrich*

Huxley, Aldous Leonard (1894–1963), English author

Huysmans, Joris-Karl (1848–1907), *recte* Charles Maria Georges, French writer

I

Ingres, Jean-August-Dominique (1780–1867), French painter

Irving, Washington (1783–1859), American writer

J

Jacqueline, Parisian milliner

Jäger, Oskar (1830–1910), teacher.

James, Thomas (1782–1847), English captain

Janin, René, unidentified, Paris

Jeanette, unidentified, Paris

Jeanne d'Arc (1412–1431), French national heroine; the "Made of Orléans"

Jeannel, Rénée Gabriel (1879–1965), French entomologist

Jean Paul (1763–1825), *recte* Jean Paul Friedrich Richter, German writer

Jeinsen, Emmy von (1879–1955), mother of Gretha Jünger

Jeinsen, Harry von (1877–1948), father of Gretha Jünger

Jeinsen, Kurt von (1902–1943), brother of Gretha von Jeinsen, first wife of Ernst Jünger, engineer

Jeinsen, Viktoria von (b. 1926), niece of Gretha Jünger, kindergarten teacher, married to Heinz Witthuhn

Jessen, Peter Jens (1895–1944), economist

Joan of Arc, see *Jeanne d'Arc*

Jodl, Alfred (1890–1946), lieutenant general, chief of Operations Staff of the Wehrmacht

Joinville, Jean de (1224–1317)

Joffre, Joseph Jacques Césaire (1852–1931), French marshal

Jomini, Antoine Henri baron de (1779–1869), general and writer on military subjects

Jordaens, Jakob (1593–1678), Flemish painter

José, see Breitbach, Joseph

Josephus, Flavius (37–100 CE), Jewish historian

Jouhandeau, Elisabeth (1888–1971), recte Elisabeth Claire Thoulemon, French dancer; wife of Marcel Jouhandeau, "Caryathis"

Jouhandeau, Marcel (1888–1979), recte M. Provence; French writer, "Calandrus"

Jünger, Alexander Carl (1934–1993), physician, E. J.'s son

Jünger, Anna Hermine Margrete (1839–1923), née Walters, E. J.'s grandmother

Jünger, Christian Jakob Friedrich "Fritz" Clamor (1840–1904), schoolteacher, E. J.'s grandfather

Jünger, Ernst Georg (1868–1943), E. J.'s father

Jünger, Ernst (1926–1944), E. J.'s son; "Ernstel"

Jünger, Friedrich Georg (1898–1977), poet and writer, E. J.'s brother

Jünger, Gretha Lidy Toni Margrete Anni (1906–1960), née von Jeinsen, E. J.'s wife; "Perpetua"

Jünger, Hans Otto (1905–1976), physicist, E. J.'s brother; "Brother Physicus"

Jünger, Johanna Hermine (1899–1984), E. J.'s sister; "Hanna"

Jünger, Karolina (1873–1950), née Lampl, E. J.'s mother; "Lily"

Jünger, Wolfgang Wilhelm (1908–1975), geographer, E. J.'s brother

Juvenal, Decimus Junius (c. 60–140 CE), Roman satirist

K

K., unidentified, major in Wehrmacht, World War II

Kafka, Franz (1883–1924), Austro-Czech author

Kang-Hsi, Emperor (1654–1722), emperor of China

Kanne, Johann Arnold (1773–1824), writer, philologist, mythographer

Kant, Immanuel (1724–1894), German philosopher

Karl XII (1682–1718), king of Sweden

Karamsin, Nikolai Michailovitch (1766–1826), Russian historian

Karsch, Ferdinand Anton Franz (1853–1936), entomologist, pseudonym "Canus"

Kastor, pseudonym for Alfred Baeumler

Keiper, Wolfgang (1911–1981), antiquarian bookseller

Keitel, Wilhelm (1882–1946), field marshal and chief of staff, Wehrmacht

Keyserling, Hermann Graf [Count] von (1880–1946), cultural historian

Keyserling, Manfred Graf [Count] von

Khayyam, Omar (1027–1123), Persian poet and naturalist

Kiderlen-Wächter, Alfred von (1852–1912), German diplomat and politician

Klaebisch, Gustav, unidentified

Klages, Ludwig (1872–1956), philosopher and psychologist

Kleist, Ewald von (1881–1954), general, field marshal

Kleist, Heinrich von (1777–1811), German author and dramatist

Klinger, Friedrich Maximilian von (1752–1831), German poet

Klostermann, Vittorio (1901–1977), publisher

Kluge, Hans Günther von (1882–1944), general, field marshal, commander-in-chief of Wehrmacht West

Kniébolo, E. J.'s pseudonym for Adolf Hitler

Konrad, Rudolf (1891–1964), general, commander of the Caucasus front (1943)

Kossmann, Karl-Richard (1899–1969), major general, chief of staff under Heinrich von Stülpnagel

Kranzberger, see Kranzbühler, Otto

Kranzbühler, Otto Heinrich (1907–2004), German Naval judge on Dönitz's staff

Kraus, ballistics expert, friends with Hans Jünger

Krause, lieutenant colonel, participant in the legendary Eichhof Conference

Kräwel, Kurt von, colonel, World War II

Kreitz, Werner (1899–1957), host of the Eichhof Conference

Kretzschmar, corporal, telephone operator, World War II

Kretszchmer, Eberhard (b. 1909), literary historian, biographer of Schiller (1938)

Krüger, professor, unidentified, France

Kubin, Alfred (1877–1959), surrealist graphic artist, writer

Kügelgen, Gerhard von (1772–1820), painter

Kuhn, Hans (1905–1991), painter, corporal, World War II

Kutscher, first lieutenant, World War II

L

L., Madame, Paris, presumably a prostitute

Labric, Roger (b. 1893), French author

Laclos, Pierre Ambroise François Choderlos de (1741–1803), French author

Ladurée, Louis Ernest (nineteenth century), innkeeper, Paris; also the name of his inn

Lady Orpington, see *Gould, Florence*

Lahmann, unidentified, neighbor in Kirchhorst

Lamarck, Jean-Baptiste Antoine de Monet de (1744–1829), French naturalist

Lampe, Ursula, art historian

Landru, Henri Désiré (1869–1922), French murderer

Lapeyre, Gabriel Guillaume (b. 1877), French historian

Lapeyrouse, unidentified

Larcher, Pierre Henri (1726–1812), French classical scholar

La Rochefoucauld, François de (1613–1680), French writer and aphorist

Latreille, Pierre Henri (1762–1833), French entomologist

Laue, Max Theodor Felix von (1879–1960), German physicist, Nobel Prize laureate

Laurencin, Marie (1885–1956), French painter and poet

Lautréamont, comte de (1847–1870), *recte* Isidore Lucien Ducasse, French poet

Laval, Pierre (1883–1945), French politician, premier

Lawrence, David Herbert (1885–1930), English novelist

Lawrence, Thomas Edward (1888–1935), English adventurer, archaeologist, and author; "Lawrence of Arabia"

Lazarillo de Tormes (sixteenth century), fictional character in an anonymous Spanish novel

Léautaud, Paul Firmin Valentin (1872–1956), French writer

Lechevalier, Paul, French publisher and bookseller, Paris

Leinert, Robert (1873–1940), mayor of Hannover

Leleu, Jean (b. 1912), French traveling cloth salesman

Lenin, Vladimir Ilyich (1870–1924), *recte* W. I. Ulyanov, architect of the Russian Revolution

Leo, Hans, major, member of the Command Staff in Paris, World War II

Leonardo da Vinci (1452–1519), Italian painter, sculptor, architect

Leopold I of Anhalt-Dessau (1676–1747), Prussian field marshal and military reformer

Lermina, Jules Hippolyte (1839–1915), French writer

Lichtenberg, Georg Christoph (1742–1799), physicist, writer, aphorist

Ligne, Charles Joseph prince de (1735–1814), Belgian officer and writer

Limojin de Saint-Didier, Alexandre Toussaint (1630–1689), French diplomat

Lindemann, Friedrich (1896–1986), writer, philosopher, and astrologer; "Fritz"

Linné, Carl von (1707–1778), Swedish doctor and naturalist; "Linnaeus"

Linné, Elisabeth Christina (1743–1782), Swedish botanist, daughter of C. Linné

Linstow, Hans Otfried von (1899–1944), colonel, chief of staff in Paris, World War II

Liszt, Franz von (1811–1886), Hungarian composer and pianist

Litzmann, Karl (1850–1936), General and politician

Loehning, Paul (1889–1971), major general
in Wehrmacht, commander of Hannover,
World War II

Longus (second or third century CE),
Greek poet, creator of the pastoral
romance

Löns, Hermann (1866–1914), German
writer

Lottner, head of the customs office, Paris

Louis IX, Saint (1214–1270), king of France

Louis XIV (1638–1715), king of France;
"Sun King"

Louis XVI (1754–1793), king of France

Ludendorff, Erich (1865–1937), German
general and politician

Luther, Martin (1483–1546), German
religious reformer

Lyautey, Louis Hubert Gonçalve (1854–1934),
French marshal and politician

M

MacDonald, James Ramsay (1866–1937),
British politician

Macrobius, Ambrosius Teodosius (fl.400),
Latin author and philosopher

Madame Scrittore, see *Gould, Florence*

Magister, see *Fischer, Ernst Hugo*

Magius, Girolamo (1523–1572), *recte* G.
Maggi, Italian writer, architect, and
mathematician

Maillol, Aristide (1861–1944), French
sculptor, painter, and graphic artist

Maiweg, Herr, engineer, leader of a
Technical Petroleum Brigade

Mallarmé, Stephane (1842–1898), French
poet

Malraux, André (1901–1976), French writer
and politician

Malthus, Thomas Robert (1766–1834),
English economist and historian

Man, Hendrik de (1885–1953), Belgian
politician and *de facto* prime minister
under the German occupation

Mann, Thomas (1875–1955), German
author and winner of Nobel Prize for
Literature, emigrated from Germany
in 1933

Mansfield, Katherine (1888–1923), New
Zealand writer

Marais, Jean (1913–1998), *recte* J. Alfred
Villain-Marais, French actor

Marat, Jean-Paul (1744–1793), radical
politician during the French Revolution

Marcus Aurelius (121–180), Roman emperor

Marckord, Justus, *recte* Karl Ley, writer
Gebete eines Ungläubigen [*Prayers of an
Unbeliever*] (1938); opponent of the NS
regime

Marcks, Otto (1905–1978), lieutenant
colonel, brother of General Marcks,
World War II

Marcu, Valeriu (1899–1942), Romanian
writer

Mariaux, Franz (1898–1986), journalist,
correspondent for *Cologne Newspaper*

Marius, Gaius (156–86 BCE), Roman
military leader

Marmontel, Jean-François (1723–1799),
French author

Marteau, de, unidentified; "Martöchen"

Marwitz, Friedrich August Ludwig von der
(1777–1837), soldier and politician

Marx, Karl (1818–1883), political
philosopher

Massenbach, unidentified

Maulnier, Thierry (1909–1988), *recte*
Jacques Louis André Tallegrand,
French writer

Maupassant, Henri-René-Albert-Guy de
(1850–1893), French writer

Maurras, Charles (1868–1952), French
writer and politician

Médan, Pierre (murdered, 1944)

Mégret, Christian (1904–1987), French
novelist

Meinert, Klaus, German soldier, World
War II

Mell, Rudolf (1878–1970), zoologist

Melville, Herman (1819–1891), American
author

Memling, Hans (c. 1433–1494), Flemish
painter

Menge, Hermann August (1841–1939),
Bible translator, school principal

Menzel, Hanne, unidentified, Paris

Mercier, Dr., unidentified, Kirchhorst

Mergener, captain, commander of combat
unit in Caucasus

Merk, Ernst (b. 1903), lieutenant colonel, quartermaster

Merline, E. J.'s pseudonym for Céline, Louis Ferdinand

Méryon, Charles (1821–1868), French engraver

Merz, unidentified, officer on the General Staff in Paris

Metternich, Franz Graf [count] Wolff (1893–1978), art historian

Meyer, Fritz, unidentified, neighbor in Kirchhorst

Michelet, Jules (1798–1874), French historian

Migot, Georges Albert (1891–1976), French composer

Millet, Jean-François (1814–1875), French painter and graphic artist

Mirabeau, Honoré Gabriel Riqueti, conte de (1749–1791), French statesman

Mirbeau, Octave (1848–1917), French writer

Mohr, Fridtjof Lous (c. 1888–c. 1942), Norwegian explorer

Molière (1622–1673), recte Jean Baptiste Poquelin, French writer of comedies

Moltke, Helmuth Graf [count] von (1800–1891), Prussian field marshal

Mommsen, Theodor (1817–1903), historian

Monet, Claude (1840–1926), French painter

Monfreid, Henry de (1879–1974), French writer and traveler

Mons, unidentified military chaplain, World War II

Montherlant, Henry Millon de (1896–1972), French writer

Morand, Hélène (1888–1975), née Chrysolevony, previously Princess Sturdzo from her first marriage, wife of Paul Morand; "F"

Morand, Paul (1888–1976), French writer and politician; "F"

More, Thomas (1478–1535), English humanist and statesman

Morin (d. 1943), antiquarian bookseller, father of Charles Morin, Le Mans

Morin, Charles, antiquarian bookseller, Paris

Morris (b. 1874), unidentified, Paris

Mortier, Edouard Adolphe Casimir Joseph duc de Trévise (1768–1835), French marshal

Moult, Eugène le (1882–1967), French entomologist

Mossakowski, see *Syben, Friedrich*

Mozart, Wolfgang Amadeus (1756–1791), Austrian composer

Mühsam, Erich (1878–1934), German writer and anarchist

Müller, Johan Ludwig (1892–1972), major general, World War II

Münchhausen, von (d. 1943), first lieutenant, stationed in France

Murat, Joachim-Napoléon (1767–1815), king of Naples, marshal of France

Murray, Thomas Boyles (1798–1860), English pastor

Mussolini, Benito (1883–1945), Italian dictator; "Il Duce"

N

N., "our old comrade," unidentified

Naisen, Monika (d. 1626), one of the "Martyrs of Japan," beatified 1867

Napoléon, see *Bonaparte*

Napoléon III (1808–1873), French emperor

Naumann, Johannes Andreas (1744–1826), naturalist, ornithologist

Nawe-Stier, unidentified

Nay, Ernst Wilhelm (1902–1968), German painter

Nebel, Gerhard (1903–1974), writer; "Outcast of the Islands"

Nebuchadnezzar II (c. 605–562 B. CE), Babylonian king

Neuhaus, Alfred Hugo (b. 1892), major on the General Staff in Paris

Neumann, Marlise (d. 1943), "Feuerblume"

Niedermayer, Oskar Ritter von (1885–1945), general, World War II

Niekisch, Anna (1892–1973), teacher, wife of Ernst Niekisch

Niekisch, Ernst August (b. 1916), physicist, son of Ernst and Anna Niekisch

Niekisch, Ernst Karl August (1889–1967), politician and journalist; "Cellaris"

Nietzsche, Friedrich Wilhelm (1844–1900), philosopher

Nigrinus, E. J.'s pseudonym for Schwarz, Manfred

Noailles, Anna-Elisabeth, Contesse de, French writer

Noël, Marie (1883–1967), *recte* Marie Mélanie Rouget, French writer

Nostitz-Walwitz, Helene von (1878–1944), née von Beneckendorff-Hindenburg, German writer

Novalis (1772–1801), *recte* Friedrich Leopold Freiherr von Hadenberg, German Romantic poet

Nüssle (d. 1943, killed in action), junior officer

O

Oertzen, Louise von (1897–1965), director, Nurses' Branch German Red Cross

Oetinger, Friedrich Christoph (1702–1782), Protestant theologian

Oldekopp (sixteenth century), city architect, Hildesheim

Oldekopp, Johannes (sixteenth century), son of the city architect, Hildesheim

Omar, Azerbaijani man, Caucasus

Oppen, Alexander (Axel) von (1906–1984), colonel, son of Gustav von Oppen

Oppen, Gustav von (1867-1918), colonel

d'Orves, Henri Louis Honoré d'Estienne (1901–1941), Naval officer, hero of French Resistance

Otte, Kurt (1902–1983), pharmacist and art collector

P

P., see *Pétain, Phillippe Henri*

Palffy, countess, see *Vilmorin, Luise de*

Parow, Johann Heinrich (d. 1936), German-Norwegian doctor

Pascal, Blaise (1623–1662), French philosopher and mathematician

Patrouix (b. c. 1862), French engineer

Paul I (1754–1801), Russian czar

Paul, Jean, see *Jean Paul*

Paulhan, Jean (1884–1968), French writer

Pégoud, Adolphe (1890–1915), French aviator

Pellegrin, Arthur Auguste (1891–1956), French author

Pellico, Silvio (1789–1854), Italian author

Pepys, Samuel (1633–1703), English diarist

Pétain, Philippe Henri (1856–1951), French marshal and president

Perpetua, E. J.'s pseudonym for his wife, see *Jünger, Gretha*

Perré, Jean-Paul (b. 1893), French battalion commander

Peter (b. 1941), child evacuee taken in by the Jüngers

Petronius, Gaius (first century CE), Roman poet

Pfaffendorf, Hermann (1896–1969), mayor of Goslar, E. J.'s comrade in World War I

Philippe II (1674–1723), Duke of Orléans, son of Liselotte von der Pfalz

Phillipps, unidentified, Paris

Philo of Alexandria (c. 20 BCE–30 CE), philosopher

Philomela, Ste., see *Philomena*

Philomena, Ste. credited with curing diseases of the heart

Picasso, Pablo Ruiz y (1881–1973), Spanish artist

Pilate, Pontius Roman procurator in Judea (New Testament).

Pillet, Maurice Pierre (1881–1964), French Egyptologist

Planck, Max Karl Ernst Ludwig (1858–1947), German theoretical physicist, Nobel Prize laureate

Platen, August Graf [count] von (1796–1835), German poet

Plato (427–347 BCE), Greek philosopher

Pliny the Younger, Plinius Gaius Caecilius Secundus (61–113 CE), Roman administrator and historian

Plon, Henri Philippe (1806–1872), French publisher

Podewils-Juncker-Bigatto, Clemens Graf [count] (1905–1978), journalist and writer

Podewils, Sophie Dorothee (1909–1979), née Baroness von Hirschberg, wife of Clemens Podewils, German writer; "The Green Princess"

Poe, Edgar Allan (1809–1849), American author

Poincaré, Raymond (1864–1934), French politician, president

Polignac, marquise de, unidentified

Popitz, Johannes (1884–1945), minister of finance for the State of Prussia, arrested and executed for his connection with the 20 July plot against Hitler

Potard, see *Silberberg*

Poupet, Georges, editor at the Plon Publishing House, Paris

Poursin, André (d. 1969), French bookdealer, Paris

Poussin, Nicolas (1594–1665), French painter

Prévaux, Blandine Ollivier de (1894–1981), great-granddaughter of Liszt

"Princess, the green," E. J's pseudonym for Podewils, Sophie Dorothee

"Princess, the black," E. J's pseudonyms for Transvaal

Profillet, Charles (b. 1824), French priest and author

Proust, Marcel (1871–1922), French novelist

Prunier, unidentified, Paris

Pückler-Muskau, Hermann, Prince of (1785–1871), landscape architect and writer

Pushkin, Alexander Sergeyevitch (1799–1837), Russian writer

Pythagoras (c. 580–496 BCE), Greek philosopher

Q

Quincey, Thomas de (1785–1859), English writer

Quintilian, Marcus Fabius (35–96 CE), Roman writer

Quinton, René (1866–1925), lieutenant colonel, French writer

R

Raabe, Wilhelm (1831–1910), German writer

Rademacher, Otfried (1905–1968), journalist; "Dr. Weber"

Rahmelow, lieutenant, World War II

Ransonnette, Pierre Nicolas (1745–1810), French illustrator

Rantzau, Abel, unidentified

Rathke, Anton (1888–1945), colonel, lieutenant general in the German Army

Ravachol (1859–1892), *recte* François Claudius Königstein, French anarchist

Ravaillac, François (1578–1610), fanatical Catholic, regicide, murderer of Henri IV

Ravoux, Sophie (1906–2001), physician; "Mme. Dancart," "Charmille," "Camilla," "Doctoresse," "Mme. D'Armenonville"

Ravoux, Paul (d. 1957), husband of Sophie Ravoux; "A," "R"

Raynal, Guillaume-Thomas-François (1713–1796), French abbé, Enlightenment thinker

Réau, Louis (1881–1961), French writer

Reese, major, World War II

Régimbart, Maurice Auguste (1852–1907), French entomologist

Rehbock, neighbor in Kirchhorst

Rehm, E. J's aide-de-camp

Reiners, Jakob (1917–1940), lieutenant

Reitter, Emmerich (1880–1929), German entomologist

Renan, Joseph Ernest (1823–1892), French orientalist and philosopher

Renée, shopkeeper in Vincennes

Reverdy, Pierre (1889–1960), French poet

Reyès, Salvador (1899–1970), Chilean writer and diplomat

Richelet, Madame, unidentified

Richelieu, Louis François Armand Vignerot du Pléssis (1696–1788), French duke, soldier, and statesman

Richet, M. (eighteenth century), parliamentary attorney, France

Rictus, Jehan (1867–1933), *recte* Gabriel Randon de Saint-Armand, French poet

Riley, James (1777–1849), American sailor and writer

Rimbaud, Jean Nicolas Arthur (1854–1891), French poet

Rinne, Friedrich Wilhelm Berthold (1863–1933), mineralogist

Rivarol, Antoine conte de (1753–1801), French writer

Rivière, Jacques (1886–1925), French author

Robespierre, Maximilian de (1758–1794), French revolutionary leader

Rochefort, Henri (1830–1913), French
   politician
Rodin, Auguste (1840–1917), French
   sculptor and graphic artist
Rodolphe, see *Schlichter, Rudolf*
Röhricht, Edgar (1892–1967), chief of the
   General Staff, commander of the First
   Army, World War II
Roland, unidentified
Rommel, Erwin (1891–1944), German field
   marshal
Romney, George (1734–1802), English
   painter
Ronneberger, Friedrich August (1886–1968),
   chaplain, Wehrmacht pastor
Röpke, Wilhelm (1899–1966), economist
Roquelaure, Gaston-Jean-Baptiste, Marquis
   (duc) de (1617–1633), French nobleman
Rosanov, Vasily Vasilievich (1856–1919),
   Russian author
Rosen, Friedrich (1856–1953), German
   diplomat, foreign minister
Rosenberg, Alfred (1893–1946), politician,
   chief ideologue of National Socialism
Rosenkranz, Wilhelm, unidentified
Rossi, Giovanni Battista de (1822–1894),
   Italian archaeologist
Rossi, Pietro (1738–1804), Italian doctor
   and entomologist
Rousseau, Henri (1844–1910), French
   painter; "The Customs Agent"
Rousseau, Jean-Jacque (1712–1778),
   French-Swiss philosopher and writer
Roussel, Napoléon Charles Louis
   (1834–1854), French artist
Rouvier, Jean, unidentified
Rozanov, Vassily Vassilievich (1856–1919),
   Russian writer
Ruge, Friedrich Oskar (1894–1985), vice
   admiral, city counselor
Rundstedt, Gerd von (1875–1953), field
   marshal, commander-in-chief of
   Wehrmacht forces in the West
Ruoff, Richard (1883–1967), lieutenant
   general, World War II
Rupp, Ernst (1892–1943), general, division
   commander, World War II
Ruysbroec, Jan van (1293–1381), Flemish
   mystic

S

Saager, Adolf (1879–1949), journalist
Sabatier, Abbé (d. 1871)
Sachot, Octave Louis Marie (b. 1824),
   French translator and journalist
Sade, Donatien-Alphonse-François,
   Marquis de (1740–1814), French author
Saint-Albin, J. S. C. (1794–1881), *recte*
   Jacques Albin Simon Collin de Plancy
Saint-Gellais, Mellin de (1491–1558), French
   poet
Saint-Réal, César Vichard abbé de
   (1639–1692), French historian
Saint-Simon, Louis de Rouvroy duc de
   (1675–1755), politician and writer
Salewski, first lieutenant, World War II
Salmanoff, Alexandre (1871–1964), French
   physician of Russian background
Salomon, Ernst von (1902–1972), German
   writer
Sarthe, René Levasseur de la (1747–1834),
   French surgeon
Sauckel, Fritz (1894–1945), National
   Socialist politician, *Gauleiter* [governor]
   of Thuringia, Reich director of labor
   (1942–1945)
Sauerbruch, Ernst Ferdinand (1875–1951),
   surgeon
Sauerwein, Jules (1880–1967), French
   journalist
Savigny, Jean Baptiste Henri (1793–1843),
   French shipwreck survivor
Schaer, Ernst, colonel, World War II,
   implicated in 20 July 1944 plot against
   Hitler as Stauffenberg's informant but
   was released
Scharnhorst, Gerhard Johann David von
   (1755–1813), Prussian general
Schede, Wolf (b. 1888–1981), lieutenant
   general
Schenk, Gustav (1905–1969), botanist and
   writer
Schery, Friedrich Franz, Viennese musician
Scheuerlen, Ernst, admiral, commander-
   in-chief of the fleet stationed on the
   German Bight, World War II
Schewen, Werner von, colonel, head of the
   ILA [trade fair of the aerospace industry]
   in Paris; brother-in-law of Neuhaus

Schiller, Johann Christoph Friedrich von
(1759–1805), German dramatist and poet

Schinderhannes, E. J.'s pseudonym for
Heinrich Himmler

Schlegel, Friedrich von (1772–1829),
German philosopher and writer

Schleier, Rudolf (1899–1959), diplomat,
ambassador in Paris

Schlichter, Rudolf (1890–1955), painter and
draftsman; "Rodolphe"

Schlumberger, Jean (1977–1968), French
writer

Schmid, Carlo (1896–1979), politician

Schmidt, captain, World War II,
unidentified

Schmitt, Carl (1888–1985), jurist; "Don
Capisco," "C. S.," "D. P.," "D. T."

Schmitt, Duschka (1903–1950), née
Todorovich, wife of Carl Schmitt

Schnath, Georg (b. 1898–1989), archivist
and historian

Schneider, dealer in musical literature,
Paris

Schnitzler, Liselelotte (Lily) von (1889–1981),
née von Malinkrodt, art collector

Scholz, unidentified

Schoor, Hilde, unidentified

Schopenhauer, Arthur (1788–1860),
philosopher

Schrader, bathhouse attendant, Hannover

Schramm, Wilhelm Ritter von (1898–1983),
writer and journalist

Schreck, Julius (1898–1936), NS functionary,
later Hitler's driver and bodyguard

Schröter, sergeant, World War II

Schubart, Walter (1897–c. 1941), German
writer

Schuchardt, Karl (1893–1943), lieutenant
colonel, World War II, on the General
Staff

Schüddekopf, gravedigger

Schulenburg, Fritz-Dietlof count von der
(1902–1944), jurist, president of the State
of Silesia, in the resistance against Hitler;
"Fritzi"

Schuler, Alfred (1865–1923), German
religious mystic and visionary,
neo-pagan

Schultz, Edmund (1901–1965), "Edmond"

Schultz, Edmund E. (b. 1931), son of
Edmund Schultz

Schultz, Fritzi (1899–1975), sister of
Edmund Schultz

Schwab, Gustav (1792–1850), German
writer

Schwarz, Manfred (1914–1988), cultural
editor for the Bavarian Broadcasting
Company; "Nigrinus"

Schwarzenberg, Felix Fürst [Prince] zu
(1800–1852), Austrian statesman

Scipio, Publius Cornelius Africanus
(235–183 BCE), Roman general

Seeckt, Hans von (1866–1936), lieutenant
general

Seidel, Ina (1885–1974), German writer

Seneca, Lucius Ennius (4 BCE–65 CE),
Roman philosopher and politician

Seydlitz-Kurzbach, Walther Kurt von
(1888–1976), general

Shakespeare, William (1564–1616), English
dramatist and poet

Shaw, George Bernard (1856–1950),
Anglo-Irish writer and playwright

Sieburg, Friedrich (1893–1964), writer and
journalist

Siedler, Dr., member of Grand Admiral
Dönitz's legal staff

Silberberg, Jewish pharmacist, Paris;
"Potard"

Sild, Meinhart (d. 1944), editor of the
journal Zeitgeschichte [Contemporary
History]

Sild, Traugott, co-editor of the journal
Zeitgeschichte [Contemporary History]

Silesius, Angelus (1624–1677), recte Johann
Scheffler, religious poet

Smend, Julius (1835–1909), clergyman

Smith, Arthur Henderson (1860–1941),
English missionary

Sommer, unidentified, restaurateur in Paris

Sommer, first lieutenant World War
II, served in Tank Brigade 106
"Feldhernhalle"

Soung-Lin, P'Ou (1640–1715), Chinese
author

Spannuth, Franz, superintendent (i.e.,
high-level Lutheran administrator),
unidentified

Speidel, Hans Emil (1897–1984), general, World War II

Speidel, Hans Helmut (b. 1938), diplomat, brigadier general, son of Hans Emil Speidel

Speidel, Ina Rose (b. 1927), daughter of Hans Speidel

Speidel, Ruth (1897–1990), née Stahl, married to Hans Speidel

Spengler, Oswald (1880–1936), philosopher

Sperling, captain, battalion commander, Caucasus (1942)

Spinoza, Benedictus (Baruch) de (1632–1677), Dutch philosopher

Sprenger, Jakob (1436–1495), inquisitor, co-author *Malleus Malificarum* [*Hammer of Witches*]

Stameroff, Kyriak, director of the publishing house Gallimard, Paris

Stapel, Wilhelm (1882–1954), journalist

Stauffenberg, Claus Graf [count] Schenk von (1907–1944), colonel, would-be assassin of Hitler

Stellar, Georg Wilhelm (1709–1746), doctor and naturalist

Stemmermann, Wilhelm (1888–1944), general, World War II

Stendhal (1783–1842), *recte* Marie-Henri Beyle, French writer

Sternberger, Dolf (1907–1989), journalist and political scientist

Sterne, Laurence (1713–1768), English novelist

Stevenson, Robert Louis Balfour (1850–1894), Scottish writer

Stifter, Adelbert (1805–1868), Austrian writer

Straub, unidentified, Nussdorf

Strauss, David Friedrich (1808–1874), philosopher and theologian

Strecker, Karl (1884–1973), general at Stalingrad, World War II

Strindberg, Johan August (1849–1912), Swedish writer and dramatist

Strubelt, first lieutenant, World War II

Strünckmann, Karl-Christoph (1872–1953), *recte* Kurt van Emsen, German psychiatrist, pioneer in alternative medicine

Stucken, Eduard (1865–1936), writer

Stülpnagel, Carl Heinrich von (1886–1944), general, commander-in-chief of German Forces in France (1942–1944)

Stülpnagel, Helene von, née Baroness von Pentz

Stülpnagel, Otto von (1878–1948), general, commander-in-chief of German Forces in France (1940–1942); "Habakuk"

Sturm, Vilma (1912–1995), journalist

Suhrkamp, Johann Heinrich Peter (1891–1959), publisher

Suire, Karl von Le (1898–1954), colonel, World War II

Sulla, Lucius Cornelius (138–78 BCE), Roman statesman and military leader

Swammerdam, Jan (1637–1680), Dutch naturalist

Swift, Jonathan (1667–1745), Anglo-Irish writer

Swinburne, Algernon Charles (1837–1909), English poet

Syben, Friedrich (1889–1969), journalist; "Mossakowski"

T

Tallemant des Réaux, Gédéon (1619–1692), French writer

Talleyrand-Périgord, Charles Maurice de (1754–1838), French statesman

Tamerlane (1336–1405), *recte* Timur-Leng, Mongolian military leader

Tassencourt, Marcelle (1914–2001), theater director, wife of Jacques Talagrand (Thierry Maulnier)

Tavernier, Jean Baptiste baron d'Aubonne (1605–1689), French writer and diamond dealer

Tempelhof, Friedrich von (1878–1941), colonel, World War II

Tennent, James Emerson (1804–1869), English writer, traveler, and politician

Tevenar, Gerhard (Gerd) von (1912–1943), member of the resistance group Hielscher

Thérouanne, Pierre de (1891–1980), French painter

Thierry-Maulnier, see *Maulnier*

Thomas, Friedrich August Wilhelm (1840–1918), author of *Das Elisabeth Linné-Phänomen (Jena, G. Fischer, 1914)*

Thomas, Henri (1912–1993), French writer and translator

Thomas, Louis Auguste Georges Marie (1885–1962), French historian and writer

Thucydides (c. 460–399 BCE), Greek historian

Tippelskirch, Kurt von (1891–1957), colonel, World War II

Tirpitz, Alfred von (1849–1930), grand admiral of the German Navy, World War II

Tirpitz, Wolfgang (Wolf) von (1887–1968), corvette captain, son of the grand admiral

Titus, Flavius Vespasianus (39–81), Roman emperor

Titian (c. 1477–1576), *recte* Tiziano Vecellio, Italian painter

Tocqueville, Alexis Clérel conte de (1805–1859), French political theorist

Toepfer, Alfred Carl (1894–1993), merchant and patron

Tolstoy, Leo Nikolaevich (1828–1910), Russian author

Trakl, Georg (1887–1914), Austrian lyric poet

Traz, Robert de (1844–1951), French writer

Trémoille, duchess de la, unidentified

Triller, Daniel Wilhelm (1695–1782), poet, doctor, philologist

Trott zu Solz, Heinrich von (1918–2009), lieutenant in the resistance against the NS regime; "Head Forester"; E. J. notes incorrectly that Heinrich von Trott zu Solz was executed after the 20 July 1944 assassination plot

Turgenev, Ivan Sergeyevich (1818–1883), Russian novelist, playwright

Turner, Joseph Mallord William (1775–1851), English painter

U

Uckel, captain, unidentified, Paris World War II

Unger, Johann Friedrich (1753–1804), book printer and calligrapher

Uslar-Gleichen, Günther Freiherr von (b. 1893), major, World War II

V

Valentiner, Klaus (d. 1945, presumed killed in action), interpreter

Valentiner, Max, antiquarian bookseller, brother of Klaus Valenteiner

Valentiner, Max (1883–1949), captain of a corvette and U-Boot commander

Valéry, Paul Ambroise (1871–1945), French poet and essayist

Valla, Laurentius (1405–1457), Italian humanist

Vallès, Jules (1832–1885), French writer

Varnhagen von Ense, Karl August (1785–1858), diplomat and writer

Velut, Pierre, unidentified acquaintance, Paris, 1944

Veressayev (1867–1945), *recte* Vikentii Vikentevich Smidovich, Russian doctor

Verlaine, Paul (1844–1896), French poet

Vernes, Arthur (1979–1976), French doctor, specialist in syphilis

Vernet, Joseph (1714–1789), French painter

Vico, Giovanni Battista (1668–1744), Italian philosopher

Victoria (b. 1926), unidentified doctor's daughter, Caucasus

Viel-Castel, Graf [count] Horace de (1802–1864), French historian

Villiers de L'Isle-Adam, Jean Marie Philippe-Auguste conte de (1838–1889), French

Vilmorin, Luise de (1902–1969), Comtesse Palffy, French author

Vincent, Dominic, unidentified

Visconti, Giovanni Battista Primi (1648–1713), Italian writer

Vogel, aircraft engineer, World War II

Vogel, Emil Wilhelm (1894–1985), major general, commander of 101st Infantry Division in the Caucasus

Volckmar-Frentzel, Theodor (b. 1892), publisher, member of the Command Staff in Paris, World War II

Volhard, Edwald (b. 1900), naturalist

Voltaire (1694–1778), *recte* François Marie Arouet, French author and philosopher

Voss, Hans-Alexander von (1907–1944), major, General Staff in Paris

W

Wagner, Richard (1813–1883), German composer

Wallenstein, Albrecht Wenzel Usebius von (1583–1634), commander of the Imperial Forces in the Thirty Years' War

Walther, Oswald Alwin (1898–1967), mathematician

Watteau, Jean-Antoine (1684–1721), French painter

Weber, Dr., see *Rademacher, Otfried*

Weckerus, Johan Jacob (1528–1586), physician and philosopher

Weihrauter, major, World War II

Weininger, Otto (1880–1903), Austrian psychologist and philosopher

Weinstock, Heinrich (1889–1960), teacher and philosopher, member of the General Staff in Paris, World War II

Weizsäcker, Viktor Freiherr [Baron] von (1886–1957), German doctor

Weniger, Erich (1894–1961), educational theorist

Werner, Carl Friedrich Heinrich (1808–1894), illustrator

Wepler, unidentified, Paris

Whitman, Walt (1819–1892), American poet

Wickenberg, Hanne, married to Hinnerk Wickenberg

Wickenberg, Hinnerk (d. 1945), neighbor in Kirchhorst

Wieland, Christoph Martin (1733–1813), German poet

Wiemer, Horst Eduard, editor

Wilde, Oscar (1854–1900), Anglo-Irish author and playwright

Wilder, Thornton (1897–1975), American writer

Wildermuth, Hermann-Eberhard (1890–1952), colonel, General Staff, Paris

Willems, Paul (1912–1997), Flemish civil servant, son of Marie Gevers

Wimpffen, Emanuel Félix de (1811–1884), French general

Winnig, August (1878–1956), German politician, participant in the Kapp putsch

Wolf, Erik (1902–1977), philosopher

Wolfe, Thomas Clayton (1900–1938), American writer

Wollny, lieutenant, World War II

Wood, Evelyn Henry (1838–1919), English field marshal

X

Xenophon (c. 430–354 BCE), Greek historian

Z

Zaïre, Le, see *Dezaïre, Joseph*

Ziegler, Benno (1894–1949), German publisher of the Hanseatischer Verlagsanstalt

Ziegler, Leopold (1881–1958), cultural historian

Zola, Jean-Baptiste (seventeenth century), Jesuit priest

INDEX